SUPER F
BOOK

1988 EDITION

Super Bowl Stories Written by
LOWELL REIDENBAUGH
PAUL ATTNER

Championship Games Section Written by
DAVE KLEIN

Editor/Super Bowl Book
BOB McCOY

Associate Editor/Super Bowl Book
HOWARD BALZER

President-Chief Executive Officer
RICHARD WATERS

Editor
TOM BARNIDGE

Director of Books and Periodicals
RON SMITH

Published by

The Sporting News

1212 North Lindbergh Boulevard
P.O. Box 56 — St. Louis, MO 63166

Copyright © 1988
The Sporting News Publishing Company

A Times Mirror
Company

ISBN 0-89204-287-7   ISSN 0275-4487

Table of Contents

Championship Games

Super Bowl and Championship Games records used through the courtesy of the National Football League.

COVER PHOTO—Washington quarterback Doug Williams threw for four touchdowns in a 35-point second quarter and won Most Valuable Player honors in the Redskins' 42-10 Super Bowl XXII victory over the Denver Broncos.

—Photo by Rich Pilling

Joe Robbie Stadium in Miami will be the site for Super Bowl XXIII on January 22, 1989.

INTRODUCTION

The year was 1966, and war was raging in professional football. It was a bidding war for talent, and it had been going on since the American Football League came onto the scene in 1960 to challenge the National Football League, 40 years its senior.

At first, the battles were waged for college players, and the AFL scored an early victory when a court ruled in favor of the Houston Oilers over the NFL's Los Angeles Rams after both clubs had signed Billy Cannon, the Heisman Trophy winning halfback at Louisiana State.

Although the leagues agreed to a "no tampering" rule on existing player contracts, the stakes became high for college talent. Bonuses went sky-high. The AFL's New York Jets signed Alabama quarterback Joe Namath in 1965 to a $400,000 contract, largest amount ever for a collegian. In 1966, the NFL's Atlanta Falcons gave Texas linebacker Tommy Nobis a $600,000 package and the Green Bay Packers forked over $711,000 to Texas Tech running back Donny Anderson.

Meanwhile, veteran players were settling for small raises on relatively small salaries. For example, John Brodie, the San Francisco 49ers quarterback, received $35,000 in 1965 and was asking for a raise to $65,000 after leading the NFL in completions, percentage, yardage and touchdown passes.

Then came a back-breaker. Buffalo placekicker Pete Gogolak, who had played out his option in 1965, signed with the NFL's New York Giants. The "no tampering" code had been broken. The conflict was in the open, and it was time for action.

On April 7, 1966, peacemaker Joe Foss resigned as AFL commissioner and the next day Al Davis, general manager of the Oakland Raiders, took over. Davis was a hawk in regard to the NFL and he had a plan.

Davis organized an AFL war chest and urged owners to start talking to established NFL stars. The NFL had bragged of its superiority because of the caliber of its quarterbacks. Davis wanted to sign those quarterbacks for the AFL.

The Raiders quickly signed Los Angeles quarterback Roman Gabriel to a commitment starting in '67. Houston offered the 49ers' Brodie $75,000, spread over 10 years, to sign a five-year deal with the Oilers. Reportedly, eight of the NFL's starting quarterbacks were dickering with the AFL.

The NFL had no choice. On June 8, 1966, two months after Davis became the AFL commissioner, a merger agreement was announced. There would be a common draft starting in 1967, interleague preseason games starting in '67 and regular-season play combining the leagues in 1970. Territorial indemnification of $18 million was to be paid to the 49ers and Giants over a 20-year period.

Most important, from the standpoint of football fans, was the immediate establishment of a championship game between the leagues. This was the AFL-NFL World Championship Game, which was popularized as the Super Bowl from its inception.

Gabriel never went to the Raiders and Brodie never left the 49ers, but he collected a million dollars on the agreement he had made in his talks with Houston.

Davis resigned as AFL commissioner a month after the merger. He clearly had won his battle.

Super Bowl XXII

Washington Skins Broncos

January 31, 1988

Doug Williams destroyed both the Denver Broncos and the black quarterback myth in Super Bowl XXII.

Quarterbacks have provided more than a few memorable performances in Super Bowls. There was Joe Namath's prickly prediction-come-true in Super Bowl III, Terry Bradshaw's four touchdown passes in Super Bowl XIII, Jim Plunkett's storybook comeback in Super Bowl XV and Phil Simms' near-perfect marksmanship in Super Bowl XXI. Based on statistics alone, Doug Williams' wonderful work in Super Bowl XXII would put him among those elite names.

But Williams' place in football history can't be based just on statistics. After 21 years of Super Bowls and another 34 years of National Football League title games before that, a black quarterback finally played in pro football's premier event. And he played sensationally, earning Most Valuable Player honors while leading the Washington Redskins to their second NFL championship in six years.

Given the social significance attached to Williams' ground-breaking role, his performance may never be equalled in pro football. Making a Namath-like prediction is one thing; carrying the hopes of an entire race into an already pressure-saturated game—and then virtually rewriting a large portion of the record book—is the stuff of fantasies, not reality.

But Williams already had tasted as many of life's joys and sorrows as he probably cared. Two years before Super Bowl XXII, he was an unemployed quarterback waiting for the telephone to ring. Once a budding NFL star, his life had been turned upside down. Shortly after he became a free agent with the Tampa Bay Buccaneers in February 1983, his wife died of a brain tumor. He was left to raise an infant daughter and to play football in a league doomed to fail. When the United States Football League folded after the 1985 season, his career seemed over.

To understand the valleys he'd visited was to remember the peaks that had come before. Williams had been a star at Grambling State

Redskins Coach Joe Gibbs diagrams a play for his offense and quarterback Doug Williams (at right) in preparation for Super Bowl XXII.

University before joining the Buccaneers, who made him a first-round draft choice (the 17th pick overall) in 1978. There were other black quarterbacks in the NFL, but Williams was the most gifted. He seemed destined to finally demolish all the stereotypes that had become associated with blacks and the quarterback position: That blacks weren't smart enough to play quarterback, weren't dependable and weren't willing to work hard enough to do the job properly.

Williams became an instant starter in the NFL, working under the guidance of Joe Gibbs, then Tampa Bay's quarterbacks coach. But the Bucs were young and struggling, and Williams was inexperienced and unsure. Although he guided them into the National Football Conference title game in 1979, where they lost to the Los Angeles Rams, 9-0, he was never given the chance to hone his skills or to play with truly outstanding offensive personnel.

Instead, his exceptionally strong but sometimes erratic throwing arm gave birth to a joke that found its humor at his expense. It was said that Williams might best serve his country if he were sent to Iran, because he was the only person capable of "overthrowing the Ayatollah." Later, he would laugh as he retold the joke. But at first it hurt, just as it hurt when the Bucs refused to satisfy his contract demands in 1983. He felt he had little choice but to move to

the USFL, his life already shattered by the shocking loss of his wife.

"I thought," he said, "that any dreams of me playing in a Super Bowl were finished."

But Williams' life took an unexpected turn in 1986 when he received a call from Gibbs, who by then was the successful head coach of the Washington Redskins. Gibbs wanted to know if Williams would be interested in joining the Redskins as an experienced backup to starter Jay Schroeder. Said Williams: "He didn't have to ask for very long. When you don't have a job, you can't be too choosy."

Williams threw only one pass in 1986 and there was no reason for him to expect 1987 to be any different. But when Schroeder was injured in the opening game, Williams was given a chance to start. Later, after Schroeder returned but played erratically, Williams was named the starter, only to lose the job because of an injury. After Williams relieved Schroeder and rallied the Redskins to victory over Minnesota in the final regular-season game, Gibbs installed Williams as his starting quarterback for the playoffs.

"The Redskins didn't bring me here to become the first black quarterback in the Super Bowl," Williams said. "They brought me here to be the quarterback of a Super Bowl team."

Even when the Redskins did get to the Super Bowl as the somewhat surprising winner of the

Denver rookie Ricky Nattiel celebrates his 56-yard touchdown catch on the Broncos' first play from scrimmage in Super Bowl XXII. The touchdown, at 1:57 of the first quarter, was the quickest score in Super Bowl history.

Broncos quarterback John Elway is pursued by the Redskins' Dexter Manley on this 21-yard, second-quarter scramble. The run was Denver's longest from scrimmage in Super Bowl XXII.

NFC title—the favored San Francisco 49ers lost a divisional playoff game to Minnesota—Williams' presence resulted in a plethora of non-sports stories. The stories involving social significance centered on Williams; the stories detailing quarterbacking talent centered on the Denver Broncos' John Elway, who dominated the pre-game hype so much it seemed at times as if he were a one-man team.

"We've got a curfew just for John," snapped Denver Coach Dan Reeves at one point. "The rest of the guys are on their own."

Elway was the league's golden boy, a $2 million-a-year star who was so good that he had carried a good-but-not-great Broncos team into the Super Bowl two straight years. He had played well against the New York Giants in Super Bowl XXI, but Denver still had been overwhelmed. But he seemed on an even higher plane this time, and the Redskins, who had been erratic all season despite easily winning the NFC East, certainly were no Giants. Denver was a 3½-point favorite, based almost solely on Elway's aura. He was John Wayne, throwing to Denver's speedy wide receivers collectively nicknamed—after a motion picture of the same title—the "Three Amigos."

But Elway alone couldn't cope with what the Redskins produced: Williams' marvelous output coupled with a 204-yard rushing performance from rookie Tim Smith and a 35-point outburst in the second quarter—the most prolific offensive performance in one quarter in Super Bowl history. Washington won easily, 42-10, before a crowd of 73,302 at San Diego's Jack Murphy Stadium. It marked the fourth straight lopsided Super Bowl victory by an NFC team.

"I'm no Jackie Robinson," protested Williams afterward, dismissing any comparison to the man who broke the color barrier in major league baseball. But Robinson would have been proud of Williams' guts and character and class. In the days preceeding the Super Bowl, the Redskins' coaching staff fretted about the pressures being placed on Williams. They believed that their team could physically overpower the quicker, smaller Broncos, but they wondered whether they could control Elway and if Williams would press too much in trying to live up to the expectations of his fans.

"Doug is the reason we are here," said one Redskins coach. "Since he became a starter, we're a different team. But you hope he doesn't go into the game feeling he's carrying all his fans on his shoulders. If he tries too hard, we could have problems."

Redskins cornerback Barry Wilburn, who was victimized by Ricky Nattiel for Denver's only touchdown, gets revenge by intercepting a John Elway pass intended for Nattiel in the second period.

After the game, after he had completed 18 of 29 attempts and had set a Super Bowl record for passing yards (340) and had tied another for touchdown passes (four), Williams was on top of the sports world, smiling broadly.

He was the missing link in the Redskins puzzle, the stabilizer on offense that enabled the coaches to take full advantage of their varied

offensive talents. Schroeder lacked a deft touch on his short passes and sometimes pressed too hard to make big plays. Williams, passing with a soft touch he had developed in the USFL, played almost flawlessly in the postseason (one interception and one sack in the first two playoff games, and one sack and one interception in the Super Bowl). He made certain that the Redskins didn't beat themselves.

"I think there were a lot of television sets turned on today and a lot of people will start to see me as a role model," he said. "But the most important thing is to be able to play well and be a role model. That's what we did today."

The saga of the Redskins, start to finish, was an unlikely tale. This was a team that grew accustomed to struggles, often forced to rally from deficits and hardly ever putting away opponents. There were controversies at quarterback and running back and wide receiver, injuries and a "replacement" team that kept the Redskins in the championship hunt by winning all three of its games during the NFL players' strike. And in the end, it was an unheralded defense that throttled Elway and an unassuming trio of Williams, Smith and receiver Ricky Sanders that produced the offensive fireworks. Those three hadn't even been starters when the season began.

In the process, the Redskins proved that not even a player as talented as Elway can overcome the burdens of a weak defense. The Broncos were outgained badly in three playoff games and, combined with their 39-20 loss to the Giants the year before, gave up 81 points in back-to-back Super Bowl losses.

"The way we've played in the two Super Bowls, I'm embarrassed for the whole organization," said Denver linebacker Jim Ryan.

It was a Super Bowl matchup without controversy—and almost without color. During the week prior to the game, the players from the two teams couldn't say enough nice things about each other. "It's like two choir boys squaring off," said Redskins tackle Mark May, shaking his head.

Gibbs and Reeves went so far as to schedule a Saturday night chapel service that players from both teams could attend. Imagine former Green Bay Packers linebacker Ray Nitschke mingling with the Kansas City Chiefs a few hours before Super Bowl I? At least some of the players from both teams got out at night, meeting unexpectedly at a local watering spot. That's where Denver safety Tony Lilly got his first up-close look at the "Hogs," the Redskins' hefty offensive linemen. "Awesome," said Lilly.

Still, Gibbs was far from overconfident. He put in a curfew, a change from his Super Bowl policy of four years earlier. He also instructed his players to wear wrong uniform numbers at practice sessions during the week. That scheme could be attributed to Gibbs' profound belief that the Raiders had spied on his practices before they beat the Redskins, 38-9, in Super Bowl XVIII.

"The guys loved it," assistant coach Dan Henning said of the Redskins' subterfuge. "Some of them wouldn't take the most prominent numbers. They said if anyone was out there sniping, they didn't want to be a target."

Denver Coach Dan Reeves could sense another Super blowout during Washington's 35-point second-quarter explosion.

Reeves contracted a case of paranoia, too. When the Broncos saw a man filming their practice from the roof of a house, Reeves said, "See if his name is Joe."

His name certainly wasn't Dexter, although that name drew plenty of attention. Dexter Manley, the Redskins' loquacious defensive end, attempted to avoid the spotlight during Super Bowl week and, instead, wound up drawing it. At one point during the pregame build-up, he said he would be unavailable to the media. On another day, he said his dream was to "catch the quarterback and hit him from behind, in between his two numbers, and cut his lights out." Reminded that Elway wore No. 7, Manley replied: "Oh." He took verbal potshots at Jimmy (The Greek) Snyder and lauded Elway, then boycotted a mandatory interview session until Gibbs made him return.

Said a Redskins teammate: "We're waiting for Dexter to explode. He's been quiet much too long."

Redskins practices were so fierce that the coaches wondered if the team was peaking too soon. Perhaps a pep talk from Ollie North before the team left Washington had got the players too psyched. "You should have seen us on Wednesday (four days before the game)," said Manley. "No one was safe on the practice field."

Washington's Doug Williams was nearly flawless in Super Bowl XXII, completing 18 of 29 passes for a record 340 yards and four touchdowns en route to the game's Most Valuable Player award.

Redskins safety Alvin Walton sacks Broncos quarterback John Elway for an 18-yard loss in the first quarter of Super Bowl XXII.

Gibbs tried to benefit from the mistakes of Washington's Super Bowl loss to the Raiders. He thought he had installed the game plan too early back then and added too much to it as the days went on. This time, the plan was implemented in stages and then reduced instead of enlarged. The coaching staff, instead of working long hours, even had evenings to relax.

"Joe's as calm and as confident as I've seen him," said Joe Bugel, the Redskins' assistant head coach/offense. "He's relaxing and it's rubbing off on everyone else." It was easy to be laid back. Magnificent weather visited San Diego in the week prior to its first Super Bowl game.

Despite the fascination with Elway and his many talents, the Redskins saw another side to the game. They were certain they could run the ball effectively against the smaller Denver defense, especially if they started Smith in-

stead of the slower George Rogers. And the coaches believed that if Williams could have just a .500 passing day, the Redskins would be able to beat a weak Broncos secondary. The game plan was to offset Denver's defensive slanting and stunting with counter run plays and to throw the ball deep against the cornerbacks. The Redskins were intent on being bold because they thought Denver would score at least three touchdowns.

Richie Petitbon, the Redskins' assistant head coach/defense, respected Elway so much that he changed his usual approach regarding blitzing. Instead of frequently sending six or seven defenders toward the quarterback, Petitbon and the other defensive coaches decided to limit the rush to the front four linemen and a fifth player, either safety Alvin Walton or one of the linebackers—Monte Coleman, Mel Kaufman or Clarence Vaughn. The idea was to have the front four rush straight ahead, forgoing any stunting that would open up scramble lanes for Elway, and then try to confuse the quarterback by blitzing from ever-changing points on the field.

"We didn't want to leave the middle of the field open, because Elway could hurt us there," said Petitbon. So free safety Todd Bowles manned the middle and Petitbon began what Bugel called "a chess game" with Elway.

The Broncos almost had a checkmate in the first quarter. Washington's cornerbacks liked to play a lot of man-to-man defense and to press receivers on the line of scrimmage. On its first play from scrimmage, Denver, which enjoyed facing man-to-man, pressing coverages, got rookie receiver Ricky Nattiel isolated on cornerback Barry Wilburn, breaking down what had started as a zone coverage scheme.

Elway kept looking away from Wilburn, who thought he wouldn't be involved in the play. Then Elway suddenly connected with Nattiel, who was five yards behind the defender. The 56-yard touchdown pass was the quickest score in Super Bowl history, coming just 1 minute and 57 seconds after the kickoff.

"He caught me asleep," Wilburn said of Elway. "Give him credit."

On Denver's next possession, a trick pass from running back Steve Sewell to Elway—imagine risking your star quarterback as a receiver—covered 32 yards and took the Broncos to the Washington 6-yard line. But Elway was stopped by tackle Dave Butz on a third-down quarterback draw and Denver settled for a 24-yard Rich Karlis field goal and a 10-0 lead.

Sanders fumbled the ensuing kickoff, but the Redskins kept possession on a recovery by Terry Orr, perhaps the game's biggest play. Had Denver recovered, Washington might have been buried under a 17-0 avalanche.

The Redskins were tentative. "We were too excited, too emotional," said defensive end Charles Mann. "Relax, relax," the players told each other on the sideline, in between some pointed yelling by the coaches. "It was like someone was kicking us in the mouth and we weren't doing anything about it," said Bugel.

Williams watched four of his passes get dropped before he suffered a twisted knee and had to leave the game for one play near the end of the first quarter. But he returned after reminding Gibbs that he had played in pain before and that this game should be no different.

Almost overlooked in Washington's inauspicious start was that one day earlier, Williams had been forced to undergo an emergency root canal. So the Redskins confronted a 10-point deficit with a gimpy, sore-mouthed quarterback, a defense stunned by Elway's early strikes and an offensive plan of run-and-ball control that suddenly looked out of place.

Things changed dramatically in the second quarter. On the Redskins' first play of the period, Williams wanted to throw a conservative, 7-yard pass called "Charlie Hitch" to Sanders. But cornerback Mark Haynes bumped Sanders at the line and Sanders adjusted by going deep. Once he got behind Haynes, Sanders caught a finely thrown, semi-soft pass at midfield and scampered in for an 80-yard touchdown which equaled the Super Bowl record for longest pass play. Time left in the period: 14:07.

"The turning point," said Gibbs. "You could feel the sidelines come alive. We caught fire."

The rest of the quarter almost defied imagination. The Redskins scored on their next four possessions, performing as if they were going up against their scout squad. Following a Denver punt, Gary Clark, running the same pattern as Sanders, got behind Steve Wilson and pulled in a 27-yard scoring pass. Time left: 10:15. "Doug was hitting everybody, no matter what you did," said Clark. "If it didn't work, it was the receiver's fault."

After Karlis missed a 43-yard field-goal try, Smith broke away on a play called "counter gap" for a 58-yard touchdown. "(Left tackle) Joe Jacoby and (left guard) Raleigh McKenzie gave me good blocks and I busted it outside," said Smith, who also was helped by an initial block from tight end Clint Didier. "I saw a tight squeeze that made me go inside, then cut back out, and their defensive backs had their hands full with our wide receivers to make it easier to run after I got through the line." Time left: 6:27.

Then Sanders beat Lilly for a touchdown on a 50-yard pass play called "double pump." Sanders said, "It was just a run-pass. They fake it to the running back, the strong safety comes up to make the tackle and I get behind him." Washington was running so well that Denver had to respect play-action fakes; that opened up the passing game. Time left: 3:42.

Following the first of two Wilburn interceptions, Didier pulled in an 8-yard touchdown pass against safety Tyrone Braxton for a 35-10 lead. "We call it 'scram,'" said Bugel. "Clint was the primary receiver, with Sanders right behind him. If they cover Didier, we just throw a short pass to Sanders." Time left: 1:04.

The Redskins' second-quarter numbers were awesome: Five straight scores for 35 points, the most ever in one quarter in *any* NFL playoff game; 356 total yards, including 228 passing by Williams on nine completions in 11 attempts; five touchdowns in 18 plays covering just 5 minutes and 47 seconds of possession time; 122 yards on five carries by Smith, and 168 yards on five receptions by Sanders.

"After the third one, it seemed like they were on a roll," said Ryan. "Your head is spinning and it's like you're in a whirlpool." Said Broncos linebacker Karl Mecklenburg: "Williams was patient. He stayed in there and looked to the second and third receivers. He took advantage of our weak points caused by

Redskins receivers Gary Clark and Eric Yarber celebrate after Clark's 27-yard touchdown catch in the second period gave Washington a lead (14-10) it never relinquished.

running plays.

"I'll take a good physical team over a good finesse team nine out of 10 times," said May.

Washington was especially effective using its counter gap play, where the running back followed the lead blocks of the right guard and tackle pulling around left end or the left guard and tackle moving to the right.

"It's the best way to neutralize a quick team like Denver that likes to slant its defense," said Jacoby. "They were guessing where we would run and they guessed right in the first quarter. But they guessed wrong in the second and we got 'em. We'd get to the hole and there would be just a linebacker left. All the back had to do was beat a safety."

The Redskins were determined to use the counter gap, their bread-and-butter running play, at least 15 times in the game. "Patience is the key," said Bugel. "A few years ago, if we lost a few yards on it, we'd give up on it. Now, we realize you might gain two with it, then four and then maybe lose two. But then it could go for 54. Give it time."

Smith's 58-yard touchdown came on a counter gap, and he later gained 43 yards on the same play, running left behind Thielemann and May. Suddenly, Smith, a fifth-round draft pick from Texas Tech who missed most of his last two college seasons with knee problems, was a Super Bowl star.

"This is an unlimited feeling," he said. "I wasn't too nervous. I made sure I felt comfortable. I let them know I was comfortable and relaxed."

Smith had run better than hobbled starter Rogers for most of the season, but Gibbs had been reluctant to make a change. An internal debate within the team hierarchy had raged for weeks, with most backing an increased use of Smith. Finally, Gibbs decided he needed more outside speed against Denver, so he switched to Smith, cementing the decision the night before the game. To keep Smith from being nervous, the Redskins didn't inform him he was starting until just before Washington's opening possession.

He obviously never got too nervous. His 204 rushing yards broke the Super Bowl record of 191 set by Marcus Allen in 1984 and were 78 yards more than he had gained during the regular season. At least Sanders, another of the Redskins' USFL refugees, had some previous NFL experience. Still, his nine catches for a Super Bowl record 193 yards also were unexpected.

"We saw things in the second quarter that we saw in the first, but we had been dropping passes and they put on the blitz early," said Williams. "But our offensive line got together and things started clicking."

Said Ryan: "They read some of the things we were doing to overload against the counter play and they ran away from us. It seemed

Washington rookie Timmy Smith scored twice and set a Super Bowl record with 204 yards rushing.

injury."

The Broncos, who had reworked six defensive positions since the previous year, couldn't stop the Redskins because they simply were unable to handle either Williams or Washington's offensive line. The Hogs gave Williams enough time to wait for receivers to come open against an average, injury-plagued secondary and also wore down the smaller Denver front seven with the relentless pounding on

Dexter Manley (left) and Doug Williams were all smiles in the locker room after the Redskins' 42-10 triumph in Super Bowl XXII.

they knew what we were doing." No one, especially Denver defensive coordinator Joe Collier, had said the Broncos played good run defense. "The last thing a defense picks up," Collier had said in the days before the game. "We are still learning to do it right."

Meanwhile, nothing was clicking for Elway. The Redskins' five-man rush got better and better, especially Walton, whose blitzing gave Elway particular problems. After a fast start (he completed three of his first four passes for 96 yards), Elway labored (11 of 34 for 161 yards, three interceptions) and Denver collapsed.

"They did a good job checking (bumping) our receivers," said Elway. "It slowed them down, it affected our timing, it was taking longer (for patterns to unfold) than it normally does." Elway was sacked five times. Just as important, the Redskins' disciplined rush prevented him from scrambling for more than 32 yards on three carries. The Broncos had 142 total yards and 10 points in the first 15 minutes; for the rest of the game, they had 185 yards and no points.

"We thought our cornerbacks could cover their wide receivers," said Petitbon. "But we had to get pressure on Elway. We gave him new stuff, with someone blitzing a lot from different spots to confuse him. He's a great player, but he had a big load to carry coming in."

Denver survives on defense by causing turnovers. But Washington made just one mistake and the Broncos had nothing to fall back on against the Redskins' onslaught, which included a Super Bowl record 280 rushing yards. The Hogs, who were outclassed by the New York Giants' defense three times the year before (twice in the regular 1986 season and again in the NFC championship game), could be justifiably proud of their performance in the playoffs after the 1987 season. In three games, they paved the way for 513 rushing yards and surrendered only three sacks.

"We caught fire," said Gibbs, a winning coach for the second time in three trips to the Super Bowl. "(The second quarter) was easily the best quarter of football I've been around.

"Maybe now, they will look at Doug for something other than his color."

Perhaps Eddie Robinson, who was Williams' coach at Grambling, put it all in context.

"I've seen him do what he did today all the time at Grambling," Robinson said. "The only difference is, today he had a much bigger audience, that's all."

Statistics of 22nd Super Bowl
WASHINGTON 42, DENVER 10

Jack Murphy Stadium, San Diego, Calif., January 31, 1988
Attendance: 73,302

WASHINGTON	Offense	DENVER
Gary Clark	WR	Mark Jackson
Joe Jacoby	LT	Dave Studdard
Raleigh McKenzie	LG	Keith Bishop
Jeff Bostic	C	Mike Freeman
R.C. Thielemann	RG	Stefan Humphries
Mark May	RT	Ken Lanier
Clint Didier	TE	Clarence Kay
Don Warren	TE	
Doug Williams	QB	John Elway
Timmy Smith	RB	Sammy Winder
	RB	Gene Lang
Ricky Sanders	WR	Ricky Nattiel

Defense

WASHINGTON		DENVER
Charles Mann	LE	Andre Townsend
Dave Butz	LT	
	NT	Greg Kragen
Darryl Grant	RT	
Dexter Manley	RE	Rulon Jones
Mel Kaufman	LLB	Simon Fletcher
Neal Olkewicz	MLB	
	ILB	Karl Mecklenburg
	ILB	Ricky Hunley
Monte Coleman	RLB	Jim Ryan
Darrell Green	LCB	Mark Haynes
Todd Bowles	RCB	Steve Wilson
Barry Wilburn	SS	Dennis Smith
Alvin Walton	FS	Tony Lilly

SUBSTITUTIONS

WASHINGTON—Offense: Receivers—Anthony Jones, Art Monk, Terry Orr, Eric Yarber. Linemen—Russ Grimm, Rick Kehr. Backs—Reggie Branch, Kelvin Bryant, Keith Griffin, George Rogers, Jay Schroeder. Kicker—Ali Haji-Sheikh. Defense: Linebackers—Ravin Caldwell, Kurt Gouveia, Rich Milot. Linemen—Dean Hamel, Steve Hamilton, Markus Koch. Backs—Brian Davis, Vernon Dean, Clarence Vaughn, Dennis Woodberry. Punter—Steve Cox. DNP—None. Inactive—Anthony Allen, Joe Caravello, Tim Morrison, Mark Rypien, Clarence Verdin.

DENVER—Offense: Receivers—Vance Johnson, Orson Mobley, Steve Watson. Linemen—Keith Kartz. Backs—Ken Bell, Tony Boddie, Gary Kubiak, Bobby Micho, Steve Sewell. Kicker—Rich Karlis. Defense: Linebackers—Michael Brooks, Rick Dennison, Bruce Klostermann, Tim Lucas. Linemen—Walt Bowyer, Freddie Gilbert. Backs—Tyrone Braxton, Jeremiah Castille, K.C. Clark, Bruce Plummer, Randy Robbins. Punter—Mike Horan. DNP—Larry Lee. Inactive—Mitch Andrews, Steve Bryan, Sam Graddy, Ken Karcher, Dan Remsberg.

— SCORE BY PERIODS —

Washington Redskins (NFC)	0	35	0	7 — 42
Denver Broncos (AFC)	10	0	0	0 — 10

— SCORING —

Denver—Nattiel 56 pass from Elway (Karlis kick).
Denver—Field goal Karlis 24.
Washington—Sanders 80 pass from Williams (Haji-Sheikh kick).
Washington—Clark 27 pass from Williams (Haji-Sheikh kick).
Washington—Smith 58 run (Haji-Sheikh kick).
Washington—Sanders 50 pass from Williams (Haji-Sheikh kick).
Washington—Didier 8 pass from Williams (Haji-Sheikh kick).
Washington—Smith 4 run (Haji-Sheikh kick).

— TEAM STATISTICS —

	Washington	Denver
Total First Downs	25	18
First Downs Rushing	13	6
First Downs Passing	11	10
First Downs Penalty	1	2
Rushes	40	17
Yards Gained Rushing (net)	280	97
Average Yards per Rush	7.0	5.7
Passes Attempted	30	39
Passes Completed	18	15
Had Intercepted	1	3
Times Tackled Attempt, Pass	2	5
Yards Lost Attempting Pass	18	50
Yards Gained Passing (net)	322	230
Total Net Yardage	602	327
Total Offensive Plays	72	61
Avg. Gain per Offensive Play	8.4	5.4
Punts	4	7
Average Distance	37.5	36.1
Punt Returns	1	2
Punt Return Yardage	0	18
Kickoff Returns	3	5
Kickoff Return Yardage	46	88
Interceptions Return Yardage	11	0
Fumbles	1	0
Opp. Fumbles Recovered	0	0
Total Return Yardage	57	106
Penalties	6	5
Yards Penalized	65	26
Total Points Scored	42	10
Touchdowns	6	1
Touchdowns Rushing	2	0
Touchdowns Passing	4	1
Touchdowns on Returns	0	0
Extra Points	6	1
Field Goals Attempted	1	2
Field Goals	0	1
Time of Possession	35:15	24:45

INDIVIDUAL STATISTICS
RUSHING

Washington	Atts.	Yds.	Lg.	TD
Sanders	1	—4	—4	0
Smith	22	204	58	2
Williams	2	—2	—1	0
Bryant	8	38	15	0
Clark	1	25	25	0
Rogers	5	17	5	0
Griffin	1	2	2	0

Denver	Atts.	Yds.	Lg.	TD
Elway	3	32	21	0
Sewell	1	—3	—3	0
Winder	8	30	13	0
Lang	5	38	13	0

PASSING

Washington	Atts.	Comp.	Yds.	Int.	TD
Williams	29	18	340	1	4
Schroeder	1	0	0	0	0

Denver	Atts.	Comp.	Yds.	Int.	TD
Elway	38	14	257	3	1
Sewell	1	1	23	0	0

Denver's Karl Mecklenburg closes in for a sack of Washington's Jay Schroeder late in the first quarter of Super Bowl XXII. Schroeder, a former starting quarterback, threw an incomplete pass on the next play.

RECEIVING

Washington	No.	Yds.	Lg.	TD
Sanders	9	193	80	2
Smith	1	9	9	0
Bryant	1	20	20	0
Monk	1	40	40	0
Warren	2	15	9	0
Clark	3	55	27	1
Didier	1	8	8	1

Denver	No.	Yds.	Lg.	TD
Nattiel	2	69	56	1
Elway	1	23	23	0
Jackson	4	76	32	0
Sewell	4	41	18	0
Winder	1	26	26	0
Lang	1	7	7	0
Kay	2	38	27	0

INTERCEPTIONS

Washington	No.	Yds.	Lg.	TD
Wilburn	2	11	11	0
Davis	1	0	0	0

Denver	No.	Yds.	Lg.	TD
Castille	1	0	0	0

PUNTING

Washington	No.	Avg.	Lg.
Cox	4	37.5	42

Denver	No.	Avg.	Lg.
Horan	7	36.1	43

PUNT RETURNS

Washington	No.	FC	Yds.	Lg.
Green	1	1	0	0
Yarber	0	1	0	0

Denver	No.	FC	Yds.	Lg.
Clark	2	0	18	9

KICKOFF RETURNS

Washington	No.	Yds.	Lg.
Sanders	3	46	16

Denver	No.	Yds.	Lg.
Bell	5	88	21

FIELD GOALS

Washington	Att.	Made
Haji-Sheikh	1	0

Denver	Att.	Made
Karlis	2	1

SCORING

Washington	TD	PAT	FG	Pts.
Smith	2	0	0	12
Sanders	2	0	0	12
Haji-Sheikh	0	6	0	6
Clark	1	0	0	6
Didier	1	0	0	6

Denver	TD	PAT	FG	Pts.
Nattiel	1	0	0	6
Karlis	0	1	1	4

FUMBLES

Washington	No.	Own Rec.	Opp. Rec.	TD
Caldwell	0	1	0	0
Sanders	1	0	0	0

Denver—None.

Packers hero Max McGee catches his second TD pass against the Chiefs.

Super Bowl I

McGee Leads the Pack

January 15, 1967

As a pass-catching end and all-night reveler, Max McGee had few equals in the history of the National Football League.

McGee could evoke laughter from so stern a disciplinarian as Green Bay Coach Vince Lombardi. He was a master of breaking curfew without detection, declaring at one point that he had "snuck out 11 straight nights after curfew without being caught. . . . I must hold the NFL record."

If Lombardi taught him one thing, McGee quipped, it was how to get along on a minimal amount of sleep.

Bright lights, broads and booze were an integral segment of Max' lifestyle, even on the eve of a Super Bowl game.

In the book "Lombardi," edited by ex-Packer teammate Jerry Kramer, McGee relates his escapade the night of January 14, 1967, less than 12 hours before Green Bay met Kansas City in Super Bowl I.

"I'd no earthly idea I'd play in that game," McGee wrote. "Neither Paul (roommate Paul Hornung) nor I expected to get off the bench. He hadn't played in about six weeks and I knew I wouldn't play unless Boyd Dowler got hurt. Vince put in a huge penalty that week, something like $5,000, and we all knew he meant it, so I didn't think anybody snuck out. The night before the game Dave Hanner checked the room at curfew and I asked Hawg if he was going to double check later. 'Yep,' he said. But then, as he started out of my room, he changed his mind for some reason. 'Nope,' Hawg said, 'I won't check your room later.' That was enough for me. I practically ran over him getting out of the room. I met some blonde the night before and I was on my way to pay my respects. I didn't feel I was letting the team down any, because I knew there wasn't a chance in hell I'd play.

"I waddled in about 7:30 in the morning

Bart Starr . . . Always cool.

and I could barely stand up for the kickoff. On the bench Paul kept needling me, 'What would you do if you had to play?' And I said, 'No way, there's no way I could make it.'

"We sat together, discussing his wedding that was coming up, and suddenly I heard Lombardi yell, 'McGee.' I figured he'd found out about my sneaking out. I figured it was about to cost me $5,000. Then he shouted, 'Get in the game.' I almost fainted.

"Boyd was hurt and I played the rest of the game and caught seven passes and scored two touchdowns and after the game dear old Vince came up to me and said, 'Nice game.'

" 'Most any end could've done the same thing,' I said.

" 'You're right,' he said.

"I looked at him and said, 'Well, you sure took the edge off that, you s.o.b.' "

The dialogue was typical of McGee-Lombardi exchanges and the performance of semi-sober Max in Green Bay's 35-10 victory over the Chiefs also was typical of the 34-year-old receiver.

The 1966 season had been hardly a vintage year for mirthful Max. In 14 games he had caught only four passes for 91 yards, earning him a reputation as "pro football's highest priced receiver, per catch."

McGee's receptions, however, had come at highly crucial moments. One, against Baltimore, set up the deciding touchdown in the divisional title game.

In the NFL championship game against the Dallas Cowboys, Max scored the touchdown that provided the margin of victory. After 11 pro seasons his twin gifts for catching thrown footballs and for catching merriment at unconventional hours were undiminished.

On January 15, 1967, Max McGee enjoyed his finest, most luminous hour.

For many weeks of the regular professional season, through weeks of playoffs and the uninterrupted ballyhoo, football devotees had awaited the initial confrontation of the two football behemoths, the champions of the youthful American Football League and the long-established National Football League.

A name for the one-day extravaganza had been coined effortlessly one day when Lamar Hunt, architect of the AFL, came across his daughter's "Super Ball."

"Why not," he wondered, "call our championship game the Super Bowl?"

The name found immediate acceptance and, appropriately, Hunt's Kansas City Chiefs represented the AFL in the first game.

En route to the climactic struggle, played before 61,946 in Los Angeles' 100,000-seat Memorial Coliseum, the Packers compiled a 13-2 record, losing only to San Francisco, 21-20, and Minnesota, 20-17, before running off five consecutive victories that included a 34-27 conquest of Dallas in the league title game.

The Chiefs were tied once, by Boston, 27-27, and beaten twice, by Buffalo, 29-14, and Oakland, 34-13, on their way to a 12-2-1 record that included a 31-7 playoff decision over Buffalo.

Television rights to the battle of titans were granted to the Columbia Broadcasting System, with 365 outlets, and the National Broadcasting Company, with 225. Estimates of the number of television viewers ranged up from 60 million.

One-minute TV commercials sold for $75,000 on the NBC network and $85,000 on CBS.

As befitted America's newest hit show, pre-game hoopla was plentiful. Bands blared, baton twirlers twirled, choral groups chorused, Al Hirt trumpeted and, just before kickoff, 4,000 pigeons were released from the floor of the stadium.

McGee gave the pigeons a quick goodbye, then returned to the bench for an afternoon of quiet reverie that lasted only until he heard Lombardi bark, "Get in the game."

Dowler, leading an end sweep by Elijah Pitts, injured his shoulder while trying to block linebacker E. J. Holub and was through for the day. McGee was on his way to headlines.

Within moments, Packers quarterback Bart Starr completed a six-play, 80-yard drive with a pass to McGee that covered the final 37 yards. The pass was a little behind McGee, but he caught the football in his right hand over safetyman Willie Mitchell and found clear sailing to the goal line.

"I think Bart intentionally threw the ball behind me so Mitchell couldn't cut across and intercept it," said Max. "When the ball stuck I almost fainted. I expected to open my left hand and find a silver dollar."

The Chiefs tied the score in the second quarter when Len Dawson passed seven yards to Curtis McClinton, culminating a six-play, 66-yard march, and Mike Mercer's conversion matched one by Don Chandler earlier.

Again Starr brought the Pack back. Brushing off an illegal procedure that wiped out a 64-yard touchdown pass to Carroll Dale, Starr used only 11 more plays to cross the goal line, Jim Taylor rushing the final 14 yards.

Mercer's 31-yard field goal made the score 14-10 at halftime and even so astute an observer as ex-NFL star Buddy Young predicted, "Old age and heat will get the Packers in the second half."

Age did, indeed, make a difference, but it

Green Bay's Max McGee hauls in a Bart Starr pass over Chiefs defensive back Willie Mitchell (left) and out runs Fred Williamson to the end zone for the first touchdown in Super Bowl history.

was the age that breeds experience which dominated the second half.

Instead of a four-man rush as in the first half, the Packers blitzed after intermission and Dawson, who had completed 11 of 15 passes for 152 yards in the first half, completed only five of 12 for 59 yards in the second.

Three times Dawson was dropped for losses and on a fourth time, trying to avoid a loss, he wobbled a pass toward the sideline that was picked off by free safety Willie Wood, who returned it 50 yards to the Kansas City 5-yard line, from where Pitts, following tackle Bob Skoronski, scampered into the end zone.

"That interception was the key play of the game," said Chiefs Coach Hank Stram. "It changed the personality of the game. Before that play, and touchdown, we were doing the things we wanted to do. You don't like to think that one play can make that much difference, but it seemed to. From that point, we had to play catch-up. We had to pass more and do things we don't normally do best. They knew we had to pass."

"That interception gave them the momentum," added Dawson. "They took the ball and shoved it down our throats."

Wood, recalling that Lombardi had chided the Packers defense at halftime for less-than-perfect play, declared, "We got the message. I was stung by the pass Otis Taylor caught against me in the first half, so I was sort of waiting for a chance. We were all anticipating a sideline pass on a third-and-five situation."

The run, said Wood, was the biggest (and perhaps the longest) of his career. "This has to be my biggest thrill in Los Angeles," said the former University of Southern California star, who was prevented from going all the way on his runback when tackled by another ex-Trojan, Mike Garrett.

Before the third quarter ended, the Packers scored a fourth touchdown, this one on a 56-yard march in which Starr hit McGee three times, for 11, 16 and 13 yards, the last good for six points.

For his day's work, McGee caught seven passes for 138 yards and two TDs. A healthy Dowler scarcely could have done better than the champion curfew breaker.

The Packers' last touchdown culminated an 80-yard drive in the fourth period, with Pitts plunging over from one yard out.

As the Green Bay offense accelerated in the second half, the Packers' defense improved upon its first-half performance. The Chiefs penetrated Packers territory only once in the second half, for four yards. Garrett, the losers' heavy-duty ball carrier, was held to 17 yards in six tries.

In completing 16 of 23 passes for 250 yards, Starr probed Mitchell's area repeatedly. The harried cornerback gained some measure of revenge late in the game when he intercepted a Starr pass, the first against the precision passer after 173 non-interceptions.

Starr was particularly devastating on third-down conversions, succeeding 10 of 13 times. The report card looked like this:

FIRST QUARTER

Third and 1 at Green Bay 34—Jim Taylor hit left tackle for three yards and first down.

Third and 20 at Green Bay 27—Starr, back to pass, was rushed by Jerry Mays and Bobby Bell, losing five yards.

Third and 3 on Kansas City 37—Starr passed complete to McGee on 19 and McGee carried it in for 37-yard touchdown.

SECOND QUARTER

Third and 7 on Green Bay 23—Starr's pass intended for Dale was juggled and fell incomplete. Penalty on Packers for illegal procedure was declined.

Third and 6 on Green Bay 41—Starr passed complete to McGee for 10 yards and first down.

Third and 10 on Kansas City 42—Starr passed complete to Dale for 15 yards and first down.

Third and 5 on Kansas City 38—Starr passed complete to tight end Marv Fleming for 11 yards and first down.

Third and 7 on Kansas City 24—Starr passed complete to Pitts for 10 yards and first down.

THIRD QUARTER

Third and 3 on Green Bay 44—Taylor swept left end for only two yards.

Third and 1 on Kansas City 47—Taylor hit left tackle for four yards and first down.

Third and 11 on Kansas City 44—Starr passed complete to McGee for 16 yards and first down.

Third and 3 on Kansas City 21—Taylor skirted left end for eight yards and first down.

FOURTH QUARTER

Third and 3 on Kansas City 11—Pitts hit right tackle for five yards and first down.

As Lombardi cuddled the game ball and basked in the glow of a fourth championship in six years, he said: "The Chiefs are a good team, but we wore 'em down. We had a little more personnel than they did.

"And what can you say about a guy like McGee. This was one of his finest games. And Bart called a perfect game, but that's not new."

Chuck Hurston, a second-year defensive end for the Chiefs, also was impressed with

The Chiefs did have their moments, like when Buck Buchanan (86) and E. J. Holub caught up with Bart Starr.

Starr. Holding his fingers one inch apart, he exclaimed: "Once I was this close to him and he threw a touchdown pass as if he didn't even notice me. I've never seen anything like it."

Stram said: "It took exceptional timing between Starr and his receivers. It took great pass blocking, and they got it. We had a variety of coverages, but the Packers were able to isolate our corner man, one on one."

If there was one sad note among the Packers, each $15,000 richer compared to $7,500 for each of the Chiefs, it lay in the fact that Hornung, who had contributed so handsomely to the creation of the Green Bay dynasty, was the only Packer who failed to see action, the result of a pinched nerve in his neck that had not healed. "He could have played," said Lombardi, "had we really needed him. His neck still bothers him and we weren't inclined to take a chance. I asked him in the fourth quarter if he wanted to get in and he said no."

Statistics of First Super Bowl
GREEN BAY 35, KANSAS CITY 10

Los Angeles Coliseum, January 15, 1967
Attendance: 61,946

KANSAS CITY	Offense	GREEN BAY
Chris Burford	LE	Carroll Dale
Jim Tyrer	LT	Bob Skoronski
Ed Budde	LG	Fuzzy Thurston
Wayne Frazier	C	Bill Curry
Curt Merz	RG	Jerry Kramer
Dave Hill	RT	Forrest Gregg
Fred Arbanas	RE	Marv Fleming
Len Dawson	QB	Bart Starr
Otis Taylor	FL	Boyd Dowler
Mike Garrett	HB	Elijah Pitts
Curtis McClinton	FB	Jim Taylor

	Defense	
Jerry Mays	LE	Willie Davis
Andy Rice	LT	Ron Kostelnik
Buck Buchanan	RT	Henry Jordan
Chuck Hurston	RE	Lionel Aldridge
Bobby Bell	LLB	Dave Robinson
Sherrill Headrick	MLB	Ray Nitschke
E. J. Holub	RLB	Lee Roy Caffey
Fred Williamson	LHB	Herb Adderley
Willie Mitchell	RHB	Bob Jeter
Bobby Hunt	LS	Tom Brown
Johnny Robinson	RS	Willie Wood

— SUBSTITUTIONS —

KANSAS CITY–Offense: Receivers–Frank Pitts, Reg Carolan. Linemen–Tony DiMidio, Dennis Biodrowski, Jon Gilliam, Al Reynolds. Backs–Bert Coan, Pete Beathard, Gene Thomas. Kickers–Jerrel Wilson, Mike Mercer. Defense: Linebackers–Walt Corey, Smokey Stover, Bud Abell. Lineman–Aaron Brown. Backs–Emmitt Thomas, Fletcher Smith, Bobby Ply.

GREEN BAY–Offense: Receivers–Max McGee, Bob Long, Bill Anderson, Red Mack. Linemen–Steve Wright, Gale Gillingham, Ken Bowman. Backs–Zeke Bratkowski, Donny Anderson, Jim Grabowski, Phil Vandersea. Kicker–Don Chandler. Defense: Linebacker–Tommy Crutcher. Linemen–Bob Brown, Jim Weatherwax. Backs–Doug Hart, Dave Hathcock.

— SCORE BY PERIODS —

Kansas City Chiefs (AFL)	0	10	0	0 – 10
Green Bay Packers (NFL)	7	7	14	7 – 35

— SCORING —

Green Bay–McGee 37 pass from Starr (Chandler kick).
Kansas City–McClinton 7 pass from Dawson (Mercer kick).
Green Bay–Taylor 14 run (Chandler kick).
Kansas City–Field goal Mercer 31.
Green Bay–Pitts 5 run (Chandler kick).
Green Bay–McGee 13 pass from Starr (Chandler kick).
Green Bay–Pitts 1 run (Chandler kick).

— TEAM STATISTICS —

	Kansas City	Green Bay
Total First Downs	17	21
First Downs Rushing	4	10
First Downs Passing	12	11

	Kansas City	Green Bay
First Downs Penalty	1	0
Rushes	19	33
Yards Gained Rushing (net)	72	130
Average Yards Per Rush	3.8	3.9
Passes Attempted	32	24
Passes Completed	17	16
Had Intercepted	1	1
Times Tackled Attemp. Pass..	6	3
Yards Lost Attempting Pass...	61	22
Yards Gained Passing (net)	167	228
Total Net Yardage	239	358
Punts	7	4
Average Distance Punts	45.3	43.3
Punt Returns	3	4
Punt Return Yardage	19	23
Kickoff Returns	6	3
Kickoff Return Yardage	130	65
Yards Interception Returned..	0	50
Fumbles	1	1
Opponents' Fum. Recovered ..	0	0
Penalties	4	4
Yards Penalized	26	40
Total Points Scored	10	35
Touchdowns	1	5
Touchdowns Running	0	3
Touchdowns Passing	1	2
Extra Points	1	5
Field Goals Attempted	2	0
Field Goals Made	1	0
Total Offensive Plays	64	64
Avg. Gain Per Offensive Play	3.7	5.6

INDIVIDUAL STATISTICS
— RUSHING —

Kansas City	Atts.	Yds.	Lg.	TD
Dawson	3	24	15	0
Garrett	6	17	9	0
McClinton	6	16	6	0
Beathard	1	14	14	0
Coan	3	1	3	0

Green Bay	Atts.	Yds.	Lg.	TD
J. Taylor	16	53	14	1
Pitts	11	45	12	2
Anderson	4	30	13	0
Grabowski	2	2	2	0

— PASSING —

Kansas City	Atts.	Comp.	Yds.	Int.	TD
Dawson	27	16	211	1	1
Beathard	5	1	17	0	0

Green Bay	Atts.	Comp.	Yds.	Int.	TD
Starr	23	16	250	1	2
Bratkowski	1	0	0	0	0

— RECEIVING —

Kansas City	No.	Yds.	Lg.	TD
Burford	4	67	27	0
O. Taylor	4	57	31	0
Garrett	3	28	17	0
McClinton	2	34	27	1
Arbanas	2	30	18	0
Carolan	1	7	7	0
Coan	1	5	5	0

Packers Coach Vince Lombardi accepts the first Super Bowl trophy from NFL Commissioner Pete Rozelle. The trophy later was renamed the Lombardi Trophy.

— RECEIVING —

Green Bay	No.	Yds.	Lg.	TD
McGee	7	138	37	2
Dale	4	59	25	0
Pitts	2	32	22	0
Fleming	2	22	11	0
J. Taylor	1	−1	−1	0

— INTERCEPTIONS —

Kansas City	No.	Yds.	Lg.	TD
Mitchell	1	0	0	0

Green Bay	No.	Yds.	Lg.	TD
Wood	1	50	50	0

— PUNTING —

Kansas City	No.	Avg.	Lg.
Wilson	7	45.3	61

Green Bay	No.	Avg.	Lg.
Chandler	3	43.3	50
D. Anderson	1	43.0	43

— PUNT RETURNS —

Kansas City	No.	FC	Yds.	Lg.
Garrett	2	0	17	9
E. Thomas	1	0	2	2

Green Bay	No.	FC	Yds.	Lg.
D. Anderson	3	0	25	15
Wood	1	1	−2	−2

— KICKOFF RETURNS —

Kansas City	No.	Yds.	Lg.
Coan	4	87	31
Garrett	2	43	23

Green Bay	No.	Yds.	Lg.
Adderley	2	40	20
D. Anderson	1	25	25

— FIELD GOALS —

Kansas City	Att.	Made
Mercer	2	1

Green Bay—None.

— FUMBLES —

Kansas City	No.	Own Rec.	Opp. Rec.	TD
McClinton	1	1	0	0

Green Bay	No.	Own Rec.	Opp. Rec.	TD
Grabowski	1	0	0	0
Skoronski	0	1	0	0

— SCORING —

Kansas City	TD	PAT	FG	Pts.
McClinton	1	0	0	6
Mercer	0	1	1	4

Green Bay	TD	PAT	FG	Pts.
McGee	2	0	0	12
Pitts	2	0	0	12
J. Taylor	1	0	0	6
Chandler	0	5	0	5

Coach Vince Lombardi had plenty to smile about as the Packers wrapped up another Super win.

Super Bowl II

Lombardi's Starr Rises

January 14, 1968

He was of Italian extraction, but his coaching style and philosophy were pure Prussian.

Adjectives described him as cruel but wonderful, demanding but dedicated, brilliant but terrible.

When he arrived at Green Bay to assume the reins of the Packers in 1959, he announced that the foremost problem was to defeat defeatism. Of his players he demanded total dedication . . . to the team, to himself and to winning.

"You're going to work as never before," the onetime lineman who was part of Fordham's "Seven Blocks of Granite" promised the players, inspiring Green Bay defensive tackle Henry Jordan to make his unforgettable observation: "He treated us all alike—like dogs."

Another Jordan gem: "When he tells you to sit down, you don't look for a chair."

Vince Lombardi had served five years (1949-53) as assistant coach at the United States Military Academy under Earl Blaik, who subscribed to General Douglas MacArthur's principle, "There is no substitute for victory," which Lombardi also followed to the fullest degree.

How quickly Lombardi translated that principle into success was demonstrated by the fact that within two years he had produced a championship team at Green Bay.

In the days preceding Super Bowl II, played in Miami's Orange Bowl on January 14, 1968, rumors circulated that Lombardi would resign as coach and general manager of the Packers after the championship contest.

Reluctant to discuss the report, Lombardi said only: "It's too early for such a decision. I'm going to give Vince Lombardi a real hard look."

Green Bay players, however, were convinced that the forthcoming engagement with the Oakland Raiders would assume all the aspects of a farewell party for the coach who had won more than 75 percent of his games and five National Football League championships in his last seven years in the league's smallest city.

"About Thursday," remembered quarterback Bart Starr, "Coach Lombardi came to our meeting dressed in a business suit, which was not at all characteristic of him. He was going to a reception and told us how much he had enjoyed coaching us and how proud he was of us. We all had lumps in our throats. He was proud of us, but we were just as proud of him."

The mutual pride was not the type that frequently precedes a fall and on Super Sunday, a clear afternoon, before a sellout crowd of 75,546, the proud Packers saw their coach off in a style befitting a royal monarch with a 33-14 victory over Oakland.

Favored by 14 points, the NFL champions forged their triumph from the matchless play selection of Starr, the faultless place-kicking of Don Chandler and the superb team-wide execution born of the dedication demanded by Lombardi.

Concluding his Green Bay career eight years after he took over a club that had finished 1-10-1 in 1958, Lombardi had observed that "to beat Oakland, you have to pick on the entire defense, not just on one man. They don't stand and take the play. They jump around and try to confuse you."

Attempts to confuse did not succeed against the well-disciplined Packers, who converted Raider mistakes into points. The Packers also took away the Raiders' most potent weapon, the power sweep.

"Anytime you take away a team's big play," noted Lombardi, "you force them into trying something they're not quite as effective in doing."

Packers guard Jerry Kramer also did something he was not accustomed to doing.

"When I got up this morning," he related, "I put my undershorts on backward. And for the first time in my career I missed a team meeting. I was having breakfast with my wife when I suddenly realized that I was supposed to be somewhere else."

Reflecting on the season, defensive end Willie Davis remarked, "I guess this season will be remembered as the one in which we won when we had to. A 9-4-1 record isn't great but nobody can say that we didn't have it when we needed it."

A 17-17 tie with Detroit opened the Green Bay schedule after which the Packers suffered losses to Minnesota, Baltimore, Los Angeles and Pittsburgh before whipping the Los Angeles Rams, 28-7, and the Dallas Cowboys, 21-17, to sew up the NFL championship.

The Raiders dropped only one regular-season game, bowing to the New York Jets, 17-14, before reeling off 11 consecutive victories that included a 40-7 trouncing of Houston in the American Football League title game.

The NFL Department of Pre-Game Entertainment presented a tableau consisting of two 30-foot-high figures, one representing a Packer, the other a Raider and each snorting smoke from three-foot nostrils.

As the two figures approached midfield in a symbolic meeting of champions, an impression arose that this moment marked the last time that these two teams, on this day, would be equally matched.

That suspicion proved eminently correct.

The Green Bay practice of calling heads on the coin toss paid off for the second consecutive Super Bowl and the Packers did not squander the opportunity to get on the board.

Moving, as one wire service reported, "with the effervescence of overworked morticians," the Packers marched from their own 34-yard line to the Raiders 32, from where, at 9:53, Chandler kicked a 39-yard field goal.

In the second quarter, an 11-play drive terminated with another Chandler field goal, this one from 20 yards away.

Featured in the drive were short runs by Ben Wilson and a 14-yard scamper by Starr in which he took a hit from defensive end Ben Davidson, then bounced free to find daylight.

Starr lost little time in mounting a third scoring foray, connecting on a 62-yard pass to Boyd Dowler, who sprinted deep down the middle, slipped by the defensive backs and romped all the way untouched.

The thrust demonstrated one of the Raiders' major concerns before the game.

"We've never before played such big receivers as Boyd Dowler (6-5) and Carroll Dale (6-4)," cornerback Kent McCloughan had noted. "They are like tight ends but with better speed. If our two outside defensive backs can hold them, we have a chance."

Free safety Howie Williams, formerly with the Packers, gave this version of the scoring play:

"We were in man-for-man coverage. I thought Kent would stay with Dowler, but he released him for me."

Added left corner McCloughan: "It was a mix-up. The way the coverage is supposed to go, if it's a play fake I go for the back and Howie goes for the receiver."

"McCloughan was playing me tight," reported Dowler. "He bumped me and I ran through him. When I got by him there was nobody left to stop me."

Trailing, 13-0, the Raiders struck back on a nine-play, 79-yard drive that included three passes by quarterback Daryle Lamonica and running yardage by Pete Banaszak and Hewritt Dixon. The payoff play was a 23-yard pass to wide receiver Bill Miller, who slipped behind safetyman Tom Brown and brushed the flag as he scored.

"I was supposed to take Miller deep," explained Brown, "but I played him too soft. Dave Robinson (left linebacker) dropped back with him as far as he could, and I should have taken him, but I didn't."

Oakland's defense, designated the "Eleven Angry Men," held the Packers on the following series of downs, forcing Donny Anderson to punt to the Raiders 45, where Rodger Bird fumbled a fair catch with 23 seconds remaining in the half.

Two long passes missed their mark before Starr completed a 12-yarder to Anderson, setting up a 43-yard Chandler field goal that gave the Packers a 16-7 cushion at intermission.

The Green Bay lead soared to 16 points early in the third period on a typical Bart Starr maneuver.

On third-and-one on his own 40, Starr faked to fullback Wilson and passed to Max McGee. The aging receiver, who left no record of his previous night's behavior as he had when he starred in the Super Bowl the preceding year, caught the football behind Bird for a 35-yard gain to the Oakland 25.

"One of the safeties woke up late," quipped Max. "He started over and Bart saw him and adjusted to throw away from him. That's why I had to turn around to catch the ball."

McGee, in his final game as a Packer, played only because of an injury to Dowler. Shades of Super Bowl I!

Green Bay Coach
Vince Lombardi
gets the traditional
post-victory ride
from Jerry Kramer
and other Packers
while Oakland
Coach John Rauch
and quarterback
Daryle Lamonica
can only bemoan
their fate.

Green Bay quarterback Bart Starr gets plenty of time to throw the football . . .

"I really didn't expect to play," said the 12-year veteran. "I kiddingly told Boyd to get hurt. Damned if he didn't. Damned if I didn't."

From Oakland's 25, Starr's short passes advanced the ball to the 2 and Anderson bulled across. Chandler's conversion gave the Packers a 23-7 advantage.

Before the period had ended, Chandler kicked a fourth field goal, from 31 yards, that struck the crossbar and flopped over.

Both teams scored touchdowns in the fourth quarter, the Packers striking first when cornerback Herb Adderley intercepted a Lamonica pass and streaked 60 yards to the goal line as defensive tackles Henry Jordan and Ron Kostelnik cleared the way with crunching blocks.

"I didn't see Adderley," moaned Lamonica. "We all knew you can't make mistakes against Green Bay and I made the big one. I got good protection, but they took away our outside running game and their secondary was going deep to take away the long pass. We got behind and then had to play their kind of football."

Adderley added, "We designed the defense to take away their runs. We wanted to make them put the ball in the air." On his interception, he said: "Lamonica was trying to hit Fred Biletnikoff on a slant-in. I played the ball and cut in front of him . . . it was no gamble."

To the question "Would you rather play in Los Angeles (site of the 1967 Super Bowl) or Miami?" Adderley replied: "I'll play anywhere for $15,000," the winning players' reward. Each Oakland player received $7,500.

When Chandler kicked the extra point, giving Green Bay its final total of 33 points, he raised his personal total for the day to 15, one more than Oakland was able to score in the game that, as in the case of McGee, marked Chandler's farewell to professional football.

The Raiders' final score came on another 23-yard pass from Lamonica to Miller after an aerial to Banaszak had consumed 41 yards.

Chandler, who had kicked 19 field goals in 26 attempts and 39 extra points in as many tries during the regular season, was one of the more exuberant Packers in the postgame celebration.

"Thankfully," he said, "this game wraps up the best season of my career. I could go on kicking for years, but I just don't have it in my heart anymore. . . . It's time to get to know my kids, build up my business and plant family roots."

Then, remembering the coach who was packing it in also as a Packer, the 33-year-old Oklahoman said, "I owe my career to that man. I owe him everything."

Chandler was remembering how, as a discouraged rookie with the New York

... and wide receiver Boyd Dowler outruns Dan Conners on a 62-yard TD play.

Giants, he had tossed his playbook on assistant coach Lombardi's desk and hitched a ride to the airport, where he was overtaken and persuaded to return to the Giants' camp in 1956.

In 1965, when Chandler had fallen out of grace with the Giants, Lombardi again came to his rescue, obtaining him for the Packers, for whom he had produced 261 points.

In the voting for the game's outstanding player, Chandler's 15 points were considered of less significance than the field generalship and uncanny marksmanship of Starr, who completed 13 of 24 passes for 202 yards. Lamonica hit on 15 of 34 aerials for 208 yards. The Packers netted 322 yards, the Raiders 293.

Summing up the Packers' performance, Lombardi observed, "We didn't miss an opportunity. When we got down there, we got points. When you do that you have no complaints.

"It wasn't our best effort. All year it seemed like as soon as we got a couple of touchdowns ahead, we let up. Maybe it's the sign of a veteran team."

One factor that pleased Oakland Coach John Rauch was "that there was never any point where we gave up. We went out there with great confidence and without hysteria. Even at halftime, we felt that we'd come back just as we did so often during the season.

"I was disappointed that we couldn't run better, particularly on sweeps that have been such an important part of our game."

The Raiders gained 107 yards rushing, led by Dixon's 54 yards in 12 carries.

"Maybe we should have run right at 'em," mused Oakland center Jim Otto, who 12 years later would join adversary Adderley in the Pro Football Hall of Fame. "One reason our sweeps didn't work was because we could pull only one guard. The other had to stay back and take care of Jordan, who was so fast."

"The Packers were good and their execution was great," conceded Oakland defensive tackle Tom Keating, a surprise starter who spent the afternoon in a life-and-death struggle with Green Bay guard Gale Gillingham.

Suffering from an inflamed, pulled Achilles tendon in his right foot, Keating earned a starting berth only because of his constant harassment of his coaches.

"I was afraid to take a shot (of pain killer) in the ankle," he said afterward, "because I was afraid I might tear it without even knowing it. I didn't see any sense sitting on the bench until someone else got hurt. The foot hurts like hell now and it will hurt even more when I take off the tape."

Understandably, Keating peeled off his silver and black uniform very, very slowly.

Statistics of Second Super Bowl
GREEN BAY 33, OAKLAND 14

Orange Bowl, Miami, January 14, 1968
Attendance: 75,546

GREEN BAY	Offense	OAKLAND
Boyd Dowler	LE	Bill Miller
Bob Skoronski	LT	Bob Svihus
Gale Gillingham	LG	Gene Upshaw
Ken Bowman	C	Jim Otto
Jerry Kramer	RG	Wayne Hawkins
Forrest Gregg	RT	Harry Schuh
Marv Fleming	TE	Billy Cannon
Bart Starr	QB	Daryle Lamonica
Carroll Dale	FL	Fred Biletnikoff
Donny Anderson	RB	Pete Banaszak
Ben Wilson	RB	Hewritt Dixon

Defense

GREEN BAY		OAKLAND
Willie Davis	LE	Isaac Lassiter
Ron Kostelnik	LT	Dan Birdwell
Henry Jordan	RT	Tom Keating
Lionel Aldridge	RE	Ben Davidson
Dave Robinson	LLB	Bill Laskey
Ray Nitschke	MLB	Dan Conners
Lee Roy Caffey	RLB	Gus Otto
Herb Adderley	LHB	Kent McCloughan
Bobby Jeter	RHB	Willie Brown
Tom Brown	LS	Warren Powers
Willie Wood	RS	Howie Williams

— SUBSTITUTIONS —

GREEN BAY—Offense: Receivers—Bob Long, Max McGee, Dick Capp. Linemen—Fuzzy Thurston, Bob Hyland. Backs—Zeke Bratkowski, Travis Williams, Chuck Mercein. Kicker—Don Chandler. Defense: Linebackers—Tommy Crutcher, Jim Flanigan. Linemen—Bob Brown, Jim Weatherwax. Backs—John Rowser, Doug Hart. DNP—Jim Grabowski, Don Horn, Steve Wright.

OAKLAND—Offense: Receivers—Warren Wells, Dave Kocourek, Ken Herock. Linemen—Bob Kruse, Jim Harvey, Dan Archer. Backs—Larry Todd, Roger Hagberg. Kickers—George Blanda, Mike Eischeid. Defense: Linebackers—John Williamson, Bill Budness, Duane Benson. Linemen—Carleton Oates, Richard Sligh. Backs—Dave Grayson, Rodger Bird. DNP—Rod Sherman.

— SCORE BY PERIODS —

Green Bay Packers (NFL)	3	13	10	7 — 33
Oakland Raiders (AFL)	0	7	0	7 — 14

— SCORING —

Green Bay—Field goal Chandler 39.
Green Bay—Field goal Chandler 20.
Green Bay—Dowler 62 pass from Starr (Chandler kick).
Oakland—Miller 23 pass from Lamonica (Blanda kick).
Green Bay—Field goal Chandler 43.
Green Bay—Anderson 2 run (Chandler kick).
Green Bay—Field goal Chandler 31.
Green Bay—Adderley 60 interception (Chandler kick).
Oakland—Miller 23 pass from Lamonica (Blanda kick).

— TEAM STATISTICS —

	Green Bay	Oakland
Total First Downs	19	16
First Downs Rushing	11	5
First Downs Passing	7	10

	Green Bay	Oakland
First Downs Penalty	1	1
Rushes	41	20
Yards Gained Rushing (net)	160	107
Average Yards Per Rush	3.9	5.3
Passes Attempted	24	34
Passes Completed	13	15
Had Intercepted	0	1
Times Tackled Att. Pass	4	3
Yards Lost Attempting Pass	40	22
Yards Gained Passing (net)	162	186
Total Net Yardage	322	293
Punts	6	6
Average Distance Punts	39.0	44.0
Punt Returns	5	5
Punt Return Yardage	35	12
Kickoff Returns	3	7
Kickoff Return Yardage	49	127
Yards Interception Returned	60	0
Fumbles	0	3
Opponents' Fumbles Rec.	2	0
Total Return Yardage	160	139
Penalties	1	4
Yards Penalized	12	31
Total Points Scored	33	14
Touchdowns	3	2
Touchdowns Running	2	0
Touchdowns Passing	1	2
Extra Points	3	2
Field Goals Attempted	4	1
Field Goals Made	4	0
Total Offensive Plays	69	57
Aver. Gain Per Offensive Play	4.7	5.1

INDIVIDUAL STATISTICS
— RUSHING —

Green Bay	Atts.	Yds.	Lg.	TD
Wilson	17	62	13	0
Anderson	14	48	8	1
Williams	8	36	18	0
Starr	1	14	14	0
Mercein	1	0	0	0

Oakland	Atts.	Yds.	Lg.	TD
Dixon	12	54	14	0
Todd	2	37	32	0
Banaszak	6	16	5	0

— PASSING —

Green Bay	Atts.	Comp.	Yds.	Int.	TD
Starr	24	13	202	0	1

Oakland	Atts.	Comp.	Yds.	Int.	TD
Lamonica	34	15	208	1	2

— RECEIVING —

Green Bay	No.	Yds.	Lg.	TD
Dale	4	43	17	0
Fleming	4	35	11	0
Anderson	2	18	12	0
Dowler	2	71	62	1
McGee	1	35	35	0

Oakland	No.	Yds.	Lg.	TD
Miller	5	84	23	2
Banaszak	4	69	41	0
Biletnikoff	2	10	6	0
Cannon	2	25	15	0
Dixon	1	3	3	0
Wells	1	17	17	0

Oakland wide receiver Bill Miller scores the Raiders' second touchdown on a 23-yard pass from Daryle Lamonica.

— INTERCEPTIONS —

Green Bay	No.	Yds.	Lg.	TD
Adderley	1	60	60	1

Oakland—None.

— PUNTING —

Green Bay	No.	Avg.	Lg.
Anderson	6	39.0	48

Oakland	No.	Avg.	Lg.
Eischeid	6	44.0	55

— PUNT RETURNS —

Green Bay	No.	FC	Yds.	Lg.
Wood	5	0	35	31

Oakland	No.	FC	Yds.	Lg.
Bird	2	1	12	12

— KICKOFF RETURNS —

Green Bay	No.	Yds.	Lg.
Adderley	1	24	24
Williams	1	18	18
Crutcher	1	7	7

Oakland	No.	Yds.	Lg.
Todd	3	63	23
*Grayson	2	61	25
Hawkins	1	3	3
*Kocourek	1	0	0

*Kocourek lateraled to Grayson, who returned 11 yards.

— FIELD GOALS —

Green Bay	Att.	Made
Chandler	4	4

Oakland	Att.	Made
Blanda	1	0

— FUMBLES —

Green Bay	No.	Own Rec.	Opp. Rec.	TD
Capp	0	0	1	0
Robinson	0	0	1	0

Oakland	No.	Own Rec.	Opp. Rec.	TD
Bird	1	0	0	0
Banaszak	1	0	0	0
Wells	1	0	0	0
Williamson	0	1	0	0

— SCORING —

Green Bay	TD	PAT	FG	Pts.
Chandler	0	3	4	15
Anderson	1	0	0	6
Dowler	1	0	0	6
Adderley	1	0	0	6

Oakland	TD	PAT	FG	Pts.
Miller	2	0	0	12
Blanda	0	2	0	2

Super Bowl III

The Broadway Joe Show

January 12, 1969

Three days before the 1969 Super Bowl, incomparable Joe Namath appeared before the Miami Touchdown Club, tossed a few footballs into the audience, jested briefly and then, growing serious, announced: "The Jets will win on Sunday, I guarantee it."

Such a pronouncement was almost without precedent in American sports, especially because the speaker represented a team that was judged an 18- to 23-point underdog against the powerful Baltimore Colts, who had been beaten only once, by Cleveland, 30-20, in the 1968 regular season before defeating Minnesota, 24-14, and Cleveland, 34-0, in the NFL playoffs.

By contrast, the New York Jets lost to Buffalo, Denver and Oakland in the regular season before defeating Oakland, 27-23, for the AFL championship.

From the day he became a Jet, richer by $400,000 and a green Lincoln convertible, ex-Alabama All-America Namath gave full rein to his opinions. A night person, he was a patron of saloons and discotheques, as well known for his white llama rug in his East Side penthouse as for the white low-cut football shoes he wore among black-shod teammates.

Wherever night life existed, Joe Namath found it, brightening dialogue with his one-liners and expressing views that were always honest, if not quite conventional.

Typically brash were his opinions on the Colts in the days immediately following the two leagues' championship games.

Earl Morrall was Joe's favorite target.

Morrall, like Namath, was the Most Valuable Player in his league, but there the similarity ceased. Morrall was 34, Namath 25. A graduate of Michigan State, Morrall was as retiring as Namath was flamboyant. A crewcut, homebody sort, Morrall had

played for San Francisco, Pittsburgh, Detroit and the New York Giants before, just prior to the start of the 1968 season, he had been obtained by the Colts as insurance for perennial quarterback star Johnny Unitas.

The deal created no stir in the NFL, but it had far-reaching effects on the fortunes of the Colts. In the last pre-season game, Unitas, in the act of passing, was knocked down, suffering a serious tear on the inside of his right elbow. His throwing motion was impaired, as was the velocity on his passes. He was handicapped throughout the season.

Coach Don Shula was acquainted with Morrall's talents. Shula had been an assistant coach on the Detroit staff when Morrall quarterbacked the Lions, and he was not reluctant to make him Baltimore's starter. Under Morrall's leadership, the Colts failed to score at least 20 points in only one game, a 16-3 victory over Green Bay.

In Namath's eyes, Morrall was not the equal of five quarterbacks in the AFL. In addition to himself, said Joe, quarterbacks superior to Morrall were Daryle Lamonica of Oakland, John Hadl of San Diego, Bob Griese of Miami and, yes, even Babe Parilli, Namath's own aging backup.

"I study quarterbacks," said Namath. "I assure you the Colts have never had to play against quarterbacks like we have in the AFL."

Indignation among the Colts was instant. "How can Namath rap Earl?" wondered Shula. "Earl is No. 1 in the NFL. He's thrown all those touchdown passes (28). He's thrown for a great percentage of completions without using those dinky flare passes. We're proud of him.

"But I guess Namath can say whatever he pleases."

Morrall refused to take the Namath bait. "He's got his newspaper space and that's

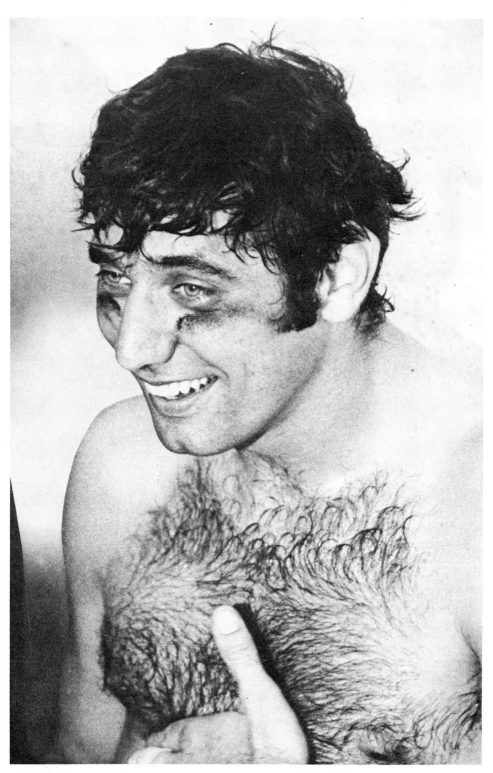

Broadway Joe Namath gives his best prediction-come-true smile.

Joe Namath and a friend he refused to identify relax in a pre-Super Bowl get-together.

what he wants," said Morrall. "A lot of players have opinions on other players that would send writers running for their typewriters if they expressed 'em.

"But players keep these opinions to themselves—at least that's the way it has been. Maybe Namath represents the new breed of athletes, the kind of athletes the coming generation wants. . . . I hope not.

"When you've been playing football for 12 years, as I have, you eventually come up against virtually every type of individual from the quiet introvert to the swinger and loudmouth. Some guys never get their name in anything but the program. Other guys would do anything or say anything to get their names in the paper. Neither characteristic, as far as I'm concerned, has any

effect on what happens on the football field."

"I have a lot of respect for Joe," added Baltimore defensive end Bubba Smith. "He's an exceptional quarterback. But a football player who's real good doesn't have to talk. The Green Bay Packers were real champions. They never talked. They never had to. That's the way I visualize all champions, dignified and humble.

"All this Namath talk isn't going to fire us up."

On that point, Namath agreed, saying, "If they need newspaper clippings to fire them up, they're in trouble."

Even when he wasn't being interviewed, Namath was making news. Shortly after he registered in room 534, the Governor's

Suite, at the Galt Ocean Mile Hotel in Fort Lauderdale, the Jets' training base, Joe was visited by two FBI agents.

Namath's life had been threatened in New York, the agents explained, and they had reason to believe that the culprit had transferred to the Miami area. They wanted to be sure that there was no exterior point of concealment that might shield a would-be sharpshooter.

On Sunday night, January 5, Namath and his roommate, safety Jim Hudson, stopped at a restaurant for a steak and a few glasses of cheer.

They were recognized by Lou Michaels, defensive end of the Colts and a younger brother of Walt Michaels, an assistant coach with the Jets. Lou was accompanied by teammate Dan Sullivan. Shortly there were four occupied chairs at Namath's table.

The conversation, reportedly, followed these lines:

"Namath," said the visitor, "Lou Michaels."

Joe nodded.

"You're doing a lot of talking," continued Michaels.

"There's a lot to talk about, we're going to beat the hell out of you," Namath promised.

"Haven't you ever heard of humility?"

Silence ensued, then Namath asked:

"You still here?"

"Damn right, I'm still here. I wanna hear everything you gotta say."

"I'm gonna pick you apart."

"You're gonna find it tough throwing out of a well," Michaels assured Namath.

"My blockers will give me time."

"I never heard Johnny Unitas or Bobby Layne talk like that."

"I believe that."

"Even if we do get in trouble we'll send in Unitas, the master."

"I hope you do because that'll mean the game is too far gone."

"Suppose we kick the hell out of you," offered Michaels, "what will you do?"

"I'll sit right down in the middle of the field and cry."

When the check arrived, Namath paid it with a $100 bill.

"You guys got a ride to the hotel?" Namath asked.

"We'll grab a cab," said Michaels.

"Don't be silly, we'll drop you off," said Namath.

Back at the Colts' hotel, the Statler-Hilton, Michaels murmured to Sullivan, "He's not such a bad kid after all."

The next day's journals carried accounts of the Namath-Michaels "brawl," with complete details.

Broadway Joe . . . Hail to the king.

Commented one amused Colt teammate, "Namath is the 837th guy that Michaels has challenged. If Lou had belted him he would have been about the 37th guy that Lou actually hit."

Added Hudson: "What else can you expect when two hard-headed coal miners from Pennsylvania get together?"

On Monday, January 6, Namath made news by sleeping late. It was picture day and Joe, along with Jets running backs Emerson Boozer and Matt Snell, failed to put in an appearance.

"I always sleep late in the morning," explained Joe limply when he showed up in early afternoon. "A fellow has to get his sleep."

Boozer and Snell heard the wakeup call, but, forgetting it was picture day, rolled over, they said, in the belief it was only a nuisance call.

The three were fined $50 apiece.

When defensive end Billy Ray Smith was asked for his opinion of Namath, the Colts' defensive captain said, "He hasn't seen defenses like ours in his league; our defenses are as complicated as some teams' offenses. We have 20 variations of our blitzes and five or six variations up front.

"That lets us do a lot of things. I think reading our defenses will be a new experience for the man.

"He's a good quarterback, but he's still a young man.

"When he gets a little older he'll get some humility."

George Sauer is tackled by Lenny Lyles after making one of his eight receptions that accounted for 133 yards.

Conspicuous by his silence in the midst of the week-long whoop-de-do was Wilbur (Weeb) Ewbank, the 61-year-old Jets coach to whom championship games were nothing new. Weeb was assistant to Paul Brown when the Cleveland Browns were annual title contenders. Also, he had guided the Colts to NFL championships in 1958 and '59. He had been released by the Colts in 1962 after finishing with a .500 record.

The preliminaries out of the way, the Colts, the Jets, the nation and the National Broadcasting Company, which paid $2.5 million for air rights, were set for the January 12 encounter between the new breed, the kids from across the tracks, who were free with their opinions, and the clean-cut wholesome fellows who practiced all of life's virtues.

Before the first fan was permitted through the gates, however, the bomb squad of the Miami Beach Police Department checked out the Orange Bowl, searching for a bomb that, according to a telephone caller, had been placed there.

Finding none, authorities gave the all-clear signal and the first of the 75,377 spectators filed into the huge horseshoe for the 3:05 p.m. (EST) kickoff.

Crowd-scanners recognized celebrities such as Richard Nixon and Spiro Agnew, newly-elected President and Vice-President; Senator Edward Kennedy and his father, Joseph P. Kennedy, former ambassador to England; comedians Bob Hope and Jackie Gleason, and astronauts Frank Borman, Bill Anders and Jim Lovell.

In preparing the Jets for the game, Ewbank had cautioned the players "not to get fancy. Let's do the things we can do best and do them well. Other AFL teams got licked in this game because they lost their poise. That happened to us once during the season (a 43-32 loss to Oakland) and we can't let it happen again."

Shula's message to the Colts was: "Don't wait for them to lose it. We've got to win it ourselves."

Shula pointed out to his players that "Namath is a great passer. He has played with the same set of receivers over a period of four years. Namath is the best pure passer in the game. He is intense on the field and prepares himself well, as is evidenced by

Jets Coach Weeb Ewbank kept a low profile during the pre-game hoopla.

the way he executes. He has a lot of (Johnny) Unitas in him. He is convinced of his own ability, and will stay in the pocket until the last possible second. He has been criticized for his lifestyle but as far as I'm concerned his personal life is his own as long as he meets the rules.''

When referee Tommy Bell signaled the team captains to the middle of the field for the pregame coin toss, Namath was warming up on the sidelines. Joe had stiff-legged his way onto the team bus for the ride to the Orange Bowl and was still trying to work out the last kinks. Several days earlier, when asked about his weak knees, he had wisecracked: "I'm not bad off, some folks don't even have knees.''

To replace Namath for the coin toss, the Jets sent in cornerback Johnny Sample, a former Colt still bitter over what he considered injustices perpetrated against him by the entire NFL.

When Sample arrived at midfield, he found old buddy Lenny Lyles, also a cornerback, representing the Colts. Calling the coin toss correctly, Sample said the Jets would receive, then needled Lyles, "The first one goes to us.''

The game had scarcely commenced before spectators recognized that they were watching a contest quite dissimilar to the first two Super Bowls. The Jets were not playing in awe of the Colts, as Kansas City and Oakland had played in awe of Green Bay.

The Jets took the game to the Colts, running into the teeth of Baltimore's veteran defense. On his third carry in the first series, Snell crashed into Rick Volk, sending the safetyman to the sideline groggy and rubber-legged.

Four minutes after gaining possession of the football, the Jets were forced to punt and the Colts took over on their own 27-yard line.

A screen pass to tight end John Mackey gained 19 yards. Tom Matte gained 10 around right end. Jerry Hill, Matte and Hill again picked up 10 yards for a third first down. A 15-yard pass to tight end Tom Mitchell gave Baltimore a first-and-10 at the New York 19.

When flanker Willie Richardson dropped a pass, another toss was overthrown and Morrall was sacked by middle linebacker Al Atkinson, the Colts went for a field goal, but Michaels' kick into the tricky winds blowing out of the end zone was wide to the right from the 27-yard line.

Late in the first quarter, pinned deep in their own territory, the Jets moved to a first down on their 17, where split end George Sauer Jr. fumbled and the Colts recovered on the 12.

Two plays consumed only six yards and on a third-and-four, Morrall fired down the middle where Atkinson flicked the ball, which bounced off Mitchell's shoulder and high into the air.

In the end zone, cornerback Randy Beverly, who had hoped that "I won't look like a clown out there,'' made a diving interception in the end zone. It was the Jets' ball on the 20.

On four consecutive plays, Snell smacked into the right side of the Colts defense, moving the ball to the Baltimore 46 as tackle Winston Hill cleared the way.

When Namath read the Colts' blitz and passed short to fullback Bill Mathis, the Jets were in enemy territory for the first time, at the 48-yard line.

Passes to Sauer for 14 and 11 yards, a two-yard burst by Boozer and a 12-yard completion to Snell carried to the 9.

Snell gained five to the right side, then smashed to the left where Winston Hill rode Michaels out of the play, Boozer erased safetyman Volk and, at the goal line, Snell bulled over middle linebacker Dennis Gaubatz. When Jim Turner converted, the Jets led, 7-0.

"That touchdown,'' wrote Larry Fox in "Broadway Joe and the Super Jets,'' "meant more than seven points, much more. The Jets had not only survived the mistake of Sauer's fumble, they had taken the ball back and rammed it under the Colts' chin straps on an 80-yard drive that took 12 plays. This is the way one football team demonstrates its superiority over another. Only one touchdown behind, the Colts and Morrall came back, trying the bomb. That's when the Jets knew they might have 'em on the run."

Once more the Colts stormed back and, with Matte eating up 58 yards on one gallop, reached the Jets 16. Again Morrall went to the air with the same calamitous results as Sample intercepted a pass intended for Richardson, blunting a Baltimore thrust that appeared certain to make points.

"Here it is, here's what you're looking for," Sample taunted Richardson, who smothered the urge to strike back.

With 43 seconds remaining in the first half, the Colts had moved to the New York 42.

Only 25 seconds showed on the scoreboard when Morrall took the snap and handed off to Matte, running to the right. Suddenly, Matte pulled up and lateraled back to Morrall. It was the ancient flea-flicker, used successfully by the Colts against Atlanta in a regular-season game.

Wide receiver Jimmy Orr was the prime target and he was standing at the 10-yard line waving frantically in an effort to attract attention. Not a single New York player was within 20 yards.

Morrall gave no heed to Orr, throwing instead in the direction of Jerry Hill on the 12-yard line, where Hudson intercepted. It was the Jets' third interception of the game.

Explaining his failure to throw to Orr, Morrall said, "As we headed for the locker room, Jimmy screamed, 'Didn't you see me? Didn't you see me?' I told him, 'No, Jimmy, I didn't.' I had to turn to the right in order to take the pass from Matte and when I looked up, Jimmy wasn't in my line of vision. Hill was, so I went to him."

Shula was perplexed himself. Walking off the field, he remarked to an aide, "Dammit, the flea-flicker is designed especially for Orr. Morrall is supposed to look for him. What in hell is happening?"

Another explanation for the Morrall-Orr misconnection, perhaps more plausible than any other, was submitted by veteran Baltimore sports journalist John Steadman. Writing in his book, "The Baltimore Colts," Steadman offered:

"No explanation was ever given for what happened. Except Morrall couldn't find Orr. It wasn't as if Jimmy had headed for the men's room or stepped out to the nearest bar for a scotch and water. It's the belief of this observer that Orr's blue jersey blended in with a marching band of musicians that was headed for the end zone to perform at the intermission. The backdrop was blue, the same color the Colts were wearing, and Morrall just couldn't pick up the primary receiver. It was almost as if he was camouflaged."

Shula's halftime speech stressed: "We're making stupid mistakes, we're stopping ourselves. You've got them believing in themselves. You've got them believing that they're better than we are."

"It really got us mad," Morrall reported. "We went out for the second half with fire pouring from our eyes."

Shula had considered turning the second-half quarterback chores over to Unitas, who was openly disappointed that he had not been given the starting assignment although conceding that he was only about 80 percent recovered from his injury.

At the final moment, however, Shula decided to give Morrall one more chance to strike a spark for the NFL champions.

When Matte fumbled on the first play from scrimmage in the second half, linebacker Ralph Baker recovered for the Jets on the Baltimore 33. Five plays later, Turner kicked a 32-yard field goal, increasing the Jets' lead to 10-0.

On the sideline, Weeb Ewbank heaved a sigh of relief. "Ten points are a helluva lot better than seven," he muttered.

Because of Matte's fumble, Shula reasoned, Morrall had not received a full-blown opportunity to exercise his talents, so Earl was still at quarterback on the Colts' next possession.

Again the chance went glimmering. One pass netted no gain, a second was overthrown and, trying to scramble, Morrall was tossed for a two-yard loss.

As Unitas warmed up for his Super Bowl baptism, the quarterback situation across the field had taken an unfavorable turn. Namath's right thumb, troublesome for two seasons, had "gone weak" and Parilli, one of the five AFL quarterbacks Namath had rated as superior to Morrall, was directing the Jets. Parilli guided the team into Baltimore territory and then spotted the football as Turner booted a 30-yard field goal. New York partisans grew more comfortable with a 13-0 cushion.

Morrall expressed no bitterness over being replaced. "If I was a coach and my team was being quarterbacked by a guy who couldn't get the ball over the goal line, I'd sure as hell do something," said Morrall, who had completed six of 17 passes for 71 yards.

The "something" that Shula did on this Sunday did not provide the answer. Unitas fared no better than Morrall and the third period ended with the Colts having run only seven plays with a net gain of 10 yards.

Two minutes into the last quarter, Turner

The Jets' Matt Snell slips from the grasp of Dennis Gaubatz and into the end zone for the Jets' second-quarter touchdown.

New York's Emerson Boozer officially meets Baltimore's Bubba Smith at the line of scrimmage.

kicked a nine-yard field goal, his third, and the Colts were now in the almost impossible situation of needing two touchdowns, two conversions and a field goal to avert one of history's most stunning upsets.

One Baltimore drive was thwarted by Beverly's interception, the cornerback's second of the game and the fourth by the Jets, but with less than four minutes remaining, Jerry Hill scored on a one-yard plunge and Michaels converted to account for the final score of 16-7.

Unitas, conqueror of countless peaks on a football field, had not been able to provide the solution that Shula had sought. On this afternoon, against a determined team led by an inspired quarterback, it is doubtful that such a miracle worker existed.

Johnny U. completed 11 of 24 passes for 110 yards, but only two of his passes traveled over 20 yards and both fell incomplete.

As the coaches met at midfield at the final gun, Ewbank said: "We got all the breaks."

"Your team played well," rejoined Shula.

In the victors' locker room, no voice rang louder than that of Johnny Sample, the ex-Colt.

"It'll take the NFL 20 years to catch up," he prophesied. "They panicked. They were so shaken up they forgot their game plan. We're the greatest team ever, better than the champion Colts of 1958 and '59 that I played on."

When Namath announced above the din that "I'm only talking to New York writers . . . they were the only ones who believed in me," Ewbank and Jets President Phil Iselin hastened to his side and dissuaded him from such a radical posture.

Recovering quickly, Broadway Joe

checked his forensic signals and quipped: "You know me, I'm a poor winner."

"This is a new era in pro football," declared Ewbank and, in truth, it was. Henceforth, the Super Bowl would rank with the World Series, the Kentucky Derby and the Indianapolis 500 as a premier event on the national sports calendar.

To Shula, the story of the game was simple. "We didn't do it and they did," he said. "We had all the opportunities, especially in the first half. We didn't make the big plays we have all season. We had a lot of dropped balls. They deserved it."

Another factor in the Colts' demise was offered by Steadman, who wrote:

"Much of the after-game second-guessing had to do with the way the Colts had prepared in the days leading up to the Super Bowl. Wives and children were invited to join the team at the Statler-Hilton Hotel . . . and the night before there was a dinner in the elegant restaurant for all to attend. Had the Colts beaten the Jets this would have been cited as the perfect way to relax a team for a major game. But the thought was introduced and unfortunately perpetuated . . . that the Colts thought they were a bunch of volunteer firemen at a beach convention. The only fault was to be found in the net result . . . they didn't win."

When the Colts returned to their Statler-Hilton headquarters they were greeted by feminine screams for a doctor. The lady was Mrs. Rick Volk, whose husband, knocked groggy early in the game and carried from the field later after a second collision, was lying on the bathroom floor in convulsions, vomiting and about to swallow his tongue.

Dr. Norman Freeman, Baltimore team physician, was close at hand and, using a ballpoint pen, freed Volk's tongue. The player was rushed to the hospital where, on regaining consciousness, he greeted his wife with, "Who won?"

Meanwhile, the Jets were enjoying victors' spoils to the fullest, starting with the $15,000 won by each player, double the amount earned by each Colt.

"Our offensive line won the game with its straight-ahead blocking," Snell informed a cheering audience.

"It was our defense that broke their back," added Boozer.

"It was execution," added assistant coach Walt Michaels, who designed the Jet defense. "And don't forget the great play of our safetymen."

"We didn't win on passing or running or defense," corrected Namath. "We beat 'em in every phase of the game. If ever there was a world champion, this is it."

Namath, completing 17 of 28 passes for

Joe Namath fires one of his 28 passes against the Colts.

208 yards, was named the game's Most Valuable Player and was presented the game ball by appreciative teammates. The ball, Joe announced to yet another wave of cheers, would be presented to the league office as a symbol of the AFL coming of age in professional football.

Savoring his finest moment, Ewbank regaled the crowd with an account of an incident that occurred prior to the game. As Shula and Colts Owner Carroll Rosenbloom strolled around the field in their customary pre-game conference, they encountered Ewbank.

"We're having a victory party at my home after the game," Rosenbloom informed Ewbank. "You know where it is. I want you and Lucy (Mrs. Ewbank) to come on over."

"Lucy and I couldn't make it," Weeb quipped. "We've got a party of our own and I'd rather be here."

As the Jets partied far into the night, a solitary policeman patrolled the Rosenbloom property. Darkness veiled the house and tent that had been erected to accommodate the party-that-never-was.

The next day, when the Jets returned to New York for a giant civic reception, it was discovered that the 21-inch sterling silver championship trophy had been left behind in the hotel vault.

No problem, somebody volunteered. The newly-won prize was placed aboard the first New York-bound jet, riding first class, presumably.

Statistics of Third Super Bowl

NEW YORK JETS 16, BALTIMORE 7

Orange Bowl, Miami, January 12, 1969
Attendance: 75,377

NEW YORK	Offense	BALTIMORE
George Sauer	LE	Jimmy Orr
Winston Hill	LT	Bob Vogel
Bob Talamini	LB	Glenn Ressler
John Schmitt	C	Bill Curry
Randy Rasmussen	RG	Dan Sullivan
Dave Herman	RT	Sam Ball
Pete Lammons	TE	John Mackey
Joe Namath	QB	Earl Morrall
Don Maynard	FL	Willie Richardson
Emerson Boozer	RB	Tom Matte
Matt Snell	RB	Jerry Hill

NEW YORK	Defense	BALTIMORE
Gerry Philbin	LE	Bubba Smith
Paul Rochester	LT	Billy Ray Smith
John Elliott	RT	Fred Miller
Verlon Biggs	RE	Ordell Braase
Ralph Baker	LLB	Mike Curtis
Al Atkinson	MLB	Dennis Gaubatz
Larry Grantham	RLB	Don Shinnick
Johnny Sample	LHB	Bob Boyd
Randy Beverly	RHB	Lenny Lyles
Jim Hudson	LS	Jerry Logan
Bill Baird	RS	Rick Volk

— SUBSTITUTIONS —

NEW YORK—Offense: Receivers—Bake Turner, Bill Rademacher, Mark Smolinski. Linemen—Jeff Richardson, Paul Crane, Sam Walton. Backs—Babe Parilli, Bill Mathis. Kickers—Jim Turner, Curly Johnson. Defense: Linebackers—John Neidert, Carl McAdams. Linemen—Steve Thompson. Backs—Earl Christy, Jim Richards, Mike D'Amato, John Dockery, Cornell Gordon.

BALTIMORE—Offense: Ray Perkins, Tom Mitchell, Alex Hawkins. Linemen—John Williams, Cornelius Johnson, Dick Szymanski. Backs—Johnny Unitas, Tim Brown, Preston Pearson, Terry Cole. Kicker—David Lee. Defense: Linebackers—Sid Williams, Ron Porter. Linemen—Lou Michaels, Roy Hilton. Backs—Charles Stukes, Ocie Austin. DNP—Jim Ward.

— SCORE BY PERIODS —

New York Jets (AFL)	0	7	6	3 – 16
Baltimore Colts (NFL)	0	0	0	7 – 7

— SCORING —

New York—Snell 4 run (Turner kick).
New York—Field goal Turner 32.
New York—Field goal Turner 30.
New York—Field goal Turner 9.
Baltimore—Hill 1 run (Michaels kick).

— TEAM STATISTICS —

	New York	Baltimore
Total First Downs	21	18
First Downs Rushing	10	7
First Downs Passing	10	9
First Downs by Penalty	1	2
Rushes	43	23
Yards Gained Rushing (net)	142	143
Average Yards per Rush	3.3	6.2
Passes Attempted	29	41

	New York	Baltimore
Passes Completed	17	17
Had Intercepted	0	4
Times Tackled Attemp. Pass..	2	0
Yards Lost Attemp. Pass	11	0
Yards Gained Passing (net)	195	181
Total Net Yardage	337	324
Punts	4	3
Average Distance Punts	38.8	44.3
Punt Returns	1	4
Punt Return Yardage	0	34
Kickoff Returns	1	4
Kickoff Return Yardage	25	105
Yards Interceptions Returned	9	0
Fumbles	1	1
Opponents' Fum. Recovered ..	1	1
Total Return Yardage	34	139
Penalties	5	3
Yards Penalized	28	23
Total Points Scored	16	7
Touchdowns	1	1
Touchdowns Running	1	1
Touchdowns Passing	0	0
Extra Points	1	1
Field Goals Attempted	5	2
Field Goals Made	3	0
Total Offensive Plays	74	64
Avg. Gain Per Offensive Play	4.6	5.1

INDIVIDUAL STATISTICS

— RUSHING —

New York	Atts.	Yds.	Lg.	TD
Snell	30	121	12	1
Boozer	10	19	8	0
Mathis	3	2	1	0

Baltimore	Atts.	Yds.	Lg.	TD
Matte	11	116	58	0
Hill	9	29	12	1
Unitas	1	0	0	0
Morrall	2	−2	0	0

— PASSING —

New York	Atts.	Comp.	Yds.	Int.	TD
Namath	28	17	206	0	0
Parilli	1	0	0	0	0

Baltimore	Atts.	Comp.	Yds.	Int.	TD
Morrall	17	6	71	3	0
Unitas	24	11	110	1	0

— RECEIVING —

New York	No.	Yds.	Lg.	TD
Sauer	8	133	39	0
Snell	4	40	14	0
Mathis	3	20	13	0
Lammons	2	13	11	0

Baltimore	No.	Yds.	Lg.	TD
Richardson	6	58	21	0
Orr	3	42	17	0
Mackey	3	35	19	0
Matte	2	30	30	0
Hill	2	1	1	0
Mitchell	1	15	15	0

Jets running back Matt Snell picks up yardage against the Colts.

— INTERCEPTIONS —

New York	No.	Yds.	Lg.	TD
Beverly	2	0	0	0
Hudson	1	9	9	0
Sample	1	0	0	0

Baltimore—None.

— PUNTING —

New York	No.	Avg.	Lg.
C. Johnson	4	38.8	39

Baltimore	No.	Avg.	Lg.
Lee	3	44.3	51

— PUNT RETURNS —

New York	No.	FC	Yds.	Lg.
Baird	1	1	0	0

Baltimore	No.	FC	Yds.	Lg.
Brown	4	0	34	21

— KICKOFF RETURNS —

New York	No.	Yds.	Lg.
Christy	1	25	25

Baltimore	No.	Yds.	Lg.
Pearson	2	59	33
Brown	2	46	25

— FIELD GOALS —

New York	Att.	Made
J. Turner	5	3

Baltimore	Att.	Made
Michaels	2	0

— FUMBLES —

New York	No.	Own Rec.	Opp. Rec.	TD
Sauer	1	0	0	0
Baker	0	0	1	0

Baltimore	No.	Own Rec.	Opp. Rec.	TD
Porter	0	0	1	0
Matte	1	0	0	0

— SCORING —

New York	TD	PAT	FG	Pts.
Snell	1	0	0	6
J. Turner	0	1	3	10

Baltimore	TD	PAT	FG	Pts.
Hill	1	0	0	6
Michaels	0	1	0	1

Kansas City quarterback Len Dawson survived this Jim Marshall sack and everything else the Vikes threw at him.

Super Bowl IV

The Survival of Len Dawson

January 11, 1970

For Len Dawson, the 1969 AFL season had consisted of misery and misfortune.

In the second game, against the Boston Patriots, he had suffered a knee injury that sidelined him for six games.

Later, his father had died and when the Kansas City Chiefs lost their final regular season game to Oakland, 10-6, a cloud of controversy swirled about the veteran quarterback because of a questionable game plan.

Harassment grew so formidable that the Dawson children were reluctant to go to school and Mrs. Dawson hesitated to mingle socially.

With it all, however, Dawson and the Chiefs had survived. After finishing second to the Raiders in the Western Division race, the Chiefs eliminated the New York Jets in the inter-divisional playoffs, 13-7, and defeated Oakland, 17-7, in the AFL championship game to qualify for their second Super Bowl appearance in four seasons.

Nothing, it seemed, could heap further grief on the Chiefs. They already had had more than their fair share.

But in the early afternoon of Tuesday, January 6, after the team had finished its noon meal at the Fontainebleau Hotel in New Orleans and as Dawson prepared to attend a quarterbacks' meeting, he was beckoned aside by Hank Stram. The news from the coach was ominous. A few hours later, the National Broadcasting Company, on its Huntley-Brinkley newscast, would report a federal investigation into sports gambling and say that Dawson and other players would be summoned to testify in Detroit.

The disclosure struck Dawson like a blind-side tackle.

Dawson's involvement, he was told, stemmed from the arrest of Donald (Dice)

QB Lenny Dawson missed six early 1969 games with a knee injury.

Dawson, who was carrying more than $400,000 as well as Lenny's telephone number.

The quarterback admitted that he had known Donald Dawson (no relation) casually for about 10 years and had received phone calls from him on several occasions, the most recent after his knee injury and the death of his father.

That evening a statement was issued by Commissioner Pete Rozelle, saying:

"It is unfortunate that any sports figures' names be mentioned loosely with an investigation of other persons, especially Len Dawson's, just prior to his playing in the world championship game. We feel the act of some individual or individuals in involving certain professional football players with this investigation by unattributable comment to news media representatives is totally irresponsible.

"More than a year ago, during the 1968 season, rumors were circulated regarding Dawson. At that time Dawson and his attorney cooperated fully with our office and Dawson volunteered to take a polygraph examination to establish his innocence in regard to the rumors. The test and our own independent examination proved to our satisfaction that the rumors were unsubstantiated. We cooperated with a federal investigative agency throughout the course of the investigation in accordance with our long-standing policy.

"While the entire matter has been under investigation by our security department for several days, we have no evidence to even consider disciplinary action against any of those publicly named."

In addition to Len Dawson those named were quarterbacks Joe Namath of the New York Jets, Karl Sweetan of the Los Angeles Rams and Bill Munson of the Detroit Lions, and tight end Pete Lammons of the Jets.

Meanwhile, in Stram's suite, the coach was in conference with Lamar Hunt, the Chiefs' owner who had founded the AFL and christened the Super Bowl; Dawson and Jim Schaaf, the team's publicity director. The purpose of the meeting was to draft a statement explaining Dawson's position in the controversy.

Eventually, a satisfactory statement was completed. The group agreed that Dawson should read the statement to the media persons assembled on another floor. "If he doesn't read it himself it will look like an admission of guilt," Schaaf contended, and the others assented.

"Okay," added Stram, "but there will be no questions. He goes in, reads the statement and leaves."

At 11 p.m., five hours after the NBC newscast, Stram and Dawson confronted the newsmen.

"Gentlemen," began Stram, "I'm sorry we've kept you waiting, Lenny has a statement to read. He will not answer questions."

In his statement, copies of which were distributed to the media, Dawson said:

"My name has been mentioned in regard to an investigation conducted by the Justice Department. I have not been contacted by any law enforcement agency or apprised of any reason why my name has been brought up. The only reason I can think of is that I have a casual acquaintance with Mr. Donald Dawson of Detroit, who I understand has been charged in the investigation. Mr. Dawson is not a relative of mine. I have known Mr. Dawson for about 10 years and have talked with him on several occasions. My only conversation with him in recent years concerned my knee injury and the death of my father. On these occasions he called me to offer his sympathy. These calls were among the many I received. Gentlemen, this is all I have to say. I have told you everything I know."

With that, Dawson retired to a room other than the one to which he was assigned, so as to avoid disturbances.

Reaction to the story among Kansas City players was hot and instant.

"We're angry as hell the story came out the way it did," snapped defensive end Jerry Mays.

"Lenny is too smart to get mixed up in something like this," said running back Mike Garrett. "To me there's nothing to it and it doesn't bother me at all."

"The club was investigated before because it was playing erratically," recalled center E.J. Holub. "We were put through the wringer pretty good. There was nothing to it then and I don't think there's anything to it now."

"You've got to believe in something and I believe in Lenny," said guard Ed Budde.

As l'affaire Dawson cooled in the following days, attention switched to the participants in Super Bowl IV, the NFL champion Minnesota Vikings and the AFL champion Chiefs.

The Vikings had lost only to the New York Giants, 24-23, in the opener, and to the Atlanta Falcons, 10-3, in the regular-season finale, while winning 12 games in between. They had allowed only 133 points while scoring 379.

The Chiefs outscored their opponents, 359 to 177 points, and had been beaten only three times, by Cincinnati, 24-19, and Oakland, 24-17 and 10-6.

The Minnesota quarterback was Joe Kapp, who had come out of the Canadian League in 1967 with the reputation of a two-

Otis Taylor (89) and tackle Dave Hill celebrate after Taylor's game-breaking touchdown catch-run.

fisted brawler.

The Vikings enjoyed telling the story of Kapp and linebacker Lonnie Warwick after the Vikings had lost a game to Green Bay in 1967.

Following an extended period drinking tequila at the bar, the two reached violent disagreement on the causes for the defeat, Kapp insisting his fumble was responsible and Warwick maintaining that the defense was at fault.

When reason could not resolve the dispute, the two adjourned to the sidewalk where Warwick's right to the eye sent Kapp sprawling on the concrete.

Finesse was not a part of Kapp's game. His passes wobbled and found their mark as if by accident. Still, he tied the NFL record with seven touchdown passes in a 52-14 rout of Baltimore, the Vikes' first victory in 1969.

Kapp welcomed contact. In the words of Coach Bud Grant: "Other quarterbacks run out of bounds. Kapp turns upfield and looks for a tackle to run into."

In the Vikings' 51-3 rout of Cleveland, Kapp barreled into Jim Houston, knocking the linebacker out.

It was Kapp who had coined the Vikes' slogan for the 1969 season: "40 for 60," meaning 40 players giving their all for the full 60 minutes. "Such inspirations come along once in a lifetime, they're no great thing," said Kapp, minimizing his contribution.

The Chiefs had the highest regard for Kapp, the former California All-America who had chosen the Canadian Football League over the Washington Redskins, who had picked him 18th in the 1959 NFL draft. He was signed as a free agent by Minnesota

A Chiefs assistant coach tries to restrain a perplexed Hank Stram.

in 1967.

"I respect him as much as any guy I've ever played against," said Jerry Mays. "He is a sorry passer and really not a great quarterback, but he's a great leader and a real fireball. I hated to play against him.

"You felt his presence no matter where he was, on the sidelines or on the field. He'd look at you and challenge you with his eyes. When I think of him, I think of his eyes."

"There's not another guy like him," asserted K.C. linebacker Jim Lynch. "He's such a threat as a passer and a runner he puts pressure not only on the pass rush but on the linebackers and secondary as well."

To all this, Kapp replied, "When you're on the field, you have to use every tool you have. I can't afford to be cautious. I prefer to pass and give the ball to the backs to run, but if a play breaks down and I have to run, yes, I enjoy running. I don't think I've called my own number 10 times this season and those have only been sneaks. The job of a quarterback is to pass and I'm a passer."

In contrast to the reckless, gambling Kapp, Dawson represented coolness and calculating conservatism.

Running into defenders was not a part of his game plan.

The onetime Purdue All-America who failed to distinguish himself with Pittsburgh and Cleveland of the NFL was sized up by one observer in this manner: "He keeps a lot to himself. He doesn't show a lot of emotion. He keeps his cool."

"Although his passes have guided the Chiefs to the AFL championship," wrote Dave Anderson in the New York Times, "Dawson's aloof manner has contributed to his relatively insignificant niche among pro football's leading quarterbacks. He doesn't possess the flair of Joe Namath or Joe Kapp or even the somewhat silent stature of Johnny Unitas or Bart Starr."

"But during his eight AFL seasons Dawson has thrown 192 touchdown passes, the most of any pro quarterback during that span.

"His manner can be as tough as his mechanical style. He was asked once why he chose to throw a pass on a critical third-and-one situation.

" 'I knew it would work,' he said.

"When he was an All-America at Purdue, an assistant coach wished him good luck on the sidelines.

" 'Luck won't win the game,' he said.

"When he was being recruited by Purdue after an outstanding schoolboy career at Alliance, O., the basketball coach attempted to entice him by saying that Len 'might be a big help' in that sport as well.

" 'You don't know that,' said Dawson. 'You've never seen me play.'

"And when he stopped smoking, someone asked him how he was able to do it so easily.

" 'I just wanted to,' he said."

With the gambling specter in recession, Hank Stram was able to concentrate on the Vikings. The Chiefs had met the Vikes in a preseason game, but now Stram was studying Minnesota game films, trying to spot a weakness that he might exploit to the advantage of the Chiefs, who had been established as 13-point underdogs.

The more he watched the movies, the more curious Stram grew over one aspect of the Vikings' defense. Why, he wondered, with Minnesota cornerbacks playing deep, did other clubs throw the short pass so sparingly?

Further analysis revealed that the Browns and Rams had employed such tactics in playoff games, but hard-charging ends Jim Marshall and Carl Eller had forced quarterbacks into hurried passes that were either deflected or intercepted. The strategy was quickly abandoned.

"Why not," mused Stram, "double-team the ends so they can't interfere with the passer, and then pass short?"

Accordingly, tight end Fred Arbanas and tackle Dave Hill were assigned the job of containing Eller while left tackle Jim Tyrer and a running back were assigned to Marshall.

Bud Grant was not so fortunate in formulating a game plan. "It's hard to plan for a team when you've only seen them on three films," he noted. "We've got nine years of Bart Starr on film. All we know about the Chiefs is that their style is similar to that of the Dallas Cowboys."

Three days before the January 11 engagement in Tulane Stadium, a wire service story out of New Orleans reported:

"Outside the Fontainebleau Hotel where the Kansas City Chiefs are lodged, there is a large fountain against a backdrop of palm trees. But today the water in the fountain was frozen and the palms were almost blue.

"The temperature is expected to drop to 24 degrees tonight matching last night's reading, a record low for January 7 here and the coldest night in seven years. The Weather Bureau has issued the following advice: 'Protect your water pipes and your tender vegetation.' "

As the day of the game drew near, offerings of Super Bowl tickets appeared more frequently in the classified sections of New Orleans dailies.

One ad offered a paint job on a pick-up truck in exchange for two tickets.

A shotgun was worth two tickets to another ducat-holder, who announced that a motor bike would be worth another pair.

Still another offered two tickets in exchange for round-trip fare to Jamaica while a fourth ad blared:

"BARGAIN: You can have my two seats to the Super Bowl in exchange for an A.K.C. registered boxer puppy with fawn coloring."

As the mercury plunged, however, the supply of tickets mushroomed. On the night before the game, one man took a position in the lobby of a midtown hotel, trying to unload ducats for $3 apiece. At a basketball game, a man strolled through the throng and gave away 24 tickets free.

A cab driver accepted two Super Bowl tickets as payment for a $5 fare. The sports editor of a Minnesota weekly was handed 50 tickets by a Vikings official with a request to peddle them. Later the newspaperman reported, "I unloaded a few of them, but it's tough, awfully tough."

But interest was still high elsewhere. Dawson received countless letters offering moral encouragement in his hour of crisis.

From his old Canadian haunts, Kapp received a telegram bearing 3,000 signatures.

"Go, go, Super Joe," it read. "You gave British Columbia its first and only Grey Cup. We know you will deliver the Super Bowl to Minnesota. We're with you all the way."

On Super Bowl Eve, while funlovers were crowding the French Quarter to gape at Ricki Corvette, 6-8 and 41-25-38, Dawson and his roommate, free safety Johnny Robinson, retired at 10:30. At midnight, Robinson was in dreamland, while Dawson contemplated the walls and what lay ahead on the following afternoon. The quarterback dozed briefly, then was awakened by cramps and nausea at 4 o'clock. He was up the rest of the night.

Before the Chiefs departed for the stadium and the 3:35 kickoff, Stram received a telephone call from Washington, D.C. "I know there is nothing to the rumors about Dawson," said President Richard Nixon. "He shouldn't be upset by them. Will you please tell him for me."

Stram promised to convey the message and then boarded the bus for Tulane Stadium, where overnight rains had made portions of the field soggy and footing a bit uncertain.

Catching sight of Bart Starr, hero of the first two Super Bowls who was on hand to conduct radio interviews, Jerry Mays introduced himself, shook hands and then quipped, "Maybe some of your poise will rub off on me."

As things developed, Mays overflowed with poise, but the same was scarcely true of other featured entertainers.

The big pre-game race between two balloons, one labeled AFL and piloted by an ersatz Indian, and the other labeled NFL and piloted by a Viking, terminated ignominiously when the NFL craft, after bobbing precariously over the field, crashed into the stands.

The NFL aerialist, an experienced hand, blamed his misadventure on an inexperienced crew that released the ropes prematurely.

"I'm hanging up in the stands and the crowd's reaction shocked me," related George Stokes of Fountain Valley, Calif. "There was no sympathy, not even laughter. The crowd was ugly. It started ripping my balloon apart, tearing at it and pulling the sign off. All I could think of was the late 1700s in France when they used to have balloon launchings and charged people to watch. Lots of times when the balloon didn't take off, the people would attack it and rip it to shreds, then go after the guy inside. But I'm saying to myself, 'This is 200 years later and this is a silly old football game. Why are these people acting this way?'

"There were several 40-foot tears in the balloon. My balloon cost $4,000 and lucky for me I was able to repair the damage myself. If I learned one thing it's never to rely on amateurs when you want a professional performance."

While Stokes cursed his luck, the AFL balloon drifted out of the stadium, a portent, Kansas City fans hoped, of what was to come on the field.

There was still one more snafu in store for the 80,988 spectators and the estimated 60 million who crowded television sets for the CBS transmission.

As Pat O'Brien recited the National Anthem to the accompaniment of Doc Severinson's trumpet, the public address system went dead. When sound was restored, spectators heard the actor recite "land of the free and the home of the brave," while the musician was in the vicinity of "the rockets' red glare."

Having dispensed with aerial mishaps and electronic failures, the Vikings and Chiefs eventually were permitted to occupy center stage.

Jan Stenerud, the Norwegian who had earned a ski scholarship to Montana State University and emerged as a soccer-style kicker, booted the opening kickoff into the end zone and the Vikings started from their own 20. The Vikes moved to the Kansas City 39, where the Chiefs, who had led the AFL in 17 of 24 defensive categories, braced, forcing a punt out of bounds on the K.C. 17.

Five plays, including two passes to wide receiver Frank Pitts, carried the Chiefs into Minnesota territory from where Stenerud booted a 48-yard field goal.

Minnesota quarterback Joe Kapp was pressured all day by the likes of Curley Culp (61).

On their second possession, the Vikings pushed to midfield and again were forced to punt, this time into the end zone.

Early in the second quarter, Stenerud kicked a 32-yard field goal to increase the Chiefs' lead to 6-0.

The Vikings' third possession was little different, only that this time the punt sailed out of bounds on the Minnesota 44. Dawson moved the Chiefs inside the 20 and Stenerud connected again, from the 25, and the AFL champions enjoyed a 9-0 cushion.

On the ensuing kickoff, Charlie West waited at the goal line for a routine return. Either a sudden gust of wind—14 mph winds were recorded out of the south—or a simple misjudgment caused West to make a sudden lunge for the ball which slipped through his hands and bounced upfield to the 19, where Remi Prudhomme fell on it for the Chiefs.

On the first play Dawson was sacked for an eight-yard loss, and yet it was not a total loss.

Dawson noted that, on the snap, tackle Alan Page had charged straight ahead. Page was ripe for a trap, concluded Dawson, who called a draw-trap on which Ed Budde cut down Page, permitting Wendell Hayes to gain 13 yards. A pass to wide receiver Otis Taylor moved the ball to the 5, from where Garrett scored through a gigantic hole created by tackle Jim Tyrer, guard Mo Moorman and tight end Arbanas. Stenerud's conversion accounted for a 16-0 halftime lead.

The Chiefs' first-half superiority was remarkable. They registered 10 first downs to only four by the Vikings, who made none by rushing. The Chiefs also had outgained their opponents, 147 yards to 95. The Vikes had crossed midfield only twice and had not advanced beyond the Chiefs' 38-yard line.

Analyzing their first-half efforts, the Chiefs found agreement on one point, the uncivilized manner in which Dawson was being assaulted by Viking defenders.

"Eller was trying to hurt Lenny," Dave

Hill, the Chiefs' 260-pound tackle, said of the Vikings' 250-pound end. "He pounced on Lenny after he had handed off one time and Eller knew he didn't have the ball. That was a cheap shot and we let him know it. Another time Page punched Lenny when he was down. That's high school stuff and I'm ashamed of them for doing it."

Meantime, on the soggy turf of the stadium, a halftime extravaganza was in progress, featuring Al Hirt, Marguerite Piazza and "The Battle of New Orleans, Part II." In this military pageant, musket-bearing individuals clad in period uniforms waged a skirmish that would have been unrecognizable to the British or their conqueror, Andy Jackson.

Battle casualties, it was announced, totaled 1,975 Britons and 13 Americans.

Stram's halftime lecture to the Chiefs emphasized: "When we defeated the Jets, we were two weeks away from our goal. When we defeated Oakland, we were one week away. Now we are only 30 minutes from being champions of the world. Go out there and give it everything you've got."

After the Chiefs controlled the ball for six minutes at the start of the second half, the Vikings mounted their most impressive offense of the day. Starting on their own 31, the Vikings moved to the Kansas City 4 in nine plays. Dave Osborn rammed over right tackle for the TD which, with the extra point, reduced the Minnesota deficit to nine points, 16-7.

The Vikes drew no closer. On their next possession, starting on their 18, the Chiefs moved to the K.C. 32, where Dawson faced a third-and-seven situation. A pass seemed to be the logical call, but Lenny crossed 'em up, calling a flanker reverse for the third time and, for as many times, it paid off as Pitts gained a first down by inches.

Although the flanker reverse had been in the Chiefs' playbook throughout the season, it was not in the films sent to the Vikings.

A 15-yard penalty for roughing Dawson set the Vikes back to their 46. When the Vikings blitzed a safetyman and linebacker, Dawson passed for six yards to Otis Taylor in the right flat. At that point things started to happen. Twisting and charging, Taylor broke from the grasp of cornerback Earsell Mackbee at the 40-yard line and headed toward strong safety Karl Kassulke at the 10. But the safetyman was no match for the 215-pound wide receiver, who stormed into the end zone. When Stenerud converted, his 11th point of the game, the Chiefs again enjoyed a 16-point advantage.

On his touchdown play, Taylor remembered, "I got hit on the left side and spun out. Then I hit the last guy downfield with my hand. I always try to punish a pass defender just as he does me. I wanted to score that touchdown because I remembered how Minnesota came back to beat the Rams and I felt we needed to continue to keep scoring today."

"I didn't know they had the safety blitz on until I saw Paul Krause coming," confessed Dawson. "If it had been a pocket pass or a play-action, I would have been hit for a loss. I was just lucky I could get the ball away quickly."

Taylor's touchdown was scored with 1:22 remaining in the third quarter, but the Vikings were unable to capitalize on any of their three remaining possessions. Twice they were halted by interceptions, by linebacker Willie Lanier and Johnny Robinson. Subsequently, Kapp was tackled hard by defensive end Aaron Brown while back to pass and left the game, his arm hanging limp at his side. Gary Cuozzo replaced him. Cuozzo also was charged with an interception, on his fourth play, concluding the Vikings' offensive activities for the afternoon.

As time was running out, Buck Buchanan, the 6-5, 276-pound defensive tackle of the Chiefs, sidled up to Pat O'Brien.

"Pat, I'm Buck Buchanan," beamed the super Chief.

"I know," responded the actor.

"How about getting a picture with you?" asked Buck. "You know, just one for the Gipper."

The laugh came easy for O'Brien, who had portrayed Notre Dame football Coach Knute Rockne in a 1940 movie, "Knute Rockne, All-American." In that film, Rockne delivers the immortal "win one for the Gipper" speech, inspiring the Irish to do their best in memory of the late fullback George Gipp.

In the Chiefs' genteel clubhouse celebration, Dawson critiqued the victory. "I don't think the victory vindicated anything," said the quarterback. "Unfortunately, the gambling report put a great deal of stress and strain on me and more so on my family. But I asked the Good Lord to give me the strength and courage to play my best and I asked Him to let the sun shine on my teammates today.

"No, the gambling thing didn't give me any extra incentive. How could it? I approached this game as a big game, as an opportunity to be the best. You don't need any outside motivation."

Later, Dawson received a phone call from the White House in which President Nixon said, "The world looks up to pro football players for courage."

"Thank you, Mr. President," replied the game's Most Valuable Player. "We try to exemplify the best in professional football. I

Chiefs safety Johnny Robinson helped stop the Vikes with an interception.

appreciate it, Mr. President, but it wasn't me, it was the whole team that did it."

The six-minute conversation, a money-minded observer estimated, cost the American taxpayers $2.68 at Sunday rates.

Because of his injury, Kapp was unable to conduct a conventional post-game interview with the media, but relayed some impressions through an intermediary.

"The Kansas City defensive line resembled a redwood forest," said Kapp. "I don't remember that one individual stood out—they were all very active. They took the running game away from us. We went into the game wanting to run the ball, and they were able to take it all away with great defensive play. We couldn't come up with the big play when we wanted to. That's what got us here, but we couldn't do it today."

Added Coach Bud Grant: "Maybe we could play better tomorrow, but today we played as well as we could.

"I can't say that Kansas City is the toughest team we've played all year, but production-wise and point-wise, they outplayed us the toughest."

"We made a batch of mistakes," added Kassulke, "more mistakes today than we made in 23 other games."

One representative of the AFL, remembering that the Chiefs had finished second in the Western Division, quipped: "Imagine what one of our first-place teams would have won by!"

Hours later, when Stram entered the Chiefs' midtown party room, he was greeted by a round of cheers and hoisted onto strong shoulders for a victory parade. Owner Hunt, a teetotaler, raised a glass of champagne with the others, toasting the club that as of this date would move with other AFC clubs into the NFL family. The AFL passed from the scene . . . departing in regal splendor.

The demise of the AFL inspired Arthur Daley, sports columnist for the New York Times, to write:

" 'Not many people realize,' said a smiling Billy Sullivan, president of the Boston Patriots, 'the extra measure of satisfaction that all American Football League owners get when one of our teams beats the Minnesota Vikings in the Super Bowl.

" 'It was great for us a year ago, of course, when the Jets beat the Colts, but there wasn't the same undercurrent that was running against the Vikings, the same deep feelings.

" 'To put it in proper perspective, I'll have to backtrack 10 years, to when we were organized as an eight-team league, and the eighth team was the Minnesota Vikings. A few days earlier, though, the Vikes had jumped to the National Football League and our dinner meeting was on the somewhat tense side when we had a confrontation with Max Winter, the president of the Vikes.

" 'We all were upset, but nobody more than Harry Wismer of the New York Titans. You know Wismer—mercurial, flighty and explosive. At the sight of Winter, Wismer really exploded. He even got a little sacrilegious.

" ' "Max, when I see you at the supper table," Harry shouted, "I can't help but think how admirably you fill the role of Judas."

" 'They almost had a fistfight. But after the AFL lost the Vikings we filled in the gap at the last minute with Oakland. At our first meeting with Wayne Valley, the president of the Raiders, he described our desperate situation best.

" ' "Gentlemen," he said, "welcome to the Foolish Club." ' "

In truth, the AFL had been a joke league at the beginning, but a decade had erased a heap of hostility. Two successive Super Bowl victories had gone far toward supplanting the sword with the olive branch.

Statistics of Fourth Super Bowl

KANSAS CITY 23, MINNESOTA 7

Tulane Stadium, New Orleans, La., January 11, 1970
Attendance 80,562

MINNESOTA	Offense	KANSAS CITY
Gene Washington....	WR	.... Frank Pitts
Grady Alderman.....	LT	..............Jim Tyrer
Jim Vellone...........	LG	..............Ed Budde
Mick Tingelhoff......	C	.............E. J. Holub
Milt Sunde..............	RG	.........Mo Moorman
Ron Yary	RT	.... Dave Hill
John Beasley..........	TE	........Fred Arbanas
John Henderson......	WR	.... Otis Taylor
Joe Kapp	QB	...........Len Dawson
Dave Osborn	RB	.........Mike Garrett
Bill Brown..............	RB	...... Robert Holmes

	Defense	
Carl Eller...............	LE	.........Jerry Mays
Gary Larsen...........	LT	............Curley Culp
Alan Page	RT	...... Buck Buchanan
Jim Marshall..........	RE	.... Aaron Brown
Roy Winston...........	LLB	.... Bobby Bell
Lonnie Warwick	MLB	.........Willie Lanier
Wally Hilgenberg....	RLB	.... Jim Lynch
Earsell Mackbee.....	LCB	.........Jim Marsalis
Ed Sharockman......	RCB	.....Emmitt Thomas
Karl Kassulke	LS	.... Jim Kearney
Paul Krause	RS	....Johnny Robinson

— SUBSTITUTIONS —

MINNESOTA–Offense: Receivers–Bob Grim, Kent Kramer. Linemen–Steve Smith, Ed White. Backs–Gary Cuozzo, Bob Lee, Clint Jones, Bill Harris, Oscar Reed, Jim Lindsey. Kicker–Fred Cox. Defense: Linebackers–Dale Hackbart, Mike McGill, Jim Hargrove. Lineman–Paul Dickson. Back–Charlie West. DNP–Doug Davis, Mike Reilly.

KANSAS CITY–Offense: Receivers–Gloster Richardson, Curtis McClinton. Linemen–George Daney, Remi Prudhomme. Backs–Mike Livingston, Warren McVea, Wendell Hayes, Ed Podolak. Kickers–Jerrel Wilson, Jan Stenerud. Defense: Linebacker–Bob Stein. Linemen–Gene Trosch, Ed Lothamer, Chuck Hurston. Backs–Goldie Sellers, Willie Mitchell, Ceasar Belser. DNP–Tom Flores.

— SCORE BY PERIODS —

Minnesota Vikings (NFL)	0	0	7	0 –	7
Kansas City Chiefs (AFL)	3	13	7	0 –	23

— SCORING —

Kansas City–Field goal Stenerud 48.
Kansas City–Field goal Stenerud 32.
Kansas City–Field goal Stenerud 25.
Kansas City–Garrett 5 run (Stenerud kick).
Minnesota–Osborn 4 run (Cox kick).
Kansas City–Taylor 46 pass from Dawson (Stenerud kick).

— TEAM STATISTICS —

	Minnesota	Kan. City
Total First Downs.................	13	18
First Downs Rushing	2	8
First Downs Passing.............	10	7
First Downs by Penalty	1	3
Rushes...............................	19	42
Yards Gained Rushing (net)...	67	151
Average Yards Per Rush	3.5	3.6
Passes Attempted.................	28	17
Passes Completed.................	17	12

	Minnesota	Kan. City
Had Intercepted.....................	3	1
Times Tackled Attemp. Pass..	3	3
Yards Lost Attempting Pass...	27	20
Yards Gained Passing (net) ...	172	122
Total Net Yardage	239	273
Punts	3	4
Average Distance Punts.........	37.0	48.5
Punt Returns........................	2	1
Punt Return Yardage.............	18	0
Kickoff Returns.....................	4	2
Kickoff Return Yardage........	79	36
Yards Interceptions Returned	0	24
Fumbles...............................	3	0
Opponents' Fum. Recovered ..	0	2
Total Return Yardage...........	97	79
Penalties.............................	6	4
Yards Penalized	67	47
Total Points Scored	7	23
Touchdowns.........................	1	2
Touchdowns Running.............	1	1
Touchdowns Passing..............	0	1
Extra Points.........................	1	2
Field Goals Attempted...........	1	3
Field Goals Made..................	0	3
Total Offensive Plays............	50	62
Avg. Gain per Offensive Play .	4.8	4.4

INDIVIDUAL STATISTICS

— RUSHING —

Minnesota	Atts.	Yds.	Lg.	TD
Brown..........................	6	26	10	0
Reed	4	17	15	0
Osborn	7	15	4	1
Kapp	2	9	7	0

Kansas City	Atts.	Yds.	Lg.	TD
Garrett	11	39	6	1
Pitts	3	37	19	0
Hayes	8	31	13	0
McVea	12	26	9	0
Dawson	3	11	11	0
Holmes	5	7	7	0

— PASSING —

Minnesota	Atts.	Comp.	Yds.	Int.	TD
Kapp.....................	25	16	183	2	0
Cuozzo	3	1	16	1	0

Kansas City	Atts.	Comp.	Yds.	Int.	TD
Dawson	17	12	142	1	1

— RECEIVING —

Minnesota	No.	Yds.	Lg.	TD
Henderson.....................	7	111	28	0
Brown..........................	3	11	10	0
Beasley........................	2	41	26	0
Reed	2	16	12	0
Osborn	2	11	10	0
Washington	1	9	9	0

Kansas City	No.	Yds.	Lg.	TD
Taylor...........................	6	81	46	1
Pitts	3	33	20	0
Garrett	2	25	17	0
Hayes	1	3	3	0

Kansas City quarterback Len Dawson hands off to back Wendell Hayes (38).

— INTERCEPTIONS —

Minnesota	No.	Yds.	Lg.	TD
Krause	1	0	0	0

Kansas City	No.	Yds.	Lg.	TD
Lanier	1	9	9	0
Robinson	1	9	9	0
Thomas	1	6	6	0

— PUNTING —

Minnesota	No.	Avg.	Lg.
Lee	3	37.0	50

Kansas City	No.	Avg.	Lg.
Wilson	4	48.5	59

— PUNT RETURNS —

Minnesota	No.	FC	Yds.	Lg.
West	2	0	18	0

Kansas City	No.	FC	Yds.	Lg.
Garrett	1	0	0	0

— KICKOFF RETURNS —

Minnesota	No.	Yds.	Lg.
West	3	46	0
Jones	1	33	

Kansas City	No.	Yds.	Lg.
Hayes	2	36	0

— FIELD GOALS —

Minnesota	Att.	Made
Cox	1	0

Kansas City	Att.	Made
Stenerud	3	3

— FUMBLES —

Minnesota	No.	Own Rec.	Opp. Rec.	TD
Henderson	1	0	0	0
West	1	0	0	0
Kapp	1	0	0	0
Vellone	0	1	0	0

Kansas City	No.	Own Rec.	Opp. Rec.	TD
Robinson	0	0	1	0
Prudhomme	0	0	1	0

— SCORING —

Minnesota	TD	PAT	FG	Pts.
Osborn	1	0	0	6
Cox	0	1	0	1

Kansas City	TD	PAT	FG	Pts.
Stenerud	0	2	3	11
Garrett	1	0	0	6
Taylor	1	0	0	6

Jim O'Brien's third field goal prompted a Super Celebration.

Super Bowl V

The Colts Get Revenge

January 17, 1971

The sting of defeat in Super Bowl III was still with the Baltimore Colts when they arrived in Miami in January, 1971, to begin preparations for Super Bowl V.

To linebacker Mike Curtis, the old wounds from the ignominious upset by the New York Jets in 1969 remained raw and painful.

"No one knows the despair, the abject humiliation we felt that day," said the player known as The Animal. "The 1968 Baltimore Colts, a perfect football machine that crushed every opponent except one in a tough schedule. . . . The Colts, the first National Football League team to lose a Super Bowl.

"I felt great anger inside me that day. Those damn Jets, for one thing, were holding as if they were never going to hold again."

Quarterback Earl Morrall conceded that he had "tried to shrug off the defeat, but I can't. I keep thinking about it and I still get flashbacks, remembering all the bad things and the turning points. I've replayed in my mind that whole game over and over again. The interceptions, the flea-flicker, the whole mess."

Tight end John Mackey remembered "sitting around in the clubhouse at halftime two years ago, and how bad it was. How unprepared we were. And, funny thing, I remember that the night before the game was the only time my wife stayed with me before a game. No, I'm not blaming the loss on her—it's just something I remember, that's all."

If cohabitation was a mistake in the 1969 game, Colts management would not commit the same blunder this year. Players were quartered at the Miami Lakes Country Club, a short distance from their practice field at Biscayne College. Wives and

Colts linebacker Mike Curtis, alias The Animal, made the big interception.

children were to arrive a day before the game and be lodged elsewhere.

There were other changes, too, since the Colts' last visit to Miami. Owner Carroll Rosenbloom, like Art Rooney in Pittsburgh and Art Modell in Cleveland, had accepted $3 million to transfer his club into the American Football Conference of the restructured NFL.

In addition, Don Shula had succumbed to the blandishments of Joe Robbie and was now coach of the Miami Dolphins. In his stead was Don McCafferty, described by one observer "as warm as a pot-bellied stove" while Shula had been "a whistling tea kettle." To the Colts players, McCafferty was referred to fondly as "Easy Rider."

Recalling the Colts' NFL championships in 1958 and '59 and the misfortune that had dogged them in the 1960s, John Steadman wrote in "The Baltimore Colts":

"But 1970, happily, turned it all around. The kicks that were off-line suddenly began to go their way, measurements that came up an inch short were now long enough. It was a year the Colts learned the breaks of football do eventually even up. The opener in San Diego against the Chargers found rookie Jim O'Brien kicking three field goals, the last one with 56 seconds remaining, to give the Colts a 16-14 win. This set the tenor of the season, close victories. The Colts didn't look impressive, but they were winning and that's what counted.

"During the '60s they were often awesome, but awfully unlucky. It was as if all those disappointments were going to even out in one year. The Colts qualified for the Super Bowl with late rallies and narrow victories during the season. They won over the Chargers by two points, the Oilers by four, the Packers by three, the Bears by one. It was almost as if it had been pre-ordained this was to be Baltimore's year."

By comparison, the Colts' Super Bowl opponents, the Dallas Cowboys, had appeared less than title aspirants early in the season. Wide receiver Bob Hayes had been benched for failure to measure up to the performance level expected by Coach Tom Landry.

Fullback Calvin Hill suffered a leg injury and was replaced by Duane Thomas. A wire service story alleged wide use of drugs on the squad, split end Lance Rentzel was found guilty on a morals charge and the quarterback situation resembled a merry-go-round between Craig Morton and Roger Staubach. Most everybody had written the Cowboys off as a legitimate title threat.

After nine games the Cowboys owned a 5-4 record. One of their defeats had been to Minnesota, 54-3, and two to St. Louis, 20-7 and 38-0.

After the second St. Louis fiasco, which had been viewed nationally on Monday night television, ex-Dallas quarterback Don Meredith, now an ABC sportscaster, remarked: "I never thought I'd see a Cowboy team lay down like that. It was obvious there was no leadership out there."

While one headline screamed "Cowboys

Are Through," Landry assumed full responsibility, saying, "It was embarrassing to all of us. You guys really didn't want to win. It was the worst performance I've ever seen."

"Everybody was down on us—friends, the media, coaches," remembered linebacker Lee Roy Jordan. "All we had was ourselves. So we pulled together. We didn't have anybody else."

The Cowboys pulled together so effectively that they won the last five games on their schedule. The defense, inspired by cornerback Herb Adderley, veteran of Green Bay's two Super Bowl championships, played 23 consecutive quarters without allowing a touchdown.

While Baltimore, 11-2-1 in the regular season, eliminated Cincinnati, 17-0, and Oakland, 27-17, in the AFC playoffs, Dallas was beating Detroit, 5-0, and San Francisco, 17-10.

When Morton was asked what had converted the Cowboys from nondescripts into conference champions, he replied: "The Cleveland game (a 6-2 victory). We had a way of going under against those guys when something went against us. In the Cleveland game, when Hayes dropped a punt for a safety, we began to get together. Before, we caved in with a bad break. But everyone sort of said, 'That's okay, we'll get it back, Bobby.' And we did, and we won and we kept on winning. I really can't explain why. We just did, that's all."

Part of the explanation lay in the emergence of Thomas as a running back. Hill, healthy once more, was unable to regain his old starting berth.

Landry's decision to entrust the quarterback chores to Morton was another factor.

"I had to either start calling plays for Morton or go with Staubach," explained Landry.

Because Morton had undergone shoulder surgery the previous winter and still was experiencing arm problems, the Cowboys de-emphasized the pass in the latter portion of the season in favor of a running game.

"In the playoffs we didn't have much of a passing game, because of Craig's arm problems," said Landry. "When we needed to pass we just dropped it off short. We did not try to go deep. We felt that our defense could hold anybody."

When the Cowboys arrived at their Fort Lauderdale camp site, one of their major concerns was disappearing rapidly. Morton was regaining his voice after a week of silence.

Morton lost his voice the day after the conference championship game. Several days of rest had effected a cure.

"I called more audibles against San Francisco than in any other game in my life,"

It was that kind of a day for the Cowboys. Lee Roy Jordan lets out a yell (above) after letting an interception get away and Larry Cole suffers (left) after Jim O'Brien's winning field goal.

explained the former University of California All-America. "I expect Baltimore will move around so much that I'll have to change a lot of plays at the scrimmage line again."

As the teams completed their preparations for the January 16 encounter at the Orange Bowl, an occasional laugh broke into the daily drudgery.

When Bob Asher, rookie defensive tackle from Vanderbilt, was asked his reaction to the crush of media persons at the Dallas camp, he replied, "I've never seen so many newspapermen in my life. Tell you the truth, I'm getting tired of answering the same question over and over."

Questions like what, he was asked.

"What's your name," said Asher straight-faced.

With a sellout guaranteed for the 80,577-seat Orange Bowl Stadium, Miami attorney Ellis Rubin filed suit in circuit court to force the NFL to lift the local television blackout. Rubin charged that since local tax money was being used to stage the game, the 2.5 million TV owners deserved the chance to watch the game.

Twenty-four hours before the game, State Circuit Judge Arthur Franza declared that he had no authority to issue an injunction although, he said, the blackout violated federal antitrust laws.

Calling the blackout "a transgression and a usurpation of the airwaves and the people who own them," Judge Franza said he would applaud a decision by Pete Rozelle to remove the blackout, but the commissioner held firm, asserting that such action would set a dangerous precedent.

"In the history of professional football there has never been a championship game televised locally," said Rozelle. "I think that's one of the reasons they continue to be sellouts."

The Cowboys having been established as one-point favorites, inquisitive folks started looking for reasons. One advantage, some concluded, was in their having played 14 of 22 games (including preseason) on artificial turf like that of the Orange Bowl.

The Colts had sampled ersatz turf only three times, once in preseason and twice during the season.

Players saw no particular significance in the situation. Baltimore quarterback John Unitas explained: "A quarterback must learn to pick up his feet when he sets up to pass. I usually slide my feet along, but on this surface you can't do that."

"It moves you fast," said Hayes quaintly, "but I don't like the burns."

"After the game," quipped Curtis, "your fingernails are clean."

Unitas and his counterpart, Morton, presented contrasting backgounds and styles. Johnny U, regarded as too skinny when he applied for a scholarship at Notre Dame, and ignored completely after he was drafted by the Pittsburgh Steelers after a successful career at the University of Louisville, was 37 and had been a topflight quarterback for more than a decade.

Early in the week, William N. Wallace related this anecdote in the New York Times:

"Sid Luckman, the Hall of Fame quarterback for the Chicago Bears, spoke recently at a dinner honoring Unitas:

"Said Luckman: 'Sammy Baugh and I made an agreement a long time ago. He would always call me the greatest pro football player of all time and I would always call him the greatest. I called Sammy this morning and told him I was sorry but I had to break the agreement because I was going to a dinner to talk about a pro football player who surely was the greatest of all time, Johnny Unitas.' "

Morton, 28, was less distinguished by many degrees. Sid Gillman, veteran coach of the San Diego Chargers, said of him: "He can only improve."

In the Cowboys' playoff victories over Detroit and San Francisco, Morton completed only 11 of 40 passes. On non-passing plays he handed off and stepped aside.

Morton, somebody wrote, was the exception to the rule that every great football team must have a great quarterback.

Despite the brickbats, Morton's sense of humor never wavered. "The only thing that gave me a lift after the St. Louis game (38-0 defeat)," he wisecracked, "was when (teammate) Ralph Neely gave me a Spiro Agnew watch."

As countdown started for the 2:10 p.m. kickoff and as scalpers outside the stadium tried to peddle tickets at face value or less, those inside sat in anticipation of pre-game entertainment, wondering how it would compare with the balloon fiasco at New Orleans in 1970. The answer wasn't long in coming.

The four Air Force jets that had been invited to buzz the stadium during the National Anthem arrived two minutes after the final strains wafted out of the stadium.

But that was not the only ill-timed event of the day. In fact, it may have set a pattern that was followed closely by the Colts and Cowboys. The two teams committed 10 turnovers. Unitas was intercepted twice and his understudy, Morrall, once. The Colts also fumbled five times, losing three of them.

The Cowboys were intercepted three times, too, but lost only one fumble.

Midway through the first quarter, Dallas linebacker Chuck Howley intercepted a

The crashing helmets of Baltimore's Norm Bulaich and Dallas' Lee Roy Jordan typified Super Bowl V.

Unitas pass and returned it to the Baltimore 46-yard line. In three plays, however, the Cowboys lost 23 yards, to their own 31, and punted to Colts safetyman Ron Gardin, who fumbled on the Baltimore 9. Cliff Harris of Dallas recovered.

Three plays later, Mike Clark gave the Cowboys a 3-0 lead with a 14-yard field goal.

Later in the period, after the Cowboys moved inside the Baltimore 10 on a roughing-the-passer penalty, Morton drew a 14-yard penalty for passing to an ineligible receiver, guard Blaine Nye, and then failed to spot an eligible receiver, Thomas, unattended on the sidelines. But the drive was not a total failure because Clark kicked a 30-yard field goal early in the second quarter, giving Dallas a 6-0 lead.

On the Colts' next possession, Unitas fired a third-down pass that just nicked the fingertips of wide receiver Eddie Hinton. Cowboys cornerback Mel Renfro also leaped, and beyond him Baltimore's tight end, Mackey, did likewise.

The ball nestled in Mackey's hands and big John romped the rest of the way to complete a 75-yard touchdown play.

"Illegal pass," screamed Dallas adherents citing the rule that makes any pass touched consecutively by two offensive players illegal. Despite Renfro's protest that he had not tipped the ball, which would have made the pass illegal, officials ruled that the cornerback had fingernailed it and allowed the play to stand. The next day game films confirmed the ruling.

With a chance to give the Colts a lead, O'Brien's extra-point attempt went squarely into the chest of Mark Washington, who had slipped the block of Tom Nowatzke.

On the Colts' next offensive series, Unitas, finding no receivers open, ran with the ball and fumbled when he was tackled by Lee Roy Jordan, the Cowboys recovering on the Baltimore 28. Quickly, the Cowboys converted the break into a touchdown. A flare pass to Dan Reeves picked up 16 yards, a running play gained a few more and then Morton passed to Thomas, who went the final seven yards for a touchdown. Clark's conversion gave Dallas a 13-6 lead.

Still more disaster lay in wait for the Colts. A Unitas pass not only was picked off by Renfro, but the quarterback, tackled by George Andre, arose unsteadily clutching his ribs. He was through for the day.

When, a few minutes later, Morrall trotted onto the field with the Colts' offensive unit, few in the crowd could ignore the reverse twist to the 1969 game in which Unitas had replaced Morrall in a futile effort to arouse the faltering Colts against the Jets.

But this clearly was not 1969, Morrall demonstrated quickly. He hit Hinton for 26 yards, then Roy Jefferson for 21 and the Colts were on the Dallas 2-yard line. This was a "new" Morrall in a "new" game-style, or was it?

Three times Norm Bulaich crashed into the line and three times he was thrown back. The 1969 specter was waving from the end zone. Morrall called time out and consulted with McCafferty.

"Go for the touchdown," advised the coach, recommending a pass to tight end Tom Mitchell in the corner of the end zone. The pass fell incomplete as the halftime gun sounded.

If the crowd of 19,204 and a record national TV audience of 64 million expected a halftime show of Anita Bryant and the Southeast Missouri State College band to produce a more tidy second half, they discovered the error of their logic when Jim Duncan fumbled the second-half kickoff and Richmond Flowers recovered for Dallas on the Colts' 31.

Duncan did not have long to wait for vindication. The Cowboys drove to the 2, from where Thomas made a second-effort dive for the goal line, only to fumble into the hands of Duncan.

Credit for the fumble-induced tackle was divided between safetyman Jerry Logan and linebacker Ray May.

"I hit him," said May, "but I think Billy Ray Smith jerked the ball loose."

"If he says I jerked the ball loose, then I guess I did," said tackle Smith.

On the first play of the fourth period, Morrall, under a heavy rush by Andre, threw still another interception, this one by Chuck Howley. It was the Colts' sixth turnover of the game.

With nine minutes remaining in the game and Dallas still protecting a 13-6 lead, Morrall remembered the ill-starred flea-flicker of two years earlier. Morrall lateraled to Sam Havrilak, but when Havrilak looked to return the ball to Morrall, his view was obstructed by the 6-6, 260-pound hulk of tackle Jethro Pugh. Undeterred, the former Bucknell quarterback sized up the situation and threw in the direction of Mackey. The football never reached Mackey. Eddie Hinton got to it first, caught the football and lit out for the goal line. En route, a strange thing happened to Hinton—although maybe it wasn't so unusual, considering the way things were going for the Colts—the ball was knocked from Hinton's grasp.

"I could see the end zone and was trying to work my way there when all of a sudden someone knocked the ball from my hands," explained Hinton. The someone was Dallas safetyman Cornell Green.

As the ball bounced toward the end zone a half-dozen players followed in mad pursuit. None succeeded in overtaking it and the ball trickled out of the end zone, a Dallas touchback.

The Cowboys did not retain possession long. From his own 20, Morton tossed a pass intended for Walt Garrison. The pass was tipped by Jim Duncan and picked off by safetyman Rick Volk, who returned the ball 30 yards, to the Dallas 3. On his second crack into the line, Nowatzke plunged into the end zone and O'Brien's conversion deadlocked the score, 13-13.

Less than two minutes showed on the clock when Morton, on his own 27, passed toward Reeves, coming out of the backfield. The pass, however, was intercepted by the Colts' Curtis and returned to the Dallas 28. Now there was less than one minute remaining. Two Bulaich smashes gained three yards and Morrall called a timeout. When he returned to the field he was accompanied by O'Brien, the long-haired rookie referred to by teammates as "Lassie."

"When we were running onto the field," recounted O'Brien, "Earl told me just to kick the ball straight, that there was no wind."

No rookie ever followed a veteran's directions more faithfully. With five seconds remaining, O'Brien's 32-yard kick sailed true and the Colts had won the world championship that eluded them two years earlier.

As time expired, veteran Dallas defensive tackle Bob Lilly heaved his helmet mightily toward the opposite goal line. It may have been the Cowboys' finest aerial of the day.

In the Baltimore locker room, after Mrs. Vince Lombardi presented the championship trophy to Colts Owner Carroll Rosenbloom, the spotlight shifted to O'Brien, the free spirit who had begun his college career at the Air Force Academy.

"I hated it there," reported O'Brien. "They recruited me pretty good and what does a kid from Cincinnati know? I lasted six months. I developed ulcers and left. I still feel the ulcers kick up once in a while. But the big reason was I didn't like anyone else telling me what to do. Not that I resent authority. It's just that there was so much Mickey Mouse stuff. I guess that you can say I'm just not shaped for the military world."

O'Brien transferred his football talents to the University of Cincinnati.

"When we lined up (for the winning field goal)," related O'Brien, "the Dallas line-

Jim O'Brien . . . Three-point plan.

men were yelling at me, trying to distract me. Other teams always do that.

"Then, for a second, I remembered our practices and how Billy Ray Smith would holler at me, and I said to myself, 'This is only Billy Ray yelling.' I knew I was either going to win or lose the game for us. Some of the fellows came over to me and started talking. Tom Mitchell said, 'Don't worry about anything. Just kick it.' It felt good going off my foot. I knew it was good."

As O'Brien talked, so did Billy Ray Smith.

"It's all over now," said the 36-year-old tackle. "I just won $15,000 (each Cowboy earned $7,500). This is my last game. What can I possibly do after this, come back and have the coaches run me out?"

Wide receiver Jimmy Orr also was talking. "Billy Ray and I started together for the Rams," recalled Orr. "Then we were traded to the Steelers, and then he was traded to the Colts. . . . He told the Colts to trade for me, so he's the one who got me here. Now we're going out together just the way we came in."

Cuddling the game ball, Coach McCafferty said that, in his opinion, the turning point of the game "was the interception by Curtis that set up the winning field goal. We had a lot of bad breaks early in the game, but those fellows hung in there."

The interception, Curtis disclosed, was made in a newly installed defensive alignment. "We put it in only three weeks ago," he said. "I had a deep drop to help out the safety on the deep pattern and when Jerry Logan hit Reeves as he was catching the pass the ball popped up and I caught it."

"A back fresh out of college could have caught the pass," grumbled Reeves. "I went as high as I could, but it went through my hands.

"I don't take the blame for the loss. We lost it as a team."

The numerous turnovers, the Colts maintained, were due to the punishing tactics by both teams.

"It may have looked sloppy, but it was a great defensive game," said Logan.

"Maybe it wasn't a good game for the fans, but it was a good physical game," added Curtis.

Landry cited Thomas' goal-line fumble as the "big play" of the game. "If he had scored, they would have had a lot of catching up to do. We would have been in firm control, but he fumbled because of his second effort.

"The ball was bouncing off us instead of them. It was a tough way to lose."

Morton, who completed 12 of 26 passes for 127 yards, blamed the Dallas defeat on too many mistakes. "Their defense didn't do anything we didn't expect," he noted. "But they shut down our run, especially in the second half. And we've been a running team. I don't know what they did, maybe they changed up front."

Unitas, completing three of nine passes for 88 yards before he was injured, could have returned to action if he had been needed.

"But Morrall (7 of 15 for 147 yards) was doing such a fine job I saw no reason to make a change," said McCafferty.

When it was suggested that luck played a dominant role in the Colts' last-minute victory, offensive tackle Bob Vogel replied with a trace of heat:

"I've had luck go against me so many times I'm sick of it. I quit being proud years ago when we lost games we should have won. The way I look at it we're going to get the Super Bowl ring because we won the game this year that counted. We deserve it."

Dallas linebacker Howley, the game's most valuable player, would willingly have changed places with Vogel.

"The award is tremendous," he conceded, "but I wish it were the world championship. They go hand in hand."

Statistics of Fifth Super Bowl

BALTIMORE 16, DALLAS 13

Orange Bowl, Miami, Fla., January 17, 1971
Attendance: 79,204

BALTIMORE	Offense	DALLAS
Eddie Hinton	WR	Bob Hayes
Bob Vogel	LT	Ralph Neely
Glenn Ressler	LG	John Niland
Bill Curry	C	Dave Manders
John Williams	RG	Blaine Nye
Dan Sullivan	RT	Rayfield Wright
John Mackey	TE	Pettis Norman
Roy Jefferson	WR	Reggie Rucker
John Unitas	QB	Craig Morton
Norm Bulaich	RB	Duane Thomas
Tom Nowatzke	RB	Walt Garrison

	Defense	
Bubba Smith	LE	Larry Cole
Billy Ray Smith	LT	Jethro Pugh
Fred Miller	RT	Bob Lilly
Roy Hilton	RE	George Andrie
Ray May	LLB	Dave Edwards
Mike Curtis	MLB	Lee Roy Jordan
Ted Hendricks	RLB	Chuck Howley
Charley Stukes	LC	Herb Adderley
Jim Duncan	RC	Mel Renfro
Jerry Logan	LS	Cornell Green
Rick Volk	RS	Charley Waters

— SUBSTITUTIONS —

BALTIMORE—Offense: Receivers—Tom Mitchell, Ray Perkins. Linemen—Sam Ball, Cornelius Johnson, Tom Goode. Backs—Earl Morrall, Sam Havrilak, Jack Maitland, Jerry Hill. Kickers—Jim O'Brien, David Lee. Defense: Linebackers—Bob Grant, Robbie Nichols. Lineman—Billy Newsome. Backs—Ron Gardin, Tom Maxwell. DNP—Jimmy Orr, George Wright.

DALLAS—Offense: Receivers—Dennis Homan, Mike Ditka. Lineman—Bob Asher. Backs—Calvin Hill, Dan Reeves, Claxton Welch. Kickers—Ron Widby, Mike Clark. Defense: Linebackers—D. D. Lewis, Tom Stincic, Steve Kiner. Linemen—Pat Toomay, Ron East. Backs—Richmond Flowers, Mark Washington, Cliff Harris. DNP—Tony Liscio, Roger Staubach.

— SCORE BY PERIODS —

Baltimore Colts (AFC)	0	6	0	10 – 16	
Dallas Cowboys (NFC)	3	10	0	0 – 13	

— SCORING —

Dallas—Field goal Clark 14.
Dallas—Field goal Clark 30.
Baltimore—Mackey 75 pass from Unitas (kick blocked).
Dallas—Thomas 7 pass from Morton (Clark kick).
Baltimore—Nowatzke 2 run (O'Brien kick).
Baltimore—Field goal O'Brien 32.

— TEAM STATISTICS —

	Baltimore	Dallas
Total First Downs	14	10
First Downs Rushing	4	4
First Downs Passing	6	5
First Downs by Penalty	4	1
Rushes	31	31
Yards Gained Rushing (net)	69	102
Average Yards per Rush	2.2	3.3
Passes Attempted	25	26

	Baltimore	Dallas
Passes Completed	11	12
Had Intercepted	3	3
Times Tackled Attemp. Pass	0	2
Yards Lost Attempting Pass	0	14
Yards Gained Passing (net)	260	113
Total Net Yardage	329	215
Punts	4	9
Average Distance Punts	41.5	41.9
Punt Returns	5	3
Punt Return Yardage	12	9
Kickoff Returns	4	3
Kickoff Return Yardage	90	34
Yards Interceptions Returned	57	22
Fumbles	5	1
Opp. Fumbles Recovered	1	3
Total Return Yardage	159	65
Penalties	4	10
Yards Penalized	31	133
Total Points Scored	16	13
Touchdowns	2	1
Touchdowns Running	1	0
Touchdowns Passing	1	1
Extra Points	1	1
Field Goals Attempted	2	2
Field Goals Made	1	2
Total Offensive Plays	56	59
Avg. Gain per Offensive Play	5.9	3.6

INDIVIDUAL STATISTICS

— RUSHING —

Baltimore	Atts.	Yds.	Lg.	TD
Nowatzke	10	33	9	1
Bulaich	18	28	8	0
Unitas	1	4	4	0
Havrilak	1	3	3	0
Morrall	1	1	1	0
Dallas	Atts.	Yds.	Lg.	TD
Garrison	12	65	19	0
Thomas	18	35	7	0
Morton	1	2	2	0

— PASSING —

Baltimore	Atts.	Comp.	Yds.	Int.	TD
Unitas	9	3	88	2	1
Morrall	15	7	147	1	0
Havrilak	1	1	25	0	0
Dallas	Atts.	Comp.	Yds.	Int.	TD
Morton	26	12	127	3	1

— RECEIVING —

Baltimore	No.	Yds.	Lg.	TD
Jefferson	3	52	23	0
Mackey	2	80	75	1
Hinton	2	51	26	0
Havrilak	2	27	25	0
Nowatzke	1	45	45	0
Bulaich	1	5	5	0
Dallas	No.	Yds.	Lg.	TD
Reeves	5	46	17	0
Thomas	4	21	7	1
Garrison	2	19	14	0
Hayes	1	41	41	0

Colts fullback Tom Nowatzke gives Dallas' Herb Adderley a free ride.

— INTERCEPTIONS —

Baltimore	No.	Yds.	Lg.	TD
Volk	1	30	30	0
Logan	1	14	14	0
Curtis	1	13	13	0
Dallas	No.	Yds.	Lg.	TD
Howley	2	22	22	0
Renfro	1	0	0	0

— PUNTING —

Baltimore	No.	Avg.	Lg.
Lee	4	41.5	56
Dallas	No.	Avg.	Lg.
Widby	9	41.9	49

— PUNT RETURNS —

Baltimore	No.	FC	Yds.	Lg.
Logan	1	0	8	8
Gardin	4	3	4	2
Dallas	No.	FC	Yds.	Lg.
Hayes	3	0	9	7

— KICKOFF RETURNS —

Baltimore	No.	Yds.	Lg.
Duncan	4	90	30
Dallas	No.	Yds.	Lg.
Harris	1	18	18
Hill	1	14	14
Kiner	1	2	2

— FIELD GOALS —

Baltimore	Att.	Made
O'Brien	2	1
Dallas	Att.	Made
Clark	2	2

— FUMBLES —

Baltimore	No.	Own Rec.	Opp. Rec.	TD
Gardin	1	0	0	0
Unitas	1	0	0	0
Duncan	1	0	1	0
Hinton	1	0	0	0
Morrall	1	1	0	0
Dallas	No.	Own Rec.	Opp. Rec.	TD
Harris	0	0	1	0
Pugh	0	0	1	0
Flowers	0	0	1	0
Thomas	1	0	0	0

— SCORING —

Baltimore	TD	PAT	FG	Pts.
Mackey	1	0	0	6
Nowatzke	1	0	0	6
O'Brien	0	1	1	4
Dallas	TD	PAT	FG	Pts.
Thomas	1	0	0	6
Clark	0	1	2	7

A jubilant Tom Landry shares a sideline smile with offensive guard John Niland.

Super Bowl VI

The Silent Cowboy

January 16, 1972

When the telephone rang at 1:30 a.m. in Don Shula's Miami Lakes, Fla., home on January 3, 1972, the coach of the Miami Dolphins was watching a videotape of the American Football Conference championship game in which Miami had defeated Baltimore, 21-0.

"Must be some nut calling at this hour," mused Shula, accustomed to interruptions at unconventional hours.

"The President is calling . . . " announced the voice on the other end of the line, bringing Shula to quick attention.

Relating the conversation later, Shula noted, "The President wanted to talk about our Super Bowl game with Dallas. He said that he's a Washington Redskins fan, but that he also has an interest in the Dolphins as a part-time resident of Florida (Key Biscayne).

"Mr. Nixon alerted me that the Cowboys are a real strong team, but he told me, 'I still think you can hit (Paul) Warfield on that down-and-in pattern.' "

President Richard M. Nixon's affection for football was well known and deep-rooted, stemming from his days as an enthusiastic bench-warmer at Whittier College. As a Redskins fan, he had appeared at a practice session before a playoff game to deliver a pep talk. He also recommended to Coach George Allen a flanker reverse play that produced a 13-yard loss.

Mr. Nixon's affinity for the Dolphins failed to ruffle the Cowboys. "Actually," said Coach Tom Landry, "the President gave them a play they run every week."

Landry thought that the President's suggested play had "a real possibility" of success. "If the play succeeds, he should get a thrill out of it," said Landry. "If it's intercepted, I'll get a thrill out of it."

The Cowboys were not without support in high places. Lyndon B. Johnson, Mr. Nixon's predecessor in the White House, assured Landry by telegram, "My prayers and my presence will be with you in New Orleans, although I don't plan to send in any plays."

The Cowboys' route to their second consecutive Super Bowl was similar to their path of the previous year. With Landry calling the plays, Roger Staubach and Craig Morton alternated at quarterback for the first seven games, three of them losses.

Once Landry settled on Staubach as his field general, things improved dramatically and the Cowboys won their last eight games, including playoff victories over Minnesota, 20-12, and San Francisco, 14-3.

Their leading ball carrier was Duane Thomas, who gained 793 yards in 175 carries during a turbulent season that began when Thomas, reacting to management's refusal to tear up the last two years of his three-year contract, missed a practice and was fined.

Thomas was traded to New England, but his career with the Patriots terminated abruptly. He was returned to the Cowboys, labeled as "uncooperative."

Thomas immediately adopted a vow of silence in his relations with the news media.

When a reporter attempted to interview him, the dialogue went something like this:

Reporter—"You were great last year, Duane. You were bright, lively, funny and talkative."

Thomas—"I don't feel like being bothered now."

Reporter—"Did someone misquote you? Is that what caused you to clam up?"

Thomas—"What time is it?"

Taking that as a signal it was time to move on, the journalist took his leave.

Asked to analyze his teammate, Calvin

Hill responded: "It would be unfair to analyze Duane because I've never considered him unusual or untalkative. I have found him cordial and warm. We've even discussed history and philosophy. That's more than you usually get in a discussion with a football player, most of whom prefer to discuss games or girls. I have never considered him a loner, but close to a lot of the guys."

Staubach expressed a similar opinion of the 6-1, 205-pound running back. "Duane is quiet, but he's intelligent and bright," the quarterback said. "He knows our plays, our formations and all of his routines perfectly. Once in a while he'll goof up a pass pattern and I chew him out just like anybody else. He knows right away when he's made a mistake."

Thomas rejoined his old mates after the third game of the season and stepped into his old role without a hitch. His return occurred at a propitious time for the Cowboys because Hill injured a knee in the fourth game and missed six weeks of action.

Hill's misfortune did not compare with that of Ralph Neely, long-time Dallas offensive tackle whose leg was fractured in a motorcycle accident prior to the start of the season. Fortunately for the Cowboys, Tony Liscio, newly retired and now a real estate executive, was just a phone call away. With only two days notice, Liscio came back as though he'd never been away.

The Dolphins, in their second season under Shula, opened the schedule with a 10-10 tie with Denver, then defeated Buffalo, lost to the Jets and ran off eight consecutive victories before suffering defeats by New England and Baltimore. In the playoffs, the Dolphins defeated the Kansas City Chiefs, 27-24, in a double overtime classic that has been called the finest football game ever played, and wrapped up the conference title with a 21-0 victory over the Colts.

The Dolphins were young and wide-eyed, with 32 of their 44 players between the ages of 24 and 26. Their ground attack revolved around "Butch Cassidy and the Sundance Kid," otherwise known as Jim Kiick and Larry Csonka. The pair, somebody thought, bore resemblances to the leading characters in a currently popular movie.

"We're two of a kind," conceded Kiick. "We enjoy running over people. We like to hit. Larry really runs over people. I feel sorry for those defensive backs who have to stop him. He destroys them. I can't really run over them because of my size.

"I get as much satisfaction when Larry has a good game running with the ball as I do myself. If he's running well it means I'm blocking well. Because Larry's so big, people get the idea that he's slow, but just watch him when he runs to the outside."

Csonka's opinion on "Butch and Sundance" was: "Jim and I are of the same mold. We're just a couple of beer drinkers who enjoy a good time. Statistics come second to us. There's only one way to gauge a runner and that's by how many yards he gains. After every season I like to feel that I've gotten every inch I possibly could get.

"The fact that Dallas resembles Kansas City doesn't make me feel too good. They have those tackles, Jethro Pugh and Bob Lilly. Lilly is so quick some people say the best thing is to run right at him, that he's so quick he sometimes jumps out of his position. The team plays great defense, but Lilly's name always comes up first when we talk about Dallas. His speed and pursuit symbolizes the entire Dallas defense."

For the season, Csonka gained 1,051 yards in 195 carries, Kiick 738 yards in 162 carries.

The Miami quarterback was Bob Griese, at 27 three years younger than Staubach. The two were alike in many respects. They were products of Ohio River Towns, Griese of Evansville, Ind., Staubach of Cincinnati. Griese was named All-America in his junior year at Purdue, Staubach in his junior year at the United States Naval Academy. Both were football, baseball and basketball stars in high school, were rejected as football players at Notre Dame and were married to nurses.

One noticeable difference was in their field conduct. Staubach was perfectly willing to scramble when conditions were right, Griese was not.

The acquisition of wide receiver Warfield from Cleveland two years earlier had opened new horizons for Griese.

"Warfield changed me as a passer," Griese explained. "When he came to Miami he brought defenses with him. I had been taught not to throw into double coverage. But Warfield always gets double coverage and he showed me he could beat it. I didn't know much about Paul at the time he joined us. I thought maybe there was something physically wrong with him or that he was over the hill and that's why he was traded."

Warfield enjoyed a remarkable 1971 season, catching 43 passes for 996 yards, an average of 23.2 yards per catch, and 11 touchdowns.

Preparing for his second Super Bowl in four years, former Colts Coach Shula observed, "We have to overcome our lack of experience with aggressiveness. The important thing is how our young people react to their offense. We don't want our aggressiveness taken away by indecision."

Shula and his aides stressed to the Dolphins that through the years the Cowboys

Duane Thomas, the silent Cowboy, scores Dallas' second touchdown as Miami defenders pursue in vain.

had boasted the best running attack in pro football. Inasmuch as the Dolphins featured a crushing attack, Shula wisely determined that his running game would have to go outside, complemented by a passing attack to exploit the chief Dallas weakness.

"We designed the game plan to pass on first down because the Cowboys stack their defense against the run on first down," explained Shula.

Landry said the Dolphins "are somewhat of a mystery to us. We haven't played them and I've seen them only a couple of times on television. I know they have excellent personnel and we know Warfield for having played against him with Cleveland. He's probably the best wide receiver in the league.

"I know nothing at all about their defense except that I do know Shula and we expect a lot of the same thing as when he was coaching Baltimore.

"If we are going to run the ball we must get somebody to block Nick Buoniconti. He has freedom back there (as middle linebacker) and he's not guessing. We don't give freedom to anybody. Buoniconti is the real key to their defense. He has the ability to read plays and get to the ball."

Landry assumed a relaxed attitude toward his players and the late-hour attractions of New Orleans. During the early part of the week he imposed no curfew, feeling that the veteran players, in their second Super Bowl in as many years, could be relied upon to exercise mature judgment.

"We've been here before, we're not quite as nervous in preparation and we have more of a matter-of-fact approach," said Landry, who set a midnight curfew as Super Sunday drew near.

Recalling the evil results of his picnic atmosphere three years earlier when he coached Baltimore, Shula was all business, devoting evenings to reviewing films with his players and establishing an 11 p.m. curfew.

Dallas cornerback Herb Adderley, on his fourth Super Bowl squad in six years, expressed doubt that the Dolphins could cope with pressure on their first venture into the big show.

"I don't know if they're prepared for what's been happening all week, the interviews with the writers, everything that's concerned with the game," said the one-time Green Bay star. "Many people don't realize this, but a lot of guys are trying to

Cowboys back Walt Garrison looks for room after ripping off a 17-yard gain.

concentrate all week on what they're going to be doing during the game. Just talking to sports writers bothers some players and breaks their concentration. Whoever withstands the pressure will play good football."

While conditions were proceeding at a fairly normal pace in New Orleans, the natives were growing restless, perhaps even a bit mutinous in Miami.

Ten thousand Super Bowl tickets were scheduled to go on sale at the Orange Bowl on Friday morning, two days before the game. In accordance with universal custom before a major sports event, thousands of fans spent the previous night camped outside the stadium.

At 8 a.m. the gates opened, at 8:28 the gates closed and a mighty roar of protest filled the morning air.

Into the Dolphins' office on Biscayne Boulevard they stormed, expressing their towering rage as best they could. The fact that Owner Joe Robbie was telephoning other clubs seeking tickets for his personal use was of little solace to the insurgents. After six hours the dissidents departed, leaving behind a harvest of half-consumed edibles and snack bar debris that caused one harried receptionist to exclaim:

"At 5 o'clock I'm going out and have a nervous breakdown."

Even if the malcontents had been able to buy tickets, it is doubtful that they would have been able to obtain housing in New Orleans, where rooms were in shorter supply than game tickets. When available, a room was going for $100 a night. Rather than battle the hotel crunch, the American Society of Refrigerating and Air Conditioning Engineers postponed its convention until the following week.

A touch of acrimony was injected into the week's proceedings when former Dolphins Coach George Wilson asserted in Miami that "Joe Doakes could have taken this Miami team to the Super Bowl."

Wilson, released as Miami coach to make way for Shula, compared the Dolphin situation to that in Green Bay some years earlier.

"Ray McLean started building the Packers the year before Vince Lombardi arrived," declared Wilson. "McLean made a halfback out of Paul Hornung and developed the offensive line and made most of the moves that Lombardi got credit for.

"I brought Don (Shula) to Detroit as an assistant when I coached the Lions," reminded Wilson. "When I was unable to accept a five-year coaching contract at Baltimore, I recommended Don for the job and helped him work out the details of his three-year revolving contract. You'd think it would have been common courtesy for Don to tell me he was being offered the Dolphins' job."

Robbie, normally of an explosive temperament, remained composed when asked about Wilson's statements. "It doesn't sound like George," he said. "We've always considered George a part of the Dolphins. We always give George season tickets for himself and his family and if he wants to see the Super Bowl he can come as our guest."

Wilson did not accept the offer.

Shula also retained his cool demeanor. When he was introduced at a press conference, he quipped, "Just call me Joe Doakes."

Soberly, he continued: "I learned a lot under George Wilson, particularly in the art of handling men. There was no better psychologist in the business. If Joe Doakes could have taken this team to the Super Bowl, well and good.

"I'm very proud of what we have accomplished and I don't think I've ever stepped forward to claim any credit."

For the 81,023 who sat in 39-degree temperature at Tulane Stadium on January 16, the NFL programmed a gigantic pre-game spectacle with a military flavor.

Roger Staubach had a few downs to go with his many ups.

There were the Tyler, Tex., marching band and the famed Apache Belles, who performed to a Dixieland tempo. The Marine Corps was represented by the Silent Drill Team from Washington. The Coast Guard and the Navy sent 20 picked personnel who formed ranks as Army men and presented a 29-by-40-foot flag from the Fifth Army garrison at San Antonio.

The 81-voice Air Force Academy chorus sang the National Anthem as 20,000 balloons were released from eight spots on the field and eight F-4 Phantom jets streaked over the stadium.

When one jet peeled off in the "Missing Man" formation, spectators were reminded of missing servicemen in Vietnam.

"You've gotta give people something fantastic these days," said Bob Cochran, in charge of entertainment for the NFL.

When the teams lined up for the 2:30 p.m. kickoff, the Cowboys were rated five-point favorites.

The first break of the contest occurred on the Dolphins' second possession when Csonka, who had not fumbled previously all season (235 rushes, 13 receptions), dropped a handoff from Griese and linebacker Chuck Howley recovered for Dallas on his own 46-yard line.

"I was reading the defense before the snap," Csonka reported. "I was a little higher than usual for the handoff and I think I hit it with my knee. If I hadn't fumbled, it would have been an easy 20- or 30-yard gain. Both tackles were stunting and we got a good block on their linebacker. That play could have given us momentum, but it gave it all to Dallas instead. I was hoping the defense would stop them but the damage was already done."

"My eyes twinged in disgust," said Shula of the fumble. "The exchange was poor. What hurt was that Griese and Csonka had executed the handoff all season with their eyes practically closed. Csonka never really had full control of the ball. The timing was just a split second off. Our tightness was beginning to show."

The Cowboys did not squander the opportunity, moving downfield so that Mike Clark could kick a nine-yard field goal with 1:02 remaining in the first quarter.

Failing to penetrate the Dallas defense on the ground, Griese launched an air offensive with even more embarrassing consequences than the Csonka mishap.

On one dropback, Griese was pursued savagely by defensive tackle Lilly. Across the field they zigzagged until Lilly finally overtook the quarterback 29 yards behind the line of scrimmage. It was, maintained some, the game's finest piece of broken field running.

The Dolphins tried the Nixon play late in the period, with Warfield running diagonally across the field pursued by Mel Renfro and Cliff Harris. When the pass arrived, Renfro flicked it aside neatly and Harris quipped, "Nixon's a great strategist, isn't he?"

The Cowboys increased their lead to 10-0 late in the second quarter. With Thomas and Hill reeling off huge gains through gaping holes, the Cowboys marched 76 yards in eight plays, Staubach culminating the drive with a seven-yard pass to Lance Alworth with 1:15 remaining and Clark converting.

On the sideline, Landry was enjoying what he was seeing. His game plan was paying off. Miami's middle linebacker, Buoniconti, was reacting so quickly that Dallas blockers could shield him off, permitting Hill and Thomas to cut back against the flow of the play.

Although only 75 seconds remained before halftime, it was enough for the Dolphins to get on the scoreboard. With one eye on the clock, Griese passed the Dolphins to the 23-yard line and Garo Yepremian, the soccer-style Cypriot kicker, booted a 31-yard field goal with only four seconds to go.

As the capacity throng was being entertained by a halftime tribute to Louis Armstrong, featuring Ella Fitzgerald, Carol Channing and Al Hirt, Shula was reflecting an air of confidence in the Miami clubhouse.

"I still felt that we could come back," he said. "Our defense had controlled Staubach. We applied good pressure on him. He had trouble trying to read the coverage and variations that we were using. Our whole idea was to hold the Cowboys after the second-half kickoff and then get our offense going."

But the Dolphins were unable to measure up to Shula's expectations. Taking the second-half kickoff, the Cowboys slashed 71 yards in eight plays. Thomas gained 37 of the yards, including 23 on an end sweep, and Bob Hayes picked up 16 on a flanker reverse. Thomas ran for the last three yards.

"That drive killed us," Shula noted.

Early in the game, facing a third and medium yardage situation, Griese had tossed a flare pass to Kiick. However, in the fourth quarter, in a similar situation on his own 49-yard line, Griese attempted the stratagem again with disastrous results. Howley leaped in front of the intended receiver, intercepted the ball and took off for the Miami goal line.

When he reached the 9-yard line, Howley stumbled and fell. Three plays later Staubach passed to tight end Mike Ditka for the last touchdown of the game.

Embarrassed by his failure to go all the way, Howley said, "Imagine, nobody

touched me. I just fell. I guess I was just amazed to have three blockers in front of me and no one between them and the goal."

After 12 years of trying and failing to capture a world championship, the Cowboys were now kings of professional football. Forgotten was the frustration created by losses to Green Bay in 1966 and '67 NFL title games, losses to the Cleveland Browns in 1968 and '69 playoff games and the Super Bowl setback by Baltimore the previous year.

"This is the successful conclusion of our 12-year plan," declared Cowboys Owner Clint Murchison.

"I feel as though I've lost two years off my age. I feel like I'm 29 again," beamed Lilly.

Even Landry shed his customary stoicism. "We were all determined nobody would stop us," announced the title-winning coach. "We ran extremely well and I've always felt that if you can run on a team you can beat that team. This is especially true when you have the great defense that we have, which we proved again today."

Landry excused himself to accept a phone call. Returning to his interviewers, he was asked about the call.

"It was from President Nixon," he replied.

"What did he say?"

"He praised our offensive line."

Staubach, the game's outstanding player, also thought well of the line that permitted him time to complete 12 of 19 passes for 119 yards and opened gaping holes that contributed to an overall gain of 252 yards.

Ignoring bruised ribs, the former Naval officer pointed out that the temporary discomfort would not interfere with the championship exhilaration. "I have a long time to recover," he noted. Half in jest, he added, "I'm going to study films more than ever. But it probably will be hard to convince Coach Landry to let me call the plays after we won 10 in a row with him calling them."

The only somber moment in the Dallas locker room was supplied by Thomas, whose 95 yards in 19 carries more than doubled the combined yards of Csonka and Kiick (40 apiece).

In the company of Jim Brown, former Cleveland Browns great and now a movie actor, Thomas was asked if he was happy.

"Never said I was mad," replied the crotchety Cowboy.

The most dejected individual among the Dolphins was Buoniconti, whom the Cowboys had to neutralize if their running game was to succeed.

"A lot of our success," said Landry, "came as a result of handling Buoniconti. You either block Nick or you don't run. I

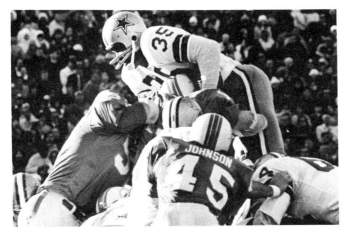

Dallas running back Calvin Hill goes over the top of the Miami defense.

was surprised with the yards we got. In the second half they came out with three men and a linebacker in a spot where we had opened holes in the first half, so we went the other way."

John Niland and Jack Manders of the Dallas offensive line did their jobs so effectively that when Buoniconti was removed from the game in the fourth quarter, he shuffled to the bench where he asked Bob Matheson, "Is the score still 10-3?" The score at the time was 24-3.

"Everything went foggy," revealed Buoniconti. "I don't remember how or when they scored.

"We weren't staying in our pursuit lanes. They just cut us off. I don't think they smashed us physically. They did a fine job of finessing us. I guess I was calling our defensive signals okay. Everything is still very hard to remember.

"I guess it didn't matter if I got zonked. The Cowboys were just great."

"We just took turns popping him," reported Niland.

"He took a terrific blow to the head," added Matheson.

Shula's greatest disappointment, the coach said, "was that we never really challenged. They completely dominated. We have a very fine football team, but we never really got untracked.

"We didn't make any positive plays that would have helped us win. Going into the game we thought only of stopping the Dallas run and that's what we were unable to do. We had good pressure on Staubach, especially early in the game, and we had his receivers covered. The run is what broke it open.

"It's unfortunate that our season had to end this way. I had hoped that there would be bigger and better things in store. The Cowboys played a near-perfect game," concluded the first coach to lose two Super Bowl games.

"Maybe I shouldn't say this because it sounds like sour grapes," offered Csonka, "but I'd rather play Dallas any day than Kansas City. The Chiefs have the best linebackers I've ever played against."

According to Dallas linebacker Dave Edwards, "The Dolphins were too young to win. Their youth kept them from being very versatile. On certain plays they ran certain formations and it was too late in the year for them to make a change. We studied every film we could get our hands on and we knew pretty well what they were going to do."

Warfield, held to four catches, only one of which—a 23-yarder—did any damage, was surprised at the double coverage he received from Cornell Green and Renfro.

"Green would just lay back and sit there waiting for the slant," he said. "I expected that once in a while, but I didn't think I'd get inside-outside coverage throughout the game."

At the height of the Cowboys' celebration, player-coach Dan Reeves spotted Tex Schramm making no particular effort to hide.

"C'mon, you're next," Reeves ordered the team's president-general manager. Schramm, suffering from the flu for a week, put up no resistance and, fully clothed, followed Reeves into the shower for his championship baptism.

After toweling off and slipping into dry clothes, Schramm received bad news. A window of his Dallas home had been jimmied, and $100 and a color television set had been stolen. Furthermore, while making a getaway in Schramm's new car, the thief had collided with another one of Schramm's cars.

Everything considered, however, it might not have been too much to pay for a world football championship.

Statistics of Sixth Super Bowl

DALLAS 24, MIAMI 3

Tulane Stadium, New Orleans, La., January 16, 1972
Attendance: 81,023

DALLAS	Offense	MIAMI
Bob Hayes	WR	Paul Warfield
Tony Liscio	LT	Doug Crusan
John Niland	LG	Bob Kuechenberg
Dave Manders	C	Bob DeMarco
Blaine Nye	RG	Larry Little
Rayfield Wright	RT	Norm Evans
Mike Ditka	TE	Marv Fleming
Lance Alworth	WR	Howard Twilley
Roger Staubach	QB	Bob Griese
Duane Thomas	RB	Jim Kiick
Walt Garrison	RB	Larry Csonka

DALLAS	Defense	MIAMI
Larry Cole	LE	Jim Riley
Jethro Pugh	LT	Manny Fernandez
Bob Lilly	RT	Bob Heinz
George Andrie	RE	Bill Stanfill
Dave Edwards	LLB	Doug Swift
Lee Roy Jordan	MLB	Nick Buoniconti
Chuck Howley	RLB	Mike Kolen
Herb Adderley	LC	Tim Foley
Mel Renfro	RC	Curtis Johnson
Cornell Green	LS	Dick Anderson
Cliff Harris	RS	Jake Scott

— SUBSTITUTIONS —

DALLAS—Offense: Receivers—Bill Truax. Lineman—John Fitzgerald. Backs—Dan Reeves, Calvin Hill, Joe Williams, Claxton Welch. Kicker—Mike Clark. Defense: Linebackers—D. D. Lewis, Tom Stincic. Linemen—Tody Smith, Bill Gregory, Pat Toomay. Backs—Isaac Thomas, Charlie Waters. Punter—Ron Widby. DNP—Gloster Richardson, Craig Morton, Forrest Gregg.

MIAMI—Offense: Receivers—Karl Noonan, Otto Stowe, Jim Mandich. Linemen—Wayne Moore, Jim Langer. Backs—Eugene Morris, Terry Cole, Hubert Ginn. Kicker—Garo Yepremian. Defense: Linebackers—Bob Matheson, Jesse Powell. Linemen—Frank Cornish, Vern Den Herder. Backs—Lloyd Mumphord, Bob Petrella. Punter—Larry Seiple. DNP—George Mira, John Richardson.

— SCORE BY PERIODS —

Dallas Cowboys (NFC)	3	7	7	7 – 24
Miami Dolphins (AFC)	0	3	0	0 – 3

— SCORING —

Dallas—Field goal Clark 9.
Dallas—Alworth 7 pass from Staubach (Clark kick).
Miami—Field goal Yepremian 31.
Dallas—D. Thomas 3 run (Clark kick).
Dallas—Ditka 7 pass from Staubach (Clark kick).

— TEAM STATISTICS —

	Dallas	Miami
Total First Downs	23	10
First Downs Rushing	15	3
First Downs Passing	8	7
First Downs by Penalty	0	0
Rushes	48	20
Yards Gained Rushing (net)	252	80
Average Yards per Rush	5.3	4.0
Passes Attempted	19	23
Passes Completed	12	12
Had Intercepted	0	1
Times Tackled Attemp. Pass	2	1
Yards Lost Attempting Pass	19	29

	Dallas	Miami
Yards Gained Passing (net)	100	105
Total Net Yardage	352	185
Punts	5	5
Average Distance Punts	37.2	40.0
Punt Returns	1	1
Punt Return Yardage	-1	21
Kickoff Returns	2	5
Kickoff Return Yardage	34	122
Yards Interception Returns	41	0
Fumbles	1	2
Opp. Fumbles Recovered	2	1
Total Return Yardage	74	143
Penalties	3	0
Yards Penalized	15	0
Total Points Scored	24	3
Touchdowns	3	0
Touchdowns Running	1	0
Touchdowns Passing	2	0
Extra Points	3	0
Field Goals Attempted	1	2
Field Goals Made	1	1
Total Offensive Plays	69	44
Avg. Gain per Offensive Play	5.1	4.2

INDIVIDUAL STATISTICS

— RUSHING —

Dallas	Atts.	Yds.	Lg.	TD
D. Thomas	19	95	23	1
Garrison	14	74	17	0
Hill	7	25	13	0
Staubach	5	18	5	0
Ditka	1	17	17	0
Hayes	1	16	16	0
Reeves	1	7	7	0
Miami	Atts.	Yds.	Lg.	TD
Csonka	9	40	12	0
Kiick	10	40	9	0
Griese	1	0	0	0

— PASSING —

Dallas	Atts.	Comp.	Yds.	Int.	TD
Staubach	19	12	119	0	2
Miami	Atts.	Comp.	Yds.	Int.	TD
Griese	23	12	134	1	0

— RECEIVING —

Dallas	No.	Yds.	Lg.	TD
D. Thomas	3	17	11	0
Alworth	2	28	21	1
Ditka	2	28	21	1
Hayes	2	23	18	0
Garrison	2	11	7	0
Hill	1	12	12	0
Miami	No.	Yds.	Lg.	TD
Warfield	4	39	23	0
Kiick	3	21	11	0
Csonka	2	18	16	0
Fleming	1	27	27	0
Twilley	1	20	20	0
Mandich	1	9	9	0

— INTERCEPTIONS —

Dallas	No.	Yds.	Lg.	TD
Howley	1	41	41	0

Miami—None.

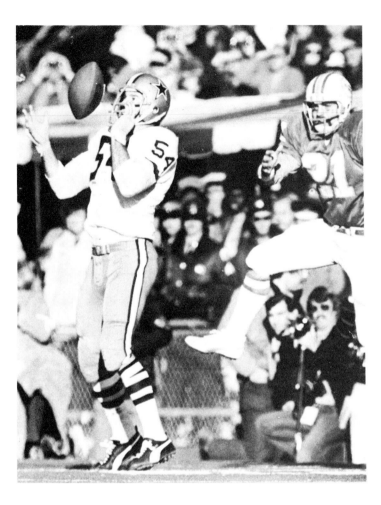

Chuck Howley picks off a Miami pass as Jim Kiick watches helplessly.

— PUNTING —

Dallas	No.	Avg.	Lg.
Widby	5	37.2	47

Miami	No.	Avg.	Lg.
Seiple	5	40.0	45

— PUNT RETURNS —

Dallas	No.	FC	Yds.	Lg.
Hayes	1	1	−1	−1
Harris	0	2	0	0

Miami	No.	FC	Yds.	Lg.
Scott	1	0	21	21

— KICKOFF RETURNS —

Dallas	No.	Yds.	Lg.
I. Thomas	1	23	23
Waters	1	11	11

Miami	No.	Yds.	Lg.
Morris	4	90	37
Ginn	1	32	32

— FIELD GOALS —

Dallas	Att.	Made
Clark	1	1

Miami	Att.	Made
Yepremian	2	1

— FUMBLES —

Dallas	No.	Own Rec.	Opp. Rec.	TD
Howley	0	0	1	0
Cole	0	0	1	0
Hill	1	0	0	0

Miami	No.	Own Rec.	Opp. Rec.	TD
Csonka	1	0	0	0
Griese	1	0	0	0
Fernandez	0	0	1	0

— SCORING —

Dallas	TD	PAT	FG	Pts.
Clark	0	3	1	6
Alworth	1	0	0	6
D. Thomas	1	0	0	6
Ditka	1	0	0	6

Miami	TD	PAT	FG	Pts.
Yepremian	0	0	1	3

Wide receiver Howard Twilley and running back Larry Csonka share a triumphant moment at the end of a perfect season.

Super Bowl VII

The Perfect Ending

January 14, 1973

In his distinguished career as a football coach, Don Shula had never faced a more difficult decision. Who should be the starting quarterback for the Miami Dolphins in Super Bowl VII against the Washington Redskins? Should it be Bob Griese, who suffered a fractured ankle in the fifth game of the season, or Earl Morrall, who led the Dolphins to nine consecutive victories and into the playoffs until Griese returned late in the AFC title game and pulled out a 21-17 triumph over the Pittsburgh Steelers?

Favoring the direct approach, Shula summoned Griese to his office in Miami and inquired, "How do you feel, how's the ankle?"

"I feel fine," Griese replied. "The ankle feels the best it's felt since I hurt it."

"I'm thinking of starting you in the Super Bowl," Shula explained.

Revealing his decision to Morrall was just as tough as making it. When a quarterback figures in 11 straight victories, he has every right to expect the starting assignment in the game that decides the championship of professional football.

"I explained to Earl that I thought the team would be stronger if we started a healthy Griese," said Shula. "We had been having some trouble scoring lately and I wanted Morrall ready to come in in case something should happen to Griese.

"I preferred having Morrall in reserve, because we couldn't be sure what Bob would do because of his inactivity."

Morrall accepted the decision in stride. At 38, Morrall had grown accustomed to such disappointments. Before he was acquired for $100 from the New York Giants two years earlier, Morrall had played for the Baltimore Colts, with whom he had experienced his share of peaks and valleys as

When Dolphins Coach Don Shula got the traditional victory ride, it was perfectly clear who was No. 1.

Bob Griese barks signals as line-backer Chris Hanburger looks on.

"the other quarterback" behind Johnny Unitas.

"Of course, I don't agree with the decision," said Morrall, "but I'll abide by it. I thought I had a good year and should get the starting spot. Coach Shula told me the staff had a meeting and agreed we'd be stronger with Bob starting. I'll be ready. I'll watch the Redskins' defense and try to figure out what they're doing. And how they're reacting to our offense. It generally takes a period or two to get the feel of the defense."

Asked why he had decided on a starting quarterback before the Dolphins enplaned for Los Angeles and their January 14, 1973, engagement, Shula responded, "Because you don't fool around with men the stature of Bob and Earl."

Was Shula prepared for the second guess?

"I'm always prepared for the second guess," said Shula. "Earl was brought here as a backup to Bob. That's the way we started the season and that's how we'll end it."

"Nobody's going to question Shula, he's made too many correct decisions," Griese observed. "Somebody might question his views on social activities, but not on football."

At the moment no NFL coach's name was more readily recognizable than that of Shula. Just four seasons after losing Super Bowl III, and one year after losing Super Bowl VI, the one-time defensive back out of Painesville, O., and John Carroll University had coached the Dolphins to 16 consecutive victories, an unprecedented feat in professional football.

In their triumphant march, there had been only two squeakers, a 24-23 decision over Buffalo and a 16-14 victory over Minnesota. Despite a 52-0 humiliation of New England, a team that defeated Washington, 24-23, the Dolphins were established initially as three-point underdogs, a line that wavered only slightly during the two weeks prior to Super Sunday.

The Dolphins' unbeaten record through the AFC championship game was as follows:

20—Kansas City	10
34—Houston	13
16—Minnesota	14
27—New York Jets	17
24—San Diego	10
24—Buffalo	23
23—Baltimore	0
30—Buffalo	16
52—New England	0
28—New York Jets	24
31—St. Louis	10
37—New England	21
23—New York Giants	13
16—Baltimore	0
20—Cleveland	14
21—Pittsburgh	17
426	202

One of the factors weighing in the Redskins' favor, many thought, was a superiority at quarterback, manned by free-spirited Billy Kilmer.

A former All-America at UCLA, Kilmer was drafted No. 1 by the San Francisco 49ers, for whom he labored as backup to John Brodie. In an expansion draft, Kilmer was selected by the New Orleans Saints, but was acquired by George Allen for the Redskins before the start of the next season.

Kilmer violated most of the accepted rules of proper training, but somehow he got the job done, leading the Skins to an 11-3 regular-season record and playoff victories over Green Bay, 16-3, and Dallas, 26-3.

"Some of his passes," joshed one journalist," "follow the wobbly pattern of a loaf of bread thrown by your maiden aunt at the church strawberry festival." Kilmer would be the last to deny such a metaphor. During the season he had thrown the football 225 times and completed 120 passes for 1,648

Dolphins linebacker Nick Buoniconti heads downfield after picking off a Washington pass.

yards and 19 touchdowns.

On or off the field, Kilmer was highly visible. He numbered among his acquaintances President Richard M. Nixon, a friendship attested to by a pin bearing the presidential seal and a letter presented by the Chief Executive to Billy's 13-year-old daughter, a cerebral palsy victim in California.

In uniform, Billy was the leader of the "Over the Hill Gang," the band of Redskin oldsters assembled by Allen in exchange for future draft choices.

Defensive tackle Diron Talbert was one of the greybeards acquired by Allen from Los Angeles after George left the Rams to accept the Redskins' post.

Like fans, Talbert could enjoy a laugh over Allen's proclivities for ice cream.

"I'm captain of the huddle," Talbert joked. "And every once in a while we'll scream. 'I scream, you scream, we all scream for ice cream.'"

Life with the "Over the Hill Gang" was a rewarding experience for the geriatric set.

"I've never been better prepared for a football game," said 34-year-old Ron McDole, a defensive end obtained from Buffalo two years earlier. In the playoff games we held Green Bay and Dallas without a touchdown. But that's expected of us. The offense expects us to do it, we expect the offense to score."

"We're older and we're expected not to make mistakes. When I was with Buffalo we had a lot of kids. One week we'd look like Superman, the next week we'd look like nothing."

The Redskins were not alone in the area of nicknames. A year earlier Tom Landry unwittingly bestowed on the Dolphins' defense a name that caught on immediately. Preparing for Super Bowl VI, the Dallas coach exclaimed, "I can't recall the names of the Miami defensive unit, but they're a big concern to me."

Overnight the Dolphins' defensive unit became the "No Names" and they reveled in the designation. When a contest was proposed to select a more colorful handle, members of the unit arose in righteous indignation and with demands to "knock it off, we're happy the way it is."

One person impressed by the unbeaten Dolphins was Allen, who proclaimed them "the soundest team we have faced in my coaching career . . . there isn't a weakness on the ball club." Allen added that "the Redskins are the strongest team we've ever had."

In returning to the Los Angeles Memorial Coliseum, site of the first Super Bowl, the Dolphins and Redskins faced logistical problems foreign to pro football teams. The Dolphins were quartered in Long Beach, 25

miles from the Coliseum, the Redskins in Santa Ana, 36 miles distant. Media headquarters were at Newport Beach, equidistant between the camps.

The Monday practice routine was interrupted by a one-hour session for photographers. Tuesday through Thursday, the coaches and players were on call for interviews. On Friday the coaches were required to be in Newport Beach for a mass media interview. Conditions were not favorable for total concentration.

The trip to Newport Beach, Allen maintained, caused him to miss his first team meeting in 25 years of coaching. Shula appeared so tense to Jim Mandich that the tight end cracked, "Can you imagine what Don will be like if he loses another Super Bowl?"

"If I had my selfish way," said Allen, "I'd have come out here on Friday (two days before the game)." Later he conceded, "But this is good for the game."

Shula was not above having a little joke at the expense of his coaching rival, noted for his extreme security measures at his own practices and alleged attempts at counterespionage at opponents' workouts.

At an interview, Shula quipped, "We've thought of moving our last practice sessions to Tijuana so that George can start now to scour the area for our practice field."

Later Shula cracked, "George says that he has never lost a game played in the rain. So, if it rains on Sunday, we plan to forfeit."

Turning serious, Shula added, "When you go against an Allen-coached team it's tough. They play strong defense. They are strong offensively, able to strike quickly, and they have a fine kicking game. This is a team that is strong in all departments, and that's our main concern. Going into the game we know that we have to scrap and battle and come up with the plays that somehow will win for us.

"We feel that the run is our main strength and even though Washington is strong against it, we think we can get our running game going. We feel we have the offensive weapons to take advantage of a five-man line if Washington plays it."

"Both teams live by the run," said Allen, whose teams had won three, lost four and tied one in eight previous engagements with Shula teams. "Both teams pass sparingly. They gave up the fewest points in their conference, and ours the fewest in our conference. The teams are almost exactly alike."

Washington's running game was spearheaded by Larry Brown, who gained 1,286 yards in 285 carries, and Charlie Harraway, with 567 yards in 148 rushes.

Miami's ground assault featured Larry Csonka, 1,117 yards in 213 carries, and Mer-

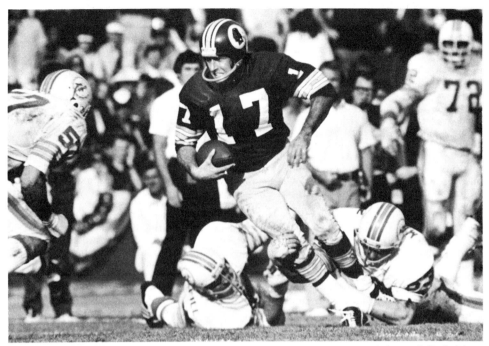

Redskins quarterback Billy Kilmer was not too mobile and found Dolphins draped all over him.

cury Morris, 1,000 yards in 190 attempts. Jim Kiick added 521 yards in 137 tries.

Allen was well aware of Morris' talents, admitting that he had discussed a possible trade for Mercury the previous winter, but added ruefully, "All I had to offer was future draft choices, and Don didn't want to wait until 1977."

In the midst of preparations for his Sunday encounter, Shula received two disturbing pieces of information. In a midweek wire service story, Carroll Rosenbloom, Shula's former boss at Baltimore, was quoted as saying, "There are two coaches who have broken all the rules of football." Allen, he said, "was guilty of nothing more than violating some waiver rules." Rosenbloom implied that Shula was guilty of a more grievous offense.

Shula fretted at length over the situation until Commissioner Pete Rozelle assured him that his fears were groundless.

On the day before the game another story surfaced, reporting that Allen had been fined $2,000 for failing to report an injury before a playoff game. Such an announcement, Shula reasoned, would serve as a unifying influence on the Redskins.

A phone call to Rozelle assured Shula that no such penalty had been assessed. If a fine were contemplated, Rozelle made it clear, it would be levied after the Super Bowl

game, not before it.

If the report had been true, Shula remarked later, "I was going to tell him it was the dumbest thing anybody ever did the day before a big game. Can you imagine Allen telling his players the day before the game, 'Look what they're doing to me and I'm only trying to protect you.'"

When the National Broadcasting Company television cameras flashed on at 12:30 p.m.—commercials went for $200,000 a minute—Memorial Coliseum showed 8,472 vacant seats among its 90,182. The no-shows, it was contended widely, resulted from the lifting of the TV blackout in the L.A. area.

After receiving the opening kickoff, the Dolphins failed to make a first down and had to punt, a development that Griese and his teammates accepted with perfect aplomb. A year earlier the reaction would have been completely different, Griese conceded.

"Last year (when the Dolphins lost to the Dallas Cowboys in the Super Bowl) we fell for the theory that the first team on the scoreboard would control the tempo of the game," he said. "Last year we departed from form to try to get a quick score. I threw on the first two downs and both times the receivers were covered. When we didn't score it hurt us psychologically. Then when Dallas scored we were really shook."

More battle-wise this time, the Dolphins awaited their turn, which came on their third possession. Starting from their own 37-yard line, and with 2:55 remaining in the first quarter the Dolphins moved to the Washington 28, where Griese faced a third-and-four situation.

Griese went to Howard Twilley, his 5-10 wide receiver, who faked Pat Fischer into a 180-degree turn at the 5-yard line, caught the pass and scored.

Garo Yepremian's conversion gave the Dolphins their first Super Bowl lead.

"On third-and-short I thought they'd be in man-for-man coverage," reported Griese. "They had (Paul) Warfield doubled. Howard and I had talked about this often. All year we had gone on a slant to the inside for the sure first down and we felt that Fischer would be expecting that. Howard made an inside move, three full steps, and Fischer went for it. Howard made a great move and Fischer did well to get back to make the tackle at the goal line.

Fischer credited Twilley with running a perfect pattern. "He kept running down and inside for about 15 yards," explained the cornerback. "Then he changed directions. He was trying to make me commit myself. When I made my move he cut to the outside. I didn't think he'd have time to do that. When the ball was coming down I thought I could get underneath him and knock the ball away. I think I could have tackled him short of the goal line, but I attempted to hit him high and dislodge the ball."

An apparent Miami touchdown, on a 47-yard pass from Griese to Warfield, was nullified by an illegal procedure penalty against wide receiver Marlin Briscoe and a promising Washington drive came up empty when Nick Buoniconti picked off a Kilmer pass and returned it 32 yards to the Washington 27.

Kiick and Csonka gained three yards apiece and Griese, who completed all six of his first-half passes, connected with tight end Jim Mandich, who rolled out of bounds on the 2-yard line. On his second smash into the line, Kiick went across and Yepremian added the extra point.

Opening the second half, the Redskins invaded Miami territory for the first time, moving from their own 30 to the Dolphins' 17 as Kilmer engineered four first downs.

The drive fell short, however, when two passes fell incomplete, Kilmer was sacked for an eight-yard loss by Manny Fernandez and Curt Knight, who had kicked seven consecutive field goals in the playoffs, missed to the right from 32 yards.

Later in the third period, the Dolphins unleashed a 78-yard march, Csonka accounting for the Dolphins' longest run of the sea-

son, a 49-yard scamper.

From the 5-yard line, Griese attempted to pass to tight end Marv Fleming, but safetyman Brig Owens intercepted in the end zone.

The Redskins' longest sustained drive in the 80-degree afternoon consumed 79 yards and more than seven minutes on the clock in the fourth quarter. From his own 11, Kilmer guided the 'Skins to the Miami 10, picking up five of the team's 16 first downs on the way.

This drive, too, failed to produce points because a Kilmer pass intended for Charlie Taylor was picked off by Jake Scott, who returned the ball from three yards deep in the end zone to the Washington 48, a 55-yard runback aided in a large measure by Bob Heinz' devastating block on Kilmer.

In five plays the Dolphins marched to the Redskins' 34, where the most bizarre play of the game took place.

Yepremian, attempting to increase the Miami lead to 17-0 with a 42-yard field goal, kicked the ball squarely into charging tackle Bill Brundige.

Instead of falling on the ball, Yepremian picked it up and made a feeble attempt to throw a forward pass. The ball was batted into the air and into the hands of cornerback Mike Bass, who sprinted 49 yards for a Washington touchdown. Knight's conversion made the score 14-7.

One minute and 57 seconds remained when the Redskins kicked off. As the Dolphins headed for their last series, Csonka addressed his teammates. "This is what we've been waiting for since last July," said Zonk. "We have to kill the clock and keep the ball away from them."

Added tackle Norm Evans: "We don't have to say it. We all know what we have to do now. So let's just do it."

Less than a minute remained when the Dolphins were forced to punt and the Redskins were about to draw their last gasp. Two Kilmer passes fell incomplete, a swing pass to Larry Brown lost four yards and then Kilmer, culminating an afternoon of frustration, was sacked for a nine-yard loss by Bill Stanfill as time ran out.

Exactly seven years, four months and 26 days after Joe Robbie was granted a franchise in the American Football League, the Dolphins were Super Bowl champions, completing the first perfect season in the history of the 53-year-old NFL.

Form had held true. The Dolphins were the fourth consecutive team to win the Super Bowl after losing on their first appearance. Others were Kansas City in 1970, Baltimore in '71 and Dallas in '72.

"There's no empty feeling this year," Exulted Shula, freed from the double-loser

One of the classic plays in Super Bowl history occurred when Garo Yepremian, his field goal attempt blocked (above), grabbed the deflection and tried to throw the infamous pass that resulted in a 49-yard Washington touchdown.

stigma.

The most popular post-game question was directed at Allen. Why did the Redskins disdain the onside kickoff after Bass' TD run?

"We had all our timeouts remaining," explained the coach, "and we couldn't run the risk of giving them good field position. We tried to kick the ball deep, hold them and come back and tie the game."

The Redskins' game strategy, Allen added, "was to get on the scoreboard early because when they get ahead they have the talent to hold the ball and grind it out.

"There was great pressure on Kilmer because we were unable to run as we would have liked to. It was a difficult day for him, but he brought us to where we are today. They stopped our running better than I thought they could.

"It doesn't do any good to play in the Super Bowl if you don't win. We just lost to a team that played a better game."

In the coach's opinion, two plays were particularly damaging. "The biggest play of the first half was our failure to recover the punt fumbled by Scott," he said. Six plays later the Dolphins scored their first touchdown.

"The other play that hurt us was the ruling against Harold McLinton (linebacker) for slapping the ball."

The action forced a fumble by center Jim Langer on a fourth down on Miami's 27 in the first quarter. An illegal procedure call restored possession to the Dolphins.

"Interceptions were the big difference," said Kilmer, who was intercepted three times while completing 14 of 28 passes for 104 yards. "Buoniconti's interception set up a touchdown for them and Scott's cost us three points, at least.

"That's a swing of 10 or 14 points and that's all it would have taken."

Kilmer admitted that "I did not throw well today, I wasn't sharp. But you know Miami has as strong a defense as any we've played against all season and their two safeties (Scott and Dick Anderson) are super athletes. They're the heart of the pass defense.

"We felt we had to run against them, but their overall defense is so good that we couldn't get anything started."

The Redskins gained 141 yards on the ground, with Brown, their leading rusher in the season with 1,217 yards, held to 72 yards in 22 rushes.

"Griese read our double coverage extremely well throughout the game," said Fischer, victim of the Twilley touchdown. "We try to conceal our coverage when we double up on certain receivers. But Griese picked it up and always seemed able to go to the man with single coverage."

"We should have whipped them by more than 30-0," declared Fernandez, richer by $15,000 as a member of the winning team. "We call ourselves the 'No Names,' but I don't think there's a defense in the league with as many guys so good at their positions."

Informed that Scott, who had two of the Dolphins' three interceptions, had been named the outstanding player of the game, Fernandez agreed wholeheartedly with the selection.

"That's great, he's the guy who stopped 'em," said the defensive tackle. "Those two interceptions, those fair catches in traffic, not letting the ball bounce around. . . .

"We call him 'Big Play Jake' and the award couldn't have gone to a more deserving fellow. He's made the big plays all season. First he gets hell knocked out of him by Bob Matheson (on a collision), then he dives

after the ball and comes up with it. Then he makes the big interception in the end zone."

Scott performed his heroics despite bone chips in his wrist that required post-season surgery and despite an injection of a painkiller in his right shoulder.

"I didn't practice for two weeks," he related, "but my shoulder hurt only once, when I fell on it while covering a pass."

Scott's ground-covering abilities should not have been surprising. A native of South Carolina, he attended school in Virginia and went to the University of Georgia. He played a season of football in Canada before joining the Dolphins at a $5,000 cut in pay.

"I was lucky on the first interception," said Jake. "I batted the ball in the air and caught it. On the second Lloyd Mumphord (cornerback) and I were covering Charlie Taylor. Kilmer didn't see me coming across and the ball came right to me."

Shula said, "This is the greatest team I've ever been associated with. It's hard to compare it with other great teams but this team has gone into an area no other team has ever gone into before. It went through the season undefeated and won it at the end. And they have to be given credit for that achievement. There was always the feeling of not having accomplished the ultimate. This is the ultimate.

"Remember, they didn't score against our defense. We knew they were tough to run against. We came out with the run, mixed in some passes to take advantage of their stacked defense. On defense, we made them lay the ball up. We figured if we made them do that we'd come down with something. Griese's fine performance (8 of 11 for 88 yards) didn't surprise me. If he were 18-for-18, I wouldn't be surprised."

Shula's lavish endorsement of the new world champions was given a hearty endorsement by tight end Marv Fleming, who had been a member of Green Bay's first two Super Bowl champions.

"This team is greater than the Packer championship teams I was on," announced the tight end. "Shula deserves a lot of credit for the way he handled the team. We never had an unbeaten season at Green Bay and that's why this is a better team."

For several heart-pounding moments in the fourth quarter, however, there were growing suspicions that the Dolphins would fail to measure up to Fleming's lofty appraisal. Yepremian's debut as a Super Bowl passer sent shock waves through Miami partisans and created fears of total disaster in the final two minutes.

"It made you sick to think about it," said Scott.

"We had the game in control, we didn't even have to use the clock."

A dejected Larry Brown leaves the field after Miami's victory.

Still shaking with relief that his boner had not cost the Dolphins the title, Yepremian admitted that "I had never prayed so much. God came through for me.

"I thought I was doing something good, something to help the team. Instead it was almost a tragedy. I almost caused a disaster."

Garo reported that he looked on "in horror" as Bass sped to the touchdown, but added that Shula never raised his voice to him when he returned to the bench, advising only that "you should have fallen on the ball."

"I thought I saw some white jerseys downfield, that's why I decided to throw the ball," Yepremian explained. "But the ball just slipped out of my fingers.

"Wouldn't it have been terrible after we

win 16 games in a row if we had lost because of that play?"

Howard Kindig's snap for the attempted field goal was low," revealed Morrall, the holder. "Garo hit it good, but they broke through to block it."

Concerning his effort to tackle Bass, Yepremian said, "Mike ran right by me, then he came over and laughed and said, 'What were you trying to do, tackle me? You know better than that.'

"Then I told him, 'You just ruined my big break.' Really we're good friends. We were teammates at Detroit."

"I heard the thump when the ball was blocked," related Bass. "And it's my job to get the ball when it's blocked.

"Then I saw Garo with the ball and I knew from our years in Detroit that he wasn't going to run with it. He picked up the ball and it slipped out of his hand when he tried to throw it. When he tried to get it back, he kinda batted it into the air. That's when I got it. Somebody threw a good block on Morrall and that opened up the way for me.

"It was pretty much a straight line after that and I knew Garo wasn't going to tackle me. I'd never let that happen to me or I'd never hear the end of it back in Detroit."

Like others, Griese could laugh at the near-calamitous moment. "I've got to work with Garo," cracked Griese. "His throwing technique isn't what it should be. I don't even think he can throw, but he sure can kick."

Both coaches received telegrams from President Nixon, who watched the telecast at Key Biscayne, Fla.

Shula's wire read: "Today's victory was a smashing climax to a truly perfect season. You and all the Dolphins have my heartiest congratulations. It was a great victory for all of your players, for all of your devoted followers throughout the country and especially for you—Don—the man who brought the Vince Lombardi Trophy to Miami. Once again, my congratulations and warmest personal regards to you and all the Dolphins."

Allen was told by the President that the defeat "was a keen disappointment to all Redskin fans but it certainly has done nothing to diminish the admiration and love for the team that you have coached so masterfully this season.

"The Redskins played gallantly from the opening kickoff this fall through the final seconds in the Coliseum, bringing a new sense of pride to the entire Washington community. You will never be 'over the hill' in our book and we'll all be in there rooting for you next season, fully confident you can go all the way."

Statistics of Seventh Super Bowl

MIAMI 14, WASHINGTON 7

Memorial Coliseum, Los Angeles, Calif., January 14, 1973
Attendance: 90,192

MIAMI	Offense	WASHINGTON
Paul Warfield	WR	Charley Taylor
Wayne Moore	LT	Terry Hermeling
Bob Kuechenberg	LG	Paul Laaveg
Jim Langer	C	Len Hauss
Larry Little	RG	John Wilbur
Norm Evans	RT	Walter Rock
Marv Fleming	TE	Jerry Smith
Howard Twilley	WR	Roy Jefferson
Bob Griese	QB	Bill Kilmer
Jim Kiick	RB	Larry Brown
Larry Csonka	RB	Charley Harraway

MIAMI	Defense	WASHINGTON
Vern Den Herder	LE	Ron McDole
Manny Fernandez	LT	Bill Brundige
Bob Heinz	RT	Diron Talbert
Bill Stanfill	RE	Verlon Biggs
Doug Swift	LLB	Jack Pardee
Nick Buoniconti	MLB	Myron Pottios
Mike Kolen	RLB	Chris Hanburger
Lloyd Mumphord	LC	Pat Fischer
Curtis Johnson	RC	Mike Bass
Dick Anderson	LS	Brig Owens
Jake Scott	RS	Roosevelt Taylor

— SUBSTITUTIONS —

MIAMI—Offense: Receivers—Jim Mandich, Marlin Briscoe. Linemen—Doug Crusan, Howard Kindig. Backs—Eugene Morris, Ed Jenkins, Hubert Ginn, Earl Morrall, Charles Leigh. Kicker—Garo Yepremian. Defense: Linebackers—Bob Matheson, Larry Ball, Jesse Powell. Lineman—Maulty Moore. Backs—Henry Stuckey, Charles Babb. Punter—Larry Seiple. DNP—Otto Stowe.

WASHINGTON—Offense: Receivers—Clifton McNeil, Mack Alston. Lineman—George Burman. Backs—Sam Wyche, Herb Mul-Key, Bob Brunet, Mike Hull. Kicker—Curt Knight. Defense: Linebackers—Rusty Tillman, Harold McLinton. Linemen—Mike Fanucci, Manuel Sistrunk. Backs—Ted Vactor, Alvin Haymond, Jeff Severson, Jon Jaqua. Punter—Mike Bragg. DNP—Ray Schoenke.

— SCORE BY PERIODS —

Miami Dolphins (AFC)	7	7	0	0 —	14
Wash. Redskins (NFC)	0	0	0	7 —	7

— SCORING —

Miami—Twilley 28 pass from Griese (Yepremian kick).
Miami—Kiick 1 run (Yepremian kick).
Washington—Bass 49 fumble recovery return (Knight kick).

— TEAM STATISTICS —

	Miami	Washington
Total First Downs	12	16
First Downs Rushing	7	9
First Downs Passing	5	7
First Downs by Penalty	0	0
Rushes	37	36
Yards Gained Rushing (net)	184	141
Average Yards per Rush	5.0	3.9
Passes Attempted	11	28
Passes Completed	8	14
Had Intercepted	1	3

	Miami	Washington
Times Tackled Att. to Pass	2	2
Yards Lost Att. to Pass	19	17
Yards Gained Passing (net)	69	87
Total Net Yardage	253	228
Punts	7	5
Average Distance Punts	43.0	31.2
Punt Returns	2	4
Punt Return Yardage	4	9
Kickoff Returns	2	3
Kickoff Return Yardage	33	45
Yards Interception Returns	95	0
Fumbles	2	1
Opponent Fumbles Recovered	0	1
Total Return Yardage	132	103
Penalties	3	3
Yards Penalized	35	25
Total Points Scored	14	7
Touchdowns	2	1
Touchdowns Running	1	1
Touchdowns Passing	1	0
Extra Points	2	1
Field Goals Attempted	1	1
Field Goals Made	0	0
Total Offensive Plays	50	66
Avg. Gain per Offensive Play	5.1	3.5

INDIVIDUAL STATISTICS

— RUSHING —

Miami	Atts.	Yds.	Lg.	TD
Csonka	15	112	49	0
Kiick	12	38	8	1
Morris	10	34	6	0

Washington	Atts.	Yds.	Lg.	TD
Brown	22	72	11	0
Harraway	10	37	8	0
Kilmer	2	18	9	0
C. Taylor	1	8	8	0
Smith	1	6	6	0

— PASSING —

Miami	Atts.	Comp.	Yds.	Int.	TD
Griese	11	8	88	1	1

Washington	Atts.	Comp.	Yds.	Int.	TD
Kilmer	28	14	104	3	0

— RECEIVING —

Miami	No.	Yds.	Lg.	TD
Warfield	3	36	18	0
Kiick	2	6	4	0
Twilley	1	28	28	1
Mandich	1	19	19	0
Csonka	1	−1	−1	0

Washington	No.	Yds.	Lg.	TD
Jefferson	5	50	15	0
Brown	5	26	12	0
C. Taylor	2	20	15	0
Smith	1	11	11	0
Harraway	1	−3	−3	0

— INTERCEPTIONS —

Miami	No.	Yds.	Lg.	TD
Scott	2	63	55	0
Buoniconti	1	32	32	0

Washington	No.	Yds.	Lg.	TD
Owens	1	0	0	0

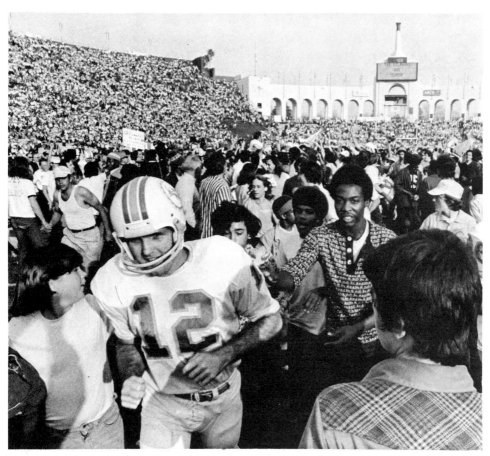

Bob Griese and other members of the winning Dolphins thread their way through the crowd at the Los Angeles Coliseum.

— PUNTING —

Miami	No.	Avg.	Lg.
Seiple	7	43.0	50

Washington	No.	Avg.	Lg.
Bragg	5	31.2	38

— PUNT RETURNS —

Miami	No.	FC	Yds.	Lg.
Scott	2	2	4	4
Anderson	0	1	0	0

Washington	No.	FC	Yds.	Lg.
Haymond	4	0	9	7
Vactor	0	2	0	0

— KICKOFF RETURNS —

Miami	No.	Yds.	Lg.
Morris	2	33	17

Washington	No.	Yds.	Lg.
Haymond	2	30	18
Mul-Key	1	15	15

— FIELD GOALS —

Miami	Att.	Made
Yepremian	1	0

Washington	Att.	Made
Knight	1	0

— FUMBLES —

Miami	No.	Own Rec.	Opp. Rec.	TD
Scott	1	0	0	0
Anderson	0	1	0	0
Yepremian	1	0	0	0

Washington	No.	Own Rec.	Opp. Rec.	TD
Brown	1	0	0	0
Bass	0	0	1	1

— SCORING —

Miami	TD	PAT	FG	Pts.
Twilley	1	0	0	6
Kiick	1	0	0	6
Yepremian	0	2	0	2

Washington	TD	PAT	FG	Pts.
Bass	1	0	0	6
Knight	0	1	0	1

Vikings quarterback Fran Tarkenton scrambled for his life most of the day while falling to the relentless Dolphins.

Super Bowl VIII

Who's the Greatest?

January 13, 1974

The major subject among the Miami Dolphins was women—their women.

The chief topic of dialogue among the Minnesota Vikings was training facilities—their own—as the champions of the American and National Football Conferences prepared for Super Bowl VIII at Rice Stadium in Houston.

The Dolphins were disturbed by club policy for transporting their womenfolk from Miami to Houston. Single players maintained that if Owner Joe Robbie paid wives' air fare from Miami to Houston, then he also should pay for the mothers of single players.

"They suggested a one-man, one-woman rule," reported Coach Don Shula. "I presented the players' views to Robbie, but he held firm and said he would pay only for wives.

"I told the players of Robbie's decision and thought that was the end of it. But, as usual at the Super Bowl, subjects such as this are frequently blown out of proportion. A few of the players discussed the subject with the press."

The matter consumed large chunks of time during Shula's early interviews, but policy prevailed. If mothers or sisters or girl friends were to attend the game, it would not be at the Dolphins' expense.

The Minnesota matter was of a more sinister nature, with the usually stoic Bud Grant firing verbal blasts at Commissioner Pete Rozelle and fellow functionaries of the NFL.

As related by Jim Klobuchar in his book "TARKENTON," "The first tremors developed on the opening practice day. Grant's team arrived at the prescribed training field quarters at Delmar School to find a locker room apparently designed for the East Dry Gulch Groundhogs. It was the first record-breaking statistic of Super Bowl week, the first locker room in Super Bowl history without a locker.

"Of the 15 shower heads in the bathing section, three revealed signs of activity. The others were arid. Two of them atoned for their derelictions by serving as a nesting grounds for a pair of sparrows.

" 'Men,' declared Jim Marshall, 'consider yourself honored. It is the first time we have ever showered in an aviary.'

"Although the room was rude and claustrophobic, it did have a certain democratic charm. The coaches had to undress right in there with the kickoff return serfs. This created no dignity gap for Grant, a distant man but never a ceremonial one. He did stalk out of the dressing room, however, with the sternly set jaw of a Norseman who has just been shafted in the fjord."

Not once, but twice, Grant stepped out of character to express his opinion of those who had reduced the Vikings to the class of galley slaves.

"This is a Super Bowl game, not a pickup game," Grant grumbled. "The league is responsible and Pete Rozelle runs the league.

"I don't think our players have seen something like this since junior high school.

"Miami can walk from its hotel to its field, but we have a 20-minute bus ride. And we don't have any blocking sleds . . . and the Dolphins do."

As the home team, the Dolphins were assigned the more pretentious facility, the practice field and dressing quarters of the Houston Oilers.

For his unprofessional behavior, Grant was fined $1,500.

Besides the female flight fare issue, Shula encountered another disrupting matter. A rumor infiltrated the Miami ranks that defensive coordinator Bill Arnsparger was headed for the New York Giants as head coach. Arnsparger's concentration was shattered daily by queries on the story, which later proved true.

Arnsparger had molded a formidable Miami defense that had limited opponents to 176 points in 16 games, including playoff victories over Cincinnati, 34-16, and Oakland, 27-10. In three consecutive games late in the regular season, the Dolphins had allowed only one touchdown, shutting out Baltimore, 44-0, and Buffalo, 17-0, before defeating Dallas, 14-7.

The Dolphins had scored 404 points while winning 14 games and losing two, to Oakland, 12-7, and Baltimore, 16-3.

The Vikings opened their season with nine consecutive victories, dropped a 20-14 decision to Atlanta, directed by their former coach, Norm Van Brocklin, then won five of their last six times, with only a 27-0 shutout by Cincinnati to mar the streak.

As in the two previous Super Bowls, Miami's ground attack featured Larry Csonka, who gained 1,003 yards in 219 carries. Mercury Morris was only slightly less devastating, gaining 965 yards in 149 rushes, an average of 6.4 yards per carry.

The Minnesota ground attack revolved around rookie Chuck Foreman, who carried 182 times for 801 yards although missing three games because of a leg injury.

The freshman out of the University of Miami also caught 37 passes for 362 yards, the second-best record in the Viking passing attack that netted 2,294 yards.

Miami gained 1,685 yards by air, with Paul Warfield accounting for 514 yards on 29 receptions.

As the countdown to Super Sunday progressed, however, Warfield suffered a pulled hamstring during a workout and was a doubtful starter against the Vikings.

The other Miami question marks were pronounced fit. Offensive guard Bob Kuechenberg, who suffered a broken arm in the next to last regular-season game and wore a cast in the playoff games, and defensive tackle Manny Fernandez, handicapped by a torn leg muscle, were reported ready for kickoff.

Because of the Dolphins' powerful running game, quarterback Bob Griese was required to do comparatively little passing in the playoff games. In the AFC championship game against Oakland, Griese passed only six times, completing three for 34 yards.

Griese's Minnesota counterpart was Fran Tarkenton, who had begun his professional career with the expansion Vikings of 1961 and later spent five seasons with the New York Giants before returning to the Vikings in 1972.

Tarkenton had played 13 years without post-season recognition. He had, however, been a spectator at New Orleans when the Vikings lost to Kansas City in Super Bowl IV.

"I went to that one because my people, the Vikings, whom I'd played with years ago, were in it," he explained. "But it was so frustrating, just sitting there."

In 1973, Tarkenton had been in Los Angeles the day before Super Sunday, but "took a 1 a.m. flight to Atlanta, because I didn't want to be there unless I was in the game myself."

Tarkenton was not only a pinpoint passer, but an accomplished runner as well, a "scrambler" in the truest sense of the word. With his receivers covered and a ray of daylight ahead, he frequently ran for crucial yardage. In the regular season Tark carried the ball 41 times for 202 yards, a 4.9-yard average, the best among six Viking ball carriers.

Because he had flouted the quarterbacks-should-not-run doctrine, Tarkenton originally was branded a loser. When Roger Staubach of Dallas and others followed in his footsteps and made significant contributions to championships, however, the football fraternity revised its views of scrambling.

"It was the greatest lie ever perpetrated on the pro football public," Tarkenton asserted.

Tarkenton enjoyed high esteem among the Dolphins. "He's a marvel, he has a sixth sense," declared Miami linebacker Nick Buoniconti. "He seems to know where the pressure is and he moves away from it so fast that he never takes a shot from the blind side.

"He does everything by instinct so that we never know where he'll be. So the whole thing has to start with our defensive ends, Bill Stanfill and Vern Den Herder. They've got to control Tarkenton. If they let him roll outside, it's going to be a long afternoon.

"Who knows what the Vikings will do? The Vikings used to have a lot of tendencies on offense. You pretty much knew when and where they'd pass and run. Now, they have no tendencies at all. Tarkenton is a great pass caller in that respect."

Declaring that he had "never been so hungry and never with a team that I thought was so ready," Tarkenton predicted a more wide-open Super Bowl "than you've seen in several years. Our team isn't afraid to gamble. I don't mean that we'll be a scatter-gun team. The team has more backfield speed than we've had before. I'll throw the ball on first down and feel I can throw deep against a zone defense."

Tarkenton anticipated little difficulty

MVP Larry Csonka gives Vikings linebacker Wally Hilgenberg that get-out-of-my-way look.

with the Dolphins' 53 defense, in which Miami substituted a linebacker for a defensive tackle. (The defense was named for Bob Matheson's uniform number.)

"The '53' is a little bit different," Tarkenton acknowledged, "but all that means to me is that it has to be approached a little bit different. Some teams defy it. They think they can run their own stuff against it. I think you've got to prepare for the 53 defense, you've got to make it so the Dolphins don't know what to expect. I'm sure we'll prepare a little bit different."

In the 1972 season, the Vikings had solved the 53 defense for a 14-6 fourth-quarter lead, only to lose, 16-14, when Garo Yepremian kicked a 51-yard field goal.

The Vikings do not play scared, Tarkenton added. Too frequently, he said, when a team plays an important game, "it's so

worried about making mistakes that it doesn't play as well as it can. It doesn't take any chances because it feels it's good enough to win if it doesn't make any mistakes.

"If passing from our end zone seems to be the thing to do, we'll do that. If taking fourth-down chances seems right, we'll do that, too. The tempo of the game often dictates different strategy. In the Dallas (playoff) game, when we went for two fourth-down plays, it was obvious that our offense was moving the ball well. If we hadn't, we might have played it differently. You don't go for a fourth-down play just for the heck of it."

One of the more fascinating confrontations of the forthcoming game featured Tarkenton and Jake Scott, Miami safetyman.

Although Tarkenton was five years Scott's senior, they shared a common denominator—Athens, Ga.

"When I was in seventh and eighth grades," Scott recalled, "Fran was the big hero on the high school football team. He was just like he is now, a real leader. I knew his two brothers, the whole family. Years later Fran recruited me for the University of Georgia."

Tarkenton remembered: "His mother taught me a course in educational psychology in college. She was a brilliant woman. I remember Jake from the kid football programs that the 'Y' conducted. I always thought that when it came to playing free safety, Willie Wood of the Green Bay Packers was the best. He set the standard. Now I consider Jake to be the equal of Willie. I can think of no higher praise."

Scott was equally lavish in his praise of Tarkenton, asserting, "Fran can turn a bad play into a good play just like that. You can't predict what he'll do. That will make it tough on me. He has so many wrinkles, he is so tough to defense."

While football fever was rising in Houston and most other sections of the country, Miami players found it difficult to get into the emotional mainstream.

"This isn't like it was the first two years," said Csonka. "I wouldn't say that we're bored, but it's just not the same exciting adventure it was in the other years.

"I came here to talk about the Super Bowl, but I have so little conversation about it, I really don't know what to say anymore. People want to hear me talk about faith and morals. That's fine, but I'm a football player. It's a livelihood and I love the game.

"I'm not worried about whether our team is the greatest of all time. That may sound funny. The object is to get to the Super Bowl. How history judges the Dolphins of the 1970s is something I don't worry about."

Super Bowl VIII, played before 68,142 on a murky, humid afternoon, was televised by the Columbia Broadcasting System to an audience estimated at 60 million. One-minute commercials sold for $210,000, an increase of $10,000 over the 1973 rate.

Pre-game entertainment featured the release of 17,000 balloons that cost $3,000 and required 40 blowers five hours with 25 tanks of helium to inflate.

When referee Ben Dreith called the captains to midfield, the Dolphins, as was their custom, called the coin toss correctly and chose to receive the opening kickoff. The coin flip was an omen of things to come for the Vikings.

Starting on his own 38-yard line, Griese alternated runs by Morris and Csonka with his own passes to Jim Mandich and Marlin

Briscoe in masterful, mechanical fashion. In 10 plays consuming five minutes and 27 seconds, Griese guided the Dolphins across 62 yards, Csonka smashing the final five yards over right guard for the touchdown.

It was a textbook demonstration at the expense of "The Purple People Eaters," the resolute defense that generated inordinate pride in the Viking family.

Three plays, two on the ground, one in the air, represented the Vikings' first possession before Mike Eischeid punted and the Dolphins resumed their relentless style from their own 34.

Four first downs, two each by rushes and passes, moved the ball to the 1-yard line, from where Jim Kiick plunged for his first touchdown of the season.

The drive consumed 5:46. In the first 13 minutes and 36 seconds, the Dolphins ran off 20 plays for 120 yards.

The Vikings failed to register a first down until the final play of the quarter when Tarkenton completed a nine-yard pass to Doug Kingsriter, moving the ball to the Minnesota 27.

That drive stalled on the 36 and the next drive, which started on the 27, came to grief when Tarkenton was sacked for a 10-yard loss.

Seven plays later the Dolphins were on the scoreboard again. Aided by a 15-yard unsportsmanlike penalty against linebacker Wally Hilgenberg, and with Csonka carrying five times, the Dolphins marched from the 35 to the Minnesota 21. Yepremian kicked a 28-yard field goal that put the Dolphins ahead, 17-0.

With 5:56 remaining in the half, the Vikes unleashed their longest drive of the day, moving from their own 20 to the Miami 6 as Tarkenton completed passes of 17 and 14 yards to Stu Voigt and of 30 yards to John Gilliam.

Facing a fourth-and-one situation and trailing by 17 points, the Vikings shunned the field goal, choosing instead a running play by Oscar Reed, who fumbled on the 6, where Scott recovered.

Should the Vikings have tried for the three points considering the score at that time? "No," insisted Tarkenton. "We had the first down, we just fumbled."

The second half provided no solace for the Vikings as the Dolphins, starting on the Minnesota 43, punched out a third touchdown. A Griese-to-Warfield pass gulped 27 yards before Csonka charged across from the 2 on a busted play.

"I confused everybody on the play," confessed Csonka. "Griese led the team out of the huddle, then forgot the count. He asked me what the count was. He'd forgotten it. He doesn't do that very often, but I guess he

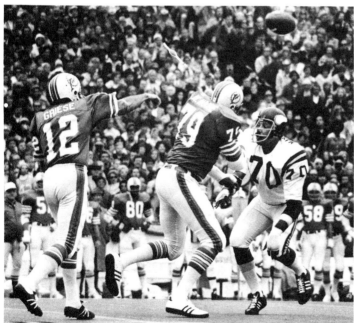

Vikings receiver John Gilliam snared this pass (above) in front of defensive back Curtis Johnson, but such occurrences were not nearly so frequent as the sight of Bob Griese connecting with Nat Moore.

was trying to figure out something about the defense. Anyway he turned around and said, 'Hey, what's the count?'

"I said, 'It's on two, isn't it?'

"Kiick heard all this and said, 'No, no, it's on one.'

"Griese glared at both of us for a second, but he believed me. He decided it was on two. He shouldn't have done that. Kiick was paying attention. The count was one."

Center Jim Langer had not heard the conversation and, to Griese's surprise, snapped the ball on the count of one. Griese handed off to Csonka, who followed Kiick, Langer, guard Larry Little and tackle Norm Evans into the end zone.

"Griese seemed to bobble the ball a little," related Csonka. "I'm just glad that I didn't confuse him so badly that he dropped the ball."

When Yepremian kicked his third extra point, the Dolphins led, 24-0.

Later, Griese could laugh about the mixup. "Coming out of the huddle, I was looking over the defense to see what I might call on the next play if we didn't score," he explained. "Then I forgot the count. I should have known that Zonk was the wrong guy to ask."

The Vikings scored their only touchdown early in the fourth period when, climaxing a 10-play, 57-yard march, Tarkenton rolled four yards around right end.

The Vikings had only one more possession and were stopped by an interception by Curtis Johnson under the Miami goalpost. The Dolphins ate up the last 6½ minutes as Kiick and Csonka alternated on 12 running plays that sealed Miami's 32nd victory in 34 games over two seasons.

The Dolphins committed virtually no mistakes. They lost no fumbles and were not intercepted. Their only penalty was for four yards.

On the rare occasions that they did err, there were no ill effects. Once, on a punt, only 10 Dolphins lined up because Ed Newman "forgot" to take the field. Result: Larry Seiple punted the ball 57 yards to the Minnesota 3.

On another occasion, Csonka charged into his own tackle, Wayne Moore, and nearly tripped. Regaining his equilibrium, Zonk charged on for an eight-yard gain.

The Vikes were penalized seven times for 65 yards and when Fred Cox booted an onside kickoff that was covered by Terry Brown following the Vikings' touchdown, that, too, was doomed for failure as Ron Porter was ruled offside. Cox then was forced to kick deep.

On the second-half kickoff, which Gilliam returned 65 yards to the Miami 34, Voigt was detected clipping and the Vikings were set back to their 10. It was that kind of day for the Norsemen.

Csonka accounted for a record 145 yards on 33 carries, breaking Matt Snell's mark of 121 yards in Super Bowl III, and was named the game's most valuable player. Reed was the Vikings' most productive ball carrier, gaining 32 yards in 11 tries. Because of Miami's steamroller offense, Griese threw only seven passes, completing six. Tarkenton threw more frequently than he had anticipated, hitting on 18 of 28 tosses for 182 yards. One was intercepted.

The Dolphins controlled the football for 33 minutes and 47 seconds, the Vikings for 26 minutes and 13 seconds. The biggest disparity was in the first quarter when the Dolphins controlled the ball for 11 minutes and 13 seconds, the Vikings for only 3:47.

While the Dolphins ground out 13 first downs by rushing, the Vikings accounted for only five, the first of which came late in the third period, after 44 minutes and 17 seconds of play.

The Vikings did not search long for reasons behind their second Super Bowl loss in as many tries.

Coach Bud Grant dismissed a suggestion that the team's week of inactivity before flying to Houston may have been responsible. What hurt the Vikings more, said Grant, was the absence of big plays. "When you face a team like Miami, you must make the big plays," he pointed out. "The main thing is that Miami came off the ball well and we didn't tackle as well as we can.

"Csonka has run that hard before. When Miami gets ahead of you, Csonka is going to carry the ball 25 times. This is one of their strengths.

"When you play the great teams, you have to break even in the turnovers and penalties. This wasn't the case. We had penalties on two kickoffs. We had a fumble on the goal line. On our onside kickoff we had a penalty. When they can back you up in bad field position, you have a hard time beating them."

Defensive line coach Jack Patera termed Miami's offensive unit "the most well coordinated" he had ever seen.

"We thought maybe other teams hadn't prepared properly for them," he said. "We took pains to prepare properly for them, but they went out and did the same thing to us."

"They're just a great team and execute well," lauded middle linebacker Jeff Siemon.

Tarkenton said, "Csonka's the strongest fullback I've ever seen," and the Minnesota quarterback added, "We gave them our best shot and weren't good enough. They played as nearly perfect a game as a team can play.

Don Shula watched stoically as the Dolphin machine hummed.

"Everything just went their way. Not only did they play very well, but every bounce of the football seemed to go their way. Scott fumbles a punt and they recover. On one of their punts the ball bounces sideways instead of going into the end zone and they down it. But the Dolphins made the most of their breaks."

One of the contest's premier matchups involved two former Notre Dame teammates, Kuechenberg of Miami and Minnesota's All-Pro defensive tackle Alan Page. "Alan was a bit annoyed," reported Kuechenberg after the game.

In the fourth quarter Page appeared to vent all his frustrations with an over-zealous charge into Griese. In defense of his action, Page explained, "When the quarterback has his back to you, you have to determine right now if he has the ball. When in doubt, you hit him. That's what I did."

The incident cost the Vikings 15 yards.

"I got plenty hot at that," reported Kuechenberg. "I let Page know I though it was a cheap shot."

Griese told Page he didn't think it was intentional malice and that "you shouldn't have been penalized."

Wide receiver Warfield also had some heated words for Minnesota cornerback Bob Bryant, quoted as saying in pregame interviews that he hoped Warfield's hamstring pull would be healed by Super Sunday "because I don't want to hear any of his excuses. I want him to be at full speed."

"I have no respect for anyone who would say that," snapped Warfield, playing at about 80 percent efficiency. "I believe in respecting the man who plays across from me."

Warfield said he had to slow down on his 27-yard, third-quarter pass play with Griese. "If I'd been perfectly healthy, it would have been a touchdown," he said.

With two consecutive Super Bowl championships, and another $15,000 payday, the Dolphins were fair game for the obvious question: "Are they the greatest team of all time, better even than the Green Bay Packers who won the first two Super Bowls?"

"Not yet, not yet," protested Owner Robbie.

Shula sidestepped the issue, announcing instead, "I can't begin to tell you how proud I am of this team. After our 17-0 season last year I didn't think anything could be better, but this team has gone one step beyond last year. There is no question in my mind that this team is better.

"This year we hung tough, had a little slump toward the end of the regular season, but when the playoffs started, we played as well as any team I ever saw. It's tougher to repeat in the Super Bowl than to get there the first time. We made it because our players are completely unselfish and entirely dedicated."

Neither wide receiver Briscoe nor Kuechenberg would express an opinion on the Dolphins' rating among the all-time best teams. But defensive tackle Manny Fernandez leaped into the discussion willingly.

"What do you think?" began Fernandez, who participated in eight tackles. "How can anyone dispute what we are after we've been to three straight Super Bowls and won two of them? We've had to prove ourselves over and over again, and we've done it."

The logical person to compare the Dolphins with the powerful Packers of the Vince Lombardi era was Bart Starr, the former Green Bay quarterback who had picked the Vikings to defeat the Dolphins.

"I can't compare 'em," hedged Starr. "The Dolphins think of themselves as the best in history and I would think less of them if they didn't. By the same token I have to think of my team as the best.

"Really, though, you can't compare teams from different eras. So much changes. If you think about it, no two plays are ever the same. Every time the ball is snapped, something is different about the play from every other play in the history of football.

"The Dolphins are a stupendously marvelous team, and the Vikings are a splendidly coached team. This just wasn't their day."

Statistics of Eighth Super Bowl
MIAMI 24, MINNESOTA 7

Rice Stadium, Houston, Texas, January 13, 1974
Attendance Paid 71,882. Actual 68,142.

MINNESOTA	Offense	MIAMI
Carroll Dale	WR	Paul Warfield
Grady Alderman	LT	Wayne Moore
Ed White	LG	Bob Kuechenberg
Mick Tingelhoff	C	Jim Langer
Frank Gallagher	RG	Larry Little
Ron Yary	RT	Norm Evans
Stu Voigt	TE	Jim Mandich
John Gilliam	WR	Marlin Briscoe
Fran Tarkenton	QB	Bob Griese
Chuck Foreman	RB	Mercury Morris
Oscar Reed	RB	Larry Csonka

	Defense	
Carl Eller	LE	Vern Den Herder
Gary Larsen	LT	Manny Fernandez
Alan Page	RT	Bob Heinz
Jim Marshall	RE	Bill Stanfill
Roy Winston	LLB	Doug Swift
Jeff Siemon	MLB	Nick Buoniconti
Wally Hilgenberg	RLB	Mike Kolen
Nate Wright	LC	Lloyd Mumphord
Bob Bryant	RC	Curtis Johnson
Jeff Wright	LS	Dick Anderson
Paul Krause	RS	Jake Scott

— SUBSTITUTIONS —

MINNESOTA—Offense: Receivers—Jim Lash, Doug Kingsriter. Lineman—Chuck Goodrum. Backs—Ed Marinaro, Bill Brown. Dave Osborn. Kicker—Fred Cox. Defense: Linebackers—Amos Martin, Ron Porter. Linemen—Bob Lurtsema, Doug Sutherland. Backs—Charlie West, Terry Brown. Punter—Mike Eischeid. DNP—Bob Berry, Godfrey Zaunbrecher, Steve Lawson, Gary Ballman.

MIAMI—Offense: Receivers—Marv Fleming, Howard Twilley. Linemen—Doug Crusan, Irv Goode, Ed Newman. Backs—Earl Morrall, Jim Kiick, Don Nottingham. Kicker—Garo Yepremian. Defense: Linebackers—Larry Ball, Bruce Bannon, Bob Matheson. Lineman—Maulty Moore. Backs—Tim Foley, Henry Stuckey, Charles Babb. Punter—Larry Seiple. DNP—Ron Sellers.

— SCORE BY PERIODS —

Minnesota Vikings (NFC)	0	0	0	7	— 7
Miami Dolphins (AFC)	14	3	7	0	— 24

— SCORING —

Miami—Csonka 5 run (Yepremian kick).
Miami—Kiick 1 run (Yepremian kick).
Miami—Field goal Yepremian 28.
Miami—Csonka 2 run (Yepremian kick).
Minnesota—Tarkenton 4 run (Cox kick).

— TEAM STATISTICS —

	Minnesota	Miami
Total First Downs	14	21
First Downs Rushing	5	13
First Downs Passing	8	4
First Downs by Penalty	1	4
Rushes	24	53
Yards Gained Rushing (net)	72	196
Average Yards per Rush	3.0	3.7
Passes Attempted	28	7
Passes Completed	18	6
Had Intercepted	1	0
Times Tackled Attemp. Pass	2	1

	Minnesota	Miami
Yards Lost Attempting Pass	16	10
Yards Gained Passing (net)	166	63
Total Net Yardage	238	259
Punts	5	3
Average Distance Punts	42.2	39.6
Punt Returns	0	3
Punt Return Yardage	0	20
Kickoff Returns	4	2
Kickoff Return Yardage	69	47
Yards Interception Returns	0	10
Fumbles	2	1
Opp. Fumbles Recovered	0	1
Total Return Yardage	69	77
Penalties	7	1
Yards Penalized	65	4
Total Points Scored	7	24
Touchdowns	1	3
Touchdowns Rushing	1	3
Touchdowns Passing	0	0
Extra Points	1	3
Field Goals Attempted	0	1
Field Goals Made	0	1
Total Offensive Plays	54	61
Avg. Gain per Offensive Play	4.4	4.2

INDIVIDUAL STATISTICS
— RUSHING —

Minnesota	Atts.	Yds.	Lg.	TD
Reed	11	32	9	0
Foreman	7	18	5	0
Tarkenton	4	17	8	1
Marinaro	1	3	3	0
B. Brown	1	2	2	0

Miami	Atts.	Yds.	Lg.	TD
Csonka	33	145	16	2
Morris	11	34	14	0
Kiick	7	10	5	1
Griese	2	7	5	0

— PASSING —

Minnesota	Atts.	Comp.	Yds.	Int.	TD
Tarkenton	28	18	182	1	0

Miami	Atts.	Comp.	Yds.	Int.	TD
Griese	7	6	73	0	0

— RECEIVING —

Minnesota	No.	Yds.	Lg.	TD
Foreman	5	27	10	0
Gilliam	4	44	30	0
Voigt	3	46	17	0
Marinaro	2	39	27	0
B. Brown	1	9	9	0
Kingsriter	1	9	9	0
Lash	1	9	9	0
Reed	1	1	1	0

Miami	No.	Yds.	Lg.	TD
Warfield	2	33	27	0
Mandich	2	21	13	0
Briscoe	2	19	13	0

— INTERCEPTIONS —

Minnesota—None.

Miami	No.	Yds.	Lg.	TD
Johnson	1	10	10	0

Dolphins running back Jim Kiick finds a nice hole in the Vikings defensive line.

<table>
<tr><td colspan="4">— PUNTING —</td></tr>
<tr><td>Minnesota</td><td>No.</td><td>Avg.</td><td>Lg.</td></tr>
<tr><td>Eischeid.................................</td><td>5</td><td>42.2</td><td>48</td></tr>
<tr><td>Miami</td><td>No.</td><td>Avg.</td><td>Lg.</td></tr>
<tr><td>Seiple....................................</td><td>3</td><td>39.7</td><td>57</td></tr>
</table>

— PUNT RETURNS —

Minnesota	No.	FC	Yds.	Lg.
Bryant	0	1	0	0
Miami	No.	FC	Yds.	Lg.
Scott	3	1	20	12

— KICKOFF RETURNS —

Minnesota	No.	Yds.	Lg.
West	2	28	15
Gilliam	2	41	21
Miami	No.	Yds.	Lg.
Scott	2	47	31

— FIELD GOALS —

Minnesota—None.

Miami		Att.	Made
Yepremian		1	1

— FUMBLES —

Minnesota	No.	Own Rec.	Opp. Rec.	TD
Tarkenton	1	1	0	0
Reed	1	0	0	0
Miami	No.	Own Rec.	Opp. Rec.	TD
Scott	1	1	1	0

— SCORING —

Minnesota	TD	PAT	FG	Pts.
Tarkenton	1	0	0	6
Cox	0	1	0	1
Miami	TD	PAT	FG	Pts.
Csonka..............................	2	0	0	12
Kiick.................................	1	0	0	6
Yepremian	0	3	1	6

Super Bowl IX

Rooney Gets His Wish

January 12, 1975

For 42 years mild-mannered Art Rooney had watched his Pittsburgh Steelers compete in the National Football League.

As four decades slipped by, he lived in the hope that he could bring a professional football championship to his native city.

At the close of every season, however, the little man with the big heart and the ever-present cigar looked back in disappointment as his team finished down the track. Eleven times they finished last, 10 times they were fourth and six times they came in second. For a man who had made his initial stake in one implausible weekend bonanza at the race track, it was beginning to appear as though the "little people" had deserted forever the non-complaining gentleman who was friend to everybody.

There had been a glimmer of hope in 1972 when the Steelers finished first in their division, their first championship of any kind, only to lose to Miami in the American Football Conference championship game.

And the following year, after qualifying as a wild card team, the Steelers were eliminated by the Dolphins in the first round of the playoffs.

Now they were back, bidding for football's brightest bauble, the Vince Lombardi Trophy emblematic of the Super Bowl championship. They had won 10 games, lost three and tied one during the 1974 AFC season before they eliminated Buffalo, 32-14, in the playoffs and then did away with Oakland, 24-13, in the conference title game as Terry Bradshaw engineered three fourth-quarter touchdowns.

The change in Rooney's football fortunes had commenced in 1969 when he hired Chuck Noll as head coach. A native of Cleveland and a graduate of Dayton University, Noll had been a defensive back with the Cleveland Browns for seven years, after which he served as an assistant coach for the San Diego Chargers and Baltimore Colts.

In Noll's three seasons at Baltimore, the Colts had lost only seven games. Noll's familiarity with a winning tradition was a big factor when Dan Rooney, son of the Steelers' owner, interviewed Chuck for the

Art Rooney finally saw his championship dream come true.

Quarterback Terry Bradshaw expresses his feeling about the Steelers.

Pittsburgh job.

"I liked his attitude and the way he evaluated our team," reported the young Rooney. "Everything he told me about our team was right on target."

Noll entertained no illusions about life with the Steelers. The team had a 2-11-1 record in 1968. In the five preceding years, they had won only 18 games and enjoyed a winning record in only four of the last 19 years. Clearly, the task facing Noll was monumental.

"The Steelers gave me everything I asked for," revealed Noll, noting that the organization, archaic in many facets of its operation prior to his arrival, took one gigantic leap forward by shifting its offices from a tired downtown hotel into spanking new Three Rivers Stadium.

Noll was only 37, but he demonstrated a solid maturity from his first day on the job. The Steelers needed help virtually everywhere and Noll might have succumbed to public clamor by starting his rebuilding program with Terry Hanratty, Notre Dame quarterback and a native of nearby Butler, Pa., as his first choice in the NFL draft.

A one-time defensive player himself, Noll recognized, however, that the Steelers' foremost need was defensive strength and, after conferring with scouting supervisor Art Rooney Jr., he chose instead Joe Greene, 6-4, 270-pound defensive tackle from North Texas State.

Hanratty was No. 2 choice, followed by defensive end L. C. Greenwood of Arkansas AM&N and offensive tackle Jon Kolb from Oklahoma State. The foundation was laid, solidly and wisely.

Noll won his first game as a head coach, defeating Detroit, 16-13, but after that the news was all bad as the Steelers lost 13 games in a row.

"We weren't being blown off the field, we were losing because of our mistakes," Noll summarized later.

The next season, 1979, playing now in the realigned Central Division of the AFC, the Steelers won five games and lost nine. In '71, they were 6-8 and the next season 11-3 as they won the division title.

Following up his initial success in the player draft, Noll selected Bradshaw, the Louisiana Tech quarterback, as first choice in the 1970 draft. Cornerback Mel Blount also was selected that year. Noll selected Jack Ham, Ernie Holmes, Dwight White and Mike Wagner in '72. When the Steelers arrived in New Orleans for their January 12, 1975, Super Bowl engagement with the Minnesota Vikings at Tulane Stadium, seven of their 11 starting defensive players had been acquired via the draft.

Despite the Steelers' 10-3-1 record, their 1974 season had been neither smooth nor straight.

Franco Harris, the third-year running back out of Penn State, gained only 125 yards in the first three games and then sat out the next two with an injury. When he returned to the lineup for the sixth game, Harris was ready to explode. In the last nine games of the regular schedule, he gained 881 yards, finishing with 1,006.

Like Harris, Bradshaw struggled in the early season. The young quarterback was on the bench at season's start as Joe Gilliam played a hot passing hand. In six preseason games, Gilliam completed 65 percent of his passes and accounted for 12 touchdowns.

On the sidelines, Bradshaw muttered about the necessity of a balanced attack that blended running and passing.

Eventually, Bradshaw was tapped for regular duty. Immediately, he demonstrated that time on the bench was not without its rewards. The Louisianian emerged as a take-charge quarterback, prepared to lead the Steelers through the playoffs and into their first Super Bowl.

The Minnesota Vikings, making their third Super Bowl appearance and second in as many years, had won their sixth division title in seven years and then brushed aside St. Louis and Los Angeles en route to New Orleans.

Foremost among the Vikings once more was Fran Tarkenton, the scrambler, who had averaged 5.7 yards on 21 carries and tossed 17 touchdown passes behind a line that allowed only 17 sacks. One of Tarkenton's adversaries would be Greene, who had acquired the unwelcomed and undeserved monicker of "Mean Joe" because of his pursuit of Tarkenton in a hounds-and-hare chase some years earlier.

Tarkenton was with the New York Giants at the time and, as Greene remembered, "I kept chasing him and when I finally hit him I didn't realize he had thrown the ball five minutes before. I got flagged for it and got escorted off the field.

"I had been called 'Mean Joe' before, but this made it even stronger. I prefer Joe," concluded Greene, christened Charles Edward.

In the days preceding the Steelers-Vikings clash, the condition of Tarkenton's shoulder caused some concern among the NFC champions, although Coach Bud Grant conceded that "Francis always has a good game when his arm is sore. He's like all the great ones when they get nicked or have a temperature. They work twice as hard."

In the Steelers' camp there was concern over the health of Harris and defensive end White.

The vaunted Steel Curtain defense took care of all challengers, such as Vikings running back Dave Osborn (above) and quarterback Fran Tarkenton.

Harris was suffering from a severe head cold in the damp and windy climate, but worked out daily.

White's condition was a more serious matter, a viral infection. A week in the hospital, "living on water and sleep," had pared 18 pounds off his 6-4 frame and he was a doubtful starter almost until game time.

"Doctors told me I might suffer some serious consequences if I got a negative reaction after playing," White reported. "But this is the Super Bowl and I wasn't going to pass it up."

White's attitude was typical of the Steelers' spirit, declared Greene. It amazed Noll.

"He was weak," said the coach. "I figured he'd take part in the pre-game workouts and then he'd keel over and we'd drag him off. But it didn't happen that way."

Preparing for the game, in which the Vikings were three-point underdogs, Grant gave his players greater freedom than in previous Super Bowls, both of which wound up in defeats. The French Quarter, with its all-night attractions, was no longer off limits and the players were also permitted to fly their wives to New Orleans for the game.

"The players are not running off at every opportunity, and we're more relaxed," Grant noted. "We're not as edgy as we were in previous Super Bowls."

As a Super Bowl novitiate, Noll was unable to gauge the mood of the Steelers. "I've given up trying to determine if the players are ready emotionally," he conceded. "I don't worry about the mental aspect. I just prepare the players for the game and what to expect from the other team. There's a lot of hoopla attached to this game, but it will all come down to blocking and tackling, that's all."

Because of the Vikings' vaunted pass rush, led by tackle Alan Page, Noll decided that the best game plan was to rush at the Vikings, sending Harris up the middle on draws and traps and then trusting to Franco to weave a path to daylight.

But the Pittsburgh defensive front four were no slouches either. "With those four going for them," cracked Tarkenton, "the Steelers may be able to play without their linebackers. Usually, I can scramble away from a strong rush, but they are so quick it would be suicide to turn it into a track meet on every play. That's why we'll use a lot of play action to slow down their pass rush."

As the 80,997 spectators attempted to find warmth in Tulane Stadium, the game, as expected, developed into a defensive struggle. In the first quarter, the Vikings registered one first down, the Steelers four. The Vikes netted no yards rushing, the Steelers 64. The Vikes gained 20 yards by passing,

Steelers Coach Chuck Noll gets the traditional victory ride.

the Steelers 15. The Vikings advanced no farther than their own 35-yard line. The Steelers twice penetrated to field goal range. On the first march, Roy Gerela missed on a 37-yard attempt. On the second, holder Bobby Walden picked up an errant snap from center and attempted to run, only to wind up with a seven-yard loss.

Crammed in their own territory on their first four possessions, the Vikings suddenly found themselves on the Pittsburgh 24-yard line early in the second quarter after Rocky Bleier fumbled and Randy Poltl recovered.

The opportunity to score fizzled, however, when Fred Cox missed a fourth-down field goal from 39 yards.

Midway through the period, on a second-and-seven situation from his own 10-yard line, Tarkenton pitched out weakly to Dave Osborn, who fumbled the ball and then fell on it in the end zone for a Pittsburgh safety. That was the only score of the first half.

The Vikings had a second chance to score before halftime, marching from their own 20 to the Pittsburgh 25 as Tarkenton mixed passes with Chuck Foreman's line smashes to pick up three first downs.

With 1:17 remaining in the half, Tarken-

Super Bowl IX MVP Franco Harris runs past Alan Page for some of the 158 yards he gained in the game.

ton passed down the middle to John Gilliam. The wide receiver caught the ball, but was hit savagely by safety Glen Edwards and fumbled, Mel Blount recovering. Instead of a first down on the Pittsburgh 5, the Vikings came away emptyhanded.

"That play could have made the difference," said Steelers linebacker Jack Ham. "Edwards and Gilliam had a little feud going. That play may have done it."

Late in the second quarter, when middle linebacker Jack Lambert limped off the field with a sprained ankle, Ed Bradley replaced him in the Steelers' lineup.

"The Vikings were calling, 'Who's this turkey?' " related Bradley. "They came right at me, but they didn't get me."

"Bradley was beautiful," lauded Noll. "He made big hits and big plays."

The third quarter was less than one minute old when the Steelers scored the game's first touchdown. Bill Brown, playing his last game for the Vikings at 37, fumbled the kickoff after returning it four yards and Marv Kellum recovered on the Minnesota 30. Harris turned left end for 24 yards, then lost three on the right side before sweeping around left end for nine yards and the TD.

Gerela's PAT increased the Steelers' lead to 9-0.

The Vikings uncorked one mild threat later in the quarter, to the Pittsburgh 47, where a Tarkenton pass was deflected and then intercepted by Greene, who returned the ball 10 yards to the Minnesota 46.

"I sort of lumbered along with that interception," reported Greene. "I would like to have gone all the way, but I just don't run fast enough."

Later in the period Pittsburgh linebacker Andy Russell limped to the sidelines with a torn hamstring. He was replaced by Loren Toews.

"I kept begging the coaches to put me back in," recounted Russell. "Then they'd ask me how I felt. I'd have to confess, 'I shouldn't be in there.' It ate my heart out. I didn't want to be isolated on Chuck Foreman or John Gilliam and get beaten for a touchdown."

By the end of the third period, the Vikings had generated only 23 yards rushing, compared to 192 for the Steelers, but had picked up 99 yards by air, more than double the 44 yards credited to the Steelers.

A Harris fumble, recovered by Paul

Krause at the Pittsburgh 47, provided the Vikings with an early fourth-quarter opportunity. An interference penalty against safety Wagner on a Tarkenton-to-Gilliam pass advanced the ball to the Pittsburgh 5, where the drive ended when Foreman fumbled on the next play and Greene recovered for the Steelers.

"That was the biggest defensive play of the day," asserted Noll. "They tried to run a counter play and Greene knocked the ball out of Foreman's hands. If they had scored then, they would have made it tough on us."

Four plays after the fumble recovery, Walden's punt was blocked by Matt Blair and recovered in the end zone by Terry Brown for a touchdown. Cox' extra-point attempt struck the left upright and bounded away, leaving the score at 9-6.

"I saw Blair coming and knew I didn't have a chance to get the kick away," said Walden. "Nobody even touched him. I never had a chance to recover the ball once it was blocked."

More than 10 minutes remained in the game, and more than seven minutes were consumed in a Bradshaw-directed march that carried from the Pittsburgh 34 to the Minnesota 4. Bradshaw's pass to tight end Larry Brown in the end zone and Gerela's PAT supplied the final points of the game.

The pass play to Brown was suggested by Joe Gilliam as he watched Bradshaw maneuver the Steelers from the position he occupied at the start of the season. "Our quarterbacks hang together," Noll noted.

"I thought I had Brown covered on the rollout play," explained free safety Krause. "But then Bradshaw pulled up and Brown got behind me. I was hoping he'd throw the ball at first, because I had Brown covered real well. He just stopped and the ball was there."

When the Vikings' defensive unit left the field for the last time, with less than a minute remaining, Page slammed his helmet to the ground in a gesture of disgust. "I didn't think I'd need it anymore," explained the tackle.

Later Page confessed, "It didn't bother me so much that we lost, but that we had some players who didn't want to win. Franco Harris is a good running back, but we have faced others who were just as good or better. We just weren't good enough today to beat them."

Harris carried the ball six times on the Steelers' final touchdown drive and 11 times during the quarter. His last carry, a 15-yard gain to the right, increased Franco's rushing production for the day to 158 yards and broke the record of 145 yards set by Larry Csonka in Super Bowl VIII.

Harris, the game's most valuable player, found his rushing total difficult to believe. "You have to be kidding," he responded. "Gaining 1,000 yards and contributing to a title and Super Bowl victory make this the most significant year of my career.

"Bradshaw had us all relaxed in the huddle. The only time we weren't in control of the situation was when I fumbled, but when I came off the field, Joe Greene told me, 'Don't worry, we'll get it back,' and they did."

By all odds, Greene was the most formidable figure in the Pittsburgh defense that held the Vikings to 23 net yards on the ground, a previously unheard of total. Foreman gained 22 yards in 12 carries and Osborn lost one in eight tries.

"I feel so good about winning I'm almost weak," quipped Greene. "Winning is a lot bigger than I thought it would be.

"It's more fun than wearing the ring and being No. 1. We've never been here before, but we never considered losing. We knew we had a job to do because the Vikings are a tough opponent."

As he trudged off the field, Greene related, he felt sorry for the Vikings after losing their third Super Bowl. "But," he amended, "rather than us."

Bud Carson, who designed the Steelers' defensive game plan, noted, "We were convinced the only way the Vikings could beat us was with Tarkenton scrambling and completing those short rollout passes. Our plan was to shut their run down early to force them to throw the football. Our front four put on too big a rush to permit Tarkenton to have success throwing the football. Our biggest problem was that regular linebackers Lambert and Russell got hurt. We didn't know how their replacements would do, but Bradley and Toews did good jobs."

After a day of trying to contain the Steelers' defensive charge, Minnesota tackle Ron Yary declared, "Their defensive line outplayed us. They beat us with their defensive line. They beat us with their linebackers. They beat us in our secondary. Today our defense played well enough to win, but our offense didn't do the job."

In the opinion of Grant, "It wasn't a very good football game and that's a shame because this is football's showcase. The kicking game was not good, with three missed field goals, some fluke interceptions, some penalties. It was not the type of game either team played to get here."

Tarkenton put it more succinctly. "They deserved to win. They did it. We didn't."

When the victorious Steelers poured into their surprisingly subdued clubhouse, they found Owner Art Rooney already on hand. "I came down early to make sure my hair was combed," wisecracked the 73-year-old

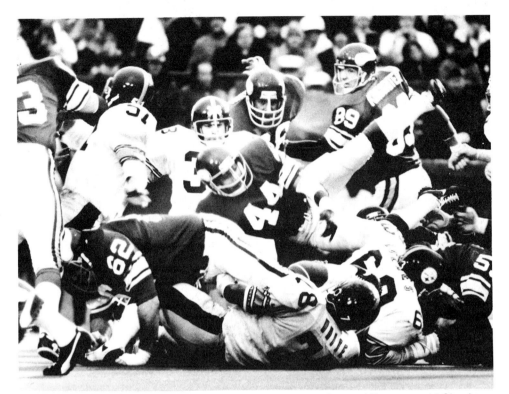

Chuck Foreman, minus football, hits the turf, courtesy of the rugged Steelers defensive line.

patriarch.

Bleier, the Vietnam hero with the Bronze Star and Purple Heart, was the first to greet the owner. "Thanks for giving me the chance to play," whispered Bleier from behind an embrace.

"Thanks for being part of the championship team," rejoined Rooney. The tears of both were genuine.

Russell presented the game ball to Rooney, exclaiming, "This one's for The Chief. It's been a long time coming."

"Thank you," murmured Rooney. "I'm proud of you and I'm grateful to you."

"Art Rooney is the greatest man who ever walked," exulted Bradshaw in a burst of hyperbole. "I'm glad our victory occurred in Louisiana. This is like the hometown boy coming home to win the Super Bowl." Bradshaw is a Shreveport native.

Terry recalled that Rooney had predicted in 1970 that the Steelers would be in the Super Bowl in five years. "I didn't believe in that stuff at the time but here we are," he said.

"As I walked off the field, I just savored it all, the noise and all the emotion. It was just a great, satisfying feeling."

As Bradshaw walked into the clubhouse,

he, like many members of the Steelers, was wearing a special type of shoe supplied by equipment manager Tony Parisi.

"I knew that the artificial surface of Tulane Stadium would be slick if it rained," reported Parisi, a transplanted Canadian. "So I called up the Weather Bureau and asked for a long-range forecast. They told me there was a good chance there would be a lot of rain before Sunday.

"Then I remembered reading something about shoes that had not yet come on the market. I did a little checking and found I could get this special type of shoe in Montreal. I phoned and ordered 75 pairs of shoes, which arrived on Wednesday.

"I don't tell the players what to wear. I only suggest and if they like the suggestion, fine."

"I don't know where he got 'em, but it was like they came from heaven," declared Russell. "They made a tremendous difference. They were absolutely fantastic."

Russell, Bradshaw and Harris were among those who wore the special shoes during the second half of the game, a game that, many contended, would not have culminated in victory without the foresight and enterprise of Tony Parisi.

Statistics of Ninth Super Bowl
PITTSBURGH 16, MINNESOTA 6

Tulane Stadium, New Orleans, La., January 12, 1975
Attendance: 80,997

PITTSBURGH	Offense	MINNESOTA
Frank Lewis	WR	Jim Lash
Jon Kolb	LT	Charles Goodrum
Jim Clack	LG	Andy Maurer
Ray Mansfield	C	Mick Tingelhoff
Gerry Mullins	RG	Ed White
Gordon Gravelle	RT	Ron Yary
Larry Brown	TE	Stu Voigt
Ron Shanklin	WR	John Gilliam
Terry Bradshaw	QB	Fran Tarkenton
Rocky Bleier	RB	Chuck Foreman
Franco Harris	RB	Dave Osborn

Defense

L. C. Greenwood	LE	Carl Eller
Joe Greene	LT	Doug Sutherland
Ernie Holmes	RT	Alan Page
Dwight White	RE	Jim Marshall
Jack Ham	LLB	Roy Winston
Jack Lambert	MLB	Jeff Siemon
Andy Russell	RLB	Wally Hilgenberg
J. T. Thomas	LCB	Nate Wright
Mel Blount	RCB	Jackie Wallace
Mike Wagner	LS	Jeff Wright
Glen Edwards	RS	Paul Krause

— SUBSTITUTIONS —

Pittsburgh—Offense: Receivers—John Stallworth, Lynn Swann, Reggie Garrett, John McMakin, Randy Grossman. Linemen—Sam Davis, Dave Reavis, Rick Druschel, Mike Webster. Backs—Preston Pearson, Steve Davis, Reggie Harrison. Kicker—Roy Gerela. Defense: Linebackers—Loren Toews, Marv Kellum, Ed Bradley. Linemen—Charlie Davis, Steve Furness. Backs—Jim Allen, Richard Conn, Donnie Shell. Punter—Bobby Walden. DNP—Joe Gilliam, Terry Hanratty, Jim Wolf.

Minnesota—Offense: Receivers—Sam McCullum, Doug Kingsriter, Steve Craig. Linemen—Grady Alderman, Scott Anderson, Steve Lawson, Milt Sunde. Backs—Bill Brown, Brent McClanahan, Oscar Reed, Ed Marinaro. Kicker—Fred Cox. Defense: Linebackers—Matt Blair, Amos Martin, Fred McNeill. Linemen—Gary Larsen, Bob Lurtsema. Backs—Terry Brown, Randy Poltl. Punter—Mike Eischeid. DNP—Bob Berry, Joe Blahak, Dave Boone, John Holland, Steve Riley.

— SCORE BY PERIODS —

Pittsburgh Steelers (AFC)	0	2	7	7 —	16
Minnesota Vikings (NFC)	0	0	0	6 —	6

— SCORING —

Pittsburgh—Safety, White downed Tarkenton in end zone.
Pittsburgh—Harris 9 run (Gerela kick).
Minnesota—T. Brown recovered blocked punt in end zone (kick failed).
Pittsburgh—L. Brown 4 pass from Bradshaw (Gerela kick).

— TEAM STATISTICS —

	Pittsburgh	Minnesota
Total First Downs	17	9
First Downs Rushing	11	2
First Downs Passing	5	5
First Downs by Penalty	1	2
Rushes	57	21
Yards Gained Rushing (net)	249	17

	Pittsburgh	Minnesota
Average Yards per Rush	4.4	0.8
Passes Attempted	14	26
Passes Completed	9	11
Had Intercepted	0	3
Times Tackled Att. to Pass	2	0
Yards Lost Att. to Pass	12	0
Yards Gained Passing (net)	84	102
Total Net Yardage	333	119
Punts	7	6
Average Distance	34.7	37.2
Punt Returns	5	4
Punt Return Yardage	36	12
Kickoff Returns	3	3
Kickoff Return Yardage	32	50
Interception Return Yardage	46	0
Fumbles	4	3
Opponent Fumbles Recovered	2	2
Total Return Yardage	107	52
Penalties	8	4
Yards Penalized	122	18
Total Points Scored	16	6
Touchdowns	2	1
Touchdowns Rushing	1	0
Touchdowns Passing	1	0
Touchdowns on Returns	0	1
Extra Points	2	0
Field Goals Attempted	2	1
Field Goals	0	0
Total Offensive Plays	73	47
Avg. Gain per Offensive Play	4.6	2.5

INDIVIDUAL STATISTICS
— RUSHING —

Pittsburgh	Atts.	Yds.	Lg.	TD
Harris	34	158	25	1
Bleier	17	65	18	0
Bradshaw	5	33	17	0
Swann	1	−7	−7	0

Minnesota	Atts.	Yds.	Lg.	TD
Foreman	12	18	12	0
Tarkenton	1	0	0	0
Osborn	8	−1	2	0

— PASSING —

Pittsburgh	Atts.	Comp.	Yds.	Int.	TD
Bradshaw	14	9	96	0	1

Minnesota	Atts.	Comp.	Yds.	Int.	TD
Tarkenton	26	11	102	3	0

— RECEIVERS —

Pittsburgh	No.	Yds.	Lg.	TD
Brown	3	49	30	1
Stallworth	3	24	22	0
Bleier	2	11	6	0
Lewis	1	12	12	0

Minnesota	No.	Yds.	Lg.	TD
Foreman	5	50	17	0
Voigt	2	31	28	0
Osborn	2	7	4	0
Gilliam	1	16	16	0
Reed	1	−2	−2	0

Terry Bradshaw fires a pass over the head of Vikings linebacker Jeff Siemon.

— INTERCEPTIONS —

Pittsburgh	No.	Yds.	Lg.	TD
Wagner	1	26	26	0
Blount	1	10	10	0
Greene	1	10	10	0

Minnesota–None.

— PUNTING —

Pittsburgh	No.	Avg.	Lg.
Walden	7	34.7	52

Minnesota	No.	Avg.	Lg.
Eischeid	6	37.2	42

— PUNT RETURNS —

Pittsburgh	No.	FC	Yds.	Lg.
Swann	3	0	34	17
Edwards	2	0	2	2

Minnesota	No.	FC	Yds.	Lg.
McCullum	3	0	11	6
N. Wright	1	0	1	1
Wallace	0	1	0	0

— KICKOFF RETURNS —

Pittsburgh	No.	Yds.	Lg.
Pearson	1	15	15
Harrison	2	17	17

Minnesota	No.	Yds.	Lg.
McCullum	1	26	26
McClanahan	1	22	22
B. Brown	1	2	2

— FIELD GOALS —

Pittsburgh	Att.	Made
Gerela	2	0

Minnesota	Att.	Made
Cox	1	0

— FUMBLES —

Pittsburgh	No.	Own Rec.	Opp. Rec.	TD
Harris	2	1	0	0
Walden	1	1	0	0
Bleier	1	0	0	0
Greene	0	0	1	0
Kellum	0	0	1	0

Minnesota	No.	Own Rec.	Opp. Rec.	TD
Tarkenton	1	1	0	0
B. Brown	1	0	0	0
Foreman	1	0	0	0
Krause	0	0	1	0
Poltl	0	0	1	0

— SCORING —

Pittsburgh	TD	PAT	FG	Pts.
Brown	1	0	0	6
Harris	1	0	0	6
Gerela	0	2	0	2
White (safety)	0	0	0	2

Minnesota	TD	PAT	FG	Pts.
T. Brown	1	0	0	6

MVP Lynn Swann was beautiful and devastating in Super Bowl X.

Super Bowl X

Swann Is Beautiful

January 18, 1976

For two nights Lynn Swann lay in a Pittsburgh hospital, the victim of a concussion that he suffered in the American Football Conference title game in which the Steelers defeated the Oakland Raiders, 16-10.

Set upon by Oakland safeties Jack Tatum and George Atkinson, the hospitalized wide receiver pondered his future, wondering if his professional career was finished, only two years after he earned All-America honors at the University of Southern California.

One week elapsed and when the Steelers arrived in Miami for their date with the Dallas Cowboys, Swann was listed as a doubtful starter.

When his teammates worked out, Swann stood on the sidelines, a spectator. Doctors examined him daily and told him at midweek that another severe blow to the head could result in permanent damage. He could play, said the medics, but the final decision was Swann's alone.

The player engaged in light workouts, mostly running and trying to perfect his timing. He continued as a questionable performer almost until the eve of the game, when his decision was made for him.

The decision-provoking incident occurred in, of all places, the camp of the Cowboys, where safetyman Cliff Harris was quoted as saying, "I'm not going to hurt anyone intentionally. But getting hit again while he's running a pass route must be in the back of Swann's mind. I know it would be in the back of my mind."

Swann read the Harris quotes and all doubts vanished. Announcing his decision to play, the swift Steeler said, "I'm still not 100 percent. I value my health, but I've had no dizzy spells. I read what Harris said. He was trying to intimidate me. He said I'd be afraid out there. He needn't worry. He doesn't know Lynn Swann. He can't scare me or the team. I said to myself, 'The hell with it, I'm gonna play.'

"Sure, I thought about the possibility of being reinjured. But it's like being thrown by a horse. You have to get up and ride again immediately or you may be scared the rest of your life."

As late as Saturday, the day before the January 18, 1976, extravaganza at the Orange Bowl, quarterback Terry Bradshaw reported that Swann was dropping passes, and that Lynn confessed, "I felt stiff. I couldn't get loose. I had no concentration."

The decision made, Swann recaptured his customary mobility, his leaping agility, his concentration and prehensile hands when the whistle sounded to signal the start of Super Bowl X.

Four times Swann caught Bradshaw passes, one on a 64-yard touchdown play, for 161 total yards.

"The first catch," wrote one journalist, "was incredible, the second unbelievable, the third was merely a standard, difficult, professional reception, but the fourth was a blazing touchdown that earned Swann most valuable player honors."

Swann's heroics also helped the Steelers engrave a second consecutive championship on the Vince Lombardi trophy in the form of a 21-17 victory before 80,187 spectators.

The first reception, a 32-yarder along the right sideline in the first quarter, was particularly significant to Swann.

"It seemed to boost me," he reported. "I never had a day in my life when I felt so loose."

In the second quarter, Bradshaw and Swann combined on a 53-yard pass play, again to the right side.

In the third quarter, Swann caught a 12-

yard pass and he completed his theatrics with 3:02 remaining in the fourth quarter by catching a 59-yard Bradshaw pass and scampering the five remaining yards to score the deciding touchdown.

Wasn't it a gamble, somebody asked Chuck Noll, throwing deep to Swann on a third-and-four situation from the Pittsburgh 36-yard line?

"We felt we could slip a few bombs in during the day," explained the Steelers' coach. "We missed by inches on a couple of others."

"Bradshaw called a pass route on the touchdown play, but I mainly just ran right up the middle," explained Swann. "I thought I could beat (cornerback) Mark Washington because I'd been beating him all day. The safetymen didn't give Washington any help. Washington played a pretty good game, but I made a couple of pretty good catches on him in the first half.

"Nobody hit me to hurt me. They just hit me hard enough to make me get up and make another catch.

"Cliff Harris came over to me once after a play and said I was lucky because he just missed me with a hard shot. He said he was going to come after me when I went across the middle and I told him to come ahead because if anyone got hurt it was going to be him. He hits hard, but there was no trouble."

The 6-foot, 180-pound speedster attributed his leaping ability to his basketball experience, revealing that he could dunk a ball when he was a junior in high school and stood only 5-10.

"It always makes me feel good when our passing game plays such a big part in a victory," said Swann. "We're a running team, we're known as a grind-it-out team and we win with that. But the passing game was really clicking today."

Bradshaw completed nine of 19 passes for 209 yards while the Cowboys' Roger Staubach hit on 15 of 24 for 204 yards.

Bradshaw did not see Swann haul down his long pass. At the snap of the ball, D.D. Lewis crashed across the line from his linebacker position. Bradshaw, anticipating the blitz, ducked under Lewis. He gained the time necessary to fire the pass, then was crushed to earth by Harris. When Swann caught the ball, Bradshaw was flat on his back, unconscious.

Revived, he was assisted from the field in an unsteady condition. Only when he reached the clubhouse did Bradshaw understand what had happened.

Thirty minutes after the game, following an extensive medical examination, Bradshaw was able to face the media.

"I got hit from the blind side and heard bells ringing," he reported. "I wanted to go deep all day. It was my call all the way. I barely got the pass away. They were coming on a double blitz. I got hit on my left cheek.

"Our strategy was to run with the ball, then mix the plays. I decided to throw more on first down and then throw some more. I had lots of time, great protection and felt we were in control of the game even though we were trailing most of the game."

Swann's performance on a sunlit, 56-degree afternoon was not extraordinary. He had caught 49 passes, more than any other player on either team, during the regular season and had scored 11 touchdowns to help the Steelers to a 12-2 record, matching the marks of Minnesota and Los Angeles.

In the AFC championship game, he caught two passes for 45 yards before he was injured.

Compared to the Steelers' methodical march to Miami, the Dallas route was less expected and far more dramatic. The Cowboys compiled a 10-4 regular-season record, second to St. Louis' 11-3 in the Eastern Division, to qualify as the NFC's wild card team.

With 24 seconds remaining in the divisional playoff game and trailing Minnesota, 14-10, the Cowboys pulled out a stunning, 17-14 upset when Staubach connected with Drew Pearson on a 50-yard "Hail Mary!" touchdown pass.

The following week, again the underdogs, the Cowboys defeated the Los Angeles Rams, 37-7, as Staubach threw four TD passes, three to Preston Pearson, in the NFC title game.

Climatic conditions in Super Bowl week commenced on a sour note. Wind and rain drove the temperature downward. Hotel pools were deserted and bars were jammed and, at Miami Lakes Inn, where the Steelers were quartered, defensive tackle Ernie Holmes was developing an advanced case of cabin fever and the mean disposition that goes with it.

"I'll be glad to leave here," he grumbled. "I feel like eating palm trees. I don't like this place. It's for people with arthritis. They come here to play golf and to die."

Holmes was not alone in his dislike of Miami conditions. The demand for Super Bowl tickets was unprecedented, NFL Commissioner Pete Rozelle announced, and some folks were paying up to $150 for tickets that turned out to be counterfeit.

Those who were swindled by fast-buck artists could sympathize with others who arrived with tour groups in the days immediately preceding the game.

An estimated 5,000 persons flew into Miami as members of junkets conducted by

Pittsburgh's Reggie Harrison (46) blocks Mitch Hoopes' punt, a play that resulted in a Steelers' safety.

Super Tours International. Air transportation, hotel accommodations and tickets to the game were wrapped up in an attractive package selling for between $375 and $500. Hotel facilities were readily available, but tickets were in short supply.

According to one visitor from Pittsburgh, "First, we were to get our game tickets when we boarded the plane. Then, they told us the tickets would be distributed the day before the game to prevent forgeries. Then, they told us the tickets would be waiting for us on the bus on the way to the stadium."

Some ticketless tourists shelled out exorbitant sums for ducats. Some slouched grumpily before hotel TV sets, assuring themselves they could have done as much at home for considerably less expense. Others angrily accosted travel agents in hotel lobbies, bringing riot squads on the double.

Authorities estimated that the swindle may have aggregated $1.5 million.

As one who had suffered at the hands of the Steelers a year earlier, Fran Tarkenton had some pre-game thoughts on the Pittsburgh defense.

"Their defense is the most dominating in football," declared the Minnesota quarterback. "It is also the most frustrating.

"I doubt they're the greatest pass-rushing line that has played the game, but against the run they might be.

"Their linebackers play the pass as well as any I've ever seen. The Cowboys are playing the best football they've ever played. They probably played their best game against the Rams, and they played very well against us.

"The Steelers have geared themselves to the offense that depends on Franco Harris. Dallas should be fairly successful in defensing the Steelers."

The Cowboys, with their celebrated "flex" defense, were considered admirably structured to halt the run. Against the Rams they had permitted only 22 net yards rushing.

To Staubach, the game shaped up as a struggle "between our offense and their defense. The Steeler defense represents the biggest challenge we've faced all year. I probably run too much, but that's just my instinct. I've always run when a play breaks down. I'd like to be more like Tarkenton. He scrambles and throws, picking receivers downfield. I don't have the ability to do that. When I scramble, I usually run."

Staubach cited the Cowboys' shotgun formation as another asset "because it gives us more time and confuses the defense. We use it only on third-down plays. I've learned to look for a receiver and hit him whenever possible. I've tried to scramble in such situations, but have come up short of a first down too often."

Bradshaw, whose season passing statistics were only a shade less imposing than those of Staubach, saw the game in this manner:

"We'll see a formation and run a play and see if they give us the defensive front four that we expect. If they do, fine; we'll know where we stand. Then we'll run another play to see how they react. If they don't react the way they normally would, we'll throw our first pass and see what they do on their coverage.

"If they do what our scouting reports say they will, fine. If they don't, we'll change things on the sideline. This could go on all afternoon."

Bradshaw planned to send Harris into the line and control the tempo of the game, which he followed faithfully on the Steelers' first possession as Harris carried on four of the first five plays before Bobby Walden attempted to punt from the Pittsburgh 40-yard line.

The snap from center was low, however. Walden bobbled the ball and was tackled on the 29 by Billy Joe DuPree, a Dallas tight end playing on the special teams.

"I just took my eyes off the ball," Walden explained. "It happens to every punter once in a while. You try not to press after something like that, but sometimes you don't succeed."

Staubach wasted no time in capitalizing on the break. On the first play he fired a 14-yard bull's-eye to Drew Pearson crossing up the middle and the wide receiver raced into the end zone without being touched. Toni Fritsch's extra point gave the Cowboys a surprisingly easy 7-0 lead with only four minutes and 35 seconds elapsed.

The touchdown marked the first time in the season that Pittsburgh had yielded points in the first quarter.

The Cowboys retained their lead for about five minutes, or only until Bradshaw, mixing running plays by Harris and Rocky Bleier with the 32-yard pass to Swann, moved the Steelers from their 33 to the Dallas 7.

On a third-and-one, Bradshaw reasoned correctly that the Cowboys anticipated a running play and called instead a pass play to Randy Grossman. The reserve tight end faked a block, then headed diagonally for the end zone where he caught a pass that, with Roy Gerela's PAT, knotted the score at 7-7.

In eight plays, the Steelers had moved 67 yards under the steady hand of Bradshaw, who had completed the only two passes he attempted.

The scoring play was a novelty for Noll.

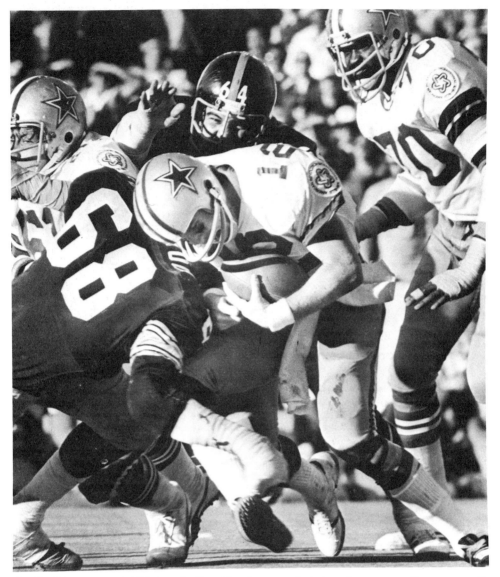

L. C. Greenwood (68) leads the Steelers sack brigade on another assault against Roger Staubach.

In his Pittsburgh coaching career, when the Steelers were deep in opponents' territory, Noll used the three tight-end offense with guard Gerry Mullins lining up in the tight end position.

"Early in the game we ran out of that formation to give them a look at it," revealed Grossman. "Then we threw the pass."

After the kickoff was returned to the Dallas 35, Staubach resorted almost exclusively to the ground attack that featured Robert Newhouse and Doug Dennison. An illegal motion penalty helped stall the drive early in the second quarter, but Fritsch kicked a 36-yard field goal to send the Cowboys ahead again, 10-7.

Midway through the quarter, Staubach mounted another Dallas drive from his 48-yard line. In six plays, four of them passes, the Cowboys advanced to the Pittsburgh 20, where the Steeler defense stiffened abruptly.

Newhouse lost three yards at left tackle and then Staubach was sacked twice, once by L. C. Greenwood for 12 yards and once by

Randy Grossman pulls in a Terry Bradshaw pass . . .

Dwight White for 10. Mitch Hoopes punted 39 yards and the Steelers took over at their 6 with 3:47 remaining until halftime. But that was time enough for Bradshaw to unleash one more threat.

In eight plays, including the 53-yard Bradshaw-to-Swann pass on a third-and-six from the 10, the Steelers drove to the Dallas 19 with 32 seconds remaining. A pass intended for John Stallworth fell incomplete and, on fourth-and-three, Gerela's 36-yard field goal attempt that would have tied the score sailed wide to the left.

Although the Cowboys enjoyed the lead at halftime, statistics favored the Steelers. The AFC champions held an edge in first downs, 10 to 8; total net yards, 194 to 98; net yards rushing, 92 to 51; net yards passing, 102 to 47. In passing, Staubach had completed six of 10, Bradshaw six of 11.

The break that the Steelers had been looking for occurred in the third quarter when cornerback J. T. Thomas intercepted a Staubach pass and returned it 35 yards to the Dallas 25. Behind three Harris smashes, the Steelers moved to a first down on the 14, but a two-yard loss by Bradshaw and two incomplete passes brought the Pittsburgh field goal unit onto the field again. Once more Gerela's 33-yard kick faded to the left.

"Nobody was more disappointed than I over mssing those two field goals," said Gerela. "The wind may have been a factor,

but I didn't hit them too good, either."

Defending his teammate, center Ray Mansfield reported: "Roy couldn't even practice before the game. He kicked about seven balls into the stands and the fans kept 'em. We finally had to steal a football from the Cowboys so he could practice."

At 3:52 of the fourth quarter, and with Dallas still leading, 10-7, the momentum of the game made a 180-degree turn in a most unexpected fashion. When Hoopes attempted to punt from the Dallas 16, reserve running back Reggie Harrison blocked the ball, which rolled out of the end zone for a Steeler safety, cutting the Cowboys' lead to 10-9.

"I don't know what happened," replied Harrison when asked to explain the play. "I just came up the middle. I knew I was going to block that one, it was mine. I was always afraid to block a kick before for fear of being kicked myself."

Harrison did not escape unscathed. Opening his mouth, he displayed a cut on his tongue. "I'm going to put a $1,000 bill on it and see what happens," he joked.

From the area of the Dallas bench, Landry saw that "they rushed 10 men and somebody missed a block. I don't know who it was. We probably just brush-blocked Harrison and he made the big play. That's what usually happens on a blocked punt."

In Harrison's football career—in high school, at Northeast Oklahoma Junior Col-

. . . and scores the Steelers' first touchdown of the game.

lege, at the University of Cincinnati and in the NFL—he had never before blocked a punt. He was astonished over his accomplishment.

"I was yelling and screaming so much that when I went to the bench I didn't realize that we got some points," he related. "We were losing and we were supposed to win and I was all messed up in my head. The next thing I remember we were lining up to kick off and I looked at the scoreboard and we were winning by 12 to 10. I asked Jimmy Allen what had happened."

What had happened was that the Steelers, after the safety, had taken the free kick and driven to the Dallas 20, from where, on fourth down, Gerela had booted a 36-yard field goal.

On the Cowboys' next possession, Staubach attempted a first-down pass to Drew Pearson that was intercepted by safetyman Mike Wagner, who returned the ball to the Dallas 7.

Three plays later, Gerela kicked an 18-yard field goal and the Steelers, with eight unanswered points, enjoyed a 15-10 lead.

Still, one touchdown was all the Cowboys needed to regain the lead and they had more than six minutes in which to do it.

They failed on their next possession and Hoopes punted to Glen Edwards, who returned the ball to the Pittsburgh 30. Two line smashes picked up six yards and then Bradshaw connected with swift-gliding Swann on the 64-yard scoring play. Gerela's conversion kick hit the upright, but the Steelers had a 21-10 lead with 3:02 remaining.

"I reached for the ball, but missed it," said Washington, placed in the uncomfortable position of trying to cover Swann singlehandedly. "You feel some pressure when the safety blitz is on and you're out there by yourself. Nobody can cover Swann adequately under those conditions."

Fighting the clock was nothing unusual for Staubach and in less than a minute, the Cowboys were on the scoreboard again. Starting on his 20-yard line, Staubach passed to Charle Young for seven yards, to Drew Pearson for 30, to Preston Pearson for 11, and then, after a two-yard sack, to Percey Howard on a 34-yard TD play. When Fritsch converted, the Cowboys were within four points, 21-17.

A Dallas on-side kick failed and the Steelers began their next series at the Cowboys' 42 with one minute and 47 seconds to be played. The Cowboys called a timeout after each play.

Franco Harris lost two yards at left guard and 1:41 remained.

Harris regained the two yards on a right end sweep and there was 1:35 to go.

Rocky Bleier hit left guard for one and the time was down to 1:28 with a fourth-and-nine situation at the Dallas 41.

Certainly, the Steelers would punt, hopeful of pinning the Cowboys deep in their own territory. But punter Walden made no move to come on the field. Noll preferred to take his chances on a running play, rather than risk a blocked punt or a long runback, and then turn the game over to the Steelers' defense.

When Bleier picked up only two, fourth-down yards, the Cowboys took over on their 39 with 1:22 remaining.

As a starter, Staubach turned left end for 11 yards, then passed to Preston Pearson for 12 and the Cowboys were at the Pittsburgh 38. Time remained for deep passes only. A receiver may be unable to get out of bounds on a sideline pattern but any completion short of the end zone could result in the receiver being tackled before he could cross the goal line. The odds against Dallas' success were astronomical.

Staubach's first pass, intended for Drew Pearson, was overthrown. The second, intended for Howard, fell incomplete. The third, intended for Drew Pearson, was intercepted by safety Glen Edwards, who returned it 30 yards to the Pittsburgh 33 as time ran out.

Postmortems were pointed and plentiful by players of both teams. Jack Lambert, middle linebacker for the Steelers, reported that "there was some rough stuff going on out there that we didn't need. After Gerela missed one of his field goal tries, Cliff Harris came over and slapped him on the helmet. Sure that stirred me up, but I was stirred up before that. In the first half we were being intimidated and the Steelers aren't supposed to be intimidated. We were just plain being pushed around. But we made some changes and took control of the game physically in the second half."

According to defensive tackle Joe Greene, "Lambert was the fellow who held us together when things weren't going good. He spearheaded us. He made the licks that got us going."

Greene was forced to sit out the second half because of a pulled groin muscle and turned the job over to Steve Furness.

Preston Pearson, a member of the Steelers' Super Bowl IX team, conceded that he had "a little dispute" with Lambert. "But Jack's always a very zealous linebacker," he noted. "You can't let him abuse you physically. I don't like to be pushed around, but nothing came of it."

Howard, whose first pass reception as a pro turned out to be a Super Bowl touchdown, expressed criticism of the officiating in the last frenzied seconds when Staubach

Pittsburgh's Mike Wagner holds up the ball after the interception that set up a Pittsburgh field goal.

fired a pass intended for him.

"The pass I'll always remember is the one I didn't catch," said the rookie from Austin Peay University. "When I saw the pass coming, I knew it was mine. But I never got to touch the ball because this guy (Mel Blount) hit me and he didn't have a chance to go for the ball. I was expecting a flag to be thrown and so was he because he got up, looking around everywhere for a flag. I guess the officials didn't call it because three Steelers were around me and they didn't see it."

Staubach, victim of a Super Bowl-record seven sacks, paid tribute to the Pittsburgh rush. "They did a good job rushing the shotgun," said Roger. "I didn't do well from it, but you're always in a negative situation when you use it. I had good protection, but their secondary and linebackers made it tough. They didn't get to me until I ran out of the pocket."

About Wagner's interception, which set up the field goal making the score 15-10, Staubach commented, "I didn't even see Wagner. He wasn't supposed to be there. I bet Golden Richards (wide receiver) was wide open, but I didn't see him either. Golden was Wagner's responsibility. Wagner just guessed, and guessed right."

In addition to the seven sacks, Staubach entered the record book with two touchdown passes, giving him four in two Super Bowl games. He also set records by fumbling three times and recovering twice.

Landry cited the blocked punt and Swann's receptions as the two major reasons for the Cowboys' second Super Bowl setback.

"The blocked punt reversed the game's momentum," said the Dallas coach.

On Noll's decision not to punt late in the game, Landry said, "It was a judgment a coach must make. Noll has always had a lot of confidence in his defense. I've seen him do it before. Of course, when they didn't make it, it gave their defense a chance since we had good field position. I was a little surprised by the move, but at the end we had no timeouts remaining and we couldn't get the ball out of bounds."

Pittsburgh players were unprepared for Noll's decision to pass up the punt. "I couldn't figure it out," conceded linebacker Andy Russell. "I didn't know what his plan was. But don't ask me to second guess the fellow. I won't do that."

Noll had his reasons.

"The move left them with no timeouts and needing a touchdown to win," he explained. "If they had needed a field goal, then it would have been different. But we had them in a must-pass situation and I like for my defense to have a team in that kind of spot.

"Our defense did just what we thought it would do. They came up with a pass interception. I would prefer to turn a situation like that over to the defense instead of taking a chance on getting a punt blocked."

When Staubach was firing last-second passes toward the end zone, somebody wanted to know, was Noll worried that the Cowboys would pull out a miracle victory as they did in the playoffs against Minnesota?

"No."

Why not?

"We're not Minnesota."

Statistics of Tenth Super Bowl

PITTSBURGH 21, DALLAS 17

Orange Bowl, Miami, Fla., January 18, 1976
Attendance: 80,187

DALLAS	Offense	PITTSBURGH
Golden Richards.....	WR	......John Stallworth
Ralph Neely	LT	.... Jon Kolb
Burton Lawless	LG	.... Jim Clack
John Fitzgerald	C	........Ray Mansfield
Blaine Nye	RG	.... Gerry Mullins
Rayfield Wright	RT	.....Gordon Gravelle
Jean Fugett............	TE	........Larry Brown
Drew Pearson	WR	...........Lynn Swann
Roger Staubach	QB	..... Terry Bradshaw
Preston Pearson.....	RB	........Rocky Bleier
Robert Newhouse ...	RB	.... Franco Harris

Defense

DALLAS	Defense	PITTSBURGH
Ed Jones	LE	.... L. C. Greenwood
Jethro Pugh	LT	.... Joe Greene
Larry Cole	RT	.........Ernie Holmes
Harvey Martin........	RE	.... Dwight White
Dave Edwards........	LLB	.... Jack Ham
Lee Roy Jordan	MLB	.... Jack Lambert
D. D. Lewis	RLB	..........Andy Russell
Mark Washington ...	LCB	..........J. T. Thomas
Mel Renfro.............	RCB	.... Mel Blount
Charlie Waters	LS	.... Mike Wagner
Cliff Harris	RS	.... Glen Edwards

— SUBSTITUTIONS —

DALLAS—Offense: Receivers—Percy Howard, Ron Howard, Billy Joe DuPree. Linemen—Kyle Davis, Pat Donovan, Herbert Scott. Backs—Doug Dennison, Charley Young. Kicker—Toni Fritsch. Defense: Linebackers—Bob Breunig, Randy White, Tom Henderson, Cal Peterson, Warren Capone. Linemen—Bill Gregory. Backs—Benny Barnes, Randy Hughes, Roland Woolsey. Punter—Mitch Hoopes. DNP—Clint Longley, Bruce Walton.

PITTSBURGH—Offense: Receivers—Frank Lewis, Randy Grossman, Reggie Garrett. Linemen—Mike Webster, Sam Davis, Dave Reavis. Backs—Terry Hanratty, John Fuqua, Mike Collier, Reggie Harrison. Kicker—Roy Gerela. Defense: Linebackers—Ed Bradley, Loren Toews, Marv Kellum. Linemen—Steve Furness, John Banaszak. Backs—Donnie Shell, Dave Brown, Jim Allen. Punter—Bobby Walden. DNP—Joe Gilliam.

— SCORE BY PERIODS —

Dallas Cowboys (NFC)	7	3	0	7 — 17
Pittsburgh Steelers (AFC)	7	0	0	14 — 21

— SCORING —

Dallas—D. Pearson 29 pass from Staubach (Fritsch kick).
Pittsburgh—Grossman 7 pass from Bradshaw (Gerela kick).
Dallas—Field goal Fritsch 36.
Pittsburgh—Safety, Harrison blocked Hoopes' punt through end zone.
Pittsburgh—Field goal Gerela 36.
Pittsburgh—Field goal Gerela 18.
Pittsburgh—Swann 64 pass from Bradshaw (kick failed).
Dallas—P. Howard 34 pass from Staubach (Fritsch kick).

— TEAM STATISTICS —

	Dallas	Pittsburgh
Total First Downs...................	14	13
First Downs Rushing	6	7
First Downs Passing.............	8	6
First Downs by Penalty	0	0
Rushes.................................	31	46
Yards Gained Rushing (net)...	108	149
Average Yards per Rush	3.5	3.2
Passes Attempted.................	24	19
Passes Completed.................	15	9
Had Intercepted....................	3	0
Times Tackled Attemp. Pass...	7	2
Yards Lost Attempting Pass...	42	19
Yards Gained Passing (net) ...	162	190
Total Net Yardage	270	339
Punts...................................	7	4
Average Distance	35.0	39.8
Punt Returns.......................	1	4
Punt Return Yardage............	5	31
Kickoff Returns...................	4	4
Kickoff Return Yardage.........	96	89
Interception Return Yardage .	0	89
Fumbles...............................	4	4
Opp. Fumbles Recovered	0	0
Total Return Yardage............	101	198
Penalties..............................	2	0
Yards Penalized	20	0
Total Points Scored	17	21
Touchdowns........................	2	2
Touchdowns Rushing	0	0
Touchdowns Passing.............	2	2
Touchdowns on Returns........	0	0
Extra Points........................	2	1
Field Goals Attempted	1	4
Field Goals...........................	1	2
Total Offensive Plays............	62	67
Avg. Gain per Offensive Play .	4.4	5.1

INDIVIDUAL STATISTICS

— RUSHING —

Dallas	Atts.	Yds.	Lg.	TD
Newhouse	16	56	16	0
Staubach	5	22	11	0
Dennison	5	16	5	0
P. Pearson	5	14	9	0
Pittsburgh	Atts.	Yds.	Lg.	TD
Harris............................	27	82	11	0
Bleier	15	51	8	0
Bradshaw.......................	4	16	8	0

— PASSING —

Dallas	Atts.	Comp.	Yds.	Int.	TD
Staubach	24	15	204	3	2
Pittsburgh	Atts.	Comp.	Yds.	Int.	TD
Bradshaw..............	19	9	209	0	2

— RECEIVING —

Dallas	No.	Yds.	Lg.	TD
D. Pearson	2	59	30	1
P. Pearson	5	53	14	0
P. Howard......................	1	34	34	1
Young............................	3	31	14	0
Newhouse	2	12	8	0
Fugett............................	1	9	9	0
Dennison........................	1	6	6	0

Dallas' D.D. Lewis closes in on Steelers' quarterback Terry Bradshaw as he sets to throw a pass.

— RECEIVING —

Pittsburgh	No.	Yds.	Lg.	TD
Swann	4	161	64	1
Harris	1	26	26	0
Stallworth	2	8	13	0
L. Brown	1	7	7	0
Grossman	1	7	7	1

— INTERCEPTIONS —

Dallas–None.

Pittsburgh	No.	Yds.	Lg.	TD
Edwards	1	35	35	0
Thomas	1	35	35	0
Wagner	1	19	19	0

— PUNTING —

Dallas	No.	Avg.	Lg.
Hoopes	7	35.0	48

Pittsburgh	No.	Avg.	Lg.
Walden	4	39.8	59

— PUNT RETURNS —

Dallas	No.	FC	Yds.	Lg.
Richards	1	3	5	5

Pittsburgh	No.	FC	Yds.	Lg.
Edwards	2	0	17	10
D. Brown	3	0	14	9

— KICKOFF RETURNS —

Dallas	No.	Yds.	Lg.
P. Pearson	4	48	24
Henderson	0	48	48

Pittsburgh	No.	Yds.	Lg.
Blount	3	64	27
Collier	1	25	25

— FIELD GOALS —

Dallas	Att.	Made
Fritsch	1	1

Pittsburgh	Att.	Made
Gerela	4	2

— FUMBLES —

Dallas	No.	Own Rec.	Opp. Rec.	TD
Staubach	3	2	0	0
Fitzgerald	0	1	0	0
P. Pearson	1	1	0	0

Pittsburgh	No.	Own Rec.	Opp. Rec.	TD
Walden	1	1	0	0
D. Brown	1	0	0	0
Thomas	0	1	0	0
Bradshaw	1	0	0	0
Harris	1	1	0	0

— SCORING —

Dallas	TD	PAT	FG	Pts.
P. Howard	1	0	0	6
D. Pearson	1	0	0	6
Fritsch	0	2	1	5

Pittsburgh	TD	PAT	FG	Pts.
Gerela	0	1	2	7
Grossman	1	0	0	6
Swann	1	0	0	6
Harrison (safety)	0	0	0	2

Super Bowl XI MVP Fred Biletnikoff (left) and Cliff Branch share an emotional moment after the Raiders' victory.

Super Bowl XI

A Silver and Black Sunday

January 9, 1977

In the Oakland Raiders' locker room, muscular athletes clad in the club's distinctive silver and black, watched with suppressed emotion as Pete Rozelle presented the silver Vince Lombardi Trophy to Al Davis, managing general partner, and Coach John Madden.

"I'm sorry the trophy isn't silver and black, but it's close," equipped the commissioner. "Your victory was one of the most impressive in Super Bowl history."

More than just a symbol of professional football's supreme accomplishment, the trophy represented to the Raiders the culmination of years of frustration, seasons of building and the death of one of the game's most vile canards: "They can't win the big one."

Oakland had just won "the big one," thrashing the Minnesota Vikings, 32-14, in a suprisingly effortless demonstration before 103,438 on the sunny, 58-degree afternoon of January 9, 1977.

The moment of triumph was particularly exhilarating to those who could remember the early years of the American Football League when the Raiders drew only curiosity seekers to nondescript Frank Youell Field, named for an undertaker and which was nothing more, one writer maintained, than "an urban playground with portable stands."

The Raiders had lost 25 of their previous 28 games when Al Davis, an assistant coach of the San Diego Chargers, assumed the coaching chores in 1963, proclaiming that "I've always gone into everything with the confidence that I could do the job."

Later, Davis recalled, "I was never concerned that we could get this thing off the ground. It was only a matter of how quickly."

At 36, Davis engineered an instant transformation on the rag-tag Raiders, who had been selected to finish last in the Western Division. The team finished second, missing the title by one game. Not surprisingly, Davis was selected AFL Coach of the Year in virtually every poll.

After laying the foundation for Raider success, Davis moved on to more prestigious chairs, turning the coaching reins over to John Rauch, who guided the Raiders to the AFL title in 1967 and into Super Bowl II. Then came John Madden, who won division titles in six of his first seven seasons as coach. In five of those championship years, the Raiders advanced to the American Football Conference title game, only to lose the big one.

But 1976 was a different story. The Raiders started off with victories over Pittsburgh, Kansas City and Houston before suffering a 48-17 wipeout at New England.

Injuries to key personnel forced the Raiders to adopt a 3-4 defense for the Patriots game and inexperience took a heavy toll.

"Everything New England did was right and everything we did was wrong," philosophized quarterback Ken Stabler. "There are some games you can't really get upset about because there is nothing you can do about it.

"New England uses the same defense we use and they knew how to take advantage of our people. Our guy in the middle had to take on their center, maybe a guard double-teaming him, and then the running back. He didn't have much chance."

After the Foxboro fiasco, it was all smooth sailing for the Raiders, the only close call a 28-27 squeaker in Chicago.

The Raiders eliminated the Patriots in the first round of the playoffs, 24-21, and then won a trip to the Super Bowl with a 24-7 triumph over the Pittsburgh Steelers, their conquerors in the two previous AFC title games.

The Oakland offense was spearheaded by Mark van Eeghen, who gained 1,012 yards, fifth highest in the conference, and Stabler, who led AFC quarterbacks with 194 pass completions in 291 attempts and accounted for 2,737 yards.

The Minnesota Vikings cakewalked to the championship of the NFC Central Division with an 11-2-1 record. Their only defeats came at the hands of the Chicago Bears, 14-13, and the San Francisco 49ers, 20-16. Los Angeles accounted for the 10-10 tie.

In the playoffs, the Vikings eliminated the Washington Redskins, 35-20, and Los Angeles, 24-13, to gain a shot at a Super Bowl championship that had eluded them three times.

As in recent seasons, the Minnesota offense revolved around Chuck Foreman (1,155 yards in 277 carries) and Fran Tarkenton, the No. 3 rated quarterback in the conference (255 completions in 412 attempts) and Fred Cox, the third highest NFC scorer among kickers with 89 points.

One of the brightest new members of the Vikings cast was Sammy White, a wide receiver out of Grambling. The swift deep threat caught 51 passes, sixth highest total in the NFC, and gained 906 yards, more than any other receiver, and averaged 17.8 yards per catch. His 10 touchdowns also led the NFC.

The fact that the game would be played in the Rose Bowl was, in itself, historic. For years directors of the Pasadena stadium had remained aloof of the professional game, preferring to limit the facility to one major football event annually, the New Year's Day extravaganza.

But NFL blandishments, plus pressure from other points, weakened the resistance and the Rose Bowl became the fifth site for football's premier attraction.

Rental for the Rose Bowl was announced as $112,000, while the City of Pasadena realized an additional $8,000 from concessions sales.

Other NFL expenses included $75,000 for the cocktail party, dinner and entertainment on the Friday night preceding the game, $25,000 for halftime entertainment, $130,000 for each club's hotels, food, practice field and security and the cash equivalent of 80 round-trip tickets to Los Angeles.

Each player, who received one-fourteenth of his annual salary for the first playoff game and $8,500 for the conference championship game, would receive $15,000 or $7,500 for the Super Bowl, depending on the outcome.

The game was not only witnessed by the first Super Bowl crowd to surpass 100,000, but approximately 78 million who watched on NBC television on 224 American channels as well as outlets in Canada, France, England, Mexico, Latin America and Japan.

To accommodate visitors from afar, two major airlines scheduled additional flights from Minneapolis to Los Angeles and the No. 1 rent-a-car agency increased its rolling stock by 20 percent.

Tourism officials estimated that more than $31 million would be poured into the city's economy by free-spending visitors.

As the two contestants engaged in Super Week drills, ripples of discontent emanated from the Viking base at Costa Mesa. Foreman was unhappy because the club refused to renegotiate his contract as he had requested before the start of the season.

"This may be the wrong time to make this public," conceded the three-year veteran, "but I'm not happy with my contract and won't play with the club again. I think I've proved myself and want to be paid as the best."

Tarkenton, among others, agreed with Foreman. "We don't give Foreman the ball to set records like Buffalo does with O.J. Simpson," declared the quarterback. "Foreman is the most valuable player on this team. In fact, he's the most valuable player in the league."

The addition of Brent McClanahan, a running back, and wide receivers Ahmad Rashad and White created, continued Tarkenton, "an obsession on this team to win the Super Bowl. It started last year in the Dallas game. This team is on fire to play the game."

Comparing the present Vikings with the model of a year earlier, Coach Bud Grant announced, "This team has a new dimension—emotion. It may have been dormant all the while. It's the kind of spirit players need to build themselves up. It can't come from the outside."

Jim Finks, general manager of the Vikes from 1964 to '73 and now front office chief of the Chicago Bears, cast a pre-game vote of confidence for the NFC champions, declaring, "I'm not convinced that Dave Rowe, Otis Sistrunk and John Matuszak (Raider front three) strike fear into the hearts of anyone. They have played all season, but I don't think they are in the same class as Carl Eller, Alan Page, Doug Sutherland and Jim Marshall (Minnesota front four).

"I believe Minnesota is the better team from player No. 1 through No. 43. Minnesota's linebackers are just as good, their front four are better and their secondary just as good.

"Minnesota also has more ways of scor-

It wasn't the best of days for Fran Tarkenton. The Vikings quarterback couldn't get away from Oakland linebacker Phil Villapiano (above) and then walked dejectedly from the field as Willie Hall celebrated his fumble recovery at the Raiders' 2-yard line.

ing. I don't think Oakland can break a play for any distance. Foreman has that ability."

Washington Redskins Coach George Allen said he had never seen a stronger Viking team, but gave a possible edge to Oakland because of its depth. "That counts in a game that figures to be so close," said Allen.

"Oakland's big threat is the bomb. Stabler can go deep and nobody has been able to stop him. The only way is with a great rush or lay off and give away the short stuff underneath. Stabler gets the best protection in football. He has time to find the open man and his receivers have the speed and knowledge to get open."

A free spirit with full appreciation of the unfettered lifestyle, Stabler was eminently qualified for distinction as a professional quarterback.

"In the NFL," he once remarked, "I bet there are 25 quarterbacks who can throw better than I can. But I can make guys win. I can motivate players and they'll tell you that. It's part of my job. Winning is what we're all here for. It cures colds, heals fever blisters, whatever's wrong with you.

"The worst thing I could do would be to let my guys see me with a worried look. I'm not a worrier anyway. I'm really relaxed and loose on the field, no matter how tense things are.

"Sometimes I think of all the things that could go wrong if I screw up. But then I know that I'm not going to, so it ain't no big deal."

Approaching his first Super Bowl, Stabler confessed that "I'd like to think that this is nothing more than a sandlot game and all we had to do is go out there and have some fun. But I can't, the game is just too big. It means too much to too many people for me to say it's just another game. It means money and job security.

"We've showed that we don't have to establish the running game before we pass. We can pass anytime we want to as long as we have good protection. Cliff Branch is our home run guy. Freddie Biletnikoff is a great clutch guy and Dave Casper is a real smart, strong guy who outmuscles people. They're very difficult to cover. People say that the zone defense has taken away the long ball, but I've seen Branch run right away from zones."

Biletnikoff did not possess the blazing speed of Branch, a world-class sprinter, but the 12-year veteran whose 43 receptions had accounted for 551 yards had developed a technique that made him one of the game's most feared wide receivers.

"I try to give the defensive back the impression that I'm on a deep pattern," he explained. "As soon as he turns his back and starts running, I plant my foot and go either back toward the line of scrimmage, or toward the middle or out toward the sideline. That gives me two chances to beat him, either by forcing him to turn and start running before I plant my foot or by coming back toward scrimmage.

"Success often depends on knowing what your own backs are doing on a certain pattern. If I'm running a hook, for instance, I know that the outside linebacker will follow our backs coming out of the backfield. So I'll slide over a few yards toward the vacated spot."

Despite his pre-eminence as a pass catcher, Biletnikoff tried continually to add refinements to his act. "I still get to the same point where I plan to break either left or right," he explained. "But getting to the spot can be done several different ways. If I run an out pattern, I can line up a lot wider so my first move is to the inside, then back outside. I get to the same spot I originally planned to go to, but I give the defender a different view from what he's accustomed to."

Unlike nine years earlier when the Raiders made their only previous Super Bowl appearance, against Green Bay, their veteran players were no longer in awe of the opposition.

Pete Banaszak capsulized the Raiders' feelings of an earlier era when he recalled: "On our first offensive play, I came out of the huddle and looked across the line at Ray Nitschke, Dave Robinson, Henry Jordan, Herb Adderley, Willie Davis, guys whose bubble gum cards I had collected as a kid. I was supposed to block Robinson and Hewritt Dixon carried the ball. I never touched Robinson. Nitschke came over to get Dixon for no gain. I had cleat marks all over my back."

Slack-jawed admiration was gone the second time around. The Raiders exuded confidence, a mood detected by Len Dawson, former Kansas City quarterback and now an NBC sportscaster who predicted, "The Raiders will kill 'em."

If the Raiders had a killer instinct, it was not readily apparent. After Carl Garrett returned the opening kickoff to the Oakland 34, Stabler guided the Raiders to the Minnesota 32, with Clarence Davis picking up 20 yards on a left end sweep.

"The only play I second-guessed myself on came just after that," Stabler disclosed. "We lost a yard on first down and then I missed on a pass on second down. Everybody in the stadium expected a pass on third down, but I decided to get fancy and call a running play. I knew everyone would be looking for a pass.

Tight end Dave Casper hauls in Ken Stabler's pass for the first Raider touchdown.

"I thought maybe I could pop a run in there and surprise the Vikings and make a good gain. But we didn't fool them. They may have been looking for a pass, but they stopped Banaszak on a running play after two yards. That made it fourth down and we went for a field goal and missed. I figured it was my fault we didn't score because of the play I called on third down."

On their third possession, the Raiders' premier punter, Ray Guy, dropped back to kick. Guy never before had had a punt blocked in his four years in the NFL, but this time he kicked the football squarely into linebacker Fred McNeill, who recovered on the Oakland 3-yard line.

"The snap was low," reported Guy. "Then I had to take steps, extra time to get the kick away. I thought I got the kick off, then I saw it in the air over my head. That's when I knew it had been blocked. McNeill got to the ball because the snap was low and we missed a blocking assignment."

The Vikings failed to capitalize on the break. On second down from the 2, McClanahan fumbled and linebacker Willie Hall recovered for Oakland.

In 12 plays, the Raiders thundered from their 3 to the Viking 7, and, with 48 seconds gone in the second quarter, Errol Mann booted a 24-yard field goal.

Oakland linebacker Phil Villapiano described McClanahan's fumble:

"On the preceding play I went in high and was sandwiched by Ron Yary and Stu Voigt. On the second down, I went in low and when I came up there was McClanahan getting the ball. I hit the ball with my helmet."

Fellow linebacker Hall "saw the ball roll through somebody's legs and I dived for it. I was lucky nobody else saw it and beat me to it."

When Stabler trotted off the field after Mann's field goal had given the Raiders their 3-0 lead, he found Madden screaming.

"He thought the score should have been 14-0," said Stabler. "He thought we should have gone in for a touchdown just as we should have done earlier. I told him, 'Don't worry, Coach, we'll get a lot more points.' "

Stabler gained almost instant stature as a prophet. The Vikings failed to make a first down and Neil Clabo punted to the Oakland 36.

In 10 plays, Stabler directed the Raiders to a touchdown, with 19 yards consumed by a pass to tight end Casper. Another toss to Casper, for one yard, completed the drive and Mann's extra point put Oakland on top, 10-0, with 7:50 elapsed in the period.

Again the Vikings failed to register a first down and again Clabo punted, Neal Colzie returning the ball 25 yards to the Minnesota 35.

Three line smashes and a 17-yard pass to Biletnikoff placed the ball on the 1-yard line, from where Banaszak plunged across. Mann's PAT attempt sailed wide to the right and it was 16-0.

The Vikings advanced no farther than the Oakland 48 the remainder of the quarter, although they did register their only third-down conversion in six tries before halftime. The Raiders' first-half record on third-down conversions was 7 of 12.

Other first-half statistics were predominantly in the Raiders' favor. First downs: 16 to 4; total net yards, 288 to 86; offensive plays, 48 to 22; net yards rushing, 166 to 27; net yards passing, 122 to 59.

With nearly 10 minutes gone in the third quarter, a 40-yard Mann field goal sent the Raiders ahead, 19-0. That score endured about five minutes, or until Tarkenton could move the Vikings 68 yards on 12 plays. Aided by a roughing the passer penalty against Ted Hendricks and a holding penalty against Colzie in the Oakland secondary, the Vikings marched from their 32 to the Oakland 8 from where Tarkenton connected with White for six points. Fred Cox' conversion gave Minnesota partisans a breath of hope, but only briefly. Early in the fourth quarter, having moved from their 22 to the Oakland 37, the Vikings were brought up short when Hall intercepted a Tarkenton pass and returned it 16 yards to the Oakland 46.

From that point Stabler needed only four plays, including a 48-yard pass-run with Biletnikoff, to travel the 54 yards. Banaszak plunged the final two yards and, as he had done on his earlier TD, heaved the football into the stands in a gesture of unrestrained delight. Mann's conversion gave the Raiders a 26-7 lead.

The quarter was now seven minutes and 21 seconds old, and before another two minutes had expired, the Raiders had scored again, raising the count to 32-7. The last Oakland TD was a lightning thrust, resulting from veteran cornerback Willie Brown's interception of a Tarkenton pass at the Oakland 25 and a 75-yard sprint to the end zone. For the second time, Mann's extra-point attempt was wide right.

Brown had no doubts that Tarkenton was planning to pass. "When they lined up without a huddle, I knew they were going to pass," said the cornerback. "I've been around 13 years, so I usually know what a team is likely to do in certain situations. We were ahead, 26-7, so they didn't have much choice.

"I could tell the way Sammy White looked at me and the way Tarkenton looked over my way. When Tarkenton was two

Fred Biletnikoff bowls over Minnesota's Bobby Bryant after catching a third-quarter pass from Ken Stabler.

steps back in the drop, I knew for sure and made my move."

After an Oakland drive bogged down on the 44-yard line at the two-minute mark, Bob Lee, who had replaced Tarkenton, completed six of seven passes, the last to Voigt, to produce the second Minnesota TD.

Biletnikoff, with four catches good for 79 yards, was named the game's most valuable player, a selection that met with almost universal approval. One complaint was filed by the wide receiver himself.

"A stick of gum would have been reward enough," he observed. "I was surprised to hear that I had won it. It's like all the rest of the guys got cheated. That makes me feel bad. The thing that makes me feel happy is that we won."

Stabler, for one, endorsed the selection of Biletnikoff, recalling that Freddie was trotting off the field as the announcement was being made to the crowd.

"Freddie started to cry," reported Stabler. "He's a very emotional fellow. The other players were hugging him and shaking his hand. Photographers were snapping his picture and the game was still going on. It really was a great experience to see

something like that because he deserved it so much."

On the 48-yard pass play, Biletnikoff revealed, "Nate Wright (cornerback) came up to bump me but I went around him on the inside. I took off and he just seemed to sit there. I got to the hole in the middle and nobody was there."

Minnesota safety Krause had this version of the long pass: "I loused up the coverage. I called one coverage to Wright and played another. It gave Biletnikoff practically the whole field and he doesn't need more than a few inches."

Biletnikoff's talents were not lost on Wright. "He almost never drops a ball," declared the cornerback in wonderment. "He catches everything catchable and some passes that aren't. Stabler throws the ball in such a way to Biletnikoff that it's almost impossible to intercept. He keeps it away. Sometimes only a great catch will keep it in play, but Biletnikoff makes those all the time. I don't think I could play him any better on the two balls he caught near the goal line to set up touchdowns. He went high for one near the sideline, and caught the other one off the ground in the middle of the field.

Dave Casper bowls over Nate Wright after a 25-yard reception.

I've never played a man with his combination of moves and catching ability.''

Madden assured the victorious Raiders, "We're No. 1. You did a great job. You had a great season. They can't say anymore that we don't win the big one.

"We had tougher games than this in the AFC. I knew last night that we were going to win big. I usually don't feel that way before a game. But·I was so sure of it I was even saying it. Everything was perfect.''

Madden's gaze shifted to the opposite side of the locker room where Clarence Davis was peeling tape from his legs. "Hooray for Clarence Davis," Madden shouted twice.

Davis had carried the ball 16 times and gained 137 yards for an 8.6-yard average. "Our offensive line just knocked people out of the way," said the six-year veteran from the University of Southern California. "We have three All-Pros up there and the other guys should be, too.

"Maybe because everyone said we'd run on them, they believed it. They didn't expect us to go wide. That may have been part

of it, but basically we just blocked them inside and outside.''

Davis, who had been plagued by a knee problem for three years, had spurts of 20, 35, 13, 18 and 16 yards.

Banaszak, asked about his throwing the football into the stands after his touchdowns, replied, "The first time, Davis said to me 'Do something, you scored.' Throwing the ball was the only thing I could think of. The second throw was better than the first, but neither was good. I hurt my arm about five years ago.''

Hall, whose fumble recovery and interception earned him recognition as the game's top defensive player, disclosed that he had changed his tactics to make the interception.

"I had been going the other way with a back and was supposed to do it again, but I hid in the traffic and Tarkenton didn't see me.''

Minnesota's 71 net yards rushing in 26 carries was the direct result of Oakland's defensive game plan, revealed Villapiano.

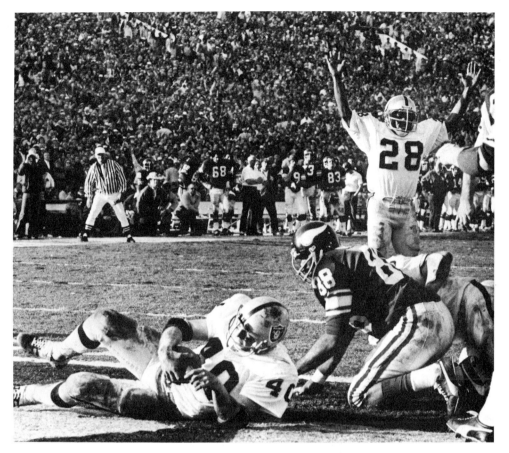

Clarence Davis signals touchdown after Pete Banaszak's 2-yard run.

"We wanted to prevent their short passes to Foreman, make them throw long and make them run with the ball."

Added linebacker Monte Johnson: "We did a couple of things differently. When they went to a double wing and put Foreman in the slot we put a strong safety (Jack Tatum) on him. That shut them down."

When Casper commented that he would have gained 40 fewer yards if the Vikings had tackled more effectively, Minnesota linebacker Hilgenberg could only agree.

"Sure, he's right, we didn't tackle well because the defense was on the field almost the entire first quarter, and most of the first half. We should have been able to control them better with our offense. I think if we had better balance in our offense, we would have done it. So Oakland moved on us and scored on us. They did that because the longer we stayed on the field, the more tired we got and the more tired we got, the worse our tackling got."

In the wake of their fourth Super Bowl defeat, the Vikings attempted to be philoso-phical.

"It's not the end of the world," proclaimed defensive end Carl Eller. "Personally, I don't feel down."

"The Raiders completely dominated us," noted Tarkenton. "We were up. We had the emotion, but you have to make the plays to keep it going. We made one play (the blocked punt) but we couldn't make the others."

After attempting to be analytical, Coach Grant quipped, "We just played them on the wrong day. Next time we'll play them on a Wednesday."

Despite the fact that the Vikings had now earned more Super Bowl money than any other team, Yary was inconsolable.

"It wasn't just the score or the way they ran us around," he moaned. "I don't know how you can play in four of these things and lose them all. Not only lose them all, but play bad football. I don't know how or why it happened, but for the first time in all the years that I've been playing football, I'm embarrassed."

Statistics of 11th Super Bowl
OAKLAND 32, MINNESOTA 14

Rose Bowl, Pasadena, Calif., January 9, 1977
Attendance: 103,438

OAKLAND	Offense	MINNESOTA
Cliff Branch	WR	Ahmad Rashad
Art Shell	LT	Steve Riley
Gene Upshaw	LG	Charles Goodrum
Dave Dalby	C	Mick Tingelhoff
George Buehler	RG	Ed White
John Vella	RT	Ron Yary
Dave Casper	TE	Stu Voigt
Fred Biletnikoff	WR	Sammy White
Ken Stabler	QB	Fran Tarkenton
Clarence Davis	RB	Brent McClanahan
Mark van Eeghen	RB	Chuck Foreman

Defense

OAKLAND		MINNESOTA
John Matuszak	LE	Carl Eller
Dave Rowe	MG-LT	Doug Sutherland
Otis Sistrunk	RE-RT	Alan Page
Phil Villapiano	LLB-RE	Jim Marshall
Monte Johnson	MB-LLB	Matt Blair
Willie Hall	MLB	Jeff Siemon
Ted Hendricks	RLB	Wally Hilgenberg
Skip Thomas	LCB	Nate Wright
Willie Brown	RCB	Bobby Bryant
George Atkinson	LS	Jeff Wright
Jack Tatum	RS	Paul Krause

— SUBSTITUTIONS —

OAKLAND—Offense: Quarterback—David Humm, Mike Rae. Punter—Ray Guy. Kicker—Errol Mann. Receivers—Warren Bankston, Morris Bradshaw, Mike Siani. Backs—Pete Banaszak, Carl Garrett, Hubie Ginn, Manfred Moore. Linemen—Steve Sylvester. Defense: Linebackers—Rodrigo Barnes, Rik Bonness, Floyd Rice. Backs—Neal Colzie, Charles Phillips. Linemen—Henry Lawrence, Herb McMath, Dan Medlin, Charles Philyaw. DNP—None.

MINNESOTA—Offense: Quarterback—Bob Lee. Punter—Neil Clabo. Kicker—Fred Cox. Receivers—Steve Craig, Bob Grim, Leonard Willis. Backs—Ron Groce, Sammy Johnson, Robert Miller. Linemen—Doug Dumler. Defense: Linebackers—Amos Martin, Fred McNeill, Roy Winston. Backs—Nate Allen, Autry Beamon, Windlan Hall. Linemen—Mark Mullaney, James White. DNP—Bob Berry (QB), Bart Buetow (T).

— SCORE BY PERIODS —

Oakland Raiders (AFC)	0	16	3	13	— 32
Minnesota Vikings (NFC)	0	0	7	7	— 14

— SCORING —

Oakland—Field goal Mann 24.
Oakland—Casper 1 pass from Stabler (Mann kick).
Oakland—Banaszak 1 run (kick failed).
Oakland—Field goal Mann 40.
Minnesota—S. White 8 pass from Tarkenton (Cox kick).
Oakland—Banaszak 2 run (Mann kick).
Oakland—Brown 75 interception (kick failed).
Minnesota—Voigt 13 pass from Lee (Cox kick).

— TEAM STATISTICS —

	Oakland	Minnesota
Total First Downs	21	20
First Downs Rushing	13	2
First Downs Passing	8	15

	Oakland	Minnesota
First Downs Penalty	0	3
Rushes	52	26
Yards Gained Rushing (net)	266	71
Average Yards per Rush	5.1	2.7
Passes Attempted	19	44
Passes Completed	12	24
Had Intercepted	0	2
Times Tackled Attemp. Pass	2	1
Yards Lost Attempting Pass	17	4
Yards Gained Passing (net)	163	282
Total Net Yardage	429	353
Punts	5	7
Average Distance	32.4	37.9
Punt Returns	4	3
Punt Return Yardage	43	14
Kickoff Returns	2	7
Kickoff Return Yardage	47	136
Interception Return Yardage	91	0
Fumbles	0	1
Opponent Fumbles Recovered	1	0
Total Return Yardage	181	150
Penalties	4	2
Yards Penalized	30	25
Total Points Scored	32	14
Touchdowns	4	2
Touchdowns Rushing	2	0
Touchdowns Passing	1	2
Touchdowns Returns	1	0
Extra Points	2	2
Field Goals	2	0
Field Goals Attempted	3	0
Total Offensive Plays	73	71
Avg. Gain Per Offensive Play	5.9	5.0

INDIVIDUAL STATISTICS
— RUSHING —

Oakland	Atts.	Yds.	Lg.	TD
Davis	16	137	35	0
van Eeghen	18	73	11	0
Garrett	4	19	13	0
Banaszak	10	19	6	2
Ginn	2	9	9	0
Rae	2	9	11	0

Minnesota	Atts.	Yds.	Lg.	TD
Foreman	17	44	7	0
Johnson	2	9	8	0
S. White	1	7	7	0
Lee	1	4	4	0
Miller	2	4	3	0
McClanahan	3	3	2	0

— PASSING —

Oakland	Atts.	Comp.	Yds.	Int.	TD
Stabler	19	12	180	0	1

Minnesota	Atts.	Comp.	Yds.	Int.	TD
Tarkenton	35	17	205	2	1
Lee	9	7	81	0	1

— RECEIVING —

Oakland	No.	Yds.	Lg.	TD
Biletnikoff	4	79	48	0
Casper	4	70	25	1
Branch	3	20	10	0
Garrett	1	11	11	0

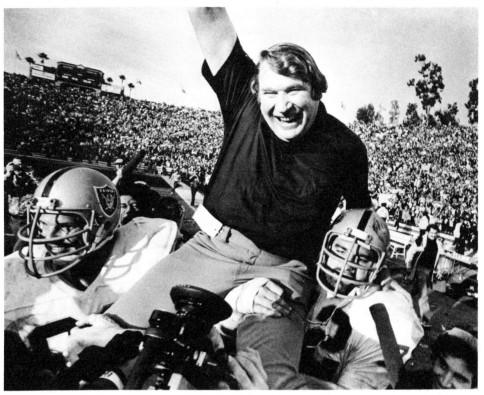

Raiders Coach John Madden enjoys his seat atop the football world.

— RECEIVING —

Minnesota	No.	Yds.	Lg.	TD
S. White	5	77	20	1
Foreman	5	62	26	0
Voigt	4	49	15	1
Miller	4	19	13	0
Rashad	3	53	25	0
Johnson	3	26	17	0

— INTERCEPTIONS —

Oakland	No.	Yds.	Lg.	TD
Brown	1	75	75	1
Hall	1	16	16	0

Minnesota—None.

— PUNTING —

Oakland	No.	Avg.	Lg.
Guy	4	40.5	51

Minnesota	No.	Avg.	Lg.
Clabo	7	37.9	46

— PUNT RETURNS —

Oakland	No.	FC	Yds.	Lg.
Colzie	4	0	43	25

Minnesota	No.	FC	Yds.	Lg.
Willis	3	0	14	8

— KICKOFF RETURNS —

Oakland	No.	Yds.	Lg.
Garrett	2	47	24

Minnesota	No.	Yds.	Lg.
S. White	4	79	26
Willis	3	57	20

— FIELD GOALS —

Oakland	Att.	Made
Mann	3	2

Minnesota—None.

— FUMBLES —

Oakland	No.	Own Rec.	Opp. Rec.	TD
Hall	0	0	1	0

Minnesota	No.	Own Rec.	Opp. Rec.	TD
McClanahan	1	0	0	0

— SCORING —

Oakland	TD	PAT	FG	Pts.
Banaszak	2	0	0	12
Mann	0	2	2	8
Brown	1	0	0	6
Casper	1	0	0	6

Minnesota	TD	PAT	FG	Pts.
Voigt	1	0	0	6
S. White	1	0	0	6
Cox	0	2	0	2

Randy White, co-MVP with teammate Harvey Martin, puts the wraps on Denver quarterback Craig Morton.

Super Bowl XII

Orange Crushed

January 15, 1978

While hordes of orange-clad loyalists shrieked their undying allegiance to the Denver Broncos, Thomas (Hollywood) Henderson of the Dallas Cowboys stood defiantly on the green carpet of the Louisiana Superdome.

As the overhead clock ticked off the final moments of Super Bowl XII, the uninhibited linebacker crumpled an orange cup in his upraised fist and shouted into the teeth of the storm: "There's your Orange Crush."

For weeks, especially after the Broncos defeated the Oakland Raiders in the American Football Conference championship game, Broncomania had raged unchecked through Rocky Mountain country.

Orange-shirted behemoths representing the Denver Broncos suddenly became known as the Orange Crush during the team's first championship season and sales of a soft drink bearing the same name skyrocketed so that suppliers were unable to meet the demand.

Any item with an Orange Crush label was guaranteed to sell. After the Broncos qualified for the Super Bowl, 65,000 Orange Crush T-shirts were sold within 48 hours. Even the Denver mayor was caught up in the contagion and displayed his shirt as proof.

The disease, said Woodrow Paige Jr., in "ORANGE MADNESS," was identified by these symptoms:

"Stiffness of the index finger—caused by repeatedly signaling No. 1; compulsion to purchase anything orange—it was estimated that 50 new items were going on sale weekly; sprained knee joints—caused by constant jumping up and down at Broncos games; irrational behavior—as evidenced by Denverites' when their team was excluded from \ABC's Monday Night football

Denver's Craig Morton gazes over fallen bodies as his hurried pass falls incomplete.

highlights; glassy eyes—a look generally associated with those dreaming about a weekend in New Orleans; unbearable foot irritation—known as the Super Bowl itch."

This was the affliction that Hollywood Henderson figuratively stomped out in the early evening of January 15, 1978, as the Cowboys were wrapping up a 27-10 victory that clinched their second NFL championship.

Dallas and Denver had compiled the best regular-season records in 1977, each winning 12 games and losing two. The Cowboys eliminated Chicago, 37-7, and Minnesota, 23-6, to earn a fourth trip to the Super Bowl.

The Broncos, 14-6 losers to the Cowboys in the regular-season finale, thumped Pittsburgh, 34-21, before edging Oakland, 20-17, in the AFC playoffs. The contest with the Raiders carried dramatic overtones for the more than 74,000 who jammed Denver's Mile High Stadium for the title struggle. Oakland, the wild-card team from the Western Division, finished one game behind the Broncos and had split its two previous games with Denver, losing at home, 30-7, and winning, 24-14, two weeks later at Mile High.

Riding highest on Denver's emotional wave was Craig Morton, 35-year-old quarterback who had thrown two touchdown passes to Haven Moses in the AFC title game and was about to face his former Dallas teammates, with whom he played nine seasons.

Morton's Dallas counterpart was Roger Staubach, the former Heisman Trophy winner at the Naval Academy who had beaten out Morton for the Dallas quarterback position some years earlier.

"We're friends now," declared Morton, who had drifted from the Cowboys to the New York Giants and then to Denver where, in Red Miller's first season as head coach, he had helped give Denver its first major sports championship.

But a nagging hip injury had restricted Morton's mobility late in the season and his state of mind took a plunge when he was forced to face batteries of reporters in the early days of workouts at Tulane Stadium.

A private sort of person, Morton was confident that the question he would be asked most frequently by media people would pertain to a recent story about a check on his tax returns by the Internal Revenue Service.

He wasn't disappointed. Steeling himself for the onslaught, Morton faced the gaggle of newsmen one morning. As Paige recorded it:

" 'Craig, what about the income tax thing,' a guy from Dallas asked. Morton smiled. Of course.

" 'Everybody come in close. I'm going to talk about this once and then I'm not going to discuss it anymore. It's all being taken care of. We've talked with the Internal Revenue Service and the matter will be settled. I've paid the taxes I thought I owed, and then another amount was added on. That's about it. It's not really that important. It's not on my mind. (But the IRS had sent him a notice about back income taxes, and the story broke the same day. He had lost some respect for the privacy the IRS reportedly keeps.) Now, any more questions?'

"A reporter walked up, managed to inch his way toward the front of the pack and speak up. 'Craig, could you tell what's going on with the income taxes?' Morton lowered his head. It wasn't going to be easy."

Staubach, in his book "ROGER STAUBACH, Time Enough to Win," with Frank Luksa, said, "The only thing that made me nervous was competing against Craig Morton. The media was into comparing us every which way. Craig was coming off a tremendous season and because I liked him personally I was happy for him.

"If anyone wanted to second guess the decision that resulted in my staying with the Cowboys and Craig's leaving, at this point they were forced to admit that it was good for both of us."

Recalling the 1977 season, Staubach continued: "We were coming off a season that left me depressed. I had a finger injury, felt that I had let the club down and even gave Tom Landry carte blanche to trade me. Our off-season attitude was good and, like 1976, we started off strong. I was confident we wouldn't fall off at the end like we did in 1976 because we'd picked up Tony Dorsett. Our running back situation hadn't been solid for a number of years because of injuries to Robert Newhouse and Preston Pearson. I really think we were the best team in football."

Las Vegas oddsmakers favored the Cowboys by five points and other reputed experts shared that opinion.

Allie Sherman, former NFL quarterback and ex-coach of the New York Giants, proclaimed, "There is no way the Broncos can run against the Cowboys' flex defense. The Broncos have to come out throwing. They have to throw on first down and use a lot of play-action passes."

Len Dawson, hero of Kansas City's victory in Super Bowl IV and now an NBC sportscaster, echoed Sherman's opinion.

"I'd throw early," said the former quarterback, "and use my tight end a lot. In Riley Odoms the Broncos have one of the best. I wouldn't hesitate to throw on first down to pick up four, five or six yards. If I'm successful, the Cowboys will have to play defense and they'll be the ones who do the guessing."

Robert (Red) Miller, the Denver coach, conceded that "on paper the Cowboys are a

Craig Morton spent much of his pre-game time answering questions about income taxes and much of the game itself on his back.

better team than we are, but we've faced that situation all year. There were a lot of teams better overall than we are.

"What usually happened is that we outplayed the teams and beat them. And we have that one big thing going for us in this game—motivation.

"Nobody expected us to be here," said Miller, hired to coach the Broncos after a player rebellion led to the dismissal of John Ralston. "We had a great training camp and I knew we had the makings of a good team.

"Nobody has given us credit. No rival coach ever congratulated us after a victory. They'd say, 'We played a bad game today,'' or 'We've sure got a lot of work ahead of us.' By the end of the season we had made believers out of just about everybody. But something's funny. All along we're winning games week after week, and nobody seems to recognize it. It's been a great season for us, the greatest in Denver history."

Landry noted, "Denver is a very emotional team. It plays each game as if it has its back to the wall. I'm very impressed. It's a team in the true sense of the word, not a bunch of individuals."

Defending his own sideline stoicism, Landry said: "I don't believe you can be emotional and concentrate the way you should to be effective. As a team, we win by concentrating, by thinking. The players don't want to see me rushing around and screaming. They want to believe I know what I'm doing."

Dallas safety Cliff Harris added one final thought on the subject of emotion.

"Emotion is great," he observed, "but they pay for execution and we've got execution."

The team with the better execution could look forward to an $18,000 payday per man; the other would receive $9,000 per player.

The Broncos were not alone in generating emotion. Patrons of a Philadelphia travel agency were also working up a good head of steam, the result of discovering that the Super Bowl tickets that had been part of their package were not available.

Approximately 1,400 tourists were in a foul mood. To pacify them, the agency paid up to $350 for tickets that sold originally for $30.

"We took a loss of between $95,000 and $100,000," disclosed a representative of Travel Leisure Concepts of Philadelphia. "These have been the most emotional days of my life. We combed every hotel lobby, every street for tickets."

Customers of a New York agency paid $450 for a full package and wound up watching the game on TV.

The game, aired by the Columbia Broadcasting System, was seen on 214 television stations in the United States and 378 in Canada. A total of 269 U.S. radio stations carried the game, which was broadcast on 70 French Language outlets.

A one-minute TV commercial sold for $344,000 and it was estimated that CBS would clear $2 million for the highest rated sports event in TV history.

Because the game was played indoors for the first time, wind was not a factor in game strategy and the Cowboys, to the surprise of nobody in the crowd of 75,804, chose to receive the opening kickoff after winning the coin toss.

Their choice of plays in the opening series did create some surprise, however.

On a double reverse, wide receiver Butch Johnson fumbled, then recovered the ball on the Dallas 20-yard line.

Landry had debated the play selection and conceded later that he had made the wrong choice.

"I probably shouldn't have called the double reverse," he said. "But I just thought it might be something that would put them off-balance early. I should have known that we would still be a little tight at that stage of the game and that a fumble could occur.

"I figured that we could not afford to play conservatively. The Broncos have such great pursuit that you can't drive 60 or 70 yards on them."

Staubach found the play altogether acceptable, declaring: "That play was well calculated. Denver's strength was its unbelievable pursuit. The Broncos flowed to the ball. It was very difficult to run wide on them. They would bottle us up. If we tried to cut back inside, the pursuit took care of the runner.

"With that reverse we told them, 'You better stay home and play your position. We have some things up our sleeves.' There wasn't any other meaning than that."

On their first possession, the Broncos drove to the Dallas 33-yard line before Morton was sacked for an 11-yard loss and Bucky Dilts punted to the 1-yard line where Tony Hill fumbled. As on the previous fumble, the Cowboys recovered, Hill snatching the ball away from onrushing Broncos.

Moments later Tony Dorsett fumbled on the 19 and Cowboys center John Fitzgerald pounced on the ball. The one break that was so essential to Denver success was painfully elusive.

When the game's first turnover occurred, it went to the Cowboys. Under heavy pressure from defensive end Harvey Martin and defensive tackle Randy White, Morton passed erratically into the hands of safety Randy Hughes on the Denver 25.

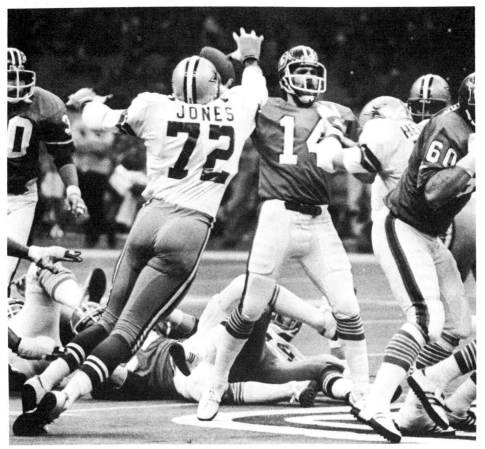

When Craig Morton went to the bench, the Cowboys defense zoomed in on Norris Weese.

In five plays, Staubach directed the Cowboys to a touchdown, Dorsett covering the last three yards on a sweep around left end.

Efren Herrera's conversion gave the Cowboys a 7-0 lead.

A second twist of good fortune produced more points for Dallas. When linebacker Bob Breunig tipped a Morton pass into the hands of Aaron Kyle, the cornerback returned the ball 19 yards to the Denver 35. Six plays later, Herrera kicked a 35-yard field goal and Dallas was on top, 10-0.

From a Denver viewpoint, matters were little better in the second quarter. Even an apparent interception worked against the Broncos. From the Denver 19, Staubach scrambled toward the sideline, then passed to the end zone where safety Bill Thompson intercepted.

Not so, ruled an official. Staubach had stepped out of bounds before releasing the football. An overhead camera cast serious doubt on the decision, but it prevailed and

the Cowboys, given a reprieve, cashed in with a 43-yard Herrera field goal to provide a 13-0 lead.

And still misfortune dogged the Broncos. After a holding penalty on a kickoff set them back to their 10-yard line, Miller decided it was time for unconventional measures—like a deep pass to Haven Moses. The wide receiver broke into the clear behind Benny Barnes, but the pass was underthrown and the Dallas cornerback intercepted at the Cowboy 40.

When Dallas punted, the ball struck John Schultz on the helmet and caromed into the hands of Bruce Huther of Dallas.

Still more misfortune lurked for the Orange Crush. A 15-yard pass to Jack Dolbin was fumbled away to Hughes and a shorter toss to Odoms met the same fate, a fumble recovery by Hughes.

During the first half, the Broncos had lost three fumbles and Morton was intercepted four times, half as many times as he was intercepted in 14 regular-season games. Had the Cowboys been executing as well as Harris predicted they would, their halftime lead would have been closer to 30-0. But Herrera missed on field goal attempts of 43, 32 and 44 yards and Billy Joe DuPree fumbled away a completed pass on the Denver 12.

"We were jittery," explained Staubach. "An indoor atmosphere is crazy and I think both teams were fighting the noise. The noise is overwhelming if you're not accustomed to playing indoors."

In the game's first 30 minutes, the Broncos registered only 72 yards total offense, 28 by passing. They made three first downs and committed the seven turnovers.

In Houston, Oilers Coach Bum Phillips looked away from his TV screen at halftime and exclaimed dolefully, "What surprises me is that the Broncos are beating themselves, something they haven't done all year."

In Los Angeles, one-time Broncos Coach Jack Faulkner expressed amazement that the Broncos were "throwing down the middle. They should be throwing on first down, and throwing to the outside. Down the middle won't beat the Cowboys."

Meanwhile, in the clubhouse, Coach Miller was trying to convince the Broncos that they were still in the game. As the players stomped out the door, he shouted after them: "You're not too tight, just too emotional. Offense, break the ice."

Then, turning to Morton, Miller said: "You'll start the second half, but if we can't get something going, we'll have to see what Norris Weese can do."

Morton replied with a knowing nod.

On their first possession of the second half, the Broncos advanced 35 yards to the Dallas 30 before they stalled and settled for a 47-yard field goal by Jim Turner.

Midway through the period, the Cowboys struck again. On third-and-10, Staubach passed deep to Butch Johnson. The wide receiver made a diving catch of the 45-yard heave, broke the goal line plane, struck the end zone turf and released the football.

To all appearances it was a routine incompletion . . . then an official signaled a touchdown.

Referee Jim Tunney offered this explanation: "Johnson caught the ball in the air in flight. He crossed the goal line in possession and came to the ground in the end zone. Then he released the ball. He didn't fumble the ball. He hit the ground and then released it."

The play had been improvised in the huddle, Staubach disclosed. "Bernard Jackson (Broncos free safety) had been hanging in the middle. He wasn't dropping into a deep zone as he should have been doing. Our receivers had mentioned it to me and I remembered it in the huddle. Butch wasn't supposed to figure in the play, but I told him 'Run a good post pattern.'

"When I faded, I saw that Jackson hadn't dropped quickly enough. Steve Foley (cornerback) did a good job, but Jackson should have stopped the play. When I threw, I thought the pass was too long. I couldn't believe it when Butch made a sensational catch."

Johnson snared the pass despite a broken right thumb, suffered while blocking in the second quarter. Ordinarily a wide receiver only, Johnson was pressed into service as a tight end after Jay Saldi was sidelined by bruised leg muscles.

"As a pass catcher," observed offensive coordinator Dan Reeves, "Butch has better concentration than any receiver I've ever seen."

Protests by Jackson and Foley that he had made an illegal catch brought only a smile to Johnson. "They were complaining about everything," he reported.

Johnson explained that he had to "catch the ball more with my left hand than with my right," because of the injury, "but when the pass is there you'd better catch it."

Trailing now, 20-3, the Broncos nearly erased six points on the ensuing kickoff, which Rick Upchurch returned a record 67 yards, to the Dallas 26.

When, on the next play, Morton's pass was almost intercepted by Ed (Too Tall) Jones, Miller made the change he had mentioned at halftime, replacing Morton with Weese. Four plays later, Rob Lytle crashed over from one yard out and, with the conversion, the Broncos were again within 10 points of the Cowboys.

"The near-interception had nothing to do with the change of quarterbacks," insisted Miller. "Weese was going in on the next play, we had already decided that."

Throughout the season the Broncos had dominated fourth-quarter action and as the last period was about to start at the Superdome, Miller held up four fingers in front of the Denver bench. The signal was unmistakably clear before Miller shouted: "We can win this thing, we're gonna win."

The Cowboys had already lost the services of Tony Dorsett because of a knee injury and when Staubach broke the tip of his right forefinger, chances for another cardiac climax by the Broncos appeared improved significantly.

Unfortunately for the Orange Crush, however, Weese fumbled and Aaron Kyle recovered. By this time, Staubach had received a shot of novocaine and was back in action although unable to throw a football with

Roger Staubach eludes Lyle Alzado's flying tackle.

any degree of accuracy.

On the Dallas sideline, Landry decided it was time to call for a big play, one that would put the game beyond Denver's reach and quash the fourth-quarter mystique enjoyed by the AFC champions.

While Staubach was unable to pass, he could hand off, or pitch out. But, said Robert Newhouse . . . well, it was time to call for the unexpected. Landry sent in a play that the Cowboys had rehearsed all week, but it was one, Newhouse had assured himself, that would not be used in Super Bowl XII.

Newhouse was so confident the play would not be called that the fullback had coated his hands generously with stickum, the better to hold on to the football. Now he was in a dilemma.

He started licking his fingers feverishly. He wiped his hands on his pants and on a towel provided by Preston Pearson, hopeful that the Broncos would not grow suspicious. He noted, happily, that nobody appeared alarmed.

Taking a Staubach pitchout on a play from the Denver 29, Newhouse glided toward the outside as though on an end sweep. The Cowboys had noticed that Steve Foley had been quick to move up on running plays and were now prepared to make the cornerback pay for his discretion.

Wide receiver Golden Richards faked a block on Foley, then sped on by. Too late, Foley realized he had been duped. As Newhouse arched a perfectly thrown pass toward the end zone, Foley made a desperate lunge but it was no contest.

"I was nervous about throwing the ball," confessed Newhouse, who had not thrown a pass since his rookie season five years earlier when he fired a TD pass against Detroit. "In practice the ball had been wobbling, but Danny (backup quarterback Danny White) told me to get my hip around it. I kept thinking about that when I got the ball."

Even after the pitchout, Newhouse was not positive he wanted to go through with the pass. "I saw all that wide-open space downfield," he said, "and I was tempted to run, but then I remembered it was one of Coach Landry's all-or-nothing plays so I threw."

As Richards clutched the football in the end zone, Miller turned to assistant coach Babe Parilli and said somberly, "That's it, Babe. It's all over."

Later, in the muffled Broncos clubhouse, Miller conceded, "Dallas is a very, very good team. The Cowboys are No. 1, I believe. They proved it because of their terrific defense.''

Defense, as exemplified by right tackle Randy White and right end Harvey Martin, co-winners of the game's Most Valuable Player award, limited the Broncos to 156 net yards and permitted them to convert only three of 14 third downs.

"We knew we had to pressure Morton," said White. "It was part of our game plan. I figured that if we didn't give them turnovers and field position we would win. Denver is a field-position team. We gave them field position only three times, and we stopped them on two of those occasions.''

"Denver was looking for the blitz," Martin added. "We showed it to them but we used just good defensive football. We wanted to give Morton something to think about, but it was just four guys rushing the passer.

"It seemed as though Morton was looking at me every time he came to the line. I think he was more concerned because he thought all of us would be coming at him.

"I guess we might have shocked a few people today. We knew there was no way that Denver was going to run on us, and Morton would have to put the ball up.''

The pressure applied by the Cowboys' defensive line produced a record four interceptions against Morton, giving him a Super Bowl record total of seven in 41 attempts. He completed only four of 15 against Dallas, for whom he had played in Super Bowl V against Baltimore.

Other records set in the NFC's first Super Bowl win in six tries included: Most penalties club, Dallas 12; most penalties both clubs, 20; most fumbles, club, Dallas, six; most fumbles, both clubs, 10, and fewest first downs passing, club, Denver, one.

The effects of the aggressive Dallas defense were particularly evident in the Broncos' performance on first-down plays. Their record, with B denoting Broncos and C denoting Cowboys, was:

B47—Jon Keyworth loses 5.

C34—Otis Armstrong gains 1.

B39—Pass incomplete; holding was called on the second play, setting up a second and 20, B29, and Dallas' rush hit Morton's arm, forcing the first interception at the Broncos 25, setting up a touchdown.

B40—Lytle gains 2; on second and eight, Broncos 42, Morton was rushed, the pass was tipped and intercepted by Dallas, setting up a field goal.

B28—Lonnie Perrin, no gain.

B10—Lytle gains 5; on the next play, Dallas intercepted.

B26—Armstrong loses 3 on third and nine from the 27, Morton passes to Dolbin, who fumbles, Dallas recovers.

B20—Morton passes to Odoms, who fumbles.

B40—Morton pass intercepted.

B35—Keyworth no gain.

C47—Pass incomplete.

C36—Pass incomplete.

B35—Pass incomplete.

C26—Pass complete, no gain.

C1—Lytle, 1 yard, touchdown.

B45—Lytle loses 8.

B2—Weese gains 9.

C42—Pass incomplete.

B24—Weese loses 1.

C47—No gain.

C29—Weese gains 9.

C11—No gain.

Landry, heralded by Dallas Owner Clint Murchison as "not only the Coach of the Year but also the Coach of the Century,'' maintained that the blocking and tackling was the hardest he had witnessed since Super Bowl V, in 1971, when the Cowboys bowed to Baltimore, 16-13.

"You had to be on the sidelines to appreciate how hard the players were hitting,'' he said. "Whenever you see players limping off the field, as they were today, you know they were hitting hard.

"I think the hard hitting had something to do with the fumbles and penalties. When you play on a synthetic surface, you can really get traction and dig in and pop someone. Also we got a little too high trying to match Denver's enthusiasm early—that caused some execution problems that resulted in penalties. But everything eventually turned out okay.''

While the Cowboys yippie-ei-ohed over their second championship, two of their numbers paused to express compassion for their one-time teammate Craig Morton.

At the close of the contest, Landry and Staubach visited with Morton on the field.

"You're a great quarterback," volunteered Landry. "Today, it just wasn't there. Good luck.''

Staubach told his old rival for the Dallas quarterback job, "You had a great season. I'm sorry it ended the way it did.''

Later Staubach added: "I mean it. I feel sorry for him. I've been there myself in a few big games. Maybe he began to second guess himself. It's no fun when there's no time for a quarterback to throw and we didn't give him time. He was on the run constantly. If Craig and I had changed places, the Cowboys still would have won.''

Morton acknowledged the pressure, saying, "They sure came after me and they got us into too many predictable situations.

"You might expect me to be more disappointed. And I am disappointed in my play. But I'm pleased to be here. We've come such a long way. I can't base my season on just one game.''

The play of the game was Butch Johnson's finger-tip grab of a Roger Staubach pass (above). Johnson lost the ball when he hit the ground in the end zone, but the referee, despite the pleas of Denver defenders, still signaled touch-down.

Statistics of 12th Super Bowl

DALLAS 27, DENVER 10

Louisiana Superdome, New Orleans, La., January 15, 1978

Attendance: 75,804

DALLAS	Offense	DENVER
Butch Johnson	WR	Jack Dolbin
Ralph Neely	LT	Andy Maurer
Herbert Scott	LG	Tom Glassic
John Fitzgerald	C	Mike Montler
Tom Rafferty	RG	Paul Howard
Pat Donovan	RT	Claudie Minor
Billy Joe DuPree	TE	Riley Odoms
Drew Pearson	WR	Haven Moses
Roger Staubach	QB	Craig Morton
Tony Dorsett	RB	Otis Armstrong
Robert Newhouse	RB	Jon Keyworth

DALLAS	Defense	DENVER
Ed Jones	LE	Barney Chavous
Jethro Pugh	LT/NT	Rubin Carter
Randy White	RT	
Harvey Martin	RE	Lyle Alzado
	LB	Bob Swenson
Tom Henderson	LB	Joe Rizzo
Bob Breunig	LB	Randy Gradishar
D.D. Lewis	LB	Tom Jackson
Benny Barnes	LCB	Louis Wright
Aaron Kyle	RCB	Steve Foley
Charlie Waters	SS	Bill Thompson
Cliff Harris	FS	Bernard Jackson

— SUBSTITUTIONS —

DALLAS—Offense: Receivers—Golden Richards, Tony Hill. Linemen—Burton Lawless, Jim Cooper, Rayfield Wright, Andy Frederick. Backs—Danny White, Preston Pearson, Scott Laidlaw, Larry Brinson, Doug Dennison. Kicker—Efren Herrera. Defense: Linebackers—Bruce Huther, Mike Hegman, Guy Brown. Linemen—Dave Stalls, Bill Gregory, Larry Cole. Backs—Mel Renfro, Mark Washington.

DENVER—Offense: Receivers—Rick Upchurch, Ron Egloff, John Schultz. Linemen—Bobby Maples, Henry Allison, Glenn Hyde. Backs—Jim Jensen, Lonnie Perrin, Rob Lytle, Norris Weese. Kickers—Bucky Dilts, Jim Turner. Defense: Linebackers—Godwin Turk, Larry Evans, Rob Nairne. Linemen—John Grant, Brison Manor, Paul Smith. Backs—Randy Rich, Randy Poltl. DNP—Craig Penrose.

— SCORE BY PERIODS —

Dallas Cowboys (NFC)	10	3	7	7	— 27
Denver Broncos (AFC)	0	0	10	0	— 10

— SCORING —

Dallas—Dorsett 3 run (Herrera kick).
Dallas—Field goal Herrera 35.
Dallas—Field goal Herrera 43.
Denver—Field goal Turner 47.
Dallas—Johnson 45 pass from Staubach (Herrera kick).
Denver—Lytle 1 run (Turner kick).
Dallas—Richards 29 pass from Newhouse (Herrera kick).

— TEAM STATISTICS —

	Dallas	Denver
Total First Downs	17	11
First Downs Rushing	8	8
First Downs Passing	8	1
First Downs by Penalty	1	2
Rushes	38	29

	Dallas	Denver
Yards Gained Rushing (net)	143	121
Average Yards per Rush	3.8	4.2
Passes Attempted	28	25
Passes Completed	19	8
Had Intercepted	0	4
Times Tackled Attemp. Pass	5	4
Yards Lost Attempting Pass	35	26
Yards Gained Passing (net)	182	35
Total Net Yardage	325	156
Total Offensive Plays	71	58
Avg. Gain per Offensive Play	4.6	2.7
Punts	5	4
Average Distance	41.6	38.2
Punt Returns	1	4
Punt Return Yardage	0	22
Kickoff Returns	3	6
Kickoff Return Yardage	51	173
Interception Return Yardage	46	0
Fumbles	6	4
Opp. Fumbles Recovered	4	2
Total Return Yardage	97	195
Penalties	12	8
Yards Penalized	94	60
Total Points Scored	27	10
Touchdowns	3	1
Touchdowns Rushing	1	1
Touchdowns Passing	2	0
Extra Points	3	1
Field Goals Attempted	5	1
Field Goals Made	2	1

INDIVIDUAL STATISTICS

— RUSHING —

Dallas	Atts.	Yds.	Lg.	TD
Dorsett	15	66	19	1
Newhouse	14	55	10	0
White	1	13	13	0
P. Pearson	3	11	5	0
Staubach	3	6	5	0
Laidlaw	1	1	1	0
Johnson	1	—9	—9	0

Denver	Atts.	Yds.	Lg.	TD
Lytle	10	35	16	1
Armstrong	7	27	18	0
Weese	3	26	10	0
Jensen	1	16	16	0
Keyworth	5	9	6	0
Perrin	3	8	4	0

— PASSING —

Dallas	Atts.	Comp.	Yds.	Int.	TD
Staubach	25	17	183	0	1
White	2	1	5	0	0
Newhouse	1	1	29	0	1

Denver	Atts.	Comp.	Yds.	Int.	TD
Morton	15	4	39	4	0
Weese	10	4	22	0	0

— RECEIVING —

Dallas	No.	Yds.	Lg.	TD
P. Pearson	5	37	11	0
DuPree	4	66	19	0
Newhouse	3	—1	5	0
Johnson	2	53	45	1
Richards	2	38	29	1
Dorsett	2	11	15	0
D. Pearson	1	13	13	0

Denver's rabid fans were literally crushed by the final result.

— RECEIVING —

Denver	No.	Yds.	Lg.	TD
Dolbin	2	24	15	0
Odoms	2	9	10	0
Moses	1	21	21	0
Upchurch	1	9	9	0
Jensen	1	5	5	0
Perrin	1	−7	−7	0

— INTERCEPTIONS —

Dallas	No.	Yds.	Lg.	TD
Washington	1	27	27	0
Kyle	1	19	19	0
Barnes	1	0	0	0
Hughes	1	0	0	0

Denver— None.

—PUNTING —

Dallas	No.	Avg.	Lg.
White	5	41.6	53

Denver	No.	Avg.	Lg.
Dilts	4	38.2	46

— PUNT RETURNS —

Dallas	No.	FC	Yds.	Lg.
Hill	1	1	0	0

Denver	No.	FC	Yds.	Lg.
Upchurch	3	0	22	8
Schultz	1	0	0	0

— KICKOFF RETURNS —

Dallas	No.	Yds.	Lg.
Johnson	2	29	15
Brinson	1	22	22

Denver	No.	Yds.	Lg.
Upchurch	3	94	67
Schultz	2	62	37
Jensen	1	17	17

— FIELD GOALS —

Dallas	Att.	Made
Herrera	5	2

Denver	Att.	Made
Turner	1	1

— FUMBLES —

Dallas	No.	Own Rec.	Opp. Rec.	TD
Johnson	2	2	0	0
Hill	1	1	0	0
Dorsett	1	0	0	0
DuPree	1	0	0	0
Staubach	1	0	0	0
Fitzgerald	0	1	0	0
Hughes	0	0	2	0
Huther	0	0	1	0
Kyle	0	0	1	0

Denver	No.	Own Rec.	Opp. Rec.	TD
Schultz	1	0	0	0
Dolbin	1	0	0	0
Odoms	1	0	0	0
Weese	1	0	0	0
T. Jackson	0	0	1	0
Carter	0	0	1	0

— SCORING —

Dallas	TD	PAT	FG	Pts.
Dorsett	1	0	0	6
Herrera	0	3	2	9
Johnson	1	0	0	6
Richards	1	0	0	6

Denver	TD	PAT	FG	Pts.
Lytle	1	0	0	6
Turner	0	1	1	4

Dallas tight end Jackie Smith shows the frustration that can accompany a dropped touchdown pass in a Super Bowl.

Super Bowl XIII

Dumb Like a F-O-X

January 21, 1979

As the Pittsburgh Steelers were rehearsing for Super Bowl XIII, somebody recalled the day when Terry Bradshaw, asked what he thought about Rhodes Scholars, resorted to a costly bit of humor and replied: "I never did care for hitch-hikers."

The remark backfired on the Pittsburgh quarterback. To many it was seen as further evidence that Bradshaw lacked gray matter beneath his rapidly receding blond hairline.

Even after he had led the Steelers to Super Bowl championships in 1975 and '76, the 6-3 Louisianian with a soul for country and western pathos was unable to shake the evil rap. Any compliments directed toward the quarterback usually were accompanied by, "Yes, but . . . ," alluding to alleged mental deficiencies.

Bradshaw rarely, if ever, offered disclaimers, although he once declared, "I'm not extremely brilliant and have never claimed to be, but I can study a tendency chart on the defense and select the plays that will work in a given situation. This isn't nuclear physics, it's a game . . . how smart do you have to be?"

Thomas Henderson, the loquacious Dallas linebacker who had christened himself "Hollywood" in recognition of his showmanship, used the word "dumb" in describing Bradshaw during Super Bowl week. The game, proclaimed Henderson, belonged to the team with the Texas-size IQs. Bradshaw, he said, couldn't spell "cat" if "you spotted him the "c" and the "a"".

Now it was early evening of January 21, 1979, and the son of the Louisiana soil was seated in the locker room beneath Miami's Orange Bowl, spitting tobacco juice into a paper cup.

Bradshaw jokingly ordered newsmen clustered about him, "Go and ask Hender-

MVP Terry Bradshaw hugs receiver Lynn Swann (88) after the Steelers had captured their third Super Bowl win.

son if I was dumb today."

Nobody stirred. The inference was clear. This day belonged to Bradshaw, named the Most Valuable Player in the Steelers' 35-31 victory over the Dallas Cowboys before a crowd of 79,484.

Bradshaw had completed 17 of 30 passes for a record 318 yards and passed for four touchdowns, another Super Bowl record. Bradshaw had to be brilliant because the Steelers' ground attack netted only 66 yards against the Doomsday II defense of the Cowboys.

While Bradshaw was hurling zingers at Henderson, the linebacker slumped dejectedly in the Dallas clubhouse, trying unsuccessfully to stem tears with a bravado that fell short of the mark.

"I'm a little sad," he confessed. "I didn't feel defeat until the game was over. Now I'm upset. I was working out there. Now I'm on the verge of a heart attack. I'm hurt that we lost. I'm hurt that I didn't make the big play to win the game."

Did Hollywood still question Bradshaw's intelligence? "I never questioned his ability," he responded, neatly sidestepping the issue.

Crushed as he was by his own shortcomings and the Cowboys' defeat, Henderson probably was crushed even more by a putdown by Joe Greene, the Steelers' defensive tackle, during the game.

After a Cowboys kickoff sailed out of bounds and the teams were returning upfield, Greene sauntered off the sideline to inquire of Henderson: "What is a super star like you doing on a kickoff team?"

Hollywood's puff was coming home to roost.

The Steelers' route to a third Super Bowl was marred by only two defeats. They suffered a 24-17 loss to Houston and a 10-7 setback at the hands of Los Angeles, after which they ran off seven consecutive victories, climaxed by a 33-10 thumping of Denver in the divisional playoff and a 34-5 whipping of Houston in the AFC title game.

The Cowboys started the season sluggishly, winning only six of their first 10 games.

Roger Staubach attributed the unimpressive record to "the Super Bowl syndrome, just not giving it everything you've got."

The quarterback said the team was inconsistent, as if each player was waiting for another to do something to end the slump.

The quarterback did not absolve himself from blame, pointing to his numerous interceptions. Running back Tony Dorsett was fumbling too frequently, Staubach said, while the offense and defense took turns playing ineffectively.

Suddenly, however, the Cowboys found the combination for success. The various units started to mesh. After a 23-16 reversal by Miami, the Cowboys won their last eight games. Included were a 27-20 decision over Atlanta in the divisional playoff and a 28-0 whitewash of Los Angeles in the NFC championship game.

In the Rams' rout, Staubach passed for two touchdowns and the Dallas defense made five interceptions, including one by Henderson that was converted into a 68-yard TD gallop finished off with Hollywood's patented slam-dunk over the crossbar.

Dallas' defense was the most stubborn in the NFC, allowing only 107.6 rushing yards per game. Pittsburgh's Steel Curtain was the stingiest in the AFC, permitting an average of 107.8 yards rushing per game.

"The first Super Bowl rematch (Pittsburgh won, 21-17, in Super Bowl X) was the game," said Dallas defensive end Harvey Martin, that "everybody's been waiting for."

Teammate Ed (Too Tall) Jones thought that the key to the contest would be the Cowboys' degree of success in controlling Bradshaw. "If we do that well," he said, "we've got a good part of the battle won."

Greene predicted that the winning team "will be the most successful at getting at the quarterback."

Dallas Coach Tom Landry predicted that the champion would be the team that scored 21 points, a total achieved 12 times by each team during the season.

As a fitting tribute to one of the NFL cofounders in 1920, the pre-game coin toss was conducted by George Halas. The legendary coach of the Chicago Bears and now the club's board chairman was transported in an antique car to midfield where he made the ceremonial flip with an 1820 gold piece for the captains of the two teams.

Calling the toss correctly, the Cowboys received the opening kickoff and launched an impressive drive, looking every inch the team that had accumulated 5,959 total yards during the season. With Dorsett ripping off huge gains, the Cowboys registered two quick first downs in moving from their 35-yard line to the Steelers 34. On a first-and-10, however, wide receiver Drew Pearson fumbled a handoff from Dorsett on a double reverse and John Banaszak recovered for the Steelers on their 47.

The play, on which Pearson was to have thrown to tight end Billy Joe DuPree, was relatively new to the Cowboys, having been installed before the conference title game against Los Angeles.

Lamented Pearson: "We practiced that play for three weeks. It is designed for me to hit Billy Joe 15 to 17 yards downfield. We practiced the play so much it was unbeliev-

Pittsburgh's John Stallworth hauls in a 28-yard Terry Bradshaw pass for the game's first touchdown.

able we could fumble it. I expected the handoff a bit lower, but I should have had it. Billy Joe was in the process of breaking into the clear when the fumble occurred.''

Six plays and two first downs after the fumble, the Steelers were on the Dallas 28, from where Bradshaw passed to wide receiver John Stallworth in the corner of the end zone for the game's first touchdown. When Roy Gerela converted, the Steelers had a 7-0 lead with 5:13 gone.

"We exploited a Cowboy weakness we spotted on film," explained Stallworth. "We saw the cornerbacks jumping around, so I took a slant, then cut back to the outside and Terry lobbed the ball to me.''

The Cowboys failed to reach their 40 on either of their next two possessions, but, with one minute remaining in the quarter, Harvey Martin sacked Bradshaw, who fumbled, and Ed Jones recovered on the Pittsburgh 41.

After a two-yard gain by Robert New-

house and an incomplete pass, Staubach found Tony Hill uncovered on the 26-yard line. Time was running out as the wide receiver tightroped the sideline for the equalizing TD. It was the initial first-quarter touchdown scored against the Steelers in the season.

After one period the teams were not only deadlocked in points, but also were virtually equal in other statistics as well. The Cowboys held a running edge, 36 yards to 23, while the Steelers excelled in passing yardage, 83 to 63, and in first downs, five to four.

With less than three minutes elapsed in the second quarter, the hard-charging Cowboys forced a second fumble by Bradshaw. On the Pittsburgh 37, Bradshaw was stripped of the football by Henderson, linebacker Mike Hegman picking up the football and racing for the touchdown. Rafael Septien's second conversion sent the Cowboys in front, 14-7.

The Dallas edge endured less than two

Steelers touchdown No. 3 came in the second quarter when Rocky Bleier hauled in a 7-yard pass from Terry Bradshaw.

minutes, or until Bradshaw connected again with Stallworth. From his 25, Bradshaw passed to the wide receiver on the 35. Stallworth broke a tackle by cornerback Aaron Kyle and cut toward the middle of the field to complete a 75-yard pass-run play. Gerela knotted the score a second time, 14-14.

Kyle offered no excuses for failing to stop Stallworth. "I just missed him," he said. "If I had been in a better position, initially, maybe I would have stopped him. Pittsburgh has two good outside receivers, but we are paid to cover them. If we don't do it well, we get beat. They get paid to catch the ball, we get paid to cover them."

Stallworth was not the primary receiver on the play, Bradshaw disclosed. "I was going to Lynn Swann on the post," he said, "but the Cowboys covered Swann and left Stallworth open. I laid the ball out there and it should have gone for about 15 yards, but Stallworth broke the tackle and went all the way."

On their subsequent possession, the Cowboys were in their two-minute drill and had reached the Pittsburgh 32 when a Staubach pass intended for Drew Pearson was intercepted by Mel Blount.

When Staubach returned to the bench, saddled with his only interception of the game, as events proved, Landry asked, "Why didn't you throw late to Billy Joe (DuPree)?"

"Why did you call that play? It's ridiculous," Staubach shot back. "We have a two-minute offense. Why were we running that play?"

Landry reasoned that the play had been successful against Pittsburgh in the past, including Super Bowl X.

Staubach figured that overuse of the play-action pass would breed familiarity among the Steelers defenders. The element of surprise would be gone.

Had Blount been playing his position properly, he should have been up short, Staubach concluded, not back where he

TD No. 4 went to Franco Harris after a 22-yard run.

could make the interception.

"Of all the passes I've ever thrown," noted Roger, "this one will haunt me the longest."

After making the interception, Blount returned the ball 13 yards to the 29.

A holding penalty set the Steelers back 10 yards, but Bradshaw put the club on the march again. Two passes to Swann put the Steelers on the Dallas 16 and, at 0:40, Franco Harris picked up nine yards against the left side. The clock showed 0:33 when Bradshaw, from the Dallas 7, arched a soft pass toward the right side of the end zone. When Rocky Bleier pulled in the pass and Gerela converted, the Steelers had a 21-14 halftime lead.

Halftime statistics strongly favored the Steelers. The AFC champions led in first downs, 13 to 7; net yards passing, 229 to 61, and net yards, 271 to 102. Only in net yards rushing (42 to 41, Steelers), were the Cowboys compatible.

Septien's 27-yard field goal with less than three minutes remaining represented all the scoring in the third period, but Dallas barely missed a touchdown that would have given the Cowboys a tie after three quarters.

The unfortunate player in the near miss was Jackie Smith, 38-year-old tight end who had retired from the St. Louis Cardinals after the previous season when a doctor informed him that a neck condition threatened paralysis if he continued to play.

When the Cowboys needed a backup tight end and made a pitch for his services, Smith consented, but only if he was able to pass the physical. Jackie surmounted that obstacle and throughout Super Bowl week had cavorted like a young colt, declaring, "I'm a very happy, fortunate old man, particularly when I think of all my old teammates who never made it to the Super Bowl."

Now, with time running out in the third period, and on a third-and-three on the Pittsburgh 10, Staubach passed to Smith, alone in the end zone, but the hands that once caught everything they touched dropped the football.

"That wasn't exactly the way we had worked on it," acknowledged Smith. "It was a good call, I just missed it. I slipped a little, but still should have caught it. I've dropped passes before, but never any that was so important.

"Maybe I should have tried to catch it with my hands only, but in that situation you try to use your chest. Then I lost my footing, my feet ended up in front of me and I think the ball went off my hip. It's hard to remember, those things happen so quickly."

Attempting to take some of the heat off Smith, Staubach said, "When I started to throw, there was no question in my mind, I knew the pass would be completed. But it wasn't a good throw. I took too much off it. If you're casting blame, it's 50 percent my fault and 50 percent Jackie's. I know one thing, the play wasn't a failure for lack of experience because we're the two oldest guys on the team.

"One call, one play doesn't make a game. The Steelers' defense made some key plays."

One of the key plays occurred early in the fourth quarter and set that period apart from any of the previous 51 Super Bowl quarters as a spawning ground for controversy.

Source of the long and loud dispute was a bumping incident between Lynn Swann of the Steelers and cornerback Benny Barnes of the Cowboys.

From his 44-yard line, Bradshaw passed to the right where Swann and Barnes col-

The controversial play occurred when Dallas defender Benny Barnes was called for interference against Lynn Swann (88) on a 33-yard fourth-quarter play.

lided and fell to the turf as the ball rolled free.

Back judge Pat Knight, standing nearby and with an unobstructed view of the play, spotted no infraction. Field judge Fred Swearingen, a 19-year veteran of NFL officiating and observing the play from a considerably greater distance than Knight, called a tripping violation on Barnes and quickly the ball was on the Dallas 23.

Shrieks of protest rose from the Dallas bench. "He missed it," stormed Landry, referring to Swearingen. "Because the safety blitz was on, all Bradshaw did was throw up an alley-oop pass, hoping Swann could run under it. Benny had taken away the inside because of the blitz (keeping Swann away from the area vacated by safety Cliff Harris) and was running with Swann when he looked back to locate he ball. The ball was inside him so Swann cut across trying to get to the ball.

"He cut across the back of Benny's legs, tripped and fell down. Benny was tripped, of course, and fell.

"When he hit the ground with his chest, his feet flopped up. That's the only thing that Swearingen could have seen. He assumed after the play that Benny tripped Swann."

Landry added, "But Knight was there, just a few feet away on Benny's side looking at the play. He called it a good play and should have argued for Benny because it was so obvious from his side. Normally, one official won't go against another's flag, but I think Knight should have done so in such a big game.

"Swearingen had no idea what had happened. He had Swann between him and Benny. He just saw Benny's feet flopping up and to him that was a tripping move. Swann was the one who did the tripping, when he cut across Benny's legs."

Barnes' version of the play was as follows: "Swann ran right up my back. When I saw the flag I knew it was on him. I couldn't believe the call. Maybe Swearingen needs glasses, maybe he's from Pittsburgh.

"I don't even know how far behind me Swann was. Then I felt hands on me, then he tripped me. The ball was catchable between us. I had the right of way, I'm told. The ball was just floating up there.

"The official said I swung my foot back to trip Swann. I didn't even see Swann."

Not unexpectedly, Pittsburgh opinions coincided with that of Swearingen.

"I didn't think there was anything controversial about the call," reported Swann. "I was tripped. I didn't see Barnes and didn't touch him. My hands are clean. I'm one of the good guys."

"There was a safety blitz and no pickup and I knew it," explained Bradshaw. "So I put the 'Hail Mary' on the ball. It was a good call by the official."

Swearingen, a Carlsbad, Calif., real estate broker, defended his call. "It was a judgment call," he explained. "The players bumped before the ball was even close to them, perhaps before the ball was thrown. They were both looking back and the defender went to the ground. The Pittsburgh receiver, in trying to get to the ball, was tripped by the defender's feet. He interfered with the receiver trying to get to the ball. It was coming to him in that direction and I threw the flag for pass interference.

Knight, a San Antonio lumber firm executive whose initial call of an incomplete pass was overruled by Swearingen, said, "I was about seven or eight yards from the play and had about a 10-degree angle. Fred's angle was a little different. We think it was a good call."

From the Dallas 23, the Steelers advanced to the 17, then were set back to the 22, from where Franco Harris broke over the left side for a touchdown, climaxing an eight-play, 84-yard drive.

"I was expecting a blitz," reported Bradshaw, "so I called for a quick off-tackle trap. You blitz on that play and Franco will bust it."

The Steelers now led, 28-17, a lead that ballooned by seven more points in less than a minute, largely because Randy White fumbled the ensuing kickoff.

The All-Pro defensive tackle of the Cowboys was wearing a cast to cover a fractured right thumb and was stationed in the middle of the field to lead the blocking charge for the kickoff return. Chances of the kickoff going to White were extremely small, except that in this instance it did. White fumbled when tackled by Tony Dungy and Dennis (Dirt) Winston recovered for Pittsburgh on the Dallas 18 with 6:57 remaining.

Roy Gerela had not intended that the kickoff should go to White. "I thought I'd kick the ball into the end zone and they would down it and bring the ball out to the 20-yard line," he said. "But the field has a sandy base. My foot slipped as I approached the ball. It wasn't the kickoff I wanted, but it worked out to our advantage."

"We had it planned that if the kick was squibbed, we would lateral it back to one of the deep backs," explained White. "But it took me so long just to pick up the ball, I had to go with it. When I started running, I fumbled the ball, that's all there was to it. I've handled a couple of kicks this year, but I fumbled this one."

Dallas Coach Tom Landry and Roger Staubach consult late in the game.

Tony Dorsett ran for a game-high 96 yards, but that wasn't enough.

On the next play, Bradshaw's 18-yard pass to Swann was caught on the rear line of the end zone and Gerela's fifth extra point gave the Steelers a 35-17 cushion.

On the Pittsburgh bench, general merriment alarmed Bradshaw.

"With more than six minutes left, our guys were celebrating," said Terry. "That made me mad because I remembered the Super Bowl three years ago when Dallas came back and threatened to pull it out.

"I looked out on the field and here was Roger scrambling well, throwing well, moving them downfield and they scored twice. I got very upset. We had scored 35 points on a team that seldom gives up that much and then it looked as though we might wind up losing it.

"And here were our fellows on the sidelines shaking hands and slapping one another on the back."

Jack Lambert was worried, too. "Fortunately," said the Steelers' middle linebacker, "we had a large enough lead so that the Cowboys' comeback didn't affect us."

The Dallas comeback commenced immediately after the kickoff. In eight plays the Cowboys marched 89 yards, with Staubach passing the last seven yards to DuPree. When Septien converted, 2:27 showed on the stadium clock and it was 35-24.

Septien's onside kickoff was bobbled by the Steelers' Dungy and recovered by Dennis Thurman of the Cowboys on the Dallas 48.

In nine plays—eight passes and a sack—the Cowboys scored again. Staubach's four-yard pass to Butch Johnson produced the TD and Septien's extra point lifted the Cowboys within four points of the Steelers, at 35-31, with 22 seconds remaining.

As the Cowboys lined up for what was certain to be another onside kick, sure-handed running back Rocky Bleier waited on the Dallas 45-yard line, reflecting on his chances if the football came to him.

"I was trying to anticipate what Septien would do," said Bleier. "If he kicked it hard and tried to bounce it off me, I was going to let it go through to Sidney Thornton rather than risk a fumble. But he decided to dribble the ball and it wasn't that hard, so I was able to get under it, and I was relieved."

Twice, Bradshaw took the snap and fell to the ground as time expired. The once ragtag Steelers, the poor relations of the National Football League, were the first team to win three Super Bowls.

Post-game paens rang loud and clear for Bradshaw, selected the MVP.

"He throws a football 20 yards like I throw a dart 15 feet," praised Charlie Waters, Dallas safety.

"Every time we got them in a third-and-eight situation, Bradshaw would throw another unbelievable pass," observed Dallas' White.

Bradshaw beamed over his record passing performance (318 yards and four TDs). "This sure was a lot of fun," he said. "I played this game just the way I hoped I would.

"The thing I didn't want to do was change the things that got us here. Play-action passes, throwing the ball, doing whatever it took to win, that was what made this team. We just needed to keep it up.

"I didn't want to come here and let the pressure of the Super Bowl dictate to me like it had dictated to some people in the past. I wanted to play my game, win or lose, and not give a hoot. I was surprised how relaxed I was. I was able to stay relaxed and not worry.

"When I left this stadium, I wanted to know I had done what I needed to do."

Swann admired the quarterback's play selection and confidence. "You couldn't ask for a finer quarterback or leader than Terry was today," said the wide receiver. "He had us tuned to just the right pitch."

The Steelers' game plan, according to Swann, was to "throw to our wide receivers so Dallas' cornerbacks would have to make the tackles. The cornerbacks don't tackle as well as the safeties."

Cliff Harris, one of the safeties (Charlie Waters was the other), had announced during the week that he planned "to hit Swann hard, not to hurt him, but that doesn't mean he might not get hurt."

Was the blast he received from Harris along the sideline early in the game unnecessarily rough? Swann was asked.

"That was a good clean shot to the chest," declared Swann, "and, anyhow, all that talk during the week . . . I'm at the point now, in my mind, where I could blast every Cowboy player who talked about me. But I prefer to let the results speak for themselves."

Nobody agonized more over the Dallas defeat than Landry. "We tried hard, but we didn't take advantage of the opportunities we had," lamented the losing coach. "I said all along that turnovers and breaks would determine the winner. That's what happened today. On any given day the Steelers are no better than we are."

Landry was not alone in his opinion.

"My teammates may not like this," said Pittsburgh defensive captain Greene, "but the Cowboys are good enough that on any given Sunday they might beat us."

"I'll think a lot about Bradshaw during the off-season," said Waters. "Unfortunately, the pain will get worse before it gets better."

Steeler Lynn Swann pops the cork and TV analyst Fran Tarkenton (left) gets a bath.

Statistics of 13th Super Bowl

PITTSBURGH 35, DALLAS 31

Orange Bowl, Miami, Fla., January 21, 1979
Attendance: 79,484

PITTSBURGH	OFFENSE	DALLAS
John Stallworth	WR	Tony Hill
Jon Kolb	LT	Pat Donovan
Sam Davis	LG	Herbert Scott
Mike Webster	C	John Fitzgerald
Gerry Mullins	RG	Tom Rafferty
Ray Pinney	RT	Rayfield Wright
Randy Grossman	TE	Billy Joe DuPree
Lynn Swann	WR	Drew Pearson
Terry Bradshaw	QB	Roger Staubach
Rocky Bleier	RB	Robert Newhouse
Franco Harris	RB	Tony Dorsett

Defense

L. C. Greenwood	LE	Ed Jones
Joe Greene	LT	Larry Cole
Steve Furness	RT	Randy White
John Banaszak	RE	Harvey Martin
Jack Ham	LLB	Thomas Henderson
Jack Lambert	MLB	Bob Breunig
Loren Toews	RLB	D. D. Lewis
Ron Johnson	LCB	Benny Barnes
Mel Blount	RCB	Aaron Kyle
Donnie Shell	SS	Charlie Waters
Mike Wagner	FS	Cliff Harris

— SUBSTITUTIONS —

PITTSBURGH—Offense: Kicker—Roy Gerela. Punter—Craig Colquitt. Running Backs—Jack Deloplaine, Rick Moser, Sidney Thornton. Wide Receivers—Theo Bell, Jim Smith. Tight End—Jim Mandich. Tackle—Larry Brown. Guard—Steve Courson. Center—Ted Peterson. Defense: Linemen—Fred Anderson, Tom Beasley, Gary Dunn, Dwight White. Linebackers—Robin Cole, Dennis Winston. Backs—Larry Anderson, Tony Dungy, Ray Oldham. DNP—Bennie Cunningham (TE), Mike Kruczek (QB), Cliff Stoudt (QB).

DALLAS—Offense: Punter-QB—Danny White. Kicker—Rafael Septien. Running Backs—Alois Blackwell, Larry Brinson, Scott Laidlaw, Preston Pearson. Wide Receivers—Butch Johnson, Robert Steele. Tight End—Jackie Smith. Tackle—Andy Frederick. Guards—Jim Cooper, Burton Lawless, Tom Randall. Defense: Linemen—Larry Bethea, Dave Stalls. Linebackers—Guy Brown, Mike Hegman, Bruce Huther. Backs—Randy Hughes, Dennis Thurman. DNP—Glenn Carano (QB), Jethro Pugh (DT), Mark Washington (CB).

— SCORE BY PERIODS —

Pittsburgh Steelers (AFC)	7	14	0	14 —	35
Dallas Cowboys (NFC)	7	7	3	14 —	31

— SCORING —

Pittsburgh—Stallworth 28 pass from Bradshaw (Gerela kick).
Dallas—Hill 39 pass from Staubach (Septien kick).
Dallas—Hegman 37 fumble recovery return (Septien kick).
Pittsburgh—Stallworth 75 pass from Bradshaw (Gerela kick).
Pittsburgh—Bleier 7 pass from Bradshaw (Gerela kick).
Dallas—Field goal Septien 27.
Pittsburgh—Harris 22 run (Gerela kick).

Pittsburgh—Swann 18 pass from Bradshaw (Gerela kick).
Dallas—DuPree 7 pass from Staubach (Septien kick).
Dallas—B. Johnson 4 pass from Staubach (Septien kick).

— TEAM STATISTICS —

	Pittsburgh	Dallas
Total First Downs	19	20
First Downs Rushing	2	6
First Downs Passing	15	13
First Downs by Penalty	2	1
Rushes	24	32
Yards Gained Rushing (net)	66	154
Average Yards per Rush	2.8	4.8
Passes Attempted	30	30
Passes Completed	17	17
Had Intercepted	1	1
Times Tackled Attemp. Pass.	4	5
Yards Lost Attempting Pass.	27	52
Yards Gained Passing (net)	291	176
Total Net Yardage	357	330
Punts	3	5
Average Distance	43.0	39.6
Punt Returns	4	2
Punt Return Yardage	27	33
Kickoff Returns	3	6
Kickoff Return Yardage	45	104
Interception Return Yardage	13	21
Fumbles	2	3
Own Fumbles Recovered	0	1
Opp. Fumbles Recovered	2	2
Total Return Yardage	85	158
Penalties	5	9
Yards Penalized	35	89
Total Points Scored	35	31
Touchdowns	5	4
Touchdowns Rushing	1	0
Touchdowns Passing	4	3
Touchdowns Returns	0	1
Extra Points	5	4
Field Goals	0	1
Field Goals Attempted	1	1
Total Offensive Plays	58	67
Avg. Gain per Offensive Play	6.2	4.9

INDIVIDUAL STATISTICS

— RUSHING —

Pittsburgh	Atts.	Yds.	Lg.	TD
Harris	20	68	22	1
Bleier	2	3	2	0
Bradshaw	2	−5	−2	0

Dallas	Atts.	Yds.	Lg.	TD
Dorsett	16	96	29	0
Staubach	4	37	18	0
Laidlaw	3	12	7	0
P. Pearson	1	6	6	0
Newhouse	8	3	5	0

— PASSING —

Pittsburgh	Atts.	Comp.	Yds.	Int.	TD
Bradshaw	30	17	318	1	4
Dallas	Atts.	Comp.	Yds.	Int.	TD
Staubach	30	17	228	1	3

Terry Bradshaw directs traffic as he prepares to unload.

— RECEIVING —

Pittsburgh	No.	Yds.	Lg.	TD
Swann	7	124	29	1
Stallworth	3	115	75	2
Grossman	3	29	10	0
Bell	2	21	12	0
Harris	1	22	22	0
Bleier	1	7	7	1

Dallas	No.	Yds.	Lg.	TD
Dorsett	5	44	13	0
D. Pearson	4	73	25	0
Hill	2	49	39	1
Johnson	2	30	26	1
DuPree	2	17	10	1
P. Pearson	2	15	8	0

Dallas	No.	Yds.	Lg.
Johnson	3	63	23
Brinson	2	41	25
R. White	1	0	0

— INTERCEPTIONS —

Pittsburgh	No.	Yds.	Lg.	TD
Blount	1	13	13	0

Dallas	No.	Yds.	Lg.	TD
Lewis	1	21	21	0

— FIELD GOALS —

Pittsburgh		Att.	Made
Gerela		1	0

Dallas		Att.	Made
Septien		1	1

— FUMBLES —

Pittsburgh	No.	Own Rec.	Opp. Rec.	TD
Bradshaw	2	0	0	0
Banaszak	0	0	1	0
Winston	0	0	1	0

Dallas	No.	Own Rec.	Opp. Rec.	TD
D. Pearson	1	0	0	0
Staubach	1	0	0	0
Rafferty	0	1	0	0
R. White	1	0	0	0
Jones	0	0	1	0
Hegman	0	0	1	1

— PUNTING —

Pittsburgh	No.	Avg.	Lg.
Colquitt	3	43.0	52

Dallas	No.	Avg.	Lg.
D. White	5	39.6	50

— PUNT RETURNS —

Pittsburgh	No.	FC	Yds.	Lg.
Bell	4	0	27	12

Dallas	No.	FC	Yds.	Lg.
Johnson	2	1	33	21

— KICKOFF RETURNS —

Pittsburgh	No.	Yds.	Lg.
L. Anderson	3	45	24

— SCORING —

Pittsburgh	TD	PAT	FG	Pts.
Stallworth	2	0	0	12
Bleier	1	0	0	6
Harris	1	0	0	6
Swann	1	0	0	6
Gerela	0	5	0	5

Dallas	TD	PAT	FG	Pts.
Septien	0	4	1	7
DuPree	1	0	0	6
Hegman	1	0	0	6
Hill	1	0	0	6
B. Johnson	1	0	0	6

Pittsburgh's Lynn Swann towers over Rams Nolan Cromwell and Pat Thomas as he pulls in Terry Bradshaw's third-quarter 47-yard TD pass.

Super Bowl XIV

The Pittsburgh Story

January 20, 1980

Almost from the moment he was drafted by the Pittsburgh Steelers, John Stallworth was the other kid on the block, the wide receiver who gained recognition only if some spilled over from heralded Lynn Swann.

A product of Alabama A&M, Stallworth was hardly a publicity match for Swann, an All-America from the University of Southern California and an acrobatic artist whose very name implied ballet-like grace.

In the 1974 draft, Swann was selected No. 1 by the Steelers, and Stallworth No. 4, which was their approximate numerical relationship five years later: one Swann was equal to four Stallworths in the minds of most observers.

In Super Bowl XIII, Stallworth caught two first-half touchdown passes against Dallas, a fact that was generally overlooked when John sat out the second half because of leg cramps and Swann stole the spotlight.

The 1979 season was pure discomfort for Stallworth. Two sprained wrists made it too painful for him to lift his infant daughter, yet he caught 70 passes good for 1,183 yards, both Steelers records.

Stallworth's day of recognition arrived eventually, before a record Super Bowl crowd of 103,985 in the Rose Bowl on January 20, 1980, when the 6-2 Alabamian caught three passes for 121 yards and scored the go-ahead touchdown on a 73-yard pass play in Pittsburgh's 31-19 victory over the Los Angeles Rams.

The play that projected the Steelers into their fourth world championship had been practiced eight times during Super Bowl week, Stallworth disclosed—and it hadn't worked once.

"It's hard to have confidence in a play that never works," said Stallworth. "But I think it didn't work because the field was soggy. Terry Bradshaw was throwing the ball long and I couldn't get to it."

The play, known to the Steelers as "60 prevent, slot, hook and go," occurred at 2:56 of the fourth quarter, after the score had already changed hands five times. Los Angeles held a 19-17 lead.

On third and eight at his 27-yard line, Stallworth, the slot man, took two defenders 15 yards downfield, hooked and then went deep, pulling in a perfectly thrown Bradshaw pass 39 yards from the line of scrimmage and raced the remaining 34 yards unmolested.

"Usually, on that play," Bradshaw noted, "the receiver hooks and slides. And that's the way the Rams defensed it."

Los Angeles strong safety Eddie Brown confessed, "I blew it. I thought we had five defensive backs on the field instead of six. I should have gone to the inside, but I took the outside receiver instead." The help that cornerback Rod Perry expected never arrived.

"Bradshaw put just enough arc on the ball to get it over my hands," noted Perry, who yielded five inches to Stallworth.

Bradshaw called the same play later in the game and Stallworth picked up 45 yards, setting up the final Pittsburgh touchdown.

"I felt all along I could deliver the big play," reported Stallworth, gifted with 4.5 speed in the 40-yard dash. "I feel that I can go deep on anybody in the NFL. We tried to beat them with the bomb and go deep on the fly pattern because they were double covering short and deep."

The selection of Bradshaw as the Most Valuable Player for the second consecutive year failed to disturb Stallworth. "I don't

Rams quarterback Vince Ferragamo avoided the rush and guided his team to a 13-10 halftime lead.

worry about things I can't control," he philosophized. "I just go with the flow."

The Steelers did not exactly "flow" to their fourth Super Bowl appearance in six years, suffering four defeats on their 16-game schedule. Their most crushing defeats were by Cincinnati, 34-10, and San Diego, 35-7. In the AFC playoffs, they eliminated Miami, 34-14, and Houston, 27-13.

For the Rams, the Super Bowl engagement was their first and capped their seventh consecutive NFC Western Division championship season. It also marked the first time an NFC West team had qualified for the title game.

The Los Angeles regular-season record of 9-7 was the poorest of any team ever to reach the Super Bowl and it was only one victory better than division runner-up New Orleans' 8-8. The Rams barely outscored their season opponents, 323 points to 309, and in midseason suffered such consecutive one-sided defeats as 30-6 to Dallas and 40-16 to San Diego. In the playoffs they squeaked by Dallas, 21-19, before beating Tampa Bay,

9-0, on three field goals by Frank Corral.

L.A. had undergone its annual quarterback crisis, with Vince Ferragamo, a third-year player, emerging as the starter at season's end. Pat Haden held the job at the beginning of the year, but was felled by a broken finger. Rookie Jeff Rutledge and veteran Bob Lee also had turns behind center before Ferragamo recovered from a broken hand and led the Rams to six victories in seven games, enough to win the NFC West.

The Rams were coached by Raymondo Giuseppi Giovanni Baptiste Malavasi, who had replaced George Allen midway through the preseason schedule in 1978.

A product of Clifton, N.J., and a graduate of Mississippi State in civil engineering, Ray Malavasi surfaced as coach of the Rams following a checkerboard career that started at Fort Belvoir, Va., while he was in military service.

He was an assistant coach at the University of Minnesota, Memphis State and Wake Forest before being hired as personnel director of the Denver Broncos in 1962.

In 1966, following the dismissal of Mac Speedie, Malavasi coached the Broncos to a 4-8 record. He was defensive coordinator of the Hamilton Tiger-Cats of the Canadian Football League the following year. In 1969, he became an assistant with the Buffalo Bills, moved to the Oakland Raiders as an assistant in 1970 and joined the Rams in 1973, serving as defensive coordinator under Coach Chuck Knox. For Allen, he was offensive coordinator and offensive coach.

Malavasi underwent quadruple bypass heart surgery early in 1978. A year later, in the spring of 1979, he was hospitalized for treatment of hypertension and, he said at the Super Bowl, he was still on medication.

Now Malavasi was ready for the Steelers. When he was asked if he thought the Rams would be satisfied to have gotten to the Super Bowl and were not 100 percent determined to win, Malavasi replied heatedly, "I don't think so. For me to get here and not win is like not getting here at all."

While Malavasi was prepared for the main event, Terry Bradshaw tossed fitfully the night before the game. Three hours after falling asleep, he was wide awake, staring at blank walls. For entertainment, he turned on the television set and listened to the whine of test patterns.

"I couldn't shake the idea of losing," related the three-time Super Bowl quarterback. "I couldn't sleep. It was the first time that's happened to me."

To Art Rooney, gentle patriarch of the Steelers, went the honor of making the traditional coin toss. Rooney nearing 79, heard the Rams' captains call the toss correctly and announce they would receive.

The NFC champions,. however, progressed no further than their 34-yard line on their first possession and the Steelers, following Ken Clark's punt and a 15-yard clipping penalty, started their first series from their 21.

Eleven plays and three first downs later, rookie Matt Bahr kicked a 41-yard field goal.

After Bahr's kickoff traveled only to the Los Angeles 41, the Rams scored in eight plays to move ahead, 7-3. Wendell Tyler accounted for 39 yards with a sweep around left end and Cullen Bryant finished off the drive with a one-yard plunge with 12:16 elasped.

Larry Anderson, who was to set a Super Bowl record by returning five kickoffs 162 yards, sprinted 45 yards with Corral's kickoff and Bradshaw needed only nine plays for Pittsburgh to regain the lead. Systematically, Terry mixed passes and line smashes until the Steelers reached the 1, from where

Terry Bradshaw and friend enjoy that post-game victory feeling.

Franco Harris circled right end for the touchdown. With 2:08 gone in the second period, the AFC champions were on top, 10-7.

The Steelers had three more possessions the remainder of the quarter. One drive stalled at midfield, another was terminated by safety Dave Elmendorf's interception of a first-down pass on the Pittsburgh 49 and the third died at the Pittsburgh 34 as time ran out.

The Rams, meanwhile scored twice on Corral field goals from 31 and 45 yards, taking a 13-10 lead into the locker room at halftime.

"It was an uneasy feeling," reported tackle Larry Brown of the mood in the Pittsburgh clubhouse. "We knew we could win the game, but we also knew we'd have to make some changes."

"We never thought we were going to lose," added defensive end Dwight White, "but it was going to be a test of maturity and character."

Middle linebacker Jack Lambert conceded that "I was scared. The Rams had the momentum. I'm never concerned about our offense, but our defense was playing poorly."

Assistant coach Woody Widenhofer minced no words, telling the defensive unit, "How can you mess up this way? Didn't we go over these things a dozen times? You guys are standing out there like statues."

Results of the censure were not immediately noticeable, although the Pittsburgh offensive unit scored three minutes into the third quarter when Bradshaw and Lynn Swann hooked up on a 47-yard play and turned a 17-13 lead over to the defense.

Along with others, Rams free safety Nolan Cromwell thought he was in ideal position to deflect the touchdown pass to Swann. "But I guess I jumped a little early," he said. "I was on the way down when the ball arrived. I think I partially deflected it, but not enough to knock it off-course."

Cornerback Pat Thomas thought that Cromwell "had the interception. He misjudged it. All I could do was try to slap the ball away from Swann."

When Swann returned to the Pittsburgh bench, teammates greeted him with backslaps and a message: "Swannie, that's what we needed."

The lead did not last long in the hands of the Steelers' defense. The Rams went 77 yards in four plays to reclaim the lead. A 50-yard pass from Ferragamo to wide receiver Billy Waddy moved the ball to the Pittsburgh 24. One play later, Lawrence McCutcheon, on a halfback option play, passed to wide receiver Ron Smith for a touchdown. When Corral's extra point try was wide left, the Rams' lead was 19-17.

"A good call," conceded Lambert of the TD play. "They'd had some success running on us, and the secondary was coming up to give support."

If there was any favorable aspect of the game's pattern, Stallworth noted, it was that "we always had time to come back.

"It wasn't like there were two minutes left and everything was at stake."

There were in fact, 10 minutes remaining in the third quarter when the Steelers commenced their next series on their 26-yard line.

Two plays later, from his 44, Bradshaw launched a bomb intended for Swann. Cromwell was positioned perfectly for the interception, but let the ball slip through his hands.

"After I dropped the ball, I looked up and saw where everyone was," related Cromwell. "I felt sick. There was one Steeler in front of me and he was blocked. I just took my eye off the ball. We could have been nine points ahead and that might have changed the result."

If the Rams missed a scoring opportunity on Cromwell's failure, the Steelers did no better with continued possession.

Their drive ended disastrously when a Bradshaw pass intended for Jim Smith was intercepted by Eddie Brown, who handed off to Pat Thomas for an overall return of 12 yards to the Rams' 39.

With less than one minute left in the quarter, and the Steelers driving inside the Rams' 20, Bradshaw attempted a pass to Stallworth on the 5, where cornerback Rod Perry batted the ball into the air and intercepted.

"I was so dad-blame mad at that interception I couldn't see straight," said Bradshaw. "In a situation like that you have to get at least three points."

At this juncture Bradshaw was 12-for-17 in passing, with three interceptions, and Ferragamo was 11-for-16 with a spotless interception record.

With less than three minutes elapsed in the fourth period, the Steelers executed the play that turned the game around, in the opinion of many observers. It was the Stallworth special that had been such an abominable failure during the week.

Bradshaw refused to call the play the first time that Coach Chuck Noll sent it in. On this occasion, Stallworth convinced the quarterback he should call it.

"I saw Rod Perry's hand over me just as I was about to catch the ball," related the wide receiver. "He came very close to making a damn good play."

With 8:29 to play and trailing 24-19, the Rams launched a drive from their 16-yard line and proceeded to the Steelers 32 when Ferragamo passed toward Smith.

Lambert beat Smith to the ball, however, and the Steelers were in control at their 16.

"The play-action pass is designed to hold the linebackers," said Ferragamo. "It held nobody. I probably should have gone to the deep man (Billy Waddy) near the goal line. Lambert is a very rangy guy."

The interception was not Lambert's first contribution to the Pittsburgh effort, of course. Late in the first half he had stepped into the defensive huddle and emitted an ear-splitting exhortation to his teammates.

"He bellowed so loud," remembered safety Donnie Shell, "that I got kinda scared. I don't recall what he said, but I can tell you I didn't say anything."

At another time, after the Rams' Tyler had broken a tackle and reversed his course across the field, Lambert suddenly appeared in his rear and threw the ball-carrier for a nine-yard loss.

"Jack has a role on this team," declared Greene. "I can't tell you what the role is, but he plays it very well."

"I did go into a tirade," Lambert admitted, "but I was very concerned the way the defense was playing. It seemed to me that we didn't have the necessary intensity. We weren't flying around the field the way we should have."

Jack Lambert jumps in front of receiver Ron Smith for the game-sealing interception (left) and then returns the ball 16 yards with a host of Rams in hot pursuit.

Inspired by Lambert, who participated in 13 tackles during the game, the Steelers put the ball in play on their 30 with 5:24 remaining. Two plays netted only three yards before Bradshaw, surveying the L. A. defense, spotted and inviting deployment. "Gol dang it," he muttered to himself, "they're in the same coverage" as in the TD bomb to Stallworth seven minutes earlier. Terry called the same play.

It was a 45-yard completion to Stallworth, who reached the Rams' 22 before he was tackled by Perry.

Rocky Bleier gained nothing at left tackle and Bradshaw went to the air again. A pass to Jim Smith in the end zone fell incomplete, but field judge Charlie Musser flagged Pat Thomas for interference, placing the ball on the L.A. 1-yard line. Two line smashes came up short before Harris plunged over tackle for an insurance touchdown with 1:49 remaining.

"It was a sorry call," snorted Thomas of the interference ruling.

Malavasi agreed. "I could see the play clearly. Thomas did not interfere. It was just a bad call."

Assistant coach Jack Faulkner of the Rams added, "I thought it was offensive interference. You don't call it that close in that situation in a game as important as this one."

Replied Musser, "Thomas had good position all the way until the last second when he played the man instead of the ball."

"Never in my life was I so happy to see a game end," said Bradshaw, who set Super Bowl records for most yards gained passing, career, and most touchdown passes, career. "There was so much more pressure than in previous Super Bowls.

"We knew how good the Rams were, and they were playing at home. I knew it would be very, very tough."

Bradshaw confessed that he was not "totally involved" in the first half. "I knew I wasn't throwing well. I could see that the team wasn't juiced. So, I did a lot of talking to a lot of guys. I feel good about that. I feel like I contributed to getting us juiced up."

Concerning his MVP honor, Bradshaw joked, "They seldom give such awards to quarterbacks who throw three interceptions."

Bradshaw was generous in his praise of Ferragamo, in the sternest test of his 21-game pro career. "I didn't believe he could play as well as he did," complimented Bradshaw. "I have great respect for him."

Describing himself as "excited but not nervous," Ferragamo observed, "I didn't do well in particular, but the whole team did well. We could have won if I hadn't thrown an interception.

"The big thing is that we've been to a Super Bowl, we've had a taste. We know what it takes to win this thing."

While Ferragamo may not have been nervous, running back Tyler was. "I had a nervous stomach," he revealed, "and was throwing up on the sidelines. I was lying down when an official wondered if I was hurt."

"We had 'em on the ropes," moaned L.A. defensive end Fred Dryer after the Rams lost to the Steelers for the first time in four meetings. "Nobody on this club is bitter, nobody's sore. We played the hell out of those guys. I guarantee those guys know they've been in a football game."

Satisfaction in their performance was general among the Rams. Said defensive tackle Larry Brooks, "There's a lot of pride on this team. A lot of people didn't respect the Rams, but who will say we didn't play admirably?"

"We were in it all the way," said Jack Youngblood, defensive end. "If anyone wants to call us dogs now, let him come to me. The Rams can play with anyone, anytime, anywhere. I'm not ashamed."

"We played as well as we could as hard as we could," added Dave Elmendorf.

"We played a damn good game. We gave them a long pass and an interception," asserted Doug France, an offensive tackle.

Rams defensive coordinator Bud Carson, a former Pittsburgh assistant, lamented, "We had them by the jugular and let them get away. They had only one receiver they wanted to throw to (after Swann suffered a mild concussion in the second half). It should have been all over."

"From the beginning I thought we were going to win," said Malavasi. "We ran on them, we threw on them. We just didn't get the big play."

Steelers players were nearly unanimous in their praise for the beaten Rams. Mel Blount was an exception. "I think they played their game in the newspapers," said the cornerback. "I was surprised at the comments they made. That told me right there they didn't have any confidence. That's the difference between a championship team with character and the team that's trying to become a champion."

Other Steelers were more charitable. "They played their hearts out," lauded Greene. "They were just outmanned. They read our blitzes well. They stayed outside well, and they ran well. We just didn't play with our usual zest in the first half.

"We were sleep-walking out there for a while. They played well enough to make us look bad. They came prepared and you've got to respect a team like that."

Offered center Mike Webster, "It took

Franco Harris (32) looks for running room against the stingy Rams defensive line.

the big play to beat them and that's what you need to beat a great defense."

Defensive end White cited the bruising physical aspects of the game, declaring, "They have the type of guys who, when we do so much stunting, can catch you moving and drive you into the stands."

With a fourth Super Bowl trophy at hand, much post-game conversation concentrated on the Steelers' ranking among the all-time great teams. Art Rooney fired the signal gun. "This might be the greatest team of all time," he said, while lamenting the fact that the referee had failed to return the gold piece used in the pre-game coin toss. "The Rams played a wonderful game. They should be proud, just as I am proud of my boys. These are the most gentlemanly fellows I've ever had. None of the team gets swell-headed."

"The facts speak for themselves," said Noll. "The victory is probably the best we've ever had."

Jack Ham, Pittsburgh linebacker who was forced to miss the game because of an ankle injury, summed it up this way:

"Comparisons are hard to make, but I think we're the greatest. The No. 1 factor is depth. We have 45 players who can play. We have much more depth than we have ever had.

"We can win a lot of different ways. We can grind it out and make the big plays. Today, it was a big-play game."

"Winning a fourth Super Bowl should put us in a special category," said Blount. "I think this is the best team ever assembled. They talk about Vince Lombardi, but I think the Chuck Noll era is even greater."

None of the Steelers demonstrated more elation over the victory than J. T. Thomas. He had been sidelined the entire 1978 season with a blood disorder and missed Super Bowl XIII. he recovered in time to play again in 1979 and got one more Super Bowl ring.

"It's something I wished for, hoped for, prayed for," bubbled the free safety. "The Rams thought they were good enough to win, but we were convinced we were good enough.

"I think we can be imitated, but I don't think we can be duplicated. We knew to beat us they had to throw the ball and we had to beat ourselves. We didn't.

"We win together, we lose together, we screw up together. The difference between the two teams is that they only thought they could beat us. We knew we could beat them."

Statistics of 14th Super Bowl

PITTSBURGH 31, LOS ANGELES 19

Rose Bowl, Pasadena, Calif., January 20, 1980
Attendance: 103,985

LOS ANGELES	Offense	PITTSBURGH
Billy Waddy	WR	John Stallworth
Doug France	LT	Jon Kolb
Kent Hill	LG	Sam Davis
Rich Saul	C	Mike Webster
Dennis Harrah	RG	Gerry Mullins
Jackie Slater	RT	Larry Brown
Terry Nelson	TE	Bennie Cunningham
Preston Dennard	WR	Lynn Swann
Vince Ferragamo	QB	Terry Bradshaw
Wendell Tyler	RB	Franco Harris
Cullen Bryant	RB	Rocky Bleier

	Defense	
Jack Youngblood	LE	L.C. Greenwood
Mike Fanning	LT	Joe Greene
Larry Brooks	RT	Gary Dunn
Fred Dryer	RE	John Banaszak
Jim Youngblood	LLB	Dennis Winston
Jack Reynolds	MLB	Jack Lambert
Bob Brudzinski	RLB	Robin Cole
Pat Thomas	LCB	Ron Johnson
Rod Perry	RCB	Mel Blount
Dave Elmendorf	SS	Donnie Shell
Nolan Cromwell	FS	J.T. Thomas

— SUBSTITUTIONS —

LOS ANGELES—Offense: Kicker—Frank Corral. Punter—Ken Clark. Running Backs—Eddie Hill, Lawrence McCutcheon, Jim Jodat. Receivers—Charle Young, Ron Smith, Drew Hill. Linemen—Dan Ryczek, Bill Bain, Gordon Gravelle. Defense: Linemen—Jerry Wilkinson, Reggie Doss. Linebackers—Joe Harris, George Andrews, Greg Westbrooks. Backs—Jackie Wallace, Eddie Brown, Dwayne O'Steen, Ivory Sully. DNP—Jeff Rutledge (QB), Bob Lee (QB), Ken Ellis (CB).

PITTSBURGH—Offense: Kicker—Matt Bahr. Punter—Craig Colquitt. Running Backs—Greg Hawthorne, Anthony Anderson, Sidney Thornton, Rick Moser. Receivers—Theo Bell, Randy Grossman, Jim Smith. Linemen—Thom Dornbrook, Ted Peterson, Steve Courson. Defense: Linemen—Steve Furness, Tom Beasley, Dwight White. Linebackers—Tom Graves, Loren Toews, Zack Valentine. Backs—Larry Anderson, Dwayne Woodruff. DNP—Mike Kruczek (QB), Cliff Stoudt (QB), Jack Ham (LB).

— SCORE BY PERIODS —

Los Angeles Rams (NFC)	7	6	6	0	— 19
Pittsburgh Steelers (AFC)	3	7	7	14	— 31

— SCORING —

Pittsburgh—Field goal Bahr 41.
Los Angeles—Bryant 1 run (Corral kick).
Pittsburgh—Harris 1 run (Bahr kick).
Los Angeles—Field goal Corral 31.
Los Angeles—Field goal Corral 45.
Pittsburgh—Swann 47 pass from Bradshaw (Bahr kick).
Los Angeles—Smith 24 pass from McCutcheon (kick failed).
Pittsburgh—Stallworth 73 pass from Bradshaw (Bahr kick).
Pittsburgh—Harris 1 run (Bahr kick).

— TEAM STATISTICS —

	Los Angeles	Pittsburgh
Total First Downs	16	19
First Downs Rushing	6	8
First Downs Passing	9	10
First Downs by Penalty	1	1
Rushes	29	37
Yards Gained Rushing (net)	107	84
Average Yards per Rush	3.7	2.3
Passes Attempted	26	21
Passes Completed	16	14
Had Intercepted	1	3
Times Tackled Attemp. Pass	4	0
Yards Lost Attempting Pass	42	0
Yards Gained Passing (net)	194	309
Total Net Yardage	301	393
Total Offensive Plays	59	58
Avg. Gain per Offensive Play	5.1	6.8
Punts	5	2
Average Distance	44.0	42.5
Punt Returns	1	4
Punt Return Yardage	4	31
Kickoff Returns	6	5
Kickoff Return Yardage	79	162
Interception Return Yardage	21	16
Fumbles	0	0
Own Fumbles Recovered	0	0
Opp. Fumbles Recovered	0	0
Total Return Yardage	104	209
Penalties	2	6
Yards Penalized	26	65
Total Points Scored	19	31
Touchdowns	2	4
Touchdowns Rushing	1	2
Touchdowns Passing	1	2
Touchdown Returns	0	0
Extra Points	1	4
Field Goals	2	1
Field Goals Attempted	2	1

INDIVIDUAL STATISTICS

— RUSHING —

Los Angeles	Atts.	Yds.	Lg.	TD
Tyler	17	60	39	0
Bryant	6	30	14	1
McCutcheon	5	10	6	0
Ferragamo	1	7	7	0

Pittsburgh	Atts.	Yds.	Lg.	TD
Harris	20	46	12	2
Bleier	10	25	9	0
Bradshaw	3	9	6	0
Thornton	4	4	5	0

— PASSING —

Los Angeles	Atts.	Comp.	Yds.	Int.	TD
Ferragamo	25	15	212	1	0
McCutcheon	1	1	24	0	1

Pittsburgh	Atts.	Comp.	Yds.	Int.	TD
Bradshaw	21	14	309	3	2

— RECEIVING —

Los Angeles	No.	Yds.	Lg.	TD
Bryant	3	21	12	0
Waddy	3	75	50	0
Tyler	3	20	11	0
Dennard	2	32	24	0
Nelson	2	20	14	0
D. Hill	1	28	28	0
Smith	1	24	24	1
McCutcheon	1	16	16	0

Linebacker Dennis Winston gives the familiar Steelers signal.

— RECEIVING —

Pittsburgh	No.	Yds.	Lg.	TD
Swann	5	79	47	1
Stallworth	3	121	73	1
Harris	3	66	32	0
Cunningham	2	21	13	0
Thornton	1	22	22	0

— INTERCEPTIONS —

Los Angeles	No.	Yds.	Lg.	TD
Elmendorf	1	10	10	0
Brown	1	6	6	0
Perry	1	−1	−1	0
Thomas	0	6	6	0
Pittsburgh	No.	Yds.	Lg.	TD
Lambert	1	16	16	0

— KICKOFF RETURNS —

Los Angeles	No.	Yds.	Lg.
E. Hill	3	47	27
Jodat	2	32	16
Andrews	1	0	0
Pittsburgh	No.	Yds.	Lg.
L. Anderson	5	162	45

— FIELD GOALS —

Los Angeles	Att.	Made
Corral	2	2
Pittsburgh	Att.	Made
Bahr	1	1

— PUNT RETURNS —

Los Angeles	No.	FC	Yds.	Lg.
Brown	1	0	4	4
Pittsburgh	No.	FC	Yds.	Lg.
Bell	2	0	17	11
Smith	2	0	14	7

— PUNTING —

Los Angeles	No.	Avg.	Lg.
Clark	5	44.0	59
Pittsburgh	No.	Avg.	Lg.
Colquitt	2	42.5	50

— FUMBLES —

Los Angeles—None.
Pittsburgh—None.

— SCORING —

Los Angeles	TD	PAT	FG	Pts.
Corral	0	1	2	7
Bryant	1	0	0	6
Smith	1	0	0	6
Pittsburgh	TD	PAT	FG	Pts.
Harris	2	0	0	12
Bahr	0	4	1	7
Stallworth	1	0	0	6
Swann	1	0	0	6

MVP Jim Plunkett arose from the NFL grave to lead the Raiders to victory.

Super Bowl XV

Eagles Go Ker-Plunk

January 25, 1981

Two years earlier he had been one step from oblivion, a one-time Heisman Trophy winner tarnished before his time.

His record for the 1978 season had been a total blank. Although on the active list for 14 games, he had not played a single down for the Oakland Raiders. In 1979 he had thrown 15 passes as Oakland's backup quarterback.

When the 1980 season started the former Stanford All-America, nearly 33, was still cast in a backup role, this time standing in for Dan Pastorini, acquired from Houston in a trade for Ken Stabler. For Jim Plunkett, the future was as unpromising as his immediate past.

Another year of bench duty was the prospect when, in the fifth game of the season, Pastorini suffered a leg fracture and went out of action for the remainder of the season. Suddenly, Plunkett was thrust into the spotlight he had known in 1971 when, as quarterback for the New England Patriots, he was acclaimed the Rookie of the Year in the American Football Conference.

The transition from Pastorini to Plunkett was accomplished without a ripple. The Raiders lost the game in which Pastorini was injured, bowing to Kansas City, 31-17, but the following Sunday, with Plunkett at quarterback, they upset San Diego, 38-24, and then beat Pittsburgh, 45-34, on Monday Night Football. Jim Plunkett and the Oakland Raiders were on their way. Losing only to Philadelphia, 10-7, and to Dallas, 19-13, the Raiders compiled an 11-5 record for the season and qualified for a wild-card berth in the AFC playoffs.

For the season, Plunkett completed 165 passes in 320 attempts, passed for 18 touchdowns and was intercepted 15 times, ranking ninth among AFC quarterbacks.

"I knew we could win with Plunkett," said Tom Flores, second-year coach of the

'Outlaw' Al Davis was not popular with other NFL officials, but the Raiders owner got the last laugh.

Raiders.

"I was tempted to call it quits and enter private business," recalled Plunkett after he was rescued from the slagpile. New England had traded him to San Francisco in 1976 and he'd been released by the 49ers two weeks before joining Oakland in '78. "But I thought, 'Well, maybe if I give it one more try, things will work out.'

"For the most part, I had faith in my ability. There was a time, after I was released by the 49ers, when I wondered if the coaches were right, that I couldn't do the job anymore. That was the low point, without a doubt.

"But I have some good friends, people I can trust, and they stayed with me. They said, 'Look, you can still play. You've just been stuck in some circumstances which weren't the best. It's just a matter of being in the right place at the right time.'

"I had received several offers, but I accepted that of the Raiders, and not necessarily because it was the best."

The 1980 season was not only a year of rebirth for Plunkett, but for the Raiders as well. Picked to finish last in the AFC West in what was to have been a year of rebuilding, the Raiders grew more impressive weekly, climaxing their remarkable development by breezing through the playoffs.

Entering each game as the underdog, the Raiders swept past Houston, 27-7, in the AFC wild-card matchup and then won at Cleveland, 14-12, and at San Diego, 34-27, to earn their third Super Bowl invitation and second in five years.

The Philadelphia Eagles, with a 12-4 season record, defeated Minnesota, 31-16, and Dallas, 20-7, to qualify for their first Super Bowl. The Eagles had not contested for a title since 1960 when they won the NFL championship.

To many, Super Bowl XV represented a clash of good and evil, the clean-cut, well-mannered Eagles against the unfettered, rowdy Raiders whose individual lifestyles covered all shades of the spectrum.

The differences in training philosophies was apparent from the start of Super Bowl week in New Orleans. While the Eagles were confined to quarters, concentrating wholly on the business at hand, the Oakland officials preferred a "situation normal" atmosphere, permitting the players to sample the nocturnal attractions in the City That Care Forgot.

After their first night on the town, Plunkett reported, "We cruised the French Quarter, but we didn't see any Eagles."

The Raiders did not intend, however, that the relaxed discipline should extend beyond the 11 p.m. curfew and embrace all-night revelries on Bourbon Street.

Shortly after arriving in New Orleans, John Matuszak proclaimed himself a one-man committee for the enforcement of good conduct and high morals.

"I'm going to see that there's no funny business," announced the 6-8, 280-pound defensive end. "I've had enough parties for 20 people's lifetimes. I've grown up. I'll keep our young fellows out of trouble. If any players want to stray, they gotta go through Ol' Tooz."

A night later, Ol' Tooz was spotted dancing with the wife of Charley Conerly, former New York Giants quarterback, at 1 a.m., and at 3 a.m., four hours after curfew, he still was going strong with another female partner. Clearly, the enforcement committee was working overtime, even though he realized an automatic $1,000 fine would follow.

But Ol' Tooz was the exception. Raymond Chester, for one, presented a different view.

"Everybody talks about how loose we are," said the veteran tight end, "but I don't think any team works harder than we do.

"I watched films in my room until 2 a.m. last night. People who call us a bunch of misfits don't know us."

Matt Millen, a rookie from Penn State, shared Chester's intensity. "I told the guys," said the inside linebacker, "I've been in the league too long to let this chance slip away. You guys better produce."

More than just a Raider success symbol, Super Bowl XV also represented a major triumph for Flores, who had graduated to the head coaching job at Oakland after seven seasons as an assistant to John Madden.

The son of Mexican-American farm laborers who followed the fruit harvests through California, Flores rode a bumpy route to the summit. A graduate of the College of the Pacific in Stockton, Calif., he failed to make the grade in the Canadian Football League and with the Washington Redskins before he was rescued by the infant American Football League in 1960.

Following a 10-year AFL career with Oakland, Buffalo and Kansas City, Flores served one season as an assistant coach at Buffalo before joining the Oakland staff.

As the first Chicano to coach in the Super Bowl, Flores felt "very good and proud" for what that accomplishment meant to other members of the Latin community. "I can sense there are people who care about what I do," he noted. "It means something to be recognized by your people, the people who share your background."

A placid, subdued type, Flores could, nevertheless, jest about the relative lack of attention shown to him. At one press interview session he began his introductory remarks with: "I'm Tom Flores, coach of the other team."

As a coach, Flores did not attempt to con-

Oakland receiver Cliff Branch outwrestles Eagles defensive back Roynell Young for the ball on his second TD reception.

vert the free-spirited Raiders into choir-boys. "Tom doesn't say much," reported Gene Upshaw, 14-year veteran who played on Oakland's first Super Bowl team in 1968. "He just cuts off your wallet. When we came to New Orleans he told us every mistake, every missed curfew, would cost us a flat one thousand dollars."

According to reports, fun-loving Raiders had their wallets trimmed by $15,000 during their stay in the Crescent City.

"We play cards in the locker room, we shoot dice," Upshaw continued. "This is a party, but if Tom sent everyone home who screwed up he'd be the only one on the side-lines when the game started. There comes a time for the party to end."

Like Flores, Eagles Coach Dick Vermeil was a Californian, a native of Calistoga. After receiving his bachelor's and master's degrees at San Jose State, Vermeil worked his way up the coaching ladder, moving from high school, to junior college, to assistant's positions at Stanford and UCLA, to three years as an aide to George Allen with the Los Angeles Rams to two years as head coach at UCLA.

He owed his position with the Eagles, according to a popular story, to the way he walked off the field after the Rose Bowl game on January 1, 1976.

Eagles Owner Leonard Tose and General Manager Jim Murray had been screening candidates to succeed Mike McCormack as coach and, to break the routine, watched UCLA upset Ohio State, 23-10, on national television. "I remember watching him walk off the field," recalled Tose. "There was something in his manner that suggested the type of leadership we were looking for."

Fortified by a five-year contract that has since been extended to "a lifetime contract," Vermeil took over a Philadelphia club that had not had a winning season since 1968, had not had a first-round draft choice since 1973 when it selected offensive lineman Jerry Sisemore of Texas and tight end Charle Young of USC, and would not have another first-round selection until 1979.

"The team's morale was low and it had very little physical talent," Vermeil remembered. "If the team had had some talent, it probably would have won some games and the job would not have been open."

In Vermeil's first season of stewardship, the Eagles matched their 4-10 record of the previous year. They finished at 5-9 in 1977, 9-7 in '78 and 11-5 in '79, when they were eliminated from the playoffs by the Tampa Bay Buccaneers.

A tyrant and slave-driver to some, a genius and miracle worker to others, Vermeil injected his own determination and dedication into a club that included 16 free agents in 1980.

An offensive coach himself, Vermeil had entrusted the team's defensive strategy to Marion Campbell, former All-Pro end with the Eagles and one-time head coach of the Atlanta Falcons. Under Campbell's direction, the Eagles' defense developed into the toughest in the NFC.

One of Vermeil's most important moves in rebuilding the Eagles occurred on March 10, 1977, when he acquired quarterback Ron Jaworski from the Los Angeles Rams. By 1980 Jaworski ranked as the No. 1 quarterback and the Player of the Year in the NFC. In the regular season, he completed 257 passes, including 27 for touchdowns, in 451 attempts.

Vermeil and Flores were not strangers. When Vermeil was a split-T quarterback at San Jose State in 1957, Flores was one of the nation's leading passers and a Vermeil rival at College of the Pacific. When Jim Plunkett was a sophomore at Stanford, in 1968, Vermeil was his quarterback coach.

The clash of the conference champions in the Superdome on January 25 shaped up, in the opinions of most observers, as a replay of the November 23 engagement in which the Eagles defeated the Raiders, 10-7, at Philadelphia.

One scout predicted, "There won't be much scoring, if any, in the first two or three periods, but eventually the Raiders will win."

Tom Landry, whose Dallas Cowboys had beaten the Raiders and lost two of three games to Philadelphia, predicted, "You won't see any scoring until one of the teams makes a breakthrough in field position. The offensive teams will be muffled until something happens."

Norm Pollom, director of scouting for the Buffalo Bills, conceded that "The Eagles have the two big guns, Wilbert Montgomery and Harold Carmichael, but the Raiders have better balance and they've been there before."

Being there before (in 1977 and '68) was regarded popularly as an edge for the Raiders, as was the fact that they had played a relatively tougher schedule, including games with Pittsburgh, Buffalo and San Diego.

In addition, the AFC teams had won the interconference series for the season, 33 to 19, and in three seasons held a superiority of 100 to 56.

In the days preceding the game, speculation grew over whether, if the Raiders won, Commissioner Pete Rozelle would present the Vince Lombardi Trophy to Al Davis, the team's managing general partner.

It was that kind of a day for Eagles quarterback Ron Jaworski, who tries to explain a second-quarter breakdown to Coach Dick Vermeil.

For months the two had been at each other's throat over Davis' efforts to move the Raiders to Los Angeles, vacated by the Rams in favor of Anaheim, 40 miles distant.

Maintaining that he needed the greater capacity of the Los Angeles Coliseum, as well as other benefits, to remain competitive, Davis challenged the NFL constitution and 27 other owners in his determination to transfer to the more lucrative market. At the time of Super Bowl XV, the case was in the courts.

Initially, said Rozelle, he regarded Davis as merely a "charming rogue." Lately, the Oakland owner had become an "outlaw."

There were some "outlaws" roaming the streets of New Orleans, too, poorly disguised as ticket scalpers. Ducats were sell-ing for $500 apiece in midweek but were available for $250 the day before the game. Face value was $40. Vice squad members made seven arrests for scalping and confiscated 17 tickets.

In addition to the 75,500 who jammed the Superdome, the game was viewed by an estimated 100 million on 222 outlets of the NBC network. Commercial time on TV sold for $350,000 a minute. Gross receipts totaled approximately $12,650,000, more than double the $6 million that NBC paid for the rights.

An extra dash of color was added to the Superdome for the championship game in the form of a yellow bow 80 feet long and 30 feet wide erected over the main entrance. This bow, and 80,000 miniature bows distributed to the spectators and media as they

Oakland linebacker Rod Martin exults over his three interceptions that helped the Raiders to their lopsided victory.

entered the stadium, commemorated the return of 52 Americans who had been held hostage for 444 days after the Iranians took over the United States embassy in Tehran and whose release had been announced on January 20, the same day that Ronald Reagan took the oath of office as 40th President of the United States.

Throughout their captivity, a yellow ribbon had served as a national symbol of remembrance for the hostages.

The honor of performing the coin flip to open the game was accorded Mrs. Vince Lombardi, widow of the coach whose Green Bay teams had won the first two Super Bowls.

Asked what she thought her late husband would have said if he had seen her at midfield, Mrs. Lombardi quipped, "He'd probably have said, 'What the hell's a woman doing on the field?' "

The Eagles called the coin toss correctly and ran off two plays from scrimmage before, on a first-and-10 at his 35-yard line, Jaworski attempted his first pass of the day. The toss was intended for tight end John Spagnola, but was picked off by Rod Martin, outside right linebacker in Oakland's 3-4 defensive alignment. Martin returned 17 yards, to the Philadelphia 30.

Like Plunkett, Martin was a San Francisco discard. He was drafted on the 12th round by the Raiders out of USC in 1977, but the Raiders, just off a Super Bowl victory, were well stocked with linebackers and traded the rookie to the 49ers.

However, he was released after two weeks. Offered jobs by several clubs, he accepted the Oakland bid "because they're the club I always wanted to play with."

After the turnover, two running plays netted the Raiders two yards, but on third down, Eagles right end Carl Hairston was ruled offside, a penalty that Oakland converted into a first down when fullback Mark van Eeghen gained four yards on the right side to the Eagles 19.

A 14-yard pass to wide receiver Cliff Branch carried to the 5-yard line and, on third-and-goal from the 2, Plunkett passed to Branch alone in the end zone for the first score of the game. Matt Bahr's conversion gave the Raiders a 7-0 lead with 6:04 elapsed.

"Bob Chandler was the primary receiver on the play," revealed Branch. "Plunkett scrambled, saw me get open and hit me."

The Eagles were unable to move past their 34 on their second possession and Max Runager's punt carried to the Oakland 20, from where Ira Matthews returned it two yards.

The Raiders were stymied on three running plays and the Eagles also came up

Raiders defensive back Mike Davis towers over a scrambling Ron Jaworski, setting the tone for the game.

short on their next possession although it appeared momentarily as though they had tied the score on a 40-yard Jaworski pass to wide receiver Rodney Parker in the end zone.

When Super Bowl IV was played at New Orleans' Tulane Stadium in 1970, Parker had been in the stands as an usher. The touchdown pass in the Super Bowl could have been the most memorable moment of his first NFL season, but the play was nullified by an illegal motion penalty against wide receiver Carmichael.

Runager's punt with 1:06 remaining in the quarter gave the Raiders the ball on their 14. Two plays gained six yards to the 20 before Plunkett, chased out of the pocket, spotted running back Kenny King near the sideline at the 39 and tossed a pass that seemed destined for interception by Herman Edwards.

The cornerback was well positioned, but the ball slipped untouched into the hands of King who, escorted by Chandler, sprinted the rest of the way to complete an 80-yard scoring play, the longest in Super Bowl history.

"The play wasn't designed for me to go deep," explained King, who had caught 22 passes during the season but none for a touchdown, although he did grab a scoring pass in the AFC championship game. "I'm supposed to go six yards upfield and cut for the sidelines, but when I saw Jim looking upfield I broke up the sideline. I didn't hear any footsteps behind me, and Chandler kept up with me stride for stride. I didn't know he was that fast."

King's touchdown and Bahr's PAT made the score 14-0 with nine seconds left in the first quarter. Tony Franklin's 30-yard field goal produced the first Philadelphia points at 4:32 of the second quarter. Neither team scored further in the period, although each drove within field goal range. Bahr missed from 45 yards away and Franklin's attempt from 28 yards out with 54 seconds left in the half was blocked by linebacker Ted Hendricks.

"That was probably the easiest blocked kick of my life," reported the 6-7 Hendricks, known as the Mad Stork. "I didn't even penetrate, just stepped up there and jumped."

The Raiders required only six plays to increase their 14-3 lead at the start of the second half. Starting on their 24, the AFC champions were forced back to their 14 on a holding penalty against tackle Henry Lawrence. The setback proved only temporary as van Eeghen gained eight yards, a pass to King picked up 13, another aerial to Chandler netted 32 and a van Eeghen run to the right added four, carrying to the Philadelphia 29.

On second down from the 29, Plunkett passed toward the goal line, and Branch outwrestled rookie cornerback Roynell Young for the football at the 1-yard line and twisted into the end zone. Bahr's third conversion gave the Raiders a comfortable 21-3 lead 2:36 gone in the period.

"I misread the coverage and threw the ball short, hoping that Cliff either would knock the ball down or make a great catch," said Plunkett.

"It was a championship catch," lauded Vermeil before expressing his disappointment that the Raiders were allowed to score so easily.

"We weren't picking on Young," declared Branch. "At Oakland we're taught to go for the football. I don't think of Young as a rookie. I think he's their best cornerback."

The next Philadelphia possession again ended in disaster, spelled Rod Martin. The linebacker intercepted a pass intended for Spagnola and stepped out of bounds at the Oakland 32 after a two-yard return.

Eight plays later, Bahr kicked his second field goal, a 46-yarder, with 10:25 elapsed, and the Raiders enjoyed a 24-3 advantage. Plunkett had passed for 16 yards to Chester and 17 yards to Chandler to set up the field goal.

With 4:35 remaining in the period, the Eagles mounted another drive and, featuring a 43-yard Jaworski pass to wide receiver Charles Smith, marched from their 12 to the Oakland 5 as the third quarter ended.

Set back by an offside penalty, the Eagles scored on the fourth play of the fourth period when Jaworski connected with tight end Keith Krepfle from eight yards out.

Bahr's 35-yard field goal climaxed a 12-play, 72-yard drive on the next Oakland series and concluded the game's scoring, although not the illustrious performance by Martin.

With less than three minutes remaining, Jaworski, forced to pass on every play, attempted to hit running back Billy Campfield, but once again Martin intervened, making a record third interception.

"If they throw the ball in my area 15 times, it figures I'll catch it two or three times," said Martin. "They stay away from Ted Hendricks (left outside linebacker) and Lester Hayes (left cornerback who led the NFL in interceptions) and I don't blame 'em."

Jaworski had been intercepted only 12 times during the 16-game regular season, but seven of his passes were picked off in three playoff games.

Candidates for the Most Valuable Player award were numerous, but the prize went to Plunkett. His 13 completions for 261 yards and three touchdowns in 21 passes overshadowed the contributions of all others.

The Eagles ran off 64 offensive plays to 55 for the Raiders and also led in time of possession. But the "big play" Raiders were, as the scout had pointed out before the game, better balanced. They gained 117 yards on the ground to 69 for the Eagles, and Plunkett's air yards were only 30 fewer than those of Jaworski.

The Raiders were champions of the football universe and now Rozelle would have to present the championship trophy to Davis in the Oakland locker room before the conquering Raiders and countless millions of TV viewers.

Despite a sportscaster's efforts to fan hostile flames, the presentation was made smoothly, although one observer noted, tongue in cheek, that Rozelle gripped the trophy with both hands so as to preclude a handshake.

The commissioner said to Davis: "As the first wild-card team to win the Super Bowl, it's a tremendous compliment to the organization because you had to win four postsea-

Eagles defensive end Carl Hairston experiences the agony of defeat.

son games. It's a great tribute to you for putting this team together and I think that Tom Flores clearly did one of the great coaching jobs in recent years. It's a credit to some marvelously dedicated athletes, especially Jim Plunkett and the offensive line. You've earned it and congratulations."

"Thank you, commissioner," began Davis. "When you look back on the glory of the Oakland Raiders, this was our finest hour. To Tom Flores, the coaches and the great athletes, you were magnificent. Your commitment to excellence and your will to win will endure forever."

To Tom Flores, the keys to the victory were the blocked Philadelphia field goal and "our scoring on the first possession of the second half. If they had made the field goal it might have given them momentum."

Flores also cited the protection (up to four seconds) that the offensive line provided Plunkett. "We felt that if we could give Jim good pass protection, we could throw the ball," he said. "We had certain things planned against Herman Edwards and Roynell Young, but we felt we could throw against the entire defense. The Eagles use the nickel defense on third down, so that's why we passed so often on first and second down.

"We also knew we had to be solid against Wilbert Montgomery and the Eagles' running game, and we used a couple of new stunts to get to Jaworski."

Jaworski was never sacked, but he had to hurry many passes and finished 18-for-38 for the game.

The difference between the Raiders' loss to the Eagles in November and their Super Bowl triumph was, said Flores, "pass blocking. It was outstanding. After the Eagles sacked us eight times, the challenge was there. The offensive line studied the films upside down and sideways. They were well prepared this time."

Dick Vermeil refused to hide behind excuses, declaring flatly, "The Raiders deserve to be world champions. They beat us soundly. They dominated us."

Vermeil was inflexible in his praise of the Raiders. When he was asked if the Raiders' Super Bowl experience might have been a factor in the outcome of the game, he snapped, "I don't buy that. That's nothing but an excuse for losing. We got our butts whipped."

While admitting he thought "the game would be tighter, more physical on our part," Vermeil added, "but I think they're just better than we are."

On several occasions, Vermeil noted, it appeared the Eagles were about to mount an offensive that might have influenced the score, if not the final result.

"We had a little something going in the second quarter," he said, "but then Tony Franklin's field goal attempt was blocked. We go in at halftime with three points instead of six.

"We had a nice play action pass to Keith Krepfle where he was wide open and ran into the umpire.

"For some reason I didn't think we were flying around the field like we usually do, but maybe that's a misjudgment. The truth probably is that individually they were doing a better job."

The players' intensity, Vermeil pointed out, was not as pronounced as he had expected, although in pregame workouts his assistants told him, "They're intense, they're banging, they're excited."

In the game, said the coach, "I didn't see us jumping up and down and flying and swarming. But maybe that's because Oakland wouldn't let us.

"A lot of credit has been given to me for getting the Eagles here, so I should assume some of the responsibility for not winning the game."

Jaworski insisted the Eagles were ready to play, "although we didn't show it." The quarterback said he "sensed a lack of emotion during the game and it never seemed to get stronger."

Of his three interceptions, Jaworski said, "Rod Martin is a good player, but he becomes even better when he doesn't have to worry about the rush."

The second of Martin's interceptions occurred when the Eagles trailed 21-3, the third when they trailed 27-10.

For Martin, his glittering performance climaxed a week of remarkable activity, starting with a three-handed card game with Hendricks and Jeff Barnes.

"We played Crazy Eights all year, all the time," he revealed. "The object is to get rid of all your cards. It's a tough game.

"If you win three games in a row, it's called a Triple Crown, which we named for John Matuszak's favorite drink.

"Last week I had two Triple Crowns and that's hard to do. Hendricks kidded me, 'Why don't you do that in the game on Sunday?' When we were getting dressed today, Ted said, 'Hey, get that Triple Crown today, this is the day.' "

Martin had other indications that his hot hand would extend into the Super Bowl. On the West Coast his sister Carolyn had a feeling that Rod would intercept a pass and, on the flight to New Orleans, a fellow passenger expressed the same hunch.

When Carolyn told her brother about the premonitions, he had replied, "Look, I don't make that many interceptions. I made only two all season."

At such moments when Martin was not playing cards or attending to football business on the practice field, he was frequently in his room watching game films long after curfew. The late-hour cramming paid off.

Martin explained his interceptions in this manner:

"On the first, Carmichael ran a streak pattern and tried to hook behind me. They threw to my inside and I caught the ball with my left hand. On the second, I just got a good jump on the ball. I knew with us in the lead they weren't going to abandon their game plan. On the third, we were in a prevent defense and all the receivers were well covered."

Of all the accolades distributed to the victorious Raiders, none were so numerous or so lavish as those bestowed on Plunkett.

"I can't say enough about him," volunteered Flores. "He met every challenge this season with style and class. He has great competitive spirit and deserves all the credit in the world.

"His career has a lot of ups and downs. During the bad years he took all the criticism and never said a word. He's not the type to point his finger and say, 'I told you so.' He has great courage."

It was Flores, then an assistant coach, who recommended that the Raiders sign Plunkett in 1978, following his release by San Francisco.

"Plunkett is the most efficient quarterback I've ever played with," offered Cliff Branch, a favorite target of Ken Stabler during The Snake's heyday with Oakland. "He can take off and scramble and that gives a team a lot of sting. Stabler could get the ball deep, but the key to stopping Stabler is putting pressure on him because he can't maneuver. Plunkett is the leader we didn't have when Pastorini was in there. Dan didn't know the Oakland system, but Plunkett knows it. He was behind Stabler for two years and learned the system.

"They said Jim didn't have it anymore, but all he needed was good people around him. We gave 'em to him."

Davis chided the media for making too big a story out of Plunkett's heroics. "Jim always was a great player," declared the Oakland owner. "What he has done is a great story, but reporters are making too big a thing out of it. He was never anything but a fine quarterback."

Modestly, Plunkett tossed compliments to his offensive line that permitted only one sack. That occurred when Plunkett, forced out of the pocket, attempted to run and was tackled a yard short of the line of scrimmage.

"I don't think I'm playing any better than

Jim Plunkett had plenty to smile about after vindicating himself and the underdog Raiders.

I did in San Francisco," he said. "I still have the same confidence, and I was just given the opportunity to play, and I'm with a better team.

"It means a lot when the defense gets you a turnover early in the game. You can start being aggressive and we were able to stay aggressive with those interceptions. Our defense won the game.

"Do I feel vindicated?" he responded to a question. "No, not really. Vindication implies bitterness and I don't feel bitterness toward anybody."

"Suppose," Plunkett was asked, "somebody had told you in September that you would be the MVP of the Super Bowl, what would you have said?"

"I wasn't even the starting quarterback then," he replied. "The idea would have been too far-fetched. I couldn't have believed it."

Nor would Plunkett have believed that he, like all Raiders, would be wealthier by $35,000 at 9 p.m. on January 25. The new world champions received $3,000 for their wild-card victory over Houston, $5,000 for beating Cleveland, $9,000 for beating San Diego in the conference playoff and $18,000 for defeating Philadelphia.

The Eagles received $23,000 apiece. Had they won Super Bowl XV, they would have received only $32,000 because they did not play a wild-card game.

Statistics of 15th Super Bowl
OAKLAND 27, PHILADELPHIA 10

Louisiana Superdome, New Orleans, La., January 25, 1981
Attendance: 75,500.

OAKLAND	Offense	PHILADELPHIA
Cliff Branch	WR	.Harold Carmichael
Art Shell	LT	.... Stan Walters
Gene Upshaw	LG	.... Pete Perot
Dave Dalby	C	...Guy Morriss
Mickey Marvin	RG	...... Woody Peoples
Henry Lawrence.....	RT	...... Jerry Sisemore
Ray Chester	TE	...... Keith Krepfle
Bob Chandler	WR/TE	........John Spagnola
Jim Plunkett	QB	.... Ron Jaworski
Mark van Eeghen ...	RB	......W. Montgomery
Kenny King	RB	.... Leroy Harris

	Defense	
John Matuszak	LE	....Dennis Harrison
Reggie Kinlaw........	MG	..... Charlie Johnson
Dave Browning.......	RE	........Carl Hairston
Ted Hendricks........	LLB	..........John Bunting
Matt Millen	ILB	.... Bill Bergey
Bob Nelson.............	ILB	....Frank LeMaster
Rob Martin.............	RLB	...... Jerry Robinson
Lester Hayes..........	LCB	...... Roynell Young
Dwayne O'Steen	RCB	... Herman Edwards
Mike Davis	SS	..........Randy Logan
Burgess Owens.......	FS	..... Brenard Wilson

— SUBSTITUTIONS —

OAKLAND—Offense: Receivers—Morris Bradshaw, Derrick Ramsey, Rich Martini, Ira Matthews. Linemen—Bruce Davis, Lindsey Mason, Steve Sylvester. Backs—Arthur Whittington, Derrick Jensen, Todd Christensen. Kicker—Chris Bahr. Defense: Linebackers—Mario Celotto, Jeff Barnes, Randy McClanahan. Linemen—Dave Pear, Joe Campbell, Cedrick Hardman, Willie Jones. Backs—Odis McKinney, Keith Moody, Monte Jackson. Punter—Ray Guy. DNP—Marc Wilson.

PHILADELPHIA—Offense: Receivers—Rodney Parker, Charlie Smith, Wally Henry. Linemen—Mark Slater, Steve Kenney, Ken Clarke, Ron Baker. Backs—Louie Giammona, Perry Harrington, Billy Campfield. Kicker—Tony Franklin. Defense: Linebackers—Al Chesley, Reggie Wilkes, Ray Phillips. Linemen—Claude Humphrey, Thomas Brown. Backs—Zac Henderson, John Sciarra, Richard Blackmore. Punter—Max Runager. DNP—Joe Pisarcik, Rob Hertel, Bob Torrey.

— SCORE BY PERIODS —

Oakland Raiders (AFC)	14	0	10	3 — 27
Philadelphia Eagles (NFC)	0	3	0	7 — 10

— SCORING —

Oakland—Branch 2 pass from Plunkett (Bahr kick).
Oakland—King 80 pass from Plunkett (Bahr kick).
Philadelphia—Field goal Franklin 30.
Oakland—Branch 29 pass from Plunkett (Bahr kick).
Oakland—Field goal Bahr 46.
Philadelphia—Krepfle 8 pass from Jaworski (Franklin kick).
Oakland—Field goal Bahr 35.

— TEAM STATISTICS —

	Oakland	Phila'phia
Total First Downs..................	17	19
First Downs Rushing	6	3
First Downs Passing..............	10	14
First Downs by Penalty	1	2
Rushes.................................	34	26

Yards Gained Rushing (net)...	117	69
Average Yards per Rush........	3.4	2.7
Passes Attempted..................	21	38
Passes Completed..................	13	18
Had Intercepted.....................	0	3
Times Tackled Attemp. Pass..	1	0
Yards Lost Attempting Pass...	1	0
Yards Gained Passing (net) ...	260	291
Total Net Yardage	377	360
Total Offensive Plays.............	56	64
Avg. Gain per Offensive Play .	6.7	5.6
Punts.....................................	3	3
Average Distance	42.0	36.7
Punt Returns..........................	2	3
Punt Return Yardage.............	1	20
Kickoff Returns......................	3	6
Kickoff Return Yardage.........	48	87
Interception Return Yardage .	44	0
Fumble..................................	0	1
Opp. Fumbles Recovered	0	1
Total Return Yardage	93	107
Penalties...............................	5	6
Yards Penalized	37	57
Total Points Scored	27	10
Touchdowns	3	1
Touchdowns Rushing	0	0
Touchdowns Passing.............	3	1
Touchdowns on Returns.........	0	0
Extra Points...........................	3	1
Field Goals Attempted	3	2
Field Goals............................	2	1

INDIVIDUAL STATISTICS
— RUSHING —

Oakland	Atts.	Yds.	Lg.	TD
van Eeghen	19	80	8	0
King	6	18	6	0
Jensen	3	12	6	0
Plunkett	3	9	5	0
Whittington	3	−2	2	0
Philadelphia	**Atts.**	**Yds.**	**Lg.**	**TD**
Montgomery...................	16	44	8	0
Harris	7	14	5	0
Giammona	1	7	7	0
Harrington	1	4	4	0
Jaworski.......................	1	0	0	0

— PASSING —

Oakland	Atts.	Comp.	Yds.	Int.	TD
Plunkett.................	21	13	261	0	3
Philadelphia	**Atts.**	**Comp.**	**Yds.**	**Int.**	**TD**
Jaworski.................	38	18	291	3	1

— RECEIVERS —

Oakland	No.	Yds.	Lg.	TD
Branch	5	67	29	2
Chandler	4	77	32	0
King	2	93	80	1
Chester	2	24	16	0
Philadelphia	**No.**	**Yds.**	**Lg.**	**TD**
Montgomery...................	6	91	25	0
Carmichael	5	83	29	0
Krepfle	2	16	8	1
Smith	2	59	43	0
Parker	1	19	19	0
Spagnola	1	22	22	0
Harris	1	1	1	0

The expected confrontation between Oakland Owner Al Davis and Commissioner Pete Rozelle became a cordial exchange of praise and thank yous.

— INTERCEPTIONS —

Oakland	No.	Yds.	Lg.	TD
Martin	3	44	25	0

Philadelphia—None.				

— PUNTING —

Oakland	No.	Avg.	Lg.
Guy	3	42.0	44

Philadelphia	No.	Avg.	Lg.
Runager	3	36.7	46

— PUNT RETURNS —

Oakland	No.	FC	Yds.	Lg.
Matthews	2	1	1	2

Philadelphia	No.	FC	Yds.	Lg.
Sciarra	2	0	18	12
Henry	1	0	2	2

— KICKOFF RETURNS —

Oakland	No.	Yds.	Lg.
Moody	1	19	19
Matthews	2	29	21

Philadelphia	No.	Yds.	Lg.
Campfield	5	87	21
Harrington	1	0	0

— FIELD GOALS —

Oakland	Att.	Made
Bahr	3	2

Philadelphia	Att.	Made
Franklin	2	1

— SCORING —

Oakland	TD	PAT	FG	Pts.
Branch	2	0	0	12
Bahr	0	3	2	9
King	1	0	0	6

Philadelphia	TD	PAT	FG	Pts.
Krepfle	1	0	0	6
Franklin	0	1	1	4

— FUMBLES —

Oakland	No.	Own Rec.	Opp. Rec.	TD
Jones	0	0	1	0

Philadelphia	No.	Own Rec.	Opp. Rec.	TD
Jaworski	1	0	0	0

Ray Wersching's toe and the powerful right arm of Joe Montana (right) helped make the 49ers No. 1.

Super Bowl XVI

49ers Strike It Rich

January 24, 1982

When Bobby Layne flipped the coin for the start of Super Bowl XVI, it logically followed that the game between the San Francisco 49ers and Cincinnati Bengals would be played along uncoventional lines.

As a Hall of Fame quarterback for the Detroit Lions in the 1950s, the Texan Layne frequently delighted in unorthodox strategy while en route to National Football League championships.

Super Bowl XVI was played to an improbable script. Three turnovers cost the Bengals 17 points in a 20-point first half that set a Super Bowl record; the 49ers staged a dramatic goal line stand that might have saved the game, and Ray Wersching kicked a record-tying four field goals.

The location of the game also set a precedent. After 15 games in warm weather climates, the 1982 championship contest was played in the Pontiac (Mich.) Silverdome, 25 miles from Detroit. While surrounding areas shivered in below zero chill factors, 81,270 enjoyed 72-degree comfort in the huge, 5-year-old stadium.

That the 49ers and Bengals were in the Super Bowl was remarkable in itself. For more than 30 years, the 49ers had strained and struggled in a bid for distinction, but their best efforts produced only three division titles. On each occasion they were eliminated by the Dallas Cowboys.

The Bengals, admitted to the American Football League in 1968, won a Central Division title in the realigned NFL in 1970, but succumbed to Baltimore in the playoffs. In 1973, the division-champion Bengals were beaten by the Miami Dolphins in the playoffs.

The emergence of the two teams into title form was unexpected and unprecedented.

During their nonproductive years, the 49ers finished last six times, including the

Bengals quarterback Ken Anderson discovered early that things would not be easy in Super Bowl XVI.

1978 season when they won only two games and lost 14 under the split leadership of Pete McCulley and Fred O'Connor.

In January of 1979, Owner Edward De-Bartolo, Jr., reached across the backyard fence to Palo Alto and secured the coaching services of Bill Walsh, who had compiled a 17-7 record in two seasons at Stanford University. His teams also won post-season games in the Sun and Bluebonnet Bowls. Previously, the 47-year-old Walsh had served as an assistant coach under Al Davis at Oakland and Paul Brown at Cincinnati, where he was instrumental in the development of Ken Anderson as a premium quarterback in the NFL.

When Brown retired as coach, Walsh moved on to the San Diego Chargers, serving as assistant to Tommy Prothro and tutoring Dan Fouts in the same fashion as he had Anderson.

Walsh's coaching talents were not immediately discernible at San Francisco in the fall of 1979. For the second consecutive season, the team finished with a 2-14 record. His initial draft yielded only two players who remained with the Niners into 1981, but they were prize picks—quarterback Joe Montana and wide receiver Dwight Clark.

In 1980 the 49ers drafted two players who stuck for more than one season, signed two key free agents, and added another key player by trade—tight end Charle Young.

Their 1981 "gold strike" included five rookies, five more acquisitons by trade and 10 free agents. Three of the rookies earned starting assignments—cornerbacks Ronnie Lott and Eric Wright and safety Carlton Williamson.

The influx of new talent helped transform the Niners from a 6-10 team in 1980 into a 13-3 team in 1981, when they compiled the best record in the NFL.

While the 49ers were foundering with 2-14 records in 1978 and '79, the Bengals were posting 4-12 records and finishing at the bottom of the AFC Central Division.

Although they finished last again in 1980, the Bengals improved their record to 6-10 under the first-year leadership of Forrest Gregg. The former offensive tackle of the Green Bay Packers in the heyday of Vince Lombardi had served as head coach of the Cleveland Browns and Toronto Argonauts of the Canadian Football League before succeeding Homer Rice at the Cincinnati helm in 1980.

Gregg, once described by Lombardi as "the finest player I've ever coached," appeared with the Packers in Super Bowls I and II and the Dallas Cowboys in VI. So when the Bengals defeated Buffalo, 28-21, and San Diego, 27-7, in the AFC playoffs, Gregg became the first ex-player to coach

49ers defensive back Lynn Thomas celebrates after recovering a Cris Collinsworth fumble.

in the Super Bowl.

Walsh, a graduate of San Jose State where he also earned a master's degree in education, was without professional playing experience. He also was without extraordinary optimism. In the club's 1981 media guide, Walsh was quoted as saying: "We have been able to add slowly potentially better athletes to our squad, especially with this year's draft, and that's working to make us potentially better overall.

"There is still a long way to go, but I am certain we have turned the corner and are becoming a well-based, more versatile team that will be a consistent contender in the years to come."

49ers Coach Bill Walsh capped a dream season with a victorious ride from the Silverdome field.

The "long way to go" that Walsh foresaw was covered in six months. The team that ranked 26th in the NFL in points allowed in 1980 soared into second place in 1981, trailing only Philadelphia. After losing two of its first three games, the team breezed the rest of the way, with only a 15-12 loss to Cleveland marring the last 13 weeks of the season. One of its victories was over Cincinnati by a 21-3 score.

Playoff wins over the New York Giants, 38-24, and the Dallas Cowboys, 28-27 on a last-minute Montana pass to Dwight Clark, earned the 49ers a trip to the Silverdome.

Meanwhile, the Bengals lost two of their first five games, then bowed only to New Orleans, 17-7, and San Francisco the rest of the way.

The 49ers, who lost 12 of 26 fumbles in their NFC title march, opened their first Super Bowl game on an inauspicious note. Amos Lawrence, after returning the kickoff 17 yards, fumbled on the 26, where John Simmons recovered for the Bengals.

The AFC champions advanced to a second-and-goal on the 5-yard line before Anderson was sacked for a six-yard loss by Jim Stuckey. On third-and-11, Anderson fired a pass intended for Isaac Curtis, but Dwight Hicks intercepted and returned the football 27 yards to the San Francisco 32.

In 11 plays, the 49ers traveled 68 yards. Two of the plays were passes, for nine and 14 yards, to wide receiver Freddie Solomon, a doubtful quantity in the 49ers' pregame plan because of a knee injury suffered three days earlier.

The second pass carried to the 1-yard line, from where Montana dived across for the first touchdown.

"This was for the world championship and there was no way I was going to miss it," explained Solomon, who caught four passes for 52 yards during the game.

On their first possession of the second quarter, the Bengals mounted another drive. They had progressed to the San Francisco 27 when Anderson completed a 19-yard pass to Cris Collinsworth. The wide receiver fumbled when tackled by Eric Wright, however, and Lynn Thomas recovered on the 8-yard line.

"I was pivoting and trying to make more yards when Wright stripped the ball from me," reported Collinsworth. "The 49ers have been doing that all season and are pretty good at it."

Again the opportunistic 49ers capitalized on the turnover. Eleven plays carried the Niners to the Cincinnati 11, from where Montana passed to Earl Cooper on the 3. The second-year running back out of Rice barrelled into the end zone, completing a Super Bowl record 92-yard march.

Explaining his role in the TD play, Cooper said, "It was a fake up the middle to the fullback. The wide receiver on the left clears out so I can come underneath the zone coverage."

Cincinnati's horrendous luck continued in the ensuing series of plays. Wersching's squib kickoff was fielded by David Verser on the 5-yard line. By the time Verser completed his lateral sprint, the ball was on the 4. An illegal chuck set the Bengals back two more yards and, six plays later, Pat McInally's punt set the 49ers up on their own 34.

With Montana passing and Cooper and Ricky Patton running, the Niners advanced to the Cincinnati 5 with 18 seconds remaining before intermission. With Montana holding, Wersching kicked a 22-yard field goal, increasing the Niners' lead to 17-0.

Wersching's kickoff was another squibbler. Archie Griffin touched the ball at the 15, but failed to grab it and watched the ball bounce to the 4, where it was downed by Milt McColl of the 49ers. An illegal procedure penalty cost five yards, but Wersching, refusing as always to look at the goal posts, got his bearings from Montana, the holder, and booted a 26-yard field goal, boosting the San Francisco lead to 20-0.

The two scoring plays within the space of 13 seconds set a Super Bowl record.

Bruce Coslet, the special teams coach for Cincinnati, welcomed the squib kicks. "I'd like to see teams squib kick against us all the time," he said. "Nine times out of 10 we'd wind up with good field position."

Griffin, who said he was surprised that the Niners would try a squib kick, revealed that "I used to have a theory on that kind of kick, that the first two bounces would be funny and the next bounce would be high. Today they all were funny."

Walsh's halftime oration to the troops emphasized that "I wasn't comfortable with the lead. I told them what to expect. We knew we were playing a great team. Maybe if it had been 24-0, the Bengals might have caved in, but not with the score 20-0."

John Ayers revealed that the coach had instructed the Niners to treat the second half as though the score was 0-0. "He told us we would have to score at least two more times," reported the left guard. "He told us we couldn't let their offense on the field too long or eventually Anderson would burn us."

Gregg's halftime pitch to the Bengals scaled no emotional peaks. "I reminded 'em," said the coach, "that we had been behind before. I referred to our first game of the season when we came from a 21-0 first-quarter deficit to beat Seattle. We didn't do anything different in the second half. We just played better."

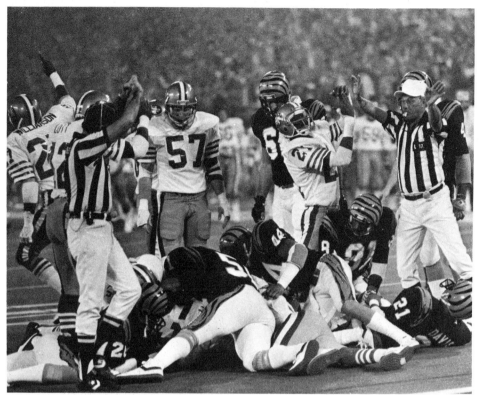

Bengals and 49ers fight for a loose ball near the Bengals' goal line at the end of the first half. Milt McColl recovered, setting up a 49er field goal.

The improvement was noticeable immediately after Wersching's second-half kickoff. Nine plays, plus two Niner face mask penalties, carried to the San Francisco 5-yard line, from where Anderson, after dropping back to pass, sprinted into the end zone.

Two possessions later, the Bengals were at midfield with 6:53 remaining in the third period. The Bengals were pushed back to their own 41 and Fred Dean, the defensive end obtained from San Diego, made matters worse by tackling Anderson for another four-yard loss, one of four Niner sacks during the game. But Anderson, on a third-and-23 situation, connected with Collinsworth for 49 yards to the San Francisco 14.

Five plays, including Johnson's fourth-and-one plunge from the 5 that netted two yards, resulted in a first-and-goal at the 3. Johnson hit center for two yards and then left guard, where he was stopped by John Harty for no gain. On third down Anderson passed to Charles Alexander in the right flat, but linebacker Dan Bunz came up fast, grabbed the receiver around the waist, and hurled him backward before he could break the plane of the goal line. Had Bunz tackled

him low, Alexander's momentum would have carried him into the end zone.

Disdaining a field goal, the Bengals gave the ball again to Johnson, who was stopped by the entire defensive line for no gain.

"It was the first time all season we were stopped on that play," asserted Forrest Gregg. "If I had to do it again, I'd still give it to Pete."

Concerning the decision to pass up the field goal, Gregg said, "I figured that even if we didn't make it, it would put the 49ers on the 1-yard line. It worked out that way. We held and they punted to us. Then we scored to make it 20-14."

According to offensive coordinator Lindy Infante, "It was a staff decision to go for the touchdown. We had run twice to the left, and David Verser missed a block on the second call because of the crowd noise. He failed to pick up an audible blocking change.

"Rather than run to the same place three times, we felt we could go to the right. We had great success with that play all season, but the 49ers got great penetration."

In Cincinnati lineman Dave Lapham's opinion, "We just didn't move anybody off

The 49er defense presses back a Bengals' charge on a key third-quarter goal line stand.

the ball. Their defense would shift as late as possible before the snap of the ball and we often didn't know who or where a guy would come into the gap. They forced us to change quite a bit on every play."

Johnson, the 249-pound battering ram who spearheaded the Cincinnati offense that ranked second best in the NFL, "saw the 49ers rise up at the snap of the ball. I figured I could go underneath. It just didn't work."

Middle linebacker Jack Reynolds, in his 12th consecutive playoff season, "thought Johnson would carry the ball in all those short-yardage situations."

As Bunz handled lead blocker Alexander on the fourth-down smash, Reynolds led the charge that snuffed out Johnson.

While Bill Walsh regarded the fourth-down stop of Johnson as "the play that won the game for us," Chuck Studley considered Bunz' tackle of Alexander more significant.

"Dan had to make a perfect tackle in the open," noted the defensive coordinator. "Here's a guy (Alexander) who weighs 220 pounds and can run and he has only a yard to go for the end zone . . . Bunz had to hit him perfectly to stop him."

Bunz thought at first that "Alexander would come up inside. I don't get but four or five good pops a game and I wasn't going to miss my chance."

Studley explained further: "The Bengals tried to shield Danny off and make him run around, but he hit Alexander quick in the flat. We worked like hell on that play."

The Bengals' second-down play from the one-yard line did not surprise Studley. "They double-teamed Archie Reese, but did not block John Choma (tackle) and ran right at the double team," said Studley. "They figured Choma would overpenetrate. What they didn't know was that we worked our tails off all week on that play, too."

Much of the post-game talk centered on the 49ers' goal line stand and the general belief that they had only 10 men on the field for two of the plays. But it was later discovered that only once did the 49ers play short-handed—and that occurred on the fourth-and-one from the 5.

It was on that play that the 49ers replaced their pass defense with their goal-line alignment. But linebacker Keena Turner never got the message as defensive coordinator Chuck Studley's call was lost in the Silver-

Cincinnati's Charles Alexander gets a rude greeting from Dan Bunz at the
goal line after catching a Ken Anderson pass. Bunz threw Alexander down,
saving a touchdown during a key 49er defensive stand.

The 49ers had some bad moments, such as Joe Montana's tumble . . .

. . . and Charle Young's rude treatment by Bo Harris (53) and Jim LeClair.

dome noise.

Fellow linebacker Craig Puki later said that he thought Turner had missed two plays, but he was in his stance and evidently did not see Turner race onto the field at the last instance for the first-down play from the 3.

"What happened," revealed Studley, "is that I called for our goal line defense to go in, but Keena Turner thought I said 'giant' defense and didn't go in.

"The coaches upstairs spotted it. I kept asking myself, 'Who's missing?' Finally Keena realized I'd called for the goal-line defense."

The touchdown denied the Bengals in the third period was scored at 4:54 of the fourth, when Anderson passed four yards to tight end Dan Ross.

With their lead pared to six points, the 49ers turned to their time-consuming ground attack. In 10 plays, seven of them rushes, the Niners advanced 50 yards and, with 5:25 remaining, Wersching kicked his third field goal, a 40-yarder that raised the NFC club's lead to 23-14.

The Bengals' next-to-last possession of the game endured for just one play, on which an Anderson pass, intended for Collinsworth, was intercepted by Wright on the Cincinnati 47 and returned to the 22, where he fumbled when trying to lateral the ball to a teammate. Willie Harper recovered, however, for the 49ers. A 16-yard drive, eating up three minutes, moved the ball to the 6 and, on fourth down, Wersching kicked a

Linebacker Keena Turner (58) celebrates the 49ers' good fortune with Amos Lawrence.

23-yard field goal with only 1:57 to go.

That was enough time for Anderson to complete six consecutive passes, none of which was run out of bounds to stop the clock.

Anderson's final pass was a three-yard heave to tight end Ross which, with Jim Breech's third extra point, narrowed the Cincinnati deficit to 26-21. When Breech's onside kickoff nestled in the arms of Dwight Clark, however, all that remained to seal the 49ers victory was for Montana to take a snap, retreat four yards and kneel gently on the synthetic turf as time expired.

After Commissioner Pete Rozelle's pre-sentation of the Vince Lombardi Trophy to 49ers Owner Edward DeBartolo, Jr., a telephone was thrust into Walsh's hand.

Clapping his other hand over an ear to muffle the shrieks of exuberant players, Walsh said, "I thought it might be you calling."

On the other end of the line, President Ronald Reagan said, "I wanted to congratulate you. Tell the fellows they really did win one for the Gipper."

Reagan, a Californian, had portrayed legendary George Gipp, a Notre Dame star of more than six decades earlier, in a 1940 movie version of the life of Knute Rockne.

"I think Joe was thinking of the Gipper when we won. Thank you very, very much," concluded Walsh.

Montana, selected the game's most valuable player, completed 14 of 22 passes, ran for 18 yards in six carries and scored a touchdown.

At 25, Montana was the same age as Joe Namath when Broadway Joe led the New York Jets to a stunning upset of the Baltimore Colts in Super Bowl III.

"Montana will be the great quarterback of the future," lauded Walsh of his third-year field general. "He is one of the coolest competitors of all time and he has just started."

Walsh and Montana denied allegations that the 49ers turned conservative during the third quarter when they had the ball for only nine plays in three possessions and failed to get beyond their 15-yard line.

"The Bengals were throwing every conceivable blitz at us," said Walsh. "We didn't want to get stopped by those blitzes. We went to our running game and our trapping game and that made the difference."

"We had our backs to the wall and bad field position hurt us," added Montana. "The only thing we could do was run the ball and hope we could get it out and punt."

Reviewing the game and the season, Gregg found much to engender optimism. "We weren't even picked for third in our division," he noted. "We lost, but there is lots to be proud of. The team was loose all week and never tensed up. I think the players started thinking about what could have been instead of what was. After that it looked as if they were trying not to make mistakes."

The difference in the game, said Gregg, "was the four turnovers. You don't help a team like San Francisco with four turnovers. You can't spot 'em 20 points."

Paul Brown, founder and long-time coach of the Bengals, attributed the defeat to "too many mistakes early against a good team."

Then, turning to Gregg, he said: "Congratulations, you had a fine, fine season."

The 49ers' Earl Cooper rushed for 39 yards and caught a pass for a TD.

Statistics of 16th Super Bowl
SAN FRANCISCO 26, CINCINNATI 21

Pontiac Silverdome, Detroit, Mich., January 24, 1982
Attendance: 81,270

SAN FRANCISCO	Offense	CINCINNATI
Dwight Clark	WR	... Cris Collinsworth
Dan Audick	LT	...... Anthony Munoz
John Ayers	LG	.........Dave Lapham
Fred Quillan	C	...... Blair Bush
Randy Cross	RG	.... Max Montoya
Keith Fahnhorst	RT	.... Mike Wilson
Charle Young	TE	.... Dan Ross
Freddie Solomon	WR	.... Isaac Curtis
Joe Montana	QB	.... Ken Anderson
Ricky Patton	RB	..Charles Alexander
Earl Cooper	FB	.... Pete Johnson

	Defense	
Jim Stuckey	LE	......Eddie Edwards
Archie Reese	NT	.... Wilson Whitley
Dwaine Board	RE	...... Ross Browner
Fred Dean	LOLB	...............Bo Harris
Jack Reynolds	LILB	.... Jim LeClair
Bobby Leopold	RILB	... Glenn Cameron
Keena Turner	ROLB	..... Reggie Williams
Ronnie Lott	LCB	........Louis Breeden
Eric Wright	RCB	...............Ken Riley
Carlton Williamson	SS	.... Bobby Kemp
Dwight Hicks	FS	...........Bryan Hicks

—SUBSTITUTIONS—

SAN FRANCISCO—Offense: Receivers—Eason Ramson, Mike Shumann, Mike Wilson. Linemen—John Choma, Walt Downing, Allan Kennedy. Backs—Amos Lawrence, Bill Ring, Johnny Davis. Kicker—Ray Wersching. Defense: Linebackers—Milt McColl, Craig Puki, Dan Bunz, Willie Harper. Linemen—Lawrence Pillers, John Harty. Backs—Lynn Thomas, Rick Gervais. Punter—Jim Miller. DNP—Guy Benjamin, Walt Easley, Lenvil Elliott, Saladin Martin.

CINCINNATI—Offense: Receivers—Steve Kreider, M.L. Harris, Don Bass, David Verser. Linemen—Blake Moore, Mike Obrovac. Backs—Jim Hargrove, Archie Griffin. Kicker—Jim Breech. Defense: Linebackers—Guy Frazier, Rick Razzano, Tom Dinkel. Linemen—Gary Burley, Rod Horn, Mike St. Clair. Backs—John Simmons, Mike Fuller, Ray Griffin, Oliver Davis. Punter—Pat McInally. DNP—Glenn Bujnoch, Turk Schonert, Jack Thompson.

— SCORE BY PERIODS —

San Francisco 49ers (NFC)	7	13	0	6 –	26
Cincinnati Bengals (AFC)	0	0	7	14 –	21

— SCORING —

San Francisco—Montana 1 run (Wersching kick).
San Francisco—Cooper 11 pass from Montana (Wersching kick).
San Francisco—Field goal Wersching 22.
San Francisco—Field goal Wersching 26.
Cincinnati—Anderson 5 run (Breech kick).
Cincinnati—Ross 4 pass from Anderson (Breech kick)./
San Francisco—Field goal Wersching 40.
San Francisco—Field goal Wersching 23.
Cincinnati—Ross 3 pass from Anderson (Breech kick).

— TEAM STATISTICS —

	San Francisco	Cincinnati
Total First Downs	20	24
First Downs Rushing	9	7
First Downs Passing	9	13
First Downs Penalty	2	4
Rushes	40	24
Yards Gained Rushing (net)	127	72
Average Yards per Rush	3.2	3.0
Passes Attempted	22	34
Passes Completed	14	25
Had Intercepted	0	2
Times Tackled Attemp. Pass	1	5
Yards Lost Attempting Pass	9	16
Yards Gained Passing (net)	148	284
Total Net Yardage	275	356
Total Offensive Plays	63	63
Avg. Gain per Offensive Play	4.4	5.7
Punts	4	3
Average Distance	46.3	43.7
Punt Returns	1	4
Punt Return Yardage	6	35
Kickoff Returns	3	7
Kickoff Return Yardage	40	52
Interception Return Yardage	52	0
Fumbles	2	2
Opp. Fumbles Recovered	1	2
Total Return Yardage	98	87
Penalties	8	8
Yards Penalized	65	57
Total Points Scored	26	21
Touchdowns	2	3
Touchdowns Rushing	1	1
Touchdowns Passing	1	2
Touchdowns on Returns	0	0
Extra Points	2	3
Field Goals Attempted	4	0
Field Goals	4	0

INDIVIDUAL STATISTICS
—RUSHING—

San Francisco	Atts.	Yds.	Lg.	TD
Patton	17	55	10	0
Cooper	9	34	14	0
Montana	6	18	7	1
Ring	5	17	7	0
Davis	2	5	4	0
Clark	1	-2	-2	0
Cincinnati	Atts.	Yds.	Lg.	TD
Johnson	14	36	5	0
Alexander	5	17	13	0
Anderson	4	15	6	1
A. Griffin	1	4	4	0

—Passing—

San Francisco	Atts.	Comp.	Yds.	Int.	TD
Montana	22	14	157	0	1
Cincinnati	Atts.	Comp.	Yds.	Int.	TD
Anderson	34	25	300	2	2

—RECEIVING—

San Francisco	No.	Yds.	Lg.	TD
Solomon	4	52	20	0
Clark	4	45	17	0
Cooper	2	15	11	1
Wilson	1	22	22	0
Young	1	14	14	0
Patton	1	6	6	0
Ring	1	3	3	0

San Francisco fans express their feelings while watching the 49ers roll past Cincinnati in Super Bowl XVI.

Cincinnati	No.	Yds.	Lg.	TD
Ross	11	104	16	2
Collinsworth	5	107	49	0
Curtis	3	42	21	0
Kreider	2	36	19	0
Johnson	2	8	5	0
Alexander	2	3	3	0

—INTERCEPTIONS—

San Francisco	No.	Yds.	Lg.	TD
Hicks	1	27	27	0
Wright	1	25	25	0
Cincinnati–None.				

—PUNTING—

San Francisco	No.	Avg.	Lg.
Miller	4	46.3	50

Cincinnati	No.	Avg.	Lg.
McInally	3	43.7	53

—PUNT RETURNS—

San Francisco	No.	FC	Yds.	Lg.
Hicks	1	0	6	6
Solomon	0	1	0	0

Cincinnati	No.	FC	Yds.	Lg.
Fuller	4	0	35	17

—KICKOFF RETURNS—

San Francisco	No.	Yds.	Lg.
Lawrence	1	17	17
Hicks	1	23	23
Clark	1	0	0

Cincinnati	No.	Yds.	Lg.
Verser	5	52	16
A. Griffin	1	0	0
Frazier	1	0	0

—FIELD GOALS—

San Francisco	Att.	Made
Wersching	4	4
Cincinnati–None.		

—SCORING—

San Francisco	TD	PAT	FG	Pts.
Wersching	0	2	4	14
Cooper	1	0	0	6
Montana	1	0	0	6

Cincinnati	TD	PAT	FG	Pts.
Ross	2	0	0	12
Anderson	1	0	0	6
Breech	0	3	0	3

—FUMBLES—

San Francisco	No.	Own Rec.	Opp. Rec.	TD
Lawrence	1	0	0	0
Harper	0	1	0	0
McColl	0	0	1	0
Thomas	0	0	1	0
Wright	1	0	0	0

Cincinnati	No.	Own Rec.	Opp. Rec.	TD
Simmons	0	0	1	0
Collinsworth	1	0	0	0
A. Griffin	1	0	0	0

The Redskins whoop it up as the clock runs down during their Super Bowl XVII victory over the Dolphins.

Super Bowl XVII

Redskins Get Revenge

January 30, 1983

Conformity and John Riggins were never meant for each other.

Riggins sings his own lyrics written to his own tempo. He hacks his own pathways while others ride the interstates.

In times past, when teammates favored the Afro hair-style, John modeled the Mohawk or had the cue-ball look.

Shortly before Super Bowl XVII, Riggins broke a two-year moratorium on interviews. Submitting to a press inquisition four days before the game in Pasadena, Calif., he delighted jaded journalists with a sprightly sense of humor.

Two nights before the Washington-Miami encounter for the championship of professional football, Redskins Owner Jack Kent Cooke played host to a party for 350. Casual attire was suggested. Riggins demonstrated his interpretation of "casual," arriving in top hat, white tie and tails and jauntily swinging a walking stick.

On another evening, Riggins and fellow revelers returned to the hotel several hours past midnight and awakened all other teammates within earshot.

That was Riggins running in the face of convention prior to kickoff on January 30, 1983, at the Rose Bowl. Once the whistle sounded, however, the 230-pound Kansan ran into the faces of the Miami Dolphins as he led the Redskins to a 27-17 victory before 103,667 sun-drenched spectators, the second largest Super Bowl crowd (Super Bowl XIV at Pasadena drew 103,985).

In avenging a 14-7 loss to Miami in Super Bowl VII, the Redskins eroded the National Football League's top-rated defense and then humbled it. Washington posted 400 total net yards compared with 176 for Miami. Riggins gained 166 yards in 38 carries, both records, and with 15 more yards on a pass outgained the entire Miami offense.

The Dolphins registered only nine first downs, tying a mark for ineptitude set by the

A dejected Kim Bokamper reflects on what went wrong for the Dolphins in Super Bowl XVII.

Miami quarterback David Woodley's frustrations began when Dexter Manley delivered a fumble-forcing hit in the second quarter.

Minnesota Vikings in Super Bowl IX, and made only two first downs in the second half. The American Conference champions invaded Washington territory only once in the last two quarters, and that was due to an interception.

Miami quarterbacks completed only four passes, an all-time low, and none in the second half. The subjugation was complete when Coach Don Shula inserted Don Strock, miracle worker of past revivals, with 2 minutes remaining. The backup quarterback contributed three incompletions to the 10 posted by David Woodley.

The victory was the Redskins' 15th in 16 games dating to the 1981 season—marred only by a December, 1982, loss to Dallas—and the championship was the club's first since 1942 when a Ray Flaherty team defeated the Chicago Bears in the title game.

While Riggins was romping to Most Valuable Player honors, Washington's teams-within-in-a-team were excelling in their own miniature arenas. The offensive line, affectionately known as the Hogs, was winning blue ribbons, opening holes and providing excellent pass protection.

The Smurfs, undersized wide receivers Alvin Garrett and Charlie Brown, caught touchdown passes that allowed the Fun Bunch, the pass-catching corps, to stage its tribal ritual in the end zone.

But the game belonged to Riggins, the former Kansas Jayhawk who might have matriculated at Colorado except that Buffalo recruiters, according to legend, were unable to locate Centralia, Kan., a pinpoint on the map near the Nebraska border.

In addition to his heavy-duty rushing, Riggins rambled 43 yards for a touchdown, the longest Super Bowl scoring run from scrimmage.

The world championship climaxed an irregular course for Riggins, a first-round draft choice by the New York Jets in 1971. After five seasons in the AFC, he played out his option and signed a five-year contract with the Redskins.

In July, 1980, Riggins reported to training camp, but left two days later when General Manager Bobby Beathard refused to renegotiate the final year of his contract. He was placed on the left camp-retired list and returned to his farm outside Lawrence, Kan.

It was there that Joe Gibbs found Riggins shortly after replacing Jack Pardee as the Redskins' coach following the 1980 season.

"I told him I wanted to help him do what he wanted to do," revealed Gibbs, the former offensive coordinator of the San Diego Chargers. "If he wanted to come back to Washington, I sure wanted him. If he wanted something else, I wanted to help him." Riggins was 31 and in no shape for the rigors of pro football.

"All I did the whole year was paint my house," Riggins said. "I'm a slow worker."

But John liked Gibbs' pitch and he rejoined the Redskins. Before long, however, Joe wondered if he had made the right move.

"We took it easy on him the first year," said the coach. "We felt he'd turn it on during the regular season, but he didn't play well in our first two games and in the fourth, against Philadelphia, he played poorly. All of us, including John, wondered if he was through." Nevertheless, Riggins gained 714 yards in 1981.

The strike-shortened 1982 season offered some encouragement. In nine games, Riggins gained 553 yards as the team posted an 8-1 record, best in the National Conference.

Before the start of the playoff tournament, Riggins thought his hour had arrived, that he was ready to demolish defenses—provided he had enough opportunity to carry the ball.

"Gimme the ball 20 to 25 times a game," he told Gibbs, a disciple of the passing school, "and we'll do it."

Gibbs consented and John delivered handsomely. He gained more than 100 yards in victories over Detroit, Minnesota and Dallas before detonating against Miami. He totaled 610 playoff yards in 136 carries.

Dolphins Coach Don Shula does a sideline dance as Jimmy Cefalo heads for the end zone with a first-quarter touchdown.

Miami's Fulton Walker stunned Washington players and fans with his 98-yard kickoff return that negated a Redskins' touchdown only seconds earlier.

Lyle Blackwood's interference on a pass intended for Washington's Nick Gia-quinto set up a Redskin scoring opportunity near the end of the half.

"I thought he could do it all year long," said tackle Joe Jacoby, one of the Hogs. "All he needed was to get the ball."

Riggins, who thought Gibbs "might have been carried away" by his request for action, was busiest against Miami in the fourth quarter when he carried the ball 13 times, three more than in the first period. His number was called seven times in the second quarter and eight in the third.

The Dolphins, seeking their third world title in four Super Bowl appearances, gave early indications that they merited their role as three-point favorites. On Miami's second possession, from a second-and-six at its 24-yard line, Woodley passed to wide receiver Jimmy Cefalo, who caught the ball at the Dolphins' 45 and out-raced safety Tony Peters to the goal line.

"I was watching to see how far Jimmy would go," explained Woodley. "If the defensive back played off him, he would stay close to the line. But the defensive back came up and Jimmy ran right by him. They should have been in double coverage with a cornerback backing up, but the corner was frozen by the fake quick pitch."

Miami's stout defense checked the Redskins on the next possession, after which the Dolphins ran off two first downs before Washington right end Dexter Manley crashed into Woodley, who fumbled. When tackle Dave Butz recovered, the Redskins had the ball at Miami's 46.

The possibility of trying to advance the fumble never occurred to Butz, a 10-year veteran.

"My job is not to run with the ball, just secure it," Butz said. "In a game as important as this, running with the ball is something I wouldn't think of trying. Securing it was my only thought."

With Riggins carrying on four consecutive plays, the Redskins moved to Miami's 14, from where Mark Moseley kicked a 31-yard field goal two plays into the second quarter.

Fulton Walker's 42-yard return of the ensuing kickoff gave the Dolphins fine field position at their 47, from where Woodley launched a 14-play, 50-yard drive featuring the running of Tony Nathan and Andra Franklin. When the Washington defense stiffened at the 3, Ewe von Schamann booted a 20-yard field goal, restoring the Dolphins' seven-point advantage.

The clock showed 5 minutes, 55 seconds remaining in the first half when the Redskins

Not everything went Joe Theismann's way during Super Bowl XVII. Earnest Rhone pulls down the Redskins quarterback (left) and Theismann frantically breaks up his own pass attempt (right) after it was blocked, nearly resulting in a Miami touchdown.

started their next offensive series from their own 20. Ten plays, including a 15-yard swing pass to Riggins and a 12-yard scramble by quarterback Joe Theismann, brought up a third-and-one at the Miami 4. It was time to call on the Smurfs.

Wide receivers Garrett and Brown dashed to the right, where Brown made a pick that freed Garrett to catch Theismann's soft pass over the head of cornerback Gerald Small.

"They were in tight coverage and I just beat my guy off the line," said Garrett, who started in the playoffs only because of injuries to Art Monk.

Only 1:51 remained in the half when Moseley's conversion kick knotted the score at 10-10.

Suddenly, the "Hail to the Redskins" fight song boomed with extra zest, and just as suddenly it went flat as Walker gathered in Jeff Hayes' kickoff at the 2. Walker, a second-year backup cornerback from West Virginia, raced to the left and broke through a large hole in the coverage wedge. At midfield he encountered Hayes, whom he faked into a turnaround. Hayes attempted a leg tackle that merely brushed Walker, who galloped all the way with the first scoring kickoff return in 17 Super Bowls. For the third time, the Dolphins enjoyed a seven-point lead when von Schamann converted.

"We had a wedge set to the left," said Walker. "I baited their guy to go to the right, then I cut back to the left as hard as I could. That's when the alley opened up, and when Hayes turned his back I knew he wasn't going to catch me."

Walker's electrifying dash put scarcely a dent in the clock and 1:34 remained when the Redskins started from their 7 with Riggins' three-yard smash up the middle. Aided by a 30-yard interference call against Lyle Blackwood on a pass intended for Nick Giaquinto, the Redskins moved to the Miami 16 with 14 seconds left.

A low-risk pass into the end zone seemed in order, but Theismann, with no timeouts remaining, passed to Garrett, who was tackled inbounds by Glenn Blackwood as time expired.

Explaining the surprise call, Gibbs said, "We called a dash that got Theismann outside. The formation gives us one guy on the sideline and another in the end zone. If Joe has nobody, he can throw it away. He went to the guy who was supposed to be on the sidelines, but they wouldn't let him get out of bounds."

Theismann was more harsh. "I made a stupid play," he muttered. "I thought we could get the play off with time to try a field goal."

"I didn't see Blackwood behind me," said Garrett. "I thought I could score by going inside, but he cut me off."

Trailing by seven points where only moments earlier his team was even, Gibbs reminded the Redskins at halftime that they had rebounded from greater deficits to win and could do so again by continuing to do what they do best.

"I told 'em a lot of things hadn't gone right for them in the first half and that they'd turn around," Gibbs said. "I said I had a good feeling about the game and they said the same thing."

Gibbs' euphoria translated into three points in the first 7 minutes of the second half. On Washington's second possession, from its 47, Garrett ran a reverse on a handoff from Riggins and raced 44 yards to the Miami 9 before he was stopped by Small.

"That's our 'X-Reverse,'" said Garrett, a ninth-round draft choice out of Angelo (Tex.) State by San Diego in 1979 who was subsequently cut by the Chargers and New York Giants. "The last time we ran it I think I lost two yards. It was the perfect time to call it (first-and-10). It was wide open and perfectly executed."

On third down, Theismann tried the same play that had produced the Redskins' first touchdown, but he overshot Garrett and Wash-

ington settled for a 20-yard Moseley field goal that cut Miami's edge to 17-13.

Action stalled for the next 4 minutes, until a Theismann pass intended for Don Warren was intercepted by linebacker A.J. Duhe at the Washington 47. An offsides penalty and a five-yard run by Woodley netted the Dolphins their ninth and last first down of the game before Woodley attempted a long pass to Cefalo. The ball was tipped by cornerback Vernon Dean and intercepted by safety Mark Murphy, who batted the ball with one had and pulled it in with the other as he fell to the ground.

Three plays later, Theismann dropped back from the 18 intending to pass to Brown. The ball had scarcely left his hand when it struck the outstretched palms of Kim Bokamper. For a split second Miami's defensive end teetered on the brink of an interception, but as he was about to clasp the ball, Theismann charged forward and slapped it to the ground.

"That was the biggest play of the game," said Theismann, not immodestly. "And I did hit the ball, I'll be honest. I had visions of Duhe last week (three interceptions in the AFC title game against the New York Jets, including a touchdown return), and I didn't want to be in Richard Todd's shoes."

Only Miami defender Don McNeal blocked John Riggins' path to the end zone and the Redskins' big running back made short work of that problem (left, above and right) en route to the winning touchdown of Super Bowl XVII.

Washington's Charlie Brown clutches the ball and Alvin Garrett celebrates the Redskins' fourth-quarter insurance touchdown.

"It was a great play," Shula agreed. "It could have put us in pretty good shape, but Theismann broke it up."

Bokamper, crestfallen over his failure to make the interception and score an easy touchdown, said, "I just came upfield on my guy (tackle George Starke) and got an opportunity to get my hand up and tip it. The ball went straight up. Theismann wasn't anywhere in sight. Then just as it came down in my hands he punched it right through."

Miami nose tackle Bob Baumhower had his own version. "Theismann's gotta be the luckiest guy in the world on that play," he snorted.

Having dodged the Bokamper bullet late in the third quarter, Theismann led the Redskins to the Miami 43 where Gibbs, who had promised he would be aggressive and "do the things we do best," dipped into his pouch of tricks.

On a first-and-10 in the early moments of the final period, Theismann handed off to Riggins, who lateraled back to the quarterback whose pass intended for Brown was picked off by a diving Lyle Blackwood at the 1. After two plays netted only three yards and a Woodley pass fell incomplete, the Dolphins gave the ball back to Washington at its 48. Three line smashes gained nine yards and placed Gibbs squarely at the crossroads of a major decision: Go for the first down or punt the ball away.

Gibbs was thinking of a specific play on third down. "We knew if we didn't make it then," he said, "it would be a risky field goal. We decided to take our best play and go at them. We didn't want to lose a Super Bowl by not being tough enough. The play was a fake zoom. I think they thought we were slanting one way and got caught when we went the other way."

The play started with Washington tight end Clint Didier in motion. Across the line of scrimmage, Miami cornerback Don McNeal kept pace until the end wheeled and headed back from whence he had come. Attempting the same move, McNeal lost his footing, but only briefly. It was, however, long enough.

To McNeal's horror, he saw Riggins heading for the area he had vacated. McNeal arrived a fraction too late. He got a hand on the runaway Riggins, but it was no contest as the Washington back ran 43 yards for a touchdown. With 4:59 elapsed in the fourth quarter, the Redskins had their first lead of the game. Moseley's conversion made it 20-17.

"The play is called 70-Chip out of the I formation," said Riggins. "It's something we've used all season. We must have run it seven or eight times against Dallas (in the NFC championship game)."

Ten minutes still remained, ample time for the Dolphins to countercharge, but the Redskins would have none of it. When Woodley threw an incompletion that terminated the next series, his futility was full-blown. His passing record for the second half was 0-for-8.

Washington was now in position to play the clock. Eight running plays consumed nearly 4 minutes. On third-and-nine at Miami's 18, Theismann rolled left and tossed to Brown at the 9. Three plays later, the same pair teamed up on a six-yard scoring play. Moseley's toe accounted for a 10-point lead at the 2-minute mark.

At that point, Theismann felt like "we were in RFK Stadium. We felt the vibrations coming from the East."

When the Dolphins began their next possession, Strock was at quarterback. But a lack of time and a hounding Washington defense made the old magician as ineffective as Woodley. A four-yard end-around and three incomplete passes represented the Dolphins' last gasp.

"I had thought about using Strock late in the third quarter," said Shula. "But when he got in he really didn't have a chance."

Of Theismann, once the property of the Dolphins, Shula said, "He was outstanding. He was going against a tough defense, yet came up with big plays. On designed rollouts, he came out of the pocket and continually made big plays."

Another candidate for big-play honors was Rick Walker, one of 26 free agents (14 of whom were not even drafted by NFL teams) on the new world champions. It was Walker's block that sprung Riggins loose on his scoring jaunt.

"I didn't see much of the run," said Walker, a member of the Hogs. "I was in the dirt as usual, blocking Larry Gordon (linebacker). When I looked up, I saw the big diesel rolling along."

Diesel or train (McNeal's description) or sycamore (Theismann's expression), it made little difference to Riggins.

"Reagan may be President, but today I'm

The strong leg of Washington's Mark Moseley put the final touch on Super Bowl XVII.

king," exulted John to his subjects in press interview quarters.

But the crown head reverted to character in the final scene. Richer by $70,000 than he had been a month before—as were all the world champions—Riggins slipped into a pair of camouflage pants and slipped out the back door of the Rose Bowl locker room.

Perched on his head where a crown should have been was a cap proclaiming, "Ducks Unlimited."

Statistics of 17th Super Bowl
WASHINGTON 27, MIAMI 17

Rose Bowl, Pasadena, Calif., January 30, 1983
Attendance: 103,667

Offense

MIAMI		WASHINGTON
Duriel Harris	WR	Alvin Garrett
Jon Giesler	LT	Joe Jacoby
Bob Kuechenberg	LG	Russ Grimm
Dwight Stephenson	C	Jeff Bostic
Jeff Toews	RG	Fred Dean
Eric Laakso	RT	George Starke
Bruce Hardy	TE	Don Warren
Jimmy Cefalo	WR	Charlie Brown
David Woodley	QB	Joe Theismann
Tony Nathan	RB	
	TE	Rick Walker
Andra Franklin	FB	John Riggins

Defense

MIAMI		WASHINGTON
Doug Betters	LE	Mat Mendenhall
Bob Baumhower	NT	
	LT	Dave Butz
	RT	Darryl Grant
Kim Bokamper	RE	Dexter Manley
Bob Brudzinski	LLB	Mel Kaufman
A.J. Duhe	ILB	
Earnie Rhone	ILB	
	MLB	Neal Olkewicz
Larry Gordon	RLB	Rich Milot
Gerald Small	LCB	Jeris White
Don McNeal	RCB	Vernon Dean
Glenn Blackwood	SS	Tony Peters
Lyle Blackwood	FS	Mark Murphy

SUBSTITUTIONS

MIAMI—Offense: Receivers—Vince Heflin, Ronnie Lee, Nat Moore, Joe Rose. Linemen—Mark Dennard, Roy Foster, Cleveland Green. Backs—Woody Bennett, Rich Diana, Eddie Hill, Jim Jensen, Don Strock, Tom Vigorito. Kicker—Uwe von Schamann. Defense: Linebackers—Charles Bowser, Ron Hester, Steve Potter, Steve Shull. Linemen—Vern Den Herder. Backs—William Judson, Mike Kozlowski, Paul Lankford, Fulton Walker. Punter—Tom Orosz. DNP—Richard Bishop, Steve Clark, Mark Duper.

WASHINGTON—Offense: Receivers—Clint Didier, Virgil Seay. Linemen—Donald Laster, Mark May. Backs—Nick Giaquinto, Clarence Harmon, Wilbur Jackson, Otis Wonsley. Kicker—Mark Moseley. Defense: Linebackers—Monte Coleman, Peter Cronan, Larry Kubin, Quentin Lowry. Linemen—Perry Brooks, Todd Liebenstein, Tony McGee. Backs—Curtis Jordan, Joe Lavender, LeCharls McDaniel, Mike Nelms, Greg Williams. Punter—Jeff Hayes. DNP—Richard Caster, Bob Holly, Tom Owen, Garry Puetz, Joe Washington.

— SCORE BY PERIODS —

Miami Dolphins (AFC)	7	10	0	0 — 17
Wash. Redskins (NFC)	0	10	3	14 — 27

— SCORING —

Miami—Cefalo 76 pass from Woodley (von Schamann kick).
Washington—Field goal Moseley 31.
Miami—Field goal von Schamann 20.
Washington—Garrett 4 pass from Theismann (Moseley kick).
Miami—Walker 98 kickoff return (von Schamann kick).
Washington—Field goal Moseley 20.
Washington—Riggins 43 run (Moseley kick).
Washington—Brown 6 pass from Theismann (Moseley kick).

— TEAM STATISTICS —

	Miami	Washington
Total First Downs	9	24
First Downs Rushing	7	14
First Downs Passing	2	9
First Downs Penalty	0	1
Rushes	29	52
Yards Gained Rushing (net)	96	276
Average Yards per Rush	3.3	5.3
Passes Attempted	17	23
Passes Completed	4	15
Had Intercepted	1	2
Times Tackled Attempt. Pass	1	3
Yards Lost Attempting Pass	17	19
Yards Gained Passing (net)	80	124
Total Net Yardage	176	400
Total Offensive Plays	47	78
Avg. Gain per Offensive Play	4.4	5.7
Punts	6	3
Average Distance	37.8	45.7
Punt Returns	2	2
Punt Return Yardage	22	52
Kickoff Returns	6	3
Kickoff Return Yardage	222	57
Interceptions Return Yardage	0	0
Fumbles	2	0
Opp. Fumbles Recovered	0	1
Total Return Yardage	244	109
Penalties	4	5
Yards Penalized	55	36
Total Points Scored	17	27
Touchdowns	2	3
Touchdowns Rushing	0	1
Touchdowns Passing	1	2
Touchdowns on Returns	1	0
Extra Points	2	3
Field Goals Attempted	1	2
Field Goals	1	2

INDIVIDUAL STATISTICS

—RUSHING—

Miami	Atts.	Yds.	Lg.	TD
Franklin	16	49	9	0
Woodley	4	16	7	0
Nathan	7	26	12	0
Harris	1	1	1	0
Vigorito	1	4	4	0

Washington	Atts.	Yds.	Lg.	TD
Riggins	38	166	43	1
Harmon	9	40	12	0
Walker	1	6	6	0
Theismann	3	20	12	0
Garrett	1	44	44	0

—PASSING—

Miami	Atts.	Comp.	Yds.	Int.	TD
Woodley	14	4	97	1	1
Strock	3	0	0	0	0

Washington	Atts.	Comp.	Yds.	Int.	TD
Theismann	23	15	143	2	2

—RECEIVING—

Miami	No.	Yds.	Lg.	TD
Cefalo	2	82	76	1
Harris	2	15	8	0

Redskins' Owner Jack Kent Cooke leaves the post-game victory party with his long-awaited treasure.

Washington	No.	Yds.	Lg.	TD
Brown	6	60	26	1
Warren	5	28	10	0
Walker	1	27	27	0
Riggins	1	15	15	0
Garrett	2	13	9	1

—INTERCEPTIONS—

Miami	No.	Yds.	Lg.	TD
Duhe	1	0	0	0
L. Blackwood	1	0	0	0

Washington	No.	Yds.	Lg.	TD
Murphy	1	0	0	0

—PUNTING—

Miami	No.	Avg.	Lg.
Orosz	6	37.8	46

Washington	No.	Avg.	Lg.
Hayes	4	42.0	54

—PUNT RETURNS—

Miami	No.	FC	Yds.	Lg.
Vigorito	2	1	22	12

Washington	No.	FC	Yds.	Lg.
Nelms	6	0	52	12

—KICKOFF RETURNS—

Miami	No.	Yds.	Lg.
L. Blackwood	2	32	17
Walker	4	190	98

Washington	No.	Yds.	Lg.
Nelms	2	44	24
Wonsley	1	13	13

—FIELD GOALS—

Miami	Att.	Made
von Schamann	1	1

Washington	Att.	Made
Moseley	2	2

—SCORING—

Miami	TD	PAT	FG	Pts.
Cefalo	1	0	0	6
Walker	1	0	0	6
von Schamann	0	2	1	5

Washington	TD	PAT	FG	Pts.
Moseley	0	3	2	9
Brown	1	0	0	6
Garrett	1	0	0	6
Riggins	1	0	0	6

—FUMBLES—

Miami	No.	Own Rec.	Opp. Rec.	TD
Woodley	1	0	0	0
L. Blackwood	1	1	0	0

Washington	No.	Own Rec.	Opp. Rec.	TD
Butz	0	0	1	0

The Los Angeles Raiders, led by the Super Bowl-record 191-yard performance of Marcus Allen, ran over, around and through the favored Redskins.

Super Bowl XVIII

Raiders Sack the Skins

January 22, 1984

In the week preceding Super Bowl XVIII, when bluster and ballyhoo were running rampant, one voice was heard above all others.

"I'm gonna take off Joe Theismann's head," glared the 34-year-old defensive end of the Los Angeles Raiders.

Nobody regarded Lyle Alzado's threat of decapitation as anything more than pregame hype, least of all Theismann, who said, "Down deep Alzado is a very fine fellow."

But the quarterback's noggin was about the only thing the Washington Redskins did not lose in their interconference contest for the championship of the National Football League.

According to all calculations, Super Bowl XVIII should have presented a memorable engagement. Without question, the participants were the best in the NFL. Washington compiled a 14-2 regular-season record, losing only to Dallas, 31-30, and Green Bay, 48-47, in nationally televised Monday night games.

Los Angeles dominated the American Football Conference with 12 victories and losses only to St. Louis, Washington and Western Division rival Seattle (twice).

On the playoff road that led to Tampa Stadium, the Raiders easily disposed of Pittsburgh and Seattle. The Redskins walloped the Los Angeles Rams, 51-7, before squeezing past San Francisco, 24-21, in a game they had led, 21-0, entering the final quarter.

The Skins were installed as three-point Super Bowl favorites. Who could question the oddsmakers' wisdom? They were, after all, the defending champions with the best record in the NFL against the rush.

Moreover, they had the Hogs, the indelicately named, hard-charging offensive line, and the Smurfs, a corps of fleet, sure-handed wide receivers, and the Fun Bunch, which reveled in the end zone after touchdown passes.

The Skins also had Theismann, who entertained with his flow of oratory and who completed about 60 percent of his passes, and run-

A dejected John Riggins tries to figure out what happened to the Redskins in Super Bowl XVIII.

Redskins punter Jeff Hayes watches helplessly as his kick sails toward the outstretched arms of onrushing Derrick Jensen.

ning back John Riggins, a juggernaut who gained huge chunks of yardage and was the Most Valuable Player in Super Bowl XVII.

In addition, the Skins already owned a regular-season win over the Raiders. On October 2 at Robert F. Kennedy Memorial Stadium, they registered a 37-35 victory by scoring 17 points in the final 6 minutes and 15 seconds. Generally overlooked in that argument, however, was that the Raiders were operating without running back Marcus Allen, wide receiver Cliff Branch and cornerback Mike Haynes.

Washington Coach Joe Gibbs echoed the opinion of many when he predicted shortly before the game that "both teams will score in the 20s and the game will go down to the wire."

So much for Gibbs' crystal ball. The Raiders scored their 20 points—21 in fact—in the first half. The Redskins never reached double digits. And the game never reached "the wire,"

although few in the capacity crowd of 72,920 would have suspected it.

Los Angeles' 38-9 conquest of the Redskins was achieved with relative ease and with first-degree shock. The Raiders scored the first time the Redskins had the ball. The Raiders also converted on their fourth possession and again on the Skins' sixth possession.

The game, played on a partly cloudy day with a 20-mph wind from the northeast, was less than 5 minutes old when misfortune dealt the Skins a mighty blow. Starting on their 19-yard line, the NFC champions advanced to only the 30 when the drive stalled. Jeff Hayes, who had punted 80 times without problems in the 18 previous games, attempted to launch No. 81. Enter Derrick Jensen.

As Hayes kicked, the special teams captain bolted up the middle, blocked the football and chased it into the end zone, where he fell on it

Los Angeles players help the official by signaling touchdown after Derrick Jensen's punt block and subsequent recovery in the Redskin end zone.

for a touchdown. The first of Chris Bahr's five point-after conversions gave Los Angeles a 7-0 lead.

"I don't know why (special teams coach) Steve Ortmayer decided to go for the block so quickly," Jensen said. "Greg Pruitt is such a good punt-return man, good enough to go to the Pro Bowl, that we've tried to block punts only about eight times all season. Usually we don't attempt to block a kick until late in the game, when we want the ball desperately."

Jensen, a five-year veteran out of Texas-Arlington, speculated that his route to the kicker was left unguarded "because the Redskins were so concerned about Lester Hayes and Odis McKinney coming off the corners, they kinda forgot about me."

Once more the Skins attempted to crack the Raider defense, moving more than 50 yards to the Los Angeles 27. On fourth down, however,

Mark Moseley, whose 161 points in 1983 established an NFL record for placekickers, missed to the left on a 44-yard field-goal try.

The second quarter was approaching the 10-minute mark when the Raiders struck again, with only slightly less suddenness.

From his own 35, quarterback Jim Plunkett connected with wide receiver Cliff Branch for 50 yards. Branch split the double coverage of Anthony Washington and Curtis Jordan for a textbook catch on the 15-yard line.

After Allen gained three yards off right tackle, the Plunkett-Branch lightning struck again.

From his position on the left side, Branch cut toward the middle, gave Washington a token fake and sprinted into the end zone for an uncomplicated catch of Plunkett's toss.

"We set up the touchdown with a play-action fake," Plunkett explained. "The free safety bit, and Cliff was able to get behind him. Cliff ate

Veteran wide receiver Cliff Branch (21) celebrates with Marcus Allen after a Super Bowl touchdown.

up the cornerback on his side, put on an outside move and broke up the middle."

The 35-year-old Branch had some words of wisdom for the 25-year-old Washington.

"I kept telling him," Branch said, "that he'd better get some help. I said, 'You know you can't cover me.' I think he got insulted because he knew I was right."

"The 49ers beat Anthony (in the NFC title game) on the corner patterns a few times," he added. "We gave him the same look but went inside. He was very vulnerable."

Before he was injured in the second half, Branch caught six passes to become the leading receiver in playoff history. His 73 catches topped the old record of 70, held by another

Raider wide receiver, Fred Biletnikoff.

The Skins unfurled their longest march of the first half on their next possession, moving 73 yards from their own 20 to the L.A. 7 before stalling. Moseley's 24-yard field goal inspired the game's first rendition of "Hail to the Redskins."

When the Raiders' subsequent drive came to a halt on the Washington 39, Ray Guy punted to the 12.

Only 12 seconds remained before halftime, and there was little doubt, even among the untutored, that the Redskins would (a) run out the clock or (b) throw a low-risk pass far down field, hoping for either a defensive penalty or a lucky-strike TD.

The Skins rejected each course of action. The normally conservative Gibbs opted for surprise.

"We wanted to get ourselves a little breathing room and get out of there," Theismann said. "It was a good call. The flaw was in the execution."

As the Redskins lined up in their Rocket Right, Screen Left formation, Raiders linebacker coach Charlie Sumner's memory clicked.

Spotting Charlie Brown, Art Monk and Clint Didier on the right and running back Joe Washington on the left, Sumner removed Matt Millen, starting inside linebacker, and replaced him with Jack Squirek.

"Don't take me out!" Millen screamed at Sumner. "They can't handle me!"

But Sumner turned a deaf ear. He remembered how, in the regular-season game between the two teams, the Redskins had used a similar formation for a screen pass to Washington that produced a 67-yard gain. The coach wanted the 6-4 Squirek on the field rather than the 6-2 Millen.

His hunch was correct. Theismann took the snap, glanced right and then arched a soft pass over Alzado in Washington's direction. But Washington was not in the clear. "Lyle Alzado held him," Theismann said. "I didn't see the linebacker (Squirek). I was expecting zone coverage, but Squirek was on man to man."

Squirek, a second-year player out of Illinois, read Theismann's moves perfectly, stepping in front of Washington for the grab and sprinting five yards into the end zone. The TD was the first for Squirek since his days as a wide receiver at Cuyahoga Heights High School in Cleveland.

"I was in shock," Squirek said of his unfamiliar role. "I felt like I was in a dream. I couldn't believe it until everybody started pounding me in the end zone."

The Redskins were rather shocked themselves heading into the locker room. Theismann, who failed to connect on his first five passes, was 6-of-18 for 78 yards, and Riggins, the super bulldozer a year earlier when his 166 yards rushing set a Super Bowl mark, had

Raiders quarterback Jim Plunkett, the MVP of Super Bowl XV, completed 16-of-25 attempts, including a 12-yard scoring strike to Cliff Branch, in Super Bowl XVIII.

The Raider defense, led (above, left to right) by Mike Davis, Lyle Alzado and Matt Millen, made short work of Redskins quarterback Joe Theismann.

gained only 37 yards in 16 tries, an unflattering 2.3 yards per carry.

The Skins' gamble at the end of the first half left them down by 18 points, 21-3, but not down in spirit. "If anything, it made us more determined," Theismann said.

There also was hope that Riggins, who traditionally improves as the game progresses, would break loose in the second half. Additional incentive was the $64,000 prize for each winning player. The Redskins were poised for a comeback.

And as the second half began, it looked like they might. For 4 minutes in the third quarter, the Redskins displayed flashes of their talent. On that first drive of the half, Theismann completed three passes, the longest to Brown for 23 yards, and Riggins picked up 20 yards on six tries, which was not vintage Riggins, but it was an improvement.

Big John's final yard was a plunge over right tackle for the touchdown. The score extended Riggins' streak for rushing touchdowns in post-season games to six, breaking the record of five set by Franco Harris of Pittsburgh.

If Moseley could convert the extra-point attempt, Washington would trail by just 11 with about 26 minutes to play.

But Moseley did not convert. The 13-year veteran, who had kicked 71 of 72 extra points since the season began, drove the ball into the onrushing form of Don Hasselbeck.

The 12-point deficit was of short duration, however. In less than 4 minutes, the Raiders moved 70 yards in nine plays, aided by a pass-interference penalty against rookie cornerback Darrell Green that accounted for 38 yards. Allen climaxed the drive with a five-yard burst up the middle.

Trailing now by three touchdowns, 28-9, the

Washington's biggest offensive weapon, running back John Riggins (44), had a long, frustrating afternoon.

Redskins failed to advance beyond the Los Angeles 41-yard line on their next two possessions. But as the third quarter wound down, Washington appeared ready for a breakthrough. Branch fumbled after catching a nine-yard pass from Plunkett, and Anthony Washington recovered it for the Skins on the L.A. 35. The Redskins advanced to the 27, where they faced a third-and-two situation.

The handoff went to Joe Washington, who was stopped a yard short by Squirek. With no choice but to go for the first down, Gibbs went to his reliable locomotive.

Fourth and one. In a similar situation in the previous year's Super Bowl, Riggins broke away for a 43-yard touchdown romp that put Washington ahead of the Miami Dolphins for good.

Not this year.

"I had been running inside all day," Riggins said, "so some of the fellows suggested I try the outside to try to find daylight, but I just couldn't find it. I guess it got to the point that we were guessing where to go."

Riggins was stopped for no gain because linebacker Rod Martin slipped a block by tight end Rick Walker.

"I sure wasn't surprised when Riggins got the ball," said Martin, who intercepted three passes in Super Bowl XV, "but I was surprised that Walker tried to block me. Don Warren usually tries to block me on that play, but this time it was Walker.

"Walker went to UCLA when I went to USC, and he hasn't blocked me yet. I forced him into the backfield and had a clear shot at Riggins."

The Washington defensive unit, which had left the field less than 2 minutes earlier, scarcely had time to settle into position before misfortune struck again.

Marcus Allen leaves Redskin defenders in his wake as he runs 74 yards for a touchdown.

The Raiders' first play began innocently enough with Allen taking the handoff and starting to his left. Spotting a horde of Redskins there, he braked and reversed direction. Suddenly, he bolted through a hole up the middle. Defenders waved weakly as Allen shot by;

he was in the clear. Redskins gave chase, but they were no match for the former USC star who, it was alleged, could not run with the pros. The period ended as Allen glided across the goal line. His 74-yard gallop set a Super Bowl record for a play from scrimmage.

"I really screwed up that play," said Allen, the game's MVP. "The play is called 17 Bob Trail. The tight end and tackle double-team the linebacker and the guard pulls. (Guard) Mickey Marvin did a good job on the block, and I should have gone inside him. Somebody grabbed me from behind, but I pulled away and there was an alley. Darrell Green did not see me go by, and I thought I could outrun the other guys. Cliff Branch brushed another fellow aside down field.

"My first thought was not to get caught, and then I hoped there was no penalty. It was the best run I've had in the NFL. I didn't think of what to do on the run; I just let instinct take over."

More disaster awaited the Skins in the fourth quarter. Theismann was intercepted once, and three times he was sacked. Linebacker Jeff Barnes threw the quarterback for a nine-yard loss. Rookie defensive end Greg Townsend dropped him for 10.

The most painful sack, however, was delivered by Mike Davis when the Skins had a first and goal at the L.A. 8. Davis blind-sided Theismann, who was setting up to pass, and the ball bounced free. Martin recovered it at the Raider 31.

The Raiders did nothing with their opportunity. The Redskins took over on their own 17 and advanced to their 32 with 7:14 remaining.

Theismann completed two short passes, then attempted to connect with Monk along the left sideline. Haynes got to the ball first, however, and made the interception at the Raider 42.

On the first play, Allen scampered 39 yards, covering more than half the distance to the goal. The Raiders then moved steadily to the 3, and Bahr kicked a 21-yard field goal with 2:24 to go.

The blowout was complete.

The final score of 38-9 staggered the defending champions, drawing blood from a proud team that had won 11 straight games and had outscored opponents by more than 250 points for the season.

The Raiders' 38 points set a Super Bowl record, surpassing the 35 registered by Green Bay in the first world championship and by Pittsburgh in Super Bowl XVIII. The 29-point margin of victory also was a new high, topping the Packers' 25 over Kansas City in game No. 1.

Allen's 191 yards on the ground set a Super Bowl record, breaking Riggins' mark.

Riggins, meanwhile, was held to 64 rushing yards, the first time in seven playoff games that he failed to reach 100 yards. "I guess I didn't have 20-20 vision today," he mumbled.

"We didn't give Riggins anywhere to run," defensive end Howie Long said. "We forced him outside."

The Raider defensive line, which also featured Alzado and tackle Reggie Kinlaw, "is custom-made for Riggins," Long said. "We are short and heavy with 30-inch thighs and are built like refrigerators."

Long took particular delight in discussing the manner in which the Raider line and linebackers handled the Hogs. "Our front seven came up with our own nickname this week, but we didn't mention it until we had won the game," Long said. "We're the Slaughterhouse Seven. We never had a hog before that tasted so good. In fact, we may market our own T-shirts."

L.A.'s defensive secondary smothered Redskin receivers with man-to-man coverage. The Raiders had planned to use that strategy about 45 percent of the time, "but by the fourth quarter that had changed to about 95 percent," cornerback Hayes said. "We made them change because the Smurfs can't function with tight, physical man-to-man coverage. Joe Gibbs is a technical genius, but looking back to the championship game of 1980 when he was with San Diego (the Raiders beat the Chargers, 34-27, for the AFC title), the schemes he was using then are the same he is using now. The only difference is they are more diversified and complex now."

Theismann completed 16 passes in 35 attempts for 243 yards, including three to Brown for 93 yards, but he tossed two interceptions and was sacked six times for 50 yards in losses. He connected only one time apiece with wide receivers Alvin Garrett and Monk, two of his favorite targets.

And for only the second time in the season— the first came in a 45-7 victory over the Cardinals—Theismann failed to throw a touchdown pass.

The game did not measure up to pregame media hype, which had billed the matchup as a classic confrontation. Washington guard Russ Grimm explained why: "The two best teams were here. It's just that one showed up and had a great day. The other didn't execute."

It was the second Super Bowl victory for Coach Tom Flores, who guided the Oakland Raiders past Philadelphia in Super Bowl XV before the franchise moved to Los Angeles.

The Raiders indeed were No. 1, as signaled by linebacker Matt Millen (above) and MVP Marcus Allen.

Al Davis, the managing general partner of the new champions, who engineered the Raiders' change in locale, was dripping with praise for Flores, his first quarterback when he took over the team two decades earlier. After the game Commissioner Pete Rozelle called Flores "one of the greatest coaches in the game today." Davis was not satisfied.

"He is one of the greatest coaches in the history of the game," Davis said, "and the Raiders team is one of the best in the history of football. I love you all."

Statistics of 18th Super Bowl

LOS ANGELES RAIDERS 38, WASHINGTON 9

Tampa Stadium, Tampa, Fla., January 22, 1984

Attendance: 72,920

WASHINGTON	Offense	L.A. RAIDERS
Charlie Brown	WR	Cliff Branch
Joe Jacoby	LT	Bruce Davis
Russ Grimm	LG	Charley Hannah
Jeff Bostic	C	Dave Dalby
Mark May	RG	Mickey Marvin
George Starke	RT	Henry Lawrence
Don Warren	TE	Todd Christensen
Rick Walker	TE	
Art Monk	WR	Malcolm Barnwell
Joe Theismann	QB	Jim Plunkett
	RB	Marcus Allen
John Riggins	FB	Kenny King

Defense

Todd Liebenstein	LE	Howie Long
	NT	Reggie Kinlaw
Dave Butz	LT	
Darryl Grant	RT	
Dexter Manley	RE	Lyle Alzado
Mel Kaufman	LLB	Ted Hendricks
Neal Olkewicz	MLB	
	ILB	Matt Millen
	ILB	Bob Nelson
Rich Milot	RLB	Rod Martin
Darrell Green	LCB	Lester Hayes
Anthony Washington	RCB	Mike Haynes
Ken Coffey	SS	Mike Davis
Mark Murphy	FS	Vann McElroy

—SUBSTITUTIONS—

WASHINGTON—Offense: Receivers—Clint Didier, Alvin Garrett, Mike Williams. Linemen—Ken Huff, Bruce Kimball, Roy Simmons. Backs—Reggie Evans, Nick Giaquinto, Joe Washington, Otis Wonsley. Kicker—Mark Moseley. Defense: Linebackers—Stuart Anderson, Monte Coleman, Peter Cronan, Larry Kubin. Linemen—Perry Brooks, Charles Mann, Tony McGee. Backs—Brian Carpenter, Vernon Dean, Curtis Jordan, Greg Williams. Punter—Jeff Hayes. DNP—Bob Holly, Babe Laufenberg, Mark McGrath, Virgil Seay.

L.A. RAIDERS—Offense: Receivers—Don Hasselbeck, Derrick Jensen, Cle Montgomery, Calvin Muhammad, Dokie Williams. Linemen—Shelby Jordan, Don Mosebar, Steve Sylvester. Backs—Frank Hawkins, David Humm, Greg Pruitt, Chester Willis, Marc Wilson. Kicker—Chris Bahr. Defense: Linebackers—Jeff Barnes, Darryl Byrd, Tony Caldwell, Jack Squirek. Linemen—Bill Pickel, Johnny Robinson, Dave Stalls, Greg Townsend. Backs—James Davis, Kenny Hill, Odis McKinney, Ted Watts. Punter—Ray Guy. DNP—None.

— SCORE BY PERIODS —

Washington Redskins (NFC)	0	3	6	0	— 9
Los Angeles Raiders (AFC)	7	14	14	3	— 38

— SCORING —

Los Angeles—Jensen recovered blocked punt in end zone (Bahr kick), 4:52 1st.

Los Angeles—Branch 12 pass from Plunkett (Bahr kick), 5:46 2nd. Drive: 3 plays, 65 yards.

Washington—Field goal Moseley 24, 11:55 2nd. Drive: 13 plays, 73 yards.

Los Angeles—Squirek 5 interception return. 14:53 2nd.

Washington—Riggins 1 run (kick blocked), 4:08 3rd. Drive: 9 plays, 70 yards.

Los Angeles—Allen 5 run (Bahr kick), 7:54 3rd. Drive: 8 plays, 70 yards.

Los Angeles—Allen 74 run (Bahr kick), 15:00 3rd. Drive: 1 play, 74 yards.

Los Angeles—Field goal Bahr 21, 12:36 4th. Drive: 8 plays, 55 yards.

— TEAM STATISTICS —

	Washington	Los Ang.
Total First Downs	19	18
First Downs Rushing	7	8
First Downs Passing	10	9
First Downs Penalty	2	1
Rushes	32	33
Yards Gained Rushing (net)	90	231
Average Yards per Rush	2.8	7.0
Passes Attempted	35	25
Passes Completed	16	16
Had Intercepted	2	0
Times Tackled Attempt. Pass	6	2
Yards Lost Attempting Pass	50	18
Yards Gained Passing (net)	193	154
Total Net Yardage	283	385
Total Offensive Plays	73	60
Avg. Gain per Offensive Play	3.9	6.4
Punts	8	7
Average Distance	32.4	42.7
Had Blocked	1	0
Punt Returns	2	2
Punt Return Yardage	35	8
Kickoff Returns	7	1
Kickoff Return Yardage	132	17
Interception Return Yardage	0	5
Fumbles	1	1
Opp. Fumbles Recovered	2	1
Total Return Yardage	167	30
Penalties	4	7
Yards Penalized	62	56
Total Points Scored	9	38
Touchdowns	1	5
Touchdowns Rushing	1	2
Touchdowns Passing	0	1
Touchdowns on Returns	0	2
Extra Points	0	5
Field Goals Attempted	2	1
Field Goals	1	1

INDIVIDUAL STATISTICS

—RUSHING—

Washington	Atts.	Yds.	Lg.	TD
Riggins	26	64	8	1
Theismann	3	18	8	0
J. Washington	3	8	5	0
Los Angeles	Atts.	Yds.	Lg.	TD
Allen	20	191	74	2
King	3	12	10	0
Hawkins	3	6	3	0
Pruitt	5	17	11	0
Plunkett	1	−2	−2	0
Willis	1	7	7	0

—PASSING—

Washington	Atts.	Comp.	Yds.	Int.	TD
Theismann	35	16	243	2	0
Los Angeles	Atts.	Comp.	Yds.	Int.	TD
Plunkett	25	16	172	0	1

Raiders Coach Tom Flores gets the traditional victory ride.

—RECEIVING—

Washington	No.	Yds.	Lg.	TD
Didier	5	65	20	0
J. Washington	3	20	10	0
Garrett	1	17	17	0
Brown	3	93	60	0
Giaquinto	2	21	14	0
Monk	1	26	26	0
Riggins	1	1	1	0

Los Angeles	No.	Yds.	Lg.	TD
Allen	2	18	12	0
King	2	8	7	0
Christensen	4	32	14	0
Branch	6	94	50	1
Hawkins	2	20	14	0

—INTERCEPTIONS—

Washington—None

Los Angeles	No.	Yds.	Lg.	TD
Squirek	1	5	5	1
Haynes	1	0	0	0

—PUNTING—

Washington	No.	Avg.	Lg.
Hayes	7	37.0	48

Los Angeles	No.	Avg.	Lg.
Guy	7	42.7	47

—PUNT RETURNS—

Washington	No.	FC	Yds.	Lg.
Giaquinto	1	2	1	1
Green	1	0	34	34

Los Angeles	No.	FC	Yds.	Lg.
Watts	1	0	0	0
Pruitt	1	3	8	8

—KICKOFF RETURNS—

Washington	No.	Yds.	Lg.
Garrett	5	100	35
Grant	1	32	32
Kimball	1	0	0

Los Angeles	No.	Yds.	Lg.
Pruitt	1	17	17

—FIELD GOALS—

Washington	Att.	Made
Moseley	2	1

Los Angeles	Att.	Made
Bahr	1	1

—SCORING—

Washington	TD	PAT	FG	Pts.
Riggins	1	0	0	6
Moseley	0	0	1	3

Los Angeles	TD	PAT	FG	Pts.
Allen	2	0	0	12
Bahr	0	5	1	8
Branch	1	0	0	6
Jensen	1	0	0	6
Squirek	1	0	0	6

—FUMBLES—

Washington	No.	Own Rec.	Opp. Rec.	TD
G. Williams	0	0	1	0
Theismann	1	0	0	0
A. Washington	0	0	1	0

Los Angeles	No.	Own Rec.	Opp. Rec.	TD
Watts	1	0	0	0
Allen	1	0	0	0
Hannah	0	1	0	0
Branch	1	0	0	0
Martin	0	0	1	0

Super Bowl XIX

49ers Harpoon Dolphins

January 20, 1985

A stiff 49er defense turned Super Bowl XIX into a nightmare for Miami Coach Don Shula.

No question about it, this was one Super Bowl that couldn't miss.

Forget about all the past Super Bowls that had turned out to be one-sided flops; not only were the two best teams in the National Football League in 1984 matched, but so were the two best quarterbacks. Surefire box office material, this one.

You wanted points? You wanted excitement? Tune in. You wanted defense? Turn the channel.

Unfortunately, real life isn't like old-time Hollywood, where dreams come true and everyone rides off into the sunset for a happy ending. Instead of getting the drama of "Gone With the Wind" and the excitement of "Ben-Hur," the largest viewing audience in television sports history was treated to a high-budget production of "Godzilla Meets the Sea Mammals." It was a laugher.

Matinee idol Dan Marino didn't win an Oscar for his performance. Nor did the Miami Dolphin defense, which found itself vastly overmatched against a quiet guy named Joe Montana and an excellent supporting cast. The Dolphins gave more than 115 million TV viewers and 84,059 spectators at Stanford Stadium a B movie at best.

Ah, but the San Francisco 49ers. What grace, what class, what an award-winning performance. They demolished the Dolphins, 38-16, in Super Bowl XIX, and in so doing taught football fans two valuable lessons: One, even the most promising of Super Bowl matchups seldom live up to expectations, and two, defenses still hold the key to these championship games.

As good as Montana was—and he was astonishingly effective and productive—it was the 49er defense that performed the miracle of Super Bowl XIX, thereby taking the luster off Marino's rising star.

This was the same Marino who had shown absolutely no respect for the NFL's regular-season record book. A second-year quarter-

Resourceful 49ers quarterback Joe Montana scrambled the Dolphins with an MVP performance in Super Bowl XIX.

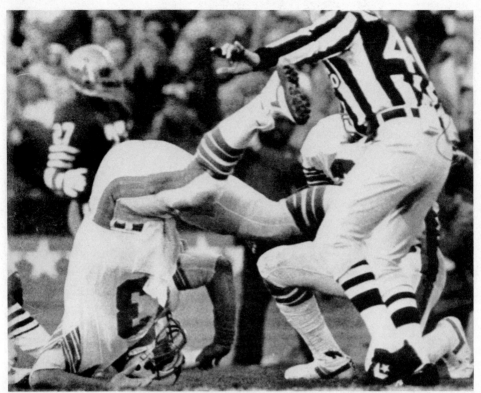

San Francisco's persistent defense made life rough for record-setting Miami quarterback Dan Marino.

back, Marino still should have been learning the game, but instead he was collecting unprecedented passing totals that pinpointed him as the best quarterback in the league.

Marino became the first player ever to throw for 5,000 yards (5,084) in a season. He shattered the NFL record for touchdown passes in a season with 48, and his 362 completions and four 400-yard games also were league records. He led the league in pass attempts, average yards per completion and efficiency rating. Entering the Super Bowl, he had passed for at least one touchdown in each of his last 22 games, including four in an overwhelming performance against Pittsburgh in the American Conference championship game.

Marino was the conductor of one of the most proficient offenses in NFL history, one that was averaging more than *four* touchdowns per game. So, it was no surprise that wherever the blond wonder boy went during Super Bowl week, he generated the kind of excitement that usually is associated with rock stars. Even the news that he was engaged failed to cool down his adoring female fans.

Stationed in Oakland, across the bay from the 49ers, the Dolphins were anything but lost amid the hometown hysteria of fans in the San Francisco area. For Montana, who is not particularly comfortable in the spotlight, it was a welcome relief to have Marino and the Dolphins capture the bulk of the pregame publicity. Yet there comes a point when enough is enough.

"You don't mind being overlooked that much, but sometimes it seemed they (reporters) forgot there were two teams in the game," Montana said. "It got to all of us after a while. But you couldn't argue with Dan's statistics. He had a great season."

The 49ers had every right to feel slighted. After all, it wasn't as if they had lucked their way into the Super Bowl. Their 15 regular-season victories constituted an NFL record, and their decisive 23-0 victory over Chicago in the National Conference title game had been impressive indeed. But there was an excitement about the Dolphins that seemed to negate anything the 49ers had accomplished.

San Francisco Coach Bill Walsh, who had spent three years reconstructing his Super Bowl XVI championship team, was not about to blow this opportunity, though. This had become a deeper, more experienced, more versatile team, and it was especially strong in two areas that Walsh deemed critical—running game and pass rush. And the 49er secondary, mostly a bunch of raw rookies in 1981, had matured into perhaps the league's best.

This wonderful 49er balance proved too much for Miami, which depended heavily on Marino not only to generate points, but also to take pressure off a defense that had struggled for much of the season.

This time, Marino couldn't save himself, much less his teammates. San Francisco turned him into a mere mortal, and a harried mortal at that. And each time that Marino was sacked or another one of his passes was batted away, it became all the more clear that another Super Bowl title would elude the Dolphins, who had been denied an NFL crown two years before by the Washington Redskins.

Montana, on the other hand, was outstanding and was named the game's Most Valuable Player, a distinction he had earned when the 49ers beat the Bengals in 1982. His 331 passing yards was a Super Bowl record, and his three touchdown passes were one off Terry Bradshaw's mark. But this multitalented athlete had another weapon, too. He was able to get outside the Dolphin pass rush, enabling him to pick up another 59 yards on the ground, which, of course, also was a record (for quarterbacks).

But every time the Dolphins tried to key on Montana, the 49ers would foul 'em up by turning to backs Wendell Tyler and Roger Craig. And they, in turn, shredded the Miami defense with their slashing runs and pass receptions.

Tyler, who had rushed for a club-record 1,262 yards in the regular season, gained 65 yards on 13 carries. Craig, a youngster from Nebraska, was even more effective, with 58 rushing yards, eight receptions for 82 yards and three touchdowns. In most years, that would have been an MVP performance.

The stunning ability of the 49ers to move the ball on the Dolphins—they gained a Super Bowl-record 537 yards—bore testimony to San Francisco's balanced attack, which was far more effective than the 49er offense had been three years before. In 1981, the 49ers could tease you with the run, but only the pass would kill you. In 1984, the run was an equally potent weapon, as the Dolphins were soon to find out.

About the only dignitary who wasn't present at Stanford Stadium on January 20, 1985, was President Reagan, but he wasn't left out entirely. Reagan, via television hookup in the White House, flipped the coin before the opening kickoff. Former 49ers halfback Hugh McElhenny helped out on the field, and San Francisco won the toss.

San Francisco immediately committed what would become one of its few mistakes. Kick returner Derrick Harmon, a rookie from Cornell, caught the opening kickoff too close to the sideline, and after trying to find his balance with both toes tickling the chalk, his momentum carried him out of bounds at the 6-yard line.

The Dolphins enjoyed the first laugh when much-maligned kicker Uwe von Schamann connected on a first-quarter field goal.

Although runs by Tyler and Craig and first-down completions to Tyler and wide receiver Dwight Clark took the 49ers to the 41, they still had to punt. Miami took over at its 36-yard line, and Marino needed only six plays, starting with an opening-down 25-yard pass to running back Tony Nathan, to put the Dolphins in position to score. Even though a third-down completion to wide receiver Mark Clayton was two yards short of a first down, it set up a 37-yard field goal by Uwe von Schamann with 7:24 left in the first quarter.

For von Schamann, that conversion was a personal triumph. He had been mired in a horrendous slump, making only two of five field goals in the playoffs and just nine of 19 in the regular season. "I certainly hope Uwe can find his range," Miami Coach Don Shula had said before the game.

Marino had made his team's first drive look so easy that even when Montana came back immediately to produce a touchdown and a 7-3 lead with 3:12 left in the period, Dolphins fans were not worried.

They should have been.

During San Francisco's eight-play, 78-yard march, Walsh revealed the basic elements of his well-conceived game plan. The 49ers wanted to take advantage of the Dolphins' linebackers, especially rookie Jay Brophy and second-year man Mark Brown on the inside, and they wanted to capitalize on what they saw as a blocking mismatch on the left side of the line, where 295-pound tackle Bubba Paris was facing 255-pound end Kim Bokamper.

"We didn't know how it would be anywhere else on the line," said Bobb McKittrick, 49ers offensive line coach, "but we definitely thought we could run behind Paris. He was just bigger and stronger than the other guy, and he should be able to win that battle."

San Francisco throws to its backs often, so it was important that the backs be able to beat the linebackers on pass coverage and continually chip away for short yardage. "We didn't intentionally set out believing that we wouldn't win without beating their linebackers," said Paul Hackett, the club's quarterbacks-receivers coach, "but it obviously worked so well for us that we kept using it until we could see if they would adjust."

On the first play of this second San Francisco possession, Montana flipped a pass behind the line to Craig, who gained six yards on coverage by outside linebacker Charles Bowser. Tyler then ran six yards for a first down. Two plays later, Tyler ran behind Paris and left guard John Ayers for six more yards and another first down at the 49er 49. After two more plays netted just three yards, Montana rolled out to his right, cut back left and scrambled 15 yards to the Miami 33, where Brown finally forced him out of bounds. This well-executed mix of plays set up the 49ers' first touchdown on the next play.

Montana rolled to his right and found reserve running back Carl Monroe free down the right sideline. His beautifully thrown pass went over Brown's head and past safety Lyle Blackwood into Monroe's arms at the 15. Monroe slipped away from Blackwood and cornerback Don McNeal and scampered into the end zone easily. Ray Wersching kicked the extra point for a 7-3 San Francisco lead.

After Marino answered with a touchdown pass of his own, this one a two-yarder to tight end Dan Johnson, it appeared that the game was shaping up as the scoring free-for-all everyone had envisioned. Three of the game's first four possessions had produced scores, and with 45 seconds to play in the first quarter, Miami was on top, 10-7. Let's see, that adds up to about 68 total points at that pace.

Marino and Shula had crossed up the 49ers by running the series of plays leading to the touchdown with hardly a huddle. The tactic was not unexpected—there had been reports all week that Miami would do it—but the ploy still worked.

The 49ers like to shuffle players in and out according to the circumstances of each down,

but the Dolphins' hurry-up tactics kept defensive coordinator George Seifert from making frequent replacements. That meant pass-rushing specialists Fred Dean and Gary (Big Hands) Johnson had to stay on the bench much of that time, taking pressure off Marino.

Marino certainly seemed unstoppable. After Nathan went up the middle for five yards to his 35-yard line on the first play of the drive, Marino completed five straight passes, including 18- and 13-yard bullets to Clayton, an 11-yarder to wide receiver Mark Duper and a 21-yarder to Johnson, who was tackled by linebacker Dan Bunz at the 49er 2-yard line. Johnson caught Marino's next pass in the right half of the end zone to give Miami its last lead of the game.

Clayton and Duper, or the Marks Brothers, as they have come to be known, had been conducting a weeklong gab session across the bay with the 49er secondary, especially cornerback Ronnie Lott. At one point, Clayton exclaimed: "All I'm hearing about is Ronnie Lott, Ronnie Lott. He's not on a pedestal, you know. He takes chances, and he can be beat. We aren't bad, either."

They certainly weren't. Although Clayton and Duper, both of whom check in at 5-foot-9, are relative midgets in this big man's game, they had whittled secondaries down to size all season. Clayton, a second-year man from Louisville, had caught 73 regular-season passes, including an NFL-record 18 TD receptions. And he did it without the speed of Duper, a former world-class sprinter who had made 71 catches.

They were matched, however, against the most aggressive secondary in the league, one that earned its many accolades, which included a trip for all four starting backs to the 1985 Pro Bowl in Honolulu. "We certainly are going to make sure they know we are there," said Lott, a tough hitter who finally had gotten over a bunch of injuries and was healthy for the first time since the opening game.

Shula had figured that if Miami's aerial threat could force the 49ers into using their nickel (five defensive back) alignment exclusively, he could generate a running game, just as the Dolphins had in a playoff game against a six-back Seattle formation. Instead, the 49ers soon found that their nickel defense had all the answers to neutralize both the runners and Marino.

"It all started from up front, with the line," said Keena Turner, who shared linebacker duties in the nickel with rookie Jeff Fuller. "Once they got pressure on Marino, he couldn't wait as long to throw, and we could do a better job of coverage."

Marino had been sacked only 13 times in the regular season and not once in the playoffs. Given enough time, he hardly seemed bothered by defensive sets that featured six and seven backs. But the 49ers' pass rush changed

Roger Craig was an offensive force for the 49ers. The youngster from Nebraska scored one of his three touchdowns (above) after taking an eight-yard pass from quarterback Joe Montana in the second period and made a circus catch (left) of a Montana pass in the first quarter.

all that in the Super Bowl; Marino was dropped a career-high four times even though the 49ers blitzed on just a handful of occasions.

It was the defensive front four that wore down Miami's fine offensive line. Dean, one of the league's premier pass rushers, usually is a spot player for the 49ers, but he stayed in the game longer than usual as part of the nickel personnel package. He teamed with Johnson, his former San Diego teammate who had been acquired in a September trade, to torment Marino.

Seifert helped by putting in some new line stunts for the game. They were designed to put pressure on center Dwight Stephenson, Miami's best lineman. "We had to tie him up on every play so we could go right up the middle on Marino," Johnson said, adding that the 49ers weren't concerned about any scrambling from the weak-kneed quarterback.

By playing a lineman directly in front of Stephenson or setting a defender just to the right or left of the Miami center and then slanting him inside, the 49ers forced Stephenson into a double-team situation. He no longer was able, as normal, to roam and help out other teammates on pass protection. That left the rest of the 49er linemen in one-on-one battles, which they won enough times to put good pressure on Marino.

"You could see him getting rattled out there," said Johnson, a former All-Pro who benefited greatly from Dean's late-season return after an 11-week contract holdout. "Marino would throw away passes or he would talk more than usual to his linemen. We could see we were getting to him, but you'd be upset, too, if you were getting hit a lot."

Going into the game, the 49ers had marked the need to harass Marino without blitzing as a key to their defensive success. Such a situation would allow them to drop more players into pass coverage. They never dreamed they'd be so effective.

"Sometimes I didn't throw the ball well, sometimes I didn't have time and sometimes guys didn't get open," a disgusted Marino said. "They played the best any team has played against us defensively. They took us out of our scheme, I think. We knew what we had to do—we had to throw the ball against a four-man line—and we didn't."

Instead, the four-man line stymied him while also shutting off the Dolphins' feeble running game, which had its lowest output of the year (25 yards). Marino was forced to throw 50 passes, completing 29—both Super Bowl records—but his 318 yards in the air, though quite respectable, was his second-lowest total of his last six games, and much of that yardage came in the fourth quarter when the 49ers eased into their "prevent" mode. Only one other time in the season had he been limited to just one TD pass.

Clayton, who said after the game that he had been sick, caught six passes for 92 yards. Nathan made 10 catches for 83 yards. Duper was limited to only one catch. Marino was having problems dissecting San Francisco's ever-changing blend of defensive coverages. "We are mainly a zone team, but we played more man than we usually do," safety Carlton Williamson said.

"We 'collisioned' them (Miami receivers) off the line," safety Dwight Hicks said. "That gave the line lots of time to rush." Marino particularly had trouble when the 49ers played man-to-man with four defensive backs and then kept two safeties in a deep zone.

In short, Marino ran out of miracles. He frequently forced the ball, causing his passes to fall short or long of his receivers or in the arms of the 49ers, who intercepted two of his passes and batted away several more.

Even though the 49er cornerbacks often dropped eight yards off the line, this quick-strike Miami offense, which relies so heavily on its receivers to get open deep, was limited to only one completion of 30 yards and just three other catches of more than 20 yards.

"He didn't have time to look us off his receiver," Hicks said. "He was getting too much pressure from our line. If he tried to go to another receiver, he would have to unload it in a hurry. We just told the line that we'd cover just tight enough to give them extra time to get in on him. We didn't care if he completed anything short. We weren't going to get beat with short passes."

The game turned on a stretch starting early in the second period and ending three Miami possessions later. In that span of 11 minutes, 55 seconds, the Dolphins had no first downs and only one net yard of offense, and Marino completed just one of six passes. San Francisco, meanwhile, scored three touchdowns in that span as its offense, led by an almost-flawless Montana, steadily improved.

The success of the 49er offense did not come as a surprise. The Miami defense, directed by ex-San Francisco coordinator Chuck Studley, had been lacking all season.

"After looking at the films," McKittrick said, "we said, 'This is a Super Bowl defense?' It's unusual for a one-dimensional team to make it to the Super Bowl, but Miami was unusual."

The Dolphins tied with the Oilers and Vikings as the league's worst defensive team against the run (4.7 yards per attempt). "We could see in the films we could run against them," McKittrick said.

The films also showed the 49ers that Miami had a soft pass rush, going with its three-man front while the other eight players dropped back in zones. Often times, they wouldn't even look back at Montana to see if he was running. And running backs coming out of the backfield often were wide open.

Running back Carl Monroe opened the 49er scoring when he took a 33-yard Joe Montana pass into the end zone and celebrated with a good spike.

It had been Studley's plan to let the 49ers peck away with short passes while protecting against the deeper pass. But that scheme played right into the hands of Walsh, who was perfectly happy to take those controlled throws and dominate the Dolphins with steady gains.

"Bill had his game plan in surprisingly early," Clark said. "We just had a lot of time to perfect it. Everything that was open on film was open in the game, especially out patterns and stuff underneath for the backs."

Studley and Walsh used to car pool to work in San Francisco, and Studley thought, "I probably know Bill as well as any man." But no matter how much he knew about Walsh's strategies, he still couldn't protect Brophy and Brown, his young inside linebackers, from Tyler and Craig (who caught 12 passes between them), and he couldn't help the weak pass rush of his front three unless he blitzed more. And the more he blitzed, the more Montana feasted on the pass defense.

Montana used play-action fakes to keep the Dolphins—especially the linebackers—off-balance all afternoon. It became a textbook display, almost as easy as working against the scout team in practice.

The 49ers began to mesh for good early in the second period after a 37-yard punt by Reggie Roby was downed at the Miami 47-yard line. Montana scrambled for 19 yards, then threw to Clark, his favorite target, for 16 yards to the Miami 12. Two plays later, Craig ran a curl over the middle after it had been cleared out by tight end Russ Francis, caught Montana's pass at the 3 and skipped past Brophy into the end zone for an eight-yard touchdown, giving San Francisco a 14-10 lead (with Wersching's kick).

Roby again had to punt, and his 40-yard kick was returned 28 yards by Dana McLemore to the 49er 45. Tyler immediately tried the right side for nine yards, and Craig ran left for six. Montana then threw to a wide-open Francis for completions of 10 and 19 yards and a first down at the 11. Craig ran over right guard for five yards before Montana spotted a blitz, saw a hole inside and scrambled up the middle six yards for a touchdown. Wersching's third extra-point conversion extended San Francisco's lead to 21-10.

Miami answered with a third straight Roby punt, which McLemore returned to the 49er 48-yard line. Following a five-yard sack by end Doug Betters, Montana threw against a blitz

Dan Johnson's two-yard touchdown pass (left) from Dan Marino lifted Miami into a 10-7 first-quarter lead, but the Dolphins' fortunes had changed by the fourth quarter, as evidenced by the expression on defensive end Doug Betters' face (right).

for 20 yards to Craig, who eluded Brophy's tackle. Montana continued to display his scrambling skills, running seven yards around right end before Brown forced him out of bounds. The officials ruled that wide receiver Freddie Solomon dropped Montana's pass on the next play, but TV replays indicated that Solomon caught and then fumbled the ball, which the Dolphins recovered. Nevertheless, Tyler then broke around left end for nine yards and another first down. Two more plays gave the 49ers a first and goal at the 5. Tyler carried the ball for three yards, and Craig then plowed in behind Tyler from the 2 for a 28-10 advantage with 2:05 left.

That's how the half should have ended. But Marino suddenly regained his accuracy and unleashed a fine two-minute drill that included seven completions. A 30-yard pass to tight end Joe Rose put the ball at the 49er 12, where the drive stalled. Two incomplete passes and a one-yard loss on a completion to Nathan followed, bringing on von Schamann, who kicked a 31-yard field goal with 12 seconds on the clock.

Even after that 72-yard drive, Miami wasn't finished yet. On the ensuing kickoff, guard Guy McIntyre picked up a bouncing ball and obviously didn't want to run with it. "I knew better," he said. But a couple of teammates urged him to run, and he started upfield, which was a

mistake. He quickly was blasted by Joe Carter and fumbled, with Jim Jensen recovering the ball for Miami at the 49er 12. With 4 seconds remaining, von Schamann nonchalantly converted another field goal, this one from 30 yards, to close the gap to 28-16 at the half.

Whatever inspiration that turn of events gave Miami was quickly doused on the first series of the third quarter, when Marino was sacked by end Dwaine Board for a nine-yard loss on third down. San Francisco responded with a 43-yard drive that set up a 27-yard Wersching field goal and gave the 49ers a 31-16 lead.

From then on, it became a matter of how many points San Francisco wanted to score. After Miami's next possession, on which two sacks of Marino put the Dolphins back on their original line of scrimmage and forced yet another Roby punt, the 49ers tallied for the last time. Starting at his own 30-yard line, Montana hit Tyler over the middle for a 40-yard gain and followed that with a 14-yarder to Francis. Three plays later, Montana threw a 16-yard TD pass to Craig. Wersching's extra point gave the 49ers their final margin of 38-16.

Interceptions thwarted the Dolphins' next two drives. Cornerback Eric Wright nabbed Marino's pass for Clayton at the 49er 1-yard line in the third quarter, and Williamson picked off a pass intended for Rose in the end

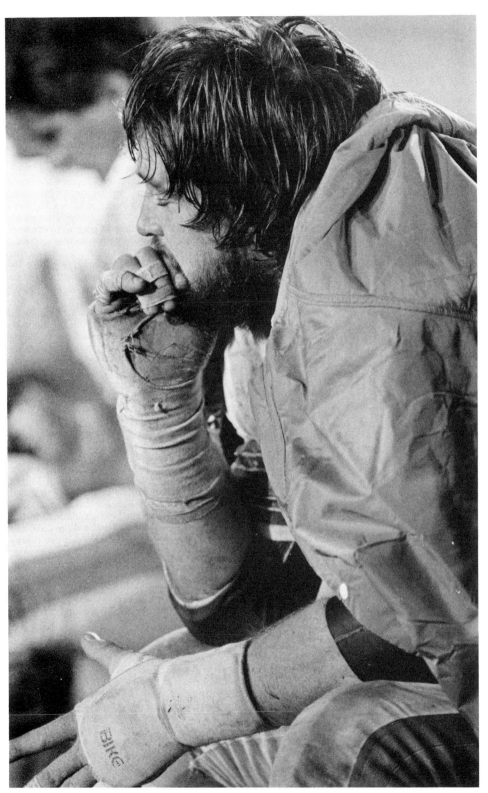

Defensive back Eric Wright hugs 49er Owner Edward DeBartolo Jr. as the final seconds tick away in Super Bowl XIX.

today, no question."

Walsh went further. "He is clearly the best quarterback in football today and maybe the best in many years," he said. "He is Number 1 in leadership, assertiveness, and he has those quick feet."

Montana is merely the NFL career leader in completion and interception percentage and overall passing rating. But he had thrown five interceptions in the first two playoff games, a statistic that clearly had San Francisco coaches worried.

They needn't have been concerned. Montana wreaked havoc on the Dolphins with both his arm and his legs, rushing for 59 yards and completing 24 of 35 passes for 331 yards, three touchdowns and no interceptions. His feel for pressure and his ability to pick out receivers on the run left the Dolphins drained and frustrated.

"We knew we had to contain him, but we couldn't," McNeal said. "You'd look up and he would be running around. They dictated to us; we never could dictate to them."

The loss was especially bitter for Shula, who had mentioned frequently during the playoffs that all of his team's accomplishments during the regular season would be tarnished by a Super Bowl defeat. Of course, he never imagined a trouncing of this magnitude.

"This is going to be tough to live with during the off-season," Shula said. "Offensively, it was our poorest game of the year. We were stopped today."

Even the game's lone controversial play—and the one that appeared to damage Miami most—was shrugged off by Shula. That was the second-quarter play when Solomon appeared to have caught a pass on the Dolphin 13 and then fumbled the ball after taking a step and being hit by Lyle Blackwood. Blackwood picked up the ball and was on his way to the end zone when a whistle blew and the pass was ruled incomplete. The 49ers scored five downs later.

"We were dominated to the point where one play didn't make much of a difference," Shula said.

His players realized that, too. "The 49ers drilled us," Betters said. "Nobody ever did what they did to us."

Walsh, who felt tremendous pressure to repeat in the years following Super Bowl XVI felt nothing but elation after winning his second NFL title.

"This is truly the greatest moment of my career," he said. "And this was the best game we ever played since I joined the 49ers."

And one other thing: "Maybe this will prove," he said, "the merits of playing with a two-dimensional offense rather than relying on a one-dimensional attack."

After the 49ers' brilliant performance in Super Bowl XIX, who could argue?

zone in the final period. The latter interception immediately followed a break for Miami when McLemore fumbled a fair catch and Vince Heflin recovered for the Dolphins at the 49er 21.

San Francisco ate up the clock on its final two drives, and the game ended as Marino recovered his own fumbled snap on a last, futile drive to the end zone.

Montana and his largely unsung comrades had thoroughly embarrassed the media darling Dolphins.

"Joe will never say it, but it's understandable that with all the talk about Marino he would like to do well," said Clark, Montana's best friend. "The talk pushed him. I know I am prejudiced, but he is the best quarterback around

One optimistic 49er fan had the Super Bowl XIX scenario mapped out from the beginning and obviously enjoyed his journalistic scoop.

Statistics of 19th Super Bowl
SAN FRANCISCO 38, MIAMI 16

Stanford Stadium, Palo Alto, Calif., January 20, 1985
Attendance: 84,059

MIAMI	Offense	SAN FRANCISCO
Mark Duper	WR	Dwight Clark
Jon Giesler	LT	Bubba Paris
Roy Foster	LG	John Ayers
Dwight Stephenson	C	Fred Quillan
Ed Newman	RB	Randy Cross
Cleveland Green	RT	Keith Fahnhorst
Bruce Hardy	TE	Russ Francis
Mark Clayton	WR	Freddie Solomon
Dan Marino	QB	Joe Montana
Tony Nathan	RB	Wendell Tyler
Woody Bennett	FB	Roger Craig

	Defense	
Doug Betters	LE	Lawrence Pillers
Bob Baumhower	NT	Manu Tuiasosopo
Kim Bokamper	RE	Dwaine Board
Bob Brudzinski	LLB	Dan Bunz
Jay Brophy	ILB	Riki Ellison
Mark Brown	ILB	Jack Reynolds
Charles Bowser	RLB	Keena Turner
Don McNeal	LCB	Ronnie Lott
William Judson	RCB	Eric Wright
Glenn Blackwood	SS	Carlton Williamson
Lyle Blackwood	FS	Dwight Hicks

SUBSTITUTIONS

MIAMI—Offense: Receivers—Jimmy Cefalo, Vince Heflin, Dan Johnson, Nat Moore, Joe Rose. Linemen—Steve Clark, Ronnie Lee, Jeff Toews. Backs—Joe Carter, Eddie Hill, Jim Jensen, Don Strock. Kicker—Uwe von Schamann. Defense: Linebackers—A.J. Duhe, Earnie Rhone, Jackie Shipp, Sanders Shiver. Linemen—Bill Barnett, Charles Benson, Mike Charles. Backs—Bud Brown, Mike Kozlowski, Paul Lankford, Robert Sowell, Fulton Walker. Punter—Reggie Roby. DNP—Pete Johnson.

SAN FRANCISCO—Offense: Receivers—Earl Cooper, Renaldo Nehemiah, Mike Wilson. Linemen—Allan Kennedy, Guy McIntyre, Billy Shields. Backs—Derrick Harmon, Carl Monroe, Bill Ring. Kicker—Ray Wesching. Defense: Linebackers—Milt McColl, Blanchard Montgomery, Todd Shell, Mike Walter. Linemen—Michael Carter, Fred Dean, Gary Johnson, Louie Kelcher, Jeff Stover, Jim Stuckey. Backs—Jeff Fuller, Tom Holmoe, Dana McLemore. Punter—Max Runager. DNP—Matt Cananaugh, Mario Clark, John Frank.

— SCORE BY PERIODS —

Miami Dolphins (AFC)	10	6	0	0	— 16
San Francisco 49ers (NFC)	7	21	10	0	— 38

— SCORING —

Miami—Field goal von Schamann 37.
San Francisco—Monroe 33 pass from Montana (Wersching kick).
Miami—D. Johnson 2 pass from Marino (von Schamann kick).
San Francisco—Craig 8 pass from Montana (Wersching kick).
San Francisco—Montana 6 run (Wersching kick).
San Francisco—Craig 2 run (Wersching kick).
Miami—Field goal von Schamann 31.
Miami—Field goal von Schamann 30.
San Francisco—Field goal Wersching 27.
San Francisco—Craig 16 pass from Montana (Wersching kick).

— TEAM STATISTICS —

	Miami	San Fran.
Total First Downs	19	31
First Downs Rushing	2	16
First Downs Passing	17	15
First Downs Penalty	0	0
Rushes	9	40
Yards Gained Rushing (net)	25	211
Average Yards per Rush	2.8	5.3
Passes Attempted	50	35
Passes Completed	29	24
Had Intercepted	2	0
Times Tackled Attempt. Pass	4	1
Yards Lost Attempting Pass	29	5
Yards Gained Passing (net)	289	326
Total Net Yardage	314	537
Total Offensive Plays	63	76
Avg. Gain per Offensive Play	5.0	7.1
Punts	6	3
Average Distance	39.3	32.7
Punt Returns	2	5
Punt Return Yardage	15	51
Kickoff Returns	7	4
Kickoff Return Yardage	140	40
Interceptions Return Yardage	0	0
Fumbles	1	2
Opp. Fumbles Recovered	2	0
Total Return Yardage	155	91
Penalties	1	2
Yards Penalized	10	10
Total Points Scored	16	38
Touchdowns	1	5
Touchdowns	0	2
Touchdowns Passing	1	3
Touchdowns on Returns	0	0
Extra Points	1	5
Field Goals Attempted	3	1
Field Goals	3	1
Time of Possession	22:49	37:11

—INDIVIDUAL STATISTICS—
—RUSHING—

Miami	Atts.	Yds.	Lg.	TD
Bennett	3	7	7	0
Nathan	5	18	16	0
Marino	1	0	0	0

San Francisco	Atts.	Yds.	Lg.	TD
Tyler	13	65	9	0
Craig	15	58	10	1
Montana	5	59	19	1
Harn	5	20	7	0
Cooper	1	4	4	0
Solomon	1	5	5	0

—PASSING—

Miami	Atts.	Comp.	Yds.	Int.	TD
Marino	50	29	318	2	1

San Francisco	Atts.	Comp.	Yds.	Int.	TD
Montana	35	24	331	0	3

—RECEIVING—

Miami	No.	Yds.	Lg.	TD
Nathan	10	83	25	0
D. Johnson	3	28	21	1
Clayton	6	92	27	0
Duper	1	11	11	0
Rose	6	73	30	0
Moore	2	17	9	0
Cefalo	1	14	14	0

Savoring the moment in the 49er locker room after Super Bowl XIX were Coach Bill Walsh, MVP Joe Montana and Owner Edward DeBartolo Jr.

San Francisco	No.	Yds.	Lg.	TD
Tyler	4	70	40	0
D. Clark	6	77	33	0
Craig	7	77	20	2
Monroe	1	33	33	1
Francis	5	60	19	0
Solomon	1	14	14	0

—INTERCEPTIONS—

Miami-1—None.

San Francisco	No.	Yds.	Lg.	TD
Wright	1	0	0	0
Williamson	1	0	0	0

—PUNTING—

Miami	No.	Avg.	Lg.
Roby	6	39.3	0

San Francisco	No.	Avg.	Lg.
Runager	3	32.7	0

—PUNT RETURNS—

Miami	No.	FC	Yds.	Lg.
Walker	2	0	15	9

San Francisco	No.	FC	Yds.	Lg.
McLemore	5	0	51	28

—KICKOFF RETURNS—

Miami	No.	Yds.	Lg.
Hardy	2	31	16
Walker	4	93	28
Hill	1	16	16

San Francisco	No.	Yds.	Lg.
Harmon	2	24	23
Monroe	1	16	16
McIntyre	1	0	0

—FIELD GOALS—

Miami	Att.	Made
Von Schamann	3	3

San Francisco	Att.	Made
Wersching	1	1

—SCORING—

Miami	TD	PAT	FG	Pts.
von Schamann	0	1	3	10
D. Johnson	1	0	0	6

San Francisco	TD	PAT	FG	Pts.
Craig	3	0	0	18
Wersching	0	5	1	8
Monroe	1	0	0	6
Montana	1	0	0	6

—FUMBLES—

Miami	No.	Own Rec.	Opp. Rec.	TD
Jensen	0	0	1	0
Marino	1	1	0	0
Heflin	0	0	1	0

San Francisco	No.	Own Rec.	Opp. Rec.	TD
McIntyre	1	0	0	0
McLemore	1	0	0	0

Super Bowl XX

The Hungry Bears Roar

January 26, 1986

Quarterback Jim McMahon and his Chicago teammates growled and manhandled the helpless Patriots in Super Bowl XX.

When the great teams in Super Bowl history are recalled, the Chicago Bears of Super Bowl XX certainly will be given a lofty spot on the list.

Rarely has any Super Bowl champion played with such intensity, power and emotion. And seldom has any Super Bowl winner had so much fun doing what comes naturally.

Even before the Bears had demolished the outclassed New England Patriots, 46-10, before an awed sellout crowd at the Louisiana Superdome in New Orleans, their defense already was being compared to some of the National Football League's all-time best. By the end of the game, the question became: What other defense has been better, especially in the last 20 years or so?

But for all the Bears' marvelous on-field talents, their off-field antics proved even more captivating. In an age of sports in which individuality seems outdated or unwanted, the Chicago players proved to be the freest of free spirits.

Imagine, for example, Vince Lombardi's Green Bay Packers being so bold as to record something called "The Super Bowl Shuffle" weeks before they even qualified for the game. The Bears did just that, and this music video became a best seller even outside Chicago.

And what about those wonderful nicknames and all those folk-hero figures, such as William (The Refrigerator) Perry, Walter (Sweetness) Payton, defensive tackle Dan Hampton and quarterback Jim McMahon, the closest the NFL has to a true punk rocker. The Bears always had a mystique, even in their inept days. This team, though, rekindled the old Monsters of the Midway image, growing more bold off the field and stronger on the field every week, until the Bears made a shambles of the NFL playoffs.

And, with one mighty Super Bowl victory, all the pent-up emotion of both a driven team and a snake-bitten city was uncorked. This was the

Super Bowl XX MVP Richard Dent (95) and teammate Dan Hampton hover over fallen New England quarterback Tony Eason in the first quarter.

climax of a five-month athletic high for a city that had known little but athletic heartbreak for so long. No one could blame the fans for dancing down Michigan Avenue, not after all the disappointment they had endured over the years at the hands of the Cubs and White Sox and Black Hawks and Bulls. The Bears, bless 'em, didn't let Chicagoans down this time. They mended all those broken hearts with an afternoon of glory and fury.

Nothing about the Bears seemed normal. Their coach, Mike Ditka, wore a tie on the sidelines so he would curb a temper that once provoked him to break his hand punching a blackboard. Their defensive coach, Buddy Ryan, almost matter-of-factly predicted what his vaunted "46" defense would do to opposing offenses—and then usually was shockingly accurate. The Chicago players thought nothing of bragging about their talents, and Ditka warned them only "to back up what you say by playing right on the field." He need not have worried.

Never were the Bears bolder or more bizarre than in the days preceding Super Bowl XX. Want to see a Bear? Try Bourbon Street after dark. "I know I was getting back to the hotel at 2 or 3 in the morning," guard Tom Thayer said. Want to know what the Bears were going to do to New England in the title game? Just ask linebacker Otis Wilson, who saw that there had never been a shutout in Super Bowl history, so he predicted one for his club.

In the midst of all this outrageousness stood quarterback McMahon. Probably not since the Super Bowl III presence of another outrageous personality, Joe Namath, has one man so dominated the NFL's premier event. McMahon came into the week riding a high, anyway, following a playoff controversy with, of all people, NFL Commissioner Pete Rozelle. It seems McMahon likes to wear head bands under his helmet, which is permitted under league rules. But McMahon added his own touch when his head band was dominated by the word, "Adidas." Can't do that, said the NFL. So McMahon was fined, and he answered back by wearing a head band saying, "Rozelle." Even the commissioner had to laugh.

McMahon then showed up in New Orleans with a sore rear end, courtesy of a hard hit in the NFC championship game against the Los Angeles Rams. He wanted an acupuncturist, Hiroshi Shiriashi, to give him treatments. The Bears refused, saying the team's medical staff could handle it. But by midweek, when McMahon hadn't responded to treatments and wasn't practicing, the Chicago hierarchy got the point and relented. Shiriashi went to work with his magic fingers and McMahon showed miraculous progress.

But there's more. One day at practice, McMahon mooned a helicopter flying overhead. Then a New Orleans sportscaster reported falsely that McMahon had made highly disparaging remarks about New Orleans women to a Chicago radio station and that he had insulted the city's men as well. Before everything was straightened out—McMahon had said no such things and the TV reporter had never verified anything—the Bears' hotel was being picketed by upset New Orleans residents. Even McMahon, whose social behavior has been unconventional since he began drinking beer in public while attending no-alcohol-allowed Brigham Young University, couldn't believe the whole episode.

"I know that some of the Patriots took offense at what we were saying," safety Gary Fencik said after the game. "They thought we felt superior to them. I guess now they know why we had reason to believe that."

The best the Patriots could come up with, headline-wise, was a small outbreak of the flu, which especially affected quarterback Tony Eason. Eason hardly practiced the last few days before the game, although he wound up starting. As it turned out, staying ill might have been a better idea than facing the mighty Bears.

Still, New England was puzzled by all the publicity surrounding the Bears. "I don't understand it," Patriots guard Ron Wooten said. "We're America's team, the Patriots, red, white and blue. They are the Russian mascot, the Bear. Who do you think President Reagan will be rooting for?"

The President's rooting interests aside, it's hard to conceive of any team dominating an opponent more than the Bears dominated New England. The largest television audience in history—for *any* event, sports or otherwise—witnessed one of those rare, magical moments when a truly gifted team peaks at just the right time.

New England couldn't match the Bears' ability, but the Patriots hardly were swiss cheese, either. Qualifying for the playoffs as a wild-card team, they had made NFL history by carving out three straight road playoff victories to get to the Super Bowl. They had found a winning formula: a low-risk, high-powered offense, an opportunistic defense and some great special-teams play. All the elements had been molded by Coach Raymond Berry, whose low-key style seemed just the correct approach for a team that over the years had repeatedly failed to live up to its potential.

"We got tired of always being branded as the great underachievers in the league," cornerback Raymond Clayborn said. "It's great to actually live up to expectations, or even exceed them for a change."

Whatever expectations the Patriots had in Super Bowl XX were doused by the end of the first quarter. What could they do against a Bear team primed and ready for a superb performance?

The Patriots got the early jump, forcing Walter Payton to fumble (above) on his second carry of the game. New England's Larry McGrew recovers (below) to set up a Patriot field goal.

Running back Matt Suhey dives across the goal line for the first of Chicago's five-touchdown blitz.

Besides, New England didn't even know what had happened the night before the game. The Chicago defense had its usual meeting, and Ryan got up to talk. It had been reported that he probably would become coach of the Philadelphia Eagles, and now he gave what the players interpreted as a farewell address. He told them, win or lose, "you'll always be my heroes." He was near tears when he finished, and there weren't many dry eyes in the house. After Ryan left the room, tackle Steve McMichael picked up a chair and threw it against the blackboard. If only Eason had known.

Eason wound up making history in Super Bowl XX, but it certainly wasn't anything he wants to remember. By the time he was replaced in the second quarter by veteran Steve Grogan, Eason had been all but driven back to Foxboro, Mass., by Chicago's unrelenting defense. He tried six passes and completed none. No previous starting Super Bowl quarterback had failed to complete a pass.

Whatever chance the Patriots had revolved around Eason, a third-year player from Illinois who began the season as a starter, then got

hurt and lost his job to Grogan, only to regain it when Grogan in turn was injured. Eason had been a pivotal part of New England's run to the Super Bowl, not throwing an interception in the first three playoff games. But he also had been asked to attempt just 42 passes; Berry wisely had based his offense on a lot of runs and a few well-timed passes.

But now the opponent was Chicago, not Miami or the Los Angeles Raiders. You don't run on the Bears, something Berry recognized in his game plan. In beating both the New York Giants and the Los Angeles Rams in the playoffs, the Bears had allowed just 118 yards rushing and no points. The Rams' Eric Dickerson, who had picked up 248 yards against the Dallas Cowboys the previous week, squeezed out 46 yards rushing against the Bears. But, of course, few offenses had done much to Chicago all season. Ditka's team led the league in both total and rushing defense and was third in passing defense. And 13 of the Bears' 18 opponents had scored 10 or fewer points.

"If we play our defense right, no one can run on us," said Wilson, reflecting on the "46" alignment that presented extraordinary one-on-one blocking problems for the opposition. "No bragging intended. I'm telling it like it is."

Berry must have been listening. "I wanted to come out throwing," Berry said. "I wanted to get their attention." Berry also knew that Miami, the only team to defeat Chicago all season, had carved out its triumph by passing. Of course, the Dolphins had Dan Marino and a pass-oriented offense; the Patriots had to change their entire offensive personality to conform to Berry's thinking.

"I'm not saying it's right or wrong, but they went away from what got them here and that is difficult to do this late in the year," Bears linebacker Mike Singletary said. Added Fencik: "They aren't the great passing team and they showed why in this game."

Maybe, just maybe, things might have been different for both Eason and his team if his first two passes had produced better endings. His first attempt came after Chicago had made a major blunder. On the game's second play, McMahon called the wrong play in the huddle and sent Payton over the weak side instead of the strong side. Payton, without proper blocking, was smacked by linebacker Don Blackmon. The ball came loose and linebacker Larry McGrew recovered at the Chicago 19.

Eason immediately dropped back after giving two play-action fakes. He lofted a pass toward tight end Lin Dawson, who was open. But Dawson tore a ligament as he was running and couldn't catch up to the ball. He was out of the game and the Patriots faced second down.

Eason again passed, this time toward wide receiver Stanley Morgan, who had cut across the middle at the goal line. Just as the ball reached Morgan, Singletary reached out and grazed the pass. "I didn't know if it was enough to deflect it or not," he said. Morgan still should have caught it, but he couldn't hang on, costing New England a sure touchdown. The Patriots finally had to settle for a 36-yard field goal by Tony Franklin and a 3-0 lead 79 seconds into in the game.

New England's last golden chance came minutes later, when McMahon's first-down pass from his 31 hit Blackmon in the chest. "I turned and didn't react quick enough to catch it," said Blackmon, who was covering tight end Emery Moorehead. If Blackmon had held on, he had a clear path to the Chicago end zone.

It could have been a 14-point New England lead. Instead, it was the Patriots' last gasp—and the game wasn't even old enough for the players to have worked up a sweat.

After the Blackmon drop, McMahon again passed, this time toward a streaking Willie Gault, who beat cornerback Ronnie Lippett for a 43-yard gain to the New England 23. The drive bogged down, but Chicago tied the score on a 28-yard field goal by Kevin Butler with 9:20 left in the first quarter.

The Bears' defense continued to play havoc with opposing quarterbacks, as New England signal callers Tony Eason (above) and Steve Grogan (below) would gladly attest. Grogan (below) was tackled by Henry Waechter for a fourth-quarter safety.

Two of Chicago's most visible stars, William Perry (left) and Jim McMahon (right), got into the scoring column with short Super Bowl runs.

"The Patriot defensive backs were a bunch of lookers," Gault said. "We noticed they always tried to cheat a little and look into the backfield to see what was going on. We wanted to take advantage of that as much as we could."

From that moment on, the game became an ordeal for New England. "It was embarrassing," Clayborn said. "I thought we would play better."

Just consider the Patriots' next three possessions: two imcomplete passes, a 10-yard sack and a punt; a Craig James rush for no gain, Eason being sacked by Richard Dent and Wilber Marshall and then fumbling, with the Bears recovering at the New England 13; James getting hit by Dent and losing the ball, with Hampton recovering at the Patriots' 13.

That meant New England had tried nine plays, lost 22 yards, given up two sacks and lost two fumbles. And it got worse for the Patriots.

Chicago had punted on its second possession. But after Eason's fumble, the Bears took the lead for good. An eight-yard pass to Moorehead moved the ball to the Patriots' 5. Then, on a second-and-goal play from the 3, Ditka sent in Perry, the 305-pound-plus Refrigerator who had captivated the country with his size, athletic ability and genial manner. This overweight rookie had become an offensive star thanks to his goal-line heroics during the season, but had been restricted to defense during the playoffs. But now Ditka put in a new wrinkle. Perry started on a sweep around right end, then pulled up and thought about passing. He couldn't find anyone open and finally was buried for a one-yard loss.

Chicago wound up with a 24-yard field goal and a 6-3 lead, and the Bears' offense had given notice that it wasn't going to be conservative in this one.

"I played it too close to the vest sometimes," said Ditka, referring to his offensive play-calling during the regular season. With two weeks to prepare for the Super Bowl, he changed his habits. He wound up throwing all types of reverses and misdirection plays at the Patriots, and even had McMahon run a veer option at the goal line.

"We had a great game plan," Chicago center

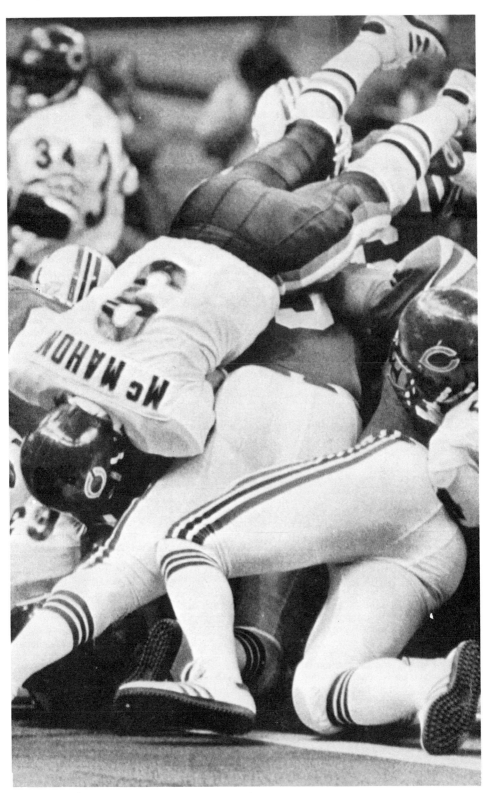

The Chicago defense made it into the scoring column when defensive back Reggie Phillips returned an interception 28 yards for a touchdown.

own game, creating six takeaways while losing the ball just twice. The Bear defense even scored twice, on a 28-yard interception return by Reggie Phillips and a safety by Henry Waechter.

New England's second turnover, caused by Dent's hit on James, set up the Bears' first touchdown. "It should never have happened," Patriots tackle Brian Holloway said of the bobble. "We should have called an audible and gotten out of the play." Eason wondered about that statement. "We never made plans to call an audible in that situation," he said.

With Payton acting as a very high-priced decoy, Matt Suhey rushed twice, the second time cutting around right end and past the overpursuing Patriot defense to score from 11 yards out. New England, which had minus 21 total yards at that point, trailed by a 13-3 score after Butler added the conversion kick.

McMahon, who finished the day with 256 yards passing on 12 completions in 20 attempts, was just warming up. He survived a vicious hit by Lippett in the first quarter to give a Most Valuable Player-type performance, even if Dent won that award on a vote of writers and broadcasters. McMahon drove Chicago 59 yards for its second touchdown, completing the march with that veer-option run from the 2. He had a 24-yard completion to Suhey in the same possession, then a 29-yarder to receiver Ken Margerum to set up a 24-yard Butler field goal as time ran out in the half.

Butler's late kick shouldn't have counted. With 21 seconds left in the second quarter, McMahon had scrambled to the New England 3. With the clock running out, Hilgenberg snapped the ball before referee Red Cashion had put it back into play. While the Bears were penalized for delay of game, NFL rules dictate that such a deliberate clock-stopping attempt in the final 2 minutes calls for a 10-second run-off from the clock. That would have left Chicago with no time to kick the field goal.

But ultimately, the botched-up play didn't affect the game's outcome. McMahon took care of that by driving the Bears 96 yards in nine plays the first time they had the ball in the third quarter. He burned New England with a 60-yard first-down pass to Gault from his end zone.

"He (McMahon) came into the huddle and said if we ran the play right, it was a touchdown," Gault said. "I got behind (safety) Fred Marion but I had to wait for the ball." McMahon had used a play fake to throw his opponents off stride.

"McMahon put a lot of critics to rest," said Ditka, who hadn't always been a McMahon fan himself. "He's our trigger man and I love him."

If nothing else, McMahon set a Super Bowl record for number of head bands worn during a game. Each one had a different lettering, and most reflected charitable causes. But New

Wally Hilgenberg said. "We especially kept them off balance with our play-action stuff. We showed we could run early and then that set up the passing."

The Bears' offense was the reason this game became a rout. It was a given that the Chicago defense would be dominant, but on this afternoon Ditka's offensive unit was just as impressive. No wonder McMahon was yelling at half-time about scoring 60 points.

To make matters worse for New England, the Patriots couldn't even get a break on turnovers. In the playoffs, they had forced 16 enemy errors, a major reason they had gotten this far. But Chicago beat New England at its

England's Clayborn wasn't impressed.

"I don't think he has any class at all," Clayborn said. "He needs to mature and grow up a little."

No matter, McMahon became quite a player in the postseason. He may have butted helmets with his offensive linemen and behaved like a punk rocker, but he also was interception-free in postseason play and wound up either running or passing for six of the Bears' eight offensive playoff touchdowns.

By the time McMahon and his friends were done, the shocked Patriots were left to assess the damage. It wasn't a pretty sight.

"It was a nightmare," Patriots fullback Mosi Tatupu said. New England, which averaged 279 yards in the first three playoff games, finished the first half of this game with minus 19 yards, one first down, two pass completions and three points. The Patriots established Super Bowl records in three categories for first-half offensive ineptness: rushing yards (minus five), passing yards (minus 14) and total offense.

Even after Eason went to the bench—"I was slightly shocked, I couldn't understand it," he said—and Grogan came in, things didn't get much better. The Patriots ended with 123 total yards, second worst in Super Bowl history, and a mere seven rushing yards, a record low. No previous Super Bowl loser had ever been beaten by as many points (36), nor had any team surrendered as many points as the Pats yielded.

"We would have liked to have hit them in the chops a few times," Wooten said of New England's offensive line and its usual spirited play. "We got here by being physical, but I think the Bears showed all year they couldn't be beaten by anyone who tried to get physical with them. We saw how Miami beat them, but I don't think we are ready yet to execute that type of offense. We let the first few blitzes and sacks demoralize us."

The Bears intended to go right after Eason, trying to shake him up. To reduce his chances of scrambling, they blitzed from the outside, pinching him in. The Patriots countered by trying to block the Bears' Wilson with a running back. It didn't work.

"You could see it in his (Eason's) eyes very early," Singletary said. "It was a look that said, 'Oh my, here we go again.'" Singletary said he saw the same look in September, when Chicago beat New England, 20-7, and Eason threw three interceptions.

Amid all the happiness among the Bears, the only twinge of sadness belonged to the great Payton, who long had waited to play in the NFL's showcase game but failed to score and rushed for only 61 yards, a small portion of Chicago's 408 total yards. "It didn't matter," the 11-year veteran said of his lack of production, although the look on his face said it did.

Bears fans turned out in force to celebrate the return of their conquering heroes.

Still, this was the Bears' triumph—and Ditka's. "We are molded in his image," Suhey said. "We win by being physical and tough and driven, but we also play with intelligence. That's him."

For the veteran Bears, who had lived through so many horrible seasons, this Super Bowl victory was hard to believe.

"We've worked so long toward a goal and to have it come true really is emotional," Fencik said. "No one can say it is a fluke."

Nearby, Payton was standing next to Suhey. He handed Suhey a lighter, so he could fire up a cigar. Payton took a puff and then coughed.

"First cigar you've smoked?" someone asked.

"Yes," Payton said. "And it will be the last. Until next year."

Statistics of 20th Super Bowl

CHICAGO 46, NEW ENGLAND 10

Louisiana Superdome, New Orleans, La., January 26, 1986
Attendance: 73,818

CHICAGO	Offense	NEW ENGLAND
Willie Gault	WR	Stanley Morgan
Jim Covert	LT	Brian Holloway
Mark Bortz	LG	John Hannah
Jay Hilgenberg	C	Pete Brock
Tom Thayer	RG	Ron Wooten
Keith Van Horne	RT	Steve Moore
Emery Moorehead	TE	Lin Dawson
Dennis McKinnon	WR	Stephen Starring
Walter Payton	RB	Tony Collins
Matt Suhey	RB	Craig James
Jim McMahon	QB	Tony Eason

Defense

CHICAGO		NEW ENGLAND
Dan Hampton	LE	Garin Veris
Steve McMichael	LT	......
William Perry	RT	
......	NT	Lester Williams
Richard Dent	RE	Julius Adams
Otis Wilson	LLB	Andre Tippett
Mike Singletary	MLB	
......	ILB	Steve Nelson
......	ILB	Larry McGrew
Wilber Marshall	RLB	Don Blackmon
Mike Richardson	LCB	Ronnie Lippett
Leslie Frazier	RCB	Raymond Clayborn
Dave Duerson	SS	Roland James
Gary Fencik	FS	Fred Marion

SUBSTITUTIONS

CHICAGO—Offense: Receivers—Ken Margerum, Keith Ortego, Tim Wrightman. Linemen—Tom Andrews, Andy Frederick, Stefan Humphries. Backs—Steve Fuller, Dennis Gentry, Thomas Sanders, Calvin Thomas, Mike Tomczak. Kicker—Kevin Butler. Defense: Linebackers—Brian Cabral, Jim Morrissey, Ron Rivera, Cliff Thrift. Linemen—Mike Hartenstine, Tyrone Keys, Henry Waechter. Backs—Shaun Gayle, Reggie Phillips, Ken Taylor. Punter—Maury Buford. DNP—None.

NEW ENGLAND—Offense: Receivers—Irving Fryar, Cedric Jones, Derrick Ramsey. Linemen—Paul Fairchild, Guy Morriss, Art Plunkett. Backs—Steve Grogan, Greg Hawthorne, Mosi Tatupu, Robert Weathers. Kicker—Tony Franklin. Defense: Linebackers—Brian Ingram, Johnny Rembert, Ed Reynolds, Ed Williams. Linemen—Smiley Creswell, Dennis Owens, Ben Thomas. Backs—Jim Bowman, Ernest Gibson, Rod McSwain. Punter—Rich Camarillo. DNP—Tom Ramsey.

— SCORE BY PERIODS —

Chicago Bears (NFC)	13	10	21	2 — 46
New England Patriots (AFC)	3	0	0	7 — 10

— SCORING —

New England—Field goal Franklin 36.
Chicago—Field goal Butler 28.
Chicago—Field goal Butler 24.
Chicago—Suhey 11 run (Butler kick).
Chicago—McMahon 2 run (Butler kick).
Chicago—Field goal Butler 24.
Chicago—McMahon 1 run (Butler kick).
Chicago—Phillips 28 interception return (Butler kick).
Chicago—Perry 1 run (Butler kick).
New England—Fryar 8 pass from Grogan (Franklin kick).

Chicago—Safety, Grogan tackled by Waechter in end zone.

— TEAM STATISTICS —

	Chicago	N. England
Total First Downs	23	12
First Downs Rushing	13	1
First Downs Passing	9	10
First Downs Penalty	1	1
Rushes	49	11
Yards Gained Rushing (net)	167	7
Average Yards per Rush	3.4	0.6
Passes Attempted	24	36
Passes Completed	12	17
Had Intercepted	0	2
Times Tackled Attempt. Pass	3	7
Yards Lost Attempting Pass	15	61
Yards Gained Passing (net)	241	116
Total Net Yardage	408	123
Total Offensive Plays	76	54
Avg. Gain per Offensive Play	5.4	2.3
Punts	4	6
Average Distance	43.3	43.8
Punt Returns	2	2
Punt Return Yardage	20	22
Kickoff Returns	4	7
Kickoff Return Yardage	49	153
Interceptions Return Yardage	75	0
Fumbles	3	4
Opp. Fumbles Recovered	4	2
Total Return Yardage	144	175
Penalties	7	5
Yards Penalized	40	35
Total Points Scored	46	10
Touchdowns	5	1
Touchdowns Rushing	4	0
Touchdowns Passing	0	1
Touchdowns on Returns	1	0
Extra Points	5	1
Field Goals Attempted	3	1
Field Goals	3	1
Time of Possession	39:15	20:45

INDIVIDUAL STATISTICS

RUSHING

Chicago	Atts.	Yds.	Lg.	TD
Payton	22	61	7	0
Suhey	11	52	11	1
McMahon	5	14	7	2
Thomas	2	8	7	0
Gentry	3	15	8	0
Perry	1	1	1	1
Fuller	1	1	1	0
Sanders	4	15	10	0

New England	Atts.	Yds.	Lg.	TD
C. James	5	1	3	0
Hawthorne	1	—4	—4	0
Collins	3	4	3	0
Weathers	1	3	3	0
Grogan	1	3	3	0

PASSING

Chicago	Atts.	Comp.	Yds.	Int.	TD
McMahon	20	12	256	0	0
Fuller	4	0	0	0	0

New England	Atts.	Comp.	Yds.	Int.	TD
Eason	6	0	0	0	0
Grogan	30	17	177	2	1

Chicago Coach Mike Ditka gets the traditional victory ride after the Bears had defeated New England in Super Bowl XX.

RECEIVING

Chicago	No.	Yds.	Lg.	TD
Gault	4	129	60	0
Moorehead	2	22	14	0
Thomas	1	4	4	0
Suhey	1	24	24	0
Gentry	2	41	27	0
Margerum	2	36	29	0

New England	No.	Yds.	Lg.	TD
Collins	2	19	11	0
C. James	1	6	6	0
Morgan	7	70	19	0
Starring	2	39	24	0
D. Ramsey	2	16	11	0
Weathers	1	3	3	0
Fryar	2	24	16	1

INTERCEPTIONS

Chicago	No.	Yds.	Lg.	TD
Phillips	1	28	28	1
Morrissey	1	47	47	0

New England—None

PUNTING

Chicago	No.	Avg.	Lg.
Buford	4	43.3	52

New England	No.	Avg.	Lg.
Camarillo	6	43.8	62

PUNT RETURNS

Chicago	No.	FC	Yds.	Lg.
Ortego	2	1	20	12

New England	No.	FC	Yds.	Lg.
Fryar	2	0	22	12

KICKOFF RETURNS

Chicago	No.	Yds.	Lg.
Gault	4	49	18

New England	No.	Yds.	Lg.
Starring	7	153	36

FIELD GOALS

Chicago	Att.	Made
Butler	3	3

New England	Att.	Made
Franklin	1	1

SCORING

Chicago	TD	PAT	FG	Pts.
Butler	0	5	3	14
McMahon	2	0	0	12
Perry	1	0	0	6
Phillips	1	0	0	6
Suhey	1	0	0	6
Waechter	0	0	0	*2

*Credited with safety

New England	TD	PAT	FG	Pts.
Fryar	1	0	0	6
Franklin	0	1	1	4

FUMBLES

Chicago	No.	Own Rec.	Opp. Rec.	TD
Payton	1	0	0	0
Suhey	1	0	0	0
Gentry	1	1	0	0
Hampton	0	0	1	0
Singletary	0	0	2	0
Marshall	0	0	*1	0

*Credited with 13 return yards

New England	No.	Own Rec.	Opp. Rec.	TD
Eason	1	0	0	0
C. James	1	0	0	0
Morgan	1	0	0	0
D. Ramsey	1	0	0	0
McGrew	0	0	1	0
Clayborn	0	0	1	0

Super Bowl XXI

A Giant Step Forward

January 25, 1987

Tight end Zeke Mowatt put the Giants on the scoreboard in the first quarter when he caught a six-yard touchdown pass from Phil Simms.

After spending the first eight years of his career shaded by the clouds of injury, inconsistency, anonymity and controversy, Phil Simms certainly had earned his day in the bright Southern California sun that towered above Super Bowl XXI.

Simms was booed even before he first put on his New York Giants uniform. When his name was announced as the team's first pick in the 1979 National Football League draft, New York fans were stunned. "Phil who?" they asked. Their downtrodden Giants had taken a little-known hick from Morehead State. The fans couldn't believe it, they sure didn't like it—and they let Simms know it. Again and again and again.

It took Simms eight often-stormy seasons to finally eliminate the sting of those boos. Before Super Bowl XXI, he had enjoyed some shining moments, but he never was completely accepted by Giants partisans, who still were searching for a reincarnation of Y.A. Tittle or Charlie Conerly. Simms could make the Pro Bowl or pass for 4,000 yards in a season, but until he quarterbacked the Giants to an NFL championship, nothing he did was good enough.

Simms, of course, wasn't the only Giant plagued by ghosts from the past.

"You get tired of hearing all the time about 23 years of suffering," linebacker Harry Carson said. "We'd like to make our own history, so maybe everyone could start talking about the present, not the past."

But since their last NFL championship game appearance in 1963, the Giants had done little to eliminate the ghosts. The proud franchise became tarnished by inept play, front-office feuding, horrible drafts and lackluster coaching. For a span, the Giants—at one time the toast of Manhattan, where the players were the glowing winter celebrities at Toots Shor's—were the worst team in the league. The Giants had even moved to New Jersey, of all places, the crowning blow in the club's downfall.

Giants quarterback Phil Simms dazzled Denver with a passing display that included 22 completions in 25 attempts for 268 yards and three touchdowns.

Denver kicker Rich Karlis watches the second of two second-quarter field-goal attempts go awry.

Nothing summed up the Giants' demise more graphically than a picture of Tittle, bloodied and bowed, kneeling on the turf near the end of their 1963 title loss to Chicago. That image, produced year after year in publication after publication, was etched painfully in the minds and hearts of all New York fans. When can we stop remembering, they kept asking?

Simms finally provided an answer in Super Bowl XXI. Instead of recalling Tittle's pain, the Giants' faithful now can recount the joy on Simms' face as he pumped his fist into the air, celebrating yet another touchdown in New York's 39-20 romp over the outclassed Denver Broncos. The brightly colored Rose Bowl in Pasadena, Calif., became Simms' stage, and no Broadway star could have sparkled any brighter than he did on January 25, 1987.

Considering the importance of the game, it is hard to imagine any quarterback ever playing better under pressure. His numbers alone give the reason: 22 completions in 25 attempts for 268 yards, three touchdowns and no interceptions. He set Super Bowl records for consecutive completions (10) and highest completion percentage (88 percent) despite throwing against one of the league's more fearsome defenses.

"This might be the best game a quarterback has ever played," Giants Coach Bill Parcells said.

Even Simms, a genial, humble man who managed to keep his sanity despite the slings and arrows of playing in New York, was stunned by his performance.

"I have to admit he's a hell of a quarterback," Simms said about himself. "There ain't no doubt about it. I can't deny it anymore."

Do you think you are underrated?

"Hell yes, I think I'm underrated."

Does this wipe out "Phil who?" for good?

"You damn well better believe it does."

Ironically, Simms received more individual recognition in other seasons, when the team was struggling and he had to pass time and again. But in the 1986 season, when New York emerged as easily the best team in the NFL, Simms didn't earn All-Pro or Pro Bowl recognition. He and the rest of the offense, even running back Joe Morris, were overshadowed by a savage defense that terrorized opponents and dominated games.

But in the biggest moment of his football life, Simms seized the spotlight and made the Giants' first NFL title victory since 1956 look incredibly easy.

Of course, that's the way the game figured to go anyway. The Broncos had a nice team, no doubt, but not in the class of the Giants. Denver quarterback John Elway was the only reason New York had emerged as no more than an eight-point favorite prior to kickoff. Could Elway, the talented ad-libber with so many impressive offensive skills, be good enough to overcome his team's deficiencies? It was the only question that kept the prognosticators guessing.

But what Elway had to face was truly impressive. The Giants' defense, anchored by one of the game's best-ever linebacking units, had dominated San Francisco and Washington in the opening games of the playoffs, shredding two of the league's best offenses with an awesome display of strength and determination. In those victories (49-3 over San Francisco and 17-0 over Washington), the Giants held the league's No. 3 and No. 5 ranked offenses to just three points.

Denver couldn't match either Washington or San Francisco in offensive talent. The Broncos could only hope that Elway was capable of the same kind of miracle he produced against Cleveland in the American Football Conference title game, when he drove the team 98 yards in the final moments to send the game

One of the key plays of Super Bowl XXI occurred in the second quarter when George Martin, part of the swarming Giants defense, tackled Broncos quarterback John Elway in the end zone for a safety.

Giants linebacker Lawrence Taylor treats Denver quarterback John Elway like a ragdoll on a fourth-quarter sack.

into overtime.

The pregame buildup centered around Elway and Giants linebacker Lawrence Taylor, the league's Most Valuable Player. Simms was a bit player, coming along for the ride.

"I really didn't mind," Simms said. "John's a great player. And it took the pressure off of me. But I really thought I was better than I was being credited for. People didn't talk about our passing game, even though we've been coming up with a lot of big plays."

Parcells began Super Bowl week by putting the Giants through what center Bart Oates termed "one of the hardest three or four practices of the year." Parcells finally had to back off by Thursday, when he figured his players realized he wasn't going to let them drift through preparations.

The Broncos also worked out so intensely that Coach Dan Reeves was afraid they'd hurt each other. On Friday, he toned down the practices. But his players remained puzzled by their role as decided underdogs against an opponent they had almost beaten (19-16) on the road in November.

"It just ticks you off," guard Keith Bishop said. "I don't know what everyone is basing their reasoning on. You don't get this far unless you are a darn good team."

Still, the teams had some fun. Reeves was given a birthday cake (he turned 43 early in the week) and Giants players either went fishing or played golf in their free time. Two days before the Super Bowl, they ate pizza supplied by Simms' favorite pizza joint, which happens to be located in Manhattan.

Mark Bavaro, the league's best tight end in 1986, normally doesn't talk to the press, but he relented under a league edict. He did his best to enhance his Rambo nickname, although he said he finds that notoriety so demeaning that he asked his teammates to drop it altogether.

Still, Sylvester Stallone he is. Here's a partial transcript of one interview:

Q. What do you like about football?
A. It's a job.
Q. Why did you go to Notre Dame?
A. Good school.
It got worse after that.

Taylor, who didn't want to talk to reporters any more than Bavaro did, was much more flamboyant.

"I can be an SOB," he explained. "Nasty, lousy, mean people are the guys who get the farthest.... I love the contact. It makes the game real enjoyable. I can go two or three games without a kill shot. That's when the snot comes from his (a quarterback's) nose and he starts quivering on the ground. You want to run that film again and again."

Maybe Taylor was kidding, but who was going to ask?

Certainly not Elway, the glamour boy from that quarterback-happy class of 1983. The best way to shut up Taylor, he reasoned, was to out-play him. And that's what the Broncos did in the opening half of the game, showing New York, as Elway put it, "everything we had."

It almost was enough. The Broncos carved out a 10-9 intermission lead, which could have been so much more if they had capitalized on Elway's stunning start (13-of-20 passing for 187 yards).

On Denver's opening possession, a 24-yard pass from Elway to wide receiver Mark Jackson set up a 48-yard Rich Karlis field goal, which equaled the longest in Super Bowl history. Simms promptly drove the Giants 78 yards to a go-ahead touchdown on a six-yard pass to tight end Zeke Mowatt, but the Broncos regained the lead when Elway countered with a four-yard quarterback draw for a score, cap-ping a 58-yard drive. After the Denver defense held New York on its next possession and forced the Giants to punt early in the second quarter, Elway eluded the rush on third-and-12 and found wide receiver Vance Johnson for a 54-yard reception ahead of free safety Herb Welch.

This early inability to contain the elusive Elway frustrated the proud Giants. They had worked all week in practice on keeping Elway in the pocket or at least forcing him to throw quickly. Welch, who was starting his fifth game in place of injured Terry Kinard, even had a nightmare in which he saw Elway running around and his receivers breaking free in the secondary.

"The worst part," Welch said, "was he's still running around and my man is out there and

Giants tight end Mark Bavaro cele-brates after scoring his team's go-ahead third-quarter touchdown.

I'm behind him and I can't catch up."

That nightmare was coming true. Six plays after the completion to Johnson, the Broncos had a first down at the Giants' one-yard line. But in one of the critical series of the game, Denver couldn't get a touchdown. Karlis then inexplicably missed a 23-yard field goal, the shortest failure in Super Bowl history.

In the earlier game between the teams, Den-ver had scored from inside the 10 by running, so the Giants were prepared this time for simi-lar tactics. On first down, Elway rolled to the right but was dropped by Taylor for a one-yard loss. On second down, the Giants stuffed a trap play and Carson stopped running back Gerald Willhite for no gain. On third down, running back Sammy Winder took a pitch and ran to the left, but linebacker Carl Banks, a standout all game, met him in the backfield for a four-yard loss, forcing the field-goal try.

The Giants had called defensive line slants on all three plays, and all three times Denver had run into the strength of the defense.

"How many times do you guess right on

Denver quarterback John Elway enjoyed early passing success and even scored the Broncos' first touchdown on a four-yard first-quarter run.

three straight plays with slants?" said an amazed Bill Belichick, the Giants' defensive coordinator.

Instead of leading, 17-7, Denver walked away from the goal-line stand ahead by just three, 10-7. The Broncos were staggering, but they still were outplaying the Giants—at least for a while.

The Giants took over at their own 20-yard line, but the Broncos again prevented them from crossing midfield, forcing another Sean Landeta punt. Denver had the ball on its own 15 with 3:33 left in the half.

But by this time, the embarrassed New York defense was warmed up. On third-and-12, veteran defensive end George Martin, who had returned an interception 78 yards for a touchdown against Denver in November, sacked Elway in the end zone for a 13-yard loss and a safety.

That safety marked the game's biggest turnaround. One play earlier, an apparent reception for a first down by tight end Clarence Kay had been ruled incomplete, a decision upheld by replay official Art McNally, who said the replays he watched "were inconclusive."

An aggravated Reeves complained that Kay had clearly made the catch, "and I wear glasses," he said. Indeed, a replay angle that was unavailable at the time of the ruling was shown later in the game, and this one indicated that Kay had caught the ball cleanly. By then, however, it was too late to help the Broncos.

The safety cut Denver's margin to 10-9, but Elway refused to surrender. After New York was forced to punt for the third consecutive time, the Broncos took over on their own 37-yard line with 65 seconds left in the half. On second down, Elway threw deep and across field to an open Steve Watson (who had beaten cornerback Elvis Patterson) for a 31-yard gain. The Broncos eventually advanced to the New York 16, where Karlis, who had been the hero of their overtime AFC title victory, failed on a 34-yard field-goal attempt.

"The key was being only one point behind at the half," Giants nose tackle Jim Burt said. "I figured they had played about as well as they could and we hadn't played very well at all."

Mowatt agreed. "If (Karlis) had made those two field goals, it could have been Denver sitting here as the world champs," he said.

A disconsolate Karlis wasn't sure why he missed the kicks. "I don't think I lost concentration," he said. "I just felt I didn't hit 'em as well as I hit the 48-yarder. I think sometimes, on a shorter kick, you have a tendency to steer the ball, and I know better than that."

The Giants didn't need to make any major

The Giants finally established their powerful running game in the second half with Joe Morris carrying much of the load.

adjustments at halftime. They already had changed slightly on defense by playing more man-to-man coverage in order to reduce Elway's effectiveness on short passes over the middle. The players were convinced they had been tentative and had worried too much about Denver's finesse offense and its changing formations. Taylor, who was limited to five tackles for the day, told his teammates to stop thinking "and kick some butt, then we'll be OK."

Simms merely pleaded for his offensive line, which Parcells called the "Suburbanites," to give him time to exploit Denver's man-to-man coverage. Simms had seen only one zone defense in the first half, and he was certain that if his receivers would run their routes at full speed and he had enough time to scan the secondary, the Broncos couldn't possibly cover all his options.

"They hadn't shown us any respect (with their man-to-man coverage) in the first game," Simms said. "We talked all week about how people were always running down our receivers. We wanted to show them they were wrong."

The Broncos had been confused in the opening half when the run-oriented Giants came out passing on opening downs. Nine of Simms' 15 first-half passes came on first down, and the

Giants had run just three times on first down.

"We didn't know if we should put our pass defense in on first down and our run defense in on second," Denver linebacker Karl Mecklenburg said. "They were outguessing us."

Even though the game plan had been to challenge the Denver secondary, Parcells didn't like what he was seeing, calling it "too helter-skelter." He ordered a return to the Giants' bread-and-butter offense: Morris running, Bavaro catching and Simms throwing off play-action.

It was a wise decision. In the second half, the Giants became more physical and unpredictable against the outmanned Broncos. Morris, who had gained 36 yards on seven carries in the first half, opened the second with a three-yard run. He gained two more yards on third down, leaving the Giants with a fourth down and half a yard to go at their own 46-yard line.

Parcells, who had made bold moves with his special teams all season, decided to go for a first down with some trickery. He sent in reserve quarterback Jeff Rutledge with the punt team. The Giants shifted from punt formation and Rutledge moved from upback to quarterback. He waited and waited, trying to decide whether or not to run a play, then took the snap and sneaked for two yards.

The Broncos claimed they recognized Rut-

Nose tackle Jim Burt and defensive coordinator Bill Belichick celebrate in the locker room after the Giants' convincing Super Bowl XXI victory over Denver.

ledge's presence and countered with most of their regular defense. But they still couldn't thwart the Giants' gamble.

"It was a big field-position swing for them," Reeves said, shaking his head.

Simms, thrilled with Parcells' decisiveness, took off. With ample time to pass, he threw to Morris for 12 yards and to running back Lee Rouson for 23. On third-and-six from the Denver 13, Bavaro ran a slant pattern against strong safety Dennis Smith, who got hung up in traffic in the end zone. Bavaro, who finished with four catches and picked particularly on Smith, grabbed Simms' bullet strike for a touchdown. The Giants had the lead for good.

Denver's first possession of the quarter ended quickly with its first punt of the game.

"You could see the whole team pick up after we drove for a touchdown and they had to punt," Simms said. "The defense had been embarrassed when they realized they (the Broncos) hadn't punted."

Phil McConkey returned Mike Horan's punt 25 yards to the Denver 36 and Simms went to work again. After Morris picked up 14 yards on three straight carries and Rouson ran for a yard, Simms connected with wide receiver Lionel Manuel for nine yards. Three more runs, including a five-yard scramble by Simms, set up Raul Allegre's 21-yard field goal, which made it 19-10.

Elway couldn't match the drive and Denver had to punt again. This time the Giants needed only five plays to cover 68 yards, with Morris scoring from the one on his third first-down carry of the march.

The key play had been a 44-yard flea flicker. Simms handed off to Morris and the running back pitched back to Simms, who waited patiently until McConkey came open at the 10. He was knocked down at the one.

"We run those flea flickers in practice, and we've never run the damn things in games," Simms said. "When I hit McConkey, I thought, 'That's it; we've won it.'"

The third quarter ended with Elway recovering his own fumble after getting sacked by defensive end Leonard Marshall. It was an appropriate finish to a dismal period for Denver. In the quarter, the Giants had gained 163 yards, the Broncos two. The Broncos, who had abandoned their running attack after being stopped at the goal line in the second quarter, called for passes on every third-quarter play. But in a wicked 19-minute stretch beginning late in the second quarter, Elway neutralized his great start by going four for 14 for 55 yards, having a pass intercepted by Patterson and getting sacked three times, including the safety.

In contrast, Simms' third quarter had been exquisite. He completed eight straight passes for 123 yards, throwing for one touchdown and setting up another 10 points to give New York

Giants Coach Bill Parcells gets a victory ride (above) after his team's Super Bowl win over Denver and then holds up the Vince Lombardi Trophy (left) during New York's postgame celebration.

a 26-10 lead.

"I was like a fastball pitcher," Simms said. "I had great location all day. Almost every pass landed exactly where I wanted it to. I've never played better. I told 'em before the game I was smoking."

Simms remained on fire into the fourth quarter, when his 36-yard completion to wide receiver Stacy Robinson set up another Giants score. Simms bounced an end zone pass off Bavaro and into McConkey's hands for yet another touchdown and a 33-10 lead.

That pass marked Simms' 10th straight completion and his last attempt for the day. Though Elway bounced back, completing his first five attempts on Denver's next possession and leading a drive that culminated with Karlis' 27-yard field goal, the Giants had a 20-point lead with 6:01 to play. It was time to run out the clock.

The Giants ate up 2:43 as they moved 46 yards for their last tally, a two-yard TD run by running back Ottis Anderson. Elway responded with a 47-yard TD pass to Johnson just before the two-minute warning. Karlis' conversion made it 39-20 and completed the scoring.

Buoyed by its running success in winning two playoff games, Denver had hoped for some success on the ground against New York. But the Giants gave up just 52 yards rushing, and the Broncos were reduced to relying on Elway's vast abilities. It was too much to ask, even of that gifted athlete.

"One guy isn't going to beat us," Taylor said. "But he never gave up. I'll give him credit for that."

Elway wound up passing for 304 yards and led Denver runners with 27 yards on six carries.

"They just got up by so much that we really didn't have the opportunity to do much offensively," Elway said. "They just seemed to sit back and play zone in the second half."

The Broncos also played more zone defense in the second half, but that was because Simms was shredding their man-to-man coverage.

"In the second half, Denver started to play some two-deep zone, which is contrary to everything they believe in on defense," Simms said. "I said to myself, 'They finally respect us.' "

And the stigma of "Phil who?" finally was erased. When the game was over and the TV cameras in the Giants' festive locker room were focusing in on the MVP of Super Bowl XXI, the man in the spotlight was Phil Simms.

Statistics of 21st Super Bowl

NEW YORK GIANTS 39, DENVER 20

Rose Bowl, Pasadena, Calif., January 25, 1987
Attendance: 101,063

DENVER	Offense	NEW YORK
Vance Johnson	WR	Lionel Manuel
Dave Studdard	LT	Brad Benson
Keith Bishop	LG	Billy Ard
Bill Bryan	C	Bart Oates
Mark Cooper	RG	Chris Godfrey
Ken Lanier	RT	Karl Nelson
Clarence Kay	TE	Mark Bavaro
Steve Watson	WR	Stacy Robinson
John Elway	QB	Phil Simms
Sammy Winder	RB	Joe Morris
Gerald Willhite	RB	Maurice Carthon

Defense

Andre Townsend	LE	George Martin
Greg Kragen	NT	Jim Burt
Rulon Jones	RE	Leonard Marshall
Jim Ryan	LOLB	Carl Banks
Karl Mecklenburg	LILB	Gary Reasons
Ricky Hunley	RILB	Harry Carson
Tom Jackson	ROLB	Lawrence Taylor
Louis Wright	LCB	Elvis Patterson
Mike Harden	RCB	Perry Williams
Dennis Smith	SS	Kenny Hill
Steve Foley	FS	Herb Welch

SUBSTITUTIONS

DENVER—Offense: Receivers—Joey Hackett, Mark Jackson, Bobby Micho, Orson Mobley, Clint Sampson. Linemen—Mike Freeman, Dan Remsberg. Backs—Ken Bell, Gary Kubiak, Gene Lang, Steve Sewell. Kicker—Rich Karlis. Defense: Linebackers—Darren Comeaux, Rick Dennison, Ken Woodard. Linemen—Tony Colorito, Simon Fletcher, Freddie Gilbert. Backs—Mark Haynes, Tony Lilly, Randy Robbins, Steve Wilson. Punter—Mike Horan. DNP—None.

NEW YORK—Offense: Receivers—Bobby Johnson, Phil McConkey, Solomon Miller, Zeke Mowatt. Linemen—Damian Johnson, Brian Johnston, William Roberts. Backs—Ottis Anderson, Tony Galbreath, Lee Rouson, Jeff Rutledge. Kicker—Raul Allegre. Defense: Linebackers—Andy Headen, Byron Hunt, Pepper Johnson, Robbie Jones. Linemen—Eric Dorsey, Erik Howard, Jerome Sally. Backs—Mark Collins, Tom Flynn, Greg Lasker. Punter—Sean Landeta. DNP—None.

— SCORE BY PERIODS —

Denver Broncos (AFC)	10	0	0	10	20
New York Giants (NFC)	7	2	17	13	39

— SCORING —

Denver—Field goal Karlis 48.
New York—Mowatt 6 pass from Simms (Allegre kick).
Denver—Elway 4 run (Karlis kick).
New York—Safety, Elway sacked by Martin in end zone.
New York—Bavaro 13 pass from Simms (Allegre kick).
New York—Field goal Allegre 21.
New York—Morris 1 run (Allegre kick).
New York—McConkey 6 pass from Simms (Allegre kick).
Denver—Field goal Karlis 28.
New York—Anderson 2 run (kick wide).
Denver—V. Johnson 47 pass from Elway (Karlis kick).

— TEAM STATISTICS —

	Denver	New York
Total First Downs	23	24
First Downs Rushing	5	10
First Downs Passing	16	13
First Downs Penalty	2	1
Rushes	19	38
Yards Gained Rushing (net)	52	136
Average Yards per Rush	2.7	3.6
Passes Attempted	41	25
Passes Completed	26	22
Had Intercepted	1	0
Times Tackled Attempt, Pass	4	1
Yards Lost Attempting Pass	32	5
Yards Gained Passing (net)	320	263
Total Net Yardage	372	399
Total Offensive Plays	64	64
Avg. Gain per Offensive Play	5.8	6.2
Punts	2	3
Average Distance	41.0	46.0
Punt Returns	1	1
Punt Return Yardage	9	25
Kickoff Returns	5	4
Kickoff Return Yardage	84	53
Interceptions Return Yardage	0	—7
Fumbles	2	0
Opp. Fumbles Recovered	0	0
Total Return Yardage	60	71
Penalties	4	6
Yards Penalized	28	48
Total Points Scored	20	39
Touchdowns	2	5
Touchdowns Rushing	1	2
Touchdowns Passing	1	3
Touchdowns on Returns	0	0
Extra Points	2	4
Field Goals Attempted	4	1
Field Goals	2	1
Time of Possession	25:21	34:39

INDIVIDUAL STATISTICS

RUSHING

Denver	Atts.	Yds.	Lg.	TD
Lang	2	2	4	0
Elway	6	27	10	1
Winder	4	0	3	0
Willhite	4	19	11	0
Sewell	3	4	12	0

New York	Atts.	Yds.	Lg.	TD
Rouson	3	22	18	0
Simms	3	25	22	0
Morris	20	67	11	1
Anderson	2	1	2	1
Carthon	3	4	2	0
Rutledge	3	0	2	0
Galbreath	4	17	7	0

PASSING

Denver	Atts.	Comp.	Yds.	Int.	TD
Elway	37	22	304	1	1
Kubiak	4	4	48	0	0

New York	Atts.	Comp.	Yds.	Int.	TD
Simms	25	22	268	0	3

Linebacker Harry Carson doused Coach Bill Parcells with a bucket of Gatorade as the Giants were putting the finishing touches on their Super Bowl XXI victory over Denver.

RECEIVING

Denver	No.	Yds.	Lg.	TD
Lang	1	4	4	0
Winder	4	34	14	0
Willhite	5	39	11	0
M. Jackson	3	51	24	0
Mobley	2	17	11	0
Sewell	2	12	7	0
V. Johnson	5	121	54	1
Watson	2	54	31	0
Sampson	2	20	11	0

New York	No.	Yds.	Lg.	TD
Rouson	1	23	23	0
Manuel	3	43	17	0
Bavaro	4	51	17	1
Morris	4	20	12	0
Robinson	3	62	36	0
Mowatt	1	6	6	1
Carthon	4	13	7	0
McConkey	2	50	44	1

INTERCEPTIONS

Denver—None

New York	No.	Yds.	Lg.	TD
Patterson	1	—7	—7	0

PUNTING

Denver	No.	Avg.	Lg.
Horan	2	41.0	42

New York	No.	Avg.	Lg.
Landeta	3	46.0	59

PUNT RETURNS

Denver	No.	FC	Yds.	Lg.
Willhite	1	1	9	9

New York	No.	FC	Yds.	Lg.
McConkey	1	1	25	25

KICKOFF RETURNS

Denver	No.	Yds.	Lg.
Lang	2	36	23
Bell	3	48	28

New York	No.	Yds.	Lg.
Rouson	3	56	22
Flynn	1	—3	—3

FIELD GOALS

Denver	Att.	Made
Karlis	4	2

New York	Att.	Made
Allegre	1	1

SCORING

Denver	TD	PAT	FG	Pts.
Karlis	0	2	2	8
Elway	1	0	0	6
V. Johnson	1	0	0	6

New York	TD	PAT	FG	Pts.
Allegre	0	4	1	7
Anderson	1	0	0	6
Bavaro	1	0	0	6
McConkey	1	0	0	6
Morris	1	0	0	6
Mowatt	1	0	0	6
Martin	0	0	0	*2

*Credited with safety

FUMBLES

Denver	No.	Own Rec.	Opp. Rec.	TD
Bell	1	0	0	0
Elway	1	1	0	0

New York—None

SUPER BOWL RECORDS

INDIVIDUAL RECORDS

SERVICE

Most Games

5—Marv Fleming, Green Bay, 1967-68; Miami, 1972-74
Larry Cole, Dallas, 1971-72, 1976, 1978-79
Cliff Harris, Dallas, 1971-72, 1976, 1978-79
D. D. Lewis, Dallas, 1971-72, 1976, 1978-79
Preston Pearson, Baltimore, 1969; Pittsburgh, 1975; Dallas, 1976, 1978-79
Charlie Waters, Dallas, 1971-72, 1976, 1978-79
Rayfield Wright, Dallas, 1971-72, 1976, 1978-79

Most Games, Coach

6—Don Shula, Baltimore, 1969; Miami, 1972-74, 1983, 1985
5—Tom Landry, Dallas, 1971-72, 1976, 1978-79
4—Bud Grant, Minnesota, 1970, 1974-75, 1977
Chuck Noll, Pittsburgh, 1975-76, 1979-80

Most Games, Winning Team, Coach

4—Chuck Noll, Pittsburgh, 1975-76, 1979-80
2—Vince Lombardi, Green Bay, 1967-68
Don Shula, Miami, 1973-74
Tom Landry, Dallas, 1972, 1978
Tom Flores, Oakland, 1981; Los Angeles Raiders, 1984
Bill Walsh, San Francisco, 1982, 1985
Joe Gibbs, Washington, 1983, 1988

SCORING
POINTS

Most Points, Career

24—Franco Harris, Pittsburgh, 4 games (4-td)
22—Ray Wersching, San Francisco, 2 games (7-pat, 5-fg)
20—Don Chandler, Green Bay, 2 games (8-pat, 4-fg)

Most Points, Game

18—Roger Craig, San Francisco vs. Miami, 1985 (3-td)
15—Don Chandler, Green Bay vs. Oakland, 1968 (3-pat, 4-fg)
14—Ray Wersching, San Francisco vs. Cincinnati, 1982 (2-pat, 4-fg)

TOUCHDOWNS

Most Touchdowns, Career

4—Franco Harris, Pittsburgh, 4 games (4-r)
3—John Stallworth, Pittsburgh, 4 games (3-p)
Lynn Swann, Pittsburgh, 4 games (3-p)
Cliff Branch, Oakland-Los Angeles Raiders, 3 games (3-p)
Roger Craig, San Francisco, 1 game (2-p, 1-r)

Most Touchdowns, Game

3—Roger Craig, San Francisco vs. Miami, 1985 (2-p, 1-r)

POINTS AFTER TOUCHDOWN

Most Points After Touchdown, Career

8—Don Chandler, Green Bay, 2 games (8 att)
Roy Gerela, Pittsburgh, 3 games (9 att)
Chris Bahr, Oakland-Los Angeles Raiders, 2 games (8 att)
7—Ray Wersching, San Francisco, 2 games (7 att)

Most Points After Touchdown, Game

6—Ali Haji-Sheikh, Washington vs. Denver (6 att)
5—Don Chandler, Green Bay vs. Kansas City, 1967 (5 att)
Roy Gerela, Pittsburgh vs. Dallas, 1979 (5 att)
Chris Bahr, Los Angeles Raiders vs. Washington, 1984 (5 att)
Ray Wersching, San Francisco vs. Miami, 1985 (5 att)
Kevin Butler, Chicago vs. New England, 1986

FIELD GOALS

Field Goals Attempted, Career

7—Roy Gerela, Pittsburgh, 3 games
6—Jim Turner, N.Y. Jets-Denver, 2 games

Most Field Goals Attempted, Game

5—Jim Turner, N.Y. Jets vs. Baltimore, 1969
Efren Herrera, Dallas vs. Denver, 1978

Most Field Goals, Career

5—Ray Wersching, San Francisco, 2 games (5 att)
4—Don Chandler, Green Bay, 2 games (4 att)
Jim Turner, N.Y. Jets-Denver, 2 games (6 att)

Most Field Goals, Game

4—Don Chandler, Green Bay vs. Oakland, 1968
Ray Wersching, San Francisco vs. Cincinnati, 1982

Longest Field Goal

48—Jan Stenerud, Kansas City vs. Minnesota, 1970
Rich Karlis, Denver vs. New York Giants, 1987

Shortest Field Goal Missed

23—Rich Karlis, Denver vs. New York Giants, 1987

SAFETIES

Most Safeties, Game

1—Dwight White, Pittsburgh vs. Minnesota, 1975
Reggie Harrison, Pittsburgh vs. Dallas, 1976
Henry Waechter, Chicago vs. New England, 1986
George Martin, New York Giants vs. Denver, 1987

RUSHING
ATTEMPTS

Most Attempts, Career

101—Franco Harris, Pittsburgh, 4 games
64—John Riggins, Washington, 2 games
57—Larry Csonka, Miami, 3 games

Most Attempts, Game

38—John Riggins, Washington vs. Miami, 1983
34—Franco Harris, Pittsburgh vs. Minnesota, 1975
33—Larry Csonka, Miami vs. Minnesota, 1974
30—Matt Snell, New York Jets vs. Baltimore, 1969

YARDS GAINED

Most Yards Gained, Career

354—Franco Harris, Pittsburgh, 4 games
297—Larry Csonka, Miami, 3 games

Most Yards Gained, Game

204—Timmy Smith, Washington vs. Denver, 1988
191—Marcus Allen, Los Angeles Raiders vs. Washington, 1984
166—John Riggins, Washington vs. Miami, 1983
158—Franco Harris, Pittsburgh vs. Minnesota, 1975
145—Larry Csonka, Miami vs. Minnesota, 1974
137—Clarence Davis, Oakland vs. Minnesota, 1977
121—Matt Snell, New York Jets vs. Baltimore, 1969
116—Tom Matte, Baltimore vs. New York Jets, 1969

Longest Run From Scrimmage

74—Marcus Allen, Los Angeles Raiders vs. Washington, 1984 (TD)
58—Timmy Smith, Washington vs. Denver, 1988 (TD)
Tom Matte, Baltimore vs. N.Y. Jets, 1969
49—Larry Csonka, Miami vs. Washington, 1973
44—Alvin Garrett, Washington vs. Miami, 1983

43—John Riggins, Washington vs. Miami, 1983 (TD)
Timmy Smith, Washington vs. Denver, 1988
39—Wendell Tyler, Los Angeles vs. Pittsburgh, 1980
Marcus Allen, Los Angeles Raiders vs. Washington, 1984
35—Clarence Davis, Oakland vs. Minnesota, 1977

Most Yards Gained, by Quarterback, Game
59—Joe Montana, San Francisco vs. Miami, 1985

AVERAGE GAIN

Highest Average Gain, Career (20 attempts)
9.5—Marcus Allen, Los Angeles Raiders, 1 game (20-191)
9.3—Timmy Smith, Washington, 1 game (22-204)
5.3—Walt Garrison, Dallas, 2 games (26-139)
5.2—Tony Dorsett, Dallas, 2 games (31-162)
Larry Csonka, Miami, 3 games (57-297)

Highest Average Gain, Game (10 attempts)
10.5—Tom Matte, Baltimore vs. N.Y. Jets, 1969 (11-116)
9.5—Marcus Allen, Los Angeles Raiders vs. Washington, 1984 (20-191)
9.3—Timmy Smith, Washington vs. Denver, 1988 (22-204)
8.6—Clarence Davis, Oakland vs. Minnesota, 1977 (16-137)
7.5—Larry Csonka, Miami vs. Washington, 1973 (15-112)

TOUCHDOWNS

Most Touchdowns, Career
4—Franco Harris, Pittsburgh, 4 games

Most Touchdowns, Game
2—Elijah Pitts, Green Bay vs. Kansas City, 1967
Larry Csonka, Miami vs. Minnesota, 1974
Pete Banaszak, Oakland vs. Minnesota, 1977
Franco Harris, Pittsburgh vs. Los Angeles, 1980
Marcus Allen, Los Angeles Raiders vs. Washington, 1984
Jim McMahon, Chicago vs. New England, 1986
Timmy Smith, Washington vs. Denver, 1988

Longest Touchdown Run, Game
74—Marcus Allen, Los Angeles Raiders vs. Washington, 1984
58—Timmy Smith, Washington vs. Denver, 1988
43—John Riggins, Washington vs. Miami, 1983

PASSING
ATTEMPTS

Most Passes Attempted, Career
98—Roger Staubach, Dallas, 4 games
89—Fran Tarkenton, Minnesota, 3 games
84—Terry Bradshaw, Pittsburgh, 4 games

Most Passes Attempted, Game
50—Dan Marino, Miami vs. San Francisco, 1985
38—Ron Jaworski, Philadelphia vs. Oakland, 1981
John Elway, Denver vs. Washington, 1988
37—John Elway, Denver vs. New York Giants, 1987
35—Fran Tarkenton, Minnesota vs. Oakland, 1977
Joe Theismann, Washington vs. Los Angeles Raiders, 1984
Joe Montana, San Francisco vs. Miami, 1985

COMPLETIONS

Most Passes Completed, Career
61—Roger Staubach, Dallas, 4 games
49—Terry Bradshaw, Pittsburgh, 4 games
46—Fran Tarkenton, Minnesota, 3 games

Most Passes Completed, Game
29—Dan Marino, Miami vs. San Francisco, 1985
25—Ken Anderson, Cincinnati vs. San Francisco, 1982
24—Joe Montana, San Francisco vs. Miami, 1985
22—Phil Simms, New York Giants vs. Denver, 1987
John Elway, Denver vs. New York Giants, 1987

Most Consecutive Completions, Game
10—Phil Simms, New York Giants vs. Denver, 1987
8—Len Dawson, Kansas City vs. Green Bay, 1967
Joe Theismann, Washington vs. Miami, 1983

COMPLETION PERCENTAGE

Highest Completion Pct., Career (40 attempts)
66.7—Joe Montana, San Francisco, 2 games (57-38)
63.6—Len Dawson, Kansas City, 2 games (44-28)
63.4—Bob Griese, Miami, 3 games (41-26)
63.0—Jim Plunkett, Oakland-Los Angeles Raiders, 2 games (46-29)
62.2—Roger Staubach, Dallas, 4 games (98-61)
61.7—Bart Starr, Green Bay, 2 games (47-29)

Highest Completion Pct., Game (20 attempts)
88.0—Phil Simms, New York Giants vs. Denver, 1987
73.5—Ken Anderson, Cincinnati vs. San Francisco, 1982 (34-25)
69.6—Bart Starr, Green Bay vs. Kansas City, 1967 (23-16)
68.6—Joe Montana, San Francisco vs. Miami, 1985 (35-24)
68.0—Roger Staubach, Dallas vs. Denver, 1978 (25-17)
66.7—Terry Bradshaw, Pittsburgh vs. Los Angeles, 1980 (21-14)
65.2—Joe Theismann, Washington vs. Miami, 1983 (23-15)

YARDS GAINED

Most Yards Gained, Career
932—Terry Bradshaw, Pittsburgh, 4 games
734—Roger Staubach, Dallas, 4 games

Most Yards Gained, Game
340—Doug Williams, Washington vs. Denver, 1988
331—Joe Montana, San Francisco vs. Miami, 1985
318—Terry Bradshaw, Pittsburgh vs. Dallas, 1979
Dan Marino, Miami vs. San Francisco, 1985
309—Terry Bradshaw, Pittsburgh vs. Los Angeles, 1980
304—John Elway, Denver vs. New York Giants, 1987
300—Ken Anderson, Cincinnati vs. San Francisco, 1982

Longest Pass Completion
80—Jim Plunkett (to King), Oakland vs. Philadelphia, 1981 (TD)
Doug Williams (to Sanders), Washington vs. Denver, 1988 (TD)
76—David Woodley (to Cefalo), Miami vs. Washington, 1983 (TD)
75—Johnny Unitas (to Mackey), Baltimore vs. Dallas, 1971 (TD)
Terry Bradshaw (to Stallworth), Pittsburgh vs. Dallas, 1979 (TD)

AVERAGE GAIN

Highest Average Gain, Career (40 attempts)
11.10—Terry Bradshaw, Pittsburgh, 4 games (84-932)
9.62—Bart Starr, Green Bay, 2 games (47-452)
9.41—Jim Plunkett, Oakland-Los Angeles Raiders, 2 games (46-433)

Highest Average Gain, Game (20 attempts)
14.71—Terry Bradshaw, Pittsburgh vs. Los Angeles, 1980 (21-309)
12.80—Jim McMahon, Chicago vs. New England, 1986 (20-256)
12.43—Jim Plunkett, Oakland vs. Philadelphia, 1981 (21-261)
11.72—Doug Williams, Washington vs. Denver, 1988 (29-340)
10.87—Bart Starr, Green Bay vs. Kansas City, 1967 (23-250)
10.72—Phil Simms, New York Giants vs. Denver, 1987
10.60—Terry Bradshaw, Pittsburgh vs. Dallas, 1979 (30-318)

TOUCHDOWNS

Most Touchdown Passes, Career
9—Terry Bradshaw, Pittsburgh, 4 games
8—Roger Staubach, Dallas, 4 games

Most Touchdown Passes, Game
　4—Terry Bradshaw, Pittsburgh vs. Dallas, 1979
　　Doug Williams, Washington vs. Denver, 1988

HAD INTERCEPTED

**Lowest Percentage, Passes Had Intercepted,
Career (40 attempts)**
　0.00—Joe Montana, San Francisco, 2 games (57-0)
　　Jim Plunkett, Oakland-Los Angeles Raiders, 2
　　games (46-0)
　2.13—Bart Starr, Green Bay, 2 games (47-1)
　4.08—Roger Staubach, Dallas, 4 games (98-4)

Most Attempts, Without Interception, Game
　35—Joe Montana, San Francisco vs. Miami, 1985
　28—Joe Namath, N.Y. Jets vs. Baltimore, 1969
　25—Phil Simms, New York Giants vs. Denver, 1987

Most Passes Had Intercepted, Career
　7—Craig Morton, Dallas-Denver, 2 games
　6—Fran Tarkenton, Minnesota, 3 games

Most Passes Had Intercepted, Game
　4—Craig Morton, Denver vs. Dallas, 1978

PASSER RATING

Highest Rating, Career (40 attempts)
　122.8—Jim Plunkett, Oakland-Los Angeles Raiders, 2
　　games
　116.7—Joe Montana, San Francisco, 2 games
　112.6—Terry Bradshaw, Pittsburgh, 4 games
　95.4—Roger Staubach, Dallas, 4 games
　95.1—Bart Starr, Green Bay, 2 games

Highest Rating, Game (20 attempts)
　150.9—Phil Simms, New York Giants vs. Denver, 1987
　145.1—Jim Plunkett, Oakland vs. Philadelphia, 1981
　128.1—Doug Williams, Washington vs. Denver, 1988
　127.3—Joe Montana, San Francisco vs. Miami, 1985
　119.3—Terry Bradshaw, Pittsburgh vs. Dallas, 1979
　116.5—Bart Starr, Green Bay vs. Kansas City, 1967

PASS RECEIVING

RECEPTIONS

Most Receptions, Career
　16—Lynn Swann, Pittsburgh, 4 games
　15—Chuck Foreman, Minnesota, 3 games
　14—Cliff Branch, Oakland-Los Angeles Raiders, 3
　　games

Most Receptions, Game
　11—Dan Ross, Cincinnati vs. San Francisco, 1982
　9—Ricky Sanders, Washington vs. Denver, 1988
　8—George Sauer, N.Y. Jets vs. Baltimore, 1969
　7—Max McGee, Green Bay vs. Kansas City, 1967
　　John Henderson, Minnesota vs. Kansas City, 1970
　　Lynn Swann, Pittsburgh vs. Dallas, 1979
　　Stanley Morgan, New England vs. Chicago, 1986

YARDS GAINED

Most Yards Gained, Career
　364—Lynn Swann, Pittsburgh, 4 games
　268—John Stallworth, Pittsburgh, 4 games

Most Yards Gained, Game
　193—Ricky Sanders, Washington vs. Denver, 1988
　161—Lynn Swann, Pittsburgh vs. Dallas, 1976
　138—Max McGee, Green Bay vs. Kansas City, 1967
　133—George Sauer, N.Y. Jets vs. Baltimore, 1969

Longest Reception
　80—Kenny King (from Plunkett), Oakland vs. Phila-
　　delphia, 1981 (TD)
　　Ricky Sanders (from Williams), Washington vs.
　　Denver, 1988 (TD)
　76—Jimmy Cefalo (from Woodley), Miami vs. Wash-
　　ington, 1983 (TD).
　75—John Mackey (from Unitas), Baltimore vs. Dallas
　　1971 (TD)
　　John Stallworth (from Bradshaw), Pittsburgh vs.
　　Dallas, 1979 (TD)

AVERAGE GAIN

Highest Average Gain, Career (8 receptions)
　24.4—John Stallworth, Pittsburgh, 4 games (11-268)
　22.8—Lynn Swann, Pittsburgh, 4 games (16-364)

Highest Average Gain, Game (3 receptions)
　40.3—John Stallworth, Pittsburgh vs. Los Angeles, 1980
　　(3-121)

TOUCHDOWNS

Most Touchdowns, Career
　3—John Stallworth, Pittsburgh, 4 games
　　Lynn Swann, Pittsburgh, 4 games
　　Cliff Branch, Oakland-Los Angeles Raiders, 3
　　games

Most Touchdowns, Game
　2—Max McGee, Green Bay vs. Kansas City, 1967
　　Bill Miller, Oakland vs. Green Bay, 1968
　　John Stallworth, Pittsburgh vs. Dallas, 1979
　　Cliff Branch, Oakland vs. Philadelphia, 1981
　　Dan Ross, Cincinnati vs. San Francisco, 1982
　　Roger Craig, San Francisco vs. Miami, 1985
　　Ricky Sanders, Washington vs. Denver, 1988

INTERCEPTIONS BY

Most Interceptions By, Career
　3—Chuck Howley, Dallas, 2 games
　　Rod Martin, Oakland, 1 game
　2—Randy Beverly, N.Y. Jets, 1 game
　　Jake Scott, Miami, 3 games
　　Mike Wagner, Pittsburgh, 3 games
　　Mel Blount, Pittsburgh, 4 games
　　Eric Wright, San Francisco, 2 games
　　Barry Wilburn, Washington, 1 game

Most Interceptions By, Game
　3—Rod Martin, Oakland vs. Philadelphia, 1981
　2—Randy Beverly, N.Y. Jets vs. Baltimore, 1969
　　Chuck Howley, Dallas vs. Baltimore, 1971
　　Jake Scott, Miami vs. Washington, 1973
　　Barry Wilburn, Washington vs. Denver, 1988

YARDS GAINED

Most Yards Gained, Career
　75—Willie Brown, Oakland, 2 games
　63—Chuck Howley, Dallas, 2 games
　　Jake Scott, Miami, 3 games

Most Yards Gained, Game
　75—Willie Brown, Oakland vs. Minnesota, 1977

Longest Return
　75—Willie Brown, Oakland vs. Minnesota, 1977 (TD)
　60—Herb Adderley, Green Bay vs. Oakland, 1968 (TD)

TOUCHDOWNS

Most Touchdowns, Game
　1—Herb Adderley, Green Bay vs. Oakland, 1968
　　Willie Brown, Oakland vs. Minnesota, 1977
　　Jack Squirek, Los Angeles Raiders vs. Washing-
　　ton, 1984
　　Reggie Phillips, Chicago vs. New England, 1986

PUNTING

Most Punts, Career
　17—Mike Eischeid, Oakland-Minnesota, 3 games
　15—Larry Seiple, Miami, 3 games

Most Punts, Game
　9—Ron Widby, Dallas vs. Baltimore, 1971

Longest Punt
　62—Rich Camarillo, New England vs. Chicago, 1986
　61—Jerrel Wilson, Kansas City vs. Green Bay, 1967

AVERAGE YARDAGE

Highest Average, Punting, Career (10 punts)
　46.5—Jerrel Wilson, Kansas City, 2 games
　41.9—Ray Guy, Oakland-Los Angeles Raiders, 3 games
　41.3—Larry Seiple, Miami, 3 games

Highest Average, Punting, Game (4 punts)
48.5—Jerrel Wilson, Kansas City vs. Minnesota, 1970

PUNT RETURNS

Most Punt Returns, Career
6—Willie Wood, Green Bay, 2 games
Jake Scott, Miami, 3 games
Theo Bell, Pittsburgh, 2 games
Mike Nelms, Washington, 1 game

Most Punt Returns, Game
6—Mike Nelms, Washington vs. Miami, 1983
5—Willie Wood, Green Bay vs. Oakland, 1968
Dana McLemore, San Francisco vs. Miami, 1985

Most Fair Catches, Game
3—Ron Gardin, Baltimore vs. Dallas, 1971
Golden Richards, Dallas vs. Pittsburgh, 1976
Greg Pruitt, Los Angeles Raiders vs. Washington, 1984

YARDS GAINED

Most Yards Gained, Career
52—Mike Nelms, Washington, 1 game
51—Dana McLemore, San Francisco, 1 game

Most Yards Gained, Game
52—Mike Nelms, Washington vs. Miami, 1983
51—Dana McLemore, San Francisco vs. Miami, 1985

Longest Return
34—Darrell Green, Washington vs. Los Angeles Raiders, 1984
31—Willie Wood, Green Bay vs. Oakland, 1968

AVERAGE YARDAGE

Highest Average, Career (4 returns)
10.8—Neal Colzie, Oakland, 1 game
10.2—Dana McLemore, San Francisco, 1 game

Highest Average, Game (3 returns)
11.3—Lynn Swann, Pittsburgh vs. Minnesota, 1975

TOUCHDOWNS

Most Touchdowns, Game
None

KICKOFF RETURNS

Most Kickoff Returns, Career
8—Larry Anderson, Pittsburgh, 2 games
Fulton Walker, Miami, 2 games
Ken Bell, Denver, 2 games
7—Preston Pearson, Baltimore-Pittsburgh-Dallas, 5 games

Most Kickoff Returns, Game
7—Stephen Starring, New England vs. Chicago, 1986
5—Larry Anderson, Pittsburgh vs. Los Angeles, 1980
Billy Campfield, Philadelphia vs. Oakland, 1981
David Verser, Cincinnati vs. San Francisco, 1982
Alvin Garrett, Washington vs. Los Angeles Raiders, 1984
Ken Bell, Denver vs. Washington, 1988

YARDS GAINED

Most Yards Gained, Career
283—Fulton Walker, Miami, 2 games
207—Larry Anderson, Pittsburgh, 2 games

Most Yards Gained, Game
190—Fulton Walker, Miami vs. Washington, 1983
162—Larry Anderson, Pittsburgh vs. Los Angeles, 1980

Longest Return
98—Fulton Walker, Miami vs. Washington, 1983 (TD)
67—Rick Upchurch, Denver vs. Dallas, 1978

AVERAGE YARDAGE

Highest Average, Career (4 returns)
35.4—Fulton Walker, Miami, 2 games
25.9—Larry Anderson, Pittsburgh, 2 games
22.5—Jim Duncan, Baltimore, 1 game

Highest Average, Game (3 returns)
47.5—Fulton Walker, Miami vs. Washington, 1983
32.4—Larry Anderson, Pittsburgh vs. Los Angeles, 1980

TOUCHDOWNS

Most Touchdowns, Game
1—Fulton Walker, Miami vs. Washington, 1983

FUMBLES

Most Fumbles, Career
5—Roger Staubach, Dallas, 4 games

Most Fumbles, Game
3—Roger Staubach, Dallas vs. Pittsburgh, 1976

RECOVERIES

Most Fumbles Recovered, Career
2—Jake Scott, Miami, 3 games (1 own, 1 opp)
Fran Tarkenton, Minnesota, 3 games (2 own)
Franco Harris, Pittsburgh, 4 games (2 own)
Roger Staubach, Dallas, 4 games (2 own)
Bobby Walden, Pittsburgh, 2 games (2 own)
John Fitzgerald, Dallas, 4 games (2 own)
Randy Hughes, Dallas, 3 games (2 opp)
Butch Johnson, Dallas, 2 games (2 own)
Mike Singletary, Chicago, 1 game (2 opp)

Most Fumbles Recovered, Game
2—Jake Scott, Miami vs. Minnesota, 1974 (1 own, 1 opp)
Roger Staubach, Dallas vs. Pittsburgh, 1976 (2 own)
Randy Hughes, Dallas vs. Denver, 1978 (2 opp)
Butch Johnson, Dallas vs. Denver, 1978 (2 own)
Mike Singletary, Chicago vs. New England, 1986 (2 opp)

YARDS GAINED

Most Yards Gained, Game
49—Mike Bass, Washington vs. Miami, 1973 (opp)

Longest Return
49—Mike Bass, Washington vs. Miami, 1973 (TD)

TOUCHDOWNS

Most Touchdowns, Game
1—Mike Bass, Washington vs. Miami, 1973 (opp 49 yards)
Mike Hegman, Dallas vs. Pittsburgh, 1979 (opp 37 yards)

COMBINED NET YARDS GAINED

ATTEMPTS

Most Attempts, Career
108—Franco Harris, Pittsburgh, 4 games
66—John Riggins, Washington, 2 games
60—Larry Csonka, Miami, 3 games

Most Attempts, Game
39—John Riggins, Washington vs. Miami, 1983
35—Franco Harris, Pittsburgh vs. Minnesota, 1975

YARDS GAINED

Most Yards Gained, Career
468—Franco Harris, Pittsburgh, 4 games
391—Lynn Swann, Pittsburgh, 4 games

Most Yards Gained, Game
235—Ricky Sanders, Washington vs. Denver, 1988
209—Marcus Allen, Los Angeles Raiders vs. Washington, 1984
192—Stephen Starring, New England vs. Chicago, 1986
190—Fulton Walker, Miami vs. Washington, 1983
181—John Riggins, Washington vs. Miami, 1983
178—Willie Gault, Chicago vs. New England, 1986

TEAM RECORDS
GAMES, VICTORIES, DEFEATS

Most Games
5—Dallas, 1971-72, 1976, 1978-79
Miami, 1972-74, 1983, 1985

Most Consecutive Games
3—Miami, 1972-74

Most Games Won
4—Pittsburgh, 1975-76, 1979-80

Most Consecutive Games Won
2—Green Bay, 1967-68
Miami, 1973-74
Pittsburgh, 1975-76, 1979-80

Most Games Lost
4—Minnesota, 1970, 1974-75, 1977

Most Consecutive Games Lost
2—Minnesota, 1974-75
Denver, 1987-88

SCORING

Most Points, Game
46—Chicago vs. New England, 1986
42—Washington vs. Denver, 1988
39—New York Giants vs. Denver, 1987
38—Los Angeles Raiders vs. Washington, 1984
San Francisco vs. Miami, 1985
35—Green Bay vs. Kansas City, 1967
Pittsburgh vs. Dallas, 1979

Largest Margin of Victory, Game
36—Chicago vs. New England, 1986

Fewest Points, Game
3—Miami vs. Dallas, 1972

Most Points, Both Teams, Game
66—Pittsburgh (35) vs. Dallas (31), 1979

Fewest Points, Both Teams, Game
21—Washington (7) vs. Miami (14), 1973

Most Points, Each Half
1st: 35—Washington vs. Denver, 1988
2nd: 30—New York Giants vs. Denver, 1987

Most Points, Each Quarter
1st: 14—Miami vs. Minnesota, 1974
Oakland vs. Philadelphia, 1981
2nd: 35—Washington vs. Denver, 1988
3rd: 21—Chicago vs. New England, 1986
4th: 14—Pittsburgh vs. Dallas, 1976; vs. Dallas, 1979; vs.
Los Angeles, 1980
Dallas vs. Pittsburgh, 1979
Cincinnati vs. San Francisco, 1982
Washington vs. Miami, 1983

Most Points, Both Teams, Each Half
1st: 45—Washington (35) vs. Denver (10), 1988
2nd: 40—New York Giants (30) vs. Denver (10), 1987

Most Points, Both Teams, Each Quarter
1st: 17—Miami (10) vs. San Francisco (7), 1985
Denver (10) vs. New York Giants (7), 1987
2nd: 35—Washington (35) vs. Denver (0), 1988
3rd: 21—Chicago (21) vs. New England (0), 1986
4th: 28—Dallas (14) vs. Pittsburgh (14), 1979

TOUCHDOWNS

Most Touchdowns, Game
6—Washington vs. Denver, 1988
5—Green Bay vs. Kansas City, 1967
Pittsburgh vs. Dallas, 1979
Los Angeles Raiders vs. Washington, 1984
San Francisco vs. Miami, 1985
Chicago vs. New England, 1986
New York Giants vs. Denver, 1987

Fewest Touchdowns, Game
0—Miami vs. Dallas, 1972

Most Touchdowns, Both Teams, Game
9—Pittsburgh (5) vs. Dallas (4), 1979

Fewest Touchdowns, Both Teams, Game
2—Baltimore (1) vs. N.Y. Jets (1), 1969

POINTS AFTER TOUCHDOWN

Most Points After Touchdown, Game
6—Washington vs. Denver, 1988
5—Green Bay vs. Kansas City, 1967
Pittsburgh vs. Dallas, 1979
Los Angeles Raiders vs. Washington, 1984
San Francisco vs. Miami, 1985
Chicago vs. New England, 1986

Most Points After Touchdown, Both Teams, Game
9—Pittsburgh (5) vs. Dallas (4), 1979

Fewest Points After Touchdown, Both Teams, Game
2—Baltimore (1) vs. N.Y. Jets (1), 1969
Baltimore (1) vs. Dallas (1), 1971
Minnesota (0) vs. Pittsburgh (2), 1975

FIELD GOALS

Most Field Goals Attempted, Game
5—N.Y. Jets vs. Baltimore, 1969
Dallas vs. Denver, 1978

Most Field Goals Attempted, Both Teams, Game
7—N.Y. Jets (5) vs. Baltimore (2), 1969

Fewest Field Goals Attempted, Both Teams, Game
1—Minnesota (0) vs. Miami (1), 1974

Most Field Goals, Game
4—Green Bay vs. Oakland, 1968
San Francisco vs. Cincinnati, 1982

Most Field Goals, Both Teams, Game
4—Green Bay (4) vs. Oakland (0), 1968
San Francisco (4) vs. Cincinnati (0), 1982
Miami (3) vs. San Francisco (1), 1985
Chicago (3) vs. New England (1), 1986

Fewest Field Goals, Both Teams, Game
0—Miami vs. Washington, 1973
Pittsburgh vs. Minnesota, 1975

SAFETIES

Most Safeties, Game
1—Pittsburgh vs. Minnesota; vs. Dallas, 1976
Chicago vs. New England, 1986
New York Giants vs. Denver, 1987

FIRST DOWNS

Most First Downs, Game
31—San Francisco vs. Miami, 1985
25—Washington vs. Denver, 1988
24—Cincinnati vs. San Francisco, 1982
Washington vs. Miami, 1983
New York Giants vs. Denver, 1987
Denver vs. New York Giants, 1987

Fewest First Downs, Game
9—Minnesota vs. Pittsburgh, 1975
Miami vs. Washington, 1983

Most First Downs, Both Teams, Game
50—San Francisco (31) vs. Miami (19), 1985
47—New York Giants (24) vs. Denver (23), 1987
44—Cincinnati (24) vs. San Francisco (20), 1982
43—Washington (25) vs. Denver (18), 1988

Fewest First Downs, Both Teams, Game
24—Dallas (10) vs. Baltimore (14), 1971

RUSHING

Most First Downs, Rushing, Game
16—San Francisco vs. Miami, 1985
15—Dallas vs. Miami, 1972

Fewest First Downs, Rushing, Game
1—New England vs. Chicago, 1986

2—Minnesota vs. Kansas City, 1970; vs. Pittsburgh, 1975
Pittsburgh vs. Dallas, 1979
Miami vs. San Francisco, 1985

Most First Downs, Rushing, Both Teams, Game
21—Washington (14) vs. Miami (7), 1983

Fewest First Downs, Rushing, Both Teams, Game
8—Baltimore (4) vs. Dallas (4), 1971
Pittsburgh (2) vs. Dallas (6), 1979

PASSING

Most First Downs, Passing, Game
17—Miami vs. San Francisco, 1985

Fewest First Downs, Passing, Game
1—Denver vs. Dallas, 1978
2—Miami vs. Washington, 1983

Most First Downs, Passing, Both Teams, Game
32—Miami (17) vs. San Francisco (15), 1985

Fewest First Downs, Passing, Both Teams, Game
9—Denver (1) vs. Dallas (8), 1978

PENALTIES

Most First Downs, Penalty, Game
4—Baltimore vs. Dallas, 1971
Miami vs. Minnesota, 1974
Cincinnati vs. San Francisco, 1982

Most First Downs, Penalty, Both Teams, Game
6—Cincinnati (4) vs. San Francisco (2), 1982
5—Baltimore (4) vs. Dallas (1), 1971
Miami (4) vs. Minnesota (1), 1974

Fewest First Downs, Penalty, Both Teams, Game
0—Dallas vs. Miami, 1972
Miami vs. Washington, 1973
Dallas vs. Pittsburgh, 1976
San Francisco vs. Miami, 1985

NET YARDS GAINED RUSHING AND PASSING

Most Yards Gained, Game
602—Washington vs. Denver, 1988
537—San Francisco vs. Miami, 1985

Fewest Yards Gained, Game
119—Minnesota vs. Pittsburgh, 1975

Most Yards Gained, Both Teams, Game
929—Washington (602) vs. Denver (327), 1988
851—San Francisco (537) vs. Miami (314), 1985

Fewest Yards Gained, Both Teams, Game
452—Minnesota (119) vs. Pittsburgh (333), 1975

RUSHING
ATTEMPTS

Most Attempts, Game
57—Pittsburgh vs. Minnesota, 1975

Fewest Attempts, Game
9—Miami vs. San Francisco, 1985

Most Attempts, Both Teams, Game
81—Washington (52) vs. Miami (29), 1983
78—Pittsburgh (57) vs. Minnesota (21), 1975
Oakland (52) vs. Minnesota (26), 1977

Fewest Attempts, Both Teams, Game
49—Miami (9) vs. San Francisco (40), 1985

YARDS GAINED

Most Yards Gained, Game
280—Washington vs. Denver, 1988
276—Washington vs. Miami, 1983.
266—Oakland vs. Minnesota, 1977

Fewest Yards Gained, Game
7—New England vs. Chicago, 1986

Most Yards Gained, Both Teams, Game
377—Washington (280) vs. Denver (97), 1988
372—Washington (276) vs. Miami (96), 1983.
337—Oakland (266) vs. Minnesota (71), 1977

Fewest Yards Gained, Both Teams, Game
171—Baltimore (69) vs. Dallas (102), 1971

AVERAGE GAIN

Highest Average Gain, Game
7.00—Los Angeles Raiders vs. Washington, 1984
Washington vs. Denver, 1988

Lowest Average Gain, Game
0.64—New England vs. Chicago, 1986

TOUCHDOWNS

Most Touchdowns, Game
4—Chicago vs. New England, 1986

Fewest Touchdowns, Game
0—By 13 teams

Most Touchdowns, Both Teams, Game
4—Miami (3) vs. Minnesota (1), 1974
Chicago (4) vs. New England (0), 1986

Fewest Touchdowns, Both Teams, Game
0—Pittsburgh vs. Dallas, 1976
Oakland vs. Philadelphia, 1981

PASSING
ATTEMPTS

Most Passes Attempted, Game
50—Miami vs. San Francisco, 1985

Fewest Passes Attempted, Game
7—Miami vs. Minnesota, 1974

Most Passes Attempted, Both Teams, Game
85—Miami (50) vs. San Francisco (35), 1985

Fewest Passes Attempted, Both Teams, Game
35—Miami (7) vs. Minnesota (28), 1974

COMPLETIONS

Most Passes Completed, Game
29—Miami vs. San Francisco, 1985
26—Denver vs. New York Giants, 1987
24—Minnesota vs. Oakland, 1977

Fewest Passes Completed, Game
4—Miami vs. Washington, 1983
6—Miami vs. Minnesota, 1974

Most Passes Completed, Both Teams, Game
53—Miami (29) vs. San Francisco (24), 1985

Fewest Passes Completed, Both Teams, Game
19—Miami (4) vs. Washington (15), 1983
20—Pittsburgh (9) vs. Minnesota (11), 1975

COMPLETION PERCENTAGE

Highest Completion Percentage, Game (20 attempts)
88.0—New York Giants vs. Denver, 1987
73.5—Cincinnati vs. San Francisco, 1982

Lowest Completion Percentage, Game (20 attempts)
32.0—Denver vs. Dallas, 1978 (25-8)

YARDS GAINED

Most Net Yards Gained, Game
326—San Francisco vs. Miami, 1985

Fewest Yards Gained, Game
35—Denver vs. Dallas, 1978

Most Yards Gained, Both Teams, Game
615—San Francisco (326) vs. Miami (289), 1985

Fewest Yards Gained, Both Teams, Game
156—Miami (69) vs. Washington (87), 1973

TACKLED ATTEMPTING PASSES

Most Times Tackled, Attempting Passes, Game
7—Dallas vs. Pittsburgh, 1976
New England vs. Chicago, 1986

Fewest Times Tackled, Attempting Passes, Game
0—Baltimore vs. N.Y. Jets, 1969; vs. Dallas, 1971
Minnesota vs. Pittsburgh, 1975
Pittsburgh vs. Los Angeles, 1980
Philadelphia vs. Oakland, 1981

Most Times Tackled, Attempting Passes, Both Teams, Game
10—New England (7) vs. Chicago (3), 1986

Fewest Times Tackled, Attempting Passes, Both Teams, Game
1—Philadelphia (0) vs. Oakland (1), 1981
2—Baltimore (0) vs. N.Y. Jets (2), 1969
Baltimore (0) vs. Dallas (2), 1971
Minnesota (0) vs. Pittsburgh (2), 1975

TOUCHDOWNS

Most Touchdowns, Game
4—Pittsburgh vs. Dallas, 1979
Washington vs. Denver, 1988

Fewest Touchdowns, Game
0—By 10 teams

Most Touchdowns, Both Teams, Game
7—Pittsburgh (4) vs. Dallas (3), 1979

Fewest Touchdowns, Both Teams, Game
0—N.Y. Jets vs. Baltimore, 1969
Miami vs. Minnesota, 1974

INTERCEPTIONS BY

Most Interceptions By, Game
4—N.Y. Jets vs. Baltimore, 1969
Dallas vs. Denver, 1978

Most Interceptions By, Both Teams, Game
6—Baltimore (3) vs. Dallas (3), 1971

YARDS GAINED

Most Yards Gained, Game
95—Miami vs. Washington, 1973

Most Yards Gained, Both Teams, Game
95—Miami (95) vs. Washington (0), 1973

TOUCHDOWNS

Most Touchdowns, Game
1—Green Bay vs. Oakland, 1968
Oakland vs. Minnesota, 1977
Los Angeles Raiders vs. Washington, 1984
Chicago vs. New England, 1986

PUNTING

Most Punts, Game
9—Dallas vs. Baltimore, 1971

Fewest Punts, Game
2—Pittsburgh vs. Los Angeles, 1980
Denver vs. New York Giants, 1987

Most Punts, Both Teams, Game
15—Washington (8) vs. Los Angeles Raiders (7), 1984
13—Dallas (9) vs. Baltimore (4), 1971
Pittsburgh (7) vs. Minnesota (6), 1975

Fewest Punts, Both Teams, Game
5—New York Giants (3) vs. Denver (2), 1987
6—Oakland (3) vs. Philadelphia (3), 1981

AVERAGE YARDAGE

Highest Average, Game (4 punts)
48.5—Kansas City, 1970

Lowest Average, Game (4 punts)
31.2—Washington, 1973

PUNT RETURNS

Most Punt Returns, Game
6—Washington vs. Miami, 1983

Fewest Punt Returns, Game
0—Minnesota vs. Miami, 1974

Most Punt Returns, Both Teams, Game
9—Pittsburgh (5) vs. Minnesota (4), 1975

Fewest Punt Returns, Both Teams, Game
2—Dallas (1) vs. Miami (1), 1972
Denver (1) vs. New York Giants (1), 1987

YARDS GAINED

Most Yards Gained, Game
52—Washington vs. Miami, 1983

Fewest Yards Gained, Game
−1—Dallas vs. Miami, 1972

Most Yards Gained, Both Teams, Game
74—Washington (52) vs. Miami (22), 1983

Fewest Yards Gained, Both Teams, Game
13—Miami (4) vs. Washington (9), 1973

AVERAGE RETURN

Highest Average, Game (3 returns)
10.8—Oakland vs. Minnesota, 1977

TOUCHDOWNS

Most Touchdowns, Game
None

KICKOFF RETURNS

Most Kickoff Returns, Game
7—Oakland vs. Green Bay, 1968
Minnesota vs. Oakland, 1977
Cincinnati vs. San Francisco, 1982
Washington vs. Los Angeles Raiders, 1984
Miami vs. San Francisco, 1985
New England vs. Chicago, 1986

Fewest Kickoff Returns, Game
1—N.Y. Jets vs. Baltimore, 1969
Los Angeles Raiders vs. Washington, 1984

Most Kickoff Returns, Both Teams, Game
11—Los Angeles (6) vs. Pittsburgh (5), 1980
Miami (7) vs. San Francisco (4), 1985
New England (7) vs. Chicago (4), 1986

Fewest Kickoff Returns, Both Teams, Game
5—N.Y. Jets (1) vs. Baltimore (4), 1969
Miami (2) vs. Washington (3), 1973

YARDS GAINED

Most Yards Gained, Game
222—Miami vs. Washington, 1983

Fewest Yards Gained, Game
17—Los Angeles Raiders vs. Washington, 1984

Most Yards Gained, Both Teams, Game
279—Miami (222) vs. Washington (57), 1983

Fewest Yards Gained, Both Teams, Game
78—Miami (33) vs. Washington (45), 1973

AVERAGE GAIN

Highest Average, Game (3 returns)
37.0—Miami vs. Washington, 1983

TOUCHDOWNS

Most Touchdowns, Game
1—Miami vs. Washington, 1983

PENALTIES

Most Penalties, Game
12—Dallas vs. Denver, 1978

Fewest Penalties, Game
0—Miami vs. Dallas, 1972
Pittsburgh vs. Dallas, 1976
Most Penalties, Both Teams, Game
20—Dallas (12) vs. Denver (8), 1978
Fewest Penalties, Both Teams, Game
2—Pittsburgh (0) vs. Dallas (2), 1976

YARDS PENALIZED
Most Yards Penalized, Game
133—Dallas vs. Baltimore, 1971
Most Yards Penalized, Both Teams, Game
164—Dallas (133) vs. Baltimore (31), 1971
Fewest Yards Penalized, Both Teams, Game
15—Miami (0) vs. Dallas (15), 1972

FUMBLES
Most Fumbles, Game
6—Dallas vs. Denver, 1978

Fewest Fumbles, Game
0—Green Bay vs. Oakland, 1968
Kansas City vs. Minnesota, 1970
Oakland vs. Minnesota, 1977
Los Angeles vs. Pittsburgh, 1980
Pittsburgh vs. Los Angeles, 1980
Oakland vs. Philadelphia, 1981
Washington vs. Miami, 1983
New York Giants vs. Denver, 1987
Most Fumbles, Both Teams, Game
10—Dallas (6) vs. Denver (4), 1978
Fewest Fumbles, Both Teams, Game
0—Los Angeles vs. Pittsburgh, 1980
Most Fumbles Lost, Game
4—Baltimore vs. Dallas, 1971
Denver vs. Dallas, 1978
New England vs. Chicago, 1986
Most Fumbles Recovered, Game
8—Dallas vs. Denver, 1978 (4 own, 4 opp)

SUPER BOWL SERVICE

The number in parentheses is the total games played.
*—Active did not play (DNP).
†—Inactive.

Abell, Bud (1)—Kansas City Chiefs 1967 (I).
Adams, Julius (1)—New England Patriots 1986 (XX).
Adderley, Herb (4)—Green Bay Packers 1967 (I), 1968 (II); Dallas Cowboys 1971 (V), 1972 (VI).
Alderman, Grady (3)—Minnesota Vikings 1970 (IV), 1974 (VIII), 1975 (IX).
Aldridge, Lionel (2)—Green Bay Packers 1967 (I), 1968 (II).
Alexander, Charles (1)—Cincinnati Bengals 1982 (XVI).
Allegre, Raul (1)—New York Giants 1987 (XXI).
Allen, Anthony (0†)—Washington Redskins 1988 (XXII-Inactive).
Allen, Jimmy (2)—Pittsburgh Steelers 1975 (IX), 1976 (X).
Allen, Marcus (1)—Los Angeles Raiders 1984 (XVIII).
Allen, Nate (1)—Minnesota Vikings 1977 (XI).
Allison, Henry (1)—Denver Broncos 1978 (XII).
Alston, Mack (1)—Washington Redskins 1973 (VII).
Alworth, Lance (1)—Dallas Cowboys 1972 (VI).
Alzado, Lyle (2)—Denver Broncos 1978 (XII); Los Angeles Raiders 1984 (XVIII).
Anderson, Anthony (1)—Pittsburgh Steelers 1980 (XIV).
Anderson, Bill (1)—Green Bay Packers 1967 (I).
Anderson, Dick (3)—Miami Dolphins 1972 (VI), 1973 (VII), 1974 (VIII).
Anderson, Donny (2)—Green Bay Packers 1967 (I), 1968 (II).
Anderson, Fred (1)—Pittsburgh Steelers 1979 (XIII).
Anderson, Ken (1)—Cincinnati Bengals 1982 (XVI).

Anderson, Larry (2)—Pittsburgh Steelers 1979 (XIII), 1980 (XIV).
Anderson, Ottis (1)—New York Giants 1987 (XXI).
Anderson, Scott (1)—Minnesota Vikings 1975 (IX).
Anderson, Stuart (1)—Washington Redskins 1984 (XVIII).
Andrews, George (1)—Los Angeles Rams 1980 (XIV).
Andrews, Mitch (0†)—Denver Broncos 1988 (XXII-Inactive)
Andrews, Tom (1)—Chicago Bears 1986 (XX).
Andrie, George (2)—Dallas Cowboys 1971 (V), 1972 (VI).
Arbanas, Fred (2)—Kansas City Chiefs 1967 (I), 1970 (IV).
Archer, Dan (1)—Oakland Raiders 1968 (II).
Ard, Billy (1)—New York Giants 1987 (XXI).
Armstrong, Otis (1)—Denver Broncos 1978 (XII).
Asher, Bob (1)—Dallas Cowboys 1971 (V).
Atkinson, Al (1)—New York Jets 1969 (III).
Atkinson, George (1)—Oakland Raiders 1977 (XI).
Audick, Dan (1)—San Francisco 49ers 1982 (XVI).
Austin, Ocie (1)—Baltimore Colts 1969 (III).
Ayers, John (2)—San Francisco 49ers 1982 (XVI), 1985 (XIX).
Babb, Charles (2)—Miami Dolphins 1973 (VII), 1974 (VIII).
Bahr, Chris (2)—Oakland Raiders 1981 (XV); Los Angeles Raiders 1984 (XVIII).
Bahr, Matt (1)—Pittsburgh Steelers 1980 (XIV).
Bain, Bill (1)—Los Angeles Rams 1980 (XIV).
Baird, Bill (1)—New York Jets 1969 (III).
Baker, Ralph (1)—New York Jets 1969 (III).
Baker, Ron (1)—Philadelphia Eagles 1981 (XV).

Ball, Larry (2)—Miami Dolphins 1973 (VII), 1974 (VIII).

Ball, Sam (2)—Baltimore Colts 1969 (III), 1971 (V).

Ballman, Gary (1)—Minnesota Vikings 1974 (VIII).

Banaszak, John (3)—Pittsburgh Steelers 1976 (X), 1979 (XIII), 1980 (XIV).

Banaszak, Pete (2)—Oakland Raiders 1968 (II), 1977 (XI).

Banks, Carl (1)—New York Giants 1987 (XXI).

Bankston, Warren (1)—Oakland Raiders 1977 (XI).

Bannon, Bruce (1)—Miami Dolphins 1974 (VIII).

Barnes, Benny (3)—Dallas Cowboys 1976 (X), 1978 (XII), 1979 (XIII).

Barnes, Jeff (2)—Oakland Raiders 1981 (XV); Los Angeles Raiders 1984 (XVIII).

Barnes, Rodrigo (1)—Oakland Raiders 1977 (XI).

Barnett, Bill (1)—Miami Dolphins 1985 (XIX).

Barnwell, Malcolm (1)—Los Angeles Raiders 1984 (XVIII).

Bass, Don (1)—Cincinnati Bengals 1982 (XVI).

Bass, Mike (1)—Washington Redskins 1973 (VII).

Baumhower, Bob (2)—Miami Dolphins 1983 (XVII), 1985 (XIX).

Bavaro, Mark (1)—New York Giants 1987 (XXI).

Beamon, Autry (1)—Minnesota Vikings 1977 (XI).

Beasley, John (1)—Minnesota Vikings 1970 (IV).

Beasley, Tom (2)—Pittsburgh Steelers 1979 (XIII), 1980 (XIV).

Beathard, Pete (1)—Kansas City Chiefs 1967 (I).

Bell, Bobby (2)—Kansas City Chiefs 1967 (I), 1970 (IV).

Bell, Ken (2)—Denver Broncos 1987 (XXI), 1988 (XXII).

Bell, Theo (2)—Pittsburgh Steelers 1979 (XIII), 1980 (XIV).

Belser, Ceaser (1)—Kansas City Chiefs 1970 (IV).

Benjamin, Guy (0*)—San Francisco 49ers 1982 (XVI-DNP).

Bennett, Woody (2)—Miami Dolphins 1983 (XVII), 1985 (XIX).

Benson, Brad (1)—New York Giants 1987 (XXI).

Benson, Charles (1)—Miami Dolphins 1985 (XIX).

Benson, Duane (1)—Oakland Raiders 1968 (II).

Bergey, Bill (1)—Philadelphia Eagles 1981 (XV).

Berry, Bob (0***)—Minnesota Vikings 1974 (VIII-DNP), 1975 (IX-DNP), 1977 (XI-DNP).

Bethea, Larry (1)—Dallas Cowboys 1979 (XIII).

Betters, Doug (2)—Miami Dolphins 1983 (XVII), 1985 (XIX).

Beverly, Randy (1)—New York Jets 1969 (III).

Biggs, Verlon (2)—New York Jets 1969 (III); Washington Redskins 1973 (VII).

Biletnikoff, Fred (2)—Oakland Raiders 1968 (II), 1977 (XI).

Biodrowski, Dennis (1)—Kansas City Chiefs 1967 (I).

Bird, Rodger (1)—Oakland Raiders 1968 (II).

Birdwell, Dan (1)—Oakland Raiders 1968 (II).

Bishop, Keith (2)—Denver Broncos 1987 (XXI), 1988 (XXII).

Bishop, Richard (0*)—Miami Dolphins 1983 (XVII-DNP).

Blackmon, Don (1)—New England Patriots 1986 (XX).

Blackmore, Richard (1)—Philadelphia Eagles 1981 (XV).

Blackwell, Alois (1)—Dallas Cowboys 1979 (XIII).

Blackwood, Glenn (2)—Miami Dolphins 1983 (XVII), 1985 (XIX).

Blackwood, Lyle (2)—Miami Dolphins 1983 (XVII), 1985 (XIX).

Blahak, Joe (0*)—Minnesota Vikings 1975 (IX-DNP).

Blair, Matt (2)—Minnesota Vikings 1975 (IX), 1977 (XI).

Blanda, George (1)—Oakland Raiders 1968 (II).

Bleier, Rocky (4)—Pittsburgh Steelers 1975 (IX), 1976 (X), 1979 (XIII), 1980 (XIV).

Blount, Mel (4)—Pittsburgh Steelers 1975 (IX), 1976 (X), 1979 (XIII), 1980 (XIV).

Board, Dwaine (2)—San Francisco 49ers 1982 (XVI), 1985 (XIX).

Boddie, Tony (1)—Denver Broncos 1988 (XXII).

Bokamper, Kim (2)—Miami Dolphins 1983 (XVII), 1985 (XIX).

Bonness, Rik (1)—Oakland Raiders 1977 (XI).

Boone, Dave (0*)—Minnesota Vikings 1975 (IX-DNP).

Boozer, Emerson (1)—New York Jets 1969 (III).

Bortz, Mark (1)—Chicago Bears 1986 (XX).

Bostic, Jeff (3)—Washington Redskins 1983 (XVII), 1984 (XVIII), 1988 (XXII).

Bowles, Todd (1)—Washington Redskins 1988 (XXII).

Bowman, Jim (1)—New England Patriots 1986 (XX).

Bowman, Ken (2)—Green Bay Packers 1967 (I), 1968 (II).

Bowser, Charles (2)—Miami Dolphins 1983 (XVII), 1985 (XIX).

Bowyer, Walt (1)—Denver Broncos 1988 (XXII).

Boyd, Bob (1)—Baltimore Colts 1969 (III).

Braase, Ordell (1)—Baltimore Colts 1969 (III).

Bradley, Ed (2)—Pittsburgh Steelers 1975 (IX), 1976 (X).

Bradshaw, Morris (2)—Oakland Raiders 1977 (XI), 1981 (XV).

Bradshaw, Terry (4)—Pittsburgh Steelers 1975 (IX), 1976 (X), 1979 (XIII), 1980 (XIV).

Bragg, Mike (1)—Washington Redskins 1973 (VII).

Branch, Cliff (3)—Oakland Raiders 1977 (XI), 1981 (XV); Los Angeles Raiders 1984 (XVIII).

Branch, Reggie (1)—Washington Redskins 1988 (XXII).

Bratkowski, Zeke (2)—Green Bay Packers 1967 (I), 1968 (II).

Braxton, Tyrone (1)—Denver Broncos 1988 (XXII).

Breech, Jim (1)—Cincinnati Bengals 1982 (XVI).

Breeden, Louis (1)—Cincinnati Bengals 1982 (XVI).

Breunig, Bob (3)—Dallas Cowboys 1976 (X), 1978 (XII), 1979 (XIII).

Brinson, Larry (2)—Dallas Cowboys 1978 (XII), 1979 (XIII).

Briscoe, Marlin (2)—Miami Dolphins 1973 (VII), 1974 (VIII).

Brock, Pete (1)—New England Patriots 1986 (XX).

Brooks, Larry (1)—Los Angeles Rams 1980 (XIV).

Brooks, Michael (1)—Denver Broncos 1988 (XXII).

Brooks, Perry (2)—Washington Redskins 1983 (XVII), 1984 (XVIII).

Brophy, Jay (1)—Miami Dolphins 1985 (XIX).

Brown, Aaron (2)—Kansas City Chiefs 1967 (I), 1970 (IV).

Brown, Bill (3)—Minnesota Vikings 1970 (IV), 1974 (VIII), 1975 (IX).

Brown, Bob (2)—Green Bay Packers 1967 (I), 1968 (II).

Brown, Bud (1)—Miami Dolphins 1985 (XIX).

Brown, Charlie (2)—Washington Redskins 1983 (XVII), 1984 (XVIII).

Brown, Dave (1)—Pittsburgh Steelers 1976 (X).

Brown, Eddie (1)—Los Angeles Rams 1980 (XIV).

Brown, Guy (2)—Dallas Cowboys 1978 (XII), 1979 (XIII).

Brown, Larry (4)—Pittsburgh Steelers 1975 (IX), 1976 (X), 1979 (XIII), 1980 (XIV).

Brown, Larry (1)—Washington Redskins 1973 (VII).

Brown, Mark (1)—Miami Dolphins 1985 (XIX).

Brown, Terry (2)—Minnesota Vikings 1974 (VIII), 1975 (IX).

Brown, Thomas (1)—Philadelphia Eagles 1981 (XV).

Brown, Tim (1)—Baltimore Colts 1969 (III).

Brown, Tom (2)—Green Bay Packers 1967 (I), 1968 (II).

Brown, Willie (2)—Oakland Raiders 1968 (II), 1977 (XI).

Browner, Ross (1)—Cincinnati Bengals 1982 (XVI).

Browning, Dave (1)—Oakland Raiders 1981 (XV).

Brudzinski, Bob (3)—Los Angeles Rams 1980 (XIV); Miami Dolphins 1983 (XVII), 1985 (XIX).

Brundige, Bill (1)—Washington Redskins 1973 (VII).

Brunet, Bob (1)—Washington Redskins 1973 (VII).

Bryan, Bill (1)—Denver Broncos 1987 (XXI).

Bryan, Steve (0†)—Denver Broncos 1988 (XXII-Inactive).

Bryant, Bobby (2)—Minnesota Vikings 1974 (VIII), 1977 (XI).

Bryant, Cullen (1)—Los Angeles Rams 1980 (XIV).

Bryant, Kelvin (1)—Washington Redskins 1988 (XXII).

Buchanan, Buck (2)—Kansas City Chiefs 1967 (I), 1970 (IV).

Budde, Ed (2)—Kansas City Chiefs 1967 (I), 1970 (IV).

Budness, Bill (1)—Oakland Raiders 1968 (II).

Buehler, George (1)—Oakland Raiders 1977 (XI).

Buetow, Bart (1)—Minnesota Vikings 1977 (XI).

Buford, Maury (1)—Chicago Bears 1986 (XX).

Bujnoch, Glenn (0*)—Cincinnati Bengals 1982 (XVI).

Bulaich, Norm (1)—Baltimore Colts 1971 (V).

Bunting, John (1)—Philadelphia Eagles 1981 (XV).

Bunz, Dan (2)—San Francisco 49ers 1982 (XVI), 1985 (XIX).

Buoniconti, Nick (3)—Miami Dolphins 1972 (VI), 1973 (VII), 1974 (VIII).

Burford, Chris (1)—Kansas City Chiefs 1967 (I).

Burley, Gary (1)—Cincinnati Bengals 1982 (XVI).

Burman, George (1)—Washington Redskins 1973 (VII).

Burt, Jim (1)—New York Giants 1987 (XXI).

Bush, Blair (1)—Cincinnati Bengals 1982 (XVI).

Butler, Kevin (1)—Chicago Bears 1986 (XX).

Butz, Dave (3)—Washington Redskins 1983 (XVII), 1984 (XVIII), 1988 (XXII).

Byrd, Darryl (1)—Los Angeles Raiders 1984 (XVIII).

Cabral, Brian (1)—Chicago Bears 1986 (XX).

Caffey, Lee Roy (2)—Green Bay Packers 1967 (I), 1968 (II).

Caldwell, Ravin (1)—Washington Redskins 1988 (XXII).

Caldwell, Tony (1)—Los Angeles Raiders 1984 (XVIII).

Camarillo, Rich (1)—New England Patriots 1986 (XX).

Cameron, Glenn (1)—Cincinnati Bengals 1982 (XVI).

Campbell, Joe (1)—Oakland Raiders 1981 (XV).

Campfield, Billy (1)—Philadelphia Eagles 1981 (XV).

Cannon, Billy (1)—Oakland Raiders 1968 (II).

Capone, Warren (1)—Dallas Cowboys 1976 (X).

Capp, Dick (1)—Green Bay Packers 1968 (II).

Carano, Glenn (0*)—Dallas Cowboys 1979

(XIII-DNP).

Caravello, Joe (0†)—Washington Redskins 1988 (XXII-Inactive).

Carmichael, Harold (1)—Philadelphia Eagles 1981 (XV).

Carolan, Reg (1)—Kansas City Chiefs 1967 (I).

Carpenter, Brian (1)—Washington Redskins 1984 (XVIII).

Carson, Harry (1)—New York Giants 1987 (XXI).

Carter, Joe (1)—Miami Dolphins 1985 (XIX).

Carter, Michael (1)—San Francisco 49ers 1985 (XIX).

Carter, Rubin (1)—Denver Broncos 1978 (XII).

Carthon, Maurice (1)—New York Giants 1987 (XXI).

Casper, Dave (1)—Oakland Raiders 1977 (XI).

Caster, Richard (0*)—Washington Redskins 1983 (XVII-DNP).

Castille, Jeremiah (1)—Denver Broncos 1988 (XXII).

Cavanaugh, Matt (0*)—San Francisco 49ers 1985 (XIX-DNP).

Cefalo, Jimmy (2)—Miami Dolphins 1983 (XVII), 1985 (XIX).

Celotto, Mario (1)—Oakland Raiders 1981 (XV).

Chandler, Bob (1)—Oakland Raiders 1981 (XV).

Chandler, Don (2)—Green Bay Packers 1967 (I), 1968 (II).

Charles, Mike (1)—Miami Dolphins 1985 (XIX).

Chavous, Barney (1)—Denver Broncos 1978 (XII).

Chesley, Al (1)—Philadelphia Eagles 1981 (XV).

Chester, Raymond (1)—Oakland Raiders 1981 (XV).

Choma, John (1)—San Francisco 49ers 1982 (XVI).

Christensen, Todd (2)—Oakland Raiders 1981 (XV); Los Angeles Raiders 1984 (XVIII).

Christy, Earl (1)—New York Jets 1969 (III).

Clabo, Neil (1)—Minnesota Vikings 1977 (XI).

Clack, Jim (2)—Pittsburgh Steelers 1975 (IX), 1976 (X).

Clark, Dwight (2)—San Francisco 49ers 1982 (XVI), 1985 (XIX).

Clark, Gary (1)—Washington Redskins 1988 (XXII).

Clark, K.C. (1)—Denver Broncos 1988 (XXII).

Clark, Ken (1)—Los Angeles Rams 1980 (XIV).

Clark, Mario (0*)—San Francisco 49ers 1985 (XIX-DNP).

Clark, Mike (2)—Dallas Cowboys 1971 (V), 1972 (VI).

Clark, Steve (1*)—Miami Dolphins 1983 (XVII-DNP), 1985 (XIX).

Clarke, Ken (1)—Philadelphia Eagles 1981 (XV).

Clayborn, Raymond (1)—New England Patriots 1986 (XX).

Clayton, Mark (1)—Miami Dolphins 1985 (XIX).

Coan, Bert (1)—Kansas City Chiefs 1967 (I).

Coffey, Ken (1)—Washington Redskins 1984 (XVIII).

Cole, Larry (5)—Dallas Cowboys 1971 (V), 1972 (VI), 1976 (X), 1978 (XII), 1979 (XIII).

Cole, Robin (2)—Pittsburgh Steelers 1979 (XIII), 1980 (XIV).

Cole, Terry (2)—Baltimore Colts 1969 (III); Miami Dolphins 1972 (VI).

Coleman, Monte (3)—Washington Redskins 1983 (XVII), 1984 (XVIII), 1988 (XXII).

Collier, Mike (1)—Pittsburgh Steelers 1976 (X).

Collins, Mark (1)—New York Giants 1987 (XXI).

Collins, Tony (1)—New England Patriots 1986 (XX).

Colfinsworth, Cris (1)—Cincinnati Bengals 1982 (XVI).

Colorito, Tony (1)—Denver Broncos 1987 (XXI).

Colquitt, Craig (2)—Pittsburgh Steelers 1979 (XIII), 1980 (XIV).

Colzie, Neal (1)—Oakland Raiders 1977 (XI).

Comeaux, Darren (1)—Denver Broncos 1987 (XXI).

Conn, Dick (1)—Pittsburgh Steelers 1975 (IX).

Conners, Dan (1)—Oakland Raiders 1968 (II).

Cooper, Earl (2)—San Francisco 49ers 1982 (XVI), 1985 (XIX).

Cooper, Jim (2)—Dallas Cowboys 1978 (XII), 1979 (XIII).

Cooper, Mark (1)—Denver Broncos 1987 (XXI).

Corey, Walt (1)—Kansas City Chiefs 1967 (I).

Cornish, Frank (1)—Miami Dolphins 1972 (VI).

Corral, Frank (1)—Los Angeles Rams 1980 (XIV).

Courson, Steve (2)—Pittsburgh Steelers 1979 (XIII), 1980 (XIV).

Covert, Jim (1)—Chicago Bears 1986 (XX).

Cox, Fred (4)—Minnesota Vikings 1970 (IV), 1974 (VIII) 1975 (IX), 1977 (XI).

Cox, Steve (1)—Washington Redskins 1988 (XXII).

Craig, Roger (1)—San Francisco 49ers 1985 (XIX).

Craig, Steve (2)—Minnesota Vikings 1975 (IX), 1977 (XI).

Crane, Paul (1)—New York Jets 1969 (III).

Creswell, Smiley (1)—New England Patriots 1986 (XX).

Cromwell, Nolan (1)—Los Angeles Rams 1980 (XIV).

Cronan, Pete (2)—Washington Redskins 1983 (XVII), 1984 (XVIII).

Cross, Randy (2)—San Francisco 49ers 1982 (XVI), 1985 (XIX).

Crusan, Doug (3)—Miami Dolphins 1972 (VI), 1973 (VII), 1974 (VIII).

Crutcher, Tommy (2)—Green Bay Packers 1967 (I), 1968 (II).

Csonka, Larry (3)—Miami Dolphins 1972 (VI), 1973 (VII), 1974 (VIII).

Culp, Curley (1)—Kansas City Chiefs 1970 (IV).

Cunningham, Bennie (1*)—Pittsburgh Steelers 1979 (XIII-DNP), 1980 (XIV).

Cuozzo, Gary (1)—Minnesota Vikings 1970 (IV).

Curry, Bill (3)—Green Bay Packers 1967 (I); Baltimore Colts 1969 (III), 1971 (V).

Curtis, Isaac (1)—Cincinnati Bengals 1982 (XVI).

Curtis, Mike (2)—Baltimore Colts 1969 (III), 1971 (V).

Dalby, Dave (3)—Oakland Raiders 1977 (XI), 1981 (XV); Los Angeles Raiders 1984 (XVIII).

Dale, Carroll (3)—Green Bay Packers 1967 (I), 1968 (II); Minnesota Vikings 1974 (VIII).

D'Amato, Mike (1)—New York Jets 1969 (III).

Daney, George (1)—Kansas City Chiefs 1970 (IV).

Davidson, Ben (1)—Oakland Raiders 1968 (II).

Davis, Brian (1)—Washington Redskins 1988 (XXII).

Davis, Bruce (2)—Oakland Raiders 1981 (XV); Los Angeles Raiders 1984 (XVIII).

Davis, Charlie (1)—Pittsburgh Steelers 1975 (IX).

Davis, Clarence (1)—Oakland Raiders 1977 (XI).

Davis, Doug (0*)—Minnesota Vikings 1970 (IV-DNP).

Davis, James (1)—Los Angeles Raiders 1984 (XVIII).

Davis, Johnny (1)—San Francisco 49ers 1982 (XVI).

Davis, Kyle (1)—Dallas Cowboys 1976 (X).

Davis, Mike (2)—Oakland Raiders 1981 (XV); Los Angeles Raiders 1984 (XVIII).

Davis, Oliver (1)—Cincinnati Bengals 1982 (XVI).

Davis, Sam (4)—Pittsburgh Steelers 1975 (IX), 1976 (X), 1979 (XIII), 1980 (XIV).

Davis, Steve (1)—Pittsburgh Steelers 1975 (IX).

Davis, Willie (2)—Green Bay Packers 1967 (I), 1968 (II).

Dawson, Len (2)—Kansas City Chiefs 1967 (I), 1970 (IV).

Dawson, Lin (1)—New England Patriots 1986 (XX).

Dean, Fred (2)—San Francisco 49ers 1982 (XVI), 1985 (XIX).

Dean, Fred (1)—Washington Redskins 1983 (XVII).

Dean, Vernon (3)—Washington Redskins 1983 (XVII), 1984 (XVIII), 1988 (XXII).

Deloplaine, Jack (1)—Pittsburgh Steelers 1979 (XIII).

DeMarco, Bob (1)—Miami Dolphins 1972 (VI).

Den Herder, Vern (4)—Miami Dolphins 1972 (VI), 1973 (VII), 1974 (VIII), 1983 (XVII).

Dennard, Mark (1)—Miami Dolphins 1983 (XVII).

Dennard, Preston (1)—Los Angeles Rams 1980 (XIV).

Dennison, Doug (2)—Dallas Cowboys 1976 (X), 1978 (XII).

Dennison, Rick (2)—Denver Broncos 1987 (XXI), 1988 (XXII).

Dent, Richard (1)—Chicago Bears 1986 (XX).

Diana, Rich (1)—Miami Dolphins 1983 (XVII).

Dickson, Paul (1)—Minnesota Vikings 1970 (IV).

Didier, Clint (3)—Washington Redskins 1983 (XVII), 1984 (XVIII), 1988 (XXII).

Dilts, Bucky (1)—Denver Broncos 1978 (XII).

DiMidio, Tony (1)—Kansas City Chiefs 1967 (I).

Dinkel, Tom (1)—Cincinnati Bengals 1982 (XVI).

Ditka, Mike (2)—Dallas Cowboys 1971 (V), 1972 (VI).

Dixon, Hewritt (1)—Oakland Raiders 1968 (II).

Dockery, John (1)—New York Jets 1969 (III).

Dolbin, Jack (1)—Denver Broncos 1978 (XII)

Donovan, Pat (3)—Dallas Cowboys 1976 (X), 1978 (XII), 1979 (XIII).

Dornbrook, Thom (1)—Pittsburgh Steelers 1980 (XIV).

Dorsett, Tony (2)—Dallas Cowboys 1978 (XII), 1979 (XIII).

Dorsey, Eric (1)—New York Giants 1987 (XXI).

Doss, Reggie (1)—Los Angeles Rams 1980 (XIV).

Dowler, Boyd (2)—Green Bay Packers 1967 (I), 1968 (II).

Downing, Walt (1)—San Francisco 49ers 1982 (XVI).

Druschel, Rick (1)—Pittsburgh Steelers 1975 (IX).

Dryer, Fred (1)—Los Angeles Rams 1980 (XIV).

Duerson, Dave (1)—Chicago Bears 1986 (XX).

Duhe, A.J. (2)—Miami Dolphins 1983 (XVII), 1985 (XIX).

Dumler, Doug (1)—Minnesota Vikings 1977 (XI).

Duncan, Jim (1)—Baltimore Colts 1971 (V).

Dungy, Tony (1)—Pittsburgh Steelers 1979 (XIII).

Dunn, Gary (2)—Pittsburgh Steelers 1979 (XIII), 1980 (XIV).

Duper, Mark (1*)—Miami Dolphins 1983 (XVII-DNP), 1985 (XIX).

DuPree, Billy Joe (3)—Dallas Cowboys 1976 (X), 1978 (XII), 1979 (XIII).

Easley, Walt (0*)—San Francisco 49ers 1982 (XVI-DNP).

Eason, Tony (1)—New England Patriots 1986 (XX).

East, Ron (1)—Dallas Cowboys 1971 (V).

Edwards, Dave (3)—Dallas Cowboys 1971 (V), 1972 (VI), 1976 (X).

Edwards, Eddie (1)—Cincinnati Bengals 1982 (XVI).

Edwards, Glen (2)—Pittsburgh Steelers 1975 (IX), 1976 (X).

Edwards, Herman (1)—Philadelphia Eagles 1981 (XV).

Egloff, Ron (1)—Denver Broncos 1978 (XII).

Eischeid, Mike (3)—Oakland Raiders 1968 (II); Minnesota Vikings 1974 (VIII), 1975 (IX).

Eller, Carl (4)—Minnesota Vikings 1970 (IV), 1974 (VIII), 1975 (IX), 1977 (XI).

Elliott, John (1)—New York Jets 1969 (III).

Elliott, Lenvil (0*)—San Francisco 49ers 1982 (XVI-DNP).

Ellis, Ken (0*)—Los Angeles Rams 1980 (XIV-DNP).

Ellison, Riki (1)—San Francisco 49ers 1985 (XIX).

Elmendorf, Dave (1)—Los Angeles Rams 1980 (XIV).

Elway, John (2)—Denver Broncos 1987 (XXI), 1988 (XXII).

Evans, Larry (1)—Denver Broncos 1978 (XII).

Evans, Norm (3)—Miami Dolphins 1972 (VI), 1973 (VII), 1974 (VIII).

Evans, Reggie (1)—Washington Redskins 1984 (XVIII).

Fahnhorst, Keith (2)—San Francisco 49ers 1982 (XVI), 1985 (XIX).

Fairchild, Paul (1)—New England Patriots 1986 (XX).

Fanning, Mike (1)—Los Angeles Rams 1980 (XIV).

Fanucci, Mike (1)—Washington Redskins 1973 (VII).

Fencik, Gary (1)—Chicago Bears 1986 (XX).

Fernandez, Manny (3)—Miami Dolphins 1972 (VI), 1973 (VII), 1974 (VIII).

Ferragamo, Vince (1)—Los Angeles Rams 1980 (XIV).

Fischer, Pat (1)—Washington Redskins 1973 (VII).

Fitzgerald, John (4)—Dallas Cowboys 1972 (VI), 1976 (X), 1978 (XII), 1979 (XIII).

Flanigan, Jim (1)—Green Bay Packers 1968 (II).

Fleming, Marv (5)—Green Bay Packers 1967 (I), 1968 (II); Miami Dolphins 1972 (VI), 1973 (VII), 1974 (VIII).

Fletcher, Simon (2)—Denver Broncos 1987 (XXI), 1988 (XXII).

Flores, Tom (0*)—Kansas City Chiefs 1970 (IV-DNP).

Flowers, Richmond (1)—Dallas Cowboys 1971 (V).

Flynn, Tom (1)—New York Giants 1987 (XXI).

Foley, Steve (2)—Denver Broncos 1978 (XII), 1987 (XXI).

Foley, Tim (2)—Miami Dolphins 1972 (VI), 1974 (VIII).

Foreman, Chuck (3)—Minnesota Vikings 1974 (VIII), 1975 (IX), 1977 (XI).

Foster, Roy (2)—Miami Dolphins 1983 (XVII), 1985 (XIX).

France, Doug (1)—Los Angeles Rams 1980 (XIV).

Francis, Russ (1)—San Francisco 49ers 1985 (XIX).

Frank, John (0*)—San Francisco 49ers 1985 (XIX-DNP).

Franklin, Andra (1)—Miami Dolphins 1983 (XVII).

Franklin, Tony (2)—Philadelphia Eagles 1981 (XV); New England Patriots 1986 (XX).

Frazier, Guy (1)—Cincinnati Bengals 1982 (XVI).

Frazier, Leslie (1)—Chicago Bears 1986 (XX).

Frazier, Wayne (1)—Kansas City Chiefs 1967 (I).

Frederick, Andy (3)—Dallas Cowboys 1978 (XII), 1979 (XIII); Chicago Bears 1986 (XX).

Freeman, Mike (2)—Denver Broncos 1987 (XXI), 1988 (XXII).

Fritsch, Toni (1)—Dallas Cowboys 1976 (X).

Fryar, Irving (1)—New England Patriots 1986 (XX).

Fugett, Jean (1)—Dallas Cowboys 1976 (X).

Fuller, Jeff (1)—San Francisco 49ers 1985 (XIX).

Fuller, Mike (1)—Cincinnati Bengals 1982 (XVI).

Fuller, Steve (1)—Chicago Bears 1986 (XX).

Fuqua, John (1)—Pittsburgh Steelers 1976 (X).

Furness, Steve (4)—Pittsburgh Steelers 1975 (IX), 1976 (X), 1979 (XIII), 1980 (XIV).

Galbreath, Tony (1)—New York Giants 1987 (XXI).

Gallagher, Frank (1)—Minnesota Vikings 1974 (VIII).

Gardin, Ron (1)—Baltimore Colts 1971 (V).

Garrett, Alvin (2)—Washington Redskins 1983 (XVII), 1984 (XVIII).

Garrett, Carl (1)—Oakland Raiders 1977 (XI).

Garrett, Mike (2)—Kansas City Chiefs 1967 (I), 1970 (IV).

Garrett, Reggie (2)—Pittsburgh Steelers 1975 (IX), 1976 (X).

Garrison, Walt (2)—Dallas Cowboys 1971 (V), 1972 (VI).

Gaubatz, Dennis (1)—Baltimore Colts 1969 (III).

Gault, Willie (1)—Chicago Bears 1986 (XX).

Gayle, Shaun (1)—Chicago Bears 1986 (XX).

Gentry, Dennis (1)—Chicago Bears 1986 (XX).

Gerela, Roy (3)—Pittsburgh Steelers 1975 (IX), 1976 (X), 1979 (XIII).

Gervais, Rick (1)—San Francisco 49ers 1982 (XVI).

Giammona, Louie (1)—Philadelphia Eagles 1981 (XV).

Giaquinto, Nick (2)—Washington Redskins 1983 (XVII), 1984 (XVIII).

Gibson, Ernest (1)—New England Patriots 1986 (XX).

Giesler, Jon (2)—Miami Dolphins 1983 (XVII), 1985 (XIX).

Gilbert, Freddie (2)—Denver Broncos 1987 (XXI), 1988 (XXII).

Gilliam, Joe (0**)—Pittsburgh Steelers 1975 (IX-DNP), 1976 (X-DNP).

Gilliam, John (2)—Minnesota Vikings 1974 (VIII), 1975 (IX).

Gilliam, Jon (1)—Kansas City Chiefs 1967 (I).

Gillingham, Gale (2)—Green Bay Packers 1967 (I), 1968 (II).

Ginn, Hubert (3)—Miami Dolphins 1972 (VI), 1973 (VII); Oakland Raiders 1977 (XI).

Glassic, Tom (1)—Denver Broncos 1978 (XII).

Godfrey, Chris (1)—New York Giants 1987 (XXI).

Goode, Irv (1)—Miami Dolphins 1974 (VIII).

Goode, Tom (1)—Baltimore Colts 1971 (V).

Goodrum, Charles (3)—Minnesota Vikings 1974 (VIII), 1975 (IX), 1977 (XI).

Gordon, Cornell (1)—New York Jets 1969 (III).

Gordon, Larry (1)—Miami Dolphins 1983 (XVII).

Gouveia, Kurt (1)—Washington Redskins 1988 (XXII).

Grabowski, Jim (1*)—Green Bay Packers 1967 (I), 1968 (II-DNP).

Graddy, Sam (0†)—Denver Broncos 1988 (XXII-Inactive).

Gradishar, Randy (1)—Denver Broncos 1978 (XII).

Grant, Bob (1)—Baltimore Colts 1971 (V).

Grant, Darryl (3)—Washington Redskins 1983 (XVII), 1984 (XVIII), 1988 (XXII).

Grant, John (1)—Denver Broncos 1978 (XII).

Grantham, Larry (1)—New York Jets 1969 (III).

Gravelle, Gordon (3)—Pittsburgh Steelers 1975 (IX), 1976 (X); Los Angeles Rams 1980 (XIV).

Graves, Tom (1)—Pittsburgh Steelers 1980 (XIV).

Grayson, Dave (1)—Oakland Raiders 1968 (II).

Green, Cleveland (2)—Miami Dolphins 1983 (XVII), 1985 (XIX).

Green, Cornell (2)—Dallas Cowboys 1971 (V), 1972 (VI).

Green, Darrell (2)—Washington Redskins 1984 (XVIII), 1988 (XXII).

Greene, Joe (4)—Pittsburgh Steelers 1975 (IX), 1976 (X), 1979 (XIII), 1980 (XIV).

Greenwood, L. C. (4)—Pittsburgh Steelers 1975 (IX), 1976 (X), 1979 (XIII), 1980 (XIV).

Gregg, Forrest (2*)—Green Bay Packers 1967 (I), 1968 (II); Dallas Cowboys 1972 (VI-DNP).

Gregory, Bill (3)—Dallas Cowboys 1972 (VI), 1976 (X), 1978 (XII).

Griese, Bob (3)—Miami Dolphins 1972 (VI), 1973 (VII), 1974 (VIII).

Griffin, Archie (1)—Cincinnati Bengals 1982 (XVI).

Griffin, Keith (1)—Washington Redskins 1988 (XXII).

Griffin, Ray (1)—Cincinnati Bengals 1982 (XVI).

Grim, Bob (2)—Minnesota Vikings 1970 (IV), 1977 (XI).

Grimm, Russ (3)—Washington Redskins 1983 (XVII), 1984 (XVIII), 1988 (XXII).

Groce, Ron (1)—Minnesota Vikings 1977 (XI).

Grogan, Steve (1)—New England Patriots 1986 (XX).

Grossman, Randy (4)—Pittsburgh Steelers 1975 (IX), 1976 (X), 1979 (XIII), 1980 (XIV).

Guy, Ray (3)—Oakland Raiders 1977 (XI), 1981 (XV); Los Angeles Raiders 1984 (XVIII).

Hackbart, Dale (1)—Minnesota Vikings 1970 (IV).

Hackett, Joey (1)—Denver Broncos 1987 (XXI).

Hagberg, Roger (1)—Oakland Raiders 1968 (II).

Hairston, Carl (1)—Philadelphia Eagles 1981 (XV).

Haji-Sheikh, Ali (1)—Washington Redskins 1988 (XXII).

Hall, Willie (1)—Oakland Raiders 1977 (XI).

Hall, Windlan (1)—Minnesota Vikings 1977 (XI).

Ham, Jack (3*)—Pittsburgh Steelers 1975 (IX), 1976 (X), 1979 (XIII), 1980 (XIV-DNP).

Hamel, Dean (1)—Washington Redskins 1988 (XXII).

Hamilton, Steve (1)—Washington Redskins 1988 (XXII).

Hampton, Dan (1)—Chicago Bears 1986 (XX).

Hanburger, Chris (1)—Washington Redskins 1973 (VII).

Hannah, Charley (1)—Los Angeles Raiders 1984 (XVIII).

Hannah, John (1)—New England Patriots 1986 (XX).

Hanratty, Terry (1*)—Pittsburgh Steelers 1975 (IX-DNP), 1976 (X).

Harden, Mike (1)—Denver Broncos 1987 (XXI).

Hardman, Cedrick (1)—Oakland Raiders 1981 (XV).

Hardy, Bruce (2)—Miami Dolphins 1983 (XVII), 1985 (XIX).

Hargrove, Jim (1)—Minnesota Vikings 1970 (IV).

Hargrove, Jim (1)—Cincinnati Bengals 1982 (XVI).

Harmon, Clarence (1)—Washington Redskins 1983 (XVII).

Harmon, Derrick (1)—San Francisco 49ers 1985 (XIX).

Harper, Willie (1)—San Francisco 49ers 1982 (XVI).

Harrah, Dennis (1)—Los Angeles Rams 1980 (XIV).

Harraway, Charley (1)—Washington Redskins 1973 (VII).

Harrington, Perry (1)—Philadelphia Eagles 1981 (XV).

Harris, Bill (1)—Minnesota Vikings 1970 (IV).

Harris, Bo (1)—Cincinnati Bengals 1982 (XVI).

Harris, Cliff (5)—Dallas Cowboys 1971 (V), 1972 (VI), 1976 (X), 1978 (XII), 1979 (XIII).

Harris, Duriel (1)—Miami Dolphins 1983 (XVII).

Harris, Franco (4)—Pittsburgh Steelers 1975 (IX), 1976 (X), 1979 (XIII), 1980 (XIV).

Harris, Joe (1)—Los Angeles Rams 1980 (XIV).

Harris, Leroy (1)—Philadelphia Eagles 1981 (XV).

Harris, M.L. (1)—Cincinnati Bengals 1982 (XVI).

Harrison, Dennis (1)—Philadelphia Eagles 1981 (XV).

Harrison, Reggie (2)—Pittsburgh Steelers 1975 (IX), 1976 (X).

Hart, Doug (2)—Green Bay Packers 1967 (I), 1968 (II).

Hartenstine, Mike (1)—Chicago Bears 1986 (XX).

Harty, John (1)—San Francisco 49ers 1982 (XVI).

Harvey, Jim (1)—Oakland Raiders 1968 (II).

Hasselbeck, Don (1)—Los Angeles Raiders 1984 (XVIII).

Hathcock, Dave (1)—Green Bay Packers 1967 (I).

Hauss, Len (1)—Washington Redskins 1973 (VII).

Havrilak, Sam (1)—Baltimore Colts 1971 (V).

Hawkins, Alex (1)—Baltimore Colts 1969 (III).

Hawkins, Frank (1)—Los Angeles Raiders 1984 (XVIII).

Hawkins, Wayne (1)—Oakland Raiders 1968 (II).

Hawthorne, Greg (2)—Pittsburgh Steelers 1980 (XIV); New England Patriots 1986 (XX).

Hayes, Bob (2)—Dallas Cowboys 1971 (V), 1972 (VI).

Hayes, Jeff (2)—Washington Redskins 1983 (XVII), 1984 (XVIII).

Hayes, Lester (2)—Oakland Raiders 1981 (XV); Los Angeles Raiders 1984 (XVIII).

Hayes, Wendell (1)—Kansas City Chiefs 1970 (IV).

Haymond, Alvin (1)—Washington Redskins 1973 (VII).

Haynes, Mark (2)—Denver Broncos 1987 (XXI), 1988 (XXII).

Haynes, Mike (1)—Los Angeles Raiders 1984 (XVIII).

Headen, Andy (1)—New York Giants 1987 (XXI).

Headrick, Sherrill (1)—Kansas City Chiefs 1967 (I).

Heflin, Vince (2)—Miami Dolphins 1983 (XVII), 1985 (XIX).

Hegman, Mike (2)—Dallas Cowboys 1978 (XII), 1979 (XIII).

Heinz, Bob (3)—Miami Dolphins 1972 (VI), 1973 (VII), 1974 (VIII).

Henderson, John (1)—Minnesota Vikings 1970 (IV).

Henderson, Thomas (3)—Dallas Cowboys 1976 (X), 1978 (XII), 1979 (XIII).

Henderson, Zac (1)—Philadelphia Eagles 1981 (XV).

Hendricks, Ted (4)—Baltimore Colts 1971 (V), Oakland Raiders 1977 (XI), 1981 (XV); Los Angeles Raiders 1984 (XVIII).

Henry, Wally (1)—Philadelphia Eagles 1981 (XV).

Herman, Dave (1)—New York Jets 1969 (III).

Hermeling, Terry (1)—Washington Redskins 1973 (VII).

Herock, Ken (1)—Oakland Raiders 1968 (II).

Herrera, Efren (1)—Dallas Cowboys 1978 (XII).

Hertel, Rob (0*)—Philadelphia Eagles 1981 (XV-DNP).

Hester, Ron (1)—Miami Dolphins 1983 (XVII).

Hicks, Bryan (1)—Cincinnati Bengals 1982 (XVI).

Hicks, Dwight (2)—San Francisco 49ers 1982 (XVI), 1985 (XIX).

Hilgenberg, Jay (1)—Chicago Bears 1986 (XX).

Hilgenberg, Wally (4)—Minnesota Vikings 1970 (IV), 1974 (VIII), 1975 (IX), 1977 (XI).

Hill, Calvin (2)—Dallas Cowboys 1971 (V), 1972 (VI).

Hill, Dave (2)—Kansas City Chiefs 1967 (I), 1970 (IV).

Hill, Drew (1)—Los Angeles Rams 1980 (XIV).

Hill, Eddie (3)—Los Angeles Rams 1980 (XIV); Miami Dolphins 1983 (XVII), 1985 (XIX).

Hill, Jerry (2)—Baltimore Colts 1969 (III), 1971 (V).

Hill, Kenny (2)—Los Angeles Raiders 1984 (XVIII); New York Giants 1987 (XXI).

Hill, Kent (1)—Los Angeles Rams 1980 (XIV).

Hill, Tony (2)—Dallas Cowboys 1978 (XII), 1979 (XIII).

Hill, Winston (1)—New York Jets 1969 (III).

Hilton, Roy (2)—Baltimore Colts 1969 (III), 1971 (V).

Hinton, Eddie (1)—Baltimore Colts 1971 (V).

Holland, John (0*)—Minnesota Vikings 1975 (IX-DNP).

Holloway, Brian (1)—New England Patriots 1986 (XX).

Holly, Bob (0**)—Washington Redskins 1983 (XVII-DNP), 1984 (XVIII-DNP).

Holmes, Ernie (2)—Pittsburgh Steelers 1975 (IX), 1976 (X).

Holmes, Robert (1)—Kansas City Chiefs 1970 (IV).

Holmoe, Tom (1)—San Francisco 49ers 1985 (XIX).

Holub, E. J. (2)—Kansas City Chiefs 1967 (I), 1970 (IV).

Homan, Dennis (1)—Dallas Cowboys 1971 (V).

Hoopes, Mitch (1)—Dallas Cowboys 1976 (X).

Horan, Mike (2)—Denver Broncos 1987 (XXI), 1988 (XXII).

Horn, Don (0*)—Green Bay Packers 1968 (II-DNP).

Horn, Rod (1)—Cincinnati Bengals 1982 (XVI).

Hornung, Paul (0*)—Green Bay Packers 1967 (I-DNP).

Howard, Erik (1)—New York Giants 1987 (XXI).

Howard, Paul (1)—Denver Broncos 1978 (XII).

Howard, Percy (1)—Dallas Cowboys 1976 (X).

Howard, Ron (1)—Dallas Cowboys 1976 (X).

Howley, Chuck (2)—Dallas Cowboys 1971 (V), 1972 (VI).

Hudson, Jim (1)—New York Jets 1969 (III).

Huff, Ken (1)—Washington Redskins 1984 (XVIII).

Hughes, Randy (3)—Dallas Cowboys 1976 (X), 1978 (XII), 1979 (XIII).

Hull, Mike (1)—Washington Redskins 1973

(VII).

Humm, David (2)—Oakland Raiders 1977 (XI); Los Angeles Raiders 1984 (XVIII).

Humphrey, Claude (1)—Philadelphia Eagles 1981 (XV).

Humphries, Stefan (2)—Chicago Bears 1986 (XX); Denver Broncos 1988 (XXII).

Hunley, Ricky (2)—Denver Broncos 1987 (XXI), 1988 (XXII).

Hunt, Bobby (1)—Kansas City Chiefs 1967 (I).

Hunt, Byron (1)—New York Giants 1987 (XXI).

Hurston, Chuck (2)—Kansas City Chiefs 1967 (I), 1970 (IV).

Huther, Bruce (2)—Dallas Cowboys 1978 (XII), 1979 (XIII).

Hyde, Glenn (1)—Denver Broncos 1978 (XII).

Hyland, Bob (1)—Green Bay Packers 1968 (II).

Jackson, Bernard (1)—Denver Broncos 1978 (XII).

Jackson, Mark (2)—Denver Broncos 1987 (XXI), 1988 (XXII).

Jackson, Monte (1)—Oakland Raiders 1981 (XV).

Jackson, Tom (2)—Denver Broncos 1978 (XII), 1987 (XXI).

Jackson, Wilbur (1)—Washington Redskins 1983 (XVII).

Jacoby, Joe (3)—Washington Redskins 1983 (XVII), 1984 (XVIII), 1988 (XXII).

James, Craig (1)—New England Patriots 1986 (XX).

James, Roland (1)—New England Patriots 1986 (XX).

Jaqua, Jon (1)—Washington Redskins 1973 (VII).

Jaworski, Ron (1)—Philadelphia Eagles 1981 (XV).

Jefferson, Roy (2)—Baltimore Colts 1971 (V); Washington Redskins 1973 (VII).

Jenkins, Ed (1)—Miami Dolphins 1973 (VII).

Jensen, Derrick (2)—Oakland Raiders 1981 (XV); Los Angeles Raiders 1984 (XVIII).

Jensen, Jim (1)—Denver Broncos 1978 (XII).

Jensen, Jim (2)—Miami Dolphins 1983 (XVII), 1985 (XIX).

Jeter, Bob (2)—Green Bay Packers 1967 (I), 1968 (II).

Jodat, Jim (1)—Los Angeles Rams 1980 (XIV).

Johnson, Bobby (1)—New York Giants 1987 (XXI).

Johnson, Butch (2)—Dallas Cowboys 1978 (XII), 1979 (XIII).

Johnson, Charlie (1)—Philadelphia Eagles 1981 (XV).

Johnson, Cornelius (2)—Baltimore Colts 1969 (III), 1971 (V).

Johnson, Curly (1)—New York Jets 1969 (III).

Johnson, Curtis (3)—Miami Dolphins 1972 (VI), 1973 (VII), 1974 (VIII).

Johnson, Damian (1)—New York Giants 1987 (XXI).

Johnson, Dan (1)—Miami Dolphins 1985 (XIX).

Johnson, Gary (1)—San Francisco 49ers 1985 (XIX).

Johnson, Monte (1)—Oakland Raiders 1977 (XI).

Johnson, Pepper (1)—New York Giants 1987 (XXI).

Johnson, Pete (1*)—Cincinnati Bengals 1982 (XVI); Miami Dolphins 1985 (XIX-DNP).

Johnson, Ron (2)—Pittsburgh Steelers 1979 (XIII), 1980 (XIV).

Johnson, Sammy (1)—Minnesota Vikings 1977 (XI).

Johnson, Vance (2)—Denver Broncos 1987 (XXI), 1988 (XXII).

Johnston, Brian (1)—New York Giants 1987 (XXI).

Jones, Anthony (1)—Washington Redskins 1988 (XXII).

Jones, Cedric (1)—New England Patriots 1986 (XX).

Jones, Clint (1)—Minnesota Vikings 1970 (IV).

Jones, Ed (3)—Dallas Cowboys 1976 (X), 1978 (XII), 1979 (XIII).

Jones, Robbie (1)—New York Giants 1987 (XXI).

Jones, Rulon (2)—Denver Broncos 1987 (XXI), 1988 (XXII).

Jones, Willie (1)—Oakland Raiders 1981 (XV).

Jordan, Curtis (2)—Washington Redskins 1983 (XVII), 1984 (XVIII).

Jordan, Henry (2)—Green Bay Packers 1967 (I), 1968 (II).

Jordan, Lee Roy (3)—Dallas Cowboys 1971 (V), 1972 (VI), 1976 (X).

Jordan, Shelby (1)—Los Angeles Raiders 1984 (XVIII).

Judson, William (2)—Miami Dolphins 1983 (XVII), 1985 (XIX).

Kapp, Joe (1)—Minnesota Vikings 1970 (IV).

Karcher, Ken (0†)—Denver Broncos 1988 (XXII-Inactive).

Karlis, Rich (2)—Denver Broncos 1987 (XXI), 1988 (XXII).

Kartz, Keith (1)—Denver Broncos 1988 (XXII).

Kassulke, Karl (1)—Minnesota Vikings 1970 (IV).

Kaufman, Mel (3)—Washington Redskins 1983 (XVII), 1984 (XVIII), 1988 (XXII).

Kay, Clarence (2)—Denver Broncos 1987 (XXI), 1988 (XXII).

Kearney, Jim (1)—Kansas City Chiefs 1970 (IV).

Keating, Tom (1)—Oakland Raiders 1968 (II).

Kehr, Rick (1)—Washington Redskins 1988 (XXII).

Kelcher, Louie (1)—San Francisco 49ers 1985 (XIX).

Kellum, Marv (2)—Pittsburgh Steelers 1975 (IX), 1976 (X).

Kemp, Bobby (1)—Cincinnati Bengals 1982 (XVI).

Kennedy, Allan (2)—San Francisco 49ers 1982 (XVI), 1985 (XIX).

Kenney, Steve (1)—Philadelphia Eagles 1981 (XV).

Keys, Tyrone (1)—Chicago Bears 1986 (XX).

Keyworth, Jon (1)—Denver Broncos 1978 (XII).

Kiick, Jim (3)—Miami Dolphins 1972 (VI), 1973 (VII), 1974 (VIII).

Kilmer, Billy (1)—Washington Redskins 1973 (VII).

Kimball, Bruce (1)—Washington Redskins 1984 (XVIII).

Kindig, Howard (1)—Miami Dolphins 1973 (VII).

Kiner, Steve (1)—Dallas Cowboys 1971 (V).

King, Kenny (2)—Oakland Raiders 1981 (XV); Los Angeles Raiders 1984 (XVIII).

Kingsriter, Doug (2)—Minnesota Vikings 1974 (VIII), 1975 (IX).

Kinlaw, Reggie (2)—Oakland Raiders 1981 (XV); Los Angeles Raiders 1984 (XVIII).

Klostermann, Bruce (1)—Denver Broncos 1988 (XXII).

Knight, Curt (1)—Washington Redskins 1973 (VII).

Koch, Marcus (1)—Washington Redskins 1988 (XXII).

Kocourek, Dave (1)—Oakland Raiders 1968 (II).

Kolb, Jon (4)—Pittsburgh Steelers 1975 (IX), 1976 (X), 1979 (XIII), 1980 (XIV).

Kolen, Mike (3)—Miami Dolphins 1972 (VI), 1973 (VII), 1974 (VIII).

Kostelnik, Ron (2)—Green Bay Packers 1967 (I), 1968 (II).

Kozlowski, Mike (2)—Miami Dolphins 1983 (XVII), 1985 (XIX).

Kragen, Greg (2)—Denver Broncos 1987 (XXI), 1988 (XXII).

Kramer, Jerry (2)—Green Bay Packers 1967 (I), 1968 (II).

Kramer, Kent (1)—Minnesota Vikings 1970 (IV).

Krause, Paul (4)—Minnesota Vikings 1970 (IV), 1974 (VIII), 1975 (IX), 1977 (XI).

Kreider, Steve (1)—Cincinnati Bengals 1982 (XVI).

Krepfle, Keith (1)—Philadelphia Eagles 1981 (XV).

Kruczek, Mike (0**)—Pittsburgh Steelers 1979 (XIII-DNP), 1980 (XIV-DNP).

Kruse, Bob (1)—Oakland Raiders 1968 (II).

Kubiak, Gary (2)—Denver Broncos 1987 (XXI), 1988 (XXII).

Kubin, Larry (2)—Washington Redskins 1983 (XVII), 1984 (XVIII).

Kuechenberg, Bob (4)—Miami Dolphins 1972 (VI), 1973 (VII), 1974 (VIII), 1983 (XVII).

Kyle, Aaron (2)—Dallas Cowboys 1978 (XII), 1979 (XIII).

Laakso, Eric (1)—Miami Dolphins 1983 (XVII).

Laaveg, Paul (1)—Washington Redskins 1973 (VII).

Laidlaw, Scott (2)—Dallas Cowboys 1978 (XII), 1979 (XIII).

Lambert, Jack (4)—Pittsburgh Steelers 1975 (IX), 1976 (X), 1979 (XIII), 1980 (XIV).

Lammons, Pete (1)—New York Jets 1969 (III).

Lamonica, Daryle (1)—Oakland Raiders 1968 (II).

Landeta, Sean (1)—New York Giants 1987 (XXI).

Lang, Gene (2)—Denver Broncos 1987 (XXI), 1988 (XXII).

Langer, Jim (3)—Miami Dolphins 1972 (VI), 1973 (VII), 1974 (VIII).

Lanier, Ken (2)—Denver Broncos 1987 (XXI), 1988 (XXII).

Lanier, Willie (1)—Kansas City Chiefs 1970 (IV).

Lankford, Paul (2)—Miami Dolphins 1983 (XVII), 1985 (XIX).

Lapham, Dave (1)—Cincinnati Bengals 1982 (XVI).

Larsen, Gary (3)—Minnesota Vikings 1970 (IV), 1974 (VIII), 1975 (IX).

Lash, Jim (2)—Minnesota Vikings 1974 (VIII), 1975 (IX).

Lasker, Greg (1)—New York Giants 1987 (XXI).

Laskey, Bill (1)—Oakland Raiders 1968 (II).

Lassiter, Ike (1)—Oakland Raiders 1968 (II).

Laster, Donald (1)—Washington Redskins 1983 (XVII).

Laufenberg, Babe (0*)—Washington Redskins 1984 (XVIII-DNP).

Lavender, Joe (1)—Washington Redskins 1983 (XVII).

Lawless, Burton (3)—Dallas Cowboys 1976 (X), 1978 (XII), 1979 (XIII).

Lawrence, Amos (1)—San Francisco 49ers 1982 (XVI).

Lawrence, Henry (3)—Oakland Raiders 1977 (XI), 1981 (XV); Los Angeles 1984 (XVIII).

Lawson, Steve (1*)—Minnesota Vikings 1974 (VIII-DNP), 1975 (IX).

LeClair, Jim (1)—Cincinnati Bengals 1982 (XVI).

Lee, Bob (2*)—Minnesota Vikings 1970 (IV), 1977 (XI); Los Angeles Rams 1980 (XIV-DNP).

Lee, David (2)—Baltimore Colts 1969 (III), 1971 (V).

Lee, Larry (0*)—Denver Broncos 1988 (XXII-DNP).

Lee, Ronnie (2)—Miami Dolphins 1983 (XVII), 1985 (XIX).

Leigh, Charles (1)—Miami Dolphins 1973 (VII).

LeMaster, Frank (1)—Philadelphia Eagles 1981 (XV).

Leopold, Bobby (1)—San Francisco 49ers 1982 (XVI).

Lewis, D. D. (5)—Dallas Cowboys 1971 (V), 1972 (VI), 1976 (X), 1978 (XII), 1979 (XIII).

Lewis, Frank (2)—Pittsburgh Steelers 1975 (IX), 1976 (X).

Liebenstein, Todd (2)—Washington Redskins 1983 (XVII), 1984 (XVIII).

Lilly, Bob (2)—Dallas Cowboys 1971 (V), 1972 (VI).

Lilly, Tony (2)—Denver Broncos 1987 (XXI), 1988 (XXII).

Lindsey, Jim (1)—Minnesota Vikings 1970 (IV).

Lippett, Ronnie (1)—New England Patriots 1986 (XX).

Liscio, Tony (1*)—Dallas Cowboys 1971 (V-DNP), 1972 (VI).

Little Larry (3)—Miami Dolphins 1972 (VI), 1973 (VII), 1974 (VIII).

Livingston, Mike (1)—Kansas City Chiefs 1970 (IV).

Logan, Jerry (2)—Baltimore Colts 1969 (III), 1971 (V).

Logan, Randy (1)—Philadelphia Eagles 1981 (XV).

Long, Bob (2)—Green Bay Packers 1967 (I), 1968 (II).

Long, Howie (1)—Los Angeles Raiders 1984 (XVIII).

Longley, Clint (0*)—Dallas Cowboys 1976 (X-DNP).

Lothamer, Ed (1)—Kansas City Chiefs 1970 (IV).

Lott, Ronnie (2)—San Francisco 49ers 1982 (XVI), 1985 (XIX).

Lowry, Quentin (1)—Washington Redskins 1983 (XVII).

Lucas, Tim (1)—Denver Broncos 1988 (XXII).

Lurtsema, Bob (2)—Minnesota Vikings 1974 (VIII), 1975 (IX).

Lyles, Lenny (1)—Baltimore Colts 1969 (III).

Lynch, Jim (1)—Kansas City Chiefs 1970 (IV).

Lytle, Rob (1)—Denver Broncos 1978 (XII).

Mack, Red (1)—Green Bay Packers 1967 (I).

Mackbee, Earsell (1)—Minnesota Vikings 1970 (IV).

Mackey, John (2)—Baltimore Colts 1969 (III), 1971 (V).

Maitland, Jack (1)—Baltimore Colts 1971 (V).

Manders, Dave (2)—Dallas Cowboys 1971 (V), 1972 (VI).

Mandich, Jim (4)—Miami Dolphins 1972 (VI), 1973 (VII), 1974 (VIII); Pittsburgh Steelers 1979 (XIII).

Manley, Dexter (3)—Washington Redskins 1983 (XVII), 1984 (XVIII), 1988 (XXII).

Mann, Charles (2)—Washington Redskins 1984 (XVIII), 1988 (XXII).

Mann, Errol (1)—Oakland Raiders 1977 (XI).

Manor, Brison (1)—Denver Broncos 1978 (XII).

Mansfield, Ray (2)—Pittsburgh Steelers 1975 (IX), 1976 (X).

Manuel, Lionel (1)—New York Giants 1987 (XXI).

Maples, Bobby (1)—Denver Broncos 1978 (XII).

Margerum, Ken (1)—Chicago Bears 1986 (XX).

Marinaro, Ed (2)—Minnesota Vikings 1974 (VIII), 1975 (IX).

Marino, Dan (1)—Miami Dolphins 1985 (XIX).

Marion, Fred (1)—New England Patriots 1986 (XX).

Marsalis, Jim (1)—Kansas City Chiefs 1970 (IV).

Marshall, Jim (4)—Minnesota Vikings 1970 (IV), 1974 (VIII), 1975 (IX), 1977 (XI).

Marshall, Leonard (1)—New York Giants 1987 (XXI).

Marshall, Wilber (1)—Chicago Bears 1986 (XX).

Martin, Amos (3)—Minnesota Vikings 1974 (VIII), 1975 (IX), 1977 (XI).

Martin, George (1)—New York Giants 1987 (XXI).

Martin, Harvey (3)—Dallas Cowboys 1976 (X), 1978 (XII), 1979 (XIII).

Martin, Rod (2)—Oakland Raiders 1981 (XV); Los Angeles Raiders 1984 (XVIII).

Martin, Saladin (0*)—San Francisco 49ers 1982 (XVI-DNP).

Martini, Rich (1)—Oakland Raiders 1981 (XV).

Marvin, Mickey (2)—Oakland Raiders 1981 (XV); Los Angeles Raiders 1984 (XVIII).

Mason, Lindsey (1)—Oakland Raiders 1981 (XV).

Matheson, Bob (3)—Miami Dolphins 1972 (VI), 1973 (VII), 1974 (VIII).

Mathis, Bill (1)—New York Jets 1969 (III).

Matte, Tom (1)—Baltimore Colts 1969 (III).

Matthews, Ira (1)—Oakland Raiders 1981 (XV).

Matuszak, John (2)—Oakland Raiders 1977 (XI), 1981 (XV).

Maurer, Andy (2)—Minnesota Vikings 1975 (IX); Dallas Cowboys 1978 (XII).

Maxwell, Tom (1)—Baltimore Colts 1971 (V).

May, Mark (3)—Washington Redskins 1983 (XVII), 1984 (XVIII), 1988 (XXII).

May, Ray (1)—Baltimore Colts 1971 (V).

Maynard, Don (1)—New York Jets 1969 (III).

Mays, Jerry (2)—Kansas City Chiefs 1967 (I), 1970 (IV).

McAdams, Carl (1)—New York Jets 1969 (III).

McClanahan, Brent (2)—Minnesota Vikings 1975 (IX), 1977 (XI).

McClanahan, Randy (1)—Oakland Raiders 1981 (XV).

McClinton, Curtis (2)—Kansas City Chiefs 1967 (I), 1970 (IV).

McCloughan, Kent (1)—Oakland Raiders 1968 (II).

McColl, Milt (2)—San Francisco 49ers 1982 (XVI), 1985 (XIX).

McConkey, Phil (1)—New York Giants 1987 (XXI).

McCullum, Sam (1)—Minnesota Vikings 1975 (IX).

McCutcheon, Lawrence (1)—Los Angeles Rams 1980 (XIV).

McDaniel, LeCharls (1)—Washington Redskins 1983 (XVII).

McDole, Ron (1)—Washington Redskins 1973 (VII).

McElroy, Vann (1)—Los Angeles Raiders 1984 (XVIII).

McGee, Max (2)—Green Bay Packers 1967 (I), 1968 (II).

McGee, Tony (2)—Washington Redskins 1983 (XVII), 1984 (XVIII).

McGill, Mike (1)—Minnesota Vikings 1970 (IV).

McGrath, Mark (0*)—Washington Redskins

1984 (XVIII-DNP).

McGrew, Larry (1)—New England Patriots 1986 (XX).

McInally, Pat (1)—Cincinnati Bengals 1982 (XVI).

McIntyre, Guy (1)—San Francisco 49ers 1985 (XIX).

McKenzie, Raleigh (1)—Washington Redskins 1988 (XXII).

McKinney, Odis (2)—Oakland Raiders 1981 (XV); Los Angeles Raiders 1984 (XVIII).

McKinnon, Dennis (1)—Chicago Bears 1986 (XX).

McLemore, Dana (1)—San Francisco 49ers 1985 (XIX).

McLinton, Harold (1)—Washington Redskins 1973 (VII).

McMahon, Jim (1)—Chicago Bears 1986 (XX).

McMakin, John (1)—Pittsburgh Steelers 1975 (IX).

McMath, Herb (1)—Oakland Raiders 1977 (XI).

McMichael, Steve (1)—Chicago Bears 1986 (XX).

McNeal, Don (2)—Miami Dolphins 1983 (XVII), 1985 (XIX).

McNeil, Clifton (1)—Washington Redskins 1973 (VII).

McNeill, Fred (2)—Minnesota Vikings 1975 (IX), 1977 (XI).

McSwain, Rod (1)—New England Patriots 1986 (XX).

McVea, Warren (1)—Kansas City Chiefs 1970 (IV).

Mecklenburg, Karl (2)—Denver Broncos 1987 (XXI), 1988 (XXII).

Medlin, Dan (1)—Oakland Raiders 1977 (XI).

Mendenhall, Mat (1)—Washington Redskins 1983 (XVII).

Mercein, Chuck (1)—Green Bay Packers 1968 (II).

Mercer, Mike (1)—Kansas City Chiefs 1967 (I).

Merz, Curt (1)—Kansas City Chiefs 1967 (I).

Michaels, Lou (1)—Baltimore Colts 1969 (III).

Micho, Bobby (2)—Denver Broncos 1987 (XXI), 1988 (XXII).

Millen, Matt (2)—Oakland Raiders 1981 (XV); Los Angeles Raiders 1984 (XVIII).

Miller, Bill (1)—Oakland Raiders 1968 (II).

Miller, Fred (2)—Baltimore Colts 1969 (III), 1971 (V).

Miller, Jim (1)—San Francisco 1982 (XVI).

Miller, Robert (1)—Minnesota Vikings 1977 (XI).

Miller, Solomon (1)—New York Giants 1987 (XXI).

Milot, Rich (3)—Washington Redskins 1983 (XVII), 1984 (XVIII), 1988 (XXII).

Minor, Claudie (1)—Denver Broncos 1978 (XII).

Mira, George (0*)—Miami Dolphins 1972 (VI-DNP).

Mitchell, Tom (2)—Baltimore Colts 1969 (III), 1971 (V).

Mitchell, Willie (2)—Kansas City Chiefs 1967

(I), 1970 (IV).

Mobley, Orson (2)—Denver Broncos 1987 (XXI), 1988 (XXII).

Monk, Art (2)—Washington Redskins 1984 (XVII), 1988 (XXII).

Monroe, Carl (1)—San Francisco 49ers 1985 (XIX).

Montana, Joe (2)—San Francisco 49ers 1982 (XVI), 1985 (XIX).

Montgomery, Blanchard (1)—San Francisco 49ers 1985 (XIX).

Montgomery, Cle (1)—Los Angeles Raiders 1984 (XVIII).

Montgomery, Wilbert (1)—Philadelphia Eagles 1981 (XV).

Montler, Mike (1)—Denver Broncos 1978 (XII).

Montoya, Max (1)—Cincinnati Bengals 1982 (PVI).

Moody, Keith (1)—Oakland Raiders 1981 (XV).

Moore, Blake (1)—Cincinnati Bengals 1982 (XVI).

Moore, Manfred (1)—Oakland Raiders 1977 (XI).

Moore, Maulty (2)—Miami Dolphins 1973 (VII), 1974 (VIII).

Moore, Nat (2)—Miami Dolphins 1983 (XVII), 1985 (XIX).

Moore, Steve (1)—New England Patriots 1986 (XX).

Moore, Wayne (3)—Miami Dolphins 1972 (VI), 1973 (VII), 1974 (VIII).

Moorehead, Emery (1)—Chicago Bears 1986 (XX).

Moorman, Mo (1)—Kansas City Chiefs 1970 (IV).

Morgan, Stanley (1)—New England Patriots 1986 (XX).

Morrall, Earl (4)—Baltimore Colts 1969 (III), 1971 (V); Miami Dolphins 1973 (VII), 1974 (VIII).

Morris, Joe (1)—New York Giants 1987 (XXI).

Morris, Mercury (3)—Miami Dolphins 1972 (VI), 1973 (VII), 1974 (VIII).

Morrison, Tim (0†)—Washington Redskins 1988 (XXII-Inactive).

Morriss, Guy (2)—Philadelphia Eagles 1981 (XV); New England Patriots 1986 (XX).

Morrissey, Jim (1)—Chicago Bears 1986 (XX).

Morton, Craig (2*)—Dallas Cowboys 1971 (V), 1972 (VI-DNP); Denver Broncos 1978 (XII).

Mosebar, Don (1)—Los Angeles Raiders 1984 (XVIII).

Moseley, Mark (2)—Washington Redskins 1983 (XVII), 1984 (XVIII).

Moser, Rick (2)—Pittsburgh Steelers 1979 (XIII), 1980 (XIV).

Moses, Haven (1)—Denver Broncos 1978 (XII).

Mowatt, Zeke (1)—New York Giants 1987 (XXI).

Muhammad, Calvin (1)—Los Angeles Raiders 1984 (XVIII).

Mul-Key, Herb (1)—Washington Redskins 1973 (VII).

Mullaney, Mark (1)—Minnesota Vikings 1977

(XI).

Mullins, Gerry (4)—Pittsburgh Steelers 1975 (IX), 1976 (X), 1979 (XIII), 1980 (XIV).

Mumphord, Lloyd (3)—Miami Dolphins 1972 (VI), 1973 (VII), 1974 (VIII).

Munoz, Anthony (1)—Cincinnati Bengals 1982 (XVI).

Murphy, Mark (2)—Washington Redskins 1983 (XVII), 1984 (XVIII).

Nairne, Rob (1)—Denver Broncos 1978 (XII).

Namath, Joe (1)—New York Jets 1969 (III).

Nathan, Tony (2)—Miami Dolphins 1983 (XVII), 1985 (XIX).

Nattiel, Ricky (1)—Denver Broncos 1988 (XXII).

Neely, Ralph (3)—Dallas Cowboys 1971 (V), 1976 (X), 1978 (XII).

Nehemiah, Renaldo (1)—San Francisco 49ers 1985 (XIX).

Neidert, John (1)—New York Jets 1969 (III).

Nelms, Mike (1)—Washington Redskins 1983 (XVII).

Nelson, Bob (2)—Oakland Raiders 1981 (XV); Los Angeles Raiders 1984 (XVIII).

Nelson, Karl (1)—New York Giants 1987 (XXI).

Nelson, Steve (1)—New England Patriots 1986 (XX).

Nelson, Terry (1)—Los Angeles Rams 1980 (XIV).

Newhouse, Robert (3)—Dallas Cowboys 1976 (X), 1978 (XII), 1979 (XIII).

Newman, Ed (2)—Miami Dolphins 1974 (VIII), 1985 (XIX).

Newsome, Billy (1)—Baltimore Colts 1971 (V).

Nichols, Robbie (1)—Baltimore Colts 1971 (V).

Niland, John (2)—Dallas Cowboys 1971 (V), 1972 (VI).

Nitschke, Ray (2)—Green Bay Packers 1967 (I), 1968 (II).

Noonan, Karl (1)—Miami Dolphins 1972 (VI).

Norman, Pettis (1)—Dallas Cowboys 1971 (V).

Nottingham, Don (1)—Miami Dolphins 1974 (VIII).

Nowatzke, Tom (1)—Baltimore Colts 1971 (V).

Nye, Blaine (3)—Dallas Cowboys 1971 (V), 1972 (VI), 1976 (X).

Oates, Bart (1)—New York Giants 1987 (XXI).

Oates, Carleton (1)—Oakland Raiders 1968 (II).

O'Brien, Jim (1)—Baltimore Colts 1971 (V).

Obrovac, Mike (1)—Cincinnati Bengals 1982 (XVI).

Odoms, Riley (1)—Denver Broncos 1978 (XII).

Oldham, Ray (1)—Pittsburgh Steelers 1979 (XIII).

Olkewicz, Neal (3)—Washington Redskins 1983 (XVII), 1984 (XVIII), 1988 (XXII).

Orosz, Tom (1)—Miami Dolphins 1983 (XVII).

Orr, Jimmy (1*)—Baltimore Colts 1969 (III), 1971 (V-DNP).

Orr, Terry (1)—Washington Redskins 1988 (XXII).

Ortego, Keith (1)—Chicago Bears 1986 (XX).

Osborn, Dave (3)—Minnesota Vikings 1970 (IV), 1974 (VIII), 1975 (IX).

O'Steen, Dwayne (2)—Los Angeles Rams 1980 (XIV); Oakland Raiders 1981 (XV).

Otto, Gus (1)—Oakland Raiders 1968 (II).

Otto, Jim (1)—Oakland Raiders 1968 (II).

Owen, Tom (0*)—Washington Redskins 1983 (XVII-DNP).

Owens, Brig (1)—Washington Redskins 1973 (VII).

Owens, Burgess (1)—Oakland Raiders 1981 (XV).

Owens, Dennis (1)—New England Patriots 1986 (XX).

Page, Alan (4)—Minnesota Vikings 1970 (IV), 1974 (VIII), 1975 (IX), 1977 (XI).

Pardee, Jack (1)—Washington Redskins 1973 (VII).

Parilli, Babe (1)—New York Jets 1969 (III).

Paris, Bubba (1)—San Francisco 49ers 1985 (XIX).

Parker, Rodney (1)—Philadelphia Eagles 1981 (XV).

Patterson, Elvis (1)—New York Giants 1987 (XXI).

Patton, Ricky (1)—San Francisco 49ers 1982 (XVI).

Payton, Walter (1)—Chicago Bears 1986 (XX).

Pear, Dave (1)—Oakland Raiders 1981 (XV).

Pearson, Drew (3)—Dallas Cowboys 1976 (X), 1978 (XII), 1979 (XIII).

Pearson, Preston (5)—Baltimore Colts 1969 (III); Pittsburgh Steelers 1975 (IX); Dallas Cowboys 1976 (X), 1978 (XII), 1979 (XIII).

Penrose, Craig (0*)—Denver Broncos 1978 (XII-DNP).

Peoples, Woody (1)—Philadelphia Eagles 1981 (XV).

Perkins, Ray (2)—Baltimore Colts 1969 (III), 1971 (V).

Perot, Petey (1)—Philadelphia Eagles 1981 (XV).

Perrin, Lonnie (1)—Denver Broncos 1978 (XII).

Perry, Rod (1)—Los Angeles Rams 1980 (XIV).

Perry, William (1)—Chicago Bears 1986 (XX).

Peters, Tony (1)—Washington Redskins 1983 (XVII).

Peterson, Cal (1)—Dallas Cowboys 1976 (X).

Peterson, Ted (2)—Pittsburgh Steelers 1979 (XIII), 1980 (XIV).

Petrella, Bob (1)—Miami Dolphins 1972 (VI).

Philbin, Gerry (1)—New York Jets 1969 (III).

Phillips, Charles (1)—Oakland Raiders 1977 (XI).

Phillips, Ray (1)—Philadelphia Eagles 1981 (XV).

Phillips, Reggie (1)—Chicago Bears 1986 (XX).

Philyaw, Charles (1)—Oakland Raiders 1977 (XI).

Pickel, Bill (1)—Los Angeles Raiders 1984 (XVIII).

Pillers, Lawrence (2)—San Francisco 49ers 1982 (XVI), 1985 (XIX).

Pinney, Ray (1)—Pittsburgh Steelers 1979

(XIII).

Pisarcik, Joe (0*)—Philadelphia Eagles 1981 (XV-DNP).

Pitts, Elijah (1)—Green Bay Packers 1967 (I).

Pitts, Frank (2)—Kansas City Chiefs 1967 (I), 1970 (IV).

Plummer, Bruce (1)—Denver Broncos 1988 (XXII).

Plunkett, Art (1)—New England Patriots 1986 ' (XX).

Plunkett, Jim (2)—Oakland Raiders 1981 (XV); Los Angeles Raiders 1984 (XVIII).

Ply, Bobby (1)—Kansas City Chiefs 1967 (I).

Podolak, Ed (1)—Kansas City Chiefs 1970 (IV).

Poltl, Randy (2)—Minnesota Vikings 1975 (IX); Denver Broncos 1978 (XII).

Porter, Ron (2)—Baltimore Colts 1969 (III); Minnesota Vikings 1974 (VIII).

Potter, Steve (1)—Miami Dolphins 1983 (XVII).

Pottios, Myron (1)—Washington Redskins 1973 (VII).

Powell, Jesse (2)—Miami Dolphins 1972 (VI), 1973 (VII).

Powers, Warren (1)—Oakland Raiders 1968 (II).

Prudhomme, Remi (1)—Kansas City Chiefs 1970 (IV).

Pruitt, Greg (1)—Los Angeles Raiders 1984 (XVIII).

Puetz, Garry (0*)—Washington Redskins 1983 (XVII-DNP).

Pugh, Jethro (4*)—Dallas Cowboys 1971 (V), 1972 (VI), 1976 (X), 1978 (XII), 1979 (XIII-DNP).

Puki, Craig (1)—San Francisco 49ers 1982 (XVI).

Quillan, Fred (2)—San Francisco 49ers 1982 (XVI), 1985 (XIX).

Rademacher, Bill (1)—New York Jets 1969 (III).

Rae, Mike (1)—Oakland Raiders 1977 (XI).

Rafferty, Tom (2)—Dallas Cowboys 1978 (XII), 1979 (XIII).

Ramsey, Derrick (2)—Oakland Raiders 1981 (XV); New England Patriots 1986 (XX).

Ramsey, Tom (0*)—New England Patriots 1986 (XX-DNP).

Ramson, Eason (1)—San Francisco 49ers 1982 (XVI).

Randall, Tom (1)—Dallas Cowboys 1979 (XIII).

Rashad, Ahmad (1)—Minnesota Vikings 1977 (XI).

Rasmussen, Randy (1)—New York Jets 1969 (III).

Razzano, Rick (1)—Cincinnati Bengals 1982 (XVI).

Reasons, Gary (1)—New York Giants 1987 (XXI).

Reavis, Dave (2)—Pittsburgh Steelers 1975 (IX), 1976 (X).

Reed, Oscar (3)—Minnesota Vikings 1970 (IV), 1974 (VIII), 1975 (IX).

Reese, Archie (1)—San Francisco 49ers 1982 (XVI).

Reeves, Dan (2)—Dallas Cowboys 1971 (V), 1972 (VI).

Reilly, Mike (0*)—Minnesota Vikings 1970 (IV-DNP).

Rembert, Johnny (1)—New England Patriots 1986 (XX).

Remsberg, Dan (1†)—Denver Broncos 1987 (XXI), 1988 (XXII-Inactive).

Renfro, Mel (4)—Dallas Cowboys 1971 (V), 1972 (VI), 1976 (X), 1978 (XII).

Ressler, Glenn (2)—Baltimore Colts 1969 (III), 1971 (V).

Reynolds, Al (1)—Kansas City Chiefs 1967 (I).

Reynolds, Ed (1)—New England Patriots 1986 (XX).

Reynolds, Jack (3)—Los Angeles Rams 1980 (XIV); San Francisco 49ers 1982 (XVI), 1985 (XIX).

Rhone, Earnie (2)—Miami Dolphins 1983 (XVII), 1985 (XIX).

Rice, Andy (1)—Kansas City Chiefs 1967 (I).

Rice, Floyd (1)—Oakland Raiders 1977 (XI).

Rich, Randy (1)—Denver Broncos 1978 (XII).

Richards, Golden (2)—Dallas Cowboys 1976 (X), 1978 (XII).

Richards, Jim (1)—New York Jets 1969 (III).

Richardson, Gloster (1*)—Kansas City Chiefs 1970 (IV); Dallas Cowboys 1972 (VI-DNP).

Richardson, Jeff (1)—New York Jets 1969 (III).

Richardson, John (1)—Miami Dolphins 1972 (VI).

Richardson, Mike (1)—Chicago Bears 1986 (XX).

Richardson, Willie (1)—Baltimore Colts 1969 (III).

Riggins, John (2)—Washington Redskins 1983 (XVII), 1984 (XVIII).

Riley, Jim (1)—Miami Dolphins 1972 (VI).

Riley, Ken (1)—Cincinnati Bengals 1982 (XVI).

Riley, Steve (1*)—Minnesota Vikings 1975 (IX-DNP), 1977 (XI).

Ring, Bill (2)—San Francisco 49ers 1982 (XVI), 1985 (XIX).

Rivera, Ron (1)—Chicago Bears 1986 (XX).

Rizzo, Joe (1)—Denver Broncos 1978 (XII).

Robbins, Randy (2)—Denver Broncos 1987 (XXI), 1988 (XXII).

Roberts, William (1)—New York Giants 1987 (XXI).

Robinson, Dave (2)—Green Bay Packers 1967 (I), 1968 (II).

Robinson, Jerry (1)—Philadelphia Eagles 1981 (XV).

Robinson, Johnny (2)—Kansas City Chiefs 1967 (I), 1970 (IV).

Robinson, Johnny (1)—Los Angeles Raiders 1984 (XVIII).

Robinson, Stacy (1)—New York Giants 1987 (XXI).

Roby, Reggie (1)—Miami Dolphins 1985 (XIX).

Rochester, Paul (1)—New York Jets 1969 (III).

Rock, Walter (1)—Washington Redskins 1973 (VII).

Rogers, George (1)—Washington Redskins

1988 (XXII).

Rose, Joe (2)—Miami Dolphins 1983 (XVII), 1985 (XIX).

Ross, Dan (1)—Cincinnati Bengals 1982 (XVI).

Rouson, Lee (1)—New York Giants 1987 (XXI).

Rowe, Dave (1)—Oakland Raiders 1977 (XI).

Rowser, John (1)—Green Bay Packers 1968 (II).

Rucker, Reggie (1)—Dallas Cowboys 1971 (V).

Runager, Max (2)—Philadelphia Eagles 1981 (XV); San Francisco 49ers 1985 (XIX).

Russell, Andy (2)—Pittsburgh Steelers 1975 (IX), 1976 (X).

Rutledge, Jeff (1*)—Los Angeles Rams 1980 (XIV-DNP); New York Giants 1987 (XXI).

Ryan, Jim (2)—Denver Broncos 1987 (XXI), 1988 (XXII).

Ryczek, Dan (1)—Los Angeles Rams 1980 (XIV).

Rypien, Mark (0†)—Washington Redskins 1988 (XXII-Inactive).

St. Clair, Mike (1)—Cincinnati Bengals 1982 (XVI).

Sally, Jerome (1)—New York Giants 1987 (XXI).

Sample, Johnny (1)—New York Jets 1969 (III).

Sampson, Clint (1)—Denver Broncos 1987 (XXI).

Sanders, Ricky (1)—Washington Redskins 1988 (XXII).

Sanders, Thomas (1)—Chicago Bears 1986 (XX).

Sauer, George (1)—New York Jets 1969 (III).

Saul, Rich (1)—Los Angeles Rams 1980 (XIV).

Schmitt, John (1)—New York Jets 1969 (III).

Schoenke, Ray (0*)—Washington Redskins 1973 (VII-DNP).

Schonert, Turk (0*)—Cincinnati Bengals 1982 (XVI-DNP).

Schroeder, Jay (1)—Washington Redskins 1988 (XXII).

Schuh, Harry (1)—Oakland Raiders 1968 (II).

Schultz, John (1)—Denver Broncos 1978 (XII).

Sciarra, John (1)—Philadelphia Eagles 1981 (XV).

Scott, Herbert (3)—Dallas Cowboys 1976 (X), 1978 (XII), 1979 (XIII).

Scott, Jake (3)—Miami Dolphins 1972 (VI), 1973 (VII), 1974 (VIII).

Seay, Virgil (1*)—Washington Redskins 1983 (XVII), 1984 (XVIII—DNP).

Seiple, Larry (3)—Miami Dolphins 1972 (VI), 1973 (VII), 1974 (VIII).

Sellers, Goldie (1)—Kansas City Chiefs 1970 (IV).

Sellers, Ron (0*)—Miami Dolphins 1974 (VIII-DNP).

Septien, Rafael (1)—Dallas Cowboys 1979 (XIII).

Severson, Jeff (1)—Washington Redskins 1973 (VII).

Sewell, Steve (2)—Denver Broncos 1987 (XXI), 1988 (XXII).

Shanklin, Ron (1)—Pittsburgh Steelers 1975 (IX).

Sharockman, Ed (1)—Minnesota Vikings 1970 (IV).

Shell, Art (2)—Oakland Raiders 1977 (XI), 1981 (XV).

Shell, Donnie (4)—Pittsburgh Steelers 1975 (IX), 1976 (X), 1979 (XIII), 1980 (XIV).

Shell, Todd (1)—San Francisco 49ers 1985 (XIX).

Sherman, Rod (0*)—Oakland Raiders 1968 (II-DNP).

Shields, Billy (1)—San Francisco 49ers 1985 (XIX).

Shinnick, Don (1)—Baltimore Colts 1969 (III).

Shipp, Jackie (1)—Miami Dolphins 1985 (XIX).

Shiver, Sanders (1)—Miami Dolphins 1985 (XIX).

Shull, Steve (1)—Miami Dolphins 1983 (XVII).

Shumann, Mike (1)—San Francisco 49ers 1982 (XVI).

Siani, Mike (1)—Oakland Raiders 1977 (XI).

Siemon, Jeff (3)—Minnesota Vikings 1974 (VIII), 1975 (IX), 1977 (XI).

Simmons, John (1)—Cincinnati Bengals 1982 (XVI).

Simmons, Roy (1)—Washington Redskins 1984 (XVIII).

Simms, Phil (1)—New York Giants 1987 (XXI).

Singletary, Mike (1)—Chicago Bears 1986 (XX).

Sisemore, Jerry (1)—Philadelphia Eagles 1981 (XV).

Sistrunk, Manny (1)—Washington Redskins 1973 (VII).

Sistrunk, Otis (1)—Oakland Raiders 1977 (XI).

Skoronski, Bob (2)—Green Bay Packers 1967 (I), 1968 (II).

Slater, Jackie (1)—Los Angeles Rams 1980 (XIV).

Slater, Mark (1)—Philadelphia Eagles 1981 (XV).

Sligh, Richard (1)—Oakland Raiders 1968 (II).

Small, Gerald (1)—Miami Dolphins 1983 (XVII).

Smith, Billy Ray (2)—Baltimore Colts 1969 (III), 1971 (V).

Smith, Bubba (2)—Baltimore Colts 1969 (III), 1971 (V).

Smith, Charles (1)—Philadelphia Eagles 1981 (XV).

Smith, Dennis (2)—Denver Broncos 1987 (XXI), 1988 (XXII).

Smith, Fletcher (1)—Kansas City Chiefs 1967 (I).

Smith, Jackie (1)—Dallas Cowboys 1979 (XIII).

Smith, Jerry (1)—Washington Redskins 1973 (VII).

Smith, Jim (2)—Pittsburgh Steelers 1979 (XIII), 1980 (XIV).

Smith, Paul (1)—Denver Broncos 1978 (XII).

Smith, Ron (1)—Los Angeles Rams 1980 (XIV).

Smith, Steve (1)—Minnesota Vikings 1970 (IV).

Smith, Timmy (1)—Washington Redskins 1988 (XXII).

Smith, Tody (1)—Dallas Cowboys 1972 (VI).

Smolinski, Mark (1)—New York Jets 1969 (III).

Snell, Matt (1)—New York Jets 1969 (III).

Solomon, Freddie (2)—San Francisco 49ers 1982 (XVI), 1985 (XIX).

Sowell, Robert (1)—Miami Dolphins 1985 (XIX).

Spagnola, John (1)—Philadelphia Eagles 1981 (XV).

Squirek, Jack (1)—Los Angeles Raiders 1984 (XVIII).

Stabler, Ken (1)—Oakland Raiders 1977 (XI).

Stalls, Dave (3)—Dallas Cowboys 1978 (XII), 1979 (XIII); Los Angeles Raiders 1984 (XVIII).

Stallworth, John (4)—Pittsburgh Steelers 1975 (IX), 1976 (X), 1979 (XIII), 1980 (XIV).

Stanfill, Bill (3)—Miami Dolphins 1972 (VI), 1973 (VII), 1974 (VIII).

Starke, George (2)—Washington Redskins 1983 (XVII), 1984 (XVIII).

Starr, Bart (2)—Green Bay Packers 1967 (I), 1968 (II).

Starring, Stephen (1)—New England Patriots 1986 (XX).

Staubach, Roger (4*)—Dallas Cowboys 1971 (V-DNP), 1972 (VI), 1976 (X), 1978 (XII), 1979 (XIII).

Steele, Robert (1)—Dallas Cowboys 1979 (XIII).

Stein, Bob (1)—Kansas City Chiefs 1970 (IV).

Stenerud, Jan (1)—Kansas City Chiefs 1970 (IV).

Stephenson, Dwight (2)—Miami Dolphins 1983 (XVII), 1985 (XIX).

Stincic, Tom (2)—Dallas Cowboys 1971 (V), 1972 (VI).

Stoudt, Cliff (0**)—Pittsburgh Steelers 1979 (XIII-DNP), 1980 (XIV-DNP).

Stover, Jeff (1)—San Francisco 49ers (XIX).

Stover, Smokey (1)—Kansas City Chiefs 1967 (I).

Stowe, Otto (1*)—Miami Dolphins 1972 (VI), 1973 (VII-DNP).

Strock, Don (2)—Miami Dolphins 1983 (XVII), 1985 (XIX).

Stuckey, Henry (2)—Miami Dolphins 1973 (VII), 1974 (VIII).

Stuckey, Jim (2)—San Francisco 49ers 1982 (XVI), 1985 (XIX).

Studdard, Dave (2)—Denver Broncos 1987 (XXI), 1988 (XXII).

Stukes, Charles (2)—Baltimore Colts 1969 (III), 1971 (V).

Suhey, Matt (1)—Chicago Bears 1986 (XX).

Sullivan, Dan (2)—Baltimore Colts 1969 (III), 1971 (V).

Sully, Ivory (1)—Los Angeles Rams 1980 (XIV).

Sunde, Milt (2)—Minnesota Vikings 1970 (IV), 1975 (IX).

Sutherland, Doug (3)—Minnesota Vikings 1974 (VIII), 1975 (IX), 1977 (XI).

Svihus, Bob (1)—Oakland Raiders 1968 (II).

Swann, Lynn (4)—Pittsburgh Steelers 1975 (IX), 1976 (X), 1979 (XIII), 1980 (XIV).

Swenson, Bob (1)—Denver Broncos 1978 (XII).

Swift, Doug (3)—Miami Dolphins 1972 (VI), 1973 (VII), 1974 (VIII).

Sylvester, Steve (3)—Oakland Raiders 1977 (XI), 1981 (XV); Los Angeles Raiders 1984 (XVIII).

Szymanski, Dick (1)—Baltimore Colts 1969 (III).

Talamini, Bob (1)—New York Jets 1969 (III).

Talbert, Diron (1)—Washington Redskins 1973 (VII).

Tarkenton, Fran (3)—Minnesota Vikings 1974 (VIII), 1975 (IX), 1977 (XI).

Tatum, Jack (1)—Oakland Raiders 1977 (XI).

Tatupu, Mosi (1)—New England Patriots 1986 (XX).

Taylor, Charley (1)—Washington Redskins 1973 (VII).

Taylor, Jim (1)—Green Bay Packers 1967 (I).

Taylor, Ken (1)—Chicago Bears 1986 (XX).

Taylor, Lawrence (1)—New York Giants 1987 (XXI).

Taylor, Otis (2)—Kansas City Chiefs 1967 (I), 1970 (IV).

Taylor, Roosevelt (1)—Washington Redskins 1973 (VII).

Thayer, Tom (1)—Chicago Bears 1986 (XX).

Theismann, Joe (2)—Washington Redskins 1983 (XVII), 1984 (XVIII).

Thielemann, R. C. (1)—Washington Redskins 1988 (XXII).

Thomas, Ben (1)—New England Patriots 1986 (XX).

Thomas, Calvin (1)—Chicago Bears 1986 (XX).

Thomas, Duane (2)—Dallas Cowboys 1971 (V), 1972 (VI).

Thomas, Emmitt (2)—Kansas City Chiefs 1967 (I), 1970 (IV).

Thomas, Gene (1)—Kansas City Chiefs 1967 (I).

Thomas, Isaac (1)—Dallas Cowboys 1972 (VI).

Thomas, J. T. (3)—Pittsburgh Steelers 1975 (IX), 1976 (X), 1980 (XIV).

Thomas, Lynn (1)—San Francisco 49ers 1982 (XVI).

Thomas, Pat (1)—Los Angeles Rams 1980 (XIV).

Thomas, Skip (1)—Oakland Raiders 1977 (XI).

Thompson, Bill (1)—Denver Broncos 1978 (XII).

Thompson, Jack (0*)—Cincinnati Bengals 1982 (XVI-DNP).

Thompson, Steve (1)—New York Jets 1969 (III).

Thornton, Sidney (2)—Pittsburgh Steelers 1979 (XIII), 1980 (XIV).

Thrift, Cliff (1)—Chicago Bears 1986 (XX).

Thurman, Dennis (1)—Dallas Cowboys 1979 (XIII).

Thurston, Fuzzy (2)—Green Bay Packers 1967 (I), 1968 (II).

Tillman, Rusty (1)—Washington Redskins 1973 (VII).

Tingelhoff, Mick (4)—Minnesota Vikings 1970 (IV), 1974 (VIII), 1975 (IX), 1977 (XI).

Tippett, Andre (1)—New England Patriots 1986 (XX).

Todd, Larry (1)—Oakland Raiders 1968 (II).

Toews, Jeff (2)—Miami Dolphins 1983 (XVII), 1985 (XIX).

Toews, Loren (4)—Pittsburgh Steelers 1975 (IX), 1976 (X), 1979 (XIII), 1980 (XIV).

Tomczak, Mike (1)—Chicago Bears 1986 (XX).

Toomay, Pat (2)—Dallas Cowboys 1971 (V), 1972 (VI).

Torrey, Bob (0*)—Philadelphia Eagles 1981 (XV-DNP).

Townsend, Andre (2)—Denver Broncos 1987 (XXI), 1988 (XXII).

Townsend, Greg (1)—Los Angeles Raiders 1984 (XVIII).

Trosch, Gene (1)—Kansas City Chiefs 1970 (IV).

Truax, Bill (1)—Dallas Cowboys 1972 (VI).

Tuiasosopo, Manu (1)—San Francisco 49ers 1985 (XIX).

Turk, Godwin (1)—Denver Broncos 1978 (XII).

Turner, Bake (1)—New York Jets 1969 (III).

Turner, Jim (2)—New York Jets 1969 (III); Denver Broncos 1978 (XII).

Turner, Keena (2)—San Francisco 49ers 1982 (XVI), 1985 (XIX).

Twilley, Howard (3)—Miami Dolphins 1972 (VI), 1973 (VII), 1974 (VIII).

Tyler, Wendell (2)—Los Angeles Rams 1980 (XIV); San Francisco 49ers 1985 (XIX).

Tyrer, Jim (2)—Kansas City Chiefs 1967 (I), 1970 (IV).

Unitas, Johnny (2)—Baltimore Colts 1969 (III), 1971 (V).

Upchurch, Rick (1)—Denver Broncos 1978 (XII).

Upshaw, Gene (3)—Oakland Raiders 1968 (II), 1977 (XI), 1981 (XV).

Vactor, Ted (1)—Washington Redskins 1973 (VII).

Valentine, Zack (1)—Pittsburgh Steelers 1980 (XIV).

Vandersea, Phil (1)—Green Bay Packers 1967 (I).

van Eeghen, Mark (2)—Oakland Raiders 1977 (XI), 1981 (XV).

Van Horne, Keith (1)—Chicago Bears 1986 (XX).

Vaughn, Clarence (1)—Washington Redskins 1988 (XXII).

Vella, John (1)—Oakland Raiders 1977 (XI).

Vellone, Jim (1)—Minnesota Vikings 1970 (IV).

Verdin, Clarence (0†)—Washington Redskins 1988 (XXII-Inactive).

Veris, Garin (1)—New England Patriots 1986 (XX).

Verser, David (1)—Cincinnati Bengals 1982 (XVI).

Vigorito, Tom (1)—Miami Dolphins 1983 (XVII).

Villapiano, Phil (1)—Oakland Raiders 1977 (XI).

Vogel, Bob (2)—Baltimore Colts 1969 (III), 1971 (V).

Voigt, Stu (3)—Minnesota Vikings 1974 (VIII), 1975 (IX), 1977 (XI).

Volk, Rick (2)—Baltimore Colts 1969 (III), 1971 (V).

von Schamann, Uwe (2)—Miami Dolphins 1983 (XVII), 1985 (XIX).

Waddy, Billy (1)—Los Angeles Rams 1980 (XIV).

Waechter, Henry (1)—Chicago Bears 1986 (XX).

Wagner, Mike (3)—Pittsburgh Steelers 1975 (IX), 1976 (X), 1979 (XIII).

Walden, Bobby (2)—Pittsburgh Steelers 1975 (IX), 1976 (X).

Walker, Fulton (2)—Miami Dolphins 1983 (XVII), 1985 (XIX).

Walker, Rick (2)—Washington Redskins 1983 (XVII), 1984 (XVIII).

Wallace, Jackie (2)—Minnesota Vikings 1975 (IX); Los Angeles Rams 1980 (XIV).

Walter, Mike (1)—San Francisco 49ers 1985 (XIX).

Walters, Stan (1)—Philadelphia Eagles 1981 (XV).

Walton, Alvin (1)—Washington Redskins 1988 (XXII).

Walton, Bruce (0*)—Dallas Cowboys 1976 (X-DNP).

Walton, Sam (1)—New York Jets 1969 (III).

Ward, Jim (0*)—Baltimore Colts 1969 (III-DNP).

Warfield, Paul (3)—Miami Dolphins 1972 (VI), 1973 (VII), 1974 (VIII).

Warren, Don (3)—Washington Redskins 1983 (XVII), 1984 (XVIII), 1988 (XXII).

Warwick, Lonnie (1)—Minnesota Vikings 1170 (IV).

Washington, Anthony (1)—Washington Redskins 1984 (XVIII).

Washington, Gene (1)—Minnesota Vikings 1970 (IV).

Washington, Joe (1*)—Washington Redskins 1983 (XVII-DNP), 1984 (XVIII).

Washington, Mark (3*)—Dallas Cowboys 1971 (V), 1976 (X), 1978 (XII), 1979 (XIII-DNP).

Waters, Charlie (5)—Dallas Cowboys 1971 (V), 1972 (VI), 1976 (X), 1978 (XII), 1979 (XIII).

Watson, Steve (2)—Denver Broncos 1987 (XXI), 1988 (XXII).

Watts, Ted (1)—Los Angeles Raiders 1984 (XVIII).

Weathers, Clarence (1)—New England Patriots 1986 (XX).

Weatherwax, Jim (2)—Green Bay Packers 1967 (I), 1968 (II).

Webster, Mike (4)—Pittsburgh Steelers 1975 (IX), 1976 (X), 1979 (XIII), 1980 (XIV).

Weese, Norris (1)—Denver Broncos 1978 (XII).

Welch, Claxton (2)—Dallas Cowboys 1971 (V), 1972 (VI).

Welch, Herb (1)—New York Giants 1987 (XXI).

Wells, Warren (1)—Oakland Raiders 1968 (II).

Wersching, Ray (2)—San Francisco 49ers 1982 (XVI), 1985 (XIX).

West, Charlie (2)—Minnesota Vikings 1970 (IV), 1974 (VIII).

Westbrooks, Greg (1)—Los Angeles Rams 1980 (XIV).

White, Danny (2)—Dallas Cowboys 1978 (XII), 1979 (XIII).

White, Dwight (4)—Pittsburgh Steelers 1975 (IX), 1976 (X), 1979 (XIII), 1980 (XIV).

White, Ed (4)—Minnesota Vikings 1970 (IV), 1974 (VIII), 1975 (IX), 1977 (XI).

White, James (1)—Minnesota Vikings 1977 (XI).

White, Jeris (1)—Washington Redskins 1983 (XVII).

White, Randy (3)—Dallas Cowboys 1976 (X), 1978 (XII), 1979 (XIII).

White, Sammy (1)—Minnesota Vikings 1977 (XI).

Whitley, Wilson (1)—Cincinnati Bengals 1982 (XVI).

Whittington, Arthur (1)—Oakland Raiders 1981 (XV).

Widby, Ron (2)—Dallas Cowboys 1971 (V), 1972 (VI).

Wilbur, John (1)—Washington Redskins 1973 (VII).

Wilburn, Barry (1)—Washington Redskins 1988 (XXII).

Wilkes, Reggie (1)—Philadelphia Eagles 1981 (XV).

Wilkinson, Jerry (1)—Los Angeles Rams 1980 (XIV).

Willhite, Gerald (1)—Denver Broncos 1987 (XXI).

Williams, Dokie (1)—Los Angeles Raiders 1984 (XVIII).

Williams, Doug (1)—Washington Redskins 1988 (XXII).

Williams, Ed (1)—New England Patriots 1986 (XX).

Williams, Greg (2)—Washington Redskins 1983 (XVII), 1984 (XVIII).

Williams, Howie (1)—Oakland Raiders 1968 (II).

Williams, Joe (1)—Dallas Cowboys 1972 (VI).

Williams, John (2)—Baltimore Colts 1969 (III), 1971 (V).

Williams, Lester (1)—New England Patriots 1986 (XX).

Williams, Mike (1)—Washington Redskins 1984 (XVIII).

Williams, Perry (1)—New York Giants 1987 (XXI).

Williams, Reggie (1)—Cincinnati Bengals 1982 (XVI).

Williams, Sid (1)—Baltimore Colts 1969 (III).

Williams, Travis (1)—Green Bay Packers 1968 (II).

Williamson, Carlton (2)—San Francisco 49ers 1982 (XVI), 1985 (XIX).

Williamson, Fred (1)—Kansas City Chiefs 1967 (I).

Williamson, John (1)—Oakland Raiders 1968 (II).

Willis, Chester (1)—Los Angeles Raiders 1984 (XVIII).

Willis, Len (1)—Minnesota Vikings 1977 (XI).

Wilson, Ben (1)—Green Bay Packers 1968 (II).

Wilson, Brenard (1)—Philadelphia Eagles 1981 (XV).

Wilson, Jerrel (2)—Kansas City Chiefs 1967 (I), 1970 (IV).

Wilson, Marc (1*)—Oakland Raiders 1981 (XV-DNP); Los Angeles Raiders 1984 (XVIII).

Wilson, Mike (2)—San Francisco 49ers 1982 (XVI), 1985 (XIX).

Wilson, Mike (1)—Cincinnati Bengals 1982 (XVI).

Wilson, Otis (1)—Chicago Bears 1986 (XX).

Wilson, Steve (2)—Denver Broncos 1987 (XXI), 1988 (XXII).

Winder, Sammy (2)—Denver Broncos 1987 (XXI), 1988 (XXII).

Winston, Dennis (2)—Pittsburgh Steelers 1979 (XIII), 1980 (XIV).

Winston, Roy (4)—Minnesota Vikings 1970 (IV), 1974 (VIII), 1975 (IX), 1977 (XI).

Wolf, Jim (0*)—Pittsburgh Steelers 1975 (IX-DNP).

Wonsley, Otis (2)—Washington Redskins 1983 (XVII), 1984 (XVIII).

Wood, Willie (2)—Green Bay Packers 1967 (I), 1968 (II).

Woodard, Ken (1)—Denver Broncos 1987 (XXI).

Woodberry, Dennis (1)—Washington Redskins 1988 (XXII).

Woodley, David (1)—Miami Dolphins 1983 (XVII).

Woodruff, Dwayne (1)—Pittsburgh Steelers 1980 (XIV).

Woolsey, Rolly (1)—Dallas Cowboys 1976 (X).

Wooten, Ron (1)—New England Patriots 1986 (XX).

Wright, Eric (2)—San Francisco 49ers 1982 (XVI), 1985 (XIX).

Wright, George (0*)—Baltimore Colts 1971 (V-DNP).

Wright, Jeff (3)—Minnesota Vikings 1974 (VIII), 1975 (IX), 1977 (XI).

Wright, Louis (2)—Denver Broncos 1978 (XII), 1987 (XXI).

Wright, Nate (3)—Minnesota Vikings 1974 (VIII), 1975 (IX), 1977 (XI).

Wright, Rayfield (5)—Dallas Cowboys 1971 (V), 1972 (VI), 1976 (X), 1978 (XII), 1979 (XIII).

Wright, Steve (1*)—Green Bay Packers 1967 (I), 1968 (II-DNP).

Wrightman, Tim (1)—Chicago Bears 1986 (XX).

Wyche, Sam (1)—Washington Redskins 1973 (VII).

Yarber, Eric (1)—Washington Redskins 1988 (XXII).

Yary, Ron (4)—Minnesota Vikings 1970 (IV), 1974 (VIII), 1975 (IX), 1977 (XI).

Yepremian, Garo (3)—Miami Dolphins 1972 (VI), 1973 (VII), 1974 (VIII).

Young, Charle (2)—Los Angeles Rams 1980 (XIV); San Francisco 49ers 1982 (XVI).

Young, Charley (1)—Dallas Cowboys 1976 (X).

Young, Roynell (1)—Philadelphia Eagles 1981 (XV).

Youngblood, Jack (1)—Los Angeles Rams 1980 (XIV).

Youngblood, Jim (1)—Los Angeles Rams 1980 (XIV).

Zaunbrecher, Godfrey (0*)—Minnesota Vikings 1974 (VIII-DNP).

Super Bowl Individual Statistics, 1967-88

SCORING

	Tds.	Td.R	Td.P	Td.M	XP-XPA	FG-FGA	Pts.
Adderley, Green Bay	1	0	0	1	0- 0	0- 0	6
Allegre, New York Giants	0	0	0	0	4- 5	1- 1	7
Allen, Los Angeles Raiders	2	2	0	0	0- 0	0- 0	12
Alworth, Dallas	1	0	1	0	0- 0	0- 0	6
Anderson, Cincinnati	1	1	0	0	0- 0	0- 0	6
Anderson, New York Giants	1	1	0	0	0- 0	0- 0	6
D. Anderson, Green Bay	1	1	0	0	0- 0	0- 0	6
Bahr, Oakland-L.A. Raiders	0	0	0	0	8- 8	3- 4	17
Bahr, Pittsburgh	0	0	0	0	4- 4	1- 1	7
Banaszak, Oakland	2	2	0	0	0- 0	0- 0	12
Bass, Washington	1	0	0	1	0- 0	0- 0	6
Bavaro, New York Giants	1	0	1	0	0- 0	0- 0	6
Blanda, Oakland	0	0	0	0	2- 2	0- 1	2
Bleier, Pittsburgh	1	0	1	0	0- 0	0- 0	6
Branch, Oakland-L.A. Raiders	3	0	3	0	0- 0	0- 0	18
Breech, Cincinnati	0	0	0	0	3- 3	0- 0	3
C. Brown, Washington	1	0	1	0	0- 0	0- 0	6
L. Brown, Pittsburgh	1	0	1	0	0- 0	0- 0	6
T. Brown, Minnesota	1	0	0	1	0- 0	0- 0	6
Brown, Oakland	1	0	0	1	0- 0	0- 0	6
Bryant, Los Angeles	1	1	0	0	0- 0	0- 0	6
Butler, Chicago	0	0	0	0	5- 5	3- 3	14
Casper, Oakland	1	0	1	0	0- 0	0- 0	6
Cefalo, Miami	1	0	1	0	0- 0	0- 0	6
Chandler, Green Bay	0	0	0	0	8- 8	4- 4	20
Clark, Dallas	0	0	0	0	4- 4	3- 3	13
Clark, Washington	1	0	1	0	0- 0	0- 0	6
Cooper, San Francisco	1	0	1	0	0- 0	0- 0	6
Corral, Los Angeles	0	0	0	0	1- 2	2- 2	7
Cox, Minnesota	0	0	0	0	4- 4	0- 1	4
Craig, San Francisco	3	1	2	0	0- 0	0- 0	18
Csonka, Miami	2	2	0	0	0- 0	0- 0	12
Didier, Washington	1	0	1	0	0- 0	0- 0	6
Ditka, Dallas	1	0	1	0	0- 0	0- 0	6
Dorsett, Dallas	1	1	0	0	0- 0	0- 0	6
Dowler, Green Bay	1	0	1	0	0- 0	0- 0	6
DuPree, Dallas	1	0	1	0	0- 0	0- 0	6
Elway, Denver	1	1	0	0	0- 0	0- 0	6
Franklin, Philadelphia-New England	0	0	0	0	2- 2	2- 3	8
Fritsch, Dallas	0	0	0	0	2- 2	1- 1	5
Fryar, New England	1	0	1	0	0- 0	0- 0	6
Garrett, Kansas City	1	1	0	0	0- 0	0- 0	6
Garrett, Washington	1	0	1	0	0- 0	0- 0	6
Gerela, Pittsburgh	0	0	0	0	8- 9	2- 7	14
Grossman, Pittsburgh	1	0	1	0	0- 0	0- 0	6
Haji-Sheikh, Washington	0	0	0	0	6- 6	0- 1	6
Harris, Pittsburgh	4	4	0	0	0- 0	0- 0	24
Harrison, Pittsburgh	0	0	0	0	0- 0	0- 0	*2
Hegman, Dallas	1	0	0	1	0- 0	0- 0	6
Herrera, Dallas	0	0	0	0	3- 3	2- 5	9
Hill, Baltimore	1	1	0	0	0- 0	0- 0	6
T. Hill, Dallas	1	0	1	0	0- 0	0- 0	6
P. Howard, Dallas	1	0	1	0	0- 0	0- 0	6
Jensen, Los Angeles Raiders	1	0	0	1	0- 0	0- 0	6
Johnson, Dallas	2	0	2	0	0- 0	0- 0	12
V. Johnson, Denver	1	0	1	0	0- 0	0- 0	6
D. Johnson, Miami	1	0	1	0	0- 0	0- 0	6
Karlis, Denver	0	0	0	0	3- 3	3- 6	12
Kiick, Miami	2	2	0	0	0- 0	0- 0	12
King, Oakland	1	0	1	0	0- 0	0- 0	6
Knight, Washington	0	0	0	0	1- 1	0- 1	1
Krepfle, Philadelphia	1	0	1	0	0- 0	0- 0	6
Lytle, Denver	1	1	0	0	0- 0	0- 0	6

SCORING—Cont.

	Tds.	Td.R	Td.P	Td.M	XP-XPA	FG-FGA	Pts.
Mackey, Baltimore	1	0	1	0	0- 0	0- 0	6
Mann, Oakland	0	0	0	0	2- 4	2- 3	8
Martin, New York Giants	0	0	0	0	0- 0	0- 0	*2
McClinton, Kansas City	1	0	1	0	0- 0	0- 0	6
McConkey, New York Giants	1	0	1	0	0- 0	0- 0	6
McGee, Green Bay	2	0	2	0	0- 0	0- 0	12
McMahon, Chicago	2	2	0	0	0- 0	0- 0	12
Mercer, Kansas City	0	0	0	0	1- 1	1- 2	4
Michaels, Baltimore	0	0	0	0	1- 1	0- 2	1
Miller, Oakland	2	0	2	0	0- 0	0- 0	12
Monroe, San Francisco	1	0	1	0	0- 0	0- 0	6
Montana, San Francisco	2	2	0	0	0- 0	0- 0	12
Morris, New York Giants	1	1	0	0	0- 0	0- 0	6
Moseley, Washington	0	0	0	0	3- 4	3- 4	12
Mowatt, New York Giants	1	0	1	0	0- 0	0- 0	6
Nattiel, Denver	1	0	1	0	0- 0	0- 0	6
Nowatzke, Baltimore	1	1	0	0	0- 0	0- 0	6
O'Brien, Baltimore	0	0	0	0	1- 2	1- 2	4
Osborn, Minnesota	1	1	0	0	0- 0	0- 0	6
D. Pearson, Dallas	1	0	1	0	0- 0	0- 0	6
Perry, Chicago	1	1	0	0	0- 0	0- 0	6
Phillips, Chicago	1	0	0	1	0- 0	0- 0	6
Pitts, Green Bay	2	0	2	0	0- 0	0- 0	12
Richards, Dallas	1	0	1	0	0- 0	0- 0	6
Riggins, Washington	2	2	0	0	0- 0	0- 0	12
Ross, Cincinnati	2	0	2	0	0- 0	0- 0	12
Sanders, Washington	2	0	2	0	0- 0	0- 0	12
Septien, Dallas	0	0	0	0	4- 4	1- 1	7
Smith, Los Angeles	1	0	1	0	0- 0	0- 0	6
Smith, Washington	2	2	0	0	0- 0	0- 0	12
Snell, N.Y. Jets	1	1	0	0	0- 0	0- 0	6
Squirek, Los Angeles Raiders	1	0	0	1	0- 0	0- 0	6
Stallworth, Pittsburgh	3	0	3	0	0- 0	0- 0	18
Stenerud, Kansas City	0	0	0	0	2- 2	3- 3	11
Suhey, Chicago	1	1	0	0	0- 0	0- 0	6
Swann, Pittsburgh	3	0	3	0	0- 0	0- 0	18
Tarkenton, Minnesota	1	1	0	0	0- 0	0- 0	6
Taylor, Green Bay	1	1	0	0	0- 0	0- 0	6
Taylor, Kansas City	1	0	1	0	0- 0	0- 0	6
D. Thomas, Dallas	2	1	1	0	0- 0	0- 0	12
J. Turner, New York Jets-Denver	0	0	0	0	2- 2	4- 6	14
Twilley, Miami	1	0	1	0	0- 0	0- 0	6
Voigt, Minnesota	1	0	1	0	0- 0	0- 0	6
von Schamann, Miami	0	0	0	0	3- 3	4- 4	15
Waechter, Chicago	0	0	0	0	0- 0	0- 0	*2
Walker, Miami	1	0	0	1	0- 0	0- 0	6
Wersching, San Francisco	0	0	0	0	7- 7	5- 5	22
White, Pittsburgh	0	0	0	0	0- 0	0- 0	*2
S. White, Minnesota	1	0	1	0	0- 0	0- 0	6
Yepremian, Miami	0	0	0	0	5- 5	2- 4	11

*Credited with safety

PASSING

(Rating figured for passers with 12 or more attempts)

	Att.	Cmp.	Pct. Cmp.	Yds.	Avg. Gain	Lg.	Td.	Pct. Td.	Int.	Pct. Int.	Rate Pts.
Anderson, Cincinnati	34	25	73.5	300	8.82	49	2	5.9	2	5.9	95.2
Beathard, Kansas City	5	1	20.0	17	3.40	17	0	0.0	0	0.0	....
Bradshaw, Pittsburgh	84	49	58.3	932	11.10	75	9	10.7	4	4.8	112.6
Bratkowski, Green Bay	1	0	0.0	0	0.00	....	0	0.0	0	0.0	....
Cuozzo, Minnesota	3	1	33.3	16	5.33	16	0	0.0	1	3.3	....
Dawson, Kansas City	44	28	63.6	353	8.02	46	2	4.5	2	4.5	84.8
Eason, New England	6	0	0.0	0	0.00	....	0	0.0	0	0.0	....
Elway, Denver	75	36	48.0	561	7.48	56	2	2.7	4	5.3	60.2
Ferragamo, Los Angeles	25	15	60.0	212	8.48	50	0	0.0	1	4.0	70.8
Fuller, Chicago	4	0	0.0	0	0.00	....	0	0.0	0	0.0	....
Griese, Miami	41	26	63.4	295	7.20	28	1	2.4	2	4.9	72.5
Grogan, New England	30	17	56.7	177	5.90	24	1	3.3	2	6.7	57.0
Havrilak, Baltimore	1	1	100.0	25	25.00	25	0	0.0	0	0.0	....
Jaworski, Philadelphia	38	18	47.4	291	7.66	43	1	2.6	3	7.9	49.3
Kapp, Minnesota	25	16	64.0	183	7.32	28	0	0.0	2	8.0	52.6
Kilmer, Washington	28	14	50.0	104	3.71	15	0	0.0	3	10.7	19.6
Kubiak, Denver	4	4	100.0	48	12.00	23	0	0.0	0	0.0	....
Lamonica, Oakland	34	15	44.2	208	6.12	41	2	5.9	1	2.9	72.0
Lee, Minnesota	9	7	77.8	81	9.00	20	1	11.1	0	0.0	....

PASSING—Cont.

	Att.	Cmp.	Pct. Cmp.	Yds.	Avg. Gain	Lg.	Td.	Pct. Td.	Int.	Pct. Int.	Rate Pts.
Marino, Miami	50	29	58.0	318	6.36	30	1	2.0	2	4.0	66.9
McCutcheon, Los Angeles	1	1	100.0	24	24.00	24	1	100.0	0	0.0	....
McMahon, Chicago	20	12	60.0	256	12.80	60	0	0.0	0	0.0	104.2
Montana, San Francisco	57	38	66.7	488	8.56	40	4	7.0	0	0.0	116.7
Morrall, Baltimore	32	13	40.6	218	6.81	45	0	0.0	4	12.5	24.7
Morton, Dallas-Denver	41	16	39.0	166	4.05	41	1	2.4	7	17.1	19.9
Namath, N.Y. Jets	28	17	60.7	206	7.36	39	0	0.0	0	0.0	83.3
Newhouse, Dallas	1	1	100.0	29	29.00	29	1	100.0	0	0.0	
Parilli, N.Y. Jets	1	0	0.0	0	0.00	....	0	0.0	0	0.0	
Plunkett, Oakland-L.A. Raiders	46	29	63.0	433	9.41	80	4	8.7	0	0.0	122.8
Schroeder, Washington	1	0	0.0	0	0.00	0	0	0.0	0	0.0	....
Sewell, Denver	1	1	100.0	23	23.00	23	0	0.0	0	0.0	....
Simms, New York	25	22	88.0	268	10.72	44	3	12.0	0	0.0	150.9
Stabler, Oakland	19	12	63.2	180	9.47	48	1	5.3	0	0.0	111.9
Starr, Green Bay	47	29	61.7	452	9.62	62	3	6.4	1	2.1	95.1
Staubach, Dallas	98	61	62.2	734	7.49	45	8	8.2	4	4.1	95.4
Strock, Miami	3	0	0.0	0	0.00	....	0	0.0	0	0.0	....
Tarkenton, Minnesota	89	46	51.7	489	5.49	30	1	1.1	6	6.7	43.8
Theismann, Washington	58	31	53.4	386	6.66	60	2	3.4	4	6.9	56.9
Unitas, Baltimore	33	14	42.4	198	6.00	75	1	3.0	3	9.1	34.5
Weese, Denver	10	4	40.0	22	2.20	9	0	0.0	0	0.0	....
D. White, Dallas	2	1	50.0	5	2.50	5	0	0.0	0	0.0	....
Williams, Washington	29	18	62.1	340	11.72	80	4	13.8	1	3.4	128.1
Woodley, Miami	14	4	28.6	97	6.93	76	1	7.1	1	7.1	50.1

RECEIVING

	No.	Yds.	Avg.	Lg.	Tds.
Alexander, Cincinnati	2	3	1.5	3	0
Allen, L.A. Raiders	2	18	9.0	12	0
Alworth, Dallas	2	28	14.0	21	1
D. Anderson, Green Bay	2	18	9.0	12	0
Arbanas, Kansas City	2	30	15.0	18	0
Banaszak, Oakland	4	69	17.3	41	0
Bavaro, N.Y. Giants	4	51	12.8	17	1
Beasley, Minnesota	2	41	20.5	26	0
Bell, Pittsburgh	2	21	10.5	12	0
Biletnikoff, Oakland	6	89	14.8	48	0
Bleier, Pittsburgh	3	18	6.0	7	1
Branch, Oakland-L.A. Raiders	14	181	12.9	50	3
Briscoe, Miami	2	19	9.5	13	0
B. Brown, Minnesota	4	20	5.0	10	0
C. Brown, Washington	9	153	17.0	60	1
L. Brown, Pittsburgh	4	56	14.0	30	1
L. Brown, Washington	5	26	5.2	12	0
Bryant, Los Angeles	3	21	7.0	12	0
Bryant, Washington	1	20	20.0	20	0
Bulaich, Baltimore	1	5	5.0	5	0
Burford, Kansas City	4	67	16.8	27	0
Cannon, Oakland	2	25	12.5	15	0
Carmichael, Philadelphia	5	83	16.6	29	0
Carolan, Kansas City	1	7	7.0	7	0
Carthon, N.Y. Giants	4	13	3.3	7	0
Casper, Oakland	4	70	17.5	25	1
Cefalo, Miami	3	96	32.0	76	1
Chandler, Oakland	4	77	19.3	32	0
Chester, Oakland	2	24	12.0	16	0
Christensen, L.A. Raiders	4	32	8.0	14	0
Clark, Washington	3	55	18.3	27	1
D. Clark, San Francisco	10	122	12.2	33	0
Clayton, Miami	6	92	15.3	27	0
Coan, Kansas City	1	5	5.0	5	0
Collins, New England	2	19	9.5	11	0
Collinsworth, Cincinnati	5	107	21.4	49	0
Cooper, San Francisco	2	15	7.5	11	1
Craig, San Francisco	7	77	11.0	20	2
Csonka, Miami	3	17	5.7	16	0
Cunningham, Pittsburgh	2	21	10.5	13	0
Curtis, Cincinnati	3	42	14.0	21	0
Dale, Green Bay	8	102	12.8	25	0
Dennard, Los Angeles	2	32	16.0	24	0
Dennison, Dallas	1	6	6.0	6	0
Didier, Washington	6	73	12.2	20	1
Ditka, Dallas	2	28	14.0	21	0
Dixon, Oakland	1	3	3.0	3	0
Dolbin, Denver	2	24	12.0	15	0
Dorsett, Dallas	7	55	7.9	15	0
Dowler, Green Bay	2	71	35.5	62	1
Duper, Miami	1	11	11.0	11	0
DuPree, Dallas	6	83	13.8	19	1
Elway, Denver	1	23	23.0	23	0
Fleming, G.Bay-Miami	7	84	12.0	27	0
Foreman, Minnesota	15	139	9.3	26	0
Francis, San Francisco	5	60	12.0	19	0
Fryar, New England	2	24	12.0	16	1
Fugett, Dallas	1	9	9.0	9	0
Garrett, Washington	3	30	10.0	17	1
Garrett, Oakland	1	11	11.0	11	0
Garrett, Kansas City	5	53	10.6	17	0
Garrison, Dallas	4	30	7.5	14	0
Gault, Chicago	4	129	32.3	60	0
Gentry, Chicago	2	41	20.5	27	0
Giaquinto, Washington	2	21	10.5	14	0
Gilliam, Minnesota	5	60	12.0	30	0
Grossman, Pittsburgh	4	36	9.0	10	1
Harraway, Washington	1	-3	-3.0	-3	0
Harris, Miami	2	15	7.5	8	0
Harris, Pittsburgh	5	114	22.8	32	0
Harris, Philadelphia	1	1	1.0	1	0
Havrilak, Baltimore	2	27	13.5	25	0
Hawkins, L.A. Raiders	2	20	10.0	14	0
Hayes, Dallas	3	64	21.3	41	0
Hayes, Kansas City	1	3	3.0	3	0
Henderson, Minnesota	7	111	15.9	28	0
C. Hill, Dallas	1	12	12.0	12	0
D. Hill, Los Angeles	1	28	28.0	28	0
Hill, Baltimore	2	1	0.5	1	0
T. Hill, Dallas	2	49	24.5	39	1
Hinton, Baltimore	2	51	25.5	26	0
P. Howard, Dallas	1	34	34.0	34	1
M. Jackson, Denver	7	127	18.1	32	0
C. James, New England	1	6	6.0	6	0
Jefferson, Balt.-Wash.	8	102	12.8	23	0
Johnson, Cincinnati	2	8	4.0	5	0
Jensen, Denver	1	5	5.0	5	0
Johnson, Cincinnati	4	83	20.8	45	2
Johnson, Minnesota	3	26	8.7	17	0
D. Johnson, Miami	3	28	9.3	21	1
V. Johnson, Denver	5	121	24.2	54	1
Kay, Denver	2	38	19.0	20	1
Kiick, Miami	5	27	5.4	11	0
King, Oakland-L.A. Raiders	4	101	25.3	80	1

RECEIVING—Cont.

	No.	Yds.	Avg.	Lg.	Tds.
Kingsriter, Minnesota	1	9	9.0	9	0
Kreider, Cincinnati	2	36	18.0	19	0
Krepfle, Philadelphia	2	16	8.0	8	1
Lammons, N.Y. Jets	2	13	6.5	11	0
Lang, Denver	2	11	5.5	7	0
Lash, Minnesota	1	9	9.0	9	0
Lewis, Pittsburgh	1	12	12.0	12	0
Mackey, Baltimore	5	115	23.0	75	1
Mandich, Miami	4	49	12.3	19	0
Manuel, N.Y. Giants	3	43	14.3	17	0
Margerum, Chicago	2	36	18.0	29	0
Marinaro, Minnesota	2	39	19.5	27	0
Mathis, N.Y. Jets	3	20	6.7	13	0
Matte, Baltimore	2	30	15.0	30	0
McClinton, Kansas City	2	34	17.0	27	1
McConkey, N.Y. Giants	2	50	25.0	44	1
McCutcheon, Los Angeles	1	16	16.0	16	0
McGee, Green Bay	8	173	21.6	37	2
Miller, Oakland	5	84	16.8	23	2
Miller, Minnesota	4	19	4.8	13	0
Mitchell, Baltimore	1	15	15.0	15	0
Mobley, Denver	2	17	8.5	11	0
Monk, Washington	2	66	33.0	40	0
Monroe, San Francisco	1	33	33.0	33	1
Montgomery, Philadelphia	6	91	15.2	25	0
Moore, Miami	2	17	8.5	9	0
Moorehead, Chicago	2	22	11.0	14	0
Morgan, New England	7	70	10.0	19	0
Morris, N.Y. Giants	4	20	5.0	12	0
Moses, Denver	1	21	21.0	21	0
Mowatt, N.Y. Giants	1	6	6.0	6	1
Nathan, Miami	10	83	8.3	25	0
Nattiel, Denver	2	69	34.5	56	1
Nelson, Los Angeles	2	20	10.0	14	0
Newhouse, Dallas	5	11	2.2	8	0
Nowatzke, Baltimore	1	45	45.0	45	0
Odoms, Denver	2	9	4.5	10	0
Orr, Baltimore	3	42	14.0	17	0
Osborn, Minnesota	4	18	4.5	10	0
Parker, Philadelphia	1	19	19.0	19	0
Patton, San Francisco	1	6	6.0	6	0
D. Pearson, Dallas	7	145	20.7	30	1
P. Pearson, Dallas	12	105	8.8	14	0
Perrin, Denver	1	−7	−7.0	−7	0
Pitts, Green Bay	2	32	16.0	22	0
Pitts, Kansas City	3	33	11.0	20	0
D. Ramsey, New England	2	16	8.0	11	0
Rashad, Minnesota	3	53	17.7	25	0
Reed, Minnesota	4	13	3.3	12	0
Reeves, Dallas	5	46	9.2	17	0
Richards, Dallas	2	38	19.0	29	1
Richardson, Baltimore	6	58	9.7	21	0
Riggins, Washington	2	16	8.0	15	0
Ring, San Francisco	1	3	3.0	3	0
Robinson, N.Y. Giants	3	62	20.7	36	0
Rose, Miami	6	73	12.2	30	0
Ross, Cincinnati	11	104	9.5	16	2
Rouson, N.Y. Giants	1	23	23.0	23	0
Sampson, Denver	2	20	10.0	11	0
Sanders, Washington	9	193	21.4	80	2
Sauer, N.Y. Jets	8	133	16.6	39	0
Sewell, Denver	6	53	8.8	18	0
Smith, Philadelphia	2	59	29.5	43	0
J. Smith, Washington	1	11	11.0	11	0
Smith, Los Angeles	1	24	24.0	24	1
T. Smith, Washington	1	9	9.0	9	0
Snell, N.Y. Jets	4	40	10.0	14	0
Solomon, San Francisco	5	66	13.2	20	0
Spagnola, Philadelphia	1	22	22.0	22	0
Stallworth, Pittsburgh	11	268	24.4	75	3
Starring, New England	2	39	19.5	24	0
Suhey, Chicago	1	24	24.0	24	0
Swann, Pittsburgh	16	364	22.8	64	3
C. Taylor, Washington	2	20	10.0	15	0
Taylor, Green Bay	1	−1	−1.0	−1	0
Taylor, Kansas City	10	138	13.8	46	1
D. Thomas, Dallas	7	38	5.4	11	1
Thomas, Chicago	1	4	4.0	4	0
Twilley, Miami	2	48	24.0	28	1
Tyler, L.A. Rams-San Fran.	7	90	12.9	40	0
Upchurch, Denver	1	9	9.0	9	0
Voigt, Minnesota	9	126	14.0	28	1
Waddy, Los Angeles	3	75	25.0	50	0
Walker, Washington	1	27	27.0	27	0
Warfield, Miami	9	108	12.0	27	0
Warren, Washington	7	43	6.1	10	0
Washington, Minnesota	1	9	9.0	9	0
J. Washington, Washington	3	20	6.7	10	0
Watson, Denver	2	54	27.0	31	0
Weathers, New England	1	3	3.0	3	0
Wells, Oakland	1	17	17.0	17	0
S. White, Minnesota	5	77	15.4	20	1
Willhite, Denver	5	39	7.8	11	0
Wilson, San Francisco	1	22	22.0	22	0
Winder, Denver	5	60	12.0	26	0
Young, Dallas	3	31	10.3	14	0
Young, San Francisco	1	14	14.0	14	0

RUSHING

	Att.	Yds.	Avg.	Lg.	Tds.
Alexander, Cincinnati	5	17	3.4	13	0
Allen, L.A. Raiders	20	191	9.5	74	2
Anderson, Cincinnati	4	15	3.8	6	1
Anderson, N.Y. Giants	2	1	0.5	2	1
D. Anderson, Green Bay	18	78	4.3	13	1
Armstrong, Denver	7	27	3.9	18	0
Banaszak, Oakland	16	35	2.2	6	2
Beathard, Kansas City	1	14	14.0	14	0
Bennett, Miami	3	7	2.3	7	0
Bleier, Pittsburgh	44	144	3.3	18	0
Boozer, N.Y. Jets	10	19	1.9	8	0
Bradshaw, Pittsburgh	14	53	3.8	17	0
B. Brown, Minnesota	7	28	4.0	10	0
L. Brown, Washington	22	72	3.3	11	0
Bryant, Los Angeles	6	30	5.0	14	1
Bryant, Washington	8	38	4.8	15	0
Bulaich, Baltimore	18	28	1.6	8	0
Carthon, N.Y. Giants	3	4	1.3	2	0
Clark, San Francisco	1	−2	−2.0	−2	0
Clark, Washington	1	25	25.0	25	0
Coan, Kansas City	3	1	0.3	3	0
Collins, New England	3	4	1.3	3	0
Cooper, San Francisco	10	38	3.8	14	0
Craig, San Francisco	15	58	3.9	10	1
Csonka, Miami	57	297	5.2	49	2
Davis, Oakland	16	137	8.6	35	0
Davis, San Francisco	2	5	2.5	4	0
Dawson, Kansas City	6	35	5.8	15	0
Dennison, Dallas	5	16	3.2	5	0
Ditka, Dallas	1	17	17.0	17	0
Dixon, Oakland	12	54	4.5	14	0
Dorsett, Dallas	31	162	5.2	29	1
Elway, Denver	9	59	6.6	21	1
Ferragamo, Los Angeles	1	7	7.0	7	0
Foreman, Minnesota	36	80	2.2	12	0
Franklin, Miami	16	49	3.1	9	0
Fuller, Chicago	1	1	1.0	1	0
Galbreath, N.Y. Giants	4	17	4.3	7	0
Garrett, Washington	1	44	44.0	44	0
Garrett, Oakland	4	19	4.8	13	0
Garrett, Kansas City	17	56	3.3	9	1
Garrison, Dallas	26	139	5.3	19	0
Gentry, Chicago	3	15	5.0	8	0
Giammona, Philadelphia	1	7	7.0	7	0
Ginn, Oakland	2	9	4.5	9	0
Grabowski, Green Bay	2	2	1.0	2	0

RUSHING—Cont.

	Att.	Yds.	Avg.	Lg.	Tds.		Att.	Yds.	Avg.	Lg.	Tds.
Griese, Miami	3	7	2.3	5	0	Patton, San Francisco	17	55	3.2	10	0
A. Griffin, Cincinnati	1	4	4.0	4	0	Payton, Chicago	22	61	2.8	7	0
Griffin, Washington	1	2	2.0	2	0	P. Pearson, Dallas	9	31	3.4	9	0
Grogan, New England	1	3	3.0	3	0	Perrin, Denver	3	8	2.7	4	0
Harmon, Washington	9	40	4.4	12	0	Perry, Chicago	1	1	1.0	1	0
Harmon, San Francisco	5	20	4.0	7	0	Pitts, Green Bay	11	45	4.1	12	2
Harraway, Washington	10	37	3.7	8	0	Pitts, Kansas City	3	37	12.3	19	0
Harrington, Philadelphia	1	4	4.0	4	0	Plunkett, Oakland-L.A. Raiders	4	7	1.8	5	0
Harris, Miami	1	1	1.0	1	0	Pruitt, L.A. Raiders	5	17	3.4	11	0
Harris, Pittsburgh	101	354	3.5	25	4	Rae, Oakland	2	9	4.5	11	0
Harris, Philadelphia	7	14	2.0	5	0	Reed, Minnesota	15	49	3.3	15	0
Havrilak, Baltimore	1	3	3.0	3	0	Reeves, Dallas	1	7	7.0	7	0
Hawkins, L.A. Raiders	3	6	2.0	3	0	Riggins, Washington	64	230	3.6	43	2
Hawthorne, New England	1	−4	−4.0	−4	0	Ring, San Francisco	5	17	3.4	7	0
Hayes, Dallas	1	16	16.0	16	0	Rogers, Washington	5	17	3.4	5	0
Hayes, Kansas City	8	31	3.9	13	0	Rouson, N.Y. Giants	3	22	7.3	18	0
C. Hill, Dallas	7	25	3.6	13	0	Rutledge, N.Y. Giants	3	0	0.0	2	0
Hill, Baltimore	9	29	3.2	12	1	Sanders, Chicago	4	15	3.8	10	0
Holmes, Kansas City	5	7	1.4	7	0	Sanders, Washington	1	−4	−4.0	−4	0
C. James, New England	5	1	0.2	3	0	Sewell, Denver	4	1	0.3	12	0
Jaworski, Philadelphia	1	0	0.0	0	0	Simms, N.Y. Giants	3	25	8.3	22	0
Jensen, Oakland	3	12	4.0	6	0	J. Smith, Washington	1	6	6.0	6	0
Jensen, Denver	1	16	16.0	16	0	T. Smith, Washington	22	204	9.3	58	2
Johnson, Cincinnati	14	36	2.6	5	0	Snell, N.Y. Jets	30	121	4.0	12	1
Johnson, Dallas	1	−9	−9.0	−9	0	Solomon, San Francisco	1	5	5.0	5	0
Johnson, Minnesota	2	9	4.5	8	0	Starr, Green Bay	1	14	14.0	14	0
Kapp, Minnesota	2	9	4.5	7	0	Staubach, Dallas	17	83	4.9	18	0
Keyworth, Denver	5	9	1.8	6	0	Suhey, Chicago	11	52	4.7	11	1
Kiick, Miami	29	88	3.0	9	2	Swann, Pittsburgh	1	−7	−7.0	−7	0
Kilmer, Washington	2	18	9.0	9	0	Tarkenton, Minnesota	5	17	3.4	8	1
King, Oakland-L.A. Raiders	9	30	3.3	10	0	C. Taylor, Washington	1	8	8.0	8	0
Laidlaw, Dallas	4	13	3.3	7	0	Taylor, Green Bay	16	53	3.3	14	1
Lang, Denver	7	40	5.7	13	0	Theismann, Washington	6	38	6.3	12	0
Lee, Minnesota	1	4	4.0	4	0	D. Thomas, Dallas	37	130	3.5	23	1
Lytle, Denver	10	35	3.5	16	1	Thomas, Chicago	2	8	4.0	7	0
Marinaro, Minnesota	1	3	3.0	3	0	Thornton, Pittsburgh	5	26	5.2	22	0
Marino, Miami	1	0	0.0	0	0	Todd, Oakland	2	37	18.5	32	0
Mathis, N.Y. Jets	3	2	0.7	1	0	Tyler, L.A. Rams-San Fran.	30	125	4.2	39	0
Matte, Baltimore	11	116	10.5	58	0	Unitas, Baltimore	2	4	2.0	4	0
McClanahan, Minnesota	3	3	1.0	2	0	van Eeghen, Oakland	37	153	4.1	11	0
McClinton, Kansas City	6	16	2.7	6	0	Vigorito, Miami	1	4	4.0	4	0
McCutcheon, Los Angeles	5	10	2.0	6	0	Walker, Washington	1	6	6.0	6	0
McMahon, Chicago	5	14	2.8	7	2	J. Washington, Washington	3	8	2.7	5	0
McVea, Kansas City	12	26	2.2	9	0	Weathers, New England	1	3	3.0	3	0
Mercein, Green Bay	1	0	0.0	0	0	Weese, Denver	3	26	8.7	10	0
Miller, Minnesota	2	4	2.0	3	0	D. White, Dallas	1	13	13.0	13	0
Montana, San Francisco	11	77	7.0	19	2	S. White, Minnesota	1	7	7.0	7	0
Montgomery, Philadelphia	16	44	2.8	8	0	Whittington, Oakland	3	−2	−0.7	2	0
Morrall, Baltimore	3	−1	−0.3	1	0	Willhite, Denver	4	19	4.8	11	0
Morris, Miami	21	68	3.2	14	0	Williams, Green Bay	8	36	4.5	18	0
Morris, N.Y. Giants	20	67	3.3	11	1	Williams, Washington	2	−2	−1.0	−1	0
Morton, Dallas	1	2	2.0	2	0	Willis, L.A. Raiders	1	7	7.0	7	0
Nathan, Miami	12	44	3.7	16	0	Wilson, Green Bay	17	62	3.6	13	0
Newhouse, Dallas	38	114	3.0	16	0	Winder, Denver	12	30	2.5	13	0
Nowatzke, Baltimore	10	33	3.3	9	1	Woodley, Miami	4	16	4.0	7	0
Osborn, Minnesota	15	14	0.9	4	1						

PUNTING

	No.	Yds.	Avg.	Lg.		No.	Yds.	Avg.	Lg.
D. Anderson, Green Bay	7	277	39.6	48	Johnson, N.Y. Jets	4	155	38.8	39
Bragg, Washington	5	156	31.2	38	Landeta, N.Y. Giants	3	138	46.0	59
Buford, Chicago	4	173	43.3	52	Lee, Minnesota	3	111	37.0	50
Camarillo, New England	6	263	43.8	62	Lee, Baltimore	7	299	42.7	56
Chandler, Green Bay	3	130	43.3	50	McInally, Cincinnati	3	131	43.7	53
Clabo, Minnesota	7	265	37.9	46	Miller, San Francisco	4	185	46.3	50
Clark, Los Angeles	5	220	44.0	59	Orosz, Miami	6	227	37.8	46
Colquitt, Pittsburgh	5	214	42.8	52	Roby, Miami	6	236	39.3	51
Cox, Washington	4	150	37.5	42	Runager, Phila.-San Fran.	6	208	34.7	46
Dilts, Denver	4	153	38.2	46	Seiple, Miami	15	620	41.3	57
Eischeid, Oak.-Minn.	17	698	41.1	55	Walden, Pittsburgh	11	402	36.5	59
Guy, Oakland-L.A. Raiders	14	587	41.9	51	D. White, Dallas	10	406	40.6	53
Hayes, Washington	11	427	38.8	54	Widby, Dallas	14	563	40.2	47
Hoopes, Dallas	7	245	35.0	48	Wilson, Kansas City	11	511	46.5	61
Horan, Denver	9	335	37.2	43					

PUNT RETURNS

	No.	FC	Yds.	Avg.	Lg.	Tds.
Anderson, Miami	0	1	0	0.0	....	0
D. Anderson, Green Bay	3	0	25	8.3	15	0
Baird, N.Y. Jets	1	1	0	0.0	0	0
Bell, Pittsburgh	6	0	44	7.3	12	0
Bird, Oakland	2	1	12	6.0	12	0
D. Brown, Pittsburgh	3	0	14	4.7	9	0
Brown, Los Angeles	1	0	4	4.0	4	0
Brown, Baltimore	4	0	34	8.5	21	0
Bryant, Minnesota	0	1	0	0.0	....	0
Clark, Washington	2	0	18	9.0	9	0
Colzie, Oakland	4	0	43	10.8	25	0
Edwards, Pittsburgh	4	0	19	4.8	10	0
Fryar, New England	2	0	22	11.0	12	0
Fuller, Cincinnati	4	0	35	8.8	17	0
Gardin, Baltimore	4	3	4	1.0	2	0
Garrett, Kansas City	3	0	17	5.7	9	0
Giaquinto, Washington	1	2	1	1.0	1	0
Green, Washington	2	1	34	17.0	34	0
Harris, Dallas	0	2	0	0.0	....	0
Hayes, Dallas	4	1	8	2.0	7	0
Haymond, Washington	4	0	9	2.3	7	0
Henry, Philadelphia	1	0	2	2.0	2	0
Hicks, San Francisco	1	0	6	6.0	6	0
T. Hill, Dallas	1	1	0	0.0	0	0
Johnson, Dallas	2	1	33	16.5	21	0
Logan, Baltimore	1	0	8	8.0	8	0
Matthews, Oakland	2	1	1	0.5	2	0
McConkey, N.Y. Giants	1	1	25	25.0	25	0
McCullum, Minnesota	3	0	11	3.7	6	0
McLemore, San Francisco	5	0	51	10.2	28	0
Nelms, Washington	6	0	52	8.7	12	0
Ortego, Chicago	2	1	20	10.0	12	0
Pruitt, L.A. Raiders	1	3	8	8.0	8	0
Richards, Dallas	1	3	5	5.0	5	0
Schultz, Denver	1	0	0	0.0	0	0
Sciarra, Philadelphia	2	0	18	9.0	12	0
Scott, Miami	6	3	45	7.5	21	0
Smith, Pittsburgh	2	0	14	7.0	7	0
Solomon, San Francisco	0	1	0	0.0	...	0
Swann, Pittsburgh	3	0	34	11.3	17	0
E. Thomas, Kansas City	1	0	2	2.0	2	0
Upchurch, Denver	3	0	22	7.3	8	0
Vactor, Washington	0	2	0	0.0	....	0
Vigorito, Miami	2	1	22	11.0	12	0
Walker, Miami	2	0	15	7.5	9	0
Wallace, Minnesota	0	1	0	0.0	0	0
Watts, L.A. Raiders	1	0	0	0.0	0	0
West, Minnesota	2	0	18	9.0	11	0
Willhite, Denver	1	1	9	9.0	9	0
Willis, Minnesota	3	0	14	4.7	8	0
Wood, Green Bay	6	1	33	5.5	31	0
N. Wright, Minnesota	1	0	1	1.0	1	0
Yarber, Washington	0	1	0	0.0	0	0

KICKOFF RETURNS

	No.	Yds.	Avg.	Lg.	Tds.
Adderley, Green Bay	3	64	21.3	24	0
D. Anderson, Green Bay	1	25	25.0	25	0
L. Anderson, Pittsburgh	8	207	25.9	45	0
Andrews, Los Angeles	1	0	0.0	0	0
Bell, Denver	8	136	17.0	28	0
L. Blackwood, Miami	2	32	16.0	17	0
Blount, Pittsburgh	3	64	21.3	27	0
Brinson, Dallas	3	63	21.0	25	0
B. Brown, Minnesota	1	2	2.0	2	0
Brown, Baltimore	2	46	23.0	25	0
Campfield, Philadelphia	5	87	17.4	21	0
Christy, N.Y. Jets	1	25	25.0	25	0
Clark, San Francisco	1	0	0.0	0	0
Coan, Kansas City	4	87	21.8	31	0
Collier, Pittsburgh	1	25	25.0	25	0
Crutcher, Green Bay	1	7	7.0	7	0
Duncan, Baltimore	4	90	22.5	30	0
Flynn, N.Y. Giants	1	−3	−3.0	−3	0
Frazier, Cincinnati	1	0	0.0	0	0
Garrett, Oakland	2	47	23.5	24	0
Garrett, Kansas City	2	43	21.5	23	0
Garrett, Washington	5	100	20.0	35	0
Gault, Chicago	4	49	12.3	18	0
Gilliam, Minnesota	2	41	20.5	21	0
Ginn, Miami	1	32	32.0	32	0
Grant, Washington	1	32	32.0	32	0
Grayson, Oakland	2	61	30.5	25	0
A. Griffin, Cincinnati	1	0	0.0	0	0
Hardy, Miami	2	31	15.5	16	0
Harmon, San Francisco	2	24	12.0	23	0
Harrington, Philadelphia	1	0	0.0	0	0
Harris, Dallas	1	18	18.0	18	0
Harrison, Pittsburgh	2	17	8.5	17	0
Hawkins, Oakland	1	3	3.0	3	0
Hayes, Kansas City	2	36	18.0	18	0
Haymond, Washington	2	30	15.0	18	0
Henderson, Dallas	0	48	....	48	0
Hicks, San Francisco	1	23	23.0	23	0
C. Hill, Dallas	1	14	14.0	14	0
E. Hill, L.A. Rams-Miami	4	63	15.8	27	0
Jensen, Denver	1	17	17.0	17	0
Jodat, Los Angeles	2	32	16.0	16	0
Johnson, Dallas	5	92	18.4	23	0
Jones, Minnesota	1	33	33.0	33	0
Kiner, Dallas	1	2	2.0	2	0
Kocourek, Oakland	1	0	0.0	0	0
Lang, Denver	2	36	18.0	23	0
Lawrence, San Francisco	1	17	17.0	17	0
Matthews, Oakland	2	29	14.5	21	0
McClanahan, Minnesota	1	22	22.0	22	0
McCullum, Minnesota	1	26	26.0	26	0
McIntyre, San Francisco	1	0	0.0	0	0
Monroe, San Francisco	1	16	16.0	16	0
Moody, Oakland	1	19	19.0	19	0
Morris, Miami	6	123	20.5	37	0
Mul-Key, Washington	1	15	15.0	15	0
Nelms, Washington	2	44	22.0	24	0
P. Pearson, Blt.-Pitt.-Dal.	7	122	17.4	33	0
Pruitt, L.A. Raiders	1	17	17.0	17	0
Rouson, N.Y. Giants	3	56	18.7	22	0
Sanders, Washington	3	46	15.3	16	0
Schultz, Denver	2	62	31.0	37	0
Scott, Miami	2	47	23.5	31	0
Starring, New England	7	153	21.9	36	0
I. Thomas, Dallas	1	23	23.0	23	0
Todd, Oakland	3	63	21.0	23	0
Upchurch, Denver	3	94	31.3	67	0
Verser, Cincinnati	5	52	10.4	16	0
Walker, Miami	8	283	35.4	98	1
Waters, Dallas	1	11	11.0	11	0
West, Minnesota	5	74	14.8	27	0
R. White, Dallas	1	0	0.0	0	0
S. White, Minnesota	4	79	19.8	26	0
Williams, Green Bay	1	18	18.0	18	0
Willis, Minnesota	3	57	19.0	20	0
Wonsley, Washington	1	13	13.0	13	0

INTERCEPTIONS

	No.	Yds.	Lg.	Tds.
Adderley, Dallas	1	60	60	1
Barnes, Dallas	1	0	0	0
Beverly, N.Y. Jets	2	0	0	0
L. Blackwood, Miami	1	0	0	0
Blount, Pittsburgh	2	23	13	0
Brown, Los Angeles	1	6	6	0
Brown, Oakland	1	75	75	1
Buoniconti, Miami	1	32	32	0
Castille, Denver	1	0	0	0
Curtis, Baltimore	1	13	13	0

INTERCEPIONS—Cont.

	No.	Yds.	Lg.	Tds.		No.	Yds.	Lg.	Tds.
Davis, Washington	1	0	0	0	Murphy, Washington	1	0	0	0
Duhe, Miami	1	0	0	0	Owens, Washington	1	0	0	0
Edwards, Pittsburgh	1	35	35	0	Patterson, N.Y. Giants	1	−7	−7	0
Elmendorf, Los Angeles	1	10	10	0	Perry, Los Angeles	1	−1	−1	0
Greene, Pittsburgh	1	10	10	0	Phillips, Chicago	1	28	28	1
Hall, Oakland	1	16	16	0	Renfro, Dallas	1	0	0	0
Haynes, L.A. Raiders	1	0	0	0	Robinson, Kansas City	1	9	9	0
Hicks, San Francisco	1	27	27	0	Sample, N.Y. Jets	1	0	0	0
Howley, Dallas	3	63	41	0	Scott, Miami	2	63	55	0
Hudson, N.Y. Jets	1	9	9	0	Squirek, L.A. Raiders	1	5	5	1
Hughes, Dallas	1	0	0	0	E. Thomas, Kansas City	1	6	6	0
Johnson, Miami	1	10	10	0	Thomas, Pittsburgh	1	35	35	0
Krause, Minnesota	1	0	0	0	Thomas, Los Angeles	0	6	6	0
Kyle, Dallas	1	19	19	0	Volk, Baltimore	1	30	30	0
Lambert, Pittsburgh	1	16	16	0	Wagner, Pittsburgh	2	45	26	0
Lanier, Kansas City	1	9	9	0	Washington, Dallas	1	27	27	0
Lewis, Dallas	1	21	21	0	Wilburn, Washington	2	11	11	0
Logan, Baltimore	1	14	14	0	Williamson, San Francisco	1	0	0	0
Martin, Oakland	3	44	25	0	Wood, Green Bay	1	50	50	0
Mitchell, Kansas City	1	0	0	0	Wright, San Francisco	2	25	25	0
Morrissey, Chicago	1	47	47	0					

FUMBLES

	No.	Own Rec.	Opp. Rec.	Tds.		No.	Own Rec.	Opp. Rec.	Tds.
Allen, L.A. Raiders	1	0	0	0	Hinton, Baltimore	1	0	0	0
Anderson, Miami	0	1	0	0	Howley, Dallas	0	0	1	0
Baker, N.Y. Jets	0	0	1	0	Hughes, Dallas	0	0	2	0
Banaszak, Pittsburgh	0	0	1	0	Huther, Dallas	0	0	1	0
Banaszak, Oakland	1	0	0	0	T. Jackson, Denver	0	0	1	0
Bass, Washington	0	0	1	1	C. James, New England	1	0	0	0
Bell, Denver	1	0	0	0	Jaworski, Philadelphia	1	0	0	0
Bird, Oakland	1	0	0	0	Jensen, Miami	0	0	1	0
L. Blackwood, Miami	1	1	0	0	Johnson, Dallas	2	2	0	0
Bleier, Pittsburgh	1	0	0	0	Jones, Dallas	0	0	1	0
Bradshaw, Pittsburgh	3	0	0	0	Jones, Oakland	0	0	1	0
Branch, Oak.-L.A. Raiders	1	0	0	0	Kapp, Minnesota	1	0	0	0
B. Brown, Minnesota	1	0	0	0	Kellum, Pittsburgh	0	0	1	0
D. Brown, Pittsburgh	1	0	0	0	Krause, Minnesota	0	0	1	0
Brown, Washington	1	0	0	0	Kyle, Dallas	0	0	1	0
Butz, Washington	0	0	1	0	Lawrence, San Francisco	1	0	0	0
Caldwell, Washington	0	1	0	0	Marino, Miami	1	1	0	0
Capp, Green Bay	0	0	1	0	Marshall, Chicago	0	0	1	0
Carter, Denver	0	0	1	0	Martin, L.A. Raiders	0	0	1	0
Clayborn, New England	0	0	1	0	Matte, Baltimore	1	0	0	0
Cole, Dallas	0	0	1	0	McClanahan, Minnesota	1	0	0	0
Collinsworth, Cincinnati	1	0	0	0	McClinton, Kansas City	1	1	0	0
Csonka, Miami	1	0	0	0	McColl, San Francisco	0	0	1	0
Dolbin, Denver	1	0	0	0	McGrew, New England	0	0	1	0
Dorsett, Dallas	1	0	0	0	McIntyre, San Francisco	1	0	0	0
Duncan, Baltimore	0	0	1	0	McLemore, San Francisco	1	0	0	0
DuPree, Dallas	1	0	0	0	Morgan, New England	1	0	0	0
Eason, New England	1	0	0	0	Morrall, Baltimore	1	1	0	0
Elway, Denver	1	1	0	0	Odoms, Denver	1	0	0	0
Fernandez, Miami	0	0	1	0	Payton, Chicago	1	0	0	0
Fitzgerald, Dallas	0	2	0	0	D. Pearson, Dallas	1	0	0	0
Flowers, Dallas	0	0	1	0	P. Pearson, Dallas	1	1	0	0
Foreman, Minnesota	1	0	0	0	Poltl, Minnesota	0	0	1	0
Gardin, Baltimore	1	0	0	0	Porter, Baltimore	0	0	1	0
Gentry, Chicago	1	1	0	0	Prudhomme, Kansas City	0	0	1	0
Grabowski, Green Bay	1	0	0	0	Pugh, Dallas	0	0	1	0
Greene, Pittsburgh	0	0	1	0	Rafferty, Dallas	0	1	0	0
Griese, Miami	1	0	0	0	D. Ramsey, New England	1	0	0	0
A. Griffin, Cincinnati	1	0	0	0	Reed, Minnesota	1	0	0	0
Hall, Oakland	0	0	1	0	Robinson, Green Bay	0	0	1	0
Hampton, Chicago	0	0	1	0	Robinson, Kansas City	0	0	1	0
Hannah, L.A. Raiders	0	1	0	0	Sanders, Washington	1	0	0	0
Harper, San Francisco	0	1	0	0	Sauer, N.Y. Jets	1	0	0	0
Harris, Dallas	0	0	1	0	Schultz, Denver	1	0	0	0
Harris, Pittsburgh	3	2	0	0	Scott, Miami	2	1	1	0
Heflin, Miami	0	0	1	0	Simmons, Cincinnati	0	0	1	0
Hegman, Dallas	0	0	1	1	Singletary, Chicago	0	0	2	0
Henderson, Minnesota	1	0	0	0	Skoronski, Green Bay	0	1	0	0
C. Hill, Dallas	1	0	0	0	Staubach, Dallas	5	2	0	0
T. Hill, Dallas	1	1	0	0	Suhey, Chicago	1	0	0	0

FUMBLES—Cont.

	No.	Own Rec.	Opp. Rec.	Tds.		No.	Own Rec.	Opp. Rec.	Tds.
Tarkenton, Minnesota	2	2	0	0	Weese, Denver	1	0	0	0
Theismann, Washington	1	0	0	0	Wells, Oakland	1	0	0	0
D. Thomas, Dallas	1	0	0	0	West, Minnesota	1	0	0	0
Thomas, Pittsburgh	0	1	0	0	R. White, Dallas	1	0	0	0
Thomas, San Francisco	0	0	1	0	G. Williams, Washington	0	0	1	0
Unitas, Baltimore	1	0	0	0	Williamson, Oakland	0	1	0	0
Vellone, Minnesota	0	1	0	0	Winston, Pittsburgh	0	0	1	0
Walden, Pittsburgh	2	2	0	0	Woodley, Miami	1	0	0	0
A. Washington, Washington	0	0	1	0	Wright, San Francisco	1	0	0	0
Watts, L.A. Raiders	1	0	0	0	Yepremian, Miami	1	0	0	0

POSTSEASON GAME COMPOSITE STANDINGS

	W.	L.	Pct.	Pts.	Opp.		W.	L.	Pct.	Pts.	Opp.
Green Bay Packers	13	5	.722	416	259	Seattle Seahawks	3	3	.500	115	118
Pittsburgh Steelers	15	8	.652	533	447	Minnesota Vikings	12	13	.480	468	478
Los Angeles Raiders‡‡	19	12	.613	761	535	Denver Broncos§	6	7	.462	252	327
Detroit Lions	6	4	.600	221	208	New England Patriots§	4	6	.400	195	258
Miami Dolphins	14	10	.583	535	468	New York Giants	10	16	.385	430	485
Philadelphia Eagles	7	5	.583	219	173	Los Angeles Rams†	11	18	.379	441	619
Washington Redskins‡	16	12	.571	569	523	Buffalo Bills	3	5	.375	138	171
Dallas Cowboys	20	16	.556	805	640	Cleveland Browns	9	16	.360	489	569
Kansas City Chiefs*	5	4	.556	159	182	San Diego Chargers††	4	8	.333	230	279
San Francisco 49ers	9	8	.529	358	373	Cincinnati Bengals	2	5	.286	137	180
Chicago Bears	11	10	.524	474	396	Atlanta Falcons	1	3	.250	85	100
Houston Oilers	7	7	.500	201	321	Tampa Bay Buccaneers	1	3	.250	41	94
Indianapolis Colts§§	8	8	.500	285	300	Phoenix Cardinals**	1	4	.200	81	134
New York Jets	5	5	.500	206	183	New Orleans Saints	0	1	.000	10	44

*One game played when franchise was in Dallas (Texans). (Won 20-17)
†One game played when franchise was in Cleveland. (Won 15-14)
‡One game played when franchise was in Boston. (Lost 21-6)
§Two games played when franchise was in Boston. (Won 26-8, lost 51-10)
**Two games played when franchise was in Chicago. (Won 28-21, lost 7-0); Three games played when franchise was in St. Louis. (Lost 35-23, lost 30-14, lost 41-16)
††One game played when franchise was in Los Angeles. (Lost 24-16)
‡‡24 games played when franchise was in Oakland. (Record 15-9)
§§15 games played when franchise was in Baltimore. (Record of 8-7)

SUPER BOWL
RESULTS

Game	Date	Winner	Loser	Site	Attendance
XXII	1-31-88	Washington (NFC) 42	Denver (AFC) 10	San Diego	73,302
XXI	1-25-87	New York (NFC) 39	Denver (AFC) 20	Pasadena	101,063
XX	1-26-86	Chicago (NFC) 46	New England (AFC) 10	New Orleans	73,818
XIX	1-20-85	San Francisco (NFC) 38	Miami (AFC) 16	Palo Alto	84,059
XVIII	1-22-84	Los Ang. Raiders (AFC) 38	Washington (NFC) 9	Tampa	72,920
XVII	1-30-83	Washington (NFC) 27	Miami (AFC) 17	Pasadena	103,667
XVI	1-24-82	San Francisco (NFC) 26	Cincinnati (AFC) 21	Pontiac	81,270
XV	1-25-81	Oakland (AFC) 27	Philadelphia (NFC) 10	New Orleans	75,500
XIV	1-20-80	Pittsburgh (AFC) 31	Los Angeles (NFC) 19	Pasadena	103,985
XIII	1-21-79	Pittsburgh (AFC) 35	Dallas (NFC) 31	Miami	79,484
XII	1-15-78	Dallas (NFC) 27	Denver (AFC) 10	New Orleans	75,583
XI	1- 9-77	Oakland (AFC) 32	Minnesota (NFC) 14	Pasadena	103,438
X	1-18-76	Pittsburgh (AFC) 21	Dallas (NFC) 17	Miami	80,187
IX	1-12-75	Pittsburgh (AFC) 16	Minnesota (NFC) 6	New Orleans	80,997
VIII	1-13-74	Miami (AFC) 24	Minnesota (NFC) 7	Houston	71,882
VII	1-14-73	Miami (AFC) 14	Washington (NFC) 7	Los Angeles	90,182
VI	1-16-72	Dallas (NFC) 24	Miami (AFC) 3	New Orleans	81,023
V	1-17-71	Baltimore (AFC) 16	Dallas (NFC) 13	Miami	79,204
IV	1-11-70	Kansas City (AFL) 23	Minnesota (NFL) 7	New Orleans	80,562
III	1-12-69	New York (AFL) 16	Baltimore (NFL) 7	Miami	75,389
II	1-14-68	Green Bay (NFL) 33	Oakland (AFL) 14	Miami	75,546
I	1-15-67	Green Bay (NFL) 35	Kansas City (AFL) 10	Los Angeles	61,946

SUPER BOWL COMPOSITE STANDINGS

	W.	L.	Pct.	Pts.	Opp.		W.	L.	Pct.	Pts.	Opp.
Pittsburgh Steelers	4	0	1.000	103	73	Washington Redskins	2	2	.500	85	79
Green Bay Packers	2	0	1.000	68	24	Dallas Cowboys	2	3	.400	112	85
San Francisco 49ers	2	0	1.000	64	37	Miami Dolphins	2	3	.400	74	103
Chicago Bears	1	0	1.000	46	10	Cincinnati Bengals	0	1	.000	21	26
New York Giants	1	0	1.000	39	20	Los Angeles Rams	0	1	.000	19	31
New York Jets	1	0	1.000	16	7	New England Patriots	0	1	.000	10	46
L.A. Raiders*	3	1	.750	111	66	Philadelphia Eagles	0	1	.000	10	27
Baltimore Colts	1	1	.500	23	29	Denver Broncos	0	3	.000	40	108
Kansas City Chiefs	1	1	.500	33	42	Minnesota Vikings	0	4	.000	34	95

*Three games played when franchise was in Oakland.
(Lost 33-14, won 32-14, won 27-10).

NFC CHAMPIONSHIP GAME
RESULTS

Sea.	Date	Winner (Share)	Loser (Share)	Score	Site	Attendance
1987	Jan. 17	Washington ($18,000)	Minnesota ($18,000)	17-10	Washington	55,212
1986	Jan. 11	New York ($18,000)	Washington ($18,000)	17-0	New York	76,633
1985	Jan. 12	Chicago ($18,000)	Los Angeles ($18,000)	24-0	Chicago	63,522
1984	Jan. 6	San Francisco ($18,000)	Chicago ($18,000)	23-0	San Francisco	61,040
1983	Jan. 8	Washington ($18,000)	San Francisco ($18,000)	24-21	Washington	55,363
1982	Jan. 22	Washington ($18,000)	Dallas ($18,000)	31-17	Washington	55,045
1981	Jan. 10	San Francisco ($9,000)	Dallas ($9,000)	28-27	San Francisco	60,525
1980	Jan. 11	Philadelphia ($9,000)	Dallas ($9,000)	20-7	Philadelphia	70,696
1979	Jan. 6	Los Angeles ($9,000)	Tampa Bay ($9,000)	9-0	Tampa Bay	72,033
1978	Jan. 7	Dallas ($9,000)	Los Angeles ($9,000)	28-0	Los Angeles	71,086
1977	Jan. 1	Dallas ($9,000)	Minnesota ($9,000)	23-6	Dallas	64,293
1976	Dec. 26	Minnesota ($8,500)	Los Angeles ($5,500)	24-13	Minnesota	48,379
1975	Jan. 4	Dallas ($8,500)	Los Angeles ($5,500)	37-7	Los Angeles	88,919
1974	Dec. 29	Minnesota ($8,500)	Los Angeles ($5,500)	14-10	Minnesota	48,444
1973	Dec. 30	Minnesota ($8,500)	Dallas ($5,500)	27-10	Dallas	64,422
1972	Dec. 31	Washington ($8,500)	Dallas ($5,500)	26-3	Washington	53,129
1971	Jan. 2	Dallas ($8,500)	San Francisco ($5,500)	14-3	Dallas	63,409
1970	Jan. 3	Dallas ($8,500)	San Francisco ($5,500)	17-10	San Francisco	59,364
1969	Jan. 4	Minnesota ($7,930)	Cleveland ($5,118)	27-7	Minnesota	46,503
1968	Dec. 29	Baltimore ($9,306)	Cleveland ($5,963)	34-0	Cleveland	78,410
1967	Dec. 31	Green Bay ($7,950)	Dallas ($5,299)	21-17	Green Bay	50,861
1966	Jan. 1	Green Bay ($9,813)	Dallas ($6,527)	34-27	Dallas	74,152
1965	Jan. 2	Green Bay ($7,819)	Cleveland ($5,288)	23-12	Green Bay	50,777
1964	Dec. 27	Cleveland ($8,052)	Baltimore ($5,571)	27-0	Cleveland	79,544
1963	Dec. 29	Chicago ($5,899)	New York ($4,218)	14-10	Chicago	45,801
1962	Dec. 30	Green Bay ($5,888)	New York ($4,166)	16-7	New York	64,892
1961	Dec. 31	Green Bay ($5,195)	New York ($3,339)	37-0	Green Bay	39,029
1960	Dec. 26	Philadelphia ($5,116)	Green Bay ($3,105)	17-13	Philadelphia	67,325
1959	Dec. 27	Baltimore ($4,674)	New York ($3,083)	31-16	Baltimore	57,545
1958	Dec. 28	Baltimore ($4,718)	New York ($3,111)	23-17*	New York	64,185
1957	Dec. 29	Detroit ($4,295)	Cleveland ($2,750)	59-14	Detroit	55,263
1956	Dec. 30	New York ($3,779)	Chi. Bears ($2,485)	47-7	New York	56,836
1955	Dec. 26	Cleveland ($3,508)	Los Angeles ($2,316)	38-14	Los Angeles	85,693
1954	Dec. 26	Cleveland ($2,478)	Detroit ($1,585)	56-10	Cleveland	43,827
1953	Dec. 27	Detroit ($2,424)	Cleveland ($1,654)	17-16	Detroit	54,577
1952	Dec. 28	Detroit ($2,274)	Cleveland ($1,712)	17-7	Cleveland	50,934
1951	Dec. 23	Los Angeles ($2,108)	Cleveland ($1,483)	24-17	Los Angeles	57,522
1950	Dec. 24	Cleveland ($1,113)	Los Angeles ($686)	30-28	Cleveland	29,751
1949	Dec. 18	Philadelphia ($1,094)	Los Angeles ($739)	14-0	Los Angeles	27,980
1948	Dec. 19	Philadelphia ($1,540)	Chi. Cardinals ($874)	7-0	Philadelphia	36,309
1947	Dec. 28	Chi. Cardinals ($1,132)	Philadelphia ($754)	28-21	Chicago	30,759
1946	Dec. 15	Chi. Bears ($1,975)	New York ($1,295)	24-14	New York	58,346
1945	Dec. 16	Cleveland ($1,469)	Washington ($902)	15-14	Cleveland	32,178
1944	Dec. 17	Green Bay ($1,449)	New York ($814)	14-7	New York	46,016
1943	Dec. 26	Chi. Bears ($1,146)	Washington ($765)	41-21	Chicago	34,320
1942	Dec. 13	Washington ($965)	Chi. Bears ($637)	14-6	Washington	36,006
1941	Dec. 21	Chi. Bears ($430)	New York ($288)	37-9	Chicago	13,341
1940	Dec. 8	Chi. Bears ($873)	Washington ($606)	73-0	Washington	36,034
1939	Dec. 10	Green Bay ($703.97)	New York ($455.57)	27-0	Milwaukee	32,279
1938	Dec. 11	New York ($504.45)	Green Bay ($368.81)	23-17	New York	48,120
1937	Dec. 12	Washington ($225.90)	Chi. Bears ($127.78)	28-21	Chicago	15,870
1936	Dec. 13	Green Bay ($250)	Boston ($180)	21-6	New York	29,545
1935	Dec. 15	Detroit ($313.35)	New York ($200.20)	26-7	Detroit	15,000
1934	Dec. 9	New York ($621)	Chi. Bears ($414.02)	30-13	New York	35,059
1933	Dec. 17	Chi. Bears ($210.34)	New York ($140.22)	23-21	Chicago	26,000

*Sudden death overtime.

NFC CHAMPIONSHIP GAME COMPOSITE STANDINGS

	W.	L.	Pct.	Pts.	Opp.		W.	L.	Pct.	Pts.	Opp.
Green Bay Packers	8	2	.800	223	116	Phoenix Cardinals*	1	1	.500	28	28
Detroit Lions	4	1	.800	129	100	Dallas Cowboys	5	7	.417	227	213
Philadelphia Eagles	4	1	.800	79	48	San Francisco 49ers	2	3	.400	85	82
Baltimore Colts	3	1	.750	88	60	Cleveland Browns	4	7	.364	224	253
Minnesota Vikings	4	2	.667	108	80	Los Angeles Rams‡	3	8	.273	120	240
Chicago Bears	7	5	.583	283	217	New York Giants	4	11	.267	225	309
Washington Redskins†	6	5	.545	181	245	Tampa Bay Buccaneers	0	1	.000	0	9

*Both games played when franchise was in Chicago. (Won 28-21, lost 7-0)
†One game played when franchise was in Boston. (Lost 21-6)
‡One game played when franchise was in Cleveland. (Won 15-14)

AFC CHAMPIONSHIP GAME
RESULTS

Sea.	Date	Winner (Share)	Loser (Share)	Score	Site	Attendance
1987	Jan. 17	Denver ($18,000)	Cleveland ($18,000)	38-33	Denver	75,993
1986	Jan. 11	Denver ($18,000)	Cleveland ($18,000)	23-20*	Cleveland	79,915
1985	Jan. 12	New England ($18,000)	Miami ($18,000)	31-14	Miami	74,978
1984	Jan. 6	Miami ($18,000)	Pittsburgh ($18,000)	45-28	Miami	76,029
1983	Jan. 8	L.A. Raiders ($18,000)	Seattle ($18,000)	30-14	Los Angeles	88,734
1982	Jan. 23	Miami ($18,000)	N.Y. Jets ($18,000)	14-0	Miami	67,396
1981	Jan. 10	Cincinnati ($9,000)	San Diego ($9,000)	27-7	Cincinnati	46,302
1980	Jan. 11	Oakland ($9,000)	San Diego ($9,000)	34-27	San Diego	52,428
1979	Jan. 6	Pittsburgh ($9,000)	Houston ($9,000)	27-13	Pittsburgh	50,475
1978	Jan. 7	Pittsburgh ($9,000)	Houston ($9,000)	34-5	Pittsburgh	50,725
1977	Jan. 1	Denver ($9,000)	Oakland ($9,000)	20-17	Denver	75,044
1976	Dec. 26	Oakland ($8,500)	Pittsburgh ($5,500)	24-7	Oakland	53,821
1975	Jan. 4	Pittsburgh ($8,500)	Oakland ($5,500)	16-10	Pittsburgh	50,609
1974	Dec. 29	Pittsburgh ($8,500)	Oakland ($5,500)	24-13	Oakland	53,800
1973	Dec. 30	Miami ($8,500)	Oakland ($5,500)	27-10	Miami	79,325
1972	Dec. 31	Miami ($8,500)	Pittsburgh ($5,500)	21-17	Pittsburgh	50,845
1971	Jan. 2	Miami ($8,500)	Baltimore ($5,500)	21-0	Miami	76,622
1970	Jan. 3	Baltimore ($8,500)	Oakland ($5,500)	27-17	Baltimore	54,799
1969	Jan. 4	Kansas City ($7,755)	Oakland ($6,252)	17-7	Oakland	53,564
1968	Dec. 29	N.Y. Jets ($7,007)	Oakland ($5,349)	27-23	New York	62,627
1967	Dec. 31	Oakland ($6,321)	Houston ($4,996)	40-7	Oakland	53,330
1966	Jan. 1	Kansas City ($5,309)	Buffalo ($3,799)	31-7	Buffalo	42,080
1965	Dec. 26	Buffalo ($5,189)	San Diego ($3,447)	23-0	San Diego	30,361
1964	Dec. 26	Buffalo ($2,668)	San Diego ($1,738)	20-7	Buffalo	40,242
1963	Jan. 5	San Diego ($2,498)	Boston ($1,596)	51-10	San Diego	30,127
1962	Dec. 23	Dallas ($2,206)	Houston ($1,471)	20-17*	Houston	37,981
1961	Dec. 24	Houston ($1,792)	San Diego ($1,111)	10-3	San Diego	29,556
1960	Jan. 1	Houston ($1,025)	Los Angeles ($718)	24-16	Houston	32,183

*Sudden death overtime

AFC CHAMPIONSHIP GAME COMPOSITE STANDINGS

	W.	L.	Pct.	Pts.	Opp.
Denver Broncos	3	0	1.000	81	70
Kansas City Chiefs‡	3	0	1.000	68	31
Cincinnati Bengals	1	0	1.000	27	7
Miami Dolphins	5	1	.833	142	86
Buffalo Bills	2	1	.667	50	38
Pittsburgh Steelers	4	3	.571	153	131
Baltimore Colts	1	1	.500	27	38
New Eng. Patriots†	1	1	.500	41	65
New York Jets	1	1	.500	27	37
Los Angeles Raiders§	4	7	.364	225	213
Houston Oilers	2	4	.333	76	140
San Diego Chargers*	1	6	.143	121	148
Seattle Seahawks	0	1	.000	14	30
Cleveland Browns	0	2	.000	53	61

*One game played when franchise was in Los Angeles. (Lost 24-16)
†Game played when franchise was in Boston. (Lost 51-10)
‡One game played when franchise was in Dallas (Texans). (Won 20-17)
§10 games played when franchise was in Oakland. (Record 3-7)

Pro Football Championship Games

This section includes championship games of the National Football League from 1933 to 1969; American Football League, 1960 to 1969; National Football Conference and American Football Conference, 1970 to the present.

Many of the names that will appear in the early games have a Hall of Fame touch, such as the Chicago Bears' Bronko Nagurski (right) and Sammy Baugh, the quarterback and head cheerleader (below) of the Washington Redskins.

The Bears' Bill Hewitt (no helmet) laterals to Billy Karr on the winning touch-down play in the 1933 NFL title game.

1933

Chicago Bears 23
New York Giants 21

It was a time and place when passes were called "forwards," when long laterals, several of them on a single play, gave professional football the look of a rugby contest.

And it was a day of forwards and laterals, December 17, 1933, when the Chicago Bears defeated the New York Giants, 23-21, in the National Football League's first championship game—a match of division winners. Before 1933, the NFL was not split into divisions and the champion was decided in regular-season play.

An estimated crowd of 26,000 in Chicago's Wrigley Field watched players who were to become legends . . . Bronko Nagurski . . . Red Grange . . . Mel Hein . . . Ken Strong . . .

Gene Ronzani . . . Harry Newman. All of them were on the field for this game, yet the most striking factor at the time was the proliferation of the forward pass. Or, as the Associated Press noted:

"The struggle was a revelation to college coaches who advocate no changes in the rules. It was strictly an offensive battle and the professional rule of allowing passes to be thrown from any point behind the line of scrimmage was responsible for most of the thrills."

Good heavens, Newman actually threw 17 forward passes for the Giants and completed a dozen of them for 201 yards.

The Giants had won the league's Eastern Division title in 1933 with an 11-3 record, and the 244 points they scored represented 74 more than the next-highest total, Green Bay's 170.

Chicago, the 10-2-1 champion of the Western Division, fared reasonably well offensively, scoring 133 points, but was recognized mostly as a defensive team, allowing just 82 points in 13 games.

And so they met, offense vs. defense, and the confrontation began to set in motion radical changes in the complexion of the league they represented and the game they espoused.

The Bears' winning touchdown was scored by end Billy Karr, who nabbed a lateral with less than one minute to play and took it 19 yards for the decisive score.

The Giants had just taken a 16-14 lead when Newman, passing on every down, finally hit Strong with an eight-yard "forward" to forge a 21-16 margin.

But the Bears battled back. Keith Molesworth, in his third season for Owner-Coach George Halas, threw to Carl Brumbaugh for 31 yards to the Giants' 32. That set up the winning play, and a strange one it was.

Nagurski, who had gained 65 yards in 14 rushing attempts, took a handoff and launched a pass 13 yards downfield to end Bill Hewitt.

Hewitt hauled in the pass and quickly lateraled the ball to Karr, who grabbed it open in the flat, got a clearing block from Ronzani (on Strong) and raced over the goal line. Karr's touchdown and the extra-point kick by Carl Brumbaugh gave Chicago a 23-21 edge and the championship.

Chicago back Jack Manders kicked three field goals in a game of six lead changes. Karr was the only player to score two touchdowns, the first an eight-yard reception on a pass from Nagurski.

For winning, each member of the Bears earned shares of the gate worth $210.34; the losing Giants realized $140.22 each.

NFL 1933 CHAMPIONSHIP GAME

Wrigley Field, Chicago, December 17, 1933

SCORE BY PERIODS

New York Giants	0	7	7	7 — 21
Chicago Bears	3	3	10	7 — 23

SCORING

Chicago—Field goal Manders 16
Chicago—Field goal Manders 40
New York—Badgro 29 pass from Newman (Strong kick)
Chicago—Field goal Manders 15
New York—Krause 1 run (Strong kick)
Chicago—Karr 8 pass from Nagurski (Manders kick)
New York—Strong 8 pass from Newman (Strong kick)
Chicago—Karr 19 lateral from Hewitt after 13-yard pass from Nagurski to Hewitt (Brumbaugh kick)

TEAM STATISTICS

	New York	Chicago
First downs	13	13
Rushing yards	80	165
Passing yards	201	160
Return yards, punts	59	58
Passes	13-19-1	7-16-1
Punts	14-31.4	10-42.0
Penalties-Yards	3-15	7-35

Attendance—26,000 (estimated).

1934

New York Giants 30
Chicago Bears 13

This championship match has been remembered as "The Sneakers Game," and credit must go to men named Abe Cohen and Gus Mauch as well as to the Giants' players for New York's 30-13 victory over the Chicago Bears.

The game on December 9, 1934, was played in frigid weather, a razor-edged wind cutting and slicing through the Polo Grounds, the field as hard and as frozen as it had ever been in the throes of a New York winter.

Prior to the game, Ray Flaherty, an All-Pro end, was standing on the field with Giants Coach Steve Owen. He kicked at the frozen turf and didn't even scratch it. "Steve," he said to the coach, "this may not matter, but we played on a field like this once in college, and we found we got better traction with basketball shoes, not cleats."

The remark slipped idly past the coach, as did the first half slip past the outmanned Giants. This was an undefeated, untied (in 13 games) Chicago squad, a team that had outscored its opponents, 286-86, a team that had twice whipped the Giants. The Bears held a 10-3 halftime advantage, built on a touchdown by Bronko Nagurski and a field goal and conversion point by Jack Manders.

During intermission, Owen mentioned Flaherty's comment about basketball shoes (right, sneakers) to Mauch, the team trainer. Mauch, in turn, called a friend at Manhattan College, received the information that a supply of sneakers was, indeed, available, and thus dispatched clubhouse attendant Cohen by subway.

The intermission ended and the Giants trudged back onto the field. Manders added a second field goal and, as the final period began, it was 13-3.

But here came Cohen, arms laden with sneakers of all sizes, protruding from his overcoat pockets, from several paper sacks. Frantically, the Giants dived into the pile on the sidelines, searching for matched pairs of the same size.

And then, presto chango!

There were only 10 minutes remaining in the game, but now the Giants were gliding gracefully over the ice, dancing and pirouetting past the ice-bound Bears.

Quarterback Eddie Danowski faded back and connected with receiver Ike Frankian for a 28-yard touchdown. Now the Bears' lead was 13-10.

On the next series, halfback Ken Strong, no longer slipping and sliding, flitted 42 yards around end, kicked the extra point and the Giants took the lead, 17-13.

Again the defense held and now the Giants had the ball once more. Keeping it on the ground, alternating running plays with Strong and Danowski, they reached the Bears' 11-yard line. Strong took it on a reverse, scored and built the lead to 23-13, the snap for the conversion having been fumbled by John Molenda.

The Giants were to score once more. Molenda intercepted a pass, lateraled the ball to Dale Burnett and before he was tackled the Giants were at Chicago's 21. Four consecutive carries by Danowski, the final one a nine-yard TD run, produced the final score, 30-13.

Amazing! The Giants had scored 27 points in 10 minutes. The crowd whooped and celebrated New York's first NFL championship.

NFL 1934 CHAMPIONSHIP GAME

Polo Grounds, New York, December 9, 1934

SCORE BY PERIODS

Chicago Bears	0	10	3	0 – 13
New York Giants	3	0	0	27 – 30

SCORING

New York—Field goal Strong 38
Chicago—Nagurski 1 run (Manders kick)
Chicago—Field goal Manders 17
Chicago—Field goal Manders 22
New York—Frankian 28 pass from Danowski (Strong kick)
New York—Strong 42 run (Strong kick)
New York—Strong 11 run (kick failed)
New York—Danowski 9 run (Molenda kick)

TEAM STATISTICS

	Chicago	New York
First downs......................	10	12
Rushing yards	93	170
Passing yards....................	76	166
Return yards, punts...........	46	12
Passes	6-13-3	7-13-2
Punts..............................	9-40.1	8-34.2
Fumbles-Lost	4-3	3-1
Penalties-Yards.................	0-0	4-30

Attendance—35,059.

1935

Detroit Lions   26
New York Giants 7

For the third year in a row, the New York Giants won the Eastern Division title and appeared in another NFL championship game, but this time their accustomed rivals, the Bears, failed to make it.

Instead of Chicago, it was a tyro, Detroit, earning not only a place in the final game of the year, but the home-field advantage as well.

Hall of Famer Bronko Nagurski scored Chicago's first TD in a 1934 loss to the New York Giants.

And, almost as if predestined, the Lions won their first-ever league title, just as, scant months earlier, Detroit's baseball Tigers had won their maiden World Series.

It was a game played in extreme and crippling weather conditions. A bitter mixture of snow, sleet and rain, whipped to a frenzy by slashing winds, tormented the estimated 15,000 spectators in the University of Detroit Stadium December 15, 1935.

All that week, Detroit Coach George (Potsy) Clark had determined that to win, the Lions would have to stop the feared air game of the bigger, burlier Giants. New York had an outstanding passer in Eddie Danowski and two remarkable receivers in Dale Burnett and rookie Todd Goodwin.

But the Giants' running game this year was ordinary. Hence Potsy's message to his men: "Keep your hands in his (Danowski's) face, make him keep the damned ball on the ground and we'll beat 'em."

Few others believed, but the Lions did, and a quick start proved to be all Detroit really needed. The Lions took the opening kickoff and marched downfield from their 39, choosing to use the pass themselves before the ball became too wet and the field too slippery. It worked. Glenn Presnell threw a 25-yarder to Frank Christensen, then Ace Gutowsky took a handoff, pulled up short and connected on another long pass, this one a 24-yarder to Ed Klewicki.

Now, with the game only minutes old, the Lions were on the Giants' 8-yard line. Two plays later, Gutowsky slipped through the line for five yards and the touchdown, and Presnell added the PAT.

A scoring drive by the Giants was snuffed when Christensen intercepted a Danowski pass and returned it 30 yards to the New York 46. Two plays netted six yards, then Dutch Clark took a handoff, started to his left, suddenly reversed his field and, getting three clearing blocks, scampered the 40 yards for another touchdown. The point kick was blocked, but Detroit held a 13-0 lead.

At the end of the half, the Giants were on the Lions' 4-yard line. It was first down. Four plays later, they were still on the 4, and that defensive stand spelled the end for New York.

A third-quarter Giants touchdown—a 42-yard pass from Danowski to Ken Strong—was all New York could manage, and Detroit added two more touchdowns in the final quarter to forge the 26-7 score.

The small turnout (this was before revenue-sharing and guaranteed shares) resulted in the minuscule checks of $313.35 to the winning Lions and $200.20 to the losing Giants.

NFL 1935 CHAMPIONSHIP GAME

University of Detroit Stadium, Detroit,
December 15, 1935

SCORE BY PERIODS

New York Giants	0	0	7	0 —	7
Detroit Lions	13	0	0	13 —	26

SCORING

Detroit—Gutowsky 5 run (Presnell kick)
Detroit—Clark 40 run (kick failed)
New York—Strong 42 pass from Danowski (Strong kick)
Detroit—Caddel 4 run (kick failed)
Detroit—Parker 4 run (Molenda kick)

TEAM STATISTICS

	New York	Detroit
First downs	9	16
Rushing yards	106	235
Passing yards	88	68
Passes	4-13-2	2-5-0
Punts	5-43.0	3-39.0
Fumbles-Lost	3-0	4-2
Penalties-Yards	2-15	3-25

Attendance—15,000 (estimated).

1936

Green Bay Packers   21
Boston Redskins   6

For the first and only time in the history of the NFL, this was a championship game in which the owner of the team with the home-field advantage, George Preston Marshall of the Boston Redskins, gladly surrendered that edge and moved the game to a neutral site, New York City's Polo Grounds.

The Redskins had been rejected by the Boston fans and, after five years of trying to make it in New England, Marshall threw in the towel—angrily.

"They don't deserve to see this championship game," he said. "They don't deserve the team, either. We will never play another game in Boston."

The next season, 1937, marked the first year of the Redskins in Washington, where they remain as one of the NFL's most popular franchises. But in 1936, only 4,813 showed up in Boston to watch the Redskins whip Pittsburgh, 30-0, in the last home game of the season.

Marshall, as the owner of the host club, shifted the championship game to New York and 29,545 fans turned out to watch the Redskins play the Green Bay Packers December 13, 1936. They saw the Packers defeat the Redskins, 21-6, in a game that contained one half of excitement and one half of rout.

Green Bay had been favored, and rightly so. Led by the Hall of Fame passing combination of quarterback Arnie Herber and receiver Don Hutson, the Packers had rolled to a 10-1-1 record. Boston had been far less impressive, finishing at 7-5, and even then only one game ahead of the .500 Pittsburgh Steelers.

Added to that inherent mediocrity was an injury suffered early in the game by Boston's star running back, Cliff Battles. As it turned out, the Redskins would gain only 130 yards in passing and rushing offense, only 39 of those yards on the ground.

Green Bay led by a single point, 7-6, at halftime. Herber connected with Hutson for a 50-yard TD only three minutes after the opening kickoff, but Boston, putting together a 73-yard thrust, countered when Pug Rentner sliced over from the Packers' 2-yard line. When Riley Smith missed the extra point, it took on the guise of a critical and costly miss.

But no sooner had the second half started than it became merely academic. Herber threw a 52-yard pass to the "old man" of the Green Bay backfield, Johnny Blood, which

1937

Washington Redskins 28
Chicago Bears 21

The 'Old man' of the backfield by 1936 was Johnny Blood, who caught a 52-yard pass that set up Green Bay's second TD in a win over Boston.

led to a TD on a pass from Herber to end Milt Gantenbein from the 5-yard line. That made it 14-6, and a final Green Bay touchdown, on a run by Bobby Monnett, really didn't matter.

NFL 1936 CHAMPIONSHIP GAME

Polo Grounds, New York, December 13, 1936

SCORE BY PERIODS

Green Bay Packers...	7	0	7	7 – 21
Boston Redskins.......	0	6	0	0 – 6

SCORING

Green Bay—Hutson 50 pass from Herber (E. Smith kick)

Boston—Rentner 2 run (kick failed)

Green Bay—Gantenbein 5 pass from Herber (E. Smith kick)

Green Bay—Monnett 3 run (E. Smith kick)

TEAM STATISTICS

	Green Bay	Boston
First downs.......................	7	6
Rushes yards.....................	67	39
Passing yards....................	153	91
Return yards, kicks	66	86
Passes	9-23-3	7-23-1
Punts................................	7-40.0	11-26.0
Fumbles-Lost	1-1	4-3
Penalties-Yards.................	3-15	3-25
Attendance—29,545.		

Sammy Baugh was to quarterback for 16 NFL seasons, and he was to appear in five championship games. But this day, December 12, 1937, marked the end of his first season, the participation in his first title game and the beginning of a legend that has stamped him as perhaps the finest quarterback of all time.

He was a rookie and, in a way, all the Washington Redskins were, too. This was their first year in Washington after moving from a red-ink situation in Boston.

And now, having played to an 8-3 record and having eliminated the New York Giants from the Eastern Division chase the week before, they were in a bitter-cold Wrigley Field in Chicago to play for the NFL championship against the haughty Bears.

The year before, as Boston Redskins, they had lost to Green Bay, 21-6, in the title game.

But there was a major change to the '37 Redskins. His name was Sam Adrian Baugh, the lanky rookie from TCU, the first of the truly gifted passers.

What Slingin' Sam did that day has been etched in glory, for it was the first time that a passer singlehandedly dominated this rock-ribbed game of pro football. He was an offensive factor that defenses were unable to fathom.

Sammy threw 35 passes against the Bears and completed 17 for 335 yards, three of them for touchdowns.

Baugh drew first blood, completing a 53-yard drive with a perfectly executed weak-side trap reverse to Cliff Battles, who sliced through the Bears' defense with a seven-yard TD.

"I was doing whatever the defense let me do," Baugh said. "The defense is always the key; it's always giving up something."

But as the game continued, the bigger Bears began to wear down the Redskins, who used finesse rather than force. As the final quarter began, Chicago held a 21-14 lead, built on a 10-yard Jack Manders run, a 37-yard pass to Manders from Bernie Masterson, and another Masterson pass, good for three yards, to rookie Ed Manske.

Yet shortly after the quarter started, Baugh almost arrogantly tied the score. From his 22, he faded back, fended off a charging George Wilson with a straight-arm, and threw to Wayne Millner at midfield. Millner gathered it in and outran Manders for the tying touchdown, a perfect 78-yard play.

Washington's Slingin' Sammy Baugh cuts loose a pass over Bears defenders during a 28-21 victory in 1937 at Wrigley Field in Chicago.

Now came the game's most dramatic moment. With time slipping away, the Redskins came up to a fourth-and-three at the Bears' 45. Punter Don Irwin lined up to kick, but ran a slant over right tackle and barely made the necessary yardage.

It was a piece of cake after that. Short ground gains put the ball on the 35, from where Baugh threw to Ed Justice for the winning points.

"I think," said the Bears' legendary Bronko Nagurski after the game, "that Sammy Baugh is going to change football with his arm."

NFL 1937 CHAMPIONSHIP GAME

Wrigley Field, Chicago, December 12, 1937

SCORE BY PERIODS

Washington Redskins	7	0	7	14 — 28
Chicago Bears	14	0	7	0 — 21

SCORING

Washington—Battles 7 run (R. Smith kick)
Chicago—Manders 10 run (Manders kick)
Chicago—Manders 37 pass from Masterson (Manders kick)
Washington—Millner 40 pass from Baugh (R. Smith kick)
Chicago—Manske 3 pass from Masterson (Manders kick)
Washington—Millner 78 pass from Baugh (R. Smith kick)
Washington—Justice 35 pass from Baugh (R. Smith kick)

TEAM STATISTICS

	Washington	Chicago
First downs	15	11
Rushing yards	76	140
Passing yards	388	203
Passes	21-41-3	8-25-3
Punts	6-30.0	6-47.0
Fumbles-Lost	3-3	3-2
Penalties-Yards	1-5	1-15

Attendance—15,870.

1938

New York Giants 23
Green Bay Packers 17

On the afternoon of December 11, 1938, the New York Giants resembled a hospital ward. Among the injured were All-Pro center Mel Hein, All-Pro guard John Dell Isola, running back Lee Shaffer, All-Pro end Jim Lee Howell and All-Pro halfback Ward Cuff.

But they all insisted on playing, even though most of them (Hein and Cuff were to spend the aftermath in a hospital) only aggravated existing injuries.

This was a "bad blood" game and they all wanted to be part of it. A fierce rivalry had emerged between these two teams and it was intensified by a 15-3 victory earned by the Giants during the regular season, one of only three defeats the Packers would endure in their 8-3 championship record in the Western Division.

So the injured and the lame limped out onto the field. New York Coach Steve Owen, aware of the fierce Green Bay defense, nevertheless devised a bit of seemingly odd strategy. "They were so good nobody tested them," he said. "I wanted to test them right away."

Hank Soar, later to be an American League umpire, was Owen's choice. He was a big, beefy man, 235 pounds, and he carried the bulk of the burden, slamming into the line, cutting back away from the sliding Packer pursuit, emerging with 63 yards in 20 carries.

Howell, later the Giants' head coach, and Jim Poole each blocked punts in the first half, and the offense cashed in these chances for a field goal and a touchdown. The extra-point try failed. Eddie Danowski's 21-yard pass to Hap Barnard accounted for another Giants touchdown and at halftime New York led, 16-14.

Early in the third quarter, after the New York defense had stymied a Green Bay drive that had reached the Giants' 5, Tiny Engebretsen kicked a 15-yard field goal, finally giving the favored Packers a 17-16 lead.

Astonishingly, those would be the Packers' final points as the game developed into a nasty defensive struggle, swinging fists and flying elbows punctuating the erupting feud.

Indeed, the go-ahead field goal seemed to arouse the Giants to heights of fury yet untapped as they drove relentlessly for 62 yards to the winning points.

The clincher was a pass from Danowski to Soar, a 23-yard play. Soar and Poole

waited for the high floater at the Packers 6, as did two Green Bay defenders. But Soar leaped and caught it, and with one of the Packers clutching his leg, he dragged himself over the goal line as a Polo Grounds crowd of 48,120 roared in celebration.

A full quarter remained, and this final period was a back-to-the-wall showcase for the proud Giants defensive unit, as four Green Bay drives were turned back, three times by deflecting end zone passes, once by causing a fumble.

With five seconds remaining, Packers quarterback Arnie Herber tried once more and spun a pass into the Giants' end zone, but Cuff knocked it away from the intended receiver, rookie Carl Mulleneaux, as the final gun sounded.

NFL 1938 CHAMPIONSHIP GAME

Polo Grounds, New York, December 11, 1938

SCORE BY PERIODS

Green Bay Packers...	0	14	3	0	– 17
New York Giants	9	7	7	0	– 23

SCORING

New York—Field goal Cuff 13
New York—Leemans 6 run (kick failed)
Green Bay—Mulleneaux 40 pass from Herber (Engebretsen kick)
New York—Barnard 21 pass from Danowski (Cuff kick)
Gren Bay—Hinkle 1 run (Engebretsen kick)
Green Bay—Field goal Engebretsen 15
New York—Soar 23 pass from Danowski (Cuff kick)

TEAM STATISTICS

	Green Bay	New York
First downs.......................	11	10
Rushing yards	148	105
Passing yards....................	213	96
Return yards, punts...........	9	42
Passes	8-19-1	8-15-1
Punts	7-30.0	7-40.4
Fumbles-Lost	3-2	1-0
Penalties-Yards.................	2-20	2-10

Attendance—48,120.

1939

Green Bay Packers 27
New York Giants 0

Green Bay Coach Curly Lambeau had to call off a team scrimmage the day before the December 11, 1939, championship game against the New York Giants. "We ran only about five plays," he said, "and I was scared to death. I was afraid a full 45-minute drill would have me without any players."

So intense were the Packers, so primed for their revenge, so single-minded, that the

Giants really never had a chance. Green Bay had been whipped into a frenzy after the previous year's 23-17 title game defeat administered by the Giants, and even the 32,279 crowd in State Fair Park at Milwaukee spent the day taunting the Eastern visitors.

That it was only 7-0 at halftime was a tribute to the Giants, but they were outmanned and outclassed, and the second half became a lesson in violence and fury.

With quarterback Cecil Isbell and the incomparable Don Hutson leading the charge, the Packers took control.

At the start of the third quarter, Tiny Engebretsen kicked a 23-yard field goal for a 10-0 lead. Moments later, the Packers having moved to the Giants 31, Isbell swept to his right, drew Giants defenders to him, and wheeled and fired a pass to halfback Joe Laws, who ran untouched down the middle of the field to make it 17-0.

The wind whistling, the crowd hooting, the Packers bent on mayhem, the New Yorkers had difficulty just playing it out. In the final quarter, even the Green Bay substitutes whirled and danced their way to 10 more points, a 42-yard field goal by Ernie Smith followed by a one-yard plunge by Eddie Jankowski.

The Giants had allowed just 85 points in romping to a 9-1-1 record for the Eastern Division championship. But here they were, surrendering almost a third of the season total.

New York had a bad day all around. Head Coach Steve Owen missed the game to attend the funeral of his mother. Waiting on the bus after the game, the Giants had to dive for cover as bottles rained down on the windows, shattering several.

Even the State Fair Park press box was a place of alarm, perched as it was high atop the stands, suspended by "little wire ropes," according to famed sportswriter Stanley Woodward, who added that "it shook and rattled all the game, terrifying the visiting press, and it tipped agonizingly whenever anyone stirred."

Woodward took stock of the onesided nature of the game, the antiquated stadium, the chaos caused by bogus tickets and insistent scalpers, the frightening press box and the folding-chair seating around the perimeter of the field and offered an opinion of doom for the National Football League:

"The league can't stand many more events of this kind and expect to be taken seriously by the public. The league revealed itself to be definitely small-time. For a day, at least, professional football slipped back into its unsavory past and did itself incalculable harm. A large share of the public was disgusted beyond words."

Don Hutson's glory years with the Packers started in 1935 and carried him into the Hall of Fame.

NFL 1939 CHAMPIONSHIP GAME

State Fair Grounds, Milwaukee,
December 10, 1939

SCORE BY PERIODS

New York Giants......	0	0	0	0 – 0
Green Bay Packers...	7	0	10	10 – 27

SCORING

Green Bay—Gantenbein 7 pass from Herber (Engebretsen kick)

Green Bay—Field goal Engebretsen 23

Green Bay—Laws 31 pass from Isbell (Engebretsen kick)

Green Bay—Field goal Smith 42

Green Bay—Jankowski 1 run (Smith kick)

TEAM STATISTICS

	New York	Green Bay
First downs......................	7	10
Rushing yards...................	56	131
Passing yards....................	93	90
Return yards, kicks...........	79	25
Passes	9-26-6	7-10-3
Punts...............................	6-31.0	6-31.0
Fumbles-Lost	1-0	2-0
Penalties-Yards................	4-20	3-45

Attendance—32,279.

The faces of Owner-Coach George Halas and quarterback Sid Luckman (right) reflect the total dominance of the Chicago Bears in their 1940 championship victory over the Washington Redskins. The 73-0 victory was sealed when the happy Bears gave Halas a post-game ride.

1940

Chicago Bears 73
Washington Redskins 0

The score was 7-0 with just 55 seconds elapsed, after Chicago's Bill Osmanski had taken a handoff from quarterback Sid Luckman, received a perfect block from George Wilson (who wiped out two Washington Redskins) and flitted down the sideline for 68 yards.

The infuriated Redskins countered immediately and in a few short plays reached the Bears 26-yard line.

Sammy Baugh dropped back, spied receiver Charlie Malone all alone in the end zone and spiraled a perfect pass.

Malone dropped it.

Later, Baugh was asked if the game would have been different had Malone caught the ball.

"Yeah," he said. "It would have been 73-7."

But it wasn't. It was 73-0, the most onesided victory in the history of the NFL, easily the most onesided championship game and a humiliating embarrassment for the Redskins at their home field, Griffith Stadium.

But perhaps the most amazing fact of all is that just a scant three weeks earlier, in a regularly-scheduled league game, Washington had endured a tight defensive struggle to beat the Bears, 7-3.

And that was the breeding ground for the Bears' fury on this Sunday afternoon, December 8, 1940.

"The Bears are crybabies," said George Preston Marshall, who owned the Redskins. "When the going gets tough, the Bears quit."

And another mistake was committed the day before the game. The Bears had arrived by train earlier in the day and were scheduled to hold a late-afternoon Saturday practice session. The Redskins, whose own practice had been held at noon, hurried to dress to be ready to see the Bears go through their drills.

Andy Farkas, an All-Pro Redskins running back, vividly recalled the sight he and his teammates witnessed.

"They came out screaming like a pack of wild men," he remembered. "They took off and ran the length of the field, then they circled the goal posts and ran all the way back. They were still screaming. I've never seen anything like it."

It was a ploy by Bears Owner-Coach George Halas, who turned to his assistant, Hunk Anderson, and said, "My, the boys are enthusiastic today. Get 'em back inside. It would be a shame to waste all this on a practice."

So the Bears didn't work out that day. They did, indeed, save it for the championship game.

First, it was 7-0 and after Malone dropped the possible Washington TD pass, it was 14-0 and then 21-0 in the first quarter. It was 28-0 at halftime. When it was 54-0 after three quarters, Halas sent in the scrubs, but the score continued to escalate. Revenge was the prize here, and Halas later admitted that "if we could've scored 100 points, I would've done it."

Want a statistic? The Bears gained 382 yards rushing. The Redskins gained 22.

The Bears, so-called "Monsters of the Midway," had held that practice session after all, with the Redskins their unwilling dupes.

NFL 1940 CHAMPIONSHIP GAME

Griffith Stadium, Washington, Dec. 8, 1940

SCORE BY PERIODS

Chicago Bears	21	7	26	19 —	73
Washington Redskins	0	0	0	0 —	0

SCORING

Chicago—Osmanski 68 run (Manders kick)
Chicago—Luckman 1 run (Snyder kick)
Chicago—Maniaci 42 run (Martinovich kick)
Chicago—Kavanaugh 30 pass from Luckman (Snyder kick)
Chicago—Pool 15 interception return (Plasman kick)
Chicago—Nolting 23 run (kick failed)
Chicago—McAfee 34 interception return (Stydahar kick)
Chicago—Turner 21 interception return (kick blocked)
Chicago—Clark 44 run (kick failed)
Chicago—Famiglietti 2 run (Maniaci pass from Sherman)
Chicago—Clark 1 run (pass failed)

TEAM STATISTICS

	Chicago	Washington
First downs	17	17
Rushing yards	382	22
Passing yards	120	223
Passes	7-10-0	20-51-8
Punts	3-46.0	3-41.3
Fumbles-Lost	2-1	4-1
Penalties-Yards	3-25	8-70

Attendance—36,034.

1941

Chicago Bears 37
New York Giants 9

Washington was anxious to gain revenge for the historic decimation by the Chicago Bears a year earlier, but first the Redskins had to beat the New York Giants in the next-to-last game of the season. They failed. New York won it, 20-13, and thus earned the somewhat dubious honor of going against the Monsters of the Midway.

The championship game was more of a contest than was generally expected and, in fact, the score at halftime showed the Bears holding only a 9-6 advantage.

This was a tired Chicago squad, one that had to endure the NFL's first divisional playoff a week earlier. The Bears routed Green Bay, 33-14, after each team had finished with a 10-1 record.

Now, in chilly Wrigley Field December 21, 1941, the effect of fatigue was weighing heavily on the Bears. Only three field goals by Bob Snyder prevented the Giants from earning the halftime lead. "You people are supposed to be champions," said Bears Coach George Halas during the break, "but you're playing like bums."

Apparently, such a reminder was enough for the Bears, who proceeded to pound out a 37-9 victory.

After Ward Cuff was successful on a field-goal try for the Giants minutes after the third period began, tying the score at 9-9, Chicago started acting like Chicago again and the Giants, who had fired all their ammunition, were little more than spectators for the rest of the game.

This was a Bears team of incredible rushing ability, with Norm Standlee, George McAfee and Hugh Gallerneau taking turns with the ball. In the first half, an eight-man defensive front had clogged all the holes, filled all gaps, but in the second half the Bears simply ran wide—and wild.

NFL 1941 CHAMPIONSHIP GAME

Wrigley Field, Chicago, December 21, 1941

SCORE BY PERIODS

New York Giants	6	0	3	0 –	9
Chicago Bears	3	6	14	14 –	37

SCORING

Chicago—Field goal Snyder 14
New York—Franck 31 pass from Leemans (kick blocked)
Chicago—Field goal Snyder 39
Chicago—Field goal Snyder 37
New York—Field goal Cuff 16
Chicago—Standlee 2 run (Snyder kick)
Chicago—Standlee 7 run (Maniaci kick)
Chicago—McAfee 5 run (Artoe kick)
Chicago—Kavanaugh 42 fumble return (McLean kick)

TEAM STATISTICS

	New York	Chicago
First downs	8	20
Rushing yards	84	192
Passing yards	73	182
Passes	3-15-3	11-19-0
Punts	5-38.6	2-53.5
Fumbles-Lost	2-2	3-1
Penalties-Yards	3-31	9-80

Attendance—13,341.

Standlee, a 230-pound rookie from Stanford, pounded over from the 2-yard line to give the Bears a 16-9 lead, then charged over again in the third quarter, this time on a seven-yard run, to make it 23-9.

In the fourth quarter, McAfee scored from the Giants 5 to make it 30-9 and finally, late in the game, New York's Andy Marefos fumbled a lateral from Hank Soar. Bears end Ken Kavanaugh picked up the ball on a bounce and sped 42 yards for the final TD.

Almost arrogantly, Halas dispatched bench-rider Scooter McLean to the field and, spurning the final placement kick, ordered the kid to dropkick the extra point.

It was good.

Strangely, and sadly, this Chicago team of the early 1940s never had the chance to prove how good it really was, even though there are still many who insist it was the finest team of all time.

This game took place exactly two weeks after the Japanese attack on Pearl Harbor, and the onrushing World War II soon broke up the Bears. One of the first to report for duty was Lt. Commander George Halas of the United States Navy.

1942

Washington Redskins 14
Chicago Bears 6

Few teams in NFL history have approached the dynastic levels reached by the Chicago Bears of the 1940s.

In 1940, the Monsters of the Midway were 8-3. In 1941, they were 10-1. And in 1942, with World War II raging, with several of their stars gone off to the service, they recorded an 11-0 season, winning by an average score of 34-7.

Naturally, here they were in yet another championship game, seeking to win their third consecutive title. And for the second time in three years, their opponents were the Washington Redskins, who had played to a 10-1 record with the superb Sammy Baugh at quarterback.

Chicago was a heavy favorite, justifiably. After all, just two years before, the Bears had inflicted the league's most embarrassing defeat on these same Redskins, the 73-0 title game.

But before 36,006 in Griffith Stadium December 13, 1942, the Redskins reached some level of vengeance with a 14-6 victory. It came after Washington almost handed the game to the Bears, courtesy of the Redskins' star running back, Andy Farkas.

The game was scoreless early in the second quarter. The Redskins had the ball and were marching through a frenzied Chicago defense. Now the snap rifled back and in the single-wing formation the Redskins used, some confusion arose. Was Farkas or Dick Todd to take the ball? Apparently, each thought it was his turn, and they collided. Farkas was charged with the fumble, a ball that was scooped up by Chicago's All-Pro tackle (and placekicker), Lee Artoe. He returned it 52 yards for a touchdown but missed the extra point and Chicago held a 6-0 lead.

But the startling touchdown only served to arouse the Redskins, who had longed for this rematch.

Baugh cranked up his arm and two minutes later passed 39 yards to end Wilbur Moore for the tying points. Bob Masterson's conversion gave Washington a 7-6 halftime cushion.

The second half belonged to Farkas, as he earned atonement for the fumble. A punt by Bears quarterback Sid Luckman to the Redskins 14 was returned by Farkas to Chicago's 44, and from there Baugh mounted a ground attack featuring Farkas.

He carried to the 32. Baugh carried to the 24. Now it was Farkas again, to the 20, to the 15, to the 8, to the 5, to the 1. Finally, it was Farkas for the touchdown, and even though he fumbled, the officials ruled that he had crossed the plane of the goal line in possession of the ball.

Masterson's conversion made it 14-6. Late in the game the inspired Redskins blunted a 78-yard Chicago drive that had reached Washington's 2-yard line.

It was over. The 73-0 slaughter was not forgotten, nor would it ever be, but it was, for many of the Redskins, softened by the championship and the largest winners' shares to date—$965 each.

NFL 1942 CHAMPIONSHIP GAME

Griffith Stadium, Washington, Dec. 13, 1942

SCORE BY PERIODS

Chicago Bears	0	6	0	0 –	6
Washington Redskins	0	7	7	0 –	14

SCORING

Chicago—Artoe 52 fumble return (kick failed)
Washington—Moore 39 pass from Baugh (Masterson kick)
Washington—Farkas 1 run (Masterson kick)

TEAM STATISTICS

	Chicago	Washington
First downs	10	10
Rushing yards	102	104
Passing yards	119	66
Return yards, kicks	82	57
Passes	8-18-3	5-13-2
Punts	6-42.0	1-52.5
Fumbles-Lost	1-1	1-1
Penalties-Yards	7-47	4-26

Attendance—36,006.

The 1943 title game belonged to strong-armed quarterback Sid Luckman, who threw five TD passes.

1943

Chicago Bears   41
Washington Redskins 21

The Chicago Bears and Washington Redskins still were the cream of the NFL's two divisions. But their superiority had become more tenuous. Chicago was only slightly better than Green Bay (8-1-1 to 7-2-1) and Washington had to engage in an Eastern Division playoff with New York (winning, 28-0) before arriving at another title confrontation.

The championship game in Chicago December 26, 1943, belonged to Bears quarterback Sid Luckman, who threw for five TD passes, two more than anyone had managed in any previous title game. He completed 15 of 27 passes for 276 yards, leading the Bears to a 41-21 victory.

Luckman's first TD pass, a 31-yarder to Harry Clark, tied the score, since the Redskins had drawn first blood with a one-yard smash by Andy Farkas.

A second Bears touchdown in the second quarter put the home team in front for good. Luckman returned George Cafego's punt to the Bears 31, then assumed his role as quarterback and strung together the go-ahead drive.

The key play was a 24-yard scramble by Luckman to the Redskins' 21. After Bronko Nagurski (who had ended a five-year retirement to bolster a war-torn roster) cracked for three, Luckman picked up 15 to the Redskins 3 on a sneak. Nagurski slammed across for the 14-7 lead, which is how the first half ended.

The second half? It was Chicago, for now the Redskins were razored into submission by Luckman's pinpoint passing. He threw a 36-yarder to Dante Magnani for a 21-7 advantage, then passed in the flat to Magnani, who ran 66 yards for a TD and a 27-7 lead (the kick was missed).

Washington interrupted the point parade with a drive of its own, achieving success on a 17-yard pass to Farkas from Sammy Baugh, who had spent the first half on the bench following a first-play concussion. But that only made it 27-14, and Chicago dominated the rest of the game.

Bears captain Bob Snyder summed up the team's attitude in the locker room.

"The championship is back where it should have stayed," he said. "What right have those Redskins to our championship, even for one season?"

NFL 1943 CHAMPIONSHIP GAME

Wrigley Field, Chicago, December 26, 1943

SCORE BY PERIODS

Chicago Bears	0	14	13	14 – 41
Washington Redskins	0	7	7	7 – 21

SCORING

Washington—Farkas 1 run (Masterson kick)
Chicago—Clark 31 pass from Luckman (Snyder kick)
Chicago—Nagurski 3 run (Snyder kick)
Chicago—Magnani 36 pass from Luckman (Snyder kick)
Chicago—Magnani 66 pass from Luckman (kick failed)
Washington—Farkas 17 pass from Baugh (Masterson kick)
Chicago—Benton 29 pass from Luckman (Snyder kick)
Chicago—Clark 16 pass from Luckman (Snyder kick)
Washington—Aguirre 25 pass from Baugh (Aguirre kick)

TEAM STATISTICS

	Washington	Chicago
First downs	11	14
Rushing yards	50	169
Passing yards	199	276
Return yards, kicks	144	81
Passes	11-24-4	15-27-0
Punts	5-40.8	5-32.0
Fumbles-Lost	1-0	0-0
Penalties-Yards	3-35	9-81

Attendance—34,320.

1944

Green Bay Packers 14
New York Giants 7

The Chicago Bears and Washington Redskins were dethroned as division champions, and the Green Bay Packers (8-2) and the New York Giants (8-1-1) met in the Polo Grounds in New York December 17, 1944, before 46,016 fans, eager not only for the spectacle but for some emotional release from the seemingly endless world war.

War was extracting service-eligible men from every walk of life and pro football proved to be no different. The replacements were over-aged or otherwise excusable athletes.

Arnie Herber, the former Packers quarterback, came out of retirement and played for the Giants. Giants halfback Ken Strong, at the age of 40, put off retirement. Don Hutson was still a Packer, and the Hall of Fame receiver played the largest role in this 14-7 championship game victory for Green Bay.

The Packers scored first, and then again, and held a 14-0 lead at halftime. The first Green Bay touchdown was scored by Ted Fritsch, the fullback, on a one-yard smash on fourth down, after the Giants had gamely held from that point three times.

This was a New York defense that had allowed only 75 points in 10 regular-season games, and the Packers realized the quality of the unit.

So, the next time they got close, they called on Hutson, first to make a circus catch of a 24-yard pass from quarterback Irv Comp, then to use his acknowledged value as a decoy.

Having reached the Giants' 26 late in the second quarter, Green Bay Coach Curley Lambeau called for the "Hutson Switch" play. The brilliant receiver, lining up on the left side of the line, ran a crossing pattern just on the other side of the line of scrimmage. He reached the right sideline and began waving his arms, drawing most of the New York defenders with him.

Comp, meanwhile, faked the pass to Hutson, then spun to his left and threw to Fritsch, who was so clear that when he caught the ball on the Giants 5, he coolly walked over, almost sauntering, for the TD and a 14-0 lead.

The Giants began to stiffen and their offense began to work more efficiently in the second half, but twice third-quarter drives were snuffed, once by an interception by Joe Laws, once after three Herber incompletions forced a punt.

Into the final quarter they went, and finally the Giants struck. A drive begun late in the third period, kept alive by a 41-yard pass from Herber to Frank Liebel, was cashed in on the first play of the fourth quarter when Ward Cuff plowed over from the 1.

But another drive in the final minutes evaporated when Paul Duhart intercepted a desperate Herber pass at the Green Bay 20.

A footnote: Giants lineman Al Blozis, playing in the game on a pass from the U.S. Army, returned overseas days after the game. He rejoined his infantry unit and a month later was killed by German fire in the Battle of the Bulge.

NFL 1944 CHAMPIONSHIP GAME

Polo Grounds, New York, December 17, 1944

SCORE BY PERIODS

Green Bay Packers...	0	14	0	0 – 14
New York Giants......	0	0	0	7 – 7

SCORING

Green Bay—Fritsch 1 run (Hutson kick)
Green Bay—Fritsch 26 pass from Comp (Hutson kick)
New York—Cuff 1 run (Strong kick)

TEAM STATISTICS

	Green Bay	New York
First downs	13	9
Rushing yards	184	101
Passing yards	74	114
Return yards, kicks	97	110
Passes	3-11-3	8-22-4
Punts	10-38.5	10-41.0
Fumbles-Lost	2-0	2-0
Penalties-Yards	4-48	11-90

Attendance—46,016.

1945

Cleveland Rams 15
Washington Redskins 14

The rule has been stricken from the books for decades now, but it was very much in force December 16, 1945, and on a frozen field in Cleveland Stadium, in sub-zero temperatures, it decided the NFL championship game.

The rule: "When a forward pass from behind the goal line strikes the goal posts or the crossbar . . . it is a safety if the pass strikes the ground in the end zone."

A safety. Two points.

In the first quarter, with the game scoreless, the Washington Redskins were backed up near their own end zone. Sammy Baugh, ever a gambler, sent end Wayne Millner far downfield, and he scampered past a startled—and beaten—Cleveland secondary.

Fading back into the end zone, Baugh threw, but the frigid wind caught the ball

In 1945, a pair of long TD passes by Cleveland rookie quarterback Bob Waterfield proved to be too much for the Redskins.

and it slapped into the goal post and bounced back into the end zone.

Cleveland 2, Washington 0. And the safety ultimately enabled the Rams to defeat the Redskins, 15-14.

In the second period, the Redskins seemed to neutralize the safety when Frank Filchock, taking over for the aging Baugh, whose ribs were bruised, completed a 38-yard TD pass to Steve Bagarus. Joe Aguirre's conversion gave the Redskins a 7-2 lead.

But in the same quarter, Rams quarterback Bob Waterfield, a rookie on his way to the Hall of Fame, struck back. He ended a march on the wings of a 37-yard scoring pass to Jim Benton, kicked the extra point and put Cleveland back in front, 9-7.

Ironically, that conversion wobbled badly from the start, finally teetering over the crossbar and actually hitting it, but falling into the end zone. An inch the other way would have produced a 14-14 final score.

The irony was accentuated in the third

quarter, when Waterfield connected with Jim Gillette for 53 yards—and then missed the extra point. Now it was Cleveland in front, but by the score of 15-7, and never did that safety look better to the 32,178 fans.

Washington finished the day's scoring in that third period, with Bob Seymour catching an eight-yard TD pass from Filchock. Aguirre made the point, forging the final score, but he missed two field goal attempts in the final quarter, of 46 and 31 yards.

Cleveland, which would move to Los Angeles the following season (and thus create a void soon filled by the fabled Cleveland Browns), had earned the championship—and player shares of $1,469 each—because of a gust of wind, a few inches and a rule long since discarded.

NFL 1945 CHAMPIONSHIP GAME

Municipal Stadium, Cleveland, Dec. 16, 1945

SCORE BY PERIODS

Washington Redskins	0	7	7	0 – 14
Cleveland Rams	2	7	6	0 – 15

SCORING

Cleveland—Safety, pass by Baugh from end zone struck goal post and became incomplete in end zone for automatic safety.
Washington—Bagarus 38 pass from Filchock (Aguirre kick)
Cleveland—Benton 37 pass from Waterfield (Waterfield kick)
Cleveland—Gillette 53 pass from Waterfield (kick failed)
Washington—Seymour 8 pass from Filchock (Aguirre kick)

TEAM STATISTICS

	Washington	Cleveland
First downs	8	14
Rushing yards	35	180
Passing yards....................	179	192
Passes	9-20-2	14-27-2
Punts	7-36.0	8-38.0
Fumbles-Lost	1	1
Penalties-Yards.................	34	60

Attendance—32,178.

1946

Chicago Bears 24
New York Giants 14

Scandal!

On the afternoon of December 14, 1946, the day before the long-awaited rematch of bitter rivals, New York Giants Owner Tim Mara received a telephone call from Mayor William O'Dwyer, summoning him and the team's coach, Steve Owen, to Gracie Mansion, the mayor's official residence.

It was bleak news. A professional gambler named Alvin Paris had offered bribes of $2,500 each to Giants quarterback Frank Filchock, obtained that year from the Redskins, and fullback Merle Hapes. In addition, he had promised to put down a $1,000 bet for each of them against the Giants if they conspired to lose the championship game.

Hapes reported the offer to Arthur Wallender, the New York Commissioner of Police. He had notified O'Dwyer, who in turn informed Mara and NFL Commissioner Bert Bell.

The players were confronted. Hapes admitted receiving the offer. Filchock did not. What was Bell to do? There were no rules covering such an event, and so he made them up. Filchock, who denied speaking with Paris, could play the next day; Hapes, because he conversed with a known gambler and "undesirable," could not play.

The story hit the town like a bombshell and when the Giants filed out onto the field, Filchock was booed. But soon after the game started, there he was at quarterback, and despite a broken nose causing pain, swelling and blinding spurts of blood, he played with uncommon courage.

But his two touchdown passes—38 yards to Frank Liebel and five yards to Steve Filipowicz to tie the game, 14-14—would go to waste.

In the fourth quarter, with the game still tied, Bears quarterback Sid Luckman conferred with coach George Halas on the sideline. Chicago would employ a trick play, one that hadn't been used during the entire season.

In the Bears' playbook, it was "97, Bingo,

NFL 1946 CHAMPIONSHIP GAME

Polo Grounds, New York, December 15, 1946

SCORE BY PERIODS

Chicago Bears	14	0	0	10 – 24
New York Giants	7	0	7	0 – 14

SCORING

Chicago—Kavanaugh 21 pass from Luckman (Maznicki kick)
Chicago—Magnani 19 interception return (Maznicki kick)
New York—Liebel 38 pass from Filchock (Strong kick)
New York—Filipowicz 5 pass from Filchock (Strong kick)
Chicago—Luckman 19 run (Maznicki kick)
Chicago—Field goal Maznicki 26

TEAM STATISTICS

	Chicago	New York
First downs	10	13
Rushing yards	101	120
Passing yards....................	144	128
Return yards, punts	13	9
Passes	9-23-2	9-29-6
Punts	7-42.3	4-31.7
Fumbles-Lost	2-1	3-2
Penalties-Yards.................	9-112	6-70

Attendance—58,346.

Keep" and it called for Luckman to fake a handoff on an apparent sweep to the left. But Luckman kept the ball, hiding it against his hip, and strode casually to his right, then suddenly took off for the goal line.

It became a 19-yard TD run that broke the Giants' backs. A 26-yard field goal by Frank Maznicki merely supplied insurance points.

At the trial of Alvin Paris, months after the game, Filchock admitted he had been offered the bribe, but said he had lied to O'Dwyer, Wallender, Bell and Mara because he wanted one more chance to play on a championship team.

Bell suspended both men indefinitely. The NFL lifted Filchock's suspension in 1950, Hapes' in 1954. Only Filchock, who attempted just three passes with the Baltimore Colts in 1950, ever played in the NFL again.

It had been the NFL's first crisis over gambling; the championship game was of almost secondary significance.

1947

Chicago Cardinals 28
Philadelphia Eagles 21

New teams, new champions.

First-time champions: The Chicago Cardinals from the Western Division and the Philadelphia Eagles from the Eastern Division. Never had either won a championship since two-conference scheduling began in 1933.

And here they were, the Eagles having had to win a playoff game with Pittsburgh, since they had tied with 8-4 records; the Cardinals barely nosing out the Chicago Bears, 9-3 to 8-4.

In the final analysis, you might say that the Cardinals won in the long run, because it was four long runs, each for a touchdown, that provided the Cardinals their 28-21 victory before 30,759 in Chicago's Comiskey Park December 28, 1947.

Elmer Angsman twice galloped 70 yards. Charley Trippi scored on long-distance trips of 75 and 44 yards—the 75-yarder with a punt.

The Cardinals, who would move to St. Louis for the 1960 season, thus kept the championship in Chicago, since the Bears had won it the year before, and in so doing they nullified a magnificent performance by several of the Eagles.

Notable among them was quarterback Tommy Thompson, who completed 27 of 44 passes for 297 yards, surpassing the previous

Former Georgia star Charley Trippi's 75-yard punt return broke the backs of the Philadelphia Eagles in 1947.

NFL title game record (1937) of Sammy Baugh (for attempts and completions).

Angsman, who gained 159 yards in just 10 carries, also set a championship game mark. Many other records, including Trippi's 75-yard punt return, also were established.

With the game less than six minutes old, Trippi took a handoff, exploded through the line and was gone on his 44-yarder, giving the Cards a 7-0 lead when Pat Harder kicked the first of four extra points. Again in the second quarter, lightning struck. Angsman capitalized on a bunched-up Eagles defense to run 70 yards, breaking a final tackle by Russ Craft.

Philadelphia countered with a 53-yard pass from Thompson to end Pat McHugh, and the 14-7 score held up at halftime.

But it was once more time for the sudden thrust, and eight minutes into the third quarter it was Trippi's turn. The former University of Georgia All-America fielded Joe Muha's punt at his 25, broke into the clear, slipped at the Eagles 30 and fell at the Eagles 33 but righted himself and scored, giving Chicago a 21-7 lead.

And here came the Eagles, driving 83 yards before fullback Steve Van Buren cracked over from the 1. Once again, Chicago's margin had been cut to one touchdown, 21-14.

But Angsman's second 70-yard run in the final period put the Eagles away for good, and Craft's one-yard plunge late in the game amounted to no more than a consolation touchdown.

Van Buren, who had become only the second player in NFL history to surpass 1,000 yards (he had 1,008 in 1947 on 217 carries), was limited to 26 yards in 18 carries by the Cardinals defense.

NFL 1947 CHAMPIONSHIP GAME

Comiskey Park, Chicago, December 28, 1947

SCORE BY PERIODS

Philadelphia Eagles..	0	7	7	7	– 21
Chicago Cardinals	7	7	7	7	– 28

SCORING

Chicago—Trippi 44 run (Harder kick)
Chicago—Angsman 70 run (Harder kick)
New York—McHugh 53 pass from Thompson (Patton kick)
Chicago—Trippi 75 punt return (Harder kick)
New York—Van Buren 1 run (Patton kick)
Chicago—Angsman 70 run (Harder kick)
New York—Craft 1 run (Patton kick)

TEAM STATISTICS

	Philadelphia	Chicago
First downs	22	11
Rushing yards	60	282
Passing yards	297	54
Return yards, punts	10	150
Passes	44-60-3	3-14-3
Punts	8-34.5	8-32.0
Fumbles-Lost	2-0	2-1
Penalties-Yards	7-55	10-97

Attendance—30,759.

1948

Philadelphia Eagles 7
Chicago Cardinals 0

It snowed.

And it continued to snow.

And by game time, the field was a white blanket, the yardlines had disappeared and the fans were indistinguishable mounds of white, huddled in the wooden stands of Shibe Park. Philadelphia had awakened to a blizzard December 19, 1948, and NFL Commissioner Bert Bell had grave misgivings about even attempting to play the game between the Chicago Cardinals and Philadelphia Eagles.

He met with the players in the morning and asked each side if it wanted to postpone the affair. Neither did.

They played it. In the snow. And the Eagles won, 7-0.

Vision was almost impossible. Hands were numb, fingers frostbitten, feet icy cold.

Eagles quarterback Tommy Thompson, still smarting from the Cards' 28-21 victory a year earlier, decided that to score at all, he would have to do it quickly, while footing and the element of surprise existed.

So he called "81 Special," a long, go-for-broke pass pattern designed for fleet end Jack Ferrante. It worked. Ferrante beat them all, hauled in the pass and scored what appeared to be a 65-yard TD.

But a red flag rested on the snow, back at the line of scrimmage. The Eagles had been offside, wiping out the dramatic play.

"Who, dammit, who was it?" Ferrante screamed at the official.

"You, that's who." It was the perfect squelch.

The game degenerated into a sliding, slipping comedy. Neither team had many true scoring opportunities. Indeed, neither team could see or feel very much of anything. As it dragged on, one thing became increasingly clear: a fumble, some sort of in-close turnover, was all that stood in the way of a scoreless tie.

And the turnover came, late in the third quarter, after a punt by Joe Muha of the Eagles had gone out of bounds at the Cards 19.

On the first play from scrimmage, Chicago quarterback Ray Mallouf attempted a handoff to Elmer Angsman, but there was a mixup on the handoff and the ball squirted to the cushiony snow. Huge Philadelphia lineman Bucko Kilroy, a 6-2, 245-pounder, pounced on the football at the Chicago 17.

The break was at hand. Bosh Pritchard ran through left tackle for six yards to bring the quarter to an end. Muha picked up three on the first play of the final period, Thompson kept on a sneak over center to the five.

Now it was Steve Van Buren's turn and the 6-0, 205-pound fullback, the NFL's leading ground-gainer a second straight year, blasted out the final five yards for the touchdown. Cliff Patton added the conversion with 1:05 elapsed in the fourth quarter.

It was the game's only score and it provided the Eagles with their first-ever championship.

Eagles quarterback Tommy Thompson keyed his team's drive to three consecutive championship game appearances.

By contrast to his 1947 performance, Thompson completed only two of 12 passes for seven yards, but the rushing of Van Buren (26 carries for 98 yards), Pritchard (16 for 67) and Thompson (11 for 50) provided all the yardage the Eagles needed in the snow.

NFL 1948 CHAMPIONSHIP GAME

Shibe Field, Philadelphia, December 19, 1948

SCORE BY PERIODS

Chicago Cardinals	0	0	0	0	– 0
Philadelphia Eagles ..	0	0	0	7	– 7

SCORING

Philadelphia—Van Buren 5 run (Patton kick)

TEAM STATISTICS

	Philadelphia	Chicago
First downs	16	6
Rushing yards	225	96
Passing yards	7	35
Return yards, kicks	40	46
Passes	2-12-2	3-11-1
Punts	5-38.6	3-37.4
Fumbles-Lost	1-1	3-2
Penalties-Yards	3-17	4-33

Attendance—36,309.

1949

Philadelphia Eagles 14
Los Angeles Rams   0

If 1948 was the Snow Bowl championship, then this first-ever championship played on the West Coast in 1949 was the Drench Bowl.

It began raining early in the morning of December 18, and it continued until the game was nearly done. The field in the Los Angeles Memorial Coliseum became a quagmire, that well-known "sea of mud," and it hurt the Los Angeles Rams far more than it did the defending champion Philadelphia Eagles.

L.A. had built its 8-2-2 record with a dizzying passing attack, with Bob Waterfield (and rookie Norm Van Brocklin) throwing to such prolific receivers as the 6-2, 216-pound Tom Fears (77 catches for 1,013 yards and nine TDs), Elroy (Crazylegs) Hirsch, Dickie Hoerner and Bob Shaw.

The Rams needed a dry field for firm, sure footing.

Philadelphia, meanwhile, passed only as a diversionary tactic. The Eagles' stock in trade was the run, and behind a tough, massive front line lurked such backs as Steve Van Buren, Bosh Pritchard, Fritz Ziegler and Jim Parmer. Van Buren had gained 1,146 yards that season in 263 carries, both figures NFL records to that date.

The Eagles didn't necessarily need a dry field. They simply needed somebody to hit, and somebody to run over and around.

The Eagles, incidentally, proved that they didn't need a dry field to pass, either. Their first touchdown, the only one in the first half, was a swiftly-completed 63-yard drive in which Tommy Thompson passed for 11 to Jack Ferrante, 15 to Ferrante and finally 31 to tight end Pete Pihos for the touchdown.

Then the Eagles resorted to the ground game and defense. Van Buren was to collect 196 yards in 31 carries, both title game records.

The Rams, who had scored 360 points in 12 league games, collected very little of anything.

Time after time, possessions had to be punted away because no offensive consistency could be mounted. In fact, the Rams punted nine times. They managed just seven first downs, none by rushing. They gained only 21 yards on the ground, 98 in the air.

Finally, one of the Rams' punts was blocked, by Leo Skladany, a defensive end and a rookie, and he returned the ball two yards for the only other touchdown of the game.

A small twist of irony: unlike 1948, when it snowed in Philadelphia, Commissioner Bert Bell didn't consider having the game postponed. But Rams Owner Daniel Reeves asked for a postponement. Bell refused, on the grounds that radio commitments of financial significance had been made.

And so it was played. Van Buren and the Eagles were the most thankful; Waterfield, Fears and Reeves the most chagrined.

NFL 1949 CHAMPIONSHIP GAME

Memorial Coliseum, Los Angeles, Dec. 18, 1949

SCORE BY PERIODS

Philadelphia Eagles..	0	7	7	0 – 14
Los Angeles Rams....	0	0	0	0 – 0

SCORING

Philadelphia—Pihos 31 pass from Thompson (Patton kick)

Philadelphia—Skladany 2 blocked punt return (Patton kick)

TEAM STATISTICS

	Los Angeles	Philadelphia
First downs	7	17
Rushing yards	21	274
Passing yards	98	68
Return yards, punts	17	14
Passes	10-27-2	5-9-1
Punts	9-38.1	6-36.3
Fumbles-Lost	1-0	4-1
Penalties-Yards	4-25	6-40

Attendance—27,980.

1950

Cleveland Browns 30
Los Angeles Rams 28

In 1946, the Cleveland Rams fled the shores of Lake Erie for the untapped riches in Los Angeles.

In 1946, a new league, the All-America Football Conference, opened for business.

The AAFC lived for only four seasons, but it prospered in Cleveland, where the Browns won each of the four championships, compiled a 47-4-3 record, went undefeated (14-0) in 1948 and introduced to the world of pro football a galaxy of stars, such as Marion Motley, Otto Graham, Mac Speedie, Dante Lavelli, Dub Jones and Lou Groza, to say nothing of its owner, general manager and coach, Paul Brown.

In 1950, the NFL absorbed three AAFC teams (Cleveland, Baltimore and San Francisco), expanding to 13 franchises.

And the Browns ruled. They were American Conference co-champions (with the Giants) at 10-2, then beat New York in a playoff, 8-3, to earn the right to a championship game. It was played in Cleveland's Municipal Stadium December 24, 1950. The Browns' opponents? The Los Angeles (nee Cleveland) Rams.

And what a game it was!

On the very first play from scrimmage, Rams quarterback Bob Waterfield connected for 82 yards and a touchdown to Glenn Davis. Three minutes later, the Browns tied it on a TD pass from Graham to Jones for 32 yards.

And then they waged war, on this day before Christmas, as the crowd alternated from agony to ecstasy with each snap of the ball.

Groza, a Hall of Fame lineman and prolific placekicker, missed an extra point after the Browns' second TD, and into the final throes of this morality play, the upstarts against the establishment, that one miss loomed in importance.

Los Angeles entered the fourth quarter with a 28-20 lead. But then Graham engineered a 65-yard march, given life by an interception by Warren Lahr at the Browns 35. That drive included nine completed passes—five in a row at one point—and was culminated by a 14-yarder to Rex Bumgardner.

The TD cut the Rams' lead to 28-27. With two minutes remaining, Waterfield punted

NFL 1950 CHAMPIONSHIP GAME

Municipal Stadium, Cleveland, Dec. 24, 1950

SCORE BY PERIODS

Los Angeles Rams....	14	0	14	0 – 28
Cleveland Browns.....	7	6	7	10 – 30

SCORING

Los Angeles—Davis 82 pass from Waterfield (Waterfield kick)

Cleveland—Jones 32 pass from Graham (Groza kick)

Los Angeles—Hoerner 3 run (Waterfield kick)

Cleveland—Lavelli 35 pass from Graham (kick failed)

Cleveland—Lavelli 39 pass from Graham (Groza kick)

Los Angeles—Hoerner 1 run (Waterfield kick)

Los Angeles—Brink 6 fumble return (Waterfield kick)

Cleveland—Bumgardner 14 pass from Graham (Groza kick)

Cleveland—Field goal Groza 16

TEAM STATISTICS

	Cleveland	Los Angeles
First downs	22	22
Rushing yards	116	106
Passing yards	298	312
Return yards, punts	22	14
Passes	22-33-1	18-32-5
Punts	5-38.4	4-50.8
Fumbles-Lost	3-3	0-0
Penalties-Yards	3-25	4-48

Attendance—29,751.

to the Browns 32.

Graham ran for 19 yards to the Rams 49. Then he threw for 10 and another first down to Bumgardner on the Rams 39. Subsequent passes to Jones and Bumgardner put the ball on the Rams 11. After a one-yard sneak to place the ball in the center of the field, the Browns called on Groza, giving him a monumental chance to wipe out the earlier failure.

The snap from Hal Herring was true. The placement by Tommy James, the holder, was swift and accurate. Groza swung his right foot, describing a short arc, and the ball soared above the frantic, grasping arms of the desperate Rams.

Good! The clock showed 28 seconds remaining. The scoreboard showed Cleveland ahead, 30-28.

Retribution had come. When the group of new team owners had approached Commissioner Bert Bell in 1946, asking for entry into the NFL, he had publicly ridiculed their fledgling league.

"I told 'em to come back when they got a football," he sneered.

The AAFC found several footballs and topped it off by finding a championship—the NFL championship.

1951

Los Angeles Rams 24
Cleveland Browns 17

The dynasty didn't exactly crumble, but it certainly did absorb a few solid jolts, as the rookie-studded Los Angeles Rams, who had barely stumbled into the championship game, registered a startling 24-17 upset of the Cleveland Browns before 57,522 fans in the Los Angeles Coliseum December 23, 1951.

The Browns had overwhelmed the American Conference with an 11-1 record, while the Rams were 8-4 in the National Conference, narrowly staggering past Detroit and San Francisco, both 7-4-1.

But now, with the score tied, 17-17, the Rams took over at their 20, midway through the fourth quarter. Quarterback Norm Van Brocklin, who had replaced incumbent Bob Waterfield, called twice for running plays. Dan Towler and Tank Younger accounted for seven yards, bringing up a third-and-three.

Later, Van Brocklin was to explain his next call. "They figured sure I'd get another running play called, just to set up a first down," he said. "It was a perfect time

Norm Van Brocklin's 73-yard TD pass doomed the Browns in 1951.

to fool somebody."

So, instead of another run, Van Brocklin decided to go for broke. He had two gifted receivers in Elroy (Crazylegs) Hirsch and Tom Fears, but the 1951 season had belonged to Hirsch.

The Browns were more concerned with this 6-2, 190-pounder, who had caught 66 passes for 1,495 yards and 17 touchdowns that season, than they were with Fears.

Naturally, Van Brocklin faked a pass to Hirsch at the right sideline, then stepped back and lofted a deep spiral downfield. Fears was waiting at the 50-yard line, sandwiched by defenders Cliff Lewis and Tommy James, but he leaped, caught the ball and was gone.

It became a 73-yard touchdown play, a spectacular and back-breaking assertion of the Rams' superiority that day.

One final bid by the Browns was thwarted when rookie Norb Hecker, one of 13 yearlings on the squad, dropped halfback Dub

Jones for a loss on a fourth-down play at the Rams 44.

Perhaps most surprising was the performance of the Rams' defense, led by rookie end Andy Robustelli, from tiny Arnold (Conn.) College, and Larry Brink, the other end. They threw Otto Graham, the Browns All-Pro quarterback, for 47 yards in losses, while the defense limited All-Pro fullback Marion Motley to 23 yards in five rushing attempts.

Yet the Browns were still—or almost—the same old Browns. Twice the Rams came up with a first down on the Cleveland 1-yard line, and twice the proud Browns held them without a point.

Fears and Hirsch were the ones who really beat the Browns. Between them, they caught eight passes for 212 yards. Fears had four for 146, including the game-winner.

Cleveland would be back, but it would take a while.

NFL 1951 CHAMPIONSHIP GAME

Memorial Coliseum, Los Angeles, December 23, 1951

SCORE BY PERIODS

Cleveland Browns.....	0	10	0	7 – 17	
Los Angeles Rams	0	7	7	10 – 24	

SCORING

Los Angeles—Hoerner 1 run (Waterfield kick)
Cleveland—Field goal Groza 52
Cleveland—Jones 17 pass from Graham (Groza kick)
Los Angeles—Towler 1 run (Waterfield kick)
Los Angeles—Field goal Waterfield 17
Cleveland—Carpenter 2 run (Groza kick)
Los Angeles—Fears 73 pass from Van Brocklin (Waterfield kick)

TEAM STATISTICS

	Los Angeles	Cleveland
First downs......................	20	22
Rushing yards	81	92
Passing yards....................	253	280
Return yards, kicks	21	146
Passes	13-30-2	19-41-3
Punts..............................	5-43.4	4-37.0
Fumbles-Lost	2-1	4-1
Penalties-Yards.................	5-25	6-41

Attendance—57,522.

1952

Detroit Lions 17
Cleveland Browns 7

It was almost a rematch of the 1951 game, but the Los Angeles Rams, with a better record than the previous year, didn't make it. Their 9-3 regular-season record was no better than that of Detroit, and the Lions, in a National Conference playoff, became

champions with a 31-21 victory.

Meanwhile, the Cleveland Browns struggled to maintain their American Conference standing and did so, but just barely, finishing at 8-4 to the 7-5 of both New York and Philadelphia.

So it was Cleveland, but not Los Angeles, back in the championship game. It was played in Cleveland December 28, 1952, before 50,934 fans, but the title went to Detroit, 17-7, the first NFL flag for that franchise since 1935.

And how was it won? By defense and an official's call.

First, the defense. Detroit gave away yards, except when the Browns got close. In the third quarter, Cleveland reached the Lions 5-yard line on first down, but was held to nothing. The Lions also forced a critical fumble on a punt return.

The Browns, too, contributed to the Detroit cause at all the wrong times. A first-quarter punt by Horace Gillom sliced off the side of his foot and was good for only 22 yards, a turn of fortune which Detroit converted into a 50-yard touchdown drive, quarterback Bobby Layne keeping for the final two yards and a 7-0 lead.

It became 14-0 in the third quarter when Layne clicked on a 67-yard play to halfback Doak Walker, handing him the ball, then watching as rookie safety Bert Rechichar allowed the 5-11, 173-pounder to slip from his arms and speed downfield for the touchdown.

But after that TD, the Browns took the kickoff and moved 67 yards to narrow the gap, fullback Chick Jagade slashing over from the 7 for the points.

Then the officials denied the Browns what would have been the tying touchdown. Cleveland had moved once again deep

NFL 1952 CHAMPIONSHIP GAME

Municipal Stadium, Cleveland, Dec. 28, 1952

SCORE BY PERIODS

Detroit Lions............	0	7	7	3 – 17	
Cleveland Browns.....	0	0	7	0 – 7	

SCORING

Detroit—Layne 2 run (Harder kick)
Detroit—Walker 67 run (Harder kick)
Cleveland—Jagade 7 run (Groza kick)
Detroit—Field goal Harder 36

TEAM STATISTICS

	Detroit	Cleveland
First downs......................	10	22
Rushing yards	199	227
Passing yards....................	59	157
Return yards, punts	18	18
Passes	7-10-0	20-36-1
Punts..............................	6-40.8	3-43.3
Fumbles-Lost	0-0	1-1
Penalties-Yards.................	3-25	7-65

Attendance—50,934.

Bobby Layne
guided the Lions
to consecutive
victories over the
Browns in 1952
and '53.

into Detroit territory and from the 7, quarterback Otto Graham lofted a pass to receiver Ray Renfro at the goal line. The ball deflected off Renfro's hands into the hands of Browns tight end Pete Brewster.

Touchdown? No, said the officials, quoting the rule (since eliminated) prohibiting two eligible receivers of the same team from touching a pass without a member of the defensive team touching it in between.

No touchdown. No tie. Detroit's Pat Harder went on to kick a 36-yard field goal to seal the victory.

1953

Detroit Lions 17
Cleveland Browns 16

An uncannily agile 300-pound man, Detroit's Les Bingaman set in motion the events of the Lions' 17-16 victory in this error-filled but fan-pleasing rematch with Cleveland, played before 54,577 in Briggs Stadium December 27, 1953.

It was early in the game, with Cleveland in possession on its 13, when LaVern Torgeson, a 6-0, 215-pound linebacker, and the monstrous Bingaman combined on a vicious tackle of quarterback Otto Graham. He fumbled, Bingaman covered the ball

with his immense body, and six plays later the Lions had the game's first blood, on a one-yard dive by halfback Doak Walker.

The half ended with Detroit in front, 10-3, as each team converted a field goal in the second quarter, a 13-yarder by the Browns' Lou Groza and a 23-yarder by the Lions' Walker.

Graham, locked in the agonies of his worst day as a professional, was to complete only two of 15 passes for a paltry 20 yards. When Ken Gorgal intercepted a Bobby Layne pass early in the third quarter, giving Cleveland possession at its 49, the Browns went into a ground-dominated attack.

They moved the 51 yards in eight plays, Graham throwing only one pass. Chick Jagade finally knotted the score with a nine-yard run.

Now, tightening their defense and running the ball to compensate for Graham's mysterious slump, the Browns broke the tie with two Groza field goals in the final period, of 43 and 15 yards, and with 10:50 elapsed, it was 16-10.

But Detroit, led by quarterback Bobby Layne, mounted a final, dramatic drive. From the Lions 20, he hit end Jim Doran for 17 yards and threw to Doran again for 18. Another receiver, Cloyce Box, caught one for nine yards. Two running plays, by Bob Hoernschemeyer and Layne, put the ball on the Browns 33.

And then it happened.

Layne faded back, saw Doran breaking clear near the end zone and fed him a pass. It was good and Walker broke the 16-16 deadlock with the extra point.

With 2:08 remaining, it was Cleveland's ball.

But on the first play, Graham went for the big play, a tendency that had terrified NFL defenses for several years. He threw deep, aiming for Dante Lavelli, but Carl Karilivacz, a rookie from Syracuse University, was waiting. He leaped, intercepted the pass and brought a second consecutive championship to Detroit.

NFL 1953 CHAMPIONSHIP GAME

Briggs Stadium, Detroit, December 27, 1953

SCORE BY PERIODS

Detroit Lions............	7	3	0	7 – 17	
Cleveland Browns.....	0	3	7	6 – 16	

SCORING

Detroit—Walker 1 run (Walker kick)
Cleveland—Field goal Groza 13
Detroit—Field goal Walker 23
Cleveland—Jagade 9 run (Groza kick)
Cleveland—Field goal Groza 15
Cleveland—Field goal Groza 43
Detroit—Doran 33 pass from Layne (Walker kick)

TEAM STATISTICS

	Detroit	Cleveland
First downs........................	18	11
Rushing yards	129	182
Passing yards.....................	164	191
Return yards, kicks	46	105
Passes	12-25-2	3-16-2
Punts................................	4-49.0	5-42.0
Fumbles-Lost	3-2	2-2
Penalties-Yards.................	4-50	4-30

Attendance—54,577.

1954

Cleveland Browns 56
Detroit Lions 10

This was the game that Otto Graham called his last. He announced that he would retire, that this would be the final time he would wear a Browns uniform, and 43,827 turned out on December 25, 1954, at Municipal Stadium in Cleveland to bid him farewell. He marked the occasion by directing the Browns to an overwhelming 56-10 triumph over the Detroit Lions.

The fans did not truly expect victory, for the Lions had become a dynasty in their own right and they seemed to hold a particularly strong jinx over the Browns, having defeated them eight consecutive times, including the last two NFL title games.

So this was a third consecutive title match, one in which Detroit was heavily favored, and Graham was still smarting over his 1953 performance against the Lions when he completed only two of 14 passes.

When his first passing attempt was intercepted and it led to a Doak Walker field goal of 36 yards for a 3-0 Detroit lead, another Lions victory seemed likely.

And then . . . well, then Graham got his act together, with an assist from the sharp-eyed Paul Brown, who "invented" film study. He noticed that when the Browns ran from a tight T-formation, without the added appendage of a wide flanker, the Lions' cornerback, rookie Billy Stits, came up close to guard against a wide running play.

Presto! The Lions were dead.

Graham, sitting on the Lions 35, called for the tight T with mercurial Ray Renfro running a deep fly pattern. Renfro passed Stits at the line of scrimmage, and the rookie suddenly realized there was nothing he could do about it.

That became a 35-yard touchdown play and a 7-3 lead, and before it was over, Graham had led the Browns to the most one-sided championship victory since the Bears' 73-0 bombing of Washington in 1940.

Otto passed for three touchdowns—the 35-yarder to Renfro, a 31-yarder to Renfro and an eight-yarder to tight end Pete Brewster —and ran for three scores himself.

In all, Graham (now 32 years old) completed nine of 12 passes for 163 yards. He added 27 yards rushing on nine tries. This

NFL 1954 CHAMPIONSHIP GAME

Municipal Stadium, Cleveland, Dec. 26, 1954

SCORE BY PERIODS

Detroit Lions............	3	7	0	0 – 10	
Cleveland Browns.....	14	21	14	7 – 56	

SCORING

Detroit—Field goal Walker 36
Cleveland—Renfro 35 pass from Graham (Groza kick)
Cleveland—Brewster 8 pass from Graham (Groza kick)
Cleveland—Graham 1 run (Groza kick)
Detroit—Bowman 5 run (Walker kick)
Cleveland—Graham 5 run (Groza kick)
Cleveland—Renfro 31 pass from Graham (Groza kick)
Cleveland—Graham 1 run (Groza kick)
Cleveland—Morrison 12 run (Groza kick)
Cleveland—Hanulak 12 run (Groza kick)

TEAM STATISTICS

	Detroit	Cleveland
First downs........................	16	17
Rushing yards	136	140
Passing yards.....................	195	163
Return yards, kicks	108	127
Passes	19-44-6	9-12-2
Punts................................	6-41.3	4-43.0
Fumbles-Lost	3-3	2-2
Penalized-Yards	5-63	4-40

Attendance—43,827.

Cleveland's Otto Graham runs one yard for the final touchdown of his illustrious career in the 1955 victory over the Rams.

might be interpreted as one of the most productive days he had ever enjoyed, for in 21 combined passes-rushes, he accounted for six touchdowns.

It was 35-10 at halftime and still Graham continued to play, wishing to purge the Detroit jinx once and for all. Two more scores in the third quarter made it 49-10 entering the final period, and rookie Chet Hanulak capped yet another Browns drive with a 12-yard scoring run.

A fearsome Cleveland defense drove Detroit quarterback Bobby Layne to distraction, intercepting six of his passes and limiting him to 18 completions in 42 passing attempts.

When Graham left the field, with only minutes remaining, the crowd gave him a standing ovation.

"That almost made me change my mind (about retiring)," he said, "but I've got to quit sometime, and I always said I'd like to go out on top."

Paul Brown changed his quarterback's mind ultimately and Otto returned for one more year.

And one more championship.

1955

Cleveland Browns 38
Los Angeles Rams 14

This was, finally, Otto Graham's last game. Coach Paul Brown had convinced him to return to the Cleveland Browns for one final season. "Why would a man who can still do what you can still do on the field want to retire?" Brown asked and, under such subtle pressure, Otto relented.

The Browns were 9-2-1 in 1955, holding off rebuilt New York and Washington teams on the strength of vintage skills. In the West, the Los Angeles Rams barely earned the division title, finishing 8-3-1 to the Chicago Bears' 8-4.

And now, in the first solid indication that pro football had entrenched itself in the nation's imagination, a startling crowd of 85,693 turned out in the Los Angeles Coliseum to witness Graham's farewell December 26, 1955.

It was a farewell party fitting for such a master. He responded with two touchdown passes, two touchdown runs and 14 completions in 25 attempts for 202 net yards as the Browns trounced the Rams, 38-14.

The Browns earned a 10-0 lead, on a 26-yard Lou Groza field goal and a 65-yard interception return by defensive back Don Paul, before the Rams were able to score. That came on a desperation heave by Norm Van Brocklin to halfback Skeet Quinlan that covered 67 yards and it shaved the Cleveland margin to 10-7.

But not for long. Graham came right back with a 50-yard pass to Dante Lavelli, making it 17-7 at halftime.

The third quarter was a study in ruthless efficiency by the Browns, who totally dominated play and scored twice—both touchdowns coming on runs by Graham of 15 yards and one yard. The Browns' final TD came on a 35-yard pass from Graham to Ray Renfro, just 11 seconds into the fourth quarter.

The Browns defense once more responded with a blue-chip performance, intercepting seven Los Angeles passes, recovering a fumble, and even overcoming a whopping 74 yards in penalties with several back-to-the-wall heroics. The seven interceptions fell one shy of a championship game record that belonging to Chicago, with eight in 1940.

And the huge throng in Los Angeles, understandably morose at the one-sided defeat of the Rams, still stood and cascaded a deafening tribute to Graham when he left

NFL 1955 CHAMPIONSHIP GAME

Los Angeles Coliseum, Los Angeles, December 26, 1955

SCORE BY PERIODS

Cleveland Browns.....	3	14	14	7 – 38
Los Angeles Rams....	0	7	0	7 – 14

SCORING

Cleveland—Field goal Groza 26
Cleveland—Paul 65 interception return (Groza kick)
Los Angeles—Quinlan 67 pass from Van Brocklin (Richter kick)
Cleveland—Lavelli 50 pass from Graham (Groza kick)
Cleveland—Graham 15 run (Groza kick)
Cleveland—Graham 1 run (Groza kick)
Cleveland—Renfro 35 pass from Graham (Groza kick)
Los Angeles—Walker 4 run (Richter kick)

TEAM STATISTICS

	Cleveland	Los Angeles
First downs	17	17
Rushing yards	169	116
Passing yards	202	143
Return yards, kicks	68	224
Passes	14-25-3	11-28-7
Punts	3-42.6	4-45.0
Fumbles-Lost	0-0	1-1
Penalties-Yards	5-74	2-10

Attendance—85,693.

the field for the final time.

"No doubt about it, I'm finished," said Otto.

He was . . . and for a while, so were the Browns.

1956

New York Giants 47
Chicago Bears 7

They had both returned, the two hoary titans of the National Football League, once the only teams, or so it seemed, qualified to meet for the league's title.

They had rebuilt and retooled, refurbished and restocked, and all at once, or so it seemed, they had exploded on the league again.

The New York Giants were 8-3-1 in 1956; the Chicago Bears 9-2-1.

Both the Browns and the Rams, last year's champions, had crumbled, Cleveland falling to 5-7, Los Angeles to 4-8.

The old order had become the new.

It came up cold, bitter cold, that December 30, 1956, in Yankee Stadium. The ground was a solid sheet of ice, and once again, returning to the famous "sneaker game" of 1934, the Giants came out in basketball shoes.

They maintained their footing, while the Bears slipped and slid, and it was never—absolutely never—a contest as the Giants rolled to a 47-7 victory.

It was 20-0 before the Bears scored, the 20-0 lead built on a 17-yard run by Mel Triplett, a three-yard run by Alex Webster and field goals of 43 and 17 yards by Ben Agajanian.

When Chicago did get its touchdown, even that was a gift. Emlen Tunnell, the safety who became the Hall of Fame's first black member, fumbled a punt on his 25. It was recovered by the Bears' John Mellekas and five plays later, Rick Casares, the Bears' workhorse fullback, pounded over from the 9.

And that was that for Chicago.

As the game continued, Webster capped a New York drive with a one-yard TD dive. Rookie defensive back Henry Moore fell on a punt blocked by Ray Beck in the Bears' end zone. Kyle Rote caught a nine-yard Conerly strike, and Frank Gifford hauled in another TD pass from Conerly, this one of 14 yards.

It was a rout, pure and simple. What made it all the more difficult to understand was that only four games earlier, the Bears had gone to New York and played to a fierce

17-17 tie with the Giants.

"I think," said Giants Coach Jim Lee Howell, "that this was the closest thing to a perfect game I've ever seen."

With the victory, the Giants would usher in an on-again, off-again dynasty that would not totally fade until 1964.

NFL 1956 CHAMPIONSHIP GAME

Yankee Stadium, New York, Dec. 30, 1956

SCORE BY PERIODS

Chicago Bears	0	7	0	0 — 7
New York Giants	13	21	6	7 — 47

SCORING

New York—Triplett 17 run (Agajanian kick)
New York—Field goal Agajanian 17
New York—Field goal Agajanian 43
New York—Webster 3 run (Agajanian kick)
Chicago—Casares 9 run (Blanda kick)
New York—Webster 1 run (Agajanian kick)
New York—Moore recovered blocked punt in end zone (Agajanian kick)
New York—Rote 9 pass from Conerly (kick failed)
New York—Gifford 14 pass from Conerly (Agajanian kick)

TEAM STATISTICS

	Chicago	New York
First downs	19	16
Rushing yards	67	126
Passing yards...................	213	222
Return yards, punts	1	46
Passes	20-47-2	11-20-0
Punts..............................	8-34.0	3-37.0
Fumbles-Lost	2-1	3-2
Penalized-Yards	4-50	6-40

Attendance—56,836.

1957

Detroit Lions 59
Cleveland Browns 14

This story started on August 12, 1957, before the NFL season had even begun. Head Coach Buddy Parker of the Detroit Lions, brooding through much of training camp, finally decided his team had no chance in the upcoming campaign. "I can't handle a losing season," he said. "This team of ours is the worst I've ever seen in training. I'm leaving Detroit . . . tonight."

So George Wilson, an assistant coach, was elevated to boss.

The next highlight occurred on December 22, 1957, when the Lions and the San Francisco 49ers met to settle their Western Conference tie after each had posted an 8-4 record. The winner of the playoff would earn the right to play the Cleveland Browns the following week for the title.

In the third quarter, the 49ers held a 27-7 lead over Detroit, but 14 minutes later, the

Lions quarterback Tobin Rote fired four TD passes in a 1957 rout of the Browns.

Lions walked off the field as 31-27 winners.

That set the scene for the championship game, and "the worst team" Parker had ever seen proceeded to carve up the Browns, 59-14, December 29.

A crowd of 55,263 gathered in Briggs Stadium, almost fearful of what might be done to the home side. Bobby Layne had been lost with two games remaining in the season, and Tobin Rote, Parker's last acquisition (from Green Bay), had taken over at quarterback.

Cleveland had rebuilt in a hurry and now offered a 9-2-1 team featuring a sensational rookie running back named Jimmy Brown, who had led the NFL with 942 yards rushing.

Jim Martin kicked a 31-yard field goal to open the scoring and then Rote finished off a drive with a one-yard TD plunge. When Gene Gedman also scored on a one-yarder, Detroit's lead after one period was 17-0.

And Cleveland came busting back, getting on the board when Brown scored on a

29-yard run, cutting the lead to 17-7. The Browns were highly potent and a 10-point deficit wouldn't mean much to them.

But the Lions soon increased their advantage to 17 points. On fourth down, Martin came in to try a field goal. Rote, the holder, took the snap—then kept it, stood up, scrambled to his left and threw a 26-yard scoring pass to rookie end Steve Junker. That was followed by a 19-yard TD on an interception return by Terry Barr and at halftime it was 31-7.

The Lions salted it away with four second-half TDs. Rote threw passes of 78 yards to Jim Doran, 23 to Junker and 32 to Dave Middleton. Rookie Jerry Reichow finished off the offensive show with a 16-yard pass to Howard (Hopalong) Cassady.

NFL 1957 CHAMPIONSHIP GAME

Briggs Stadium, Detroit, December 29, 1957

SCORE BY PERIODS

Cleveland Browns.....	0	7	7	0 – 14
Detroit Lions............	17	14	14	14 – 59

SCORING

Detroit—Field goal Martin 31
Detroit—Rote 1 run (Martin kick)
Detroit—Gedman 1 run (Martin kick)
Cleveland—Brown 29 run (Groza kick)
Detroit—Junker 26 pass from Rote (Martin kick)
Detroit—Barr 19 interception return (Martin kick)
Cleveland—Carpenter 5 run (Groza kick)
Detroit—Doran 78 pass from Rote (Martin kick)
Detroit—Junker 23 pass from Rote (Martin kick)
Detroit—Middleton 32 pass from Rote (Martin kick)
Detroit—Cassady 16 pass from Reichow (Martin kick)

TEAM STATISTICS

	Cleveland	Detroit
First down	17	22
Rushing yards	218	137
Passing yards....................	95	296
Return yards, kicks	184	98
Passes	9-21-4	13-21-0
Punts	4-35.0	4-36.0
Fumbles-Lost	2-2	3-1
Penalties-Yards.................	4-60	7-52

Attendance—55,263.

1958

Baltimore Colts   23
New York Giants   17

It has been called the greatest game ever played. But was it? Certainly not in terms of classic domination or perfect execution or stifling defense.

What it really was, what grabbed the country by the nape and shook and shook, was the excitement, the drama, the visceral, nail-biting emotion of what these two teams accomplished. It was the first sud-

den-death overtime period in NFL history and when it was finally over and the Baltimore Colts had defeated the New York Giants, 23-17, pro football had become a force to be reckoned with.

The timing couldn't have been better. The game was played in New York City, the media center of the nation. Such exposure, with such fabled players for the national telecast, made it a classic.

For the Giants, the season had already been dramatic. Despite twice beating Cleveland, the Giants finished the regular season in a tie with the Browns at 9-3 and had to beat them a third time, 10-0, in a playoff for the Eastern Conference championship.

And then it was on to the title game, to the Baltimore Colts, to quarterback Johnny Unitas, to running backs Alan Ameche and Lenny Moore and to end Raymond Berry. The date was December 28, 1958, in Yankee Stadium.

Pat Summerall gave New York an early 3-0 lead with a 36-yard field goal, but the remainder of the first half had Baltimore's potent hoofprints stamped all over it.

The incomparable Unitas was about to enjoy one of his best days, completing 26 of 40 passes for 349 yards. His favorite receiver, the gritty Berry, set playoff records with 12 catches for 178 yards. After one drive had been capped by a powerful two-yard plunge by fullback Ameche, Unitas put together another march and climaxed it with a 15-yard scoring toss to Berry. And so it was 14-3 at halftime.

The Giants came back. First, their fabled defense held when the Colts had a first down on the New York 3. A series of four running plays netted minus-2 yards, and the Giants took over on their 5, as the crowd of 64,185 howled in frenzy.

Gifford ran for five, Webster for three and then old Charley Conerly, the grizzled quarterback, crossed up the Colts. He passed deep downfield to Kyle Rote, who caught the ball, ran with it and was finally tackled on the Colts 25, where he fumbled. But Alex Webster, the halfback, had trailed on the play and he picked up the ball without breaking stride, taking it down to the Colts 1.

Mel Triplett bulled over from there and it was 14-10.

The tide had turned. Another drive, from the Giants 19, spilled into the final quarter. From the New York 39, Conerly faked a toss to flanker Frank Gifford, spun and threw to tight end Bob Schnelker for 46 yards to the Colts 15. Then Conerly hit Gifford for the rest, and the Giants, with 14:07 remaining, finally had the lead, 17-14.

Now an official's critical decision put Bal-

The Colts' Alan Ameche lies on his back in the end zone after scoring Baltimore's first touchdown in the 1958 title game against the Giants.

timore back in it. The Giants had a third-and-four situation on their 40. Conerly faked a handoff to Triplett going up the middle, then gave it to Gifford, slanting to his right. He gained yardage . . . he was stopped . . . an immense pileup of bodies froze at the official's whistle.

Referee Ron Gibbs took apart the tangled bodies and placed the ball on the ground . . . inches short.

The Giants had to punt and Don Chandler got off a beauty, a wondrously high spiral back to the Colts' 14. It was 86 yards away from the Giants' end zone, with 1:56 to play.

Dead? The Colts were just starting.

Unitas, on third down, hit Moore for 11. He found Berry for 25 to midfield. He hit Berry again for 15 to the Giants 35. And Berry again, this time for 22 to the Giants 13. Three consecutive passes to Berry had netted 62 yards.

Steve Myhra came on, with seven seconds left, and his field goal knotted it.

The overtime was a Baltimore excursion. The Giants won the toss, kept the ball for three plays and punted. Baltimore took possession at the 20. It would soon be over.

Unitas got a key first down on a pass to Ameche for eight to the Baltimore 41. Now, on third and 15, he went to Berry again for 21 yards to the Giants 43.

Ameche cracked the middle on a draw for 23 more to the Giants 20. Unitas went to

Berry again for 12 yards to the Giants 8 and to tight end Jim Mutscheller for seven yards to the 1.

And finally, on third-and-one, Ameche slammed over the middle for the touchdown after 8:15 of the overtime period.

The greatest game ever played was over, at last.

NFL 1958 CHAMPIONSHIP GAME

Yankee Stadium, New York, Dec. 28, 1958

SCORE BY PERIODS

Baltimore Colts...........	0	14	0	3	6 — 23
New York Giants	3	0	7	7	0 — 17

SCORING

New York—Field goal Summerall 36
Baltimore—Ameche 2 run (Myhra kick)
Baltimore—Berry 15 pass from Unitas (Myhra kick)
New York—Triplett 1 run (Summerall kick)
New York—Gifford 15 pass from Conerly (Summerall kick)
Baltimore—Field goal Myhra 20
Baltimore—Ameche 1 run (no extra-point try attempted)

TEAM STATISTICS

	Baltimore	New York
First downs	27	10
Rushing yards	138	88
Passing yards	322	178
Return yards, kicks	69	73
Passes..	26-40-1	12-15-0
Punts..	4-50.8	6-45.6
Fumbles-Lost................................	2-2	6-4
Penalties-Yards	3-15	2-22

Attendance—64,185.

New York halfback Frank Gifford runs into the Colts' Bill Pellington (36) and
Gino Marchetti in the 1959 title game.

1959

Baltimore Colts 31
New York Giants 16

Nothing could come close to equaling their 1958 NFL title game, but the Baltimore Colts and the New York Giants tried mightily.

It came down to an awesome burst of points—24 of them, all in the fourth quarter —before the Colts were able to repeat as league champions with a 31-16 victory over the Giants before 57,545 at Baltimore December 27, 1959.

The Giants, on the strength of three Pat Summerall field goals (of 23, 37 and 22 yards) and fierce defensive stands, held a 9-7 lead entering the final period.

But perhaps the turning point occurred late in that third quarter. The Giants, marching to what appeared to be the decisive touchdown, found themselves on the Colts 28-yard line with fourth down and only inches to go.

Quarterback Charley Conerly called on the Giants' pile-driver running back, Alex Webster, but the Colts' famed defensive end, Gino Marchetti, leveled Webster at the line of scrimmage.

Momentum turned and in the fourth period quarterback Johnny Unitas scored on a four-yard run to put Baltimore in front, 14-9. Andy Nelson then picked off a Conerly pass

and returned it 17 yards to the New York 14. Unitas hit Willie Richardson with a 12-yard pass to make it 21-9.

Then, 2:10 later, cornerback Johnny Sample picked off a Conerly pass and took it back 42 yards for a third TD, making the score 28-9 and giving the game the coloration of a rout. Another Sample interception led to Steve Myhra's 25-yard field goal, which finished the Baltimore scoring.

Only 32 seconds were left when the Giants got on the scoreboard again, on a 32-yard pass from Conerly to tight end Bob Schnelker.

The Giants' defense limited the Colts' feared running game to a paltry 73 yards in 25 carries and restricted fullback Alan Ameche, the team's leading rusher all season, to 30 yards in nine carries.

But there was very little the defense could do about Unitas, who completed 18 of 29 passes for 265 yards and two TDs, one a 59-yarder to halfback Lenny Moore in the first period.

Moore, whose dangerous running was neatly nullified (he carried four times and gained eight yards), caught three passes for 127 yards.

"We didn't win it easily," said Baltimore General Manager Don Kellet, "but we won it convincingly."

NFL 1959 CHAMPIONSHIP GAME

Memorial Stadium, Baltimore, Dec. 27, 1959

SCORE BY PERIODS

New York Giants	3	3	3	7 — 16
Baltimore Colts	7	0	0	24 — 31

SCORING

Baltimore—Moore 59 pass from Unitas (Myhra kick)
New York—Field goal Summerall 23
New York—Field goal Summerall 37
New York—Field goal Summerall 22
Baltimore—Unitas 4 run (Myhra kick)
Baltimore—Richardson 12 pass from Unitas (Myhra kick)
Baltimore—Sample 42 interception return (Myhra kick)
Baltimore—Field goal Myhra 25
New York—Schnelker 32 pass from Conerly (Summerall kick)

TEAM STATISTICS

	New York	Baltimore
First downs	16	13
Rushing yards	118	73
Passing yards	205	207
Return yards, kicks	123	135
Passes	17-38-3	18-29-0
Punts	6-47.9	6-37.0
Fumbles-Lost	1-0	1-0
Penalties-Yards	3-23	4-20

Attendance—57,545.

NFL 1960

Philadelphia Eagles 17
Green Bay Packers 13

Vince Lombardi arrived after the 1958 season to direct the fortunes of the Packers, a team beset with defeats, dissension and inexperience.

"Gentlemen," said the tough-minded former New York Giants aide, "I have never been associated with a losing team, and I do not intend to start now."

In '59, he took a 1-10-1 team and turned it into a 7-5 club with potential. In '60, the potential was fulfilled.

The Packers surprised the Western Conference with an 8-4 record and a one-game edge over Detroit and San Francisco. The Packers' appearance in the championship game was their first since 1944, and the opponent was Philadelphia, the easy (10-2) winner of the Eastern Conference.

The Packers were almost complete, almost ready to become the dominant dynasty of the 1960s, and they played the stronger

Eagles on better than even terms before losing the title, 17-13, before 67,325 in Philadelphia's Franklin Field December 26, 1960.

Paul Hornung, Green Bay's all-purpose back, kicked a 20-yard field goal in the first period and a 23-yarder in the second, building a 6-0 margin for the Packers.

But the lead went up in smoke when quarterback Norm Van Brocklin, who had been traded to the Eagles by the Los Angeles Rams in 1958, countered with a 35-yard TD pass to flanker Tommy McDonald. Minutes before the half came to a close, Bobby Walston booted a 15-yard field goal and the Eagles had a 10-6 advantage.

The teams battled through a scoreless third period, and early in the final period the Packers scored what looked to be the winning touchdown.

It was a 12-play, 80-yard march, culminated by a seven-yard pass from quarterback Bart Starr to wide receiver Max McGee. Hornung's conversion gave Green Bay a 13-10 lead with 1:53 elapsed in the quarter.

Sometimes such pressure brings out the best in certain athletes, and rookie Ted Dean was one of those. He took the ensuing kickoff back 58 yards to the Packers 39.

Van Brocklin dropped back to pass, but ran instead, and while he gained nothing, the Packers were flagged for defensive holding. First down on the Green Bay 32. Now Dean ripped off six yards and fullback Billy Barnes tore up the middle for six more.

From the 20, Van Brocklin was dumped for a seven-yard loss, but he countered with a 13-yard pass to Barnes, who then ran for five yards and a first down at the 9. Dean

NFL 1960 CHAMPIONSHIP GAME

Franklin Field, Philadelphia, Dec. 26, 1960

SCORE BY PERIODS

Green Bay Packers...	3	3	0	7 – 13
Philadelphia Eagles..	0	10	0	7 – 17

SCORING

Green Bay—Field goal Hornung 20
Green Bay—Field goal Hornung 23
Philadelphia—McDonald 35 pass from Van Brocklin (Walston kick)
Philadelphia—Field goal Walston 15
Green Bay—McGee 7 pass from Starr (Hornung kick)
Philadelphia—Dean 5 run (Walston kick)

TEAM STATISTICS

	Green Bay	Philadelphia
First downs	22	13
Rushing yards	223	197
Passing yards	178	204
Return yards, kicks	67	101
Passes	21-35-0	9-20-1
Punts	5-45.0	6-39.5
Fumbles-Lost	1-1	0-0
Penalties-Yards	4-27	0-0

Attendance—67,325.

ran for four and then for the remaining five, around left end to give the Eagles their victory.

The Packers almost pulled it out in the last three minutes, driving to the Eagles 22. With seconds to go, Starr threw to fullback Jim Taylor, who was tackled on the 9. Middle linebacker Chuck Bednarik sat on Taylor as the seconds disappeared and the Eagles, barely, were champions.

Of interest in this game was Bednarik's 60-minute performance, the last time such a feat was to be accomplished. He had played center on offense as well as going all the way at linebacker.

AFL
1960

Houston Oilers 24
Los Angeles Chargers 16

This was the culmination of the first season played by the American Football League, an eight-team grouping that had begun an effort that in less than 10 years would achieve parity with the older NFL.

In the beginning, the NFL had nothing but scorn and ridicule for the under-manned, under-financed AFL. But time would bring about several dramatic changes.

On New Year's Day of 1961, however, there was nothing for the NFL to worry about. The AFL teams were all doused in red ink and this championship game, played in Houston with the Oilers defeating the Los Angeles Chargers, 24-16, drew a "cut-rate" crowd of 32,183 to Jeppessen Stadium.

Los Angeles, which had won the Western Division title with a 10-4 record, scored first on a 38-yard Ben Agajanian field goal and made it 6-0 in the first quarter when Agajanian hit again for a 22-yarder.

But Houston, with George Blanda (who was 32 years old even then) at quarterback, took a second-quarter lead when fullback Dave Smith capped a long drive by catching Blanda's 17-yard TD pass.

That made it 7-6. Blanda's 18-yard field goal pushed it to 10-6, but with only five seconds remaining in the first half, Los Angeles narrowed it on a 27-yard Agajanian field goal, making the score 10-9 at the intermission.

Blanda's passing opened up in the second half and he widened the Oilers' lead to 17-9 when he hit Bill Groman with a seven-yard

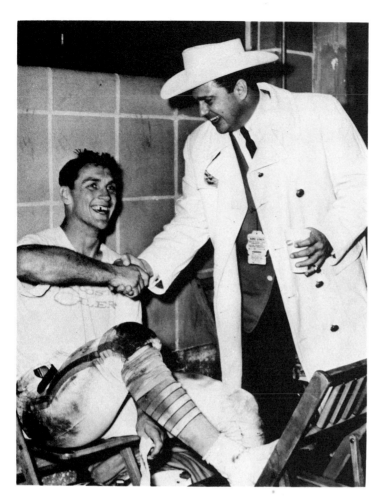

Houston Oilers Owner K. S. (Bud) Adams congratulates Billy Cannon after the halfback had teamed with George Blanda to lead the Oilers to the first AFL title in 1960. Cannon gained 259 yards in total offense, including an 88-yard TD catch.

scoring throw, but the Chargers countered on their next series, moving almost the length of the field before Paul Lowe slammed across from two yards out and cut the gap to 17-16.

They went into the final period that way, the game clearly up for grabs, and that's when Blanda pulled one of his patented passing plays to clinch it.

The Oilers were on their own 12-yard line. It was third down. Blanda, expected to call a running play, faked the handoff to his fullback, Billy Cannon, then took it back, waited until Cannon broke through the line of scrimmage and flipped him a short pass. It caught the Chargers in too tight and the LSU All-America took it all the way for an 88-yard TD and a 24-16 lead.

But the AFL had the two-point rule after touchdowns and Los Angeles had ample time to force a tie.

To no avail, the Chargers twice drove deep into Houston territory, only to lose the ball on downs at the Houston 35 and 22.

AFL 1960 CHAMPIONSHIP GAME

Jeppesen Stadium, Houston, January 1, 1961

SCORE BY PERIODS

Los Angeles Chargers	6	3	7	0 – 16
Houston Oilers	0	10	7	7 – 24

SCORING

Los Angeles—Field goal Agajanian 38
Los Angeles—Field goal Agajanian 22
Houston—Smith 17 pass from Blanda (Blanda kick)
Houston—Field goal Blanda 18
Los Angeles—Field goal Agajanian 27
Houston—Groman 7 pass from Blanda (Blanda kick)
Los Angeles—Lowe 2 run (Agajanian kick)
Houston—Cannon 88 pass from Blanda (Blanda kick)

TEAM STATISTICS

	Los Angeles	Houston
First downs.........................	21	17
Rushing yards	162	100
Passing yards....................	171	301
Return yards, kicks	165	128
Passes	21-41-2	16-32-0
Punts.................................	4-41.0	5-34.0
Fumbles-Lost	2-0	0-0
Penalties-Yards..................	3-15	4-54

Attendance—32,183.

Curly-haired Paul Hornung (right) watches action during the 1961 NFL title game. Hornung accounted for 19 points on his running and kicking, inspiring victorious Packer fans to celebrate in Green Bay's City Stadium.

NFL
1961

Green Bay Packers 37
New York Giants 0

The Green Bay Packers were rolling. They had swamped the West with an 11-3 record, scoring a league-high 391 points, and for Coach Vince Lombardi, this would be an emotional game. He would coach against the New York Giants—"my next favorite team"—for the championship. Indeed, the Giants had tried to hire him at the start of the season, but he could not get out of his Green Bay contract.

The Giants had rebuilt with a fury. Quarterback Y. A. Tittle came from San Francisco, split end Del Shofner from Los Angeles, tight end Joe Walton from Washington, cornerback Erich Barnes from Chicago.

Under new Coach Allie Sherman, an offensive innovator, the Giants became a high-powered team that retained its vicious defense, and they romped to a 10-3-1 regular-season record.

This was the first title game ever played in Green Bay and it was looked upon as "too close to call."

But the Giants never had a chance in a 37-0 trouncing by the Packers.

It was brutal cold for the game at Green Bay December 31, 1961. In the first period, Giants flanker Kyle Rote dropped a sure touchdown pass. In the second period, he dropped another certain TD pass, on an option toss from rookie halfback Bobby Gaiters.

And that would be as close as the Giants would come.

Four seconds into the second quarter, Paul Hornung scored for Green Bay on a six-yard run. Quarterback Bart Starr followed with a 13-yard TD pass to flanker Boyd Dowler. Six minutes after that, tight end Ron Kramer caught a 14-yard pass from Starr and dragged three Giants five yards over the goal line. Finally, five minutes later, Hornung booted a 17-yard field goal for a 24-point quarter.

Things only got worse in the second half. Hornung kicked a 22-yard field goal, and then Kramer scored again, this time on a 13-yard Starr pass.

Hornung's 19-yard field goal in the fourth quarter ended the day's scoring, and the 39,029 in attendance at City Stadium (now Lambeau Field) celebrated into the night, hailing their city, smallest in the NFL (then and now), as "Titletown, U.S.A."

Hornung, on leave from Army duty, set a championship game record by scoring 19 points—one touchdown, three field goals and four extra points.

The Giants, totally demoralized, gained virtually nothing. Tittle was 6-for-20 and 65 yards passing, with four interceptions; the ground game gained 31 yards in 14 carries. The offense had six first downs and five fumbles. The defense gave up 345 yards.

"We'll be back," Sherman fumed, "and I only hope they make it to next year's game."

They did. Both of them.

NFL 1961 CHAMPIONSHIP GAME

City Stadium, Green Bay, Wis., Dec. 31, 1961

SCORE BY PERIODS

New York Giants......	0	0	0	0 – 0
Green Bay Packers...	0	24	10	3 – 37

SCORING

Green Bay—Hornung 6 run (Hornung kick)
Green Bay—Dowler 13 pass from Starr (Hornung kick)
Green Bay—Kramer 14 pass from Starr (Hornung kick)
Green Bay—Field goal Hornung 17
Green Bay—Field goal Hornung 22
Green Bay—Kramer 13 pass from Starr (Hornung kick)
Green Bay—Field goal Hornung 19

TEAM STATISTICS

	New York	Green Bay
First downs........................	6	19
Rushing yards....................	31	181
Passing yards.....................	119	164
Return yards, kicks...........	130	22
Passes..............................	10-29-4	10-19-0
Punts................................	5-39.0	5-42.0
Fumbles-Lost....................	5-1	1-0
Penalties-Yards.................	4-38	4-16

Attendance—39,029.

AFL
1961

Houston Oilers 10
San Diego Chargers 3

A rematch? Sure it was, but the Chargers had moved down the California coast from Los Angeles to set up permanent residence in San Diego and they celebrated by playing to a 12-2 record, best in the eight-team AFL.

Once again, the Houston Oilers won in the East. They had a 10-3-1 record and set a pro football record that still stands with 513 points for the season.

It was an obvious offensive-minded matchup, but a funny thing happened on the way to bushels of points: The two teams played defense as the Oilers defeated the Chargers, 10-3, at Balboa Stadium in San Diego December 24, 1961.

San Diego intercepted six passes, Houston four. San Diego was held to 79 yards rushing, Houston 96. There was a total of seven fumbles in the game, three of which were recovered by the opposition.

After most of three quarters, Houston held a 3-0 lead, George Blanda having boomed a 46-yard field goal in the first period.

Then Houston added to it when Billy Cannon caught a 35-yard TD pass from Blanda to run the score to 10-0.

It was third and five, and Blanda, back to pass, was under extreme pressure. As he was hit, he spotted Cannon on the Chargers 17-yard line and flipped the ball as he fell. It was far from being an accurate pass, but Cannon leaped for the ball, sidestepped a tackler as he came down and raced in for the points.

San Diego, with Jack Kemp at quarterback, moved downfield after that and averted the shutout on a 12-yard field goal by George Blair.

Now the Chargers defense stiffened and Houston was forced to turn over the ball. Kemp, throwing to Dave Kocourek (who would show seven receptions and 123 yards for the day), moved the Chargers downfield once more until they reached the Houston 30.

There, Julian Spence, a flanker who sometimes played as a defensive back, registered only his second interception of the season to clinch a second consecutive league crown for the Oilers.

The Chargers could only take consolation in the fact that they had won the statistical battle.

AFL 1961 CHAMPIONSHIP GAME

Balboa Stadium, San Diego, Dec. 24, 1961

SCORE BY PERIODS

Houston Oilers	0	3	7	0 — 10
San Diego Chargers ..	0	0	0	3 — 3

SCORING

Houston—Field goal Blanda 46
Houston—Cannon 35 pass from Blanda (Blanda kick)
San Diego—Field goal Blair 12

TEAM STATISTICS

	Houston	San Diego
First downs......................	15	18
Rushing yards	96	79
Passing yards....................	160	226
Return yards, kicks	0	66
Passes	18-41-6	17-32-4
Punts..............................	4-41.5	6-33.3
Fumbles-Lost	5-1	2-2
Penalties-Yards.................	5-66	10-106

Attendance—29,556.

NFL 1962

Green Bay Packers 16
New York Giants 7

It was a rematch between the Green Bay Packers and New York Giants, this time in New York's Yankee Stadium December 30, 1962. A crowd of 64,892 endured biting, slicing cold winds which raced through the stadium at 35 mph, creating a chill factor far below the actual frigid reading of 20 degrees.

The field was as hard as concrete and the revenge-minded Giants, who had clearly dominated the East with a 12-2 record, were ready for anything, if it would enable them to win.

Green Bay, just as devastating, and perhaps more so, had lost only one of 14 regular-season games and had scored 415 points while surrendering only 148.

It was a dramatic scene. The Giants were said to have the faster scoring offense. Quarterback Y. A. Tittle threw 33 TD passes during the season, including seven in one game. Green Bay's offense was a relentless ground attack, led by fullback Jim Taylor, who had ousted Cleveland's Jim Brown as NFL rushing leader (1,474 yards) and scored 19 touchdowns along the way.

The tackling was vicious, the intensity unimaginable.

Green Bay scored first on a 26-yard Jerry Kramer field goal. Green Bay scored again in the second quarter, after a fumble by

NFL 1962 CHAMPIONSHIP GAME

Yankee Stadium, New York,
December 30, 1962

SCORE BY PERIODS

Green Bay Packers...	3	7	3	3 — 16
New York Giants	0	0	7	0 — 7

SCORING

Green Bay—Field goal Kramer 26
Green Bay—Taylor 7 run (Kramer kick)
New York—Collier recovered blocked punt in end zone (Chandler kick)
Green Bay—Field goal Kramer 29
Green Bay—Field goal Kramer 30

TEAM STATISTICS

	Green Bay	New York
First downs......................	18	18
Rushing yards	148	94
Passing yards....................	96	197
Return yards, punts...........	36	0
Passes	10-22-0	18-41-1
Punts..............................	6-25.5	7-42.0
Fumbles-Lost	2-0	3-2
Penalties-Yards.................	5-44	4-62

Attendance—64,892.

fullback Phil King was recovered on the Giants 28.

On the first play, Hornung threw the halfback option pass to Boyd Dowler for 21 yards. On the next play, Taylor smashed through the line seven yards for the touchdown and the Packers took a 10-0 lead into halftime.

It had now been six championship quarters in which the Giants hadn't scored against Green Bay, but that changed when the second half began.

Max McGee was back in his end zone to punt for Green Bay, but Erich Barnes slammed through the line and blocked the kick. Rookie Jim Collier covered the ball for a Giants touchdown and suddenly it was a 10-7 game.

Now the Giant defense, playing with cruel efficiency, held on downs and the Packers once again had to punt. But the Giants' Sam Horner fumbled the ball on the New York 40, Green Bay recovered and that led to a 29-yard Kramer field goal.

The Packers added yet a third Kramer field goal, of 30 yards, in the fourth quarter and held on for a 16-7 victory.

"If it hadn't been so damned windy," Green Bay Coach Vince Lombardi said, "Tittle would have done a lot more. But, then, so would have Bart Starr."

Tittle completed 18 of 41 passes, Starr nine of 21.

AFL
1962

Dallas Texas 20
Houston Oilers 17 (OT)

This was the longest AFL game, going through regulation time in a 17-17 tie, through a scoreless overtime period and then being decided at 2:54 of a second sudden death when the Dallas Texans defeated the Houston Oilers, 20-17, at Houston's Jeppessen Stadium.

Dallas, who the next year would become the Kansas City Chiefs, failed to hold a 17-7 lead, built on two Abner Haynes touchdowns (one on a two-yard run and the other on a 28-yard pass from quarterback Len Dawson) and a 16-yard Tommy Brooker field goal. Houston scored on a 15-yard pass from George Blanda to wide receiver Willard Dewveall in the third quarter.

A 10-point final period gave the Oilers a tie. Blanda kicked a 31-yard field goal and stumpy (5-7, 200) Charlie Tolar, the Oilers'

A young Len Dawson combined with Abner Haynes to lead the Dallas Texans to victory in 1962.

fullback, knotted it with a one-yard plunge.

Now the players and officials assembled at midfield for the flip of a coin to start the first overtime session. Haynes, the Dallas captain, had been instructed by Coach Hank Stram to try for the wind advantage, naturally, but only if he lost the flip.

Abner became confused when he won the flip and inadvertently elected to kick off. Houston, taking the wind advantage, still couldn't score, but neither could Dallas, and the game went into the sixth quarter. Dallas was in possession, thanks to an interception by Bill Hull near the end of the first sudden-death period, and the Texans finally began to sniff the end of the marathon.

Getting key gains by Jack Spikes, both as a rusher and an out-of-the-backfield receiver, Dawson drove the Texans to the Houston 19-yard line, from where Brooker kicked a 25-yard field goal to win it, ending pro foot-

Bears defensive end Ed O'Bradovich carries Giants tacklers after intercepting a second-half Y. A. Tittle pass in 1963.

ball's longest game to that point.

For the Oilers, playing before a home crowd of 37,981 December 23, 1962, the defeat was doubly difficult to take, since they not only lost a heartbreaker, but also missed what could have been a third straight title.

AFL 1962 CHAMPIONSHIP GAME

Jeppesen Stadium, Houston, Dec. 23, 1962

SCORE BY PERIODS

Dallas	3	14	0	0	0	3 — 20
Houston	0	0	7	10	0	0 — 17

SCORING

Dallas—Field goal Brooker 16
Dallas—Haynes 28 pass from Dawson (Brooker kick)
Dallas—Haynes 2 run (Brooker kick)
Houston—Dewveall 15 pass from Blanda (Blanda kick)
Houston—Field goal Blanda 31
Houston—Tolar 1 run (Blanda kick)
Dallas—Field goal Brooker 25

TEAM STATISTICS

	Dallas	Houston
First downs	19	21
Rushing yards	199	98
Passing yards	88	261
Return yards, kicks	88	139
Passes	9-14-0	23-46-5
Punts	8-31.2	3-39.9
Fumbles-Lost	2-1	0-0
Penalties-Yards	6-42	6-50

Attendance—37,981.

NFL 1963

Chicago Bears   14
New York Giants   10

For the sixth time since 1933 (when the NFL adopted the format of divisional winners playing for the league title), the Chicago Bears and New York Giants battled for the crown.

The Bears had finally slipped past Green Bay, their 11-1-2 record just a touch better than the Packers' 11-2-1.

The Giants, 11-3 in the East, had overwhelmed most opponents en route to a 448-point season, with Y. A. Tittle throwing 36 TD passes and gaining 3,145 aerial yards.

The weather for the title game at Chicago December 29, 1963, was bitter cold, with the mercury dipping to eight degrees by kickoff, and that cold was to play a major role.

The Giants struck first, on a 14-yard TD pass from Tittle to Frank Gifford, capping an 83-yard drive set in motion when Bears quarterback Billy Wade fumbled on the Giants 17.

It suddenly looked as though the Giants would coast when on the next Chicago series halfback Willie Galimore fumbled and the Giants' Dick Pesonen recovered on the Bears 31. On the first play, Tittle sent the slender Del Shofner down and deep. He was free in the end zone, unattended, but his frigid fingers could not handle the accurate pass. He dropped it and the Bears had new life.

To their credit, they took advantage of the opportunity.

On the next play, Tittle tried a screen pass to fullback Phil King, but Chicago linebacker Larry Morris intercepted it and returned the ball 61 yards to the Giants 5. Two plays later, Wade sneaked over from two yards out and the score was tied.

The half ended with the Giants in front, 10-7, the lead restored on a 13-yard Don Chandler field goal.

But disaster struck for the Giants in the second half. Tittle, who had wrenched a knee in the second quarter, found his mobility seriously diminished and that, in turn, affected his accuracy. Defensive end Ed O'Bradovich picked off another screen pass and rumbled 10 yards to the Giants 14.

A short pass from Wade to tight end Mike Ditka accounted for 13 of the remaining yards, and Wade kept again to put the Bears in front, 14-10.

Although Tittle stayed in (rookie quarterback Glynn Griffing was embarrassingly inept and had to come out), the Giants would not score again. Interceptions (in all, Tittle threw five of them) continued to thwart the Giants and finally, with the ball on Chicago's 39 and 10 seconds left, Tittle threw high and deep to Shofner.

The pass was intercepted by Richie Petitbon. The game was over.

NFL 1963 CHAMPIONSHIP GAME

Wrigley Field, Chicago, December 29, 1963

SCORE BY PERIODS

New York Giants	7	3	0	0 – 10
Chicago Bears	7	0	7	0 – 14

SCORING

New York—Gifford 14 pass from Tittle (Chandler kick)
Chicago—Wade 2 run (Jencks kick)
New York—Field goal Chandler 13
Chicago—Wade 1 (Jencks kick)

TEAM STATISTICS

	New York	Chicago
First downs	17	14
Rushing yards	128	93
Passing yards	140	129
Return yards, punts	21	5
Passes	11-30-5	10-28-0
Punts	4-43.3	7-41.0
Fumbles-Lost	2-1	2-2
Penalties-Yards	3-25	5-35

Attendance—45,801.

AFL 1963

San Diego Chargers 51
Boston Patriots   10

Boston came into this game with the reputation of being a dynamite defensive team; indeed, only two points separated the Patriots from the AFL's lowest points-allowed figure.

But the defense crumbled, the Patriots fell behind the San Diego Chargers early, and it was virtually over after the first period.

San Diego had a new quarterback, Tobin Rote, because a clerical error in the front office had exposed Jack Kemp to waivers, and before it could be corrected, Kemp (now a U.S. Representative from New York) was a member of the Buffalo Bills.

Ironically, Buffalo and Boston finished with 7-6-1 records that season, but Boston won a 26-8 playoff game to gain the championship berth, only to be clobbered for the title by the Chargers, 51-10, at San Diego's Balboa Stadium January 5, 1964.

Rote scored the first touchdown on a two-yard keeper. Then he handed off to halfback Keith Lincoln and watched him go 67 yards for a 14-0 lead.

Boston came back, briefly, when Babe Parilli engineered a drive that was capped by fullback Larry Garron's seven-yard run.

AFL 1963 CHAMPIONSHIP GAME

Balboa Stadium, San Diego, January 5, 1964

SCORE BY PERIODS

Boston Patriots	7	3	0	0 – 10
San Diego Chargers	21	10	7	13 – 51

SCORING

San Diego—Rote 2 run (Blair kick)
San Diego—Lincoln 67 run (Blair kick)
Boston—Garron 7 run (Cappelletti kick)
San Diego—Lowe 58 run (Blair kick)
Boston—Field goal Cappelletti 15
San Diego—Norton 14 pass from Rote (Blair kick)
San Diego—Alworth 48 pass from Rote (Blair kick)
San Diego—Lincoln 25 pass from Hadl (pass failed)
San Diego—Hadl 1 run (Blair kick)

TEAM STATISTICS

	Boston	San Diego
First downs	14	21
Rushing yards	75	318
Passing yards	228	305
Return yards, kicks	112	70
Passes	17-37-2	16-25-0
Punts	7-46.9	2-43.5
Fumbles-Lost	1-0	1-1
Penalized-Yards	1-16	6-30

Attendance—30,127.

Forget it. The other San Diego running back, Paul Lowe, tore off a 58-yard run for another TD and a 21-7 San Diego lead after just one quarter.

It was 31-10 at halftime. George Blair of San Diego and Gino Cappelletti of Boston exchanged short field goals early in the second quarter before Don Norton scored for the Chargers on a 14-yard pass from Rote.

In the second half, San Diego scored 20 more points while shutting out the weary Patriots.

Lance Alworth, now a Hall of Fame wide receiver, hauled in a 48-yard scoring pass from Rote in the third period, and in the fourth quarter Lincoln added a 25-yard TD on a pass from John Hadl, who relieved Rote at quarterback.

Hadl himself finished the day's scoring by capping a long march with a one-yard keeper for the final points.

Between them, Rote and Hadl completed 16 of 25 passes for 285 yards and three TDs. They threw no interceptions.

Lincoln caught seven passes for 123 yards and rushed for 206 yards in only 13 carries. He also completed one pass for 20 yards. So complete was the San Diego domination that Chargers punter Paul Maguire was called upon to kick only twice.

Cleveland's Gary Collins reaches for and grabs a 42-yard TD bomb from Frank Ryan, the second of his three TD catches in a 1964 win over the Colts.

NFL
1964

Cleveland Browns 27
Baltimore Colts   0

Cleveland had arrived, with the help of the incomparable Jim Brown, a rookie receiver named Paul Warfield, a veteran receiver named Gary Collins and quarterback Frank Ryan.

Baltimore, as always, had Johnny Unitas, Lenny Moore, Raymond Berry and an old but solid defense.

And Baltimore, a 12-2 team, was favored to win, but as a huge crowd of 79,544 watched in Cleveland Municipal Stadium December 27, 1964, the first half was a scoreless defensive struggle.

Then, almost instantly, the underdog Browns blew it open and won the championship, 27-0.

Lou Groza, the 40-year-old placekicker, finally broke the ice with a 43-yard field goal early in the third quarter. On Cleveland's next possession, Brown took a pitchout and raced 46 yards, and on the next play,

Ryan hit Collins with an 18-yard touchdown pass.

Then, just prior to the end of the period, Ryan went to Collins again, throwing deep, and it turned into a 42-yard scoring play, giving Cleveland an unexpected and comfortable 17-0 lead.

Baltimore never recovered. The Browns' defense played flawless pass coverage, frustrating Unitas all day. Meanwhile, in the fourth quarter a nine-yard Groza field goal was followed by another bomb from Ryan to Collins, a 51-yarder, to arrive at the final onesided score.

Technically, the Browns were successful in taking away the Colts' short passing game and forcing Unitas to either call running plays or go deep in the air. Once that was accomplished, they rushed their defensive linemen from the outside in, forcing Unitas to run up the middle. He did carry six times and gain 30 yards, but Unitas running was far less a threat than Unitas passing.

Finally, on offense, the Browns tried yet another unexpected tactic. A team so feared on the ground would be expected to stay there on crucial downs, which was exactly the reason Ryan threw so often on third-down plays.

Ryan collected nine first downs passing as he hit on 11 of 18 attempts for 206 yards. Every one of Collins' five receptions (for 130 yards) was either for a touchdown or a first down.

"They took it away from us," said Colts Coach Don Shula. "They were better prepared than we were."

The underdog Browns managed nine more first downs than the Colts, outrushed them, 142-92, and outgained them in the air, 206-89.

NFL 1964 CHAMPIONSHIP GAME

Municipal Stadium, Cleveland, Dec. 27, 1964

SCORE BY PERIODS

Baltimore Colts	0	0	0	0 – 0
Cleveland Browns	0	0	17	10 – 27

SCORING

Cleveland—Field goal Groza 43
Cleveland—Collins 18 pass from Ryan (Groza kick)
Cleveland—Collins 42 pass from Ryan (Groza kick)
Cleveland—Field goal Groza 9
Cleveland—Collins 51 pass from Ryan (Groza kick)

TEAM STATISTICS

	Baltimore	Cleveland
First downs	11	20
Rushing yards	92	142
Passing yards	89	206
Return yards, punts	18	13
Passes	12-20-2	11-18-1
Punts	4-33.8	3-44.0
Fumbles-Lost	2-2	0-0
Penalties-Yards	5-48	7-59
Attendance—79,544.		

Jack Kemp, who led Buffalo to victory in the 1964 AFL title game, later traded in his cleats for a seat in the U.S. House of Representatives.

AFL 1964

Buffalo Bills   20
San Diego Chargers 7

Things improved dramatically for the struggling AFL. The National Broadcasting Co. paid $36 million for the right to televise its games and since all the teams would share equally, there would be no instant replay of bouncing checks and red ink.

The New York Titans were taken over by the league after Harry Wismer could no longer afford them. A group headed by show business mogul Sonny Werblin purchased the team and moved it into new

Shea Stadium as co-tenant with the base-ball Mets.

It would be a while before the Jets would become potent, but the league was on firm ground now and the title game in Buffalo December 26, 1964, at War Memorial Stadium drew a crowd of 40,242. The throng was rewarded when the Bills defeated the San Diego Chargers, 20-7.

For a while, it appeared as if San Diego was headed for a repeat of its 1963 championship. The Chargers scored on their first possession, driving 80 yards in four plays. Keith Lincoln ran 38 yards to set up a 26-yard pass from Tobin Rote to Dave Kocourek.

But a smashing tackle on Lincoln by Buffalo linebacker Mike Stratton later in the quarter broke one of Lincoln's ribs and put him out of the game. Without him, the Chargers stalled and when they did, the Bills were able to win the city's first championship in any major league sport.

Pete Gogolak, a Hungarian refugee, provided Buffalo with its first points on a 12-yard field goal in the first quarter.

The Bills made it 13-7 at halftime on Wray Carlton's four-yard TD run and Gogolak's 17-yard field goal.

The teams fought through a scoreless third period, but Jack Kemp drove the Bills downfield for one final score late in the final quarter. A 48-yard pass to Glenn Bass put the ball on the San Diego one-yard line and Kemp scored on a quarterback sneak for the 20-7 advantage.

Cookie Gilchrist, the Bills' 250-pound fullback, gained 122 yards in 16 carries and accounted for all but three of Buffalo's 12 first downs rushing.

NFL 1965

Green Bay Packers 23
Cleveland Browns 12

First, the Green Bay Packers had to survive a sudden-death overtime playoff game with Baltimore to emerge as Western Conference champions and that was accomplished, 13-10, on a field goal by Don Chandler with 13:39 elapsed in the "fifth quarter."

Now came the Browns, 11-3 runaway champions in the East, still featuring Jimmy Brown, Gary Collins and Frank Ryan.

It snowed in Green Bay on the morning of January 2, 1966, but the underground electrical coils at Lambeau Field turned it to slush, which in turn became grasping, clutching, slippery mud.

It thus became a primitive battle of straight-ahead runs and denying defense, the sort of game both teams played well, but the Packers finally outkicked the Browns, 23-12.

The Packer defense was so dominant that Brown, the great running back, was held to 50 yards rushing and Ryan had to go to the air.

After Green Bay quarterback Bart Starr crossed up the Browns with a 47-yard touchdown pass to Carroll Dale on a third-and-one in the first quarter, Ryan came firing back. He moved the Browns 66 yards in

AFL 1964 CHAMPIONSHIP GAME

War Memorial Stadium, Buffalo, Dec. 26, 1964

SCORE BY PERIODS

San Diego Chargers ..	7	0	0	0 – 7
Buffalo Bills	3	10	0	7 – 20

SCORING

San Diego—Kocourek 26 pass from Rote (Lincoln kick)
Buffalo—Field goal Gogolak 12
Buffalo—Carlton 4 run (Gogolak kick)
Buffalo—Field goal Gogolak 17
Buffalo—Kemp 1 run (Gogolak kick)

TEAM STATISTICS

	San Diego	Buffalo
First downs	15	21
Rushing yards	124	219
Passing yards	149	168
Return yards, kicks	233	50
Passes	13-36-3	10-20-0
Punts	5-36.4	5-46.8
Fumbles-Lost	1-0	0-0
Penalties-Yards.................	3-20	3-45

Attendance—40,242.

NFL 1965 CHAMPIONSHIP GAME

Lambeau Field, Green Bay, January 2, 1966

SCORE BY PERIODS

Cleveland Browns.....	9	3	0	0 – 12
Green Bay Packers...	7	6	7	3 – 23

SCORING

Green Bay—Dale 47 pass from Starr (Chandler kick)
Cleveland—Collins 17 pass from Ryan (kick failed)
Cleveland—Field goal Groza 24
Green Bay—Field goal Chandler 15
Green Bay—Field goal Chandler 23
Cleveland—Field goal Groza 28
Green Bay—Hornung 13 run (Chandler kick)
Green Bay—Field goal Chandler 29

TEAM STATISTICS

	Cleveland	Green Bay
First downs	8	21
Rushing yards	64	204
Passing yards	97	128
Return yards, punts	11	−10
Passes	8-18-2	10-19-1
Punts	4-46.0	3-38.3
Fumbles-Lost	0-0	0-0
Penalties-Yards.................	2-20	3-35

Attendance—50,777.

The incomparable Jimmy Brown led Cleveland into the 1965 title game, but it was all Packers once the hitting began.

three plays—all passes—and hit Collins for the TD with a 17-yarder. But the conversion attempt failed and the Packers retained a slim 7-6 lead.

But not for long, as Lou Groza kicked a 24-yard field goal late in the first quarter and gave Cleveland a 9-7 cushion.

In the second quarter, the field goal was the only successful weapon for either side. Chandler kicked a pair (15 and 23 yards) and Groza cut the ensuing 13-9 lead to 13-12 with a 28-yarder near the end of the half.

The missed extra point loomed large, but Green Bay erased all doubts in the second half, holding the Browns scoreless while adding a Paul Hornung touchdown run of 13 yards in the third period and a 29-yard Chandler field goal in the fourth quarter.

The final Cleveland chance in the second half, to get the ball and keep trying to break Brown loose, was denied when the Packers were able to maintain possession, several times holding the ball for three, four and five-minute periods, effectively keeping it away from the Browns.

As evidence of this dominance, the Browns gained 135 yards in the first half but only 26 in the second.

AFL 1965

Buffalo Bills 23
San Diego Chargers 0

There had not been a shutout in the five previous AFL championship games, but the surgical precision of the Buffalo Bills managed that accomplishment while winning a second consecutive league crown.

The Bills had a ferocious defense. They had allowed the least number of points in the league, while relying on quarterback Jack Kemp, running back Wray Carlton, receiver Bo Roberson and a hulking offensive line to ring up 313 points en route to a 10-3-1 record.

It was never a contest as the Bills beat the San Diego Chargers, 23-0, in the title game at San Diego's Balboa Stadium December 26, 1965.

Kemp hit Ernie Warlick with a touchdown pass of 18 yards in the second quarter and then Butch Byrd made it 14-0 at halftime with a 74-yard punt return.

The rest of the game was all Buffalo and all Pete Gogolak, who completed the scoring with second-half field goals of 11, 39 and 32 yards.

The drubbing was deceptive if one peered only at the statistics, for there the teams were close enough to suggest a tightly-fought contest.

San Diego rushed for 104 yards, Buffalo for 108. San Diego's passing game accounted for 119 net yards, Buffalo's for 152. In fact, the difference showed most in the category of first downs, Buffalo pounding out 23 to only 12 for San Diego.

But Buffalo had inflicted the first (and only) AFL championship game shutout, without realizing that its dynasty had peaked, regrettably, a year before the pot of gold would be discovered.

AFL 1965 CHAMPIONSHIP GAME

Balboa Stadium, San Diego, Dec. 26, 1965

SCORE BY PERIODS

Buffalo Bills.............	0	14	6	3 – 23
San Diego Chargers ..	0	0	0	0 – 0

SCORING

Buffalo—Warlick 18 pass from Kemp (Gogolak kick)
Buffalo—Byrd 74 punt return (Gogolak kick)
Buffalo—Field goal Gogolak 11
Buffalo—Field goal Gogolak 39
Buffalo—Field goal Gogolak 32

TEAM STATISTICS

	Buffalo	San Diego
First downs......................	23	12
Rushing yards	108	104
Passing yards...................	152	119
Return yards, kicks	104	109
Passes	9-20-1	12-25-2
Punts................................	4-46.3	7-40.7
Fumbles-Lost	0-0	4-2
Penalties-Yards.................	2-21	2-41

Attendance—30,361.

NFL 1966

Green Bay Packers 34
Dallas Cowboys 27

The first Super Bowl was the prize for these two teams, and of equal fascination was the meeting of two distinctly different eras—the old, traditional Green Bay dynasty vs. the young, exciting and about-to-bloom Dallas dynasty.

This was the Cowboys' first-ever championship appearance and a crowd of 74,152 jammed into the Cotton Bowl at Dallas January 1, 1967, to witness the coming of age.

What the Texans saw was a heart-stopping drama, which wasn't over until the final seconds, a game that ebbed and flowed with maddening capriciousness and finally

Dallas quarterback Don Meredith, in the grasp of Green Bay linebacker Dave Robinson, throws a desperation pass that was intercepted by Tom Brown, sealing the Packers' 1966 victory.

ended with the Packers outscoring the Cowboys, 34-27.

In the first quarter, Green Bay scored two quick touchdowns and before the Cowboys even had the chance to run a play, they trailed, 14-0.

The Packers' first TD capped a 76-yard drive in eight plays, quarterback Bart Starr hitting halfback Elijah Pitts on a 17-yard scoring pass. Then, on the ensuing kickoff, Mel Renfro of the Cowboys fumbled, the ball bounced into the hands of Green Bay's Jim Grabowski and he loped in for an 18-yard tally.

But the young Cowboys fought back, getting scoring runs of three yards by halfback Danny Reeves and 23 yards from fullback Don Perkins. Green Bay scored on a 51-yard pass from Bart Starr (he had four TD strikes on the day) to Dale, while Dallas countered with an 11-yard Danny Villanueva field goal. The half ended with Green Bay ahead, 21-17.

Villanueva closed it to 21-20 in the third quarter with a 32-yard field goal, but then Green Bay apparently broke it wide open, scoring in the third quarter on a 16-yard

NFL 1966 CHAMPIONSHIP GAME

Cotton Bowl, Dallas, January 1, 1967

SCORE BY PERIODS

Green Bay Packers...	14	7	7	6 – 34
Dallas Cowboys	14	3	3	7 – 27

SCORING

Green Bay—Pitts 17 pass from Starr (Chandler kick)
Green Bay—Grabowski 18 fumble recovery return (Chandler kick)
Dallas—Reeves 3 run (Villanueva kick)
Dallas—Perkins 23 run (Villanueva kick)
Green Bay—Dale 51 pass from Starr (Chandler kick)
Dallas—Field goal Villanueva 11
Dallas—Field goal Villanueva 32
Green Bay—Dowler 16 pass from Starr (Chandler kick)
Green Bay—McGee 28 pass from Starr (kick blocked)
Dallas—Clarke 68 pass from Meredith (Villanueva kick)

TEAM STATISTICS

	Green Bay	Dallas
First downs	19	23
Rushing yards	102	187
Passing yards	265	231
Return yards, punts	0	–9
Passes	19-28-0	15-31-2
Punts	4-40.0	4-32.2
Fumbles-Lost	1-1	3-1
Penalties-Yards	2-23	6-29

Attendance—74,152.

INDIVIDUAL STATISTICS

Rushing—Dallas, Perkins 17-108, Reeves 17-47, Meredith 4-22, Norman 2-10; Green Bay, Pitts 12-66, Taylor 10-37, Starr 2-minus 1.

Passing—Dallas, Meredith 15-31-1—238; Green Bay, Starr 19-28-0—304.

Receiving—Dallas, Reeves 4-77, Norman 4-30, Clarke 3-102, Gent 3-28, Hayes 1-1; Green Bay, Dale 5-128, Taylor 5-23, Fleming 3-50, Dowler 3-49, McGee 1-28, Pitts 1-17, Long 1-9.

Starr pass to Boyd Dowler and again early in the fourth when Starr found Max McGee for 28 yards and a 34-20 lead. It was 34-20, not 35-20, because the extra-point attempt after the final Packers TD had been blocked.

But what did it matter? There was a 14-point spread, and the game was winding down.

Then, Dallas quarterback Don Meredith hit tight end Frank Clarke for a 68-yard TD, and suddenly it was 34-27. Another touchdown—and the PAT—wound send this game into sudden-death overtime.

And here came the Cowboys. Meredith moved the team downfield, and when linebacker Dave Robinson was guilty of pass interference on Clarke, the Cowboys had a first down at the Packers 2.

Four plays to get two yards . . . four plays to tie it. Reeves smashed into the line for one yard. Tackle Jim Boeke then was flagged for illegal procedure, setting Dallas back to the 6. Meredith threw incomplete, then on third down hit Pettis Norman for four yards. It was fourth and two.

Meredith's call was a pass to Bob Hayes, a fleet wide receiver. But Hayes was supposed to block down on Robinson, then release into the end zone. He didn't and simply ran the pattern, leaving the linebacker free to harass Meredith into a hasty and wild pass.

The throw was intercepted in the end zone by safety Tom Brown. By the barest of margins, Green Bay had earned the right to play in Super Bowl I against the AFL's Kansas City Chiefs.

AFL 1966

Kansas City Chiefs 31
Buffalo Bills 7

Merger . . . amalgamation . . . absorption. Call it what you will, but on June 8, 1966, the NFL and the AFL agreed to become one league (i.e., have a common draft of college players), while also agreeing to play separate schedules until 1970.

The most important short-term development, on the other hand, was the announcement that, beginning with the 1966 season, the two league champions would meet in a World Championship Game, later to be called the Super Bowl.

So Kansas City and Buffalo had much to play for when the two clubs met for the

AFL title at Buffalo January 1, 1967. The game was all Kansas City as the Chiefs defeated the Bills, 31-7.

The Chiefs were caught in a 7-7 deadlock after the first quarter, having scored first on a 29-yard pass from quarterback Len Dawson to tight end Fred Arbanas, only to have Buffalo strike for a 69-yard TD pass from Jack Kemp to Elbert Dubenion.

And then the Bills disappeared.

Otis Taylor caught a 29-yard TD pass from Dawson early in the second quarter. Mike Mercer added a 32-yard field goal before halftime, and it was 17-7. The field goal was far more costly to Buffalo than just three points because it came after an interception when the Bills were on the Chiefs 10-yard line and were threatening to score a touchdown.

Johnny Robinson filched a pass by Kemp in the Kansas City end zone and returned it 72 yards, paving the way for Mercer's field goal.

There was no scoring in the third period, but precious time had been lost by Buffalo— and gained by the Chiefs.

AFL 1966 CHAMPIONSHIP GAME
War Memorial Stadium, Buffalo, Jan. 1, 1967

SCORE BY PERIODS

Kansas City Chiefs ...	7	10	0	14 –	31
Buffalo Bills	7	0	0	0 –	7

SCORING

Kansas City—Arbanas 29 pass from Dawson (Mercer kick)
Buffalo—Dubenion 69 pass from Kemp (Lusteg kick)
Kansas City—Taylor 29 pass from Dawson (Mercer kick)
Kansas City—Field goal Mercer 32
Kansas City—Garrett 1 run (Mercer kick)
Kansas City—Garrett 18 run (Mercer kick)

TEAM STATISTICS

	Kansas City	Buffalo
First downs	14	9
Rushing yards	113	40
Passing yards	227	253
Return yards, kicks	65	115
Passes	16-24-0	12-27-2
Punts	6-42.3	8-39.3
Fumbles-Lost	1-0	3-2
Penalties-Yards.................	4-40	3-23

Attendance—42,080.

INDIVIDUAL STATISTICS

Rushing—Buffalo, Carlton 9-31, Burnett 3-6, Kemp 1-3; Kansas City, Garrett 13-39, McClinton 11-38, Dawson 5-28, Coan 2-6, Eu. Thomas 2-2.

Passing—Buffalo, Kemp 12-27-2—253; Kansas City, Dawson 16-24-0—227.

Receiving—Buffalo, Burnett 6-127, Dubenion 2-79, Bass 2-26, Crockett 1-16, Carlton 1-5; Kansas City, Taylor 5-78, Burford 4-76, Garrett 4-16, Arbanas 2-44, McClinton 1-13.

Kickoff Returns—Buffalo, Warner 5-91, Meredith 1-8; Kansas City, Coan 1-35, Garrett 1-30.

Punt Returns—Buffalo, Byrd 3-0, Rutkowski 2-16; Kansas City, Garrett 3-37.

Interceptions—Kansas City, Robinson 1-72, Em. Thomas 1-26.

Finally, a one-yard TD run by halfback Mike Garrett made the score 24-7, and later in the fourth quarter Garrett broke loose for an 18-yard TD jaunt that locked it up.

NFL 1967

Green Bay Packers 21
Dallas Cowboys   17

It was Green Bay weather and it was on Green Bay's field, but it wasn't until 13 seconds were left to play that Green Bay was assured of a 21-17 victory over the Dallas Cowboys.

This was the famous Ice Bowl on December 31, 1967, with a kickoff-time temperature of minus 13 degrees and with a 14-knot wind making it feel like minus 35.

And this was the greatest moment in the Green Bay era, the Packers' finest accomplishment.

This was vintage Green Bay, charging ahead, 14-0, early in the second quarter on two passes from Bart Starr to Boyd Dowler. And this was dogged Dallas, flying back, making it 14-7 when defensive end George Andrie picked up a Starr fumble and returned it seven yards for a touchdown.

And Dallas cut it again, to 14-10, when Willie Wood's fumbled punt gave the Cowboys the chance for a field goal, a 21-yarder in the third quarter by Danny Villanueva.

Finally, this was Dallas, with a characteristic flashy play, quarterback Don Meredith tossing a pitchout to halfback Danny Reeves, who rolled to his left, suddenly braked and threw a perfect 50-yard touchdown pass to wide receiver Lance Rentzel.

And it was Dallas, ahead by 17-14, hands and feet frozen, staving off the veteran Packers, who had never in their time at the top had to overcome so much in so short a span.

When they took over at their own 31, the Packers saw that only 4:50 remained in the game. Surely this was a goal too far, an impossible dream even for the NFL's greatest team.

But there was Starr, throwing short passes to his backs, Donny Anderson and Chuck Mercein; short passes, in front of the Dallas linebackers, "because they didn't have any traction," he said.

There was a pass to Anderson for six and another for 12. At the Dallas 30, with the clock ticking, a big one to Mercein gained 19. A run by Mercein brought the ball to the 3.

— 341 —

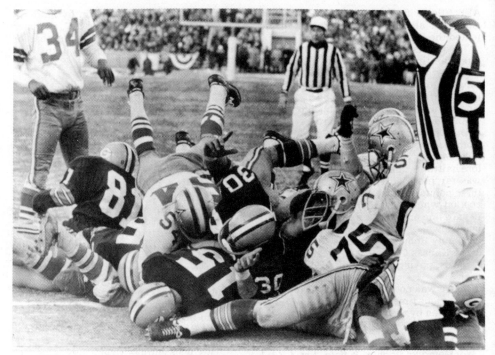

Packers quarterback Bart Starr (15) plunges over for the winning TD with only seconds remaining in the 1967 'Ice Bowl.'

Now Anderson failed twice to dent the Dallas line and Starr twice called time out. That was the last one left for the desperate Packers. Surely they would go for the short field goal, for the tie, for the sudden-death overtime.

But no! Starr lined them up . . . Starr kept the ball . . . Starr got a blasting block from guard Jerry Kramer. He dived, hit the ground and looked up. He had barely crossed the goal line.

No overtime. And the only sudden death was suffered by the Cowboys. Yet again as 50,861 shrieking believers in Lambeau Field celebrated, the Green Bay Packers were NFL champions and had another date in the Super Bowl.

"Those last five minutes," Coach Vince Lombardi said, "are what the Packers are all about."

NFL 1967 CHAMPIONSHIP GAME

Lambeau Field, Milwaukee, Dec. 31, 1967

SCORE BY PERIODS

Dallas Cowboys	0	10	0	7 — 17
Green Bay Packers	7	7	0	7 — 21

SCORING

Green Bay—Dowler 8 pass from Starr (Chandler kick)

Green Bay—Dowler 43 pass from Starr (Chandler kick)

Dallas—Andrie 7 fumble recovery return (Villanueva kick)

Dallas—Field goal Villanueva 21

Dallas—Rentzel 50 pass from Reeves (Villanueva kick)

Green Bay—Starr 1 run (Chandler kick)

TEAM STATISTICS

	Dallas	Green Bay
First downs	11	18
Rushing yards	92	80
Passing yards	100	191
Return yards, kicks	43	29
Passes	11-26-1	14-24-0
Punts	8-39.0	8-28.8
Fumbles-Lost	3-1	3-2
Penalties-Yards	7-58	2-10

Attendance—50,861.

INDIVIDUAL STATISTICS

Rushing—Green Bay, Anderson 18-35, Mercein 6-20, Williams 4-13, Wilson 3-11, Starr 1-1; Dallas, Perkins 17-51, Reeves 13-42, Meredith 1-9, Baynham 1-minus 2, Clarke 1-minus 8.

Passing—Green Bay, Starr 14-24-0—191; Dallas, Meredith 10-25-1—59, Reeves 1-1-0—50.

Receiving—Green Bay, Dowler 4-77, Anderson 4-44, Dale 3-44, Mercein 2-22, Williams 1-4; Dallas, Hayes 3-16, Reeves 3-11, Rentzel 2-61, Clarke 2-24, Baynham 1-minus 3.

Kickoff Returns—Green Bay, Caffey 1-7, Crutcher 1-3, Weatherwax 1-0; Dallas, Stevens 2-15, Stokes 1-28.

Punt Returns—Green Bay, Wood 4-21, Brown 1-minus 2.

Punting—Green Bay, Anderson 8-29.0; Dallas, Villanueva 8-39.1.

The leg of George Blanda and the arm of 'Mad Bomber' Daryle Lamonica (shown holding for a Blanda kick) lifted Oakland to the AFL title in 1967.

AFL 1967

Oakland Raiders 40
Houston Oilers 7

The Houston Oilers, 3-11 the season before, suddenly caught fire, ran up a record of 9-4-1 and edged the New York Jets (8-5-1) in the Eastern Division.

The Oakland Raiders, easily the cream of the league, ran off and hid in the West, finishing with a 13-1 mark and scoring 468 points in outdistancing Kansas City (9-5).

This was a pass-happy Oakland team, but Coach Johnny Rauch crossed up Houston by sticking to the ground. Hewritt Dixon responded with 144 yards in 21 carries, including a 69-yard second-quarter TD run, while

Pete Banaszak added 116 yards in 15 carries.

Oakland built a 27-0 lead before Houston was able to score and breezed to a 40-7 victory in the game at the Oakland Coliseum December 31, 1967.

The departure from the passing game fooled the Oilers and the fury of the Oakland running game cracked what had been a sound Houston defense.

Quarterback Daryle Lamonica, nicknamed "The Mad Bomber," had passed 425 times during the season for Oakland, more than 30 attempts per game. Yet on this day, he threw only 24 passes, completing 10, while the Raiders practiced ball control with 48 rushing plays.

Oakland built a 10-0 lead on a 37-yard field goal by George Blanda and the 69-yard run by Dixon. The Raiders then rubbed it in just before the first half ended. With 18 seconds remaining, they lined up for a field goal attempt by Blanda, only to have Lamonica, the holder, jump up and pass to tight end Dave Kocourek for a 17-yard TD and a 17-0 lead.

Houston's hopes of getting back into the game were killed when Zeke Moore fumbled the opening kickoff in the second half. Oakland recovered deep in Houston territory and scored in seven plays with Lamonica sneaking over from one yard out. Blanda kicked a 40-yard field goal before the period ended and added another from 42 yards in the fourth quarter.

The Oilers finally got on the scoreboard with a five-yard pass from Pete Beathard to Charlie Frazier. But Blanda kicked his fourth field goal for the Raiders, this one from 36 yards, and Lamonica threw a 12-yard scoring pass to Bill Miller.

AFL 1967 CHAMPIONSHIP GAME

Oakland-Alameda County Coliseum, Oakland, December 31, 1967

SCORE BY PERIODS

Houston Oilers	0	0	0	7 – 7
Oakland Raiders.......	3	14	10	13 – 40

SCORING

Oakland—Field goal Blanda 37
Oakland—Dixon 69 run (Blanda kick)
Oakland—Kocourek 17 pass from Lamonica (Blanda kick)
Oakland—Lamonica 1 run (Blanda kick)
Oakland—Field goal Blanda 40
Oakland—Field goal Blanda 42
Houston—Frazier 5 pass from Beathard (Wittenborn kick)
Oakland—Field goal Blanda 36
Oakland—Miller 12 pass from Lamonica (Blanda kick)

TEAM STATISTICS

	Houston	Oakland
First downs.........................	11	18
Rushing yards	38	263
Passing yards.....................	142	111
Return yards, kicks	215	126
Passes	15-35-1	10-26-0
Punts.................................	11-38.5	4-44.3
Fumbles-Lost	4-2	0-0
Penalties-Yards..................	7-45	4-69

Attendance—53,330.

INDIVIDUAL STATISTICS

Rushing—Oakland, Dixon 21-144, Banaszak 15-116, Lamonica 5-22, Hagberg 2-minus 1, Todd 4-minus 8, Biletnikoff 1-minus 10; Houston, Granger 14-19, Campbell 6-15, Blanks 1-6, Beathard 1-minus 2.

Passing—Oakland, Lamonica 10-24-0—111, Blanda 0-2-0—0; Houston, Beathard 15-35-1—142.

Receiving—Oakland, Miller 3-32, Cannon 2-31, Biletnikoff 2-19, Kocourek 1-17, Dixon 1-8, Banaszak 1-4; Houston, Frazier 7-81, Reed 4-60, Campbell 2-5, Taylor 1-6, Granger 1-minus 10.

Kickoff Returns—Oakland, Grayson 1-47, Todd 1-32; Houston, Jancik 4-100, Moore 3-87, Burrell 1-28, Suggs 1-0.

Punt Returns—Oakland, Bird 5-49, Sherman 1-minus 2.

Interceptions—Oakland, Brown 1-2.

Punting—Oakland, Eischeid 4-44.3; Houston, Norton 11-38.5.

Tom Matte's three touchdowns led the Colts past the Browns in the 1968 title game.

NFL 1968

Baltimore Colts   34
Cleveland Browns   0

In 1964, the Cleveland Browns had humiliated the Baltimore Colts, 27-0, in the NFL championship game. Now, four years later, the scene was set for Baltimore to gain revenge and vindication.

The game was in Cleveland before 78,410 fans December 29, 1968.

That only made the embarrassment worse for the Browns, who were trounced, 34-0.

The Colts, who had a 13-1 regular-season record, struck with a quick and early vengeance, built a 17-0 halftime lead and totally dominated the proud Browns.

So complete was the beating that the Browns reached into Baltimore territory only twice and never got beyond the Colts 33. The Browns became Baltimore's fourth shutout victim of the season, a season in which the Colts had allowed only 144 points while scoring 402 in their 14 regulation games.

The game started out deceptively, with no scoring in the first period. When the Colts finally did get on the board, it was merely a 28-yard Lou Michaels field goal.

But then came the explosion. A 60-yard, 10-play drive was capped by a one-yard Tom Matte run, making it 10-0, and minutes later linebacker Mike Curtis intercepted a Bill Nelsen pass on the Browns 33.

It took the Colts only three plays to cash in on that turnover. Matte ran for 12, Jerry Hill for nine and Matte again for the final dozen and a 17-0 lead.

Matte scored his third TD in the third quarter, a two-yard run to climax another long, time-consuming ground thrust, and Baltimore managed 10 more points in the final quarter, on a 10-yard Michaels field goal and a four-yard run by Timmy Brown.

Ironically, the victory also avenged the only loss of the season, a 30-20 Cleveland decision that prevented the Colts from achieving a perfect year.

NFL 1968 CHAMPIONSHIP GAME

Municipal Stadium, Cleveland, Dec. 29, 1968

SCORE BY PERIODS

Baltimore Colts	0	17	7	10 –	34
Cleveland Browns.....	0	0	0	0 –	0

SCORING

Baltimore—Field goal Michaels 28
Baltimore—Matte 1 run (Michaels kick)
Baltimore—Matte 12 run (Michaels kick)
Baltimore—Matte 2 run (Michaels kick)
Baltimore—Field goal Michaels 10
Baltimore—Brown 4 run (Michaels kick)

TEAM STATISTICS

	Baltimore	Cleveland
First downs	22	12
Rushing yards	184	56
Passing yards.....................	169	151
Return yards, kicks	21	95
Passing..............................	11-25-1	13-32-2
Punts	2-37.0	5-33.4
Fumbles-Lost	2-1	2-1
Penalties-Yards..................	3-15	7-54

Attendance—78,410.

INDIVIDUAL STATISTICS

Rushing—Cleveland, Kelly 13-28, Harraway 6-26, Green 1-2; Baltimore, Matte 17-88, Hill 11-60, Brown 5-18, Cole 3-14, Mackey 2-4, Morrall 1-0.

Passing—Cleveland, Nelsen 11-26-2–132, Ryan 2-6-0 –19; Baltimore, Morrall 11-25-1–169.

Receiving—Cleveland, Harraway 4-40, Morin 3-41, Kelly 3-27, Warfield 2-30, Collins 1-13; Baltimore, Richardson 3-78, Mackey 2-34, Orr 2-33, Matte 2-15, Mitchell 1-7, Cole 1-2.

Kickoff Returns—Cleveland, Morrison 3-51, Davis 3-40; Baltimore, Pearson 1-21.

Punt Returns—Cleveland, Davis 1-4; Baltimore, Brown 1-0.

Interceptions—Cleveland, Davis 1-0; Baltimore, Volk 1-26, Curtis 1-0.

Punting—Cleveland, Cockroft 5-33.4; Baltimore, Lee 2-37.0.

Joe Namath threw two TD passes to Don Maynard in the Jets' 1968 win over the Raiders.

AFL 1968

New York Jets 27
Oakland Raiders 23

In 1964, the New York Jets had signed a rookie quarterback from the University of Alabama for a staggering $400,000. His name was Joe Namath.

And on December 29, 1968, Namath hooked up with Daryle Lamonica, "The Mad Bomber" of the Oakland Raiders, to provide the AFL with its most exciting championship game. It was, in the tradition of the AFL, an all-out passing game, one in which Lamonica completed 20 of 47 passes, Namath 19 of 49.

Lamonica gained 401 yards, but threw only one TD pass, while Namath, whose passes accounted for 266 yards, connected for three TDs, including the ultimate game-winner, a six-yarder to wide receiver Don Maynard late in the fourth quarter to produce a 27-23 victory in the game before 62,627 at Shea Stadium.

The Jets scored first on a 14-yard Namath-to-Maynard connection and made it 10-0 after one quarter on a 33-yard field goal by Jim Turner.

Now the Raiders stormed back, capping a thrust with a 29-yard pass from Lamonica to his favorite wide receiver, Fred Biletnikoff. After Turner countered with a 36-yard field goal, George Blanda, now 40, did the same for Oakland with a 26-yarder, and the

AFL 1968 CHAMPIONSHIP GAME

Shea Stadium, New York, December 29, 1968

SCORE BY PERIODS

Oakland Raiders.......	0	10	3	10 – 23
New York Jets..........	10	3	7	7 – 27

SCORING

New York—Maynard 14 pass from Namath (Turner kick)
New York—Field goal Turner 33
Oakland—Biletnikoff 29 pass from Lamonica (Blanda kick)
New York—Field goal Turner 36
Oakland—Field goal Blanda 26
Oakland—Field goal Blanda 9
New York—Lammons 20 pass from Namath (Turner kick)
Oakland—Field goal Blanda 20
Oakland—Banaszak 4 run (Blanda kick)
New York—Maynard 6 pass from Namath (Turner kick)

TEAM STATISTICS

	Oakland	New York
First downs.........................	18	25
Rushing yards	50	144
Passing yards.....................	401	266
Return yards, kicks	146	118
Passes	20-47-0	19-49-1
Punts.................................	7-42.7	10-41.5
Fumbles-Lost	2-0	1-1
Penalties-Yards..................	2-23	4-26

Attendance—62,627.

INDIVIDUAL STATISTICS

Rushing—New York, Snell 19-71, Boozer 11-51, Namath 1-14, Mathis 3-8; Oakland, Dixon 8-42, Banaszak 3-6, Lamonica 3-1, Smith 5-1.
Passing—New York, Namath 19-49-1—266; Oakland, Lamonica 20-47-0—401.
Receiving—New York, Sauer 7-70, Maynard 6-118, Lammons 4-52, Snell 1-15, Boozer 1-11; Oakland, Biletnikoff 7-190, Dixon 5-48, Cannon 4-69, Wells 3-83, Banaszak 1-11.
Kickoff Returns—New York, Christy 3-86, B. Turner 1-24; Oakland, Atkinson 4-112, Smith 1-17.
Punt Returns—New York, Baird 2-8, Christy 1-0; Oakland, Atkinson 2-11, Bird 2-6.
Interceptions—Oakland, Atkinson 1-32.
Punting—New York, Johnson 10-41.5; Oakland, Eischeid 7-42.7.

Jets held a slim 13-10 halftime lead.

When the second half began, Lamonica hit long bombs to Warren Wells and Biletnikoff, taking the Raiders to the Jets 6. From there, the going became increasingly more difficult, and on fourth down Blanda's nine-yard field goal tied the score at 13-13.

But the Jets countered. Namath took his team 80 yards, the final 20 of them consumed by a touchdown pass to tight end Pete Lammons, good for a 20-13 lead as the third period expired.

Oakland seemed about to tie the score, but deep in the Jets territory a drive fizzled and Blanda shaved the lead to 20-16 with a 20-yard field goal.

Then safety George Atkinson intercepted a Namath pass at the Jets 37, returned it 32 yards and two plays later, fullback Pete Banaszak scored from the 4 to put the Raiders ahead, 23-20.

It was up to Namath and Namath was up to it. He found Maynard for a 52-yard aerial gain to set up a six-yard go-ahead TD pass to Maynard.

But Oakland drove again, moving to the Jets 24. Then Lamonica attempted a swing pass to Charlie Smith. The ball fell harmlessly. But the officials ruled that it had been a lateral and thus was still in play, which was a nice thing for Jets linebacker Ralph Baker to hear, since he had covered the ball. That was a game-saver for the Jets.

NFL 1969

Minnesota Vikings 27
Cleveland Browns 7

Few teams like to play when the weather is bitterly cold. Those few, probably, are Green Bay and Minnesota.

As the Packers formerly stamped their dynasty on the NFL by winning all those frozen-field championships, so did the Minnesota Vikings less than a decade later.

And in 1969, the Vikings were the NFL's best. They were 12-2 behind a rough, tough, free-spirited quarterback named Joe Kapp, who didn't really throw the ball but launched it like he was shot putting. The Canadian League refugee, 6-2 and 215, had a style that seemed to be "knock me down, I love it."

Minnesota eased past Los Angeles, 23-20, for the Western Conference championship, and on January 4, 1970, entertained the

Viking Joe Kapp goes down, courtesy of Deacon Jones, in 1969 game.

Cleveland Browns, who had defeated Dallas, 38-14, to win the East.

The temperature was 8 degrees. A raging wind dropped the true degree level even further. Snow fell and piled up on the sidelines.

On the field, it turned out to be all Minnesota in a 27-7 victory as a home crowd of 46,503 delighted in the Vikings' first-ever NFL crown.

In the first quarter, Kapp scored on a seven-yard run, a busted play set in motion when he missed the handoff to his fullback, Bill Brown, and was forced to keep the ball and charge straight up the middle.

Less than four minutes later, Cleveland cornerback Erich Barnes slipped on the treacherous turf, allowing Kapp to complete a 75-yard pass to wide receiver Gene Washington for a 14-0 lead.

The game would never come back to the Browns. Minnesota, using a primeval running attack and violently effective defense, kept possession. The lead became 17-0 in the second quarter after a 30-yard field goal by Fred Cox, and then Dave Osborn broke off a 20-yard off-tackle slant to make it 24-0 at halftime.

When it was 27-0, on a 32-yard field goal by Cox, the Browns finally averted a shutout, scoring with just 1:24 remaining in the game on a three-yard pass from Bill Nelsen to Gary Collins.

Statistically, the victory was obvious. Minnesota had churned out 222 yards rushing to 97 for Cleveland.

This was the ninth year of the Minnesota franchise and the Vikings were the first "expansion" team to win the championship.

1969 NFL CHAMPIONSHIP GAME
Metropolitan Stadium, Bloomington, Minn., January 4, 1970.

SCORE BY PERIODS

Cleveland Browns.....	0	0	0	7 —	7
Minnesota Vikings	14	10	3	0 —	27

SCORING

Minnesota—Kapp 7 run (Cox kick)
Minnesota—Washington 75 pass from Kapp (Cox kick)
Minnesota—Field goal Cox 30
Minnesota—Osborn 20 run (Cox kick)
Minnesota—Field goal Cox 32
Cleveland—Collins 3 pass from Nelsen (Cockroft kick)

TEAM STATISTICS

	Cleveland	Minnesota
First downs	14	18
Rushing yards	97	222
Passing yards	181	169
Return yards, kicks	104	43
Passing	17-33-2	7-13-0
Punting	3-33.0	3-41.0
Fumbles-Lost	2-1	0-0
Penalties-Yards.................	1-5	3-33

Attendance—46,503.

INDIVIDUAL STATISTICS

Rushing—Minnesota, Osborn 18-108, Kapp 8-57, Brown 12-43, Reed 5-7, Jones 2-7; Cleveland, Kelly 15-80, Scott 6-17.

Passing—Minnesota, Kapp 7-13-0—169; Cleveland, Nelsen 17-33-2—181.

Receiving—Minnesota, Washington 3-120, Henderson 2-17, Brown 1-20, Beasley 1-12; Cleveland, Scott 5-56, Collins 5-43, Warfield 4-47, Kelly 2-17, Morin -18.

Kickoff Returns—Minnesota, West 1-22, Jones 1-20; Cleveland, Scott 4-60, Morrison 1-11.

Punt Returns—Minnesota, West 1-1; Cleveland, Kelly 2-10, Morrison 1-11.

Interceptions—Minnesota, Hilgenberg 1-0, Krause 1-0.

Punting—Minnesota, Lee 3-41.0; Cleveland, Cockroft 3-33.0.

AFL
1969

Kansas City Chiefs 17
Oakland Raiders 7

The AFL, in its final year of independent operation, had installed a crossover playoff system with its two division winners meeting the runners-up from opposite divisions.

The East champion New York Jets lost to the West runner-up Kansas City Chiefs, while the West champion Oakland Raiders beat Houston, second in the East.

The result was that the Western teams met in the AFL's final championship game played in Oakland on January 4, 1970, before a capacity crowd of 53,564. The Raiders had won both regular-season meetings against the Chiefs and were heavily favored.

It looked good when the Raiders scored in the first quarter, Charlie Smith going over from the 3-yard line.

AFL 1969 CHAMPIONSHIP GAME

**Oakland-Alameda County Coliseum,
Oakland, January 4, 1970**

SCORE BY PERIODS

Kansas City Chiefs ...	0	7	7	3 – 17
Oakland Raiders	7	0	0	0 – 7

SCORING

Oakland—Smith 3 run (Blanda kick)
Kansas City—Hayes 1 run (Stenerud kick)
Kansas City—Holmes 5 run (Stenerud kick)
Kansas City—Field goal Stenerud 22

TEAM STATISTICS

	Kansas City	Oakland
First downs	13	18
Rushing yards	86	79
Passing yards	129	191
Return yards, kicks	52	111
Passes	7-17-0	17-45-4
Punts	8-42.9	6-48.5
Fumbles-Lost	5-4	1-0
Penalties-Yards	5-43	5-45

Attendance—53,564.

INDIVIDUAL STATISTICS

Rushing—Oakland, Dixon 12-36, Smith 12-31, Banaszak 2-8, Todd 2-4; Kansas City, Hayes 8-35, Garrett 7-19, Holmes 18-14, McVea 3-13, Dawson 3-5.

Passing—Oakland, Lamonica 15-39-3–167, Blanda 2-6-1–24; Kansas City, Dawson 7-17-0–129.

Receiving—Oakland, Smith 8-86, Sherman 3-45, Cannon 2-22, Banaszak 2-13, Wells 1-24, Dixon 1-1; Kansas City, Taylor 3-62, Holmes 2-16, Pitts 1-41, Arbanas 1-10.

Kickoff Returns—Oakland, Atkinson 3-95, Sherman 1-17; Kansas City, Holmes 1-26, Hill 1-0, Hayes 0-17.

Punt Returns—Oakland, Atkinson 2-minus 1; Kansas City, Garrett 4-9.

Interceptions—Kansas City, Thomas 2-69, Marsalis 1-23, Kearney 1-17.

Punting—Oakland, Eischeid 6-48.5; Kansas City, Wilson 8-42.9.

But late in the second period, Chiefs quarterback Len Dawson began to solve the Oakland defense. He hit wide receiver Frank Pitts for 41 yards to the Raider 1, from where Wendell Hayes charged across to tie the game at halftime. Kansas City went on to post a 17-7 victory.

Early in the third quarter, Lamonica banged his passing hand against a Chiefs' helmet and had to leave. Old George Blanda replaced him, but was ineffective. After a Blanda pass had been intercepted in the end zone by Emmitt Thomas, who took it out to the Kansas City 6, Dawson moved the Chiefs 94 yards to crack open the game.

He did it in the air, throwing to wide receiver Otis Taylor and running back Robert Holmes. A pass interference call against the Raiders put the Chiefs on the Oakland 7.

It took three consecutive carries by Holmes, a fireplug at 5-9 and 220, before he scored from the 5, making the score 14-7.

Jan Stenerud kicked a 22-yard field goal in the fourth quarter, and the Chiefs' defense intercepted three more passes (they had a total of four) when Lamonica had to come back, each theft snuffing out a frantic Oakland bid to get back into the game.

With the game, the AFL in large measure was history.

NFC
1970

Dallas Cowboys 17
San Francisco 49ers 10

The Dallas Cowboys had a four-year record of two playoff defeats and two more NFL championship game losses. The San Francisco 49ers didn't have as much.

But it became a whale of a game when the clubs met for the NFC title in San Francisco January 3, 1971.

Dallas quarterback Craig Morton hit only seven of 22 passing attempts in windy Kezar Stadium. But one of his completions was a five-yard touchdown strike to fullback Walt Garrison. In all, Morton gained only 101 aerial yards.

Rookie running back Duane Thomas made much more by using his feet. He carried the ball 27 times for 143 yards and scored the other Cowboys TD on a 13-yard sweep as Dallas defeated the 49ers, 17-10.

This was the first year of conference playoffs involving three division winners and a wild-card team. Dallas eliminated the wild-card Detroit Lions by the strange score

tion an eight-play drive that climaxed with Morton's pass to Garrison.

Involved in that series was a crucial 26-yard pass interference call against safety Mel Phillips, who crashed Cowboys receiver Bob Hayes to the ground at the 49ers' 5.

The 49ers fought back, reducing the Dallas lead to 17-10 on a 26-yard pass from Brodie to receiver Dick Witcher.

1970 NFC CHAMPIONSHIP GAME

Kezar Stadium, San Francisco, January 3, 1971

SCORE BY PERIODS

Dallas Cowboys	0	3	14	0 – 17
San Francisco 49ers ..	3	0	7	0 – 10

SCORING

San Francisco—Field goal Gossett 16
Dallas—Field goal Clark 21
Dallas—Thomas 13 run (Clark kick)
Dallas—Garrison 5 pass from Morton (Clark kick)
San Francisco—Witcher 26 pass from Brodie (Gossett kick)

TEAM STATISTICS

	Dallas	San Fran.
First downs	22	15
Rushing yards	229	61
Passing yards	101	262
Return yards, kicks	54	94
Passes	7-22-0	19-40-2
Punts	6-40.2	5-41.0
Fumbles-Lost	4-1	1-0
Penalties-Yards	7-75	5-51

Attendance—59,364.

INDIVIDUAL STATISTICS

Rushing—San Francisco, Willard 13-42, Cunningham 5-14, Thomas 1-5; Dallas, Thomas 27-143, Garrison 17-71, Welch 5-27, Reeves 2-minus 12.

Passing—San Francisco, Brodie 19-40-2—262; Dallas, Morton 7-22-0—101.

Receiving—San Francisco, Washington 6-88, Cunningham 4-34, Windsor 3-70, Witcher 3-41, Willard 2-22, Kwalick 1-7; Dallas, Garrison 3-51, Thomas 2-24, Rucker 1-21, Ditka 1-5.

Kickoff Returns—San Francisco, Thomas 3-66, Tucker 1-23; Dallas, Washington 1-20, Waters 1-16, Kiner 1-10.

Punt Returns—San Francisco, B. Taylor 2-5; Dallas, Hayes 1-8, Reeves 1-0.

Interceptions—Dallas, Renfro 1-19, Jordan 1-4.

Punting—San Francisco, Spurrier 5-41.0; Dallas, Widby 6-40.2.

Duane Thomas' 143 yards and one touchdown helped Dallas past the 49ers and into the Super Bowl.

of 5-0 and San Francisco beat the Minnesota Vikings, 17-14, in first-round games.

The first half of the NFC title game amounted to an exchange of field goals, the 49ers drawing first blood on a 16-yarder by Bruce Gossett, then Dallas countering in the second quarter when Mike Clark chipped in a 21-yarder.

Into the second half they went, playing as evenly as the score, when Dallas' Doomsday Defense began to take charge.

John Brodie, the veteran 49ers quarterback, faded back from his 14 and looked over the middle. He was rushed, threw too quickly (and too high) and the ball was intercepted by middle linebacker Lee Roy Jordan at the 49ers' 13.

On the first play from scrimmage, Morton handed off to Thomas and got out of the way. Duane got a clearing block from guard Blaine Nye and was in the end zone, giving Dallas a 10-3 lead.

Now Brodie, trying to catch up too quickly, began to throw long and deep, and this time it was cornerback Mel Renfro who made a key interception, returning the ball from the Dallas 19 to the 38, setting in mo-

AFC
1970

Baltimore Colts 27
Oakland Raiders 17

Johnny Unitas was 37 years old, George Blanda was 43. Yet these two relics of the NFL, the league's two oldest active quarterbacks, hooked up once more in a dandy of a game, one that would send the survivor to the Super Bowl.

It wasn't Oakland's intention to start Blanda, who had played only briefly during the 8-4-2 season. But in the second quarter, Daryle Lamonica's thigh was injured on a tackle by defensive end Bubba Smith, forcing him to the sideline.

At that point, Baltimore held a 10-3 lead, built on a 16-yard Jim O'Brien field goal and a two-yard touchdown run by fullback Norm Bulaich, countered only by a Blanda field goal of 48 yards.

This was the first year of integrated scheduling. In the realignment, Baltimore, an NFL team, had been moved into the American Conference (with Cleveland and Pittsburgh) to join the 10 original AFL clubs in a 13-team conference.

So the Colts, the NFL's losing representative in Super Bowl II, now were attempting to make it back as an AFC team.

But first they had to contend with Cincinnati in the first round of the playoffs and

1970 AFC CHAMPIONSHIP GAME

Memorial Stadium, Baltimore, January 3, 1971

SCORE BY PERIODS

Oakland Raiders.......	0	3	7	7 – 17
Baltimore Colts	3	7	10	7 – 27

SCORING

Baltimore–Field goal O'Brien 16
Baltimore–Bulaich 2 run (O'Brien kick)
Oakland–Field goal Blanda 48
Oakland–Biletnikoff 38 pass from Blanda (Blanda kick)
Baltimore–Field goal O'Brien 23
Baltimore–Bulaich 11 run (O'Brien kick)
Oakland–Wells 15 pass from Blanda (Blanda kick)
Baltimore–Perkins 68 pass from Unitas (O'Brien kick)

TEAM STATISTICS

	Oakland	Baltimore
First downs........................	16	18
Rushing yards...................	107	126
Passing yards....................	277	245
Return yards, kicks	70	106
Passing.............................	18-36-3	11-30-0
Punting.............................	5-40.0	6-45.3
Fumbles-Lost	1-1	0-0
Penalties-Yards.................	2-20	2-10

Attendance–54,799.

INDIVIDUAL STATISTICS

Rushing–Baltimore, Bulaich 22-71, Nowatzke 8-32, Hill 5-12, Unitas 2-9, Havrilak 1-2; Oakland, Dixon 10-51, Smith 9-44, Hubbard 3-12.

Passing–Baltimore, Unitas 11-30-0–245; Oakland, Blanda 17-32-3–271, Lamonica 1-4-0–6.

Receiving–Baltimore, Hinton 5-115, Jefferson 3-36, Perkins 2-80, Mackey 1-14; Oakland, Wells 5-108, Biletnikoff 5-92, Dixon 3-15, Chester 2-36, Smith 2-21, Hubbard 1-5.

Kickoff Returns–Baltimore, Duncan 4-105; Oakland, Atkinson 3-37, Sherman 1-23.

Punt Returns–Baltimore, Gardin 2-1; Oakland, Atkinson 2-10.

Interceptions–Baltimore, Logan 1-16, May 1-0, Volk 1-0.

Punting–Baltimore, Lee 6-45.3; Oakland, Eischeid 5-40.0.

they shut out the Bengals, 17-0. The Raiders defeated the wild-card Miami Dolphins, 21-14. That set up the title game in Baltimore January 3, 1971.

After the Colts took their 10-3 lead, the Raiders tied the game early in the third quarter on a 38-yard pass from Blanda to wide receiver Fred Biletnikoff.

It was 10-10, but Unitas calmly directed a counteroffensive that reached the Raiders' 16, and O'Brien kicked a 23-yard field goal to give the Colts a 13-10 cushion.

Once again, Unitas rallied Baltimore, driving the Colts deep downfield, and saw that thrust cashed in when Bulaich slanted over on an 11-yard run. The Colts' lead was 20-10.

But Blanda wasn't finished. Early in the fourth quarter he moved the Raiders 80 yards, the final 15 on a pass to wide receiver Warren Wells. The score now was 20-17.

The tide appeared to have turned, as the Colts were forced to punt twice. Each time Blanda whipped the Raiders downfield, only to snuff rallies by throwing interceptions.

Finally, the Colts tried a trick play, using four wide receivers, and Unitas hit Ray Perkins with a 68-yard TD bomb for the final score.

NFC 1971

Dallas Cowboys   14
San Francisco 49ers   3

George Andrie, the Dallas Cowboys' 6-7, 250-pound defensive end, was just doing his job, watching for running backs trying to slip out around end.

"I smelled a rat," Andrie said, "so I stayed put."

What he sniffed out was a screen pass, John Brodie aiming for fullback Ken Willard. Andrie picked off the ball at the 49ers' 8-yard line, chugged and lumbered to the 1, and on the next play halfback Calvin Hill scored.

This occurred in the second quarter of a scoreless game and gave the Cowboys a 7-0 lead. The half ended with the score 7-3, the 49ers scoring on a 28-yard Bruce Gossett field goal.

In the fourth quarter, the Cowboys drove 80 yards for the insurance points in their 14-3 victory. Quarterback Roger Staubach four times converted third-down situations into first downs and Duane Thomas finally

The Dallas defense kept quarterback John Brodie and the 49ers bottled up throughout the 1971 title game.

scooted in from the 2-yard line.

The 14-3 lead stood up as Dallas' third interception of the day killed the 49ers' last hope. For the game, the Cowboys surrendered only 61 yards rushing and nine first downs.

Dallas had advanced to the title game by beating the Vikings, 20-12, in a Minnesota snowstorm. San Francisco had eliminated the wild-card Washington Redskins, 24-20.

The fact that Dallas found it so difficult to get past the 49ers centered, interestingly enough, on a unique teacher-student relationship between head coaches, the Cowboys' Tom Landry and the 49ers' Dick Nolan.

Landry, the creator of the flex defense, taught it to Nolan when he was an aide on the Dallas staff. Upon taking the San Francisco job, Nolan became the only other coach in the league to use the alignment.

"Tom knew what we were doing," Nolan once said, "but I think I saw a few new wrinkles he never taught me."

1971 NFC CHAMPIONSHIP GAME

Texas Stadium, Irving, Tex., January 2, 1972

SCORE BY PERIODS

San Francisco 49ers..	0	0	3	0 –	3
Dallas Cowboys	0	7	0	7 –	14

SCORING

Dallas—Hill 1 run (Clark kick)
San Francisco—Field goal Gossett 28
Dallas—Thomas 2 run (Clark kick)

TEAM STATISTICS

	San Fran.	Dallas
First downs	9	16
Rushing yards	61	172
Passing yards...................	184	103
Return yards, kicks	66	23
Passes	14-30-3	9-18-0
Punts	6-38.2	6-45.0
Fumbles-Lost	0-0	2-1
Penalties-Yards...............	1-12	2-30

Attendance—63,409.

INDIVIDUAL STATISTICS

Rushing—Dallas, Staubach 8-55, Garrison 14-52, D. Thomas 15-44, Hill 9-21; San Francisco, V. Washington 10-58, Willard 6-3.

Passing—Dallas, Staubach 9-18-0—103; San Francisco, Brodie 14-30-3—184.

Receiving—Dallas, Truax 2-43, Hayes 2-22, Alworth 1-17, Reeves 1-17, D. Thomas 1-7, Ditka 1-5, Garrison 1-minus 8; San Francisco, G. Washington 4-88, Kwalick 4-52, V. Washington 3-28, Willard 1-6, Witcher 1-6, Cunningham 1-4.

Kickoff Returns—Dallas, Harris 1-19; San Francisco, V. Washington 2-35, Cunningham 1-21.

Punt Returns—Dallas, Hayes 1-3, Harris 1-1; San Francisco, Fuller 2-10, Taylor 1-0.

Interceptions—Dallas, Jordan 1-23, Andrie 1-7, Harris 1-2.

Punting—Dallas, Widby 6-45.0; San Francisco, Spurrier 6-38.2.

AFC
1971

Miami Dolphins 21
Baltimore Colts 0

Don Shula, the Dolphins' head coach, had been the Colts' head man in 1969, before leaving for Miami and precipitating a protest that resulted in Baltimore receiving the Dolphins' No. 1 draft choice for 1970 as compensation.

There was bad blood between Shula and Colts Owner Carroll Rosenbloom, and more than a few of the Colts had accused Shula of deserting them callously.

Miami, one of the newer expansion teams, had won its first Eastern Division title with a 10-3-1 record, just one-half game better than Baltimore's 10-4. But the Colts entered the playoffs as a wild-card team and beat Cleveland in the first round, 20-3.

Miami had a tougher time in its first round, going into double overtime before

1971 AFC CHAMPIONSHIP GAME

Orange Bowl, Miami, January 2, 1972

SCORE BY PERIODS

Baltimore Colts	0	0	0	0 – 0
Miami Dolphins	7	0	7	7 – 21

SCORING

Miami—Warfield 75 pass from Griese (Yepremian kick)
Miami—Anderson 62 interception return (Yepremian kick)
Miami—Csonka 5 run (Yepremian kick)

TEAM STATISTICS

	Baltimore	Miami
First downs	16	13
Rushing yards	93	144
Passing yards	224	158
Return yards, kicks	78	42
Passes	20-36-3	4-8-1
Punts	3-45.3	6-42.7
Fumbles-Lost	1-0	0-0
Penalties-Yards	2-20	1-12

Attendance—76,622.

INDIVIDUAL STATISTICS

Rushing—Miami, Kiick 18-66, Csonka 15-63, Griese 1-12, Morris 1-3; Baltimore, McCauley 15-50, Nottingham 11-33, Nowatzke 2-5, Unitas 1-5.

Passing—Miami, Griese 4-8-1—158; Baltimore, Unitas 20-36-3—224.

Receiving—Miami, Warfield 2-125, Twilley 2-33; Baltimore, Hinton 6-98, Nottingham 4-26, Perkins 3-19, Havrilak 2-31, McCauley 2-24, Mitchell 1-14, Mackey 1-6, Matte 1-6.

Kickoff Returns—Miami, Morris 1-22; Baltimore, Pittman 2-58.

Punt Returns—Miami, Scott 2-20; Baltimore, Volk 5-20.

Interceptions—Miami, Anderson 1-62, Kolen 1-11, Scott 1-0; Baltimore, Logan 1-0.

Punting—Miami, Seiple 6-42.7; Baltimore, Lee 3-45.3.

edging Kansas City, 27-24.

In the title game, the Colts were fresh and had the incentive of revenge on their side. But it didn't matter. In the first quarter, a bomb from quarterback Bob Griese to wide receiver Paul Warfield covered 75 yards and gave Miami a 7-0 lead.

The Dolphins' famed "No Name Defense," meanwhile, stifled the Colts and that was the only score at halftime.

In the third quarter, Colts quarterback Johnny Unitas decided to abandon a nonproductive running game and strike quickly. But when he threw deep for wide receiver Eddie Hinton, the ball was intercepted by Dolphins safety Dick Anderson, who returned it 62 yards for a TD and a 14-0 bulge.

With a huge crowd of 76,622 cheering on the Dolphins in the game at Miami January 2, 1972, a long drive which bridged the third and fourth quarters struck paydirt when fullback Larry Csonka crashed over from five yards out, enabling Miami to reach its 21-0 lead and assuring the defeat of the Colts.

The drive had been ignited by a 50-yard pass completion to Warfield, only his second catch of the game. But the two receptions accounted for 125 yards.

NFC
1972

Washington Redskins 26
Dallas Cowboys 3

The rivalry simmered and finally boiled over, enveloping both teams and both cities in a scalding fever.

The Washington Redskins had won the NFC's Eastern Division title with an 11-3 record; the Dallas Cowboys were a game behind, at 10-4, but qualified for the playoffs as a wild-card.

In the first round of the playoffs, Dallas rallied for 17 points in the final period on the passing of Roger Staubach to edge the San Francisco 49ers, 30-28, and Washington wiped out the Green Bay Packers, 16-3. So now, in their third meeting of the year, a Super Bowl trip was on the line as the Redskins and Cowboys squared off December 31, 1972, at RFK Stadium in Washington.

The Redskins played with intensity and humbled the defending Super Bowl champions, 26-3. Washington won its first league crown in 30 years on the strength of a rugged defense, a powerful inside running

Redskins quarterback Billy Kilmer threw for a pair of touchdowns in a 1972 victory over Dallas.

game and a busted-up, broken-down quarterback named Billy Kilmer.

It was 10-3 at halftime, still anybody's game, and the one obvious factor was that Dallas was coming on. The Redskins had shot out to a 10-0 lead on an 18-yard Curt Knight field goal and a 15-yard pass from Kilmer to wide receiver Charley Taylor, who caught seven passes that day for 146

yards and two touchdowns.

The 10-3 lead might have been reduced to 10-7, but at the conclusion of a long Cowboys drive, halfback Calvin Hill overthrew fullback Walt Garrison on an option pass when Garrison was standing clear and open in the Redskins' end zone.

In the third quarter, the Washington defense clamped down, and the offense got another break when Dallas defensive back Charlie Waters suffered a broken arm. Little-used Mark Washington came in to replace him and the Redskins took advantage with a 45-yard TD pass to Taylor that virtually locked it up, making it 17-3. Knight spent the rest of the half kicking long field goals, adding nine points on boots of 46, 45 and 39 yards.

The "Over The Hill Gang" had finally reached the top of the mountain, and on a misty, clammy New Year's Eve, the fervent hometown fans had more reason than ever to celebrate.

NFC 1972 CHAMPIONSHIP GAME

Robert F. Kennedy Stadium, Washington, December 31, 1972

SCORE BY PERIODS

Dallas Cowboys	0	3	0	0 — 3
Washington Redskins	0	10	0	16 — 26

SCORING

Washington—Field goal Knight 18
Washington—Taylor 15 pass from Kilmer (Knight kick)
Dallas—Field goal Fritsch 35
Washington—Taylor 45 pass from Kilmer (Knight kick)
Washington—Field goal Knight 39
Washington—Field goal Knight 46
Washington—Field goal Knight 45

TEAM STATISTICS

	Dallas	Washington
First downs......................	8	16
Rushing yards	96	122
Passing yards...................	98	194
Return yards, kick.............	49	10
Passes	9-21-0	14-18-0
Punts...............................	7-43.1	4-36.0
Fumbles-Lost	1-1	2-1
Penalties-Yards................	4-30	4-38

Attendance—53,129.

INDIVIDUAL STATISTICS

Rushing—Washington, Brown 30-88, Harraway 11-19, Kilmer 3-15; Dallas, Staubach 5-59, Hill 9-22, Garrison 7-15.

Passing—Washington, Kilmer 14-18-0—194; Dallas, Staubach 9-20-0—98, Hill 0-1-0—0.

Receiving—Washington, Taylor 7-146, Harraway 3-13, Jefferson 2-19, Brown 2-16; Dallas, Sellers 2-29, Garrison 2-18, Hill 2-11, Parks 1-21, Alworth 1-15, Ditka 1-4.

Kickoff Returns—Dallas, Harris 2-29, Newhouse 1-25.

Punt Returns—Washington, Haymond 4-10; Dallas, Waters 3-minus 5.

Punting—Washington, Bragg 4-36.0; Dallas, Bateman 7-43.1.

AFC
1972

Miami Dolphins 21
Pittsburgh Steelers 17

This was the perfect season. Miami had gone through the regular schedule with a 14-0 record, allowing only 171 points, an average of just 12 a game.

The first-round playoff game had been a 20-14 victory over the wild-card Cleveland Browns for win No. 15.

And now, poised to repeat as the AFC's Super Bowl representative, Miami had to get past a rock-ribbed Pittsburgh team. The Steelers had earned this spot on a miracle play against Oakland in the first round, a last-second pass that had ricocheted off Raiders safety Jack Tatum into the arms of

1972 AFC CHAMPIONSHIP GAME

Three Rivers Stadium, Pittsburgh, Dec. 31, 1972

SCORE BY PERIODS

Miami Dolphins........	0	7	7	7 – 21
Pittsburgh Steelers...	7	0	3	7 – 17

SCORING

Pittsburgh—Mullins fumble recovery in end zone (Gerela kick)
Miami—Csonka 9 pass from Morrall (Yepremian kick)
Pittsburgh—Field goal Gerela 14
Miami—Kiick 2 run (Yepremian kick)
Miami—Kiick 3 run (Yepremian kick)
Pittsburgh—Young 12 pass from Bradshaw (Gerela kick)

TEAM STATISTICS

	Miami	Pittsburgh
First downs......................	19	13
Rushing yards	193	128
Passing yards....................	121	137
Return yards, kicks	23	90
Passes	10-16-1	10-20-2
Punts	4-35.5	4-51.3
Fumbles-Lost	0-0	2-0
Penalties-Yards.................	2-19	4-30

Attendance—50,845.

INDIVIDUAL STATISTICS

Rushing—Pittsburgh, Harris 16-76, Fuqua 8-47, Bradshaw 2-5; Miami, Morris 16-76, Csonka 24-68, Seiple 1-37, Kiick 8-12.

Passing—Pittsburgh, Bradshaw 5-10-2–80, Hanratty 5-10-0–57; Miami, Morrall 7-11-1–51, Griese 3-5-0–70.

Receiving—Pittsburgh, Young 4-54, Shanklin 2-49, Harris 2-3, McMakin 1-22, Brown 1-9; Miami, Fleming 5-50, Warfield 2-63, Csonka 1-9, Mandich 1-5, Morris 1-minus 6.

Kickoff Returns—Pittsburgh, P. Pearson 2-63, S. Davis 1-22; Miami, Morris 1-23.

Punt Returns—Pittsburgh, Edwards 1-5.

Interceptions—Pittsburgh, Edwards 1-28; Miami, Buoniconti 106, Kolen 1-5.

Punting—Pittsburgh, Walden 4-51.3; Miami, Seiple 4-35.5.

fullback Franco Harris, who took it in to complete a 60-yard TD play and give Pittsburgh a 13-7 victory.

But the Pittsburgh magic faded in the face of the Miami miracle in the title game at Pittsburgh December 31, 1972, although the Steelers scored first when offensive lineman Gerry Mullins recovered a Terry Bradshaw fumble in the Miami end zone early in the first quarter.

Miami tied it in the second period, after punter Larry Seiple ran on a fake punt and gained 37 yards to the Pittsburgh 12. Two plays later Earl Morrall, filling in for the injured Bob Griese, struck with a nine-yard pass to fullback Larry Csonka.

The Steelers held a brief lead after a 14-yard Roy Gerela field goal in the third quarter, but Griese came in for his first action since October (when he suffered a broken leg), and hit on a 52-yard pass to Paul Warfield to keep a drive alive.

Shortly thereafter, halfback Jim Kiick carried it in from the 2 and he added another TD run of three yards in the fourth quarter to build the Miami lead to 21-10.

Bradshaw, the Steeler quarterback who had been knocked out in the first quarter, when his fumble became a Pittsburgh touchdown, returned in the final seven minutes of the game.

He pulled the Steelers closer with a drive leading to a 12-yard TD pass to wide receiver Al Young, but 21-17 was as close as he would get. He threw two interceptions, to linebackers Nick Buoniconti and Mike Kolen, and Miami kept its perfect season alive.

NFC
1973

Minnesota Vikings 27
Dallas Cowboys 10

The Minnesota Vikings' game was ball control, with running backs Chuck Foreman and Oscar Reed combining for 37 carries and quarterback Fran Tarkenton throwing short, high-percentage passes.

Dallas was hurt by the absence of star defensive tackle Bob Lilly and running back Calvin Hill, both sidelined by injuries. As a result, the Vikings dominated the statistics, outgaining the Cowboys in total yardage, 306 to 153, and won the championship, 27-10, before 64,422 at Irving, Tex., December 30, 1973.

Fred Cox put the Vikings on the board in

Minnesota's Carl Eller wraps up Dallas quarterback Roger Staubach during the 1973 championship game.

the first quarter with a 44-yard field goal. In the second period, an 86-yard drive culminated in a five-yard Foreman run and a 10-0 lead.

The half ended that way, but suddenly the Cowboys struck when Golden Richards returned a Mike Eischeid punt 63 yards for a touchdown, paring the Vikings' lead to 10-7.

It was time for Dallas to turn the game around, and Tarkenton knew it. He also realized that something different was needed and so, after faking a handoff to Foreman, he suddenly straightened up and threw a 54-yard strike to wide receiver John Gilliam, good for a demoralizing touchdown.

Toni Fritsch cut Dallas' deficit to 17-10 when he converted a 17-yard field goal with a few minutes left in the third quarter, but then the Minnesota defense took charge.

First, cornerback Bobby Bryant picked off a Roger Staubach pass on the Vikings' 37 and sped 63 yards for a touchdown that produced a 24-10 lead.

Then Jeff Wright picked off a Staubach pass, setting up a brief Minnesota march that led to a 34-yard Cox field goal for the final points.

Capping the futility of the day for Dallas, fullback Walt Garrison fumbled the ball away at the Vikings' 2-yard line in the final minutes.

Minnesota had marched into the NFC championship game as Tarkenton threw two TD passes to Gilliam in a 27-20 victory over the wild-card Washington Redskins. Staubach rifled two scoring passes to Drew Pearson as Dallas eliminated the Los Angeles Rams, 27-16.

1973 NFC CHAMPIONSHIP GAME

Texas Stadium, Irving, Tex., December 30, 1973

SCORE BY PERIODS

Minnesota Vikings	3	7	7	10	– 27
Dallas Cowboys	0	0	10	0	– 10

SCORING

Minnesota—Field goal Cox 44
Minnesota—Foreman 5 run (Cox kick)
Dallas—Richards 63 punt return (Fritsch kick)
Minnesota—Gilliam 54 pass from Tarkenton (Cox kick)
Dallas—Field goal Fritsch 17
Minnesota—Bryant 63 interception return (Cox kick)
Minnesota—Field goal Cox 34

TEAM STATISTICS

	Minnesota	Dallas
First downs	20	9
Rushing yards	203	80
Passing yards....................	133	89
Return yards, kicks	66	135
Passes	10-21-1	10-21-4
Punts	3-43.3	4-39.5
Fumbles-Lost	4-3	2-2
Penalties-Yards.................	3-33	2-20

Attendance—64,422.

INDIVIDUAL STATISTICS

Rushing—Dallas, Newhouse, 14-40, Staubach 5-30, Garrison 5-9, Fugett 1-1; Minnesota, Foreman 19-76, Reed 18-75, Osborn 4-27, Tarkenton 4-16, Brown 2-19.

Passing—Dallas, Staubach 10-21-4—89; Minnesota, Tarkenton 10-21-1—133.

Receiving—Dallas, Hayes 2-25, Pearson 2-24, Montgomery 2-15, DuPree 1-20, Garrison 1-10, Fugett 1-minus 1, Newhouse 1-minus 4; Minnesota, Foreman 4-28, Gilliam 2-63, Voigt 2-23, Lash 1-11, Reed 1-8.

Kickoff Returns—Dallas, Harris 2-54, Waters 1-18; Minnesota, West 2-45, Gilliam 1-21.

Punt Returns—Dallas, Richards 1-63; Minnesota, Bryant 1-0.

Interceptions—Dallas, Waters 1-1; Minnesota, Bryant 2-63, J. Wright 1-13, Siemon 1-0.

Punting—Dallas, Bateman 4-39.5; Minnesota, Eischeid 3-43.3.

AFC 1973

Miami Dolphins 27
Oakland Raiders 10

The Miami Dolphins returned. They weren't perfect this time, but they were 12-2, bringing their two-season record to 26-2.

They won their first-round game easily, beating the Cincinnati Bengals, 34-16, and now they were ready to clinch their third consecutive Super Bowl appearance.

All they had to do was defeat the Oakland Raiders, a team fresh from the emotional charge of a 33-14 victory over Pittsburgh in the first round of the playoffs.

Both sides lived and died with ball control. Oakland had used it to grind down the Steelers. Miami had used it to drub the Bengals.

AFC 1973 CHAMPIONSHIP GAME

Orange Bowl, Miami, December 30, 1973

SCORE BY PERIODS

Oakland Raiders.......	0	0	10	0 – 10
Miami Dolphins	7	7	3	10 – 27

SCORING

Miami–Csonka 11 run (Yepremian kick)
Miami–Csonka 2 run (Yepremian kick)
Oakland–Field goal Blanda 21
Miami–Field goal Yepremian 42
Oakland–Siani 25 pass from Stabler (Blanda kick)
Miami–Field goal Yepremian 26
Miami–Csonka 2 run (Yepremian kick)

TEAM STATISTICS

	Oakland	Miami
First downs	15	21
Rushing yards	107	266
Passing yards	129	34
Return yards, kicks	89	100
Passes	15-23-1	3-6-1
Punts	2-51.0	1-39.0
Fumbles-Lost	1-0	1-0
Penalties-Yards.................	3-35	3-26

Attendance–79,325.

INDIVIDUAL STATISTICS

Rushing–Miami, Csonka 29-117, Morris 14-86, Griese 3-39, Kiick 6-12, Nottingham 1-12; Oakland, Hubbard 10-54, C. Smith 10-35, C. Davis 4-15, Banaszak 2-3.

Passing–Miami, Griese 3-6-1–34; Oakland, Stabler 15-23-1–129.

Receiving–Miami, Warfield 1-27, Briscoe 1-6, Kiick 1-1; Oakland, C. Smith 5-43, Siani 3-45, Biletnikoff 2-15, Hubbard 2-11, Moore 2-9, C. Davis 1-6.

Kickoff Returns–Miami, Leigh 1-52, Morris 1-19, Nottingham 1-19; Oakland, C. Davis 3-68, C. Smith 1-21.

Punt Returns–Miami, Scott 2-10; Oakland, Atkinson 1-0.

Interceptions–Miami, Matheson 1-29; Oakland, W. Brown 1-0.

Punting–Miami, Seiple 1-39.0; Oakland, Guy 2-51.0.

Mercury Morris supported leading rusher Larry Csonka with 86 yards in Miami's 1973 win over Oakland.

But Miami was the one able to do it again, beating the Raiders, 27-10, on the strength of Larry Csonka, the fullback, and Mercury Morris and Jim Kiick, the interchangable halfbacks, in the championship game December 30, 1973, in Miami.

It was a big day for Csonka, who gained 117 yards in 29 carries and scored Miami's first two touchdowns. His runs of 11 yards in the first quarter and two yards in the second was all the scoring in the first half as Miami sped to a 14-0 lead.

But now Oakland made it a game, getting 10 points in the third quarter on a 21-yard field goal by George Blanda and a 25-yard pass from Ken Stabler to wide receiver

Mike Siani.

The Raiders' defense, meanwhile, held the Dolphins to a 42-yard field goal by Garo Yepremian, giving Miami a 17-10 lead entering the fourth quarter.

But champions are made in the fourth quarter of pressure games, and Miami was one of the game's greatest champions.

Yepremian converted a 26-yard field goal to give the Dolphins a 20-10 lead and then came the game's most dramatic play.

Oakland was moving. It came up to fourth down, inches to go with no choice but to go for it.

But the Dolphin defense held. Miami took over and Csonka and company ground out a classic ball-control drive that resulted in Csonka's third TD of the day, a two-yard run.

Csonka had scored all the Miami touchdowns and had gained more ground yardage than all the Raiders' running backs together.

NFC 1974

Minnesota Vikings 14
Los Angeles Rams 10

The game was in the third quarter. The Los Angeles Rams, trailing 7-3, finally appeared to have broken the heart of a valiant Minnesota defense.

It was second down, the ball inches from the Vikings' goal line. With running backs Lawrence McCutcheon and John Cappelletti and quarterback James Harris, all of them 200 pounds or more, the Rams' fortunes looked good.

But then All-Pro guard Tom Mack moved, just a fraction of a second before the snap, drawing Vikings defensive tackle Alan Page offside.

The resulting five-yard penalty put the ball back on the Vikings' 5-yard line, and Harris ran a bootleg for three. A third-down pass for tight end Pat Curran was deflected by cornerback Jackie Wallace into the arms of linebacker Wally Hilgenberg in the end zone for a touchback.

The interception was the key play as the Vikings defeated the Rams, 14-10, at Bloomington, Minn., December 29, 1974.

Having foiled the Rams' threat, the Vikings wrapped it up with a time-consuming drive that ate up almost eight minutes of the fourth quarter and resulted in a Dave Osborn TD plunge from less than a yard

away.

The Rams weren't finished, but now they had to fight the clock as well as the Vikings' defense. Harris went for all the numbers right away and clicked when wide receiver Harold Jackson split two defenders, Nate and Jeff Wright, for a 44-yard TD.

That cut the Vikings' lead to 14-10 and with 7:15 remaining, the Rams got the ball only once more, on the Minnesota 45. But the Vikings' defense rose up a final time. A sack, good for 17 yards, set Harris back on his own 28 on a third-down play. The Rams had to punt and the Vikings held on to run out the clock, putting themselves in another Super Bowl.

Minnesota used two Fran Tarkenton-to-John Gilliam TD passes and Nate Wright's 20-yard fumble return for a score to down the St. Louis Cardinals, 30-14, in the first round of the playoffs. A 59-yard interception return by linebacker Isiah Robertson provided the clinching TD as Los Angeles beat the wild-card Washington Redskins, 19-10.

NFC 1974 CHAMPIONSHIP GAME

Metropolitan Stadium, Bloomington, Minn., December 29, 1974

SCORE BY PERIODS

Los Angeles Rams....	0	3	0	7	– 10
Minnesota Vikings....	0	7	0	7	– 14

SCORING

Minnesota—Lash 29 pass from Tarkenton (Cox kick)
Los Angeles—Field goal Ray 27
Minnesota—Osborn 1 run (Cox kick)
Los Angeles—Jackson 44 pass from Harris (Ray kick)

TEAM STATISTICS

	Los Angeles	Minnesota
First downs	15	18
Rushing yards	121	164
Passing yards	248	123
Return yards, kicks	76	101
Passes	13-23-2	10-20-1
Punts	5-43.8	6-39.2
Fumbles-Lost	3-3	5-2
Penalties-Yards	7-70	2-20

Attendance—48,444.

INDIVIDUAL STATISTICS

Rushing—Los Angeles, Bertelsen 14-65, McCutcheon 12-32, Harris 3-17, Cappelletti 3-8, Baker 1-minus 1; Minnesota, Foreman 22-80, Osborn 20-76, Tarkenton 4-5, Marinaro 1-3.

Passing—Los Angeles, Harris 13-23-2-248; Minnesota, Tarkenton 10-20-1-123.

Receiving—Los Angeles, Bertelsen 5-53, Jackson 3-139, McCutcheon 2-22, Snow 1-19, Klein 1-10, Cappelletti 1-5; Minnesota, Voigt 4-43, Lash 2-40, Gilliam 2-33, Marinaro 1-6, Osborn 1-1.

Kickoff Returns—Los Angeles, Bryant 3-57; Minnesota, McClanahan 2-55, McCullum 1-23.

Punt Returns—Los Angeles, Bryant 3-18, Scribner 1-1, Bertelsen 1-0; Minnesota, McCullum 3-20, N. Wright 1-3.

Interceptions—Los Angeles, Stukes 1-0; Minnesota, Poltl 1-16, Hilgenberg 1-0.

Punting—Los Angeles, Burke 5-43.8; Minnesota, Eischeid 6-39.2.

Steelers running back Franco Harris accounted for 111 yards in Pittsburgh's 1974 win over Oakland.

AFC
1974

Pittsburgh Steelers 24
Oakland Raiders 13

The Pittsburgh Steelers had been in the NFL for 42 years. Finally, they produced their first conference title.

The game was played in Oakland December 29, 1974, and the Raiders were a slight favorite. But once Terry Bradshaw came in at quarterback for Pittsburgh in the second half (he had warmed the bench the first two quarters), Oakland was blown away.

Bradshaw guided the Steelers to a 21-point fourth quarter, throwing one touchdown pass (six yards to wide receiver Lynn Swann) and directing two other ball-control marches that resulted in touchdown runs by fullback Franco Harris of eight yards (the TD that tied the game at 10-10) and 21

yards (the one that provided all the insurance the Steelers needed).

The Steelers defeated Buffalo, 32-14, in the first round of the playoffs, while the Raiders edged Miami, 28-26, on a last-second pass from Ken Stabler to Clarence Davis.

For the first three periods, the championship game was a ferocious defensive struggle and the Raiders held a slim 10-3 lead.

Oakland scored in the first period on a 40-yard field goal by George Blanda and that was matched by Pittsburgh's Roy Gerela, who was accurate from 23 yards in the second quarter.

When Oakland managed to score a touchdown in the third quarter on a 38-yard pass from Stabler to Cliff Branch, it seemed almost certain the 10-3 lead would stand up.

But only six seconds into the final period, Harris' eight-yard TD tied it. An interception by linebacker Jack Ham set in motion Pittsburgh's drive to the go-ahead touchdown. Ham returned the ball to the Oakland

1974 AFC Championship Game
Oakland-Alameda County Coliseum, Oakland, December 29, 1974

SCORE BY PERIODS

Pittsburgh Steelers...	0	3	0	21	— 24
Oakland Raiders.......	3	0	7	3	— 13

SCORING

Oakland—Field goal Blanda 40
Pittsburgh—Field goal Gerela 23
Oakland—Branch 38 pass from Stabler (Blanda kick)
Pittsburgh—Harris 8 run (Gerela kick)
Pittsburgh—Swann 6 pass from Bradshaw (Gerela kick)
Oakland—Field goal Blanda 24
Pittsburgh—Harris 21 run (Gerela kick)

TEAM STATISTICS

	Pittsburgh	Oakland
First downs	20	15
Rushing yards	210	29
Passing yards...................	95	271
Return yards, kicks	149	105
Passes	8-17-1	19-39-3
Punts...............................	4.41.0	5-43.4
Fumbles-Lost	3-2	0-0
Penalties—Yards	4-30	5-60

Attendance—53,800.

INDIVIDUAL STATISTICS

Rushing—Pittsburgh, Harris 29-111, Bleier 18-98, Bradshaw 4-1; Oakland, Davis 10-16, Banaszak 3-7, Hubbard 7-6, Stabler 1-0.

Passing—Pittsburgh, Bradshaw 8-17-1—95; Oakland, Stabler 19-36-3—271.

Receiving—Pittsburgh, Brown 2-37, Bleier 2-25, Swann 2-17, Stallworth 2-16; Oakland, Branch 9-186, Moore 4-32, Biletnikoff 3-45, Davis 2-8, Banaszak 1-0.

Kickoff Returns—Pittsburgh, S. Davis 3-76, Pearson 1-28; Oakland, Hart 3-63, R. Smith 2-42.

Punt Returns—Pittsburgh, Swann 3-30, Edwards 1-15.

Interceptions—Pittsburgh, Ham 2-19, Thomas 1-37; Oakland, Wilson 1-37.

Punting—Pittsburgh, Walden 4-41.0; Oakland, Guy 5-43.4.

nine, from where a holding call on corner-back Skip Thomas gave Pittsburgh a first down on the 4.

Rocky Bleier got nothing and Harris lost two before Bradshaw found Swann, running a right-to-left slant pattern, and it was 17-10 for the Steelers.

The Steelers' defense put pressure on Stabler, forcing him to pass on the run, and the best the Raiders could do was retaliate with a 24-yard field goal by Blanda. But the Steelers made it 24-13, when Harris scored his last TD of the game, running it in from the 21.

The rest was history, and no one was happier than Art Rooney, the venerable Pittsburgh owner who surely waited well beyond reasonable expectations.

NFC 1975

Dallas Cowboys   37
Los Angeles Rams   7

The Dallas Cowboys turned up their wild card in the final winner-take-all game and it was an ace.

The Cowboys, who had finished second to St. Louis in the NFC East, had qualified as a playoff team with a 10-4 record.

They beat the Vikings in Minnesota, 17-14, on Roger Staubach's 50-yard "Hail Mary!" pass to Drew Pearson in the final seconds, and the Los Angeles Rams downed the Cardinals, 35-23, scoring on interception returns of 47 yards by Jack Youngblood and 65 yards by Bill Simpson.

The NFC championship game was January 4, 1976, in the Los Angeles Coliseum. Only it wasn't a game—it was a rout. The Cowboys rode roughshod over the Rams, 37-7.

"I never realized how satisfying a win could be," said Cowboys guard John Niland. "When I looked up at the scoreboard and we were ahead, 34-0, I figured it was okay to count on it."

The Rams had surrendered only 135 points in 14 games and compiled a record of 21-2 at home.

But this was to be just another disappointment for the Rams, who tripped on the threshold of the Super Bowl again.

The game, played before 88,919 fans, began with a Rams' error. On the first Los Angeles play, a pass by James Harris was intercepted by linebacker D. D. Lewis, who

returned it 12 yards to the L.A. 18. On the next play, Staubach fed Preston Pearson with a screen pass. It went for a touchdown and a lightning-quick 7-0 lead.

It was all downhill from there. Staubach hit Golden Richards with a four-yard TD pass and Preston Pearson again for a 15-yard score in the second quarter, bringing the halftime score to 21-0.

In the third quarter, Staubach found Preston Pearson again, this time with a 19-yard pass. For the game, the running back caught seven passes for 123 yards and three TDs, and this latest one made it 28-0.

Toni Fritsch kicked field goals of 40 and 26 yards, bringing the score to 34-0. Another Fritsch field goal and a meaningless one-yard run by the Rams' John Cappelletti finished up the scoring.

NFC 1975 CHAMPIONSHIP GAME

Memorial Coliseum, Los Angeles, Jan. 4, 1976

SCORE BY PERIODS

Dallas Cowboys	7	14	13	3 – 37
Los Angeles Rams	0	0	0	7 – 7

SCORING

Dallas—P. Pearson 18 pass from Staubach (Fritsch kick)
Dallas—Richards 4 pass from Staubach (Fritsch kick)
Dallas—P. Pearson 15 pass from Staubach (Fritsch kick)
Dallas—P. Pearson 19 pass from Staubach (Fritsch kick)
Dallas—Field goal Fritsch 40
Dallas—Field goal Fritsch 26
Los Angeles—Cappelletti 1 run (Dempsey kick)
Dallas—Field goal Fritsch 26

TEAM STATISTICS

	Dallas	Los Angeles
First downs	24	9
Rushing yards	195	22
Passing yards	246	96
Return yards	68	40
Passes	18-28-1	11-24-3
Punts	4-34.8	7-35.4
Fumbles-Lost	1-0	1-0
Penalties-Yards	5-59	4-25

Attendance—88,919.

INDIVIDUAL STATISTICS

Rushing—Dallas, Newhouse 16-64, Staubach 7-54, Dennison 13-35, P. Pearson 7-20, Young 6-17, Fugett 1-5; Los Angeles, Jaworski 2-12, McCutcheon 11-10, Cappelletti 1-1, Scribner 1-1, Bryant 1-minus 2.

Passing—Dallas, Staubach 16-26-1–200, Longley 2-2-0–26; Los Angeles, Jaworski 11-22-2–147, Harris 0-2-1–0.

Receiving—Dallas, P. Pearson 7-123, D. Pearson 5-46, Richards 2-46, Fugett 2-5, Young 1-15, Dennison 1-11; Los Angeles, Jessie 4-52, McCutcheon 3-39, T. Nelson 3-28, Bryant 1-28.

Kickoff Returns—Dallas, Dennison 2-47; Los Angeles, McGee 5-103, Bryant 2-49, Jessie 1-15.

Punt Returns—Dallas, Richards 3-17, Harris 1-9; Los Angeles, Scribner 2-3.

Interceptions—Dallas, Lewis 2-20, C. Harris 1-22; Los Angeles, Simpson 1-37.

Punting—Dallas, Hoopes 4-34.8; Los Angeles, Carrell 7-35.4.

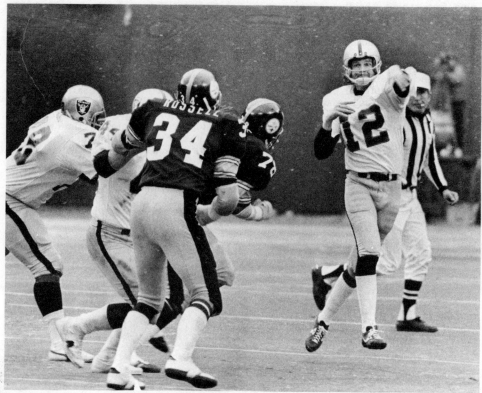

Oakland quarterback Ken Stabler fires a pass as the Steelers defense closes in during the 1975 championship game.

AFC
1975

Pittsburgh Steelers 16
Oakland Raiders   10

By now, the defending Super Bowl champion Pittsburgh Steelers were acknowledged as one of the NFL's top teams in history.

Pittsburgh had a 12-2 regular-season record, having allowed only 162 points, and they wiped out the Baltimore Colts, 28-10, in first-round playoff action.

Once again it was Oakland providing the title competition after the Raiders eliminated the wild-card Cincinnati Bengals, 31-28.

The title game this time was in Three Rivers Stadium in Pittsburgh on an 18-degree day with snow in the air and ice on the field.

The elements combined to make this a less than sharp effort, but in the end the Steelers' quality came through.

Roy Gerela started the scoring with a 36-yard field goal for Pittsburgh and in the third period middle linebacker Jack Lambert, who set a playoff record with three fumble recoveries, grabbed his second at the Pittsburgh 30. This turnover was converted into a 70-yard touchdown drive. Fullback Franco Harris scored with 54 seconds elapsed in the final quarter on a 25-yard run.

Oakland came back with a 14-yard scoring pass from Ken Stabler to wide receiver Mike Siani.

But Lambert recovered another fumble and quarterback Terry Bradshaw passed 20 yards to wide receiver John Stallworth for a 16-7 Pittsburgh lead.

Only 18 seconds remained in the game when George Blanda kicked a 41-yard field goal for Oakland. Because Pittsburgh had failed to convert the extra point on the Stallworth TD, the score was 16-10 and Oakland could win it with a touchdown and PAT.

The only choice was to try an onside kickoff, which Oakland did. And the Raiders'

Marv Hubbard made the recovery, after the Steelers' Reggie Garrett touched the ball but let it squirt away.

The clock showed nine seconds and Stabler threw to wide receiver Cliff Branch along the left sideline. Branch squirmed for 37 yards to the Steelers' 15, but failed to get out of bounds in time and the clock ran out.

AFC 1975 CHAMPIONSHIP GAME

Three Rivers Stadium, Pittsburgh, Jan. 4, 1976

SCORE BY PERIODS

Oakland Raiders.......	0	0	0	10 –	10
Pittsburgh Steelers...	0	3	0	13 –	16

SCORING

Pittsburgh—Field goal Gerela 36
Pittsburgh—Harris 25 run (Gerela kick)
Oakland—Siani 14 pass from Stabler (Blanda kick)
Pittsburgh—Stallworth 20 pass from Bradshaw (kick failed)
Oakland—Field goal Blanda 41

TEAM STATISTICS

	Oakland	Pittsburgh
First downs......................	18	16
Rushing yards	93	117
Passing yards...................	228	215
Return yards....................	90	121
Passes	18-42-2	15-25-3
Punts.............................	8-37.8	4-38.5
Fumbles-Lost	4-3	5-5
Penalties-Yards.................	4-40	3-32

Attendance—50,609.

INDIVIDUAL STATISTICS

Rushing—Oakland, Banaszak 8-33, Hubbard 10-30, Davis 13-29, J. Phillips 1-1; Pittsburgh, Harris 27-79, Bradshaw 2-22, Bleier 10-16.

Passing—Oakland, Stabler 18-42-2—246; Pittsburgh, Bradshaw 15-25-3—215.

Receiving—Oakland, Siani 5-80, Casper 5-67, Branch 2-56, Banaszak 2-12, Moore 2-12, Hart 1-16, Davis 1-3; Pittsburgh, Harris 5-58, Grossman 4-36, Swann 2-45, Stallworth 2-30, Lewis 1-33, L. Brown 1-13.

Kickoff Returns—Oakland, Davis 3-56, Banaszak 1-15; Pittsburgh, Collier 2-57, Harrison 1-2.

Punt Returns—Oakland, Siani 1-0; Pittsburgh, D. Brown 2-28, Collier 1-0.

Interceptions—Oakland, Tatum 2-8, M. Johnson 1-11; Pittsburgh, Wagner 2-34.

Punting—Oakland, Guy 8-37.8; Pittsburgh, Walden 4-38.5.

NFC
1976

Minnesota Vikings 24
Los Angeles Rams 13

It was a game of big plays in frigid, 8-degree temperature. Los Angeles made the mistakes, Minnesota got the breaks and in the end, it was the same story—for the third time in three meetings, the Rams lost in the

NFC playoff to the Vikings.

This time, the errors counted for everything as the Vikings defeated the Rams, 24-13, in the December 26, 1976, game at Bloomington, Minn.

In the first quarter, an attempted field goal by Tom Dempsey of the Rams was blocked. The ball bounced into the hands of cornerback Bobby Bryant at the Vikings' 10 and he returned it 90 yards for a Minnesota touchdown.

In the second quarter, an attempted punt by the Rams' Rusty Jackson was blocked and recovered on the Los Angeles 8-yard line by Minnesota linebacker Matt Blair. That led to a 25-yard Fred Cox field goal and a 10-0 halftime lead.

Vikings quarterback Fran Tarkenton, the chief proponent of the short-pass offense, proved his point early in the third period. Having used it most of the first half, Tarkenton now pump-faked another short pass, drawing the defense in tight. Then he hand-

1976 NFC CHAMPIONSHIP GAME

Metropolitan Stadium, Bloomington, Minn., December 26, 1976

SCORE BY PERIODS

Los Angeles Rams	0	0	13	0 –	13
Minnesota Vikings	7	3	7	7 –	24

SCORING

Minnesota—Bryant 90 blocked field goal return (Cox kick)
Minnesota—Field goal Cox 25
Minnesota—Foreman 1 run (Cox kick)
Los Angeles—McCutcheon 10 run (kick failed)
Los Angeles—H. Jackson 5 pass from Haden (Dempsey kick)
Minnesota—Johnson 12 run (Cox kick)

TEAM STATISTICS

	Los Angeles	Minnesota
First downs.......................	21	13
Rushing yards	193	158
Passing yards...................	143	109
Return yards....................	129	106
Passes	9-22-2	12-27-1
Punts.............................	7-29.4	8-35.1
Penalties-Yards.................	3-33	4-32

Attendance—48,379.

INDIVIDUAL STATISTICS

Rushing—Los Angeles, McCutcheon 26-128, Cappelletti 16-59, Jessie 1-3, Haden 3-3; Minnesota, Foreman 15-118, Miller 10-28, Johnson 2-12, McClanahan 1-2, Tarkenton 1-minus 2.

Passing—Los Angeles, Haden 9-22-2—161; Minnesota, Tarkenton 12-27-1—143.

Receiving—Los Angeles, H. Jackson 4-70, Jessie 2-60, McCutcheon 2-18, Cappelletti 1-13; Minnesota, Foreman 5-81, Rashad 3-28, Miller 3-24, Grim 1-10.

Kickoff Returns—Los Angeles, Geredine 3-50, C. Bryant 1-21, Scribner 1-8; Minnesota, Willis 3-69.

Punt Returns—Los Angeles, C. Bryant 4-31, Bertelsen 3-19; Minnesota, Willis 3-20.

Interceptions—Los Angeles, M. Jackson 1-0; Minnesota, B. Bryant 2-17.

Punting—Los Angeles, R. Jackson 7-29.4; Minnesota. Clabo 8-35.1.

Vikings quarterback Fran Tarkenton gets a little help from a friend as he looks for a receiver during the 1976 game against the Rams.

ed off to halfback Chuck Foreman, who zoomed 62 yards to the Rams' 1-yard line. From there, Foreman took it over on the next play to inflate the Vikings' lead to 17-0.

Now the Rams fought back, with Pat Haden at quarterback. A 10-yard run by halfback Lawrence McCutcheon made it 17-6 (the PAT failing). A five-yard pass to wide receiver Harold Jackson made it 17-13, and it stayed that way into the final moments of the game.

That's when the Rams threatened to win. They reached the Vikings' 39 and, with 2:40 left they came up to a fourth-and-10 situation. The Vikings, expecting a short "down and distance" pass, were fooled when Haden went deep for the points instead of the yards. He aimed for wide receiver Ron Jessie, who had beaten cornerback Nate Wright.

But Bryant, the other cornerback, read the play and left his man, Harold Jackson. He just got to the ball in time, swatted it away and snatched an almost sure touchdown from the Rams.

With less than two minutes to play, Tarkenton flipped a little pass to Foreman and it went for 57 yards. Sammy Lee Johnson, a reserve running back, sliced away the final 12 yards for the clinching TD.

Minnesota had moved into the championship game with a 35-20 victory over Washington as Tarkenton threw two TD passes to Sammy White, one for 70 yards. The Rams had beaten Dallas, 14-12. The Cowboys were trailing, 14-10, when Charlie Waters blocked a punt and Dallas took over on the Los Angeles 17. But a fourth-down pass play to Billy Joe DuPree was stopped inches short of a first down and the Rams moved the ball out of danger by taking a safety as time ran out.

AFC
1976

Oakland Raiders 24
Pittsburgh Steelers 7

Without Franco Harris and Rocky Bleier, the Pittsburgh Steelers' running game was lost. Both were out with injuries and they were the No. 3 and No. 4 rushers in the AFC during the Steelers' 10-4 season, Harris with 289 carries for 1,128 yards and 14 touchdowns, Bleier with 220 carries for 1,036 yards and five TDs.

"I won't risk their careers by playing them," said Steelers Coach Chuck Noll, "though we're terribly handicapped without them."

Both Harris (bruised ribs) and Bleier (toe) were hurt in the first round of the playoffs when the Steelers smashed Baltimore, 40-14. Quarterback Terry Bradshaw started the game against the Colts with a 76-yard TD pass to Frank Lewis and later threw a pair of scoring passes to Lynn Swann.

The Oakland Raiders, meanwhile, reached the championship game by pulling out a nail-biting 24-21 victory over New England with two fourth-quarter touchdowns. The winning score came on a one-yard rollout by quarterback Ken Stabler in the final minute.

The Raiders scored first against the Steelers on a 39-yard Errol Mann field goal in the first quarter of the December 26, 1976, game at Oakland and they built their lead to 10-0 when running back Clarence Davis pounded over from one yard out in the second period.

The Steelers, operating basically a passing game, moved downfield after that and finally got on the scoreboard when reserve fullback Reggie Harrison crashed over from the Raiders 3.

That made the score 10-7, and the half almost ended that way. But the fact that it didn't proved to be disastrous for the proud Steelers.

Oakland had the ball on the Steelers 4-yard line with only 19 seconds left in the half. The Raiders sent in a three-tight end formation, a sure sign of a run. It was first down with no time for much more than one running play.

So the Steelers decided to go with a goal-line defense, plugging the line with two additional linemen to set up an eight-man front.

At the snap of the ball, Stabler faked a running play to the right. Warren Bankston, one of the three tight ends, paused, faked a block, then slipped off into the left corner of the end zone. He was all alone when he caught Stabler's pass, giving the Raiders a 17-7 lead.

The Raiders used another big play to record their final touchdown in the third quarter.

It was fourth-and-one at the Pittsburgh 24. Stabler, using the same formation that had produced Bankston's touchdown, threw to the reserve tight end once more. It was a seven-yard gain to the 17, and fullback Pete Banaszak soon cashed it in with a five-yard TD reception from Stabler.

That score was the result of a 12-play, 63-yard drive and it was indicative of Oakland's ball-control style that day. Stabler threw only 16 passes, completing 10 for 88 yards, while the runners accounted for 157 yards.

And at the time they took their 24-7 lead, the Raiders had run 52 of the game's 81 plays.

1976 AFC CHAMPIONSHIP GAME

Oakland-Alameda County Coliseum,
Oakland, December 26, 1976

SCORE BY PERIODS

Pittsburgh Steelers...	0	7	0	0 —	7
Oakland Raiders.......	3	14	7	0 —	24

SCORING

Oakland—Field goal Mann 39
Oakland—Davis 1 run (Mann kick)
Pittsburgh—Harrison 3 run (Mansfield kick)
Oakland—Bankston 4 pass from Stabler (Mann kick)
Oakland—Banaszak 5 pass from Stabler (Mann kick)

TEAM STATISTICS

	Pittsburgh	Oakland
First downs	13	15
Rushing yards	72	157
Passing yards	165	71
Return yards	115	79
Passes	14-35-1	10-16-0
Punts	7-37.3	7-44.0
Fumbles-Lost	1-0	2-0
Penalties-Yards	5-29	7-34

Attendance—53,821.

INDIVIDUAL STATISTICS

Rushing—Pittsburgh, Harrison 11-44, Fuqua 8-24, Bradshaw 1-4, Cunningham 1-0; Oakland, van Eeghen 22-66, Davis 11-54, Banaszak 15-46, Garrett 2-4, Casper 1-minus 13.

Passing—Pittsburgh, Bradshaw 14-35-1-176; Oakland, Stabler 10-16-0-88.

Receiving—Pittsburgh, Cunningham 4-36, Swann 3-58, Fuqua 2-11, Harrison 2-10, Brown 1-32, Stallworth 1-18, Lewis 1-11; Oakland, Branch 3-46, Bankston 2-11, Davis 2-7, van Eeghen 1-14, Banaszak 1-5, Casper 1-5.

Kickoff Returns—Oakland, Garrett 2-35; Pittsburgh, Pough 3-65, Bell 1-16, Blount 1-16.

Punt Returns—Oakland, Colzie 2-19; Pittsburgh, Bell 2-14, Swann 1-4.

Interceptions—Oakland, Hall 1-25.

Punting—Oakland, Guy 7-44.0; Pittsburgh, Walden 7-37.3.

Hard-charging Harvey Martin's two fumble recoveries helped lift the Cowboys past the Vikings in 1977.

NFC 1977

Dallas Cowboys   23
Minnesota Vikings 6

Minnesota had never lost an NFC championship game, but records are made to be broken.

This was a meeting of young and old: the hot and electric Dallas Cowboys; the old, aging and stoic Vikings. Dallas had compiled the best record in the NFC, a 12-2 gem. Minnesota was a 9-5 "co-champion" in its division, a team that had scored only four points more than it had surrendered.

Dallas breezed, taking away even the dignity of Minnesota's grizzled veterans, as the Cowboys beat the Vikings, 23-6, in the game at Texas Stadium January 1, 1978.

It started quickly, with Dallas quarterback Roger Staubach finding wide receiver Golden Richards for a 32-yard touchdown pass in the first quarter after defensive end Harvey Martin recovered a Robert Miller fumble. The kick failed and the lead was 6-0.

Another fumble recovery by Martin set up another TD drive, given extra impetus when punter Danny White ran 22 yards on a fake. That enabled fullback Robert Newhouse to score on a five-yard slant for a 13-0 advantage.

The teams waged a scoreless war in the third quarter, but it was merely a holding action for the Vikings. In the fourth quarter, linebacker Thomas Henderson, on the field as part of the Cowboys' punt coverage team, tackled Manfred Moore savagely, causing a fumble recovered by tight end Jay Saldi and setting up an eventual 11-yard TD scamper by halfback Tony Dorsett.

Three Vikings' errors had led to three Cowboy touchdowns. There was no excuse, no alibi. The better team had won.

Minnesota had upset the Rams, 14-7, in the mud at Los Angeles in the first round of the playoffs. Dallas had advanced with a 37-7 breeze over the Chicago Bears.

NFC 1977 CHAMPIONSHIP GAME

Texas Stadium, Irving, Tex., January 1, 1978

SCORE BY PERIODS

Minnesota Vikings	0	6	0	0 –	6
Dallas Cowboys	6	10	0	7 –	23

SCORING

Dallas—Richards 32 pass from Staubach (kick failed)
Dallas—Newhouse 5 run (Herrera kick)
Minnesota—Field goal Cox 32
Minnesota—Field goal Cox 37
Dallas—Field goal Herrera 21
Dallas—Dorsett 11 run (Herrera kick)

TEAM STATISTICS

	Minnesota	Dallas
First downs	12	16
Rushing yards	66	170
Passing yards....................	148	158
Return yards	113	94
Passes	14-31-1	12-23-1
Punts	8-34.7	8-36.6
Fumbles-Lost	5-3	1-1
Penalties-Yards.................	5-32	5-24

Attendance—64,293.

INDIVIDUAL STATISTICS

Rushing—Minnesota, Foreman 21-59, Miller 8-5, Johnson 1-2; Dallas, Newhouse 15-81, Dorsett 19-71, White 1-14, Staubach 4-4.

Passing—Minnesota, Lee 14-31-1—158; Dallas, Staubach 12-23-1—165.

Receiving—Minnesota, White 3-46, Miller 2-39, Foreman 5-36, Voigt 1-19, Rashad 3-18; Dallas, D. Pearson 4-62, P. Pearson 3-48, Richards 2-34, DuPree 1-16, Newhouse 2-5.

Kickoff Returns—Minnesota, Moore 3-74, S. White 1-37, Kellar 1-11; Dallas, Brinson 3-36.

Punt Returns—Minnesota, Moore 3-2; Dallas, Hill 3-44, B. Johnson 2-13.

Interceptions—Minnesota, N. Wright 1-0; Dallas, Henderson 1-1.

Punting—Minnesota, Clabo 8-34.7; Dallas, D. White 8-36.6.

AFC
1977

Denver Broncos 20
Oakland Raiders 17

This was a year of fourth-quarter magic for the Denver Broncos, who outscored their regular-season opponents, 74-17, in the final period. And they came up with more magic in the first round of the playoffs, scoring 13 points in the fourth quarter on two Jim Turner field goals and a 34-yard pass from Craig Morton to Jack Dolbin to defeat Pittsburgh, 34-21. Oakland, meanwhile, won the third longest game in pro football history, going 53 seconds into a second overtime period before beating Baltimore, 37-31, on a 10-yard scoring pass from quarterback Ken Stabler to tight end Dave Casper.

The championship game at Denver January 1, 1978, must be recorded as unique. Near the middle of the second quarter, the Raiders had run 30 plays to only five for Denver. Yet the Broncos held a 7-3 lead, built on one electrifying pass from Morton to wide receiver Haven Moses, good for 74 yards in the first quarter.

It wiped out a 3-0 Oakland lead, the result of a 20-yard field goal by Errol Mann.

With Morton throwing at will, the Broncos mounted several other scoring threats, but the half ended on that 7-3 note. Then, midway through the third quarter, Denver recovered a fumble on the Raiders' 17 to set in motion a short drive capped by a one-yard TD run by fullback Jon Keyworth.

Oakland's Jack Tatum jarred the ball loose from halfback Rob Lytle on the play preceding the TD, and the Raiders recovered, but the officials ruled that the play had been blown dead and the fumble didn't count.

So the 14-3 lead was taken into the final quarter. Then, after Stabler's seven-yard TD pass to Casper cut the Denver margin to four, another big break put the Broncos safely ahead. Stabler's third-down pass was intercepted by Denver linebacker Bob Swenson, who returned it 14 yards to the Raiders' 17. On third-and-five from the 12, Morton found Moses again and the 12-yard TD put Denver in a 20-10 driver's seat (the PAT kick failed). With 3:16 left, Stabler cashed in with a 17-yard TD pass to Casper, paring the Broncos' lead to 20-17.

But with several key gains, Denver maintained ball control the rest of the game and ran out the clock.

Morton, who had spent some of the previous week in a hospital with a virus, and was also hobbled by a painful hip injury, passed for 224 yards with 168 of them accounted for by Moses on five receptions.

AFC 1977 CHAMPIONSHIP GAME

Mile High Stadium, Denver, January 1, 1978

SCORE BY PERIODS

Oakland Raiders.......	3	0	0	14 – 17
Denver Broncos........	7	0	7	6 – 20

SCORING

Oakland—Field goal Mann 20
Denver—Moses 74 pass from Morton (Turner kick)
Denver—Keyworth 1 run (Turner kick)
Oakland—Casper 7 pass from Stabler (Mann kick)
Denver—Moses 12 pass from Morton (pass failed)
Oakland—Casper 17 pass from Stabler (Mann kick)

TEAM STATISTICS

	Oakland	Denver
First downs......................	20	16
Rushing yards...................	94	91
Passing yards...................	204	217
Return yards....................	152	93
Passes............................	17-35-1	10-20-1
Punts.............................	5-36.0	4-40.8
Fumbles-Lost....................	2-2	0-0
Penalties-Yards................	2-6	8-46
Attendance—75,044.		

INDIVIDUAL STATISTICS

Rushing—Oakland, van Eeghen 20-71, Banaszak 7-22, Davis 9-1; Denver, Perrin 11-42, Lytle 7-26, Keyworth 8-19, Armstrong 7-16, Jensen 1-2, Morton 2-minus 4, Moses 1- minus 10.

Passing—Oakland, Stabler 17-35-1-215; Denver, Morton 10-20-1-224.

Receiving—Oakland, Casper 5-71, Branch 3-59, Biletnikoff 4-38, Bradshaw 1-25, Siani 1-12, van Eeghen 2-8, Banaszak 1-2; Denver, Moses 5-168, Perrin 2-20, Jensen 1-20, Odoms 1-13, Keyworth 1-3.

Kickoff Returns—Oakland, Garrett 3-111, Davis 1-25; Denver, Upchurch 2-33, Schultz 1-20, Lytle 1-14.

Punt Returns—Oakland, Garrett 2-5; Denver, Upchurch 2-12.

Interceptions—Oakland, Rice 1-11; Denver, Swenson 1-14.

Punting—Oakland, Guy 5-36.0; Denver, Dilts 4-40.8.

NFC
1978

Dallas Cowboys 28
Los Angeles Rams 0

This would be the fourth time in five years that the Los Angeles Rams had played for the NFC championship. And, for the fourth time in five years, they not only lost, but they were humiliated in a 28-0 defeat by the Dallas Cowboys.

A pair of third-quarter touchdowns, both set up on interceptions by safety Charlie Waters, put the January 7, 1979, game at Los Angeles out of the Rams' reach.

The first interception, on a pass by Pat Haden intended for tight end Terry Nelson, enabled Dallas to take a 7-0 lead on a five-yard run by Tony Dorsett with 5:49 remaining in the third quarter.

Later, Waters picked off another Haden-to-Nelson attempt, and 58 seconds into the fourth period quarterback Roger Staubach found fullback Scott Laidlaw with a four-yard TD pass.

Waters' first theft gave the Cowboys the ball on the Rams 10; the second presented Dallas with possession on the Los Angeles 20.

An 11-yard pass from Staubach to tight end Billy Joe DuPree made it 21-0, and the final touchdown came as the result of a 68-yard pass interception return by linebacker Thomas Henderson.

The shutout was the first in an NFC (nee NFL) title game since 1968, when the Balti-more Colts blanked the Cleveland Browns, 34-0.

"It was a defensive struggle, regardless of the score," said Cowboys Coach Tom Landry, "and Waters made the big plays you need against a great offense. He won the game for us."

The Rams helped mightily with seven turnovers. Pat Haden threw three interceptions, and Vince Ferragamo, his replacement, threw two. Dallas also profited from two Los Angeles fumbles.

This was the first year two wild-card teams qualified for the playoffs. The Atlanta Falcons rallied to beat the Philadelphia Eagles, 14-13, in the meeting of the wild cards. Then, Atlanta raced to 20-13 lead against Dallas and knocked Staubach out of the game with a concussion. However, the Cowboys rebounded for a 27-20 victory, with a TD pass from reserve quarterback Danny White to reserve tight end Jackie Smith a key play. The Rams reached the title game with a 34-10 rout of Minnesota.

NFC 1978 CHAMPIONSHIP GAME

Memorial Coliseum, Los Angeles, January 7, 1979

SCORE BY PERIODS

Dallas Cowboys	0	0	7	21 — 28
Los Angeles Rams	0	0	0	0 — 0

SCORING

Dallas—Dorsett 5 run (Septien kick)
Dallas—Laidlaw 4 pass from Staubach (Septien kick)
Dallas—DuPree 11 pass from Staubach (Septien kick)
Dallas—Henderson 68 interception return (Septien kick)

TEAM STATISTICS

	Dallas	Los Angeles
First downs	16	15
Rushing yards	126	81
Passing yards	109	96
Return yards	163	22
Passes	13-25-2	14-35-5
Punts	8-35.0	5-39.0
Fumbles-Lost	2-1	3-2
Penalties-Yards	10-85	5-40

Attendance—71,086.

INDIVIDUAL STATISTICS

Rushing—Dallas, Dorsett 17-101, Laidlaw 10-20, Staubach 3-7, Newhouse 1-4, DuPree 1-3, Smith 1-minus 9; Los Angeles, Bryant 20-52, Haden 2-20, Cappelletti 3-19, Phillips 3-2, Jodat 2- minu 5, Waddy 1-minus 7.

Passing—Dallas, Staubach 13-25-2-126; Los Angeles, Haden 7-19-3-76, Ferragamo 7-16-2-130.

Receiving—Dallas, DuPree 3-48, Johnson 2-19, D. Pearson 2-19, Dorsett 2-15, P. Pearson 2-12, Hill 1-9, Laidlaw 1-4; Los Angeles, Jessie 4-42, Miller 3-96, Waddy 2-23, Bryant 2-2, Scales 1-18, Cappelletti 1-15, Nelson 1-10.

Kickoff Returns—Los Angeles, Jodat 3-59, Marshall 2-47.

Punt Returns—Dallas, Johnson 4-40; Los Angeles, Wallace 2-22.

Interceptions—Dallas, Waters 2-49, Henderson 1-68, Harris 1-5, Hughes 1-1; Los Angeles, Thomas 1-0, Cromwell 1-0.

Punting—Dallas, D. White 8-35.0; Los Angeles, Walker 5-39.0.

AFC 1978

Pittsburgh Steelers 34
Houston Oilers 5

In the last 48 seconds of the second quarter, the Pittsburgh Steelers blew out the Houston Oilers by scoring 17 points and taking a 31-3 lead at halftime. That proved to be more than enough for a 35-5 victory.

The Steelers had been almost as dominant in their semifinal game, whipping the Denver Broncos, 33-10, as John Stallworth set a playoff record with 10 receptions for 156 yards. The Oilers had won the AFC wild-card game from the Miami Dolphins, 17-9, as Dan Pastorini passed for 306 yards, and then blasted the New England Patriots, 31-14, as Pastorini, wearing a flak jacket to protect injured ribs, threw three TD passes in the second quarter.

The weather for the championship game at Pittsburgh January 7, 1979, provided the breaks. In a steady downpour, on a field made slick and slippery by sub-freezing temperature, Pittsburgh achieved a 14-3 lead. Franco Harris ran seven yards for the first TD and Rocky Bleier went 15 for the second.

The Oilers could counter only with a 19-yard field goal by Toni Fritsch.

And then came the other deluge.

Steeler Rich Moser (39) recovers a Johnnie Dirden fumble in the rain-marred 1978 AFC title game.

Pittsburgh, on its 31, moved to the 50 on pass interference against Oilers defensive back Bill Currier. Two plays later, quarterback Terry Bradshaw connected with Lynn Swann for 29 yards and the TD.

It was 21-3.

Pittsburgh kicked off. Houston's Johnnie Dirden failed to hold the slick ball. The Steelers' Rick Moser recovered on the Houston 17 and Bradshaw immediately hit Stallworth with a 17-yard TD pass.

It was 28-3.

Pittsburgh kicked off again. Houston handled the chance. But on the first play from scrimmage, halfback Ronnie Coleman fumbled. Defensive tackle Steve Furness recovered and two plays later, with the clock ticking away the first half, Roy Gerela was good on a 37-yard field goal.

It was 31-3.

The weather was so inclement that it adversely affected the game on both sides. In all, there were 14 turnovers (nine by the Oilers), but a projected battle of premier running backs, Earl Campbell of Houston and the Steelers' Harris, was also washed away.

On treacherous footing, Campbell managed 62 yards in 22 carries, Harris 51 yards in 20 carries.

AFC 1978 CHAMPIONSHIP GAME

Three Rivers Stadium, Pittsburgh, Jan. 7, 1979

SCORE BY PERIODS

Houston Oilers	0	3	2	0 —	5
Pittsburgh Steelers	14	17	3	0 —	34

SCORING

Pittsburgh—Harris 7 run (Gerela kick)
Pittsburgh—Bleier 15 run (Gerela kick)
Houston—Field goal Fritsch 19
Pittsburgh—Swann 29 pass from Bradshaw (Gerela kick)
Pittsburgh—Stallworth 17 pass from Bradshaw (Gerela kick)
Pittsburgh—Field goal Gerela 37
Pittsburgh—Field goal Gerela 22
Houston—Safety, Bleier tackled in end zone

TEAM STATISTICS

	Houston	Pittsburgh
First downs	10	21
Rushing yards	72	179
Passing yards	70	200
Return yards	179	217
Passes	12-26-5	11-19-2
Punts	6-39.5	1-53.0
Fumbles-Lost	6-4	6-3
Penalties-Yards	5-48	4-32

Attendance—50,725.

INDIVIDUAL STATISTICS

Rushing—Houston, Campbell 22-62, Woods 1-9, T. Wilson 2-6, Coleman 1- minus 5; Pittsburgh, Harris 20-51, Bleier 10-45, Bradshaw 7-29, Deloplaine 3-28, Thornton 3-22, Moser 3-7, Kruczek 1-minus 3.

Passing—Houston, Pastorini 12-26-5—96; Pittsburgh, Bradshaw 11-19-2—200.

Receiving—Houston, Caster 5-44, T. Wilson 5-33, Coleman 1-15, Campbell 1-4; Pittsburgh, Swann 4-96, Bleier 4-42, Grossman 2-43, Stallworth 1-17.

Kickoff Returns—Houston, Dirden 3-72, Merkens 2-57, Woods 2-33, Duncan 1-17; Pittsburgh, Deloplaine 1-21, L. Anderson 1-15.

Punt Returns—Pittsburgh, Bell 6-91.

Interceptions—Houston, Alexander 1-0, Stemrick 1-0; Pittsburgh, Toews 1-35, Johnson 1-34, Blount 1-16, Shell 1-5, Ham 1-0.

Punting—Houston, Parsley 6-39.5; Pittsburgh, Colquitt 1-53.0.

The Rams' Cullen Bryant fights through the Tampa Bay defense for a first-quarter TD that was called back in the 1979 title game.

NFC
1979

| Los Angeles Rams | 9 |
| Tampa Bay Buccaneers | 0 |

The Tampa Bay Buccaneers, born only four years earlier and the team that lost the first 26 games of its existence, were the darlings of the nation. But the Cinderella expansion team failed to fit the golden slipper and lost to the Los Angeles Rams, 9-0, in the

NFC title game at Tampa January 6, 1980.

It was an old-fashioned defensive struggle, the kind that drew paeans of praise in the 1930s when the players wore leather helmets—or none at all.

All the scoring can be easily stated: Rams placekicker Frank Corral kicked three field-goals—a 19-yarder in the second quarter, a 21-yarder in the second quarter and a 23-yarder in the fourth quarter.

But there was more. There was drama and there was dissent. There were nullified touchdowns, one for each side.

In the end, there was the feeling that, against any other team, the Rams might have failed as they had four times previously in title games.

Los Angeles fumbled the ball away at the Bucs 16 in the first quarter and had a four-yard TD run by fullback Cullen Bryant wiped out by a penalty. In the final quarter, the Bucs' substitute quarterback, Mike Rae, having replaced an injured Doug Williams, threw a 27-yard pass to tight end Jimmie Giles for an apparent touchdown. But that, too, was erased on an illegal procedure call.

The third quarter was scoreless, Corral missing the only opportunity when a 37-yard field goal try was wide.

In the final quarter, with Rae executing with far more precision than had Williams (who completed only two of 13 passes for 12 yards), the Bucs made a move to threaten.

A razzle-dazzle halfback option pass clicked for 42 yards, Jerry Eckwood throwing to wide receiver Larry Mucker at the Rams 34. That threat fizzled in the face of the Rams' defense, and when Corral kicked his final field goal, the scoring was done.

The Bucs had won the first playoff game in their history, beating the Philadelphia Eagles, 24-17, in the semifinals as Ricky Bell ran for 142 yards. Los Angeles advanced with a 21-19 upset of the Dallas Cowboys.

NFC 1979 CHAMPIONSHIP GAME

Tampa Stadium, Tampa, January 6, 1980

SCORE BY PERIODS

Los Angeles Rams....	0	6	0	3	– 9
Tampa Bay Bucs	0	0	0	0	– 0

SCORING

Los Angeles—Field goal Corral 19
Los Angeles—Field goal Corral 21
Los Angeles—Field goal Corral 23

TEAM STATISTICS

	Los Angeles	Tampa Bay
First downs	23	7
Rushing yards	216	92
Passing yards	153	85
Return yards	104	120
Passes	12-23-0	5-27-1
Punts	5-37.2	8-37.1
Fumbles-Lost	1-1	1-0
Penalties-Yards	3-20	4-45

Attendance—72,033.

INDIVIDUAL STATISTICS

Rushing—Los Angeles, Bryant 18-106, Tyler 28-86, McCutcheon 6-26, Ferragamo 1- minus 2; Tampa Bay, Bell 20-59, Mucker 1-24, Eckwood 2-5, J. Davis 2-4, Rae 1-0.

Passing—Los Angeles, Ferragamo 12-23-0-163; Tampa Bay, Williams 2-13-1–12, Rae 2-13-0-42, Eckwood 1-1-0–42.

Receiving—Los Angeles, Dennard 3-56, Bryant 4-39, Young 3-39, Nelson 1-15, Tyler 1-14; Tampa Bay, Hagins 2-42, Mucker 1-42, Bell 2-12.

Kickoff Returns—Los Angeles, E. Hill 1-27; Tampa Bay, Hagins 4-106.

Punt Returns—Los Angeles, Brown 6-67; Tampa Bay, Reece 2-14, Johnson 1-0.

Interceptions—Los Angeles, Jim Youngblood 1-10.

Punting—Los Angeles, Clark 5-37.2; Tampa Bay, Blanchard 8-37.1.

AFC 1979

Pittsburgh Steelers 27
Houston Oilers 13

Vernon Perry, a Houston safety, stunned the favored Pittsburgh Steelers early in the first quarter when he intercepted a Terry Bradshaw pass and returned it 75 yards for a touchdown.

Just 2:30 had elapsed and the Oilers had a 7-0 lead.

But when it was all over, Houston proved no match for Pittsburgh, losing to the Steelers, 27-13.

The Steelers had rolled over the Miami Dolphins, 34-14, in their first playoff game after jumping to a 20-0 lead in the first quarter on a TD run by Sidney Thornton and two Terry Bradshaw scoring passes. Houston had beaten the Denver Broncos, 13-7, in the wild-card game and then surprised the San Diego Chargers, 17-14, as the Oilers operated without three of their top offensive players.

Running back Earl Campbell and quarterback Dan Pastorini went out of the Denver game with groin injuries and wide receiver Ken Burrough suffered a back injury. However, the Oilers beat San Diego as backup quarterback Gifford Nielsen threw a 47-yard scoring pass to Mike Renfro and Perry intercepted four passes and blocked a field-goal attempt.

After Houston's quick score on Perry's interception in the championship game at Pittsburgh January 6, 1980, the Steelers countered with a 21-yard field goal by Matt Bahr, cutting the lead to 7-3. But Houston's Toni Fritsch hit a 21-yarder of his own and it was 10-3.

The Steelers exerted their superiority, scoring two touchdowns in the second quarter, both on passes by Bradshaw. First, he hit tight end Bennie Cunningham with a 16-yarder, then he found wide receiver John Stallworth for 20 yards, and it was 17-10 in favor of Pittsburgh at halftime.

With less than two minutes remaining in the third period, the Oilers were camped on the Steelers 6-yard line. Pastorini called a "go-get-it" pass pattern to the right side for wide receiver Renfro.

"I take two steps and throw for the end zone," Pastorini explained, "and Mike . . . well, he has to go get it."

Pastorini threw. Renfro got it, beating cornerback Ron Johnson, coming down with his right foot in bounds, then falling out of the end zone—but not before brushing

Houston's Mike Renfro tries to hold the football as Steelers defender Ron Johnson looks over his shoulder on a controversial nontouchdown play in the 1979 AFC Championship game.

The Steelers' superiority was obvious, but the memorable part of this game was the non-catch by Renfro in which the Oilers lost a tying touchdown. The debates raged on through the winter.

AFC 1979 CHAMPIONSHIP GAME

Three Rivers Stadium, Pittsburgh, Jan. 6, 1980

SCORE BY PERIODS

Houston Oilers	7	3	0	3 – 13
Pittsburgh Steelers...	3	14	0	10 – 27

SCORING

Houston—Perry 75 interception return (Fristch kick)
Pittsburgh—Field goal Bahr 21
Houston—Field goal Fritsch 21
Pittsburgh—Cunningham 16 pass from Bradshaw (Bahr kick)
Pittsburgh—Stallworth 20 pass from Bradshaw (Bahr kick)
Houston—Field goal Fritsch 23
Pittsburgh—Field goal Bahr 39
Pittsburgh—Bleier 4 run (Bahr kick)

TEAM STATISTICS

	Houston	Pittsburgh
First down	11	22
Rushing yards	24	161
Passing yards....................	203	197
Return yards....................	147	90
Passes	20-29-1	18-30-1
Punts................................	4-30.0	3-51.0
Fumbles-Lost	4-2	1-1
Penalties-Yards................	2-10	5-34

Attendance—50,475.

INDIVIDUAL STATISTICS

Rushing—Houston, Campbell 17-15, Wilson 4-9, Caster 1-0; Pittsburgh, Harris 21-85, Bleier 13-52, Bradshaw 1-25, Thornton 1- minus 1.

Passing—Houston, Pastorini 19-28-1-203, Nielsen 1-1-0—9; Pittsburgh, Bradshaw 18-30-1—219.

Receiving—Houston, Wilson 7-60, Coleman 2-46, Carpenter 5-23, Renfro 3-52, Campbell 1-11, Merkens 1-12, Barber 1-8; Pittsburgh, Swann 4-64, Stallworth 3-52, Harris 6-50, Bleier 3-39, Cunningham 2-14.

Kickoff Returns—Houston, Ellender 4-47, Hartwig 1-13, Carpenter 1-4; Pittsburgh, L. Anderson 4-82.

Punt Returns—Houston, Ellender 3-8; Pittsburgh, Bell 3-8.

Interceptions—Houston, Perry 1-75; Pittsburgh, Woodruff 1-0.

Punting—Houston, Parsley 4-30.0; Pittsburgh, Colquitt 3-51.0.

---

fair territory with his other foot.

Touchdown?

No. Side judge Donald Orr, after conferring with the rest of the officiating crew, ruled that Renfro "came down in bounds with both feet, but he didn't have the possession that he must have until after he came down."

So an apparent 17-17 tie remained a 17-10 Pittsburgh lead, soon sliced to 17-13 on a 23-yard Fritsch field goal.

But Pittsburgh scored 10 more points in the fourth quarter, on a 39-yard field goal by Bahr and a time-consuming drive culminated when halfback Rocky Bleier skipped over from the 4-yard line.

NFC
1980

Philadelphia Eagles 20
Dallas Cowboys   7

This wasn't supposed to happen. This game was to be merely the preliminary for yet another appearance in the Super Bowl by the Cowboys, who had already made five such trips, tops in the NFL.

Three weeks earlier, Dallas had bombed the Eagles (in the final week of the regular season) and thereby, they thought, established superiority that would only increase because of the Cowboys' experience in pressure-cooker situations such as conference championship games.

But the Eagles, playing before a frenzied home crowd in sub-zero weather, took control from the start behind the running of halfback Wilbert Montgomery and never let go.

Montgomery, a four-year veteran who had been nursing a knee injury the week before the game, gained an astounding 194 yards in 26 carries, just two yards short of the NFL's championship game record. He broke free for a 42-yard TD jaunt on the second play of the game.

But Dallas fought back to tie the score early in the second quarter, moving 68 yards in 10 plays, a drive ending when halfback Tony Dorsett churned over from three yards out.

The Cowboys seemingly had the upper

NFC 1980 CHAMPIONSHIP GAME

Veterans Stadium, Philadelphia, Pa.
January 11, 1981

SCORE BY PERIODS

Dallas Cowboys	0	7	0	0 — 7
Philadelphia Eagles ..	7	0	10	3 — 20

SCORING

Philadelphia—Montgomery 42 run (Franklin kick)
Dallas—Dorsett 3 run (Septien kick)
Philadelphia—Field goal Franklin 26.
Philadelphia—Harris 9 run (Franklin kick)
Philadelphia—Field goal Franklin 20.

TEAM STATISTICS

	Dallas	Philadelphia
First downs	14	24
Rushing yards	86	263
Passing yards	127	91
Return yards	108	114
Passes	12-32-1	2-29-2
Punts	7-33.7	4-34.3
Fumbles-Lost	5-3	4-0
Penalties-Yards	5-40	5-45

Attendance—70,696.

INDIVIDUAL STATISTICS

Rushing—Dallas, Dorsett 13-41, Newhouse 7-44, Johnson 1-5, White 1-minus 4; Philadelphia, Montgomery 26-194, Jaworski 2-2, Harris 10-60, Campfield 1-3, Harrington 1-4.

Passing—Dallas, White 12-31-1—127, D. Pearson 0-1-0—0; Philadelphia, Jaworski 9-29-2—91.

Receiving—Dallas, Springs 2-minus 2, D. Pearson 2-15, Johnson 2-27, Dorsett 3-27, Saldi 1-28, P. Pearson 2-32; Philadelphia, Carmichael 1-7, Parker 4-31, Montgomery 1-14, Campfield 1-17, Krepfle 2-22.

Kickoff Returns—Dallas, Jones 3-70, Wilson 1-19, Newsome 1-15; Philadelphia, Campfield 2-40.

Punt Returns—Dallas, Jones 3-4; Philadelphia, Sciarra 6-69.

Interceptions—Dallas, Dickerson 1-0, Mitchell 1-0; Philadelphia, Young 1-5.

Punting—Dallas, White 7-33.7; Philadelphia, Runager 4-34.3

Dejected Cowboys quarterback Danny White reflects after his team's 1980 NFL playoff loss to the Eagles.

hand at halftime because their first half had been filled with mistakes and missed opportunities, and yet they were sitting in the locker room with a tie score.

It would be inconceivable to suggest that the Cowboys had already scored all the points they were going to get, but it worked out that way.

The Eagles won the game in the third quarter; or, more accurately, the third quarter is when the Cowboys lost it.

An interception by linebacker Anthony Dickerson gave Dallas the ball on its own 23. But on third down, defensive end Carl Hairston sacked quarterback Danny White, who fumbled. The other end, Dennis Harrison, recovered at the Dallas 11 and, four plays later, a field goal by Tony Franklin put the Eagles ahead, 10-7.

On the next Dallas possession, Dorsett fumbled. Eagle linebacker Jerry Robinson recovered, returned the ball 22 yards to the Cowboys 38 and, six plays later, fullback Leroy Harris ran up the middle for nine yards and a TD, making the Eagle lead 17-7.

Franklin sealed the verdict in the fourth quarter with a 20-yard field goal.

Both quarterbacks experienced difficulty in the swirling wind conditions. Philadelphia's Ron Jaworski completed only nine of 29 passes for 91 yards and was intercepted twice. White, the Cowboys' replacement for the retired Roger Staubach, managed only 12 completions in 31 tries for 127 yards and one interception.

"The Eagles were ready to win the championship," said Dallas Coach Tom Landry. "We knew that. We were just waiting to see whether they realized it. They proved everything that had to be proved, and they beat us soundly."

A Dallas victory would have set up an all-wild-card Super Bowl, matching the Cowboys against the Oakland Raiders. The Cowboys had convincingly dispatched of the Los Angeles Rams, 34-13, in their wild-card encounter and then slipped past Atlanta, 30-27, on the strength of three fourth-quarter touchdowns that erased a 14-point Falcon lead.

The heroes of the victory were White and Drew Pearson, who combined on a 14-yard pass play with 3:40 remaining and another (23 yards) with 42 seconds left that pulled out the victory.

The Eagles had advanced at the expense of the Minnesota Vikings, who fell, 31-16, January 3. The victory over Dallas lifted the Eagles to their first-ever Super Bowl appearance.

AFC
1980

Oakland Raiders 34
San Diego Chargers 27

For the first time since the merger of the NFL with the old American Football League, a team that had failed to win its division championship became a Super Bowl winner.

The Oakland Raiders, entering the playoffs on a runner-up basis, turned over their wild-card and showed an ace.

This was against the most prolific passing offense in the history of professional football. San Diego quarterback Dan Fouts had set piles of records by passing to wide receivers John Jefferson and Charlie Joiner and tight end Kellen Winslow.

The game was in San Diego and the Chargers were big favorites. Oakland didn't even have the quarterback with which it started the season. Dan Pastorini had been lost in the fifth game with a broken leg and the only replacement was former Heisman Trophy winner Jim Plunkett, a 10-year veteran who had been traded once, released outright once and entered the 1980 season with thoughts of retirement.

But he proved to be the necessary ingredient throughout the season and, when coupled with halfbacks Kenny King and Mark

1980 AFC CHAMPIONSHIP GAME

Jack Murphy-San Diego Stadium, San Diego, Calif., January 11, 1981.

SCORE BY PERIODS

Oakland Raiders.......	21	7	3	3 – 34
San Diego Chargers ..	7	7	10	3 – 27

SCORING

Oakland—Chester 65 pass from Plunkett (Bahr kick)
San Diego—Joiner 48 pass from Fouts (Benirschke kick)
Oakland—Plunkett 5 run (Bahr kick)
Oakland—King 21 pass from Plunkett (Bahr kick)
Oakland—van Eeghen 3 run (Bahr kick)
San Diego—Joiner 8 pass from Fouts (Benirschke kick)
San Diego—Field goal Benirschke 26
San Diego—Muncie 6 run (Benirschke kick)
Oakland—Field goal Bahr 27
Oakland—Field goal Bahr 33
San Diego—Field goal Benirschke 27

TEAM STATISTICS

	Oakland	San Diego
First downs	21	26
Rushing yards	138	83
Passing yards	224	351
Return yards	164	140
Passes	14-18-0	23-46-2
Punts	4-56.0	2-40.5
Fumbles-Lost	0-0	5-1
Penalties-Yards	7-54	6-45

Attendance—52,428.

INDIVIDUAL STATISTICS

Rushing—Oakland van Eeghen 20-85, King 11-35, Plunkett 4-6, Whittington 5-5, Jensen 2-7; San Diego, Muncie 9-34, Smith 1-minus 1, Thomas 12-48, Fouts 1-2.

Passing—Oakland, Plunkett 14-18-0-261; San Diego, Fouts 22-45-2-336, Winslow 1-1-0-28.

Receiving—Oakland, Chester 5-102, Branch 3-78, Chandler 2-27, King 2-43, Whittington 2-11; San Diego, Smith 3-76, Jefferson 4-71, Joiner 6-130, Muncie 2-5, Thomas 5-40, Winslow 3-42.

Kickoff Returns—Oakland, Moody 2-36, Whittington 4-67; San Diego, Bauer 5-89, Duncan 1-10.

Punt Returns—Oakland, Matthews 2-20; San Diego, Fuller 2-41.

Interceptions—Oakland, Hayes 1-16, Owens 1-25.

Punting—Oakland, Guy 4-56.0; San Diego, Partridge 2-40.5.

Mark van Eeghen, whose ball-control running helped the Oakland Raiders hold off San Diego in the 1980 AFC title game, finds running room during the Raiders' playoff victory over Cleveland.

van Eeghen and an opportunistic defense led by linebacker Ted Hendricks, cornerback Lester Hayes and end John Matuszak, he was too much for the Chargers.

Plunkett was superb, completing 14 of 18 passes for 261 yards and a pair of touchdowns. So unprepared for the Oakland attack was San Diego that the Chargers quickly fell behind, 28-7. By the time the first period had ended, Plunkett had connected with Raymond Chester on a 65-yard touchdown pass, King on a 21-yarder and scored himself on a five-yard run. Plunkett directed another drive in the second quarter that ended with van Eeghen's three-yard run, giving the Raiders a 28-14 halftime margin.

"We never gave them a fight in the first quarter . . . or in the first half," said Chargers Coach Don Coryell. "We were stunned."

Once the lead was established, Oakland had to control the clock and did so effectively with van Eeghen and King running behind a superior interior line anchored by guard Gene Upshaw and tackle Art Shell.

"If there was anything we could do for our defense after the great season those guys had, it was the second half," said Raiders Coach Tom Flores. "We made the big plays at the right time and we gained tough yards against a very good San Diego defense."

Van Eeghen led the Oakland running game with 85 yards in 20 carries; in all the Raiders rushed 42 times for 138 yards.

The vaunted San Diego passing attack did have its moments, however.

Fouts, who completed 22 of 45 attempts for 336 yards, had connected with Joiner on touchdowns of 48 and 8 yards in the first half. In the third quarter, he directed the Chargers on a pair of drives that resulted in a 26-yard Rolf Benirschke field goal and a six-yard TD run by Chuck Muncie, cutting the Raiders' lead to 28-24.

But Oakland reasserted control, with the running of van Eeghen and King and a pair of Chris Bahr field goals sealing the Chargers' fate.

The Oakland offense literally ran off the final 6:43 of the game.

"I don't know what our defense was thinking of during that time," van Eeghen said. "But they must have been pretty happy. For a change, we didn't ask them to keep it safe—we did it on offense."

That wasn't the case, however, in the Raiders' road to the title game. After dispensing of Houston, 27-7, in their wild-card game, the Raiders traveled to Cleveland for what was to be the second-coldest NFL playoff game ever. The temperature was one degree at kickoff and the two defenses, naturally, controlled the game.

As the game entered its final dramatic moments, the Raiders clung to a 14-12 lead and the Oakland defense was holding on for dear life as the Browns faced a second down at the Raiders 9 with less than a minute to play.

But the Browns, passing up a chip-shot field goal attempt in favor of a pass by quarterback Brian Sipe, watched as Mike Davis picked it off in the end zone, giving the Raiders a victory.

San Diego's path to the championship game was just as dramatic. The Chargers ended Buffalo's season with 2:08 remaining in a first-round game when Fouts connected on a 50-yard bomb to unexpected target Ron Smith, giving San Diego a 20-14 victory.

NFC
1981

San Francisco 49ers 28
Dallas Cowboys 27

Quarterback Joe Montana looked up and surveyed the scene coolly. The 49ers trailed, 27-21, and there were still almost five minutes to play. And the goal line was 89 yards away.

But that did not deter Montana. He deftly led San Francisco on a game-winning march that culminated with a six-yard pass to Dwight Clark for the tying points. Kicker Ray Wersching calmly booted the extra point that would provide the margin of victory.

The drive began with 4:54 to play and ended with 51 seconds remaining. In those four minutes, the 49ers proved they were more than a match for the Dallas Cowboys.

San Francisco had taken an early 7-0 lead when Montana connected for eight yards to Freddie Solomon. The Cowboys rebounded in typical fashion to gain a 10-7 lead on a 44-yard field goal by Rafael Septien and a 26-yard pass from Danny White to Tony Hill. After the 49ers regained the lead at 14-10, on a 20-yard pass from Montana to Clark, Dallas took a 17-14 halftime lead, aided by a questionable interference call against 49ers cornerback Ronnie Lott.

The penalty nullified an interception by Lott and gave Dallas a first down at the 49ers' 12-yard line. Three plays later, Tony Dorsett ran in from the 5 for the Cowboys' lead.

The game continued its see-saw pattern in the second half. The 49ers took the lead, 21-17, on a 2-yard run by backup fullback Johnny Davis. And that was the score as the contest entered the dramatic final 15 minutes. Septien kicked a 22-yard field goal that brought the Cowboys within one point, but the 49ers then launched a drive that looked as though it would put Dallas away. However, rookie running back Walt Easley fumbled, Cowboy cornerback Everson Walls recovered, and Dallas started marching the other way.

Just four plays after the fumble, White hit tight end Doug Cosbie with a 21-yard pass and the Cowboys led, 27-21. On the next series, Montana threw his third interception—the second for Walls—and it appeared San Francisco's dream had died. The interception was the 49ers' sixth turnover of the day, a statistic that kept the game as close as it was.

But the 49ers held the Cowboys on a key

Dwight Clark gets a big hug from a 49er teammate after catching a second-quarter TD pass against Dallas.

third-down play, Dallas punted, and the 49ers took control on their own 11-yard line. That set the stage for a drive that will be remembered for the coaching mastery of Bill Walsh. The Cowboys, expecting passes

Cowboys back Tony Dorsett scores a second-quarter TD against the 49ers.

from the 49ers, went to a defense that featured six defensive backs.

But San Francisco countered by running the ball. Veteran Lenvil Elliott rushed for key yardage and Solomon gained 14 yards on a reverse. The ground game got the 49ers down the field and Elliott's final rush advanced the ball from the Dallas 13 to the 6. After a timeout, Montana rolled right but was in danger. Three Cowboys, led by Ed (Too Tall) Jones, bore down on him. As he approached the sideline, Montana let loose with a pass off his wrong foot that appeared headed for the stands.

Suddenly, seemingly out of nowhere, the 6-4 Clark leaped high and snared the ball in front of a stunned Walls. The 49ers had their lead, and after Lawrence Pillers sacked White and Jim Stuckey recovered the fumbled ball, they had their victory.

1981 NFC CHAMPIONSHIP GAME

Candlestick Park, San Francisco, Calif.,
January 10, 1982

SCORE BY PERIODS

Dallas	10	7	0	10	27
San Francisco	7	7	7	7	28

SCORING

San Francisco—Solomon 8 pass from Montana (Wersching kick).
Dallas—Field goal Septien 44.
Dallas—Hill 26 pass from D. White (Septien kick).
San Francisco—Clark 20 pass from Montana (Wersching kick).
Dallas—Dorsett 5 run (Septien kick).
San Francisco—Davis 2 run (Wersching kick).
Dallas—Field goal Septien 22.
Dallas—Cosbie 21 pass from D. White (Septien kick).
San Francisco—Clark 6 pass from Montana (Wersching kick).

TEAM STATISTICS

	Dallas	San Fran.
First Downs	16	26
Rushing Yards	115	127
Passing Yards	135	266
Return Yards	102	136
Passes	16-24-1	22-35-3
Punts	6-39.3	3-35.7
Fumbles-Lost	4-2	3-3
Penalties-Yards	5-39	7-106
Attendance—60,525.		

INDIVIDUAL STATISTICS

Rushing—Dallas, Dorsett 22-91, J. Jones 4-14, Springs 5-10, D. White 1-0; San Francisco, Elliott 10-48, Cooper 8-35, Ring 6-27, Solomon 1-14, Easley 2-6, Davis 1-2, Montana 3-minus 5.

Passing—Dallas, D. White 16-24-1—173; San Francisco, Montana 22-35-3—286.

Receiving—Dallas, J. Jones 3-17, DuPree 3-15, Springs 3-13, Hill 2-43, Pearson 1-31, Cosbie 1-21, Johnson 1-20, Saldi 1-9, Donley 1-4; San Francisco, Clark 8-120, Solomon 6-75, Young 4-45, Cooper 2-11, Elliott 1-24, Shumann 1-11.

Kickoff Returns—Dallas, J. Jones 3-56, Newsome 2-33; San Francisco, Lawrence 3-60, Ring 3-47.

Punt Returns—Dallas, J. Jones 3-13; San Francisco, Hicks 5-21, Solomon 1-3.

Interceptions—Dallas, Walls 2-0, R. White 1-0; San Francisco, Leopold 1-5.

Punting—Dallas, D. White 6-39.3; San Francisco, Miller 3-35.7.

AFC 1981

Cincinnati Bengals 27
San Diego Chargers 7

How cold was it? It was so cold that NFL Commissioner Pete Rozelle briefly considered postponing the game. However, the league consulted with an expert on environmental medicine from the U.S. Army Research Institute—and the game went on.

How cold was it? Of the 59,579 Cincinnati faithful who had purchased tickets, more than 20 percent, or 13,277, decided against braving the elements and stayed home.

But, really, how cold was it? For the record, the temperature read 9 degrees below zero, winds gusted up to 35 mph out of the northwest, and the all-important wind-chill factor read 59 degrees below zero. It was a day not meant for championship football.

And on that day, the Bengals persevered, stopping San Diego, 27-7. It was the second consecutive year the Chargers were halted one game short of the Super Bowl.

While the final score makes the game look like a runaway, a key play late in the first half may have doomed the Chargers. Cincinnati had taken a 10-0 lead on a 31-yard field goal by Jim Breech and an 8-yard pass from Ken Anderson to M. L. Harris. The TD toss came two plays after James Brooks fumbled on a kickoff return and Don Bass recovered on the Chargers' 12-yard line.

San Diego cut the lead to 10-7 on a 33-yard pass from Dan Fouts to Kellen Winslow. But again the Chargers' special teams defied them when David Verser returned the ensuing kickoff 40 yards. The Bengals then went 55 yards in seven plays to score on Pete Johnson's 1-yard run.

Still, the Chargers wouldn't quit, even though Fouts was having all kinds of trouble throwing the ball in the swirling wind. San Diego drove to Cincinnati's 21-yard line and there was a little over one minute to play. Fouts went back to pass and moved right as the field opened up for him. He could have run for good yardage but opted for an end zone pass to Winslow.

Fouts hoped to throw the ball high and have the 6-5 Winslow out-jump his defenders. But the ball fluttered and died in the wind, coming down short of Winslow and into the hands of Bengals safety Bobby Kemp. Kemp returned the ball 24 yards out of danger and Cincinnati had protected its 17-7 lead.

The second half saw more frustration for the Chargers. They couldn't get on the

Chargers Coach Don Coryell checked out the playing conditions before his team's AFC title game in Cincinnati and didn't like what he saw.

A jubilant M.L. Harris celebrates Cincinnati's first touchdown after catching a short pass from quarterback Ken Anderson.

scoreboard and the Bengals padded their lead on a 38-yard field goal by Breech and a 3-yard pass from Anderson to Bass for the final points.

In addition to the cold, this game will also be remembered for Riverfront Stadium's "open door policy." Chargers Coach Don Coryell mentioned after the game that an open door may have hindered his team in the first half. The door, at the west end of the stadium, was open during the first quarter when San Diego had to drive toward it. When open, wind whips through the stadium. However, in the second quarter, when the Bengals were driving in that direction, the door was closed.

Finally, the Chargers requested that the door remain closed. By then it was too late.

Anderson had the final word on the elements, however. How cold was it, Ken? "It really wasn't all that bad," he said. "I've been colder at other times." He just didn't say when.

1981 AFC CHAMPIONSHIP GAME

Riverfront Stadium, Cincinnati, Ohio,
January 10, 1982

SCORE BY PERIODS

San Diego	0	7	0	0 —	7
Cincinnati	10	7	3	7 —	27

SCORING

Cincinnati—Field goal Breech 31.
Cincinnati—M. L. Harris 8 pass from Anderson (Breech kick).
San Diego—Winslow 33 pass from Fouts (Benirschke kick).
Cincinnati—Johnson 1 run (Breech kick).
Cincinnati—Bass 3 pass from Anderson (Breech kick).

TEAM STATISTICS

	San Diego	Cincinnati
First Downs	18	19
Rushing Yards	128	143
Passing Yards	173	175
Return Yards	139	64
Passes	15-28-2	13-25-0
Punts	2-29.5	3-30.6
Fumbles Lost	4-2	3-1
Penalties Yards	2-15	3-25

Attendance—46,302.

INDIVIDUAL STATISTICS

Rushing—San Diego, Muncie 23-94, Brooks 6-23, Cappelletti 1-5, Fouts 1-6; Cincinnati, Johnson 21-80, Alexander 9-22, Anderson 5-39, Collinsworth 1-2.

Passing—San Diego, Fouts 15-28-2-185; Cincinnati, Anderson 14-22-0-161, Thompson 1-1-0-14.

Receiving—San Diego, Winslow 3-47, Chandler 6-79, Joiner 3-41, Brooks 2-5, Sievers 1-13; Cincinnati, Alexander 3-25, Ross 5-69, M. L. Harris 1-8, Collinsworth 2-28, Curtis 2-28, Johnson 1-14, Bass 1-3.

Kickoff Returns—San Diego, Brooks 4-87, Shaw 1-7, Beaudoin 2-38; Cincinnati, Verser 1-40.

Punt Returns—San Diego, Chandler 1-7; Cincinnati, None.

Interceptions—San Diego, None; Cincinnati, Breeden 1-0, Kemp 1-24.

Punting—San Diego, Roberts 2-29.5; Cincinnati, McInally 3-30.6.

Washington's John Riggins goes over and through the Cowboy defense for a touchdown in the 1982 NFC title game.

NFC
1982

Washington Redskins 31
Dallas Cowboys 17

The Dallas Cowboys saw enough of Dexter Manley in the National Conference championship game to last the entire off-season. And, fittingly, the play of the Washington Redskins' right defensive end was instrumental in sending the Cowboys into their off-season lull eight days ahead of Dallas' projected date for the end of the season.

Manley, a second-year player from Oklahoma State, knocked Dallas quarterback Danny White—the NFC's second-ranked passer in 1982—out of the NFC title game late in the first half with a bruising sack. Then, with fewer than 7 minutes remaining in the game, Manley tipped a Gary Hogeboom pass into the hands of tackle Darryl Grant, who ran 10 yards for an insurance touchdown as Washington nailed down a 31-17 victory and a berth in Super Bowl XVII.

For Washington, the victory meant vindication and revenge. Despite an NFC-best mark of 8-1 in the strike-shortened regular season and victories over Detroit and Minnesota in the first two rounds of the Super Bowl tournament, the Redskins still had their skeptics entering the January 22 showdown at Robert F. Kennedy Memorial Stadium.

Detractors pointed to the mini-season (was it a real measure of the teams' relative strengths?) and Washington's success—or lack of it—against Dallas. The Redskins had lost six straight regular-season games to their hated rival, including their lone meeting in 1982, and were bent on extracting revenge as well as gaining respect. Washington succeeded on both counts.

For Dallas, the defeat was particularly frustrating. It marked the third straight time the Cowboys had inched within one victory of the Super Bowl and lost. Three turnovers and a sputtering ground game—Tony Dorsett managed only 57 yards—contributed heavily to the Cowboys' undoing.

"All that was," Washington Coach Gibbs said after the game, "was the whole world rolled into one game. This was the way it was supposed to be, the Redskins vs. Dallas, in RFK, for the NFC title, with the Super Bowl at stake. How can you top that?"

Washington, behind quarterback Joe Theismann, worked its game plan to perfection, emphasizing the run and avoiding turnovers. John Riggins, who rushed for 119 and 185 yards against the Lions and Vikings in the expanded playoffs (which, because of the strike, featured eight teams from each conference), gained 140 against Dallas and scored two touchdowns.

Manley, though, was the big-play man. While Dallas' high-powered offense seemingly is never out of a game, Manley went a long way toward short-circuiting the Cowboys' attack when he slammed into White. With Dallas trailing, 14-3, and 23 seconds remaining in the first half, White was through for the day because of a concussion. Enter Hogeboom, who had thrown only eight passes in his National Football League career.

Hogeboom's six-yard touchdown pass to Drew Pearson in the third quarter cut Washington's lead to 14-10. However, a four-yard scoring run by Riggins and a 29-yard Mike Moseley field goal—sandwiched around Hogeboom's 23-yard touchdown strike to Butch Johnson—left Washington ahead, 24-17, with 6:55 to play in the game.

Manley then deflected Hogeboom's pass, Grant lumbered into the end zone with the interception and the stadium was bedlam.

"Beating Dallas was Super Bowl One. Now we go on to Super Bowl Two," said Redskins tackle George Starke, looking ahead to a January 30 date in Pasadena, Calif., against the American Conference champion.

1982 NFC CHAMPIONSHIP GAME

Robert F. Kennedy Stadium, Washington, D.C., January 22, 1983

SCORE BY PERIODS

Dallas	3	0	14	0 — 17
Washington	7	7	7	10 — 31

SCORING

Dallas—Field goal Septien 27.
Washington—Brown 19 pass from Theismann (Moseley kick).
Washington—Riggins 1 run (Moseley kick).
Dallas—Pearson 6 pass from Hogeboom (Septien kick).
Washington—Riggins 4 run (Moseley kick).
Dallas—Johnson 23 pass from Hogeboom (Septien kick).
Washington—Field goal Moseley 29.
Washington—Grant 10 interception return (Moseley kick).

TEAM STATISTICS

	Dallas	Wash.
First Downs	21	18
Rushing Yards	65	137
Passing Yards	275	123
Return Yards	104	154
Passes	23-44-2	12-20-0
Punts	3-31.0	5-40.2
Fumbles-Lost	2-1	1-0
Penalties-Yards	3-15	3-25

Attendance—55,045.

INDIVIDUAL STATISTICS

Rushing—Dallas, Dorsett 15-57, Springs 4-15, T. Hill 1-

minus 6, Pearson 1-minus 1; Washington, Riggins 36-140, Washington 2-2, Garrett 1-minus 2, Theismann 1-minus 3.
Passing—Dallas, D. White 9-15-0—113, Hogeboom 14-29-2—162; Washington, Theismann 12-20-0—150.
Receiving—Dallas, T. Hill 5-59, Dorsett 2-29, Pearson 5-55, Johnson 5-73, Newsome 3-24, Cosbie 2-26, DuPree 1-9; Washington, Brown 3-54, Warren 2-24, Garrett 4-46, Washington 1-13, Walker 1-9, Harmon 1-4.
Kickoff Returns—Dallas, R. Hill 2-45, Fellows 1-15, Cosbie 1-12, Donley 1-22; Washington, Nelms 4-128.
Punt Returns—Dallas, R. Hill 1-0, Donley 2-10; Washington, Nelms 2-14.
Interceptions—Dallas, none; Washington, Kaufman 1-2, Grant 1-10.
Punting—Dallas, D. White 3-31.0; Washington, Hayes 5-40.2.

AFC
1982

Miami Dolphins   14
New York Jets   0

The New York Jets were coming off impressive road playoff victories against the Cincinnati Bengals, defending American Conference champions, and the Los Angeles Raiders, whose 8-1 regular-season record was the AFC's top mark in 1982.

Miami's Dolphins, spurred by their Killer Bees defense, had shut down the New England Patriots and San Diego Chargers in the playoffs and extended their overall winning streak to five games.

So, something had to give in the AFC championship game. That "something" was the Jets.

Don Shula's Dolphins made life miserable for the New Yorkers, stopping the Jets' offense in its tracks in the muck at the Orange Bowl and prevailing, 14-0. The game wasn't as close as the score might have indicated.

While the last two survivors of the AFC's eight-team Super Bowl tournament slugged it out to a 0-0 halftime deadlock, the Dolphins clearly were dominating play. And Miami finally broke through in the third quarter, scoring on Woody Bennett's seven-yard run and Uwe von Schamann's conversion kick. Bennett's touchdown proved more than enough to offset any threat that New York's bumbling offense might mount.

The Jets, in fact, seemed hopelessly grounded. Quarterback Richard Todd, harassed all afternoon, threw five interceptions and completed only 15 of 37 passes for 103 yards. Freeman McNeil, the National Football League's 1982 rushing champion, gained only 46 yards in 17 carries.

A.J. Duhe, a linebacker who loves to roam,

Miami linebacker A.J. Duhe celebrates his good fortune after returning an interception 35 yards for a fourth-quarter touchdown against the Jets.

was a particular pain to the Jets, intercepting three of Todd's passes and supplying the coup de grace.

Barely 2 minutes into the fourth quarter, Duhe diagnosed a New York screen pass and picked it off. Bobbling the ball twice, Duhe retained possession and ran 35 yards for a touchdown, Von Schamann added the placement and it was 14-0, Dolphins.

Duhe, who said he played six positions during the game, lined up at left defensive end on the play and rushed Todd. Seeing Bruce Harper positioning himself to receive the pass, Duhe stepped up and made the inter-ception.

If ever a two-touchdown lead appeared insurmountable, it was on this day.

"They played better than we did and we didn't play very well at all," understated Todd, whose Jets had lost to Miami twice during the regular season. "If somebody else has to go to the Super Bowl, I'm glad it's them."

Going to the Super Bowl would be nothing new for the Dolphins, who had earned their fourth appearance in pro football's title game. Their last appearance (1974) resulted in a 24-7 victory over Minnesota.

San Francisco's Freddie Solomon eludes Washington's Darrell Green after catching a 76-yard TD pass in the fourth quarter of the 1983 NFC title game.

1982 AFC CHAMPIONSHIP GAME

Orange Bowl, Miami, Florida, January 23, 1983

SCORE BY PERIODS

New York Jets	0	0	0	0	— 0
Miami	0	0	7	7	— 14

SCORING

Miami—Bennett 7 run (von Schamann kick).
Miami—Duhe 35 interception return (von Schamann kick).

TEAM STATISTICS

	New York	Miami
First Downs	10	13
Rushing Yards	62	138
Passing Yards	77	60
Return Yards	97	88
Passes	15-37-5	9-21-3
Punts	10-35.7	10-33.3
Fumbles-Lost	1-0	3-1
Penalties-Yards	6-42	3-15

Attendance—67,396.

INDIVIDUAL STATISTICS

Rushing—New York, McNeil 17-46, Augustyniak 2-5, Todd 4-10, Dierking 1-1; Miami, Nathan 7-24, Franklin 13-44, Bennett 13-24, Woodley 8-46.

Passing—New York, Todd 15-37-5—103; Miami, Woodley 9-21-3—87.

Receiving—New York, L. Jones 3-35, Harper 4-14, Gaffney 1-7, Barkum 2-20, Augustyniak 2-12, McNeil 1-9, Dierking 1-6, Walker 1-0; Miami, Nathan 2-4, Harris 2-28, Vigorito 3-29, Rose 1-20, Lee 1-6.

Kickoff Returns—New York, Sohn 1-31; Miami, Walker 1-20.

Punt Returns—New York, Sohn 6-65; Miami, Vigorito 3-20.

Interceptions—New York, Buttle 1-0, Schroy 2-1; Miami, G. Blackwood 1-4, Duhe 3-36, Small 1-8.

Punting—New York, Ramsey 9-39.7; Miami, Orosz 10-33.3.

NFC
1983

Washington Redskins   24
San Francisco 49ers   21

After scoring more points during the regular season than any team in history and losing only two games (by a total of two points), the Washington Redskins needed a good deal of both luck and controversy to escape the National Football Conference championship game January 8 with a 24-21 victory over the San Francisco 49ers.

Two years ago, the 49ers had been propelled to the Super Bowl by The Catch. This year it took The Fake, The Pass, The Hit and The Call for the Redskins to keep San Francisco from pulling The Upset.

The game had obviously slipped into the surreal when Washingtonians were frightened silly that Mark Moseley, one of the greatest pressure kickers in history, might shank a field-goal attempt from the 15-yard line in the final minute with the game on the line.

It had appeared earlier that the game would not be close. Taking a 7-0 halftime lead into the third quarter, thanks to a four-yard burst by running back John Riggins, the Redskins extended their lead. A one-yard Riggins touchdown run and a 70-yard TD pass from quarterback Joe Theismann to wide receiver Charlie Brown put the Redskins on top, 21-0, with one quarter to play. Washington fans figured the game was over; in fact, it hardly had begun.

San Francisco struck back. Quarterback Joe Montana completed a 79-yard drive with a five-yard scoring pass to Mike Wilson with 23 seconds gone in the final quarter. After Moseley missed his fourth field-goal attempt, this time from 41 yards—he had missed earlier from 45, 34 and 38 yards—wide receiver Freddie Solomon sprinted past cornerback Darrell Green, a former world-class dash man, gathered Montana's marvelous throw over his shoulder and raced the final 30 yards after shaking the diving Green to complete a 76-yard drive in 10 seconds—and one play.

Doubts began to plague the Redskins faithful among the crowd of 55,363 at Robert F. Kennedy Memorial Stadium in Washington. Doubt turned to disgust when Montana connected with Wilson from the 12 and tied the score at 21 with 7:08 left. No team in NFC championship game history had blown such a lead in the fourth quarter.

The Redskins were working on it.

Then, the Redskins passed the sort of character check required of champions and got the sort of luck winners also need. In all, the push for Moseley's victory-clinching field goal with 40 seconds left covered 78 yards and took more than 6 minutes. The first big play, a third-down completion to Art Monk with cornerback Tim Collier leaping over his falling frame, brought oohs; the second brought screams from the 49ers.

On second and 10 from the San Francisco 45, Theismann threw long down the left sideline toward Monk, who was stride for stride with cornerback Eric Wright. Monk seemed to have no chance for the ball, but Wright was called for pass interference at the 18.

"The rule says interference can be called (only) if the ball is catchable," Wright argued. "There's no way he could have caught the ball. I pushed him, but it was after the ball was way overthrown."

"That ball could not have been caught by a 10-foot Boston Celtic," 49ers Coach Bill Walsh said.

Two plays fetched five yards; the next had the 49ers even more outraged. On third and five from the 13, cornerback Ronnie Lott was called for holding on what seemed a harmless bit of waltzing with Brown far from where a pass fell incomplete.

"Charlie and I had quit on the ball," Lott said. "We were both watching to see if the pass would be complete. You just don't expect those kind of calls in a playoff game."

Redskins Coach Joe Gibbs wanted to talk about the drive to the field goal. "I don't think we had anything left at the end," Gibbs said, "but our guys responded. They came through."

Of the Redskins' final drive, Walsh fumed: "Final drive? Their final drive was two penalties."

The 49ers were still confident, but by the time Riggins stopped running and Theismann stopped throwing, by the time the officials stopped dropping their hankies and Moseley started kicking, by the time the 49ers did get the ball one last time, they had almost no time to do anything with it.

Montana's final pass was intercepted by defensive back Vernon Dean, and the Redskins had their ticket to Tampa.

1983 NFC CHAMPIONSHIP GAME

Robert F. Kennedy Stadium,
Washington, D.C.,
JANUARY 8, 1984

SCORE BY PERIODS

San Francisco	0	0	0	21	— 21
Washington	0	7	14	3	— 24

SCORING

Washington—Riggins 4 run (Moseley kick), 8:44 2nd. Drive: 64 yards, 6 plays.

Washington—Riggins 1 run (Moseley kick), 11:15 3rd. Drive: 36 yards, 5 plays.

Washington—Brown 70 pass from Theismann (Moseley kick), 13:58 3rd. Drive: 80 yards, 2 plays.

San Francisco—Wilson 5 pass from Montana (Wersching kick), 0:23 4th. Drive: 79 yards, 9 plays.

San Francisco—Solomon 76 pass from Montana (Wersching kick), 5:12 4th. Drive: 76 yards, 1 play.

San Francisco—Wilson 12 pass from Montana (Wersching kick), 7:52 4th. Drive: 53 yards, 4 plays.

Washington—Field goal Moseley 25, 14:20 4th. Drive: 78 yards, 13 plays.

TEAM STATISTICS

	San Francisco	Washington
First Downs	19	24
Rushing Yards	80	172
Passing Yards	345	238
Return Yards	105	84
Passes	27-48-1	15-27-1
Punts	7-33.6	5-40.2
Fumbles-Lost	4-2	2-1
Penalties-Yards	6-72	4-35

Attendance—55,363. No-shows—0.

INDIVIDUAL STATISTICS

Rushing—San Francisco, Tyler 9-35, Craig 3-3, Montana 3-42; Washington, Riggins 36-123, J. Washington 6-23, Hayes 1-14, Theismann 2-12.

Passing—San Francisco, Montana 27-48-1—347; Washington, Theismann 14-26-1—229, Riggins 1-1-0—36.

Receiving—San Francisco, Wilson 8-57, Craig 3-15, Francis 4-48, Solomon 4-106, Nehemiah 3-46, Tyler 1-17, Cooper 1-11, Ramson 3-47; Washington, Brown 5-137, Monk 3-35, Didier 3-61, J. Washington 3-21, Walker 1-11.

Interceptions—San Francisco, Wright 1-0; Washington, Dean 1-5.

Punting—San Francisco, Orosz 7-33.6; Washington, Hayes 5-40.2.

Punt Returns—San Francisco, McLemore 2-7; Washington, Giaquinto 4-31.

Kickoff Returns—San Francisco, McLemore 5-98; Washington, Evans 1-8, Garrett 2-31, Coleman 1-9.

Field Goals—San Francisco, Wersching 0-2 (missed: 55, 50); Washington, Moseley 1-5 (missed: 45, 34, 38, 41).

Raiders running back Frank Hawkins cuts through the Seattle defense on a one-yard touchdown run in the second period of the 1983 AFC title game.

AFC
1983

Los Angeles Raiders 30
Seattle Seahawks   14

In the end, the Seattle Seahawks looked something like one set of goal posts at the Los Angeles Memorial Coliseum—battered and beaten.

The goal posts had come down after the Raiders earned the fourth trip to the Super Bowl in the franchise's history. But this was the first trip carrying the flag of Los Angeles, and residents of the City of Angels celebrated the occasion by pouring onto the field to do battle with the goal posts, police and security forces ill-prepared to deal with a turnout of 88,734.

Afterward, 13 fans clad in black-and-silver costumes were wearing handcuffs, and one set of goal posts had been spared. That's better than the Seahawks fared.

Seattle wasn't defeated in the American Football Conference championship game January 8. It was beaten. Beaten on the head and

shoulders, on the line of scrimmage and, most importantly, on the scoreboard, 30-14.

"The Raiders' defense," explained linebacker Matt Millen, "is based on the three Ps: pointing, pushing and punching."

The Raiders applied that philosophy all over the bodies of the Seahawks. In the first two minutes of play, there were a handful of fights, there was a booming running-into-the-punter penalty and there were all sorts of terrible things being done and said to the Seahawks.

But the main mission of this always-angry football team was to stop Curt Warner, for to stop the Seahawks' talented rookie running back was to stop Coach Chuck Knox's ground-oriented offense.

To accomplish that task, the Raiders split their ends a bit farther than normal. They brought their cornerbacks up to the line of scrimmage. They squeezed their inside linebackers over the middle and then gang-tackled Warner into oblivion. Warner, the leading rusher in the AFC, ran for just 26 yards on 11 carries.

With Warner shut down, the Seahawks were forced to throw. Dave Krieg, the Cinderella story of the last half of the season, quickly discovered he was going to get no better treatment than Warner.

The Raiders grounded Krieg, hitting hard,

often and sometimes late. After he threw his third interception—to go along with being sacked a couple of times and fumbling once—he was replaced by Jim Zorn. But by that time, early in the third quarter, the Raiders were holding a 20-0 lead.

While the Raider defense was pounding the hope out of the Seattle offense, the Raider offense was saving its turnovers for late in the game and enjoying the spectacle of Marcus Allen sliding and gliding all over the field.

In losing two regular-season games to the Seahawks, the Raiders had committed 13 turnovers. They had four more in the championship game, but those came after they had built their huge lead.

Most of the lead came thanks to Allen, who rushed for 154 yards on 25 carries and caught seven passes for 62 more yards and a touchdown. Meanwhile, quarterback Jim Plunkett was 17-of-24 for 214 yards passing. Malcolm Barnwell caught five passes for 116 yards. Frank Hawkins ran for two touchdowns. Chris Bahr kicked three field goals, the first after a 44-yard interception return by Lester Hayes.

And for the fourth time in his coaching career, Knox was stopped a step short of the Super Bowl. This time he was stopped by a powerful Raider team that was just as tough—or tougher—than the teams that represented Oakland in the Super Bowl in 1968, 1977 and 1981.

1983 AFC CHAMPIONSHIP GAME

Los Angeles Coliseum, Los Angeles, Calif., JANUARY 8, 1984

SCORE BY PERIODS

Seattle	0	0	7	7 — 14
Los Angeles Raiders	3	17	7	3 — 30

SCORING

Los Angeles—Field goal Bahr 20, 6:13 1st. Drive: 23 yards, 6 plays.
Los Angeles—Hawkins 1 run (Bahr kick), 10:43 2nd. Drive: 61 yards, 9 plays.
Los Angeles—Hawkins 5 run (Bahr kick), 13:54 2nd. Drive: 60 yards, 4 plays.
Los Angeles—Field goal Bahr 45, 14:57 2nd. Drive: 33 yards, 5 plays.
Los Angeles—Allen 3 pass from Plunkett (Bahr kick), 8:11 3rd. Drive: 46 yards, 2 plays.
Seattle—Doornink 11 pass from Zorn (N. Johnson kick), 10:59 3rd. Drive: 74 yards, 10 plays.
Los Angeles—Field goal Bahr 35, 11:03 4th. Drive: 19 yards, 7 plays.
Seattle—Young 9 pass from Zorn (N. Johnson kick), 13:44 4th. Drive: 71 yards, 9 plays.

TEAM STATISTICS

	Seattle	Los Angeles
First Downs	16	21
Rushing Yards	65	205
Passing Yards	102	196
Return Yards	144	100
Passes	17-36-5	17-24-2
Punts	5-32.0	2-34.0
Fumbles-Lost	1-0	3-2
Penalties-Yards	2-20	7-53

Attendance—88,734. No-shows—3,601.

Raiders defensive back Mike Davis is tackled after making one of his team's five interceptions against Seattle.

INDIVIDUAL STATISTICS

Rushing—Seattle, Warner 11-26, Hughes 3-14, Dixon 3-24, C. Bryant 1-1; Los Angeles, Allen 25-154, Hawkins 10-24, Plunkett 7-26, Pruitt 1-4, King 2-0, Wilson 1-minus 3.

Passing—Seattle, Krieg 3-9-3—12, Zorn 14-27-2—134; Los Angeles, Plunkett 17-24-2—214.

Receiving—Seattle, Largent 2-25, Warner 2-10, Doornink 6-48, Johns 5-49, H. Jackson 1-5, Young 1-9; Los Angeles, Allen 7-62, Barnwell 5-116, Christensen 3-14, Branch 2-22.

Interceptions—Seattle, G. Johnson 1-0, Scholtz 1-8; Los Angeles, Hayes 1-44, M. Davis 2-2, Millen 1-13, McElroy 1-minus 6.

Punting—Seattle, West 5-32.0; Los Angeles, Guy 2-34.0.

Punt Returns—Los Angeles, Pruitt 1-1.

Kickoff Returns—Seattle, Hughes 2-60, Dixon 3-54, Lane 1-10, Scholtz 1-12; Los Angeles, Montgomery 2-46.

Field Goals—Seattle, none attempted; Los Angeles, Bahr 3-3.

NFC
1984

San Francisco 49ers   23
Chicago Bears   0

Most of the talk before this National Football Conference championship game between the 49ers and Bears centered on the Chicago defense, which entered the contest ranked No. 1 overall (first against the rush, second against the pass) in the league. While they weren't exactly the Monsters of the Midway of the Bears' glory years, they were a sound defensive team. Chicago set an NFL record for quarterback sacks with 72 during the regular season in winning the NFC Central Division crown. With an offense that could be described as adequate at best—with the exception of the fabulous Walter Payton at running back—there was little doubt that the defense was primarily responsible for the Bears' most successful season since their 1963 championship year.

The week prior to their meeting with the Niners, the Bears stunned the Redskins, 23-19, in a playoff game at RFK Stadium in Washington. The defense tormented Redskins quarterback Joe Theismann all afternoon, sacking him seven times and forcing three Washington turnovers. It was perhaps Chicago's best overall performance of the 1984 season, and it gave the Bears plenty of confidence for their title-game showdown with the 49ers at Candlestick Park.

"We belong in this game," said Bears Coach Mike Ditka, refusing to concede that the game might be no more than a Super Bowl warmup for San Francisco, a club that in '84 became the first in league history to win 15 regular-season games in one season. "We can play with anybody because of a great defense and the fact we can run the football. No matter what, this game is still basic. If you do the basic things right, you can win."

Unfortunately for Ditka and his team, one of the basics is scoring points, and the Bears didn't score any against the 49ers.

In one of the most lopsided Championship Games ever, the Niners' defense completely shut down the Chicago offense. The Bears didn't gain a yard in the second quarter and their running game, ranked first in the league coming into the contest, had compiled only seven yards on first down when San Francisco held a 20-0 fourth-quarter advantage. The passing game, which was almost a non-entity in Chicago with Payton having another outstanding season, was invisible in this game. Quarterback Steve Fuller had just 37 net yards passing and was sacked nine times by the hard-charging 49ers defensive front. Seven different play-

The sign in the background and the disappointment of Chicago running back Walter Payton tell the story of the 49ers' 23-0 NFC championship game victory over the Bears.

ers came up with at least one sack for San Francisco as the defense ran its string of not allowing a touchdown to 10 quarters. They had led the NFL in fewest points allowed during the regular season.

"This was the most pressure I've faced all season," said Fuller, who was acquired by the Bears during the previous offseason from the Rams as a backup for Jim McMahon. But Fuller found himself playing regularly during the '84 campaign when McMahon went down with lacerated kidneys. "They just kept coming and coming. We weren't able to make the yardage on first down. That was our downfall."

The 49ers' offense, however, was different from the Bears' in one important respect: it was well-balanced. With Joe Montana, Dwight Clark and Freddie Solomon leading the passing attack and Wendell Tyler and Roger Craig running out of the backfield, the Chicago defense couldn't key on one aspect of the attack without leaving open the other. And the offense was anchored up front by three Pro Bowlers—tackle Keith Fahnhorst, guard Randy Cross and center Fred Quillan.

But the unit started the title game very slowly. After marching to the Chicago 2-yard line on its first possession, with Montana completing five of six passes in the drive, the 49ers had to settle for a Ray Wersching field goal after Montana fumbled the snap on third down.

Then, after the Niners got the ball back on an interception by safety Dwight Hicks, Montana promptly threw a floater in the Bears end zone that Chicago safety Gary Fencik intercepted for a touchback.

Later, the 49ers tried Solomon at quarterback for one play (with Montana lining up at wide receiver), but the Bears stopped the option run for no gain. Then, two Montana passes of 14 yards each against Bear blitzes gave San Francisco a first down at the Chicago 4. But Bears defensive end Dan Hampton knocked down a third-down pass and San Francisco had to settle for a 22-yard field goal. The heavily-favored 49ers were clearly struggling on offense but, then again, so were the Bears.

In the second half the 49ers turned it around. They scored their first touchdown on their opening possession—despite Montana's being sacked twice—when Tyler scored from nine yards out. It was a particularly sweet touchdown for Tyler, who only one year earlier was benched by Coach Bill Walsh because of his fumbling in a 13-3 loss to the Bears in Chicago.

It was all downhill from there for San Francisco. The Niners added 10 fourth-quarter points and held the Bears scoreless to register the first shutout in a Championship Game since Miami whitewashed the New York Jets, 14-0, in 1983. And it was the Dolphins who the 49ers would next face in Super Bowl XIX.

1984 NFC CHAMPIONSHIP GAME

Candlestick Park, San Francisco, Calif.
JANUARY 6, 1985

SCORE BY PERIODS

Chicago	0	0	0	0 — 0
San Francisco	3	3	7	10 — 23

SCORING

San Francisco—Field goal Wersching 21, 10:39 1st. Drive: 73 yards, 10 plays.

San Francisco—Field goal Wersching 22, 7:03 2nd. Drive: 65 yards, 13 plays.

San Francisco—Tyler 9 run (Wersching kick), 6:33 3rd. Drive: 35 yards, 5 plays.

San Francisco—Solomon 10 pass from Montana (Wersching kick), 3:45 4th. Drive: 88 yards, 8 plays.

San Francisco—Field goal Wersching 34, 13:03 4th. Drive: 36 yards, 8 plays.

TEAM STATISTICS

	Chicago	San Francisco
First downs	13	25
Rushing yards	149	159
Passing yards	37	228
Return yards	74	84
Passes	13-22-1	19-35-2
Punts	7-43.1	3-39.0
Fumbles-Lost	1-0	1-0
Penalties-Yards	7-50	3-20
Attendance—61,040. No-shows—296.		

Rushing—Chicago, Payton 22-92, Fuller 6-39, Suhey 3-16, C. Thomas 1-2; San Francisco, Tyler 10-68, Craig 8-44, Montana 5-22, Harmon 3-18, Ring 2-5, Cavanaugh 1-2.

Passing—Chicago, Fuller 13-22-1—87; San Francisco, Montana 18-34-2—233, Cavanaugh 1-1-0—3.

Receiving—Chicago, McKinnon 3-48, Moorehead 2-14, Suhey 4-11, Payton 3-11, Dunsmore 1-3; San Francisco, D. Clark 4-83, Solomon 7-73, Wilson 2-25, Tyler 2-22, Francis 2-20, Nehemiah 1-10, Harmon 1-3.

Interceptions—Chicago, Fencik 2-5; San Francisco, Hicks 1-0.

Punting—Chicago, Finzer 7-43.1; San Francisco, Runager 3-39.0.

Punt Returns—Chicago, Fisher 2-12; San Francisco, McLemore 4-69.

Kickoff Returns—Chicago, Gentry 3-49, Gault 1-18; San Francisco, Harmon 1-15.

Field Goals—Chicago, B. Thomas 0-1 (missed: 41); San Francisco, Wersching 3-3.

Sacks—Chicago, Wilson, Keys, McMichael ½, Hampton ½; San Francisco, Johnson 2, Carter 2, Board, Dean, Stuckey, Pillers ½, Williamson ½.

AFC
1984

Miami Dolphins   45
Pittsburgh Steelers 28

It was a question Pittsburgh Coach Chuck Noll was asked so many times during the 1984 season that his patience was near its end. The question: Why didn't the Steelers draft hometown star Dan Marino of the University of Pittsburgh with their first-round pick in the 1983 NFL draft? Marino was terrorizing NFL secondaries so much during his short pro career that someone in the Steelers organization had to know that what Marino was doing—48 touchdown passes in '84 alone—while highly unlikely, was at least possible.

During the week leading up to the American Football Conference championship game between the Steelers and Miami Dolphins, Noll was asked the question again. This time, his anger showed.

"Scouts are human, too," he snapped. "They make mistakes." Noll left his interrogators with little doubt that, if they could have the draft to do again, Marino would be their man.

But a lot of NFL teams also felt that way, especially after Marino's fantastic first two years. Instead, he ended up in Miami, and led the Dolphins to a 45-28 AFC title-game rout of the franchise he grew up idolizing. Marino had better statistical games during the '84 season, but no victory was more important.

"What more can you say about Danny?" asked Miami Coach Don Shula. "He continues to rise to the occasion. He continually picked up the fact the Steelers would be blitzing and he made the adjustments. When you catch their defense in a situation where the blitzes can be picked up, you can really hurt them. And he did."

Marino passed for AFC title-game records of 421 yards and four touchdowns as the Miami offensive machine, ranked No. 1 in the NFL during the regular season, rolled up 569 yards against an outmanned Steelers defense. Marino could have easily broken Dan Fouts' all-time playoff game record of 433 yards (set against the Dolphins in a double-overtime victory in 1982) had not Shula called off the dogs in the final 11 minutes with the outcome no longer in doubt.

Earlier in the game, however, the outcome was very much in doubt. Although the Dolphins struck quickly with a 40-yard Marino-to-Mark Clayton touchdown pass midway through the opening period, Pittsburgh responded with a score of its own. Rookie running back Rich Erenberg carried over from seven yards out with 3:30 left in the quarter to climax a 66-yard drive and knot the score at 7-7.

After Uwe von Schamann kicked a 26-yard field goal to enable Miami to regain the lead, the Steelers showed a little quick-strike capability of their own. With less than three minutes left in the first half, perennial All-Pro receiver John Stallworth broke loose in the Dolphins secondary and hauled in a 65-yard touchdown pass from Mark Malone. The long score stunned the Orange Bowl crowd and gave the Steelers a 14-10 lead. But it turned out to be Pittsburgh's only lead of the day.

"We did get burned a couple of times on defense," admitted Shula. "But, each time, our offense was able to answer the challenge." They answered it with two touchdowns in less than a minute. First, Marino hooked up with Mark Duper for a 41-yard score as Miami regained the lead for good.

Then, after Dolphins safety Lyle Blackwood intercepted a Malone pass at the Pittsburgh 35, Marino and Co. needed just three plays to score again, Tony Nathan doing the honors as Miami took a 24-14 lead into the locker room at the half.

If there was any doubt at the intermission as to which team would be making the journey to Palo Alto, California for a date in Super Bowl XIX, it ended just four plays into the second half. The Dolphins scored again, this time on a 36-yard Marino-to-Duper hookup, as the advantage grew to 17 points.

The only thing that remained to be seen was how many points the Dolphins would score or whether Pittsburgh could make it close. Stallworth's NFL-record 12th career touchdown reception in postseason play, a 19-yard pass from Malone, cut the Steelers' deficit to 31-21. But the Dolphins scored two more touchdowns to set a Championship Game record of 45 points —and it probably would have been more had Shula allowed Marino to throw a pass in the

final 11 minutes.

"The Dolphins have a helluva passing game," said Steelers safety Donnie Shell, who had seen quite a few good passing teams in his 11-year NFL career. "It's well-designed, but it's not the design that makes it go—it's No. 13 (Marino)."

Chuck Noll would whole-heartedly agree.

1984 AFC CHAMPIONSHIP GAME
Orange Bowl, Miami, Fla.
JANUARY 6, 1985

SCORE BY PERIODS

Pittsburgh	7	7	7	7 — 28
Miami	7	17	14	7 — 45

SCORING

Miami—Clayton 40 pass from Marino (von Schamann kick), 7:15 1st. Drive: 67 yards, 4 plays.

Pittsburgh—Erenberg 7 run (Anderson kick), 11:30 1st. Drive: 66 yards, 7 plays.

Miami—Field goal von Schamann 26, 5:56 2nd. Drive: 55 yards, 8 plays.

Pittsburgh—Stallworth 65 pass from Malone (Anderson kick), 12:08 2nd. Drive: 71 yards, 3 plays.

Miami—Duper 41 pass from Marino (von Schamann kick), 13:30 2nd. Drive: 77 yards, 5 plays.

Miami—Nathan 2 run (von Schamann kick), 14:24 2nd. Drive: 35 yards, 3 plays.

Miami—Duper 36 pass from Marino (von Schamann kick), 1:48 3rd. Drive: 78 yards, 4 plays.

Pittsburgh—Stallworth 19 pass from Malone (Anderson kick), 7:05 3rd. Drive: 72 yards, 9 plays.

Miami—Bennett 1 run (von Schamann kick), 13:20 3rd. Drive: 80 yards, 10 plays.

Miami—Moore 6 pass from Marino (von Schamann kick), 3:55 4th. Drive: 66 yards, 9 plays.

Pittsburgh—Capers 29 pass from Malone (Anderson kick), 14:35 4th. Drive: 84 yards, 5 plays.

TEAM STATISTICS

	Pittsburgh	Miami
First downs	22	28
Rushing yards	143	134
Passing yards	312	435
Return yards	105	42
Passes	20-36-3	22-33-1
Punts	3-43.7	2-42.5
Fumbles-Lost	2-1	1-1
Penalties-Yards	3-30	3-25

Attendance—76,029. No-shows—None.

INDIVIDUAL STATISTICS

Rushing—Pittsburgh, Abercrombie 15-68, Pollard 11-48, Erenberg 6-27; Miami, Nathan 19-64, P. Johnson 10-39, Bennett 8-33, Strock 1-minus 2.

Passing—Pittsburgh, Malone 20-36-3—312; Miami, Marino 21-32-1—421, Nathan 1-1-0—14.

Receiving—Pittsburgh, Stallworth 4-111, Lipps 3-45, Sweeney 3-42, Pollard 3-13, Erenberg 5-59, Capers 1-29, Abercrombie 1-13; Miami, Nathan 8-114, Duper 5-148, Clayton 4-95, Moore 2-34, Hardy 2-16, Rose 1-28.

Interceptions—Pittsburgh, Shell 1-18; Miami, Judson 1-34, G. Blackwood 1-4, L. Blackwood 1-4.

Punting—Pittsburgh, Colquitt 3-43.7; Miami, Roby 2-42.5.

Punt Returns—Pittsburgh, Lipps 1-7; Miami, Walker 2-10, Kozlowski 1-2.

Kickoff Returns—Pittsburgh, Erenberg 5-106; Miami, Walker 3-62.

Field Goals—Pittsburgh, Anderson 0-1 (missed: 53); Miami, von Schamann 1-2 (missed: 52).

Jim McMahon listens to some friendly coaching advice during Chicago's NFC Championship Game victory over the Los Angeles Rams.

NFC 1985

Chicago Bears	**24**
Los Angeles Rams	**0**

When the Chicago Bears lost to the San Francisco 49ers, 23-0, in the 1984 National Football Conference championship game, few people were surprised. The 49ers, destiny's darlings, had ravaged the National Football League en route to a final 18-1 record and Super Bowl XIX championship. No one—certainly not the up-and-coming Bears—were going to keep the 49ers from their appointed glory.

A year later, the shoe was on the other foot. Having used that humiliating shutout loss as their impetus, the Bears vowed that 1985 would be different.

And it was.

In eerie resemblance to the 49ers, the Bears rolled through the regular season with only one loss, scoring 456 points and yielding a league-low 198—a difference of 16 points a game. They crushed the New York Giants, 21-

0, in their first playoff game before advancing to the conference title game for the second straight year. But this time, destiny was on Chicago's side.

The Bears beat the Los Angeles Rams, 24-0, and it could have been much worse. Swirling 20-mile-per-hour winds, freezing temperatures and a suffocating Chicago defense made life miserable for the Rams all afternoon. The West Coast visitors never came close to cracking the Chicago goal line and the Bears recorded an NFL-record second consecutive playoff shutout.

"I don't care how many points we might have scored," Chicago Coach Mike Ditka said. "Los Angeles wasn't going to score. I don't know how our guys could have played any better than they did."

All-Pro middle linebacker Mike Singletary, however, wasn't convinced. The defensive co-captain thought there was room for improvement.

"I would only rate the defense a 95 instead of a perfect 100," he said. "I don't think we'll be great until after the Super Bowl. This week was a 95 and we have an opportunity to be perfect at Super Bowl time."

You would have a tough time convincing the Rams that the Chicago defense could play any better. The Rams were held to 130 total yards on 60 plays—an average of 2.2 yards each down—and running back Eric Dickerson, who had set a single-game playoff rushing record with 248 yards against Dallas the previous week, was held to 46 yards on 17 carries. Dickerson's longest run of the day was nine yards and one of his two fumbles led to a 52-yard scoring drive that stretched the Bears' lead to 17-0 in the third quarter.

"Our defense took the game away from Eric Dickerson," Ditka said. "And when they took the game away from Dickerson, the game was ours."

Ditka's inference was clear. Without Dickerson as a threat, the Rams were forced to rely on the right arm of quarterback Dieter Brock, a 34-year-old Canadian Football League refugee who was brought in before the season to give L.A. some semblance of a passing attack. He was ineffective in the title game when his passes fluttered around windy Soldier Field. He completed just 10 of 31 attempts for 66 yards and threw one interception.

"I can't think of any quarterback who wouldn't have problems being down 10-0 against that defense and throwing into that wind," Rams Coach John Robinson said.

"Dieter's a tough guy, a good quarterback," said Ditka. "But he had some trouble keeping his passes on line in this wind; he just wasn't used to it."

Chicago quarterback Jim McMahon, however, was used to the blustery conditions and performed well. McMahon completed 16 of 25 passes for 164 yards and one touchdown and scored the Bears' first touchdown on a 16-yard run on the club's first possession. McMahon carried the ball four times for 28 yards.

"The wind must not have bothered him too much," Ditka said. "He was our leading rusher,

1985 NFC CHAMPIONSHIP GAME

Soldier Field, Chicago

JANUARY 12, 1986

SCORE BY PERIODS

Los Angeles Rams	0	0	0	0 —	0
Chicago	10	0	7	7 —	24

SCORING

Chicago—McMahon 16 run (Butler kick), 5:25 1st. Drive: 56 yards, 5 plays.

Chicago—Field goal Butler 34, 10:34 1st. Drive: 33 yards, 7 plays.

Chicago—Gault 22 pass from McMahon (Butler kick), 8:04 3rd. Drive: 52 yards, 8 plays.

Chicago—Marshall 52 fumble return (Butler kick), 12:23 4th.

TEAM STATISTICS

	Los Angeles	Chicago
FIRST DOWNS	9	13
By rushing	5	5
By passing	3	8
By penalty	1	0
3RD DOWN EFFICIENCY	2-14	4-16
TOTAL NET YARDS	130	232
Offensive plays	60	61
Average gain per play	2.2	3.8
NET YARDS RUSHING	86	91
Total rushes	26	33
Average gain per rush	3.3	2.8
NET YARDS PASSING	44	141
Sacked-Yards lost	3-22	3-23
Gross yards passing	66	164
PASSES	10-31-1	16-25-0
Average gain per pass	1.3	5.0
PUNTS	11-39.2	10-36.3
Had blocked	0	0
TOTAL RETURN YARDAGE	92	40
Punt returns	4-16	5-21
Kickoff returns	4-76	1-22
Interception returns	0-0	1- minus 3
PENALTIES-YARDS	4-25	6-48
FUMBLES-LOST	4-2	3-1
TIME OF POSSESSION	25:33	34:27

Attendance—63,522. No-shows—2,580.

INDIVIDUAL STATISTICS

Rushing—Los Angeles, Dickerson 17-46, Redden 9-40; Chicago, Payton 18-32, Suhey 6-23, McMahon 4-28, Thomas 3-minus 1, Gentry 2-9.

Passing—Los Angeles, Brock 10-31-1—66; Chicago, McMahon 16-25-0—164.

Receiving—Los Angeles, Hunter 3-29, Brown 2-14, Dickerson 3-10, Ellard 1-5, Duckworth 1-8; Chicago, Moorehead 2-28, Gault 4-56, Payton 7-48, Wrightman 1-8, Suhey 1-7, McKinnon 1-17.

Interceptions—Chicago, Frazier 1-minus 3.

Punting—Los Angeles, Hatcher 11-39.2; Chicago, Buford 10-36.3.

Punt Returns—Los Angeles, Ellard 1-6, Johnson 2-6, Irvin 1-4; Chicago, Ortego 4-21, Phillips 1-0.

Kickoff Returns—Los Angeles, Redden 1-13, Brown 3-63; Chicago, Gentry 1-22.

Field Goals—Los Angeles, none attempted; Chicago, Butler 1-1.

Sacks—Los Angeles, Doss, Reed 2; Chicago, Hampton, Perry, Dent.

our leading passer and he scored as many points as anybody else."

McMahon, who didn't play in the '84 title-game loss to San Francisco because of injury, surprised the Rams. With the Bears' running game effectively shut down (91 yards), McMahon put the ball up with regularity. The Bears passed on 12 of 22 first-down plays and completed 10 of those against a defense that had been gearing itself for the run all week.

"We can throw the ball as well as anyone and open it up when we have to," McMahon said. "We can be 'Air Ditka' if we have to."

Although McMahon's first-quarter touchdown run gave Chicago all the points it would need, his biggest contribution came midway through the third period with the Bears leading, 10-0. Faced with a second-and-10 situation at the Rams' 22-yard line, Ditka ordered a running play. McMahon, sensing the Bears offense would live or die with the pass on this day, overruled his coach.

"I didn't agree with the coach. I just didn't think the draw would get us enough yards," McMahon said, smiling. "So I called my own play."

McMahon rolled to his left and spotted fleet wide receiver Willie Gault breaking for the corner of the L.A. end zone. He drilled Gault with a perfect pass and the Bears had themselves a 17-point lead.

"Mike's reaction? Well, he congratulated me for my play selection," McMahon said.

There was little, in fact, for the Bears' fiery coach to complain about. His defense was fearsome, his offense was superb and the franchise he once gave his blood, sweat and tears for as a player was headed for its first-ever Super Bowl game. The game in New Orleans two weeks hence would be the Bears' first appearance in the NFL's title game since 1963, when a 24-year-old firebrand named Mike Ditka was the team's tight end.

"It was the way we won all year," said Ditka. "You saw it. It was unbelievable. I don't know if we can play much better."

AFC
1985

New England Patriots   31
Miami Dolphins   14

The odds were overwhelmingly against the New England Patriots when they traveled to Miami to take on the Dolphins in the 1985 American Football Conference championship game. The Pats had not won a game at the

Orange Bowl since 1966, the Dolphins' first season. Included in those 18 consecutive Miami losses was a 30-27 setback just four weeks earlier, a loss that cost New England a chance to clinch the AFC Eastern Division crown. The Dolphins eventually won the division title for the third straight season.

The Patriots were facing a team that had not lost in nine 1985 home games. And the Dolphins, riding an eight-game winning streak, had never lost a conference championship game in five tries under Coach Don Shula.

So what happened? The Patriots won, 31-14. The key was six Miami turnovers (four fumbles and two interceptions), four of which the Pats converted into 24 points. For the third successive week, New England pulled off an upset, becoming the first wild-card entry in league history to win three straight playoff games on the road.

"I'm not an oddsmaker, but what we've done must be against incredible odds," said New England Coach Raymond Berry.

The Pats forced 10 turnovers (leading to 37 points) in victories over the Jets and Raiders before getting the Dolphins to cough it up six times. The Patriots rolled up an 11-5 regular-season record largely because of the conference-leading 47 turnovers forced by their defense.

"We put the ball on the ground too often," said Miami quarterback Dan Marino, who completed 20 of 48 attempts for 248 yards and two touchdowns. "It seemed like they scored almost every time we turned it over. They have that type of team. That's why they're going to the Super Bowl."

The tone of the game was set on Miami's first play from scrimmage when running back Tony Nathan fumbled after a hard hit by linebacker Steve Nelson. Rookie defensive end Garin Veris recovered for the Pats at the Miami 20, leading to Tony Franklin's 23-yard field goal and a 3-0 New England lead.

"They were going for the football," said Nathan, who rushed only one more time but caught five passes for 57 yards. "We knew they were going to do it, but we couldn't wrap it up."

The Dolphins responded to Franklin's field goal by marching 80 yards late in the first period, with Marino completing five passes for 62 yards, including a 10-yard touchdown strike to tight end Dan Johnson. Miami had its only lead of the game.

Another key to New England's success was a running game that tied Miami's defense in knots all day. The Dolphins knew what was coming, but were powerless to stop it.

"It was no mystery what they were going to do," said Miami defensive end Doug Betters. "We just couldn't stop them. They don't do any high-tech stuff. They just blow you off the ball and run it down your throat."

The Pats ran it down the Dolphins' throat 59

times for 255 yards, with Craig James (105 yards) and Robert Weathers (87 yards) both rushing for more yards than the entire Miami team (68 yards). Quarterback Tony Eason attempted just 12 passes and completed 10, including touchdown passes of four, one and two yards. The conservative Patriots threw the ball only when they had to.

"Every time we got into a scoring battle with them, we came out a loser," said guard Ron Wooten. "With the way our defense is playing, we figured we could hold them to a reasonable number of points. If that happened, we knew we could win."

Because of their running game, the Pats maintained possession nearly twice as long as the Dolphins (39:51 to 20:09) and kept the ball away from Marino and the high-scoring Miami offense. Mark Duper and Mark Clayton, the Dolphins' two deep threats, combined for only six catches for 86 yards.

When Miami played Cleveland in its first playoff game a week earlier, the Browns employed a similar strategy. Cleveland rushed the ball 37 times for 251 yards and forced Marino to complete the majority of his passes (20 of 25) to either running backs or tight ends. The Browns collapsed late, however, yielding three touchdowns in the final 21 minutes and losing, 24-21. It was the biggest comeback in AFC playoff history.

"After studying what Cleveland did, we figured we had good enough corners to do the same things," said Pats safety Fred Marion, who had one interception.

"We felt Cleveland had just run out of gas the week before," said James. "We're in great condition and we told each other at halftime not to let up or get worn down."

Instead, it was the Dolphins who were worn down, unable to move consistently or effectively on an Orange Bowl turf that became soft and slow because of heavy rain. A muffed punt by the Pats' Roland James set up the Dolphins' final score—a 10-yard pass from Marino to Nathan—in the first minute of the fourth quarter, but there would be no miraculous Miami rally this week.

"We had a chance to get back into the game in the fourth quarter, but we didn't get it done," said Shula. "We had a chance to make it interesting, but we didn't."

Shula missed a record seventh trip to the Super Bowl, a trip that went instead to Berry, a former Hall of Fame receiver with the Baltimore Colts. Shula coached Berry during his final five seasons as a player (1963-67), but the AFC championship game was one time when the student taught the teacher a lesson.

"We knew that if we were going to make it to the Super Bowl, we'd have to get there through Miami," said Wooten. "This is like a dream come true, winning it down here, in this place, against this team."

1985 AFC CHAMPIONSHIP GAME
Orange Bowl, Miami, Fla.

JANUARY 12, 1986

SCORE BY PERIODS

New England	3	14	7	7 — 31
Miami	0	7	0	7 — 14

SCORING

New England—Field goal Franklin 23, 6:40 1st. Drive: 14 yards, 5 plays.

Miami—Johnson 10 pass from Marino (Reveiz kick), 0:21 2nd. Drive: 80 yards, 11 plays.

New England—Collins 4 pass from Eason (Franklin kick), 4:50 2nd. Drive: 66 yards, 8 plays.

New England—D. Ramsey 1 pass from Eason (Franklin kick), 9:35 2nd. Drive: 36 yards, 7 plays.

New England—Weathers 2 pass from Eason (Franklin kick), 3:02 3rd. Drive: 25 yards, 6 plays.

Miami—Nathan 10 pass from Marino (Reveiz kick), 0:32 4th. Drive: 10 yards, 1 play.

New England—Tatupu 1 run (Franklin kick), 7:26 4th. Drive: 45 yards, 9 plays.

TEAM STATISTICS

	New England	Miami
FIRST DOWNS	21	18
By rushing	15	3
By passing	6	15
By penalty	0	0
3RD DOWN EFFICIENCY	7-16	3-10
TOTAL NET YARDS	326	302
Offensive plays	71	62
Average gain per play	4.6	4.9
NET YARDS RUSHING	255	68
Total rushes	59	13
Average gain per rush	4.3	5.2
NET YARDS PASSING	71	234
Sacked-Yards lost	0-0	1-14
Gross yards passing	71	248
PASSES	10-12-0	20-48-2
Average gain per pass	5.9	4.8
PUNTS	5-40.2	4-41.3
Had blocked	0	0
TOTAL RETURN YARDAGE	90	99
Punt returns	2-2	1-8
Kickoff returns	3-67	6-91
Interception returns	2-21	0-0
PENALTIES-YARDS	2-15	4-35
FUMBLES-LOST	2-2	5-4
TIME OF POSSESSION	39:51	20:09

Attendance—74,978. No-shows—1,292.

INDIVIDUAL STATISTICS

Rushing—New England, C. James 22-105, Weathers 16-87, Collins 12-61, Tatupu 6-9, Eason 3-minus 7; Miami, Carter 6-56, Davenport 3-6, Nathan 2-4, Bennett 1-2, Marino 1-0.

Passing—New England, Eason 10-12-0—71; Miami, Marino 20-48-2—248.

Receiving—New England, Collins 3-15, D. Ramsey 3-18, Morgan 2-30, Tatupu 1-6, Weathers 1-2; Miami, Nathan 5-57, Hardy 3-52, Duper 3-45, Clayton 3-41, Davenport 3-23, Johnson 1-10, N. Moore 1-10, Rose 1-10.

Interceptions—New England, Marion 1-21, Clayborn 1-0.

Punting—New England, Camarillo 5-40.2; Miami, Roby 4-41.3.

Punt Returns—New England, R. James 2-2; Miami, Vigorito 1-8.

Kickoff Returns—New England, Starring 3-67; Miami, Hampton 6-91.

Field Goals—New England, Franklin 1-2 (missed: 41); Miami, Reveiz 0-1 (missed: 31).

Sacks—New England, Veris.

NFC
1986

New York Giants   17
Washington Redskins   0

In the week leading up to the 1986 National Football League title game between the New York Giants and Washington Redskins, the talk coming out of New York didn't revolve around the Giants' spectacular defense, the exploits of running back Joe Morris or the Redskins' outstanding passing trio of quarterback Jay Schroeder and wide receivers Art Monk and Gary Clark.

Most of the talk in the Big Apple revolved around Mayor Ed Koch's refusal to host and pick up the tab for a Giants' victory parade, the one that would follow their inevitable triumph in Super Bowl XXI.

The Super Bowl? The Giants hadn't even won the NFC championship, yet their fans were worried about where to celebrate a Super Bowl victory.

It was a classic case of putting the cart before the horse. But then it really didn't matter. The Giants systematically destroyed Washington, 17-0, with an awesome display of offense, defense and special teams play. The win was New York's 11th straight in a 16-2 season and third against the Redskins, who had finished two games behind the Giants in the NFC Eastern Division during the regular season.

"This was our game to win, on our field, in front of our fans," said Giants quarterback Phil Simms. "I'm not surprised by what happened. We felt we should win."

On a cold, windy, blustery day before 76,633 fans at Giants Stadium—"It was the windiest I've ever seen it," said Simms, an eight-year veteran—a New York victory was never in doubt. The Giants won the coin flip, elected to kick off with the 32 mile-per-hour wind and, 10 minutes later, owned a 10-0 lead.

"The coin toss was probably one of the biggest turning points," admitted Washington's Joe Gibbs, who suffered the first shutout in his six-year tenure as the Redskins' coach.

Punter Steve Cox was only able to launch 23- and 27-yard kicks after Washington was stymied by a juiced-up Giants defense on its first two possessions. New York's offense took over at the Redskin 47 and 38-yard lines and scored on Raul Allegre's 47-yard field goal after 3:22 of the first period and Simms' 11-yard touchdown pass to Lionel Manuel 6:06 later.

"I wanted the defense to go out there and take control," said linebacker Harry Carson, an 11-year veteran and inspirational leader. "We were just so antsy before the game, it was

like everyone was revving up their engines. I knew we could set the tempo if we got out there first."

Few teams have defenses good enough to dominate games. The Giants do. The Redskins mustered just 12 first downs and three of those came on penalties. Washington was a shocking 0 for 18 on third and fourth-down.

"The game was decided in the first quarter,"

1986 NFC CHAMPIONSHIP GAME

Giants Stadium, East Rutherford, N.J.,
JANUARY 11, 1987

SCORE BY PERIODS

Washington	0	0	0	0 — 0
New York Giants	10	7	0	0 — 17

SCORING

New York—Field goal Allegre 47, 3:22 1st. Drive: 17 yards, 6 plays.

New York—Manuel 11 pass from Simms (Allegre kick), 9:28 1st. Drive: 38 yards, 8 plays.

New York—Morris 1 run (Allegre kick), 8:04 2nd. Drive: 49 yards, 6 plays.

TEAM STATISTICS

	Washington	New York
FIRST DOWNS	12	12
By rushing	2	8
By passing	7	3
By penalty	3	1
3rd DOWN EFFICIENCY	0-14	3-13
TOTAL NET YARDS	190	199
Offensive plays	70	61
Average gain per play	2.7	3.7
NET YARDS RUSHING	40	117
Total rushes	16	46
Avg. gain rushing	2.5	2.5
NET YARDS PASSING	150	82
Sacked-Yards lost	4-45	1-8
Gross yards passing	195	90
PASSES	20-50-1	7-14-0
Avg. gain per pass	2.8	5.5
PUNTS	13-35.6	6-42.3
Had blocked	0	0
TOTAL RETURN YARDAGE	34	42
Punt returns	3-19	5-27
Kickoff returns	2-15	0-0
Interception returns	0-0	1-15
PENALTIES-YARDS	3-15	6-48
FUMBLES-LOST	3-1	4-3
TIME OF POSSESSION	26:56	33:04

Attendance—76,633. No-shows—258.

INDIVIDUAL STATISTICS

Rushing—Washington, Rogers 9-15, Bryant 6-25, Schroeder 1-0; New York, Morris 29-87, Carthon 7-28, Simms 7-minus 2, Galbreath 1-minus 1, Rouson 1-2, Anderson 1-3.

Passing—Washington, Schroeder 20-50-1—195; New York, Simms 7-14-0—90.

Receiving—Washington, Monk 8-126, Bryant 7-45, Warren 3-9, Didier 1-7, Griffin 1-8; New York, Carthon 3-18, Manuel 2-36, Bavaro 2-36.

Interceptions—New York, Reasons 1-15.

Punting—Washington, Cox 9-35.6; New York, Landeta 6-42.3.

Punt Returns—Washington, Yarber 3-19; New York, McConkey 5-27.

Kickoff Returns—Washington, Orr 1-10, Branch 1-5.

Field Goals—Washington, none attempted; New York, Allegre 1-1.

Sacks—Washington, Butz; New York, Reasons, Marshall, Dorsey, Martin.

said safety Kenny Hill. "We knew we had to get up on them early, because we had the wind advantage and the field position. If we could get some quick points, they'd have to throw a lot, and that was going to be hard to do."

It was hard to do, but Schroeder gallantly gave it his best. The Redskin quarterback put the ball up 50 times, completed 20 and held up well until Washington's final offensive play of the game, when he suffered a mild concussion after a hit by Jim Burt. Of Washington's final 44 offensive plays, 42 were passes.

The Giants, on the other hand, didn't throw much and didn't have to. Simms attempted only 14 passes—two in the second half—and completed seven. Morris rushed 29 times for 87 yards and scored New York's final touchdown on a one-yard run midway through the second quarter. The Giants ran the ball on 27 of 29 second-half plays.

The Giants' victory marked the third consecutive NFC title game to be won by a shutout. The trip to Pasadena for Super Bowl XXI would be the Giants' first appearance in an NFL title game since 1963. But there were surprisingly few high-fives, cheers or celebrating in the New York locker room after the game.

"You know, maybe if the wind hadn't been blowing, we still would have won the game," Carson said with tongue in cheek. "We do have a pretty good ball club."

AFC
1986

Denver Broncos 23
Cleveland Browns 20 (OT)

It took 68 National Football League games, but John Elway finally convinced skeptics that his vast physical abilities could be used to win big games on a football field.

Elway, a consensus All-America at Stanford for three years despite playing on losing teams, led the Denver Broncos to a 23-20 overtime victory against the Cleveland Browns in the 1986 American Football Conference title game. Elway, the first player chosen in the 1983 NFL draft, had never lived up to the broad expectations that preceded him into professional football. But in the biggest game of his four-year career, he led the Broncos on a 98-yard drive in the final minute to tie the game and on a 60-yard drive in overtime to win it.

"You can't believe the pressure John has been under ever since he joined our team," Denver Coach Dan Reeves said. "His buildup was so big that people expected every pass he threw to go for a touchdown.

"He's had his ups and downs, but he's a tough person."

"Before the game, I was thinking that great quarterbacks come through in situations and make great plays in big games," Elway said. "You know, when the going gets tough, the tough get going."

The going got tough when Denver rookie Ken Bell mishandled a Cleveland kickoff at his own 2-yard line with 5:34 left in regulation, giving the Broncos bad field position in a must situation. The Browns had just taken a 20-13 lead on a 48-yard touchdown pass from Bernie Kosar to Brian Brennan that was made easier when the Bronco defender on the play, cornerback Dennis Smith, fell down. Brennan caught the pass at the Denver 10-yard line and pranced into the end zone past the fallen Smith. The partisan crowd of 79,915 at cold, windy Cleveland Stadium went wild.

"When our backs are to the wall, we always seem to come out of it," said Elway, whose 34-yard scramble to the Browns' 3-yard line had set up Denver's first touchdown. "Our backs couldn't have been any closer to the wall than they were on the 1-yard line.

"We knew there weren't going to be a whole lot of people in the stands rooting for us."

With the clock, the crowd and the cold going against him, Elway methodically led the Broncos on a 15-play drive to tie the game. On first down, he hit running back Sammy Winder for a five-yard gain. Winder then carried the ball on the next two plays for five yards and a first down at the 12-yard line.

Winder carried for three more yards before Elway scrambled 11 yards for a first down at the 26. Elway then threw a 22-yard swing pass to Steve Sewell and a 12-yarder over the middle to Steve Watson to give Denver a first down at the Cleveland 40-yard line with two minutes left.

Browns tackle Dave Puzzuoli sacked Elway for an eight-yard loss to set up a third-and-18 situation at the Cleveland 48 with 1:47 left. Reeves wanted his quarterback to play it conservatively.

"I told him just to try and get half of it," Reeves said. "We would go for the rest on fourth down."

Elway agreed—until he saw the play unfold. Browns strong safety Ray Ellis was giving rookie wide receiver Mark Jackson a big cushion, too big to be ignored.

"Their safety was real deep," Elway said, "so I just took a shot at it." Elway hit the streaking Jackson for a 20-yard gain and a first down at the Cleveland 28-yard line with 1:19 left.

After throwing the ball away to stop the clock, Elway completed a 14-yard pass to Sewell and scrambled nine yards to the Browns 5-yard line with 42 seconds left. He then drilled a bullet pass low to a sliding Jack-

1986 AFC CHAMPIONSHIP GAME

Cleveland Stadium, Cleveland, Ohio
JANUARY 11, 1987
SCORE BY PERIODS

Denver	0	10	3	7	3 — 23
Cleveland	7	3	0	10	0 — 20

SCORING

Cleveland—Fontenot 6 pass from Kosar (Moseley kick), 9:41 1st. Drive: 86 yards, 14 plays.

Denver—Field goal Karlis 19, 2:53 2nd. Drive: 8 yards, 4 plays.

Denver—Willhite 1 run (Karlis kick), 4:24 2nd. Drive: 37 yards, 5 plays.

Cleveland—Field goal Moseley 29, 14:40 2nd. Drive: 53 yards, 9 plays.

Denver—Field goal Karlis 26, 12:10 3rd. Drive: 61 yards, 11 plays.

Cleveland—Field goal Moseley 24, 2:22 4th. Drive: 76 yards, 10 plays.

Cleveland—Brennan 48 pass from Kosar (Moseley kick), 9:17 4th. Drive: 52 yards, 3 plays.

Denver—M. Jackson 5 pass from Elway (Karlis kick), 14:23 4th. Drive: 98 yards, 15 plays.

Denver—Field goal Karlis 33, 5:48 OT. Drive: 60 yards, 9 plays.

TEAM STATISTICS

	Denver	Cleveland
FIRST DOWNS	22	17
By rushing	6	4
By passing	13	12
By penalty	3	1
3rd DOWN EFFICIENCY	5-18	5-13
TOTAL NET YARDS	374	356
Offensive plays	77	66
Average gain per play	4.9	5.4
NET YARDS RUSHING	149	100
Total rushes	37	33
Avg. gain rushing	4.0	3.0
NET YARDS PASSING	225	256
Sacked-Yards lost	2-19	1-3
Gross yards passing	244	259
PASSES	22-38-1	18-32-2
Avg. gain per pass	5.6	7.8
PUNTS	7-37.6	6-43.2
Had blocked	0	0
TOTAL RETURN YARDAGE	50	37
Punt returns	3-10	3-37
Kickoff returns	5-33	6-105
Interception returns	2-40	1-0
PENALTIES-YARDS	6-39	9-76
FUMBLES-LOST	2-0	3-1
TIME OF POSSESSION	34:05	31:43

Attendance—79,915. No-shows—58.

INDIVIDUAL STATISTICS

Rushing—Denver, Elway 4-56, Winder 26-83, Willhite 3-0, Sewell 1-1, Lang 3-9; Cleveland, Mack 26-94, Kosar 4-3, Fontenot 3-3.

Passing—Denver, Elway 22-38-1—244; Cleveland, Kosar 18-32-2—259.

Receiving—Denver, Willhite 2-20, Watson 3-55, Winder 3-2, Johnson 3-25, Mobley 3-36, Sampson 1-10, Kay 2-23, Lang 1-1, Sewell 3-47, M. Jackson 2-25; Cleveland, Langhorne 2-35, Fontenot 7-66, Brennan 4-72, Mack 2-20, Byner 1-4, Weathers 1-42, Slaughter 1-20.

Interceptions—Denver, Hunley 1-14, Ryan 1-26; Cleveland, Harper 1-0.

Punting—Denver, Horan 6-40.7, Elway 1-19.0; Cleveland, Gossett 6-43.2.

Punt Returns—Denver, Willhite 3-10; Cleveland, McNeil 3-37.

Kickoff Returns—Denver, Bell 2-10, Freeman 1-9, Lang 2-14; Cleveland, Fontenot 2-25, McNeil 4-80.

Field Goals—Denver, Karlis 3-3; Cleveland, Moseley 2-2.

Sacks—Denver, Jones; Cleveland, Clancy, Puzzuoli.

son in the end zone with 37 seconds left. Rich Karlis' extra point tied the game at 20-20.

"I could see the determination in his eyes today like I've never seen before," Reeves said. "He wanted to play well so badly."

But Elway was not finished. The Browns were forced to punt after failing to get a first down on the first possession of overtime. The Broncos took over on their own 25-yard line and, nine plays later, Karlis hit a 33-yard field goal that put Denver in the Super Bowl for the first time in nine years. Elway completed a 22-yard pass to tight end Orson Mobley on the first play of the drive and later hooked up with Watson for a 28-yard gain. The Browns at this point were on the ropes, and they knew it.

"After they scored that touchdown (to tie the game), we were down and didn't have the same intensity for the overtime," said defensive end Sam Clancy.

It marked the first time since the NFL-AFL merger in 1970 that a conference championship game went into overtime. It was only the third NFL title game to go into overtime and the first since 1962.

Ironically, the Browns had beaten the New York Jets in a playoff game by an identical 23-20 score in two overtimes the week before. The AFC title game was Cleveland's fourth overtime game in seven weeks and their first to end in defeat.

"I can't express the disappointment that I feel," said linebacker Clay Matthews. "It had become so ingrained in all of us that I just expected to win the game."

Defensive end Carl Hairston, however, echoed the sentiments of many of his teammates in the locker room post-mortem.

"Elway, he did a helluva job. Without him, they can't win it."

NFC
1987

Washington Redskins 17
Minnesota Vikings 10

Heading into the 1987 National Football Conference championship game, about the only thing that had been predictable about the NFC playoffs was their unpredictability. The visiting team had won each of the three playoff games played to that point, including the Minnesota Vikings' stunning 44-10 wild-card game victory at New Orleans and 36-24 thumping of the 49ers at San Francisco the following week. The Washington Redskins, on the other hand, had surprised observers by beating the Bears in Chicago for the second straight postseason, this time 21-17.

But when the Vikings and Redskins met Jan-

Linebacker Ravin Caldwell sacks Vikings quarterback Wade Wilson for one of Washington's eight sacks in the NFC championship game.

uary 17 in Washington for the conference title, the road magic came to an end. The 'Skins won, 17-10, for their ninth win in 10 playoff games at RFK Stadium since 1982. And it was the Redskins' fifth straight victory over the Vikes, including overtime triumphs in 1986 at RFK and in the 1987 regular-season finale just three weeks earlier in Minneapolis.

The Vikings' Traveling Road Show simply ran out of gas.

"Nobody expected us to be here," said Vikings wide receiver Anthony Carter, the team's playoff star. "Our heads will be up."

The Redskins won largely because of their defense, which played well enough to offset numerous offensive breakdowns. The 'Skins defense sacked Minnesota quarterback Wade Wilson eight times—one short of the playoff record—and forced him to hurry his passes on at least a half-dozen other occasions. Excluding their four-play, 71-yard touchdown drive in

the second quarter, the Vikings had just 47 yards on 25 first-down plays. They converted just three of 16 third- and fourth-down tries.

"We couldn't hear the audibles," said offensive tackle Gary Zimmerman, alluding to the crowd noise at jam-packed RFK Stadium. "Linebackers were moving around and the inside guys (offensive linemen) couldn't hear the line calls. We couldn't talk to each other along the line."

But the Vikings were not the only ones to have offensive problems. Washington never seemed to get untracked behind quarterback Doug Williams. Williams drove the Redskins 98 yards in eight plays for a touchdown on the team's first possession—throwing 42 yards to Kelvin Bryant for the score—but completed just nine of 26 attempts overall.

Redskins Coach Joe Gibbs, who had summoned Williams from the bench to relieve Jay Schroeder on numerous occasions during the

Redskins cornerback Barry Wilburn separates Vikings receiver Anthony Carter from the football in the NFC title game.

regular season, briefly contemplated making the reverse move.

"Jay wanted in there, and I think he could have done well," said the coach. "But you have to stay with your gut feeling."

Gibbs' patience paid off. With the game tied 10-10, Washington took over on its own 30-yard line with 9:57 remaining. After four running plays, Williams hit wide receiver Gary Clark for a 43-yard gain to the Vikes' 11-yard line. On a third-and-seven from the 8, Williams fired a low pass between two defenders into the hands of Clark, who fell into the Minnesota end zone for what proved to be the game-winning points.

Clark messed up by running the wrong route, but Williams adjusted in time to complete the seven-yard scoring pass with 5:15 left.

"That was a great throw," Clark said, "because I wasn't where I was supposed to be and Doug had to look for me."

But the Vikings, who had played near-perfect games in their victories over the Saints and 49ers, weren't finished yet. They took possession at their own 33-yard line with 5:04 left and moved to the Redskin 6 with a little over a minute to go. Wilson then threw three straight incompletions, the last one when running back Darrin Nelson dropped what appeared to be a certain touchdown at the 1-yard line with 52 seconds left.

"The ball hit my hands, and then it was knocked away (by cornerback Darrell Green)," Nelson said. "Anytime the ball hits your hands, you should catch it."

The Washington defense, which had been a dominant force most of the game, was hanging on at the end.

"We were all in the huddle, telling each

other to give it everything we had on the last play," said defensive end Dexter Manley. "There was a lot of talking. I guess I was doing most of it. I get excited in those moments."

"It felt like my heart stopped during that play," said 37-year-old tackle Dave Butz, who had two sacks and tipped a pass that was intercepted by teammate Mel Kaufman.

But the Redskins survived, thus earning a trip to San Diego for Super Bowl XXII, which would mark Washington's third appearance in the NFL title game in six years. They had come close in 1986, when they reached the conference championship game only to be whitewashed, 17-0, by the New York Giants.

"We didn't want to get this far again and blow the chance," Manley said. "You don't want to live a year with that hurt again."

1987 NFC CHAMPIONSHIP GAME

Robert F. Kennedy Memorial Stadium, Washington, D. C.
JANUARY 17, 1988

SCORE BY PERIODS

Minnesota	0	7	0	3 — 10
Washington	7	0	3	7 — 17

SCORING

Washington—Bryant 42 pass from Williams (Haji-Sheikh kick), 10:53 1st. Drive: 98 yards, 8 plays.

Minnesota—Lewis 23 pass from Wilson (C. Nelson kick), 13:00 2nd. Drive: 71 yards, 4 plays.

Washington—Field goal Haji-Sheikh 28, 10:30 3rd. Drive: 6 yards, 4 plays.

Minnesota—Field goal C. Nelson 18, 4:54 4th. Drive: 52 yards, 10 plays, 1 penalty.

Washington—Clark 7 pass from Williams (Haji-Sheikh kick), 9:45 4th. Drive: 70 yards, 8 plays.

TEAM STATISTICS

	Minnesota	Washington
FIRST DOWNS	16	11
By rushing	5	7
By passing	10	4
By penalty	1	0
3rd DOWN EFFICIENCY	3-15	5-16
TOTAL NET YARDS	259	280
Offensive plays	68	60
Average gain per play	3.8	4.7
NET YARDS RUSHING	76	161
Total rushes	21	34
Avg. gain rushing	3.6	4.7
NET YARDS PASSING	183	119
Sacked-Yards lost	8-60	0-0
Gross yards passing	243	119
PASSES	19-39-1	9-26-0
Avg. gain per pass	3.9	4.6
PUNTS	10-33.2	8-39.1
Had blocked	0	0
TOTAL RETURN YARDAGE	115	74
Punt returns	4-57	4-10
Kickoff returns	3-58	3-54
Interception returns	0-0	1-10
PENALTIES-YARDS	2-10	3-18
FUMBLES-LOST	0-0	0-0
TIME OF POSSESSION	33:02	26:58

Attendance—55,212. No-shows—345.

INDIVIDUAL STATISTICS

Rushing—Minnesota, D. Nelson 8-15, Anderson 4-25, Dozier 2-minus 2, Rice 1-8, Wilson 4-28, Fenney 2-2; Washington, Rogers 12-46, Bryant 3-3, Sanders 1-28, Smith 13-72, Clark 1-5, Williams 4-7.

Passing—Minnesota, Wilson 19-39-1—243; Washington, Williams 9-26-0—119.

Receiving—Minnesota, Carter 7-85, Jordan 3-56, Lewis 4-54, D. Nelson 3-25, Anderson 1-8, Rice 1-15; Washington, Clark 3-57, Bryant 4-47, Allen 1-9, Warren 1-6.

Interceptions—Washington, Kaufman 1-10.

Punting—Minnesota, Scribner 10-33.2; Washington, Cox 8-39.1.

Punt Returns—Minnesota, Carter 4-57; Washington, Dean 1-0, Green 1-1, Davis 1-0, Yarber 1-9.

Kickoff Returns—Minnesota, D. Nelson 2-43, Rice 1-15; Washington, Sanders 2-30, Smith 1-24.

Field Goals—Minnesota, C. Nelson 1-1; Washington, Haji-Sheikh 1-3 (missed: 38, 47).

Sacks—Washington, Butz 2, Manley 1½, Walton, Caldwell, Vaughn, Gouveia, Mann ½.

AFC
1987

Denver Broncos   38
Cleveland Browns   33

As the Denver Broncos and Cleveland Browns were preparing for their showdown in the 1987 American Football Conference championship game, much time was spent looking back rather than ahead. At issue was Denver's 23-20 overtime victory in the 1986 AFC title game, made possible when Broncos quarterback John Elway engineered a dramatic 98-yard drive in the final minutes of regulation to tie the score.

The loss was particularly painful for Cleveland players and fans, who were hungry for the team's first-ever Super Bowl appearance.

"I'm sorry, but I just don't understand their so-called 'revenge' factor," said Elway. "They say they feel like we almost stole that game from them, as if we threw a 'Hail Mary' pass with two seconds left and it bounced off three Browns and we caught it and scored. I think the bottom line is that we played well on the drive and then we won in overtime."

The bottom line in '87 was the same even if the final score was different: Denver 38, Cleveland 33. The Broncos thus became the first team to win back-to-back AFC title games since the 1978-79 Pittsburgh Steelers (who, ironically, also beat the same team—the Houston Oilers—in both their wins).

"This doesn't hurt any more than last year," said Cleveland Coach Marty Schottenheimer. "They all hurt. When you lose, they all hurt."

The Broncos jumped out to a big lead by scoring touchdowns on their first three possessions, the first two set up by turnovers. A pass by quarterback Bernie Kosar on Cleveland's first possession was deflected and intercepted by Denver's Freddie Gilbert at the Browns' 18-yard line. Four plays later, rookie wide receiver Ricky Nattiel split between safeties Ray Ellis and Felix Wright and hauled in an eight-yard scoring pass from Elway.

Less than four minutes later, Denver safety Tony Lilly stripped the ball from Browns fullback Kevin Mack and Steve Wilson recovered for the Broncos at his own 40-yard line. Eight running plays and 60 yards later, Steve Sewell's one-yard dash gave Denver a 14-0 lead.

The Broncos led by 18 points at the intermission, and with 75,993 fans at Mile High Stadium cheering their every move, the prospects were bleak at best for the visiting Browns.

"At halftime, we didn't make any major strategic changes," said Schottenheimer. "Instead, we leaned on the most important thing that any good football team must have, and that's the character of the players."

And the character of the three-time Central Division champion Browns came through loud and clear. Wright picked off an Elway pass on Denver's first second-half possession and returned it 13 yards to the Broncos 35. Three plays later, Kosar threw an 18-yard touchdown pass to Reggie Langhorne to cut the Denver lead to 21-10.

"We decided we'd go out attacking in the second half, that we'd really throw it around," Kosar said. "We've lived and died with that all season. We didn't make it this far this season by quitting when we got behind."

Elway and wide receiver Mark Jackson hooked up for an 80-yard touchdown on Denver's next possession to restore the Broncos' 18-point advantage, but Kosar drove the Browns 80 yards in five plays, connecting with running back Earnest Byner for a 32-yard touchdown to make the score 28-17.

Byner scored another touchdown on a four-yard run to cut the Browns' deficit to four. But a 38-yard field goal by Rich Karlis on the final play of the third period lifted Denver to a 31-24 lead.

Kosar responded by driving the Browns 86 yards on nine plays, including a 53-yard pass play to Byner. The touchdown came on a four-yard pass to Webster Slaughter, tying the game at 31-31 with 10:48 remaining.

The Browns, who appeared in need of life-support systems at the half, had scored touchdowns on four straight possessions in less than 16 minutes. Three of the touchdowns were on passes from Kosar, who completed 16 of 22 attempts for 246 yards on the four scoring drives.

"I knew we had to get some points on the board at that point, because Bernie was throwing the ball all over the place," Elway said.

The Broncos did just that. Taking over on his own 25 with 5:14 left, Elway guided his club 75 yards on five plays for what proved to be the game-winning score. He completed two 26-yard passes to Nattiel and then hooked up with Sammy Winder for a 20-yard touchdown with 4:01 left.

Like two punch-drunk fighters in a bar room brawl, Elway had responded in kind to Kosar's heavy blows. Now it was Kosar's chance once again.

Taking over at his own 25, Kosar handed to Byner on first down for a 17-yard gain. He then completed consecutive passes of 14 and 19 yards to wide receiver Brian Brennan before Byner ripped off another six-yard gain.

Cleveland worked the ball to the Denver 8 with 1:12 left, but disaster struck on second-and-five.

Byner, who would amass 120 receiving yards and 67 rushing, fumbled inside the Denver 5-yard line as he appeared headed for the go-ahead touchdown. Reserve defensive back Jeremiah Castille knocked the ball from Byner's grasp at the 3 and recovered it there with just 1:05 remaining.

"The play was supposed to go inside, but I saw that (Karl) Mecklenburg was plugging up the hole, so I slid to the outside," Byner said. "And I had daylight, too. There was no doubt in my mind that we were going to score."

But Byner and the Browns didn't score, and for the second straight season they were denied a trip to the Super Bowl.

"Last year I was elated at the end of the game," Denver Coach Dan Reeves said. "This year I'm just numb."

1987 AFC CHAMPIONSHIP GAME

Mile High Stadium, Denver, Colo.
JANUARY 17, 1988

SCORE BY PERIODS

Cleveland	0	3	21	9 —	33
Denver	14	7	10	7 —	38

SCORING

Denver—Nattiel 8 pass from Elway (Karlis kick), 3:38 1st. Drive: 18 yards, 4 plays.

Denver—Sewell 1 run (Karlis kick), 11:06 1st. Drive: 60 yards, 8 plays.

Cleveland—Field goal Bahr 24, 1:41 2nd. Drive: 64 yards, 13 plays.

Denver—Lang 1 run (Karlis kick), 6:59 2nd. Drive: 80 yards, 11 plays.

Cleveland—Langhorne 18 pass from Kosar (Bahr kick), 3:44 3rd. Drive: 35 yards, 3 plays.

Denver—Jackson 80 pass from Elway (Karlis kick), 5:03 3rd. Drive: 80 yards, 3 plays.

Cleveland—Byner 32 pass from Kosar (Bahr kick) 8:10 3rd. Drive: 80 yards, 5 plays.

Cleveland—Byner 4 run (Bahr kick), 11:15 3rd. Drive: 42 yards, 4 plays.

Denver—Field goal Karlis 38, 14:50 3rd. Drive: 59 yards, 9 plays.

Cleveland—Slaughter 4 pass from Kosar (Bahr kick), 4:12 4th. Drive: 86 yards, 9 plays.

Denver—Winder 20 pass from Elway (Karlis kick), 10:59 4th. Drive: 75 yards, 5 plays.

Cleveland—Safety, Horan ran out of endzone, 14:52 4th.

TEAM STATISTICS

	Cleveland	Denver
FIRST DOWNS	25	24
By rushing	8	10
By passing	15	11
By penalty	2	3
3rd DOWN EFFICIENCY	8-14	7-14
TOTAL NET YARDS	464	412
Offensive plays	70	67
Average gain per play	6.6	6.1
NET YARDS RUSHING	128	156
Total rushes	27	39
Avg. gain per rush	4.7	4.0
NET YARDS PASSING	336	256
Sacked-Yards lost	2-20	2-25
Gross yards passing	356	281
PASSES	26-41-1	14-26-1
Avg. gain per pass	7.8	9.1
PUNTS	2-48.0	3-33.7
Had blocked	0	0
TOTAL RETURN YARDAGE	131	56
Punt returns	2-24	2-13
Kickoff returns	5-94	3-43
Interception returns	1-13	1-0
PENALTIES-YARDS	7-59	7-44
FUMBLES-LOST	3-3	2-0
TIME OF POSSESSION	31:37	28:23

Attendance—75,993. No-shows—204.

INDIVIDUAL STATISTICS

Rushing—Cleveland, Byner 15-67, Mack 12-61; Denver, Winder 20-72, Lang 5-51, Elway 11-36, Boddie 1-8, Sewell 1-1, Horan 1-minus 12.

Passing—Cleveland, Kosar 26-41-1—356; Denver, Elway 14-26-1—281.

Receiving—Cleveland, Byner 7-120, Slaughter 4-53, Brennan 4-48, Mack 4-28, Newsome 3-35, Langhorne 2-48, Weathers 1-19, Tennell 1-5; Denver, Nattiel 5-95, Jackson 4-134, Winder 3-34, Sewell 1-10, Mobley 1-8.

Interceptions—Cleveland, Wright 1-13; Denver, Gilbert 1-0.

Punting—Cleveland, L. Johnson 2-48.0; Denver, Horan 2-41.5, Elway 1-18.0.

Punt Returns—Cleveland, McNeil 2-24; Denver, Clark 2-13.

Kickoff Returns—Cleveland, McNeil 5-94; Denver, Bell 3-43.

Field Goals—Cleveland, Bahr 0-1 (missed: 45); Denver, Karlis 1-2 (missed: 50).

Sacks—Cleveland, Baker 1-7, Clancy 1-18; Denver, Fletcher 1-9, Jones 1-11.

NFL Faced Challenges

When World War II came to an end, hundreds of former football players, who had either lost their jobs or had just peaked in time to help Uncle Sam, returned.

They were looking for work and that led to the creation of the All-America Football Conference.

The league lasted four seasons, and its ultimate contribution was the "donation" of three cities where proud NFL traditions would be built.

When the AAFC folded after the 1949 season, the NFL agreed to absorb the Cleveland Browns, Baltimore Colts and San Francisco 49ers. Those Colts folded after one season, but Baltimore received a new NFL franchise in 1953 and the reborn Colts became a league power by the late-'50s.

In the case of the Browns, the older league was accepting the only champion the AAFC ever knew. The Browns won all four league crowns and they won immediately in the NFL in 1950. In fact, they played in the NFL championship game in each of their first six years in the league, winning titles in 1954 and '55 in addition to '50.

In 1946, the Browns beat the New York Yankees, 14-9, in the AAFC championship. The next year was a rematch, which the Browns won again, 14-3. The most one-sided Cleveland victory occurred in 1948, when the Browns destroyed Buffalo, 49-7. The final AAFC championship, naturally won by Cleveland, was by the score of 21-7 over San Francisco.

These were the same Browns who soon came to dominate the NFL. They included Otto Graham, Marion Motley, Lou Groza, Mac Speedie and Dante Lavelli. The owner, general manager and coach was Paul Brown.

The war that developed between the NFL and AAFC need never have happened. A handful of prospective team owners had approached NFL Commissioner Bert Bell and asked for consideration as expansion teams. But Bell, who otherwise made very few mistakes, chose this time to reject a sincere offer —and he did it publicly.

"These men have asked me for permission to join our league," Bell said. "I told them to come back when they got themselves a football."

The insults were a strong incentive for the creation of the new league that cost the established NFL far more money in paper salaries than the owners had expected.

Money also was the incentive more than 25 years later, when another group of ambitious businessmen created the World Football League which began play in the summer of 1974 while the NFL players were on strike dur-

Cleveland's Mac Speedie grabs an Otto Graham pass over a New York defender during an AAFC game.

ing their training camp period.

This was less than a decade after the successful fight waged by the AFL, and such success was envied by those who had the money but not the teams.

So raiding of rosters and the hiring of former NFL scouts, coaches and players began.

The most incredible accomplishment of the WFL was Toronto's signing of Larry Csonka, Jim Kiick and Paul Warfield, all from the roster of the NFL Super Bowl champion Miami Dolphins. John Bassett's Canadian entry was transferred to Memphis and became the Southmen.

Things quickly went downhill after that.

There was only one WFL championship game, called World Bowl I. The numerical designation need not have been applied. It was the only championship game, played on December 15, 1974, in Birmingham, Ala.

The Birmingham Americans were the only WFL champions, defeating the Florida Blazers, 22-21.

Midway through the 1975 season, insurmountable debts and a decided lack of interest offered the WFL no choice but to disband.

Former NFL Commissioner Bert Bell made a big mistake when he ridiculed the fledgling AAFC.

Yankee defenders hang onto Dub Jones after he catches an Otto Graham pass in an AAFC game.